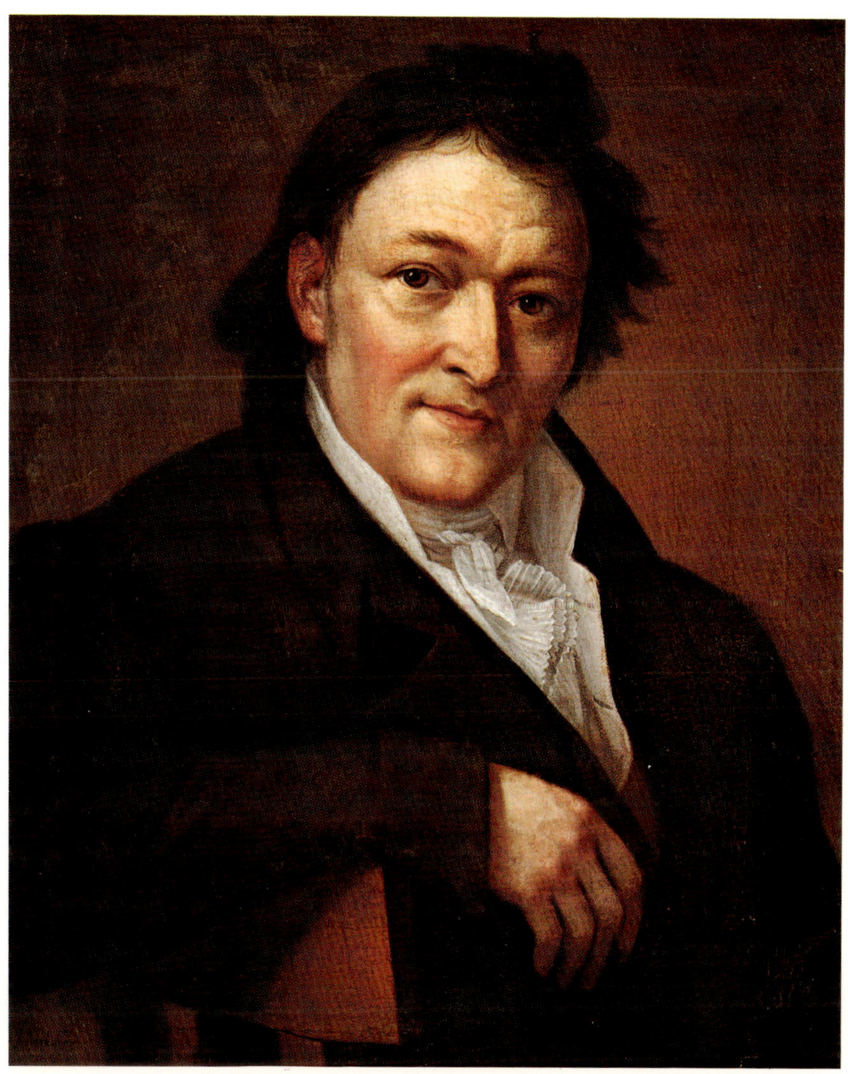

ALOIS SENEFELDER

Portrait painted in 1829 by Professor Joseph Hauber.
The original painting is in the *Deutsches Museum,* Munich.
This illustration was reproduced in four-color lithography
by the Litho-Krome® Company, Columbus, Georgia.
A subsidiary of Hallmark Cards, Inc.

THE LITHOGRAPHERS MANUAL

Ninth Edition

Dedication

The Lithographers Manual is one of the primary reference books for the printing industry. This book combined with the other texts, seminars, quality control devices, plant and environmental audits offered by the Graphic Arts Technical Foundation, provides the Printing Industry a uniquely important set of products and services at a time when all companies are in transition and need the most current information.

Craftsmen at R. R. Donnelley have benefitted for many years from the availability of GATF products and services. Donnelley is pleased to contribute production of the 9th edition of the Lithographers Manual to continue this long, productive tradition.

John R. Walter
Chairman and Chief Executive Officer
R. R. Donnelley and Sons Company

THE LITHOGRAPHERS MANUAL

Ninth Edition

Thomas M. Destree, Editor in Chief

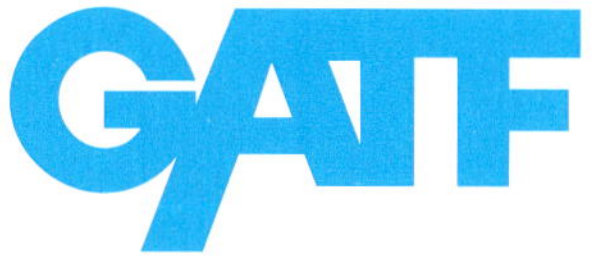

THE GRAPHIC ARTS TECHNICAL FOUNDATION, INC.
FORTY-SIX FIFTEEN FORBES AVENUE
PITTSBURGH, PENNSYLVANIA
15213

Library of Congress Catalog Card Number: 93-78999
International Standard Book Number: 0-88362-169-X

Printed in the United States of America

Ninth Edition
First Edition 1937
Order No. 1407

A catalog of GATF text and reference books, Learning Modules, and audiovisuals may be obtained on request from the Graphic Arts Technical Foundation at the address given at the bottom of the title page.

Printing compliments of
R. R. Donnelley & Sons Co., Inc.

Bound using Holly and Blue Spruce Crown Linen cloth, donated by Holliston

INTERNATIONAL PAPER

Paper courtesy of International Paper Coated Papers Division:
70# Miraweb II Matte Coated Free Sheet containing
a minimum of 10% postconsumer fiber.
Other high-quality groundwood web offset products
from International Paper are Adirondack, Saratoga, Hudson Web Gloss,
PBG-74, Liberty Hi-Brite, Educator IV, Hi-Brite Roto and Publication Gloss.

Table of Contents

Chapter One—The History of Lithography

Chapter Two—GATF: Trailblazer in the Graphic Arts

Chapter Three—The Lithographic Process

Chapter Four—Planning and Control

Chapter Five—Type and Typography

Chapter Six—Art and Copy Preparation

Chapter Seven—Basic Camera Operation

Chapter Eight—Color Separation and Correction

Chapter Nine—Film Image Assembly

Chapter Ten—Proofing

Chapter Eleven—Platemaking

Chapter Twelve—Electronic Prepress Production

Chapter Thirteen—Ink

Chapter Fourteen—Paper

Chapter Fifteen—Presswork

Chapter Sixteen—Finishing

Foreword

When the eighth edition of the *Lithographers Manual* was published in 1988, the electronic revolution in the graphic communications had already made headway into the average printing plant. Now, computer-based technology permeates the printing plant, from estimating and prepress to press and the bindery.

The ninth edition of the *Lithographers Manual* continues the general style and organizational structure of previous recent editions, but a totally new chapter on electronic prepress production has been added to the book. All existing chapters have been updated.

The technical editors in the GATF Technical Information Group—Pamela J. Groff, Ann L. Mertz, Robert J. Schneider, Jr., and Deborah L. Stevenson—not only edited the manuscript but also paginated the book using computer software and performed additional prepress functions.

Thomas M. Destree
Editor in Chief

Chapter 1

The History of Lithography

The Invention of Lithography

Lithography was invented in 1798 by Alois Senefelder. Senefelder had been experimenting with various printing plates, printing inks, and treatments of printing surfaces in order to discover an inexpensive but reliable method of printing his dramatic compositions, since he could not afford to have them printed by an established printer. In 1798, he was involved in etching copper plates; however, he was practicing the necessary reverse writing on the cheaper, more easily handled limestone. According to Senefelder (*The Invention of Lithography*), he had "just ground a stone plate smooth in order to treat it with etching fluid and to pursue on it my practice in reverse writing, when my mother asked me to write a laundry list for her. Without bothering to look for writing materials, I wrote the list hastily on the clean stone, with my prepared stone ink of wax, soap, and lampblack, intending to copy it as soon as paper was supplied."

Later, Senefelder became curious to see what would happen if the stone were etched with nitric acid. As he suspected, the acid ate into that part of the plate that was not protected by his specially developed ink. Thus, the writing stood about "the thickness of a playing card in relief." Senefelder found that this plate was much easier to ink than the etched plates and "hardly one quarter of the force was necessary for making impressions." This became known as shallow-relief printing.

Senefelder had much trouble financing his endeavors, bad luck with presses and workers, and difficulty with the artistry so intrinsic to printing at the time; thus, he continued to experiment with stone printing, hoping to make it cheaper, easier to use, and capable of good-quality printing. His lack of skill in writing on stone, which is much more difficult than writing on paper due to the requisite reverse writing and the material itself, led him to experiment with transferring. He developed an ink of linseed oil, soap, and lampblack with which he wrote on paper; then, he placed the paper face down on the stone plate and passed it through a press, producing an accurate, reversed image on the stone. "But," he wondered, "why could I not invent an ink that would serve on the stone without making it necessary to trace over it with the stone ink? Why not make an ink that would leave the paper under pressure and transfer itself to the stone entirely? Could one give the paper itself some property so that it would let go of the ink under given conditions?"

This led to more experiments, in the course of which he observed that "if there happened to be a

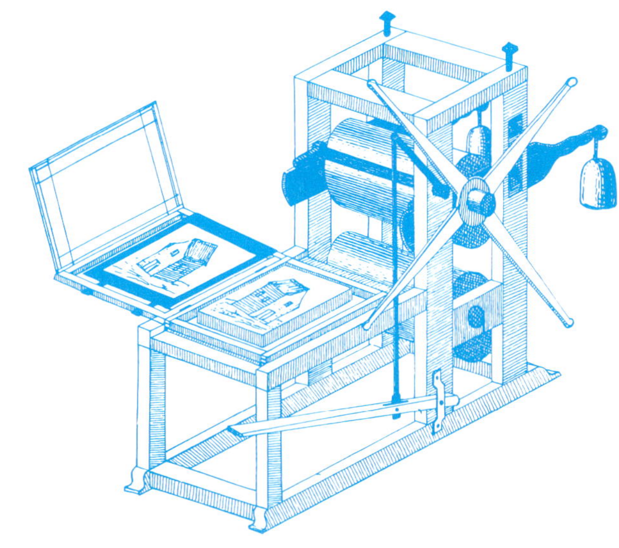

Senefelder's first lithographic press.

few drops of oil in the water into which I dipped paper inscribed with my greasy stone-ink, the oil would distribute itself evenly over all parts of the writing, whereas the rest of the paper would take no oil, and especially so if it had been treated with gum solution or very thin starch paste."

Next, Senefelder drew a sheet of an old book through a thin gum solution and then sponged it with a thin oil color, which adhered only to the printed letters. He laid a clean sheet on top of the page and put both through a press, obtaining a "very good transfer, in reverse, of course." This transfer, when treated in the same manner, could produce right-reading copies. What was significant, though, was that "this process, depending solely on chemical action, was totally, fundamentally different from all other processes of printing." Senefelder also found that this process worked well with the limestone plate, which readily absorbed the fatty ink and was much sturdier than paper. It is from this stone that lithography gets its name (meaning, literally, stone writing).

Senefelder continued to have business troubles, but in 1799 the Kurfuerst (Prince-Elector) Maximilian Joseph of Bavaria gave him an exclusive privilege lasting fifteen years for the exploitation of his invention. In 1809, the King of Bavaria appointed Senefelder to the post of Royal Inspector of Lithography at the Lithographic Institute operated by the Crown. His salary of 1,500 gulden permitted a very comfortable life.

The life of Senefelder was devoted to lithography. In the interests of lithography, he traveled to Vienna, Paris, and London. He was engaged in various business enterprises, had legal and family trouble, but kept on improving lithography as long as he lived. In 1817, he submitted a model of a lithographic press, with automatic inking and dampening, to the Royal (Bavarian) Academy, which gave him a gold medal in recognition of this invention. At about the same time, he invented the first paper plates with which he wanted to replace the heavy lithographic stones.

The Lithographic Principle

The principle on which lithography is based is the mutual repellence of water and greasy substances. The limestone used by Senefelder was porous and particularly well suited to lithography. Stone, however, was not the essence of the process. Senefelder preferred the term "chemical printing" for his invention and used this term as a generic one; stone printing (in German Steindruck), or lithography, was for him only one branch of many possible in chemical printing.

Terminology has been neither generally accepted nor consistent throughout history. At certain times and in certain countries, a distinction was made, for example, between lithography and zincography (lithography from zinc plates). The term chemical printing was less used in the Anglo-American orbit than planography, and planography, too, has been used by different people with differing connotations. In the course of this century, the term lithography has lost its meaning as stone printing and is in our day more or less generally used in the same sense in which Senefelder used chemical printing.

Lithography and Copperplate Engraving

The original method of stone printing was slow and cumbersome compared with contemporary lithographic techniques, but it was very fast and simple compared with copperplate engraving, the method with which lithography competed most vigorously.

The superiority of lithography—at least costwise—is set forth in a cost comparison of lithography and copperplate engraving in the English translation of Antoine Raucourt's treatise on lithography, published in 1821. There, it is shown that "lithography is about seven times cheaper than copperplate engraving, if plate costs of both processes are compared. The printing costs show much less of a difference, but lithographic printing costs only a little more than half of the printing of copperplate engravings."

Lithography as a Duplicating Process

The growing popularity of lithography could be explained by those cost figures. Lithography was also considered ideal as a "duplicating process." Under the title *Every man his own printer; or, lithography made easy,* a book was published anonymously in 1854 in London, Manchester, and Edinburgh. This

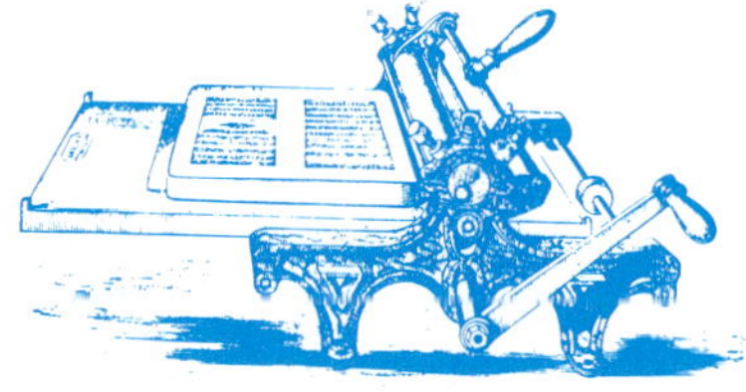

The Autographic Press, possibly the first lithographic duplicating machine.

efforts of two Frenchmen, Louis Jacques Nandé Daguerre (1789–1851) and Joseph Nicéphore Niepce (1765–1833). Daguerreotypy produced photographic images in a camera obscura on silvered copper plates. The silver was made light sensitive with iodine. Exposure originally took from 15 to 30 min., but it was later considerably reduced. The silver was developed with fumes of mercury.

Daguerreotypy, however, was not nearly as important for lithography as the development of heliography, which is considered by some to be the true invention of photography. This process was developed by Joseph Nicéphore Niepce in 1822. In this year, Niepce made a contact print of an engraving representing Pope Pius VII, which he oiled and thereby made more or less transparent on a glass plate coated with a solution of bitumen. Exposure time was 2–3 hours, and the plate was developed with a solvent consisting of a mixture of lavender oil and petroleum. The exposed areas became insoluble, while the unexposed areas remained soluble and so were washed out during development.

Heliography plays an important role in the history of graphic reproduction. In 1826, Niepce made the first experimental photoengraving by using metal instead of glass and by etching the photoprinted and developed plate. The first successful photolithographic process was based on the same material, bitumen. This process was developed in Paris by the optician Lerebours and the lithographer Lemercier in 1852. A grained lithographic stone was coated with a solution of bitumen of Judea in ether, contact printed, and developed with ether. In 1853, prints made by this process were published, but the process was later abandoned in favor of Poitevin's, because only a limited number of prints could be made. Lemercier and Lerebours were not the only ones to use the bitumen process. Helmut Gernsheim's *History of Photography* lists several others, though none in the United States.

Bichromated Colloids

Bitumen or asphalt processes, as they are also called, were considerably refined in the course of the nineteenth century, but they were completely superseded by a group of processes all based on bichromates and colloids.

Mungo Ponton, the Secretary of the Bank of Scotland and an amateur photographer, discovered in 1839 that bichromate of potassium spread on paper was light sensitive. He thought that the much cheaper bichromate could replace the expensive silver salts used in daguerreotypy.

The French physicist Edmond Becquerel experimented with variations of Ponton's process on different kinds of papers, and in 1840 established that it was not the bichromate of potash that was very light sensitive, but that the size in the paper greatly increased the light sensitivity.

The effect of bichromates on various colloids was studied by several people. In 1852, the English inventor William Henry Fox Talbot (1800–1877) discovered the light sensitivity of a mixture of potassium bichromate and gelatin. He was granted an English patent in 1852 for the process of photographic etching on steel with the aid of this chromate mixture.

Another investigator, French chemist and civil engineer Alphonse Louis Poitevin (1819–1882), one of the greatest contributors to photomechanical reproduction processes. Poitevin was the inventor of collotype and several carbon processes. To him, we also owe the invention of the first successful photolithographic process.

Poitevin invented photolithography based on bichromated albumin in August 1855. He designated his process photolithography but was not necessarily the first to use this term. According to Josef Maria Eder's *History of Photography*, "Poitevin coated the stone (grained for halftone pictures) with a solution of potassium and albumin, equalized the coating with a tampon, dried, exposed under a negative, washed with water, rolled up with greasy ink (or rolled up first and then washed), which only adhered to the parts which had become insoluble by exposure to light but did not adhere to the moist parts. The stone was then etched and printed by the usual lithographic method."

In 1855, Poitevin started his own lithographic business in Paris. He printed 300 impressions from a stone, but two years later he sold his process to the well-known Parisian lithographer Lemercier, who got up to 700 impressions from a stone.

Photolithographic Transfer Processes

Sensitizing a lithographic stone and photoprinting directly on it was not a practical procedure. It was all but impossible to obtain uniform coatings, and it was equally difficult to provide flawless contact during exposure. In the hands of very skilled craftsmen, and under the most favorable conditions, direct sensitization of stones could possibly work. Photolithography, however, needed a different technique if it was to be commonly used. This technique consisted of making photolithographic transfers.

According to Eder, "the photolithographic transfer process from chromated papers was invented by Eduard Isaak Asser (1809–1894), in 1857, at Amsterdam. . . . He was the first to make photographic prints with greasy ink on paper coated with starch paste and sensitized with bichromate for transfer on stone."

Photolithographic transfer processes were improved in 1859 by J. W. Osborn, head of the Government Survey Office in Melbourne, Australia, and independently in the same year by Colonel Sir Henry James (1803–1877), head of the Ordnance Survey, Southampton, England. According to Gernsheim, Osborn's method "allowed a much greater number of impressions to be taken—an edition of 2,000 to 3,000 against Lemercier's 700 by the Poitevin process."

Osborn and James also made transfers to zinc. They both, because of their positions, were most interested in cartography (i.e., map printing). As reported in Stephen H. Horgan's *Halftone and Photomechanical Processes,* "the rights for the United States of Osborn's process were secured by the American Photolithographic Company of New York, and thus began in the seventies the use of photolithography for reproducing government maps, Patent Office drawings, and the reproduction of steel engravings, which were so popular for home decoration at the time."

The Development of the Halftone Process

Two problems dominate the history of picture reproduction. One is the rendering of tonal values; the other is the combination of reading matter and pictures for printing in one pressrun. Invention of the halftone process was the first effective solution. It was developed for letterpress printing and made possible the reproduction of photographs and other tonal pictures together with reading matter.

Beaumont Newhall, in *The History of Photography from 1839 to the Present Day,* says that it was not by chance that "this important invention was perfected at precisely the time that the technical revolution in photography was taking place. Dry plates, flexible film, anastigmatic lenses, and hand cameras made it possible to produce negatives more quickly, more easily, and of a greater variety of subjects than ever before. The halftone enabled these photographs to be reproduced economically and in limitless quantity in books, magazines, and newspapers."

The development of the halftone process took place outside of lithography. In the 1880s, when the revolution in photography occurred, lithography was utterly unsuitable for mass production printing. Nothing illustrates this backwardness better than the story of the New York *Daily Graphic.* On March 4, 1873, the *Graphic* published the first issue of the first illustrated daily newspaper in the world. It was an eight-page paper. The pictorial four pages were printed first, by a lithographic stone transfer process, and the inside four pages were run off by letterpress. Production on the lithographic presses was between 700 and 800 sheets per hour, a rate much too slow to satisfy the demand. Lithographic stone presses were completely outdistanced by letterpress machinery. Letterpress, however, had no satisfactory means for reproducing continuous-tone pictures. The photoengraved halftone process was developed to overcome this deficiency of letterpress reproduction. In photoengraving, letterpress found an excellent process of reproducing pictures.

The development of photoengraving may not appear to belong in this history, but since the use of halftone dots was later adapted to lithography, photoengraving was a prelude to modern means of reproducing continuous-tone pictures lithographically. In 1851, Frederick Scott Archer, an Englishman (1813–1857), published a description of the wet collodion process, which was the basis of most graphic arts photography until the middle of the twentieth century. In 1855, Archer made his second great contribution to graphic arts photography by inventing the stripping of collodion film. Many people worked on the problem of making tonal pictures reproducible by breaking them up into very small units. Frederick Eugene Ives (1856–1937) of Philadelphia solved the problem of tonal reproduction in 1886 by introducing the glass cross-line screen. Max Levy of Philadelphia succeeded in 1890 in developing a precision manufacturing process for these screens. These contributions were by no means the only ones that made photoengraving into the leading reproduction process. Lithography stagnated technically until it received its next great impulse through the offset press, as described in the next section, "The Offset Press."

The offset press revived the interest in photolithography; however, conditions had vastly changed compared to the 1870s, when photolithography had been a contact printing transfer process for line work. During the time of the broad new interest in photolithography, which may be placed arbitrarily at the period shortly after the first World War, graphic arts photography had immensely advanced. Photolithography acquired a different meaning. It

stood for offset lithographic printing in which the camera and, where necessary, the halftone screen were used for converting line and tone originals by means of photography into printable form. This new photolithography could and did draw on the knowledge developed since the 1890s.

Process Color Printing

The thought of producing a wide gamut of color by printing with only three inks was first conceived and executed by James Christopher Le Blon (1667–1741), a painter and etcher. Le Blon based his process on Newton's theory of color. He made his color separations by eye and his plates by the mezzo-tinto process, then a very popular gravure reproduction method. In 1704, he was ready for commercialization of his process. Three-color printing is a product of the nineteenth and twentieth centuries; it is closely related to color photography.

The first major event in this area took place on May 17, 1861, in Great Britain. On this day, James Clerk Maxwell lectured on the theory of primary colors and demonstrated a photograph in color.

The next movement toward color photography and printing came from two Frenchmen, Louis Ducos du Hauron and Charles Cros, who, in 1868 and 1869, independently conceived the idea of producing objects in their natural colors by the superimposition of three photographically produced pictures in blue, yellow, and red. From a lithographic stone print made in three colors, we know that Du Hauron experimented with three-color lithography. A process-color stone-lithograph was presented by him to Stephen H. Horgan, who dated it 1870.

Furthermore, in 1869, Du Hauron also described not only full-color printing but also pointed to the importance of color balance. According to Eder, "Du Hauron was the first to describe the screen colorplate process. He also pointed out the necessity of adjusting the screen by such an arrangement of color elements that it would appear gray."

Another basic contribution to photography and process color reproduction is the discovery of photographic color sensitizers made by Dr. Herman Wilhelm Vogel (1834–1898), published in 1873. His discovery paved the way for color reproduction.

Much more work was necessary before process color printing became practical. However, by the end of the nineteenth century, this result had been achieved. The lead was with letterpress printing; gravure followed in second place. Collotype was the only branch of Senefelder's chemical printing that counted in process color reproduction. Lithography lay dormant; color process work was plainly beyond the scope of stone lithography.

The Offset Press

The offset press and photomechanics are the foundation of contemporary lithography. Of these two, the offset press is the more important contribution because without it, photomechanics would not have been nearly as successful. Direct rotary presses established themselves for general use but died out once the offset press had found acceptance. Direct printing put a much too heavy burden on the photomechanical plates. Only indirect printing made modern long-run lithography from photomechanical plates possible.

The Origin of the Offset Press

The basic offset principle was known for a long time before the paper offset press was introduced. In fact, offset presses were used for metal lithography long before they were adapted to paper use.

The first metal decorating presses were lithographic stone presses equipped with an intermediate cylinder. In 1875, an English patent was granted to R. Barclay, of Barclay & Fry, for such a press. The intermediate cylinder had a surface of specially treated cardboard for transferring the inked design to the sheet metal. Shortly thereafter a rubber blanket was substituted for the cardboard. Such presses were made in England around 1880.

There were also offset presses that could be used for either paper or metal, but strangely enough the offset method was never used for paper lithographing by the owners of these machines.

Harry A. Porter, retired senior vice president of the (then) Harris-Seybold Co., who not only participated in the early days of offset printing but also collected much valuable historical data, discussed the early days of offset printing at a meeting of the Detroit Litho Club on December 14, 1950. The following section is largely based on his notes.

Ira Rubel Develops the First Paper Offset Press

It is generally agreed that Ira W. Rubel was the first to develop an offset lithographic press specifi-

cally for the printing of paper. According to Porter, Ira Rubel operated a small paper mill in Nutley, N.J. There he made sulfite bond and converted it lithographically into bank deposit slips.

At the time Rubel developed his offset press, presumably during 1904 and 1905, lithographic stone presses had a rubber blanket on the surface of their impression cylinder. Whenever the feeder operator, missed feeding a sheet when the press was operating, the ink image was transferred to the rubber blanket from the stone. The following sheet would then be printed on both sides because the rubber blanket transferred the ink image to the back side of the sheet. This unintentionally made transfer produced a print superior to that made directly from stone, because the soft blanket conformed to the contours of the paper surface while the hard stone did not. Rubel noticed this and decided to use it as the basis of a printing press.

Like many other inventors, Ira Rubel had insufficient capital. He joined forces with a Chicago lithographer, A. B. Sherwood, forming the Sherbel Syndicate. The policy of the syndicate was to admit only one lithographer in a territory and thereby to monopolize the new invention. Approximately twelve presses were placed in this manner. These presses were built by the Potter Printing Press Co. of Plainfield, N.J. The Potter Printing Press Co. was merged in 1927 with Harris, and the company name was changed to Harris-Seybold-Potter Co. The engineer who redesigned the original Rubel Press at Potter was Irving F. Niles, later chief engineer of the Harris Automatic Press Co.

Apparently, there was internal trouble in the Sherbel Syndicate. In 1906, Rubel went to England and took an offset press along, the first ever installed there. The manufacture of this machine was undertaken by a firm of Lancashire engineers, but Rubel died in 1908 and the project didn't prosper.

The plan to monopolize the offset press proved unworkable. Competition was keen; those who had offset presses took advantage of them and made their competitors who were outside the syndicate look for an independent source of supply. They found it in the Harris Automatic Press Co.

Harris Enters the Picture

According to Porter, who was then working for the Harris Automatic Press Co., some time prior to June 1906, a Harris salesman tried to sell a rotary stone press, developed by Harris, to the Goes Lithograph Co. in Chicago. Charles B. Goes was not at all interested in this type of machine but said that if Harris could make him a machine such as he described, he would be interested.

The salesman returned with Charles G. Harris, who was the inventive genius of the Harris Company at that time. They then returned to Niles, the seat of the Harris Company, and from the ideas developed, work was immediately started on an offset press designed and built around the sheetfed letterpress machine that was known as the S4, the same size as the S4L 22×30. Different frames were designed, using three cylinders instead of two.

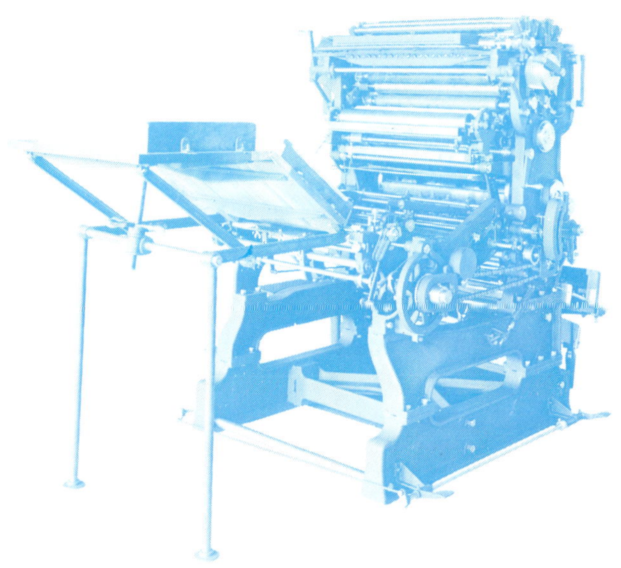

The first Harris offset press.

A. F. Harris had witnessed the offset effect in 1898 while installing a Harris Envelope Press in the plant of the Enterprise Printing Co. in Cleveland, Ohio. The feeder missed a sheet, and Harris, who was at that time not conversant with lithography, got a demonstration of offset printing then and there. He remembered this incident when his company was asked to build an offset press. The Harris brothers were builders of rotary letterpress equipment and thus experienced in the design of rotary printing machinery. Starting in October, four presses were shipped by Harris during 1906; six more presses were shipped in 1907.

The Impact of the Offset Press

The offset press was the talk of lithography, as can be seen from the trade press. Beginning in September 1906, the *National Lithographer* ran various

articles inquiring about, repeating rumors about, speculating about, and quoting others concerning the "rubber blanket off-set press." The main mystery was that if these new presses printed as quickly and cleanly as everybody reported, then why were the manufacturers "keeping so quiet about them"?

Then, in April 1907, the *National Lithographer* announced, under the headline "Off-set Press a Success," that the rubber blanket offset press was no longer a mystery. "We have finally been able to get a practical demonstration of its workings." The job being run was a fine letterhead on a good quality of bond paper. It had been engraved for a stone press, and therefore had to be retransferred to the zinc plate of the offset press. An attempt had previously been made, the magazine said, to print this job from the stone on dry paper, but the attempt was unsuccessful. It was then put on the offset press and run at the rate of more than 4,000 sheets per hour. "The finished product was as good as could possibly be done from stone with damped paper. comparable to a piece of work as the writer ever saw turned out lithographically."

This same press, on another job of bond paper, was speeded up to 7,200 sheets per hour and ran beautifully. "This settles the question of the practicability of the offset press for commercial work—at least as far as the Harris Automatic model is concerned. A press that will turn out over 7,000 sheets of bond paper in an hour, printed dry, and bring out every line and letter perfectly, has certainly passed the experimental stage. The Harris Automatic Rubber Blanket Off-Set Press has revolutionized commercial lithography."

Naturally, the offset press was not welcomed with the same enthusiasm by everybody in the lithographic industry. The subject was quite controversial and, as is often the case, also emotional. The *National Lithographer* was criticized for "booming" the offset press even though its "columns do not contain the advertisement of such a press, but, on the other hand, do contain advertisements of other styles of presses" (December 1907). The editor answered that "the editorial pages of this paper are not controlled by the advertisers." As for the offset press, "We believe it to be the salvation of the commercial lithographer." The offset press, no doubt, in part owed its acceptance to the favorable articles written in the *National Lithographer* by its editor, Warren C. Browne.

Commercial and Color Lithography

The offset press was originally intended for commercial lithography but not for color lithography. According to the then-accepted definitions, commercial lithographic originals were "engraved on stone or sheet," whereas color lithography was the appropriate designation when the original was "drawn on stone, zinc, or aluminum" (Porter).

Commercial lithography produced business and bank stationery, mainly in black and white; color lithography produced greeting cards, labels, posters, etc. It wasn't very long until the offset press was very successfully used for color work. Its advantage over the stone and direct rotary presses was thereby established in both branches of lithography. As time passed, the offset press became the dominant lithographic printing machine.

The Growth of the Offset Press

According to Harry Porter, 560 offset presses were in operation at the end of 1912. These presses had been built by eight different concerns and were of at least ten different sizes. *The Lithographers Journal* (Vol. II, June 1916, p. 9) states that 847 offset presses were in operation in the United States and Canada by the middle of 1916.

Every element of the press has been developed since the beginning of the twentieth century. The first offset presses were hand-fed; mechanical feeders followed several years later; then came proof presses. In 1914, Walter Scott & Co. installed perfecting offset presses for the printing of newspaper supplements in New York. Web offset presses and multicolor presses followed. Now the offset lithographic press is a marvel of efficiency and perfection, second to no other printing machine.

Lithography in the Twentieth Century

The lithographic offset press made modern lithography possible, and photomechanics made it practical; together they account for much of its success. It took some time until modern offset lithography became generally accepted. Approximately twenty-five years after the introduction of the offset press, it dominated the field almost completely. Stone lithography had ceased to exist as a commercial

printing process and was mainly used as an artistic medium. Direct lithography from metal plates, never too successful as an all-around method, was more and more replaced by the offset press. The offset press grew and developed at an increasing rate. Press sizes and running speed increased; multicolor presses as well as perfectors became available.

Huebner, the most prolific inventor of the graphic arts in the first half of the twentieth century.

Huebner and the Photocomposer

William C. Huebner, an American lithographer, was the first to grasp the full potential of offset lithography combined with photomechanics. From 1906 to 1912, Huebner invented many machines and processes that have since become commonly used in lithography.

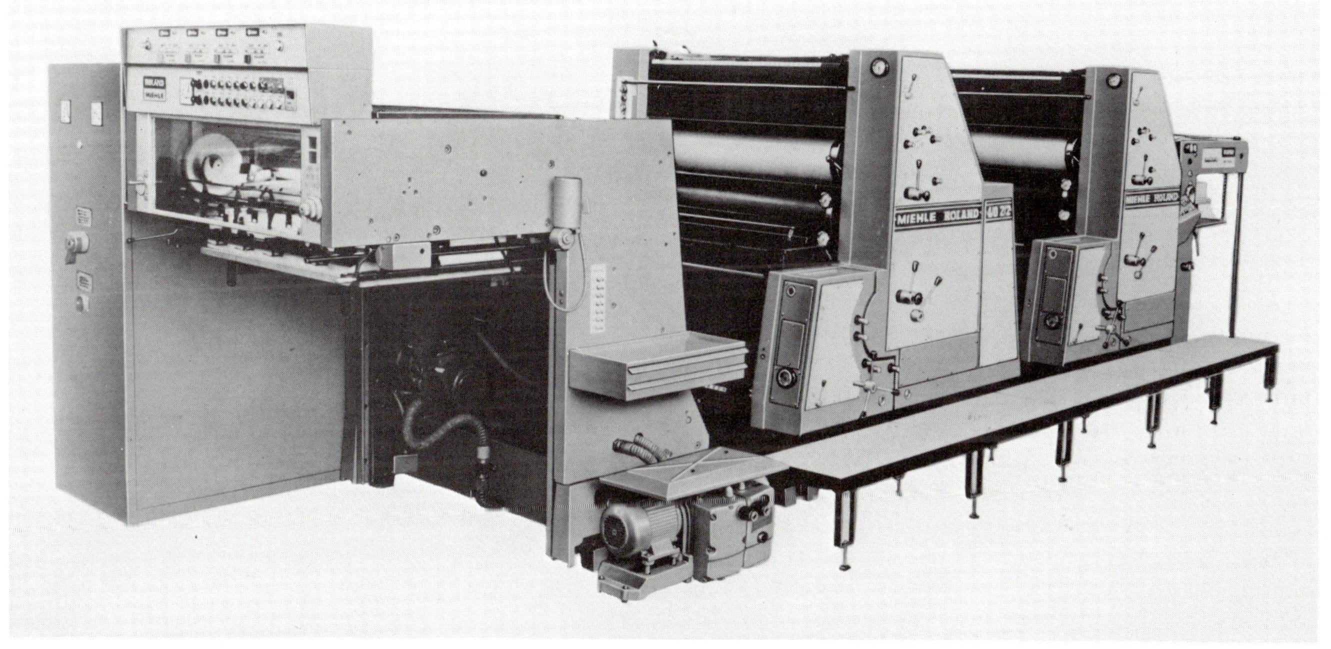

Courtesy Rockwell International

Miehle-Roland 40-in. sheetfed perfecting press, convertible to print four colors on one side of the sheet or two on each side.

The Nature of Lithographic Progress

The continued growth of lithography is not the result of a single advance; it is due to many improvements in every phase of the process. Many people and companies played, and continue to play, important roles in this process. Constant improvements in photographic materials and techniques, papers, inks, rollers, and blankets, as well as in plates and presses, have made lithography what it is now. More recently, advancements in computer hardware and software, specifically desktop publishing technologies, have had the greatest impact on the industry.

Most of these improvements are made outside of the lithographic shop or plant and are therefore too easily overlooked. Understand, however, that it takes a long time and a sizable investment before an improvement of lasting value is created. It is, unfortunately, not possible to go into the wide variety of improvements in all fields that have contributed so much to lithographic technology. No sketch of lithographic history can omit William C. Huebner, the most prolific inventor of the graphic arts in the first half of the twentieth century.

The invention of the photocomposing, or step-and-repeat, machine in 1906 is one of Huebner's major contributions to lithography. This invention made it possible to produce press plates bearing multiple images with a precision never before considered possible. Huebner made multiple-image process color plates in 1907. Huebner was one of the pioneers of lithographic process color reproduction. In 1910, he reproduced a photograph of orchids in four colors. The separations had been made direct from the object.

The Lithographic Plate and the Founding of LTF

At first, it may seem odd that the lithographic plate and the founding of the Lithographic Technical Foundation (LTF) are discussed under the same heading, but these subjects are very closely related.

The plate was the most important source of problems in lithography during the first half of this century. The plate was also the problem source closest to the printer. All other elements in lithography were either not at all or only to a very small degree subject to change by the average printer. Presses, paper, ink, photographic materials, rollers, and blankets are all manufactured by specialized industries, but the plate was made in the lithographic shop. It was possible to purchase plates from firms specializing in platemaking, but these firms were not much better equipped to cope with the problems of the lithographic plate than many printing shops.

The quality of the plate is important in many respects. For one, it is decisive for the quality of the final lithographic print. Another point is plate life, which has a great influence on run length and costs. Photomechanical platemaking is a complex process. The effort necessary to control this process could never be made by an individual lithographic shop of average size. The solution to the plate problem had to wait until the industry began to do cooperative research—until LTF was in existence.

Two kinds of photomechanically made plates were used in lithography up to the end of the Second World War: albumin plates and deep-etch plates. Albumin was first used by Poitevin as already mentioned; deep-etch plates have a long history in which many inventors participated. J. S. Mertle, in *Photolithography and Offset Printing,* credits the Reverend Hannibal Goodwin with having made "one of the first attempts toward the reversal of photomechanical images on metal plates," which he patented in 1881. Many other inventors did further work on lithographic deep-etch plates.

The real change in platemaking techniques, however, had to wait for LTF, which was founded in the early 1920s. (For further details see Chapter 2.) Not all plate problems were eliminated from lithography, but the plate ceased to be the problem child of lithography through the efforts of LTF. In the middle of the twentieth century, lithographic platemaking became a field of activity for the supply industry.

Chronologically, deep-etch and bimetallic plates preceded presensitized plates, which appeared in the 1950s. In the 1960s, "wipe-on" plates came into commercial use, and it was in the 1960s that lithography overtook letterpress to become the predominant printing process.

Chapter 2

GATF: Trailblazer in the Graphic Arts

History of the Foundation

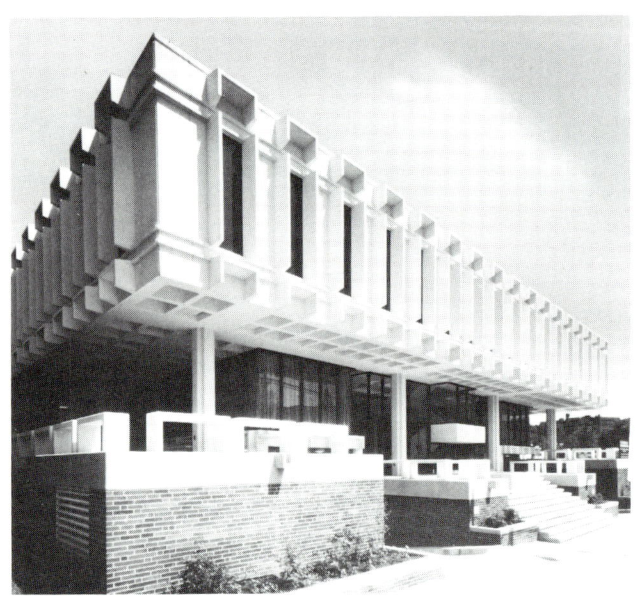

GATF Technical Center in Pittsburgh.

In the early 1920s, lithography was a small, struggling part of the printing industry. In 1923, only 328 plants in the entire United States, ones largely engaged in specialty printing, could be classified as lithographic. Most of these shops were still printing from stone, and the offset press was still relatively new. Lithography was an unwieldy process that was difficult to master; it was an art craft, the chemistry and physics of which remained to be explored.

The Founding of LTF

The idea of a cooperative research and educational effort by the lithographic industry was first voiced in 1921 by William H. Merten at the annual convention of the National Association of Employing Lithographers (NAEL). At the 1923 NAEL convention, Alfred B. Rode followed up on the idea, proposing the formation of the Lithographic Technical Foundation, whose "principal purposes and objects" would be the "training and education of lithographic workmen, the promotion and maintenance of lithographic trade schools, the investigation of subjects of a scientific or technical character which relate to lithographic processes, and other similar purposes and objects." The proposal was received with such great enthusiasm that, within one half hour, over $100,000 was pledged to support LTF.

On April 21, 1924, the Lithographic Technical Foundation (LTF) was incorporated. It was the job of Alfred Rode, the first president of LTF, and the twelve directors to raise funds for the fledgling organization. The industry continued to respond enthusiastically, contributing, by the close of the fund-raising campaign, approximately three-quarters of a million dollars. This money comprised the Foundation's endowment, the interest from which would be used for operating expenses.

Research beginnings. Research work began in March 1925 at the University of Cincinnati under the direction of Robert F. Reed. It was the first organized research effort in the graphic arts; thus, there was no background of scientific knowledge on which to build. Reed began with the basics, identifying precisely the physical and chemical requirements that the lithographic process placed on paper. Before the end of the year, he completed the first Foundation bulletin, "The Characteristics of Paper," which was published in 1926. The relationship between paper, relative humidity, and temperature was established, leading to the development

of the paper hygroscope, the first in what was to become a long line of devices and materials directly resulting from LTF research.

Another early concern was that of plates and platemaking. After studying the light sensitivity of bichromated coatings, Reed arrived at a single coating formula that would yield optimum results. He also began researching plate processing procedures and techniques, which remained a major research concern for the next thirty years. The deep-etch process, a method for increasing plate life, was also investigated, and a copper-aluminum deep-etch plate, called Lithengrave, was perfected. On another front, the Research Department developed Lithotine, a washup solvent that does not cause dermatitis or destroy litho blankets.

The major development in ink studies was simply a change in the understanding of lithographic inks. Robert Reed and others began explaining the performance of lithographic inks in terms of tack, or the way in which ink splits, which explained the causes and influences of many lithographic press problems. Ink research led to the development of the Bench Inkometer, which measured the tack of a given sample of ink.

Research in the early years progressed rapidly even though there were never more than four full-time researchers for the first twenty years. Many problems yielded to solution simply because all they required was an analysis conducted in an orderly fashion.

First education office. On September 1, 1925, an education office was opened in New York City under the direction of Dr. Layton S. Hawkins. Initially, publication of the results of LTF research was the extent of LTF education activities. This situation existed partly because of limited resources, but mostly because of inadequate knowledge of the technology. It must be remembered that before the formation of the LTF Research Department, no organization was subjecting lithographic technical problems to continuous investigation.

A major obstacle to lithographic education was the lack of textbooks and training materials. Hawkins tackled this problem by hiring Dr. David J. McDonald (who later became education director) to write some texts. McDonald began by making an analysis of the single-color offset press operator's trade, which served as the basis for a seven-unit textbook entitled *The Single-Color Offset Press.* He also wrote a text on hand transferring and one on color correcting. When the first textbook was published in 1928, the covers, design, paper, plates, printing, and binding were contributed by members, setting a precedent for subsequent Foundation publications.

In the late 1920s, the Education Department arranged with New York University to conduct a series of evening courses in lithography that covered a range of subjects, including management, sales, science, and technology. The courses consisted of both lectures and plant visits. Other "hands-on" courses, principally in platemaking and camera work, were added later. In the summer of 1936, the Foundation conducted a ten-week intensive course in lithography for college graduates and undergraduates preparing for careers in lithography. Some of the participants in the course subsequently became industry leaders. The course continued to be offered throughout the next decade.

Reorganization

The stock market crash in 1929 and the subsequent depression hit LTF hard. Some companies that had pledged contributions to be paid in five equal annual installments were unable to complete their payments and some of the Foundation's investments stopped paying dividends or interest. It was necessary to dip into the endowment itself, and the directors and a few other good friends of LTF were frequently called upon for special contributions to make up deficits. The Foundation also entered into a contract in 1940 for the compounding, packaging, marketing, and distribution of several of its original formulae. Still, income was insufficient to cover even the modest budgets of those years (about $38,000 per annum).

During this period, Alfred Rode submitted his resignation, and Edward H. Wadewitz, who had been a director, was elected president in 1944. In his new position, Wadewitz led a major reorganization effort, doubling the Foundation's endowment, substantially increasing its operating budget, and laying the groundwork for the numerous research and educational programs developed in the postwar period. Many of these achievements were a result of the ten-point program that he developed on the basis of an extensive survey of the industry. This program was used as the principal selling tool in a highly successful fund-raising effort.

Another result of his program was increased geographic and industry representation, bringing in new people, new ideas, and new interests. The position of executive director was also created and first filled by Wade Griswold, who served in that capacity for twelve years.

In the fund-raising campaign of 1944, LTF sought not only contributions to the endowment but also, for the first time, membership support in the form of annual dues, which would be used for current operating expenses. Also, the endowment funds were separated from the operating funds.

In 1945, through an agreement with Armour Research Foundation of Illinois Institute of Technology, the Foundation moved its Research Department to Glessner House in Chicago with new and improved equipment and an expanded staff. Postwar research shifted back into gear under the direction of Michael H. Bruno, the new research manager. (Robert Reed had become a research consultant.) New plate surface treatments were investigated, and the Cronak and Brunak treatments were developed. Further improvements were made in the processing of deep-etch plates, and standards for plate graining were established. A stopping-out solution that simplified the processing of positive-working plates was also developed. Two new instruments of fundamental importance came out of LTF during this period: a packing gauge to aid press operators in controlling cylinder pressures and a sensitivity guide that permits evaluation of exposure and development before mounting a plate on the press. A cellulose gum substitute for gum arabic was developed, and investigation of ink drying mechanisms began.

Between 1923 and 1953, the lithographic industry grew tenfold. The entire industry had become more conscious of the importance of research. Suppliers began to create in-house research departments, and printers began to assemble sophisticated technical staffs in their plants. Out of postwar Germany came the concept of a revolutionary image carrier: the presensitized plate. These developments and others caused the lithographic dollar volume to increase two and one-half times between 1950 and 1957.

The fifties were a golden age for LTF research. There was also a gradual shift in emphasis from the constituents of the process (paper, ink, plates, press) to the way in which these elements interact. An example is the development of the Press Inkometer, a refinement of the Bench Inkometer, which is a highly effective monitor of ink/water balance. Another device developed in the fifties was the pick tester, which evaluated a sheet of paper's potential for picking before it was run on the press. A study of doubling and slurring led to the design of the Star Target, the first of a series of test images.

Postwar consumer demand led to heavier competition in consumer markets, creating a sharp increase in demand for color printing, especially full-color process work. The Research Department responded to the growth in color printing by promoting a photographic masking system that eliminated much of the need for laborious manual methods of color correcting and by developing the LTF color chart.

It was after the move to Chicago that technical services started gradually and rather informally as the Research Department began to receive letters and calls from member plants for help with technical problems. Because of limited resources, answering technical inquiries had to take second place to the research that was to benefit the whole industry. However, as lithography grew in the postwar period, the rapidly increasing number of technical inquiries could be neither ignored nor handled effectively without changing the structure of the organization. By 1960, the number of inquiries was doubling annually. Answering them often involved extensive testing and sometimes required traveling to the plant site, all of which was handled by research personnel who were involved in other projects. The decision was made to create a Technical Services Division, staffed by its own personnel, to relieve the other research divisions of the burden of these services.

Another division, the Reduction to Practice Division, was responsible for translating research findings into practical procedures to be used in plants. Headed by Edward J. Martin, it was in charge of platemaking, press testing, materials testing, and printing research publications.

Lithographic Technical Forums also evolved at Glessner House and became so popular that they began to be held all over the United States. These one-and-a-half-day programs were designed for large audiences and covered all major aspects of the lithographic process. The first Color Seminars were given in 1957 and, likewise, became so popular that they were immediately expanded both in the number offered and in the subjects covered. The seminars were small, three-day, intensive educational programs designed for limited audiences (ten to twenty) that focused on a specific technical aspect of printing.

The Administration and Education Departments also moved, locating in a building purchased by the Foundation in New York City. At about this time, Charles Shapiro began his long association with the Foundation, first as education director. Because of the rapid growth of the lithographic industry, training became a major focus of the Education staff. Craft tests, textbooks, manuals, complete courses,

and teaching and training materials poured out of the department to fill the existing void.

In addition, alternatives to printed media were explored with the intent of improving the total effectiveness of training and education. Some of these were pioneering efforts in the industrial application of audiovisual media. In 1949, the Research Department, still somewhat involved in education, sponsored one of the earliest closed-circuit television technical education programs. The use of filmstrips in education was also developed at this time.

Broadening the Scope

In 1959, when William Webber took the helm as executive director, the Foundation entered a period of sustained growth. This growth was marked by many changes, both in the industry and in the direction of the Foundation. By this time, lithography was no longer a minor printing process. In fact, its growth rate outstripped that of the two other major processes, becoming the dominant process, for which much of the credit belongs to LTF. Many of the problems specific to lithography had been solved, and research was inevitably leading into areas that were common to all printing processes. In addition, both the Research and the Education departments were outgrowing their facilities.

In 1961, a long-range plans committee was set up to study the direction of the Foundation and determine what changes would make it more effective. After two years of careful analysis, the committee presented its conclusions and recommendations, which were unanimously approved by the board of directors. Thus, in 1963, the Lithographic Technical Foundation officially became the Graphic Arts Technical Foundation, a name that reflected its broadening scope. Another recommendation was the consolidation of the Research, Education, and Administration departments under one roof to increase efficiency. Accordingly, a search for an appropriate location for the new headquarters building and a fund-raising drive to finance its construction were begun. The site finally chosen, in Pittsburgh, Pennsylvania, had much to recommend it: 135 research and technical organizations in the vicinity, a large number of scientific and technical personnel, several major scientific libraries, and a variety of specialized laboratories and research instruments.

William Webber retired in 1974 and Gilbert W. Bassett took over as executive director. In his fourteen year stint, Bassett established the Marketing and Production Departments and increased the functions of the Education Department to include specialized teacher education programs for graphic arts teachers: teacher institutes (two-week intensive courses held at GATF's Technical center), Teacher Internships, Teacher Conferences (two-and-one-half-day events held at Graph Expo and Print shows), and Teacher Seminars (one-day programs held at various locations around the country). Bassett also spearheaded Project 80, which was an $868,000 renovation of GATF's technical center and the addition of $2.8 million in equipment. Renovations included construction of a Color Center, Web Center, and new lecture hall with tiered seating. Under Bassett's direction, the Foundation grew from an organization with an operating budget of $1.4 million and 1,000 corporate members to $5.3 million and over 3,000 corporate members.

The Foundation Today

GATF's Mission:

> *"To serve the graphic communications community as the major resource for technical information and services through research and education."*

Today, GATF is a member-supported, nonprofit, scientific, technical, and educational organization that serves the international graphic communications industries. Its fundamental purpose is to continue the scientific progress of those industries that are basic to the graphic communication of information, ideas, and knowledge.

Programs at GATF cover all major graphic processes and related areas, including environmental control, training and education, statistical process control, and occupational health and safety, to name a few.

The industry, as a whole, benefits from GATF in four basic areas: research; scientific, technical, and craft education; technical services; and technical information. Each area encompasses a variety of activities.

GATF's facilities feature a wide range of scientific instruments, tools, and machinery for studies and instruction in electronic imagesetting, photography, image assembly, platemaking, color reproduction,

press operation, ink and paper chemistry, and quality control. The Foundation's pressroom is one of the most complete of any research center in the world. The E. H. Wadewitz Memorial Library houses one of the most extensive collections of technical literature in the field of graphic communications. Many educational seminars and workshops are conducted every year both at the Technical Center in Pittsburgh and at various locations around the world. The Foundation publishes books on just about every aspect of printing at various levels of difficulty; learning modules (step-by-step instructional booklets); audiovisuals (slide and audiocassette programs and videotapes); and scientific, technical, and educational reports. The Foundation also publishes a bimonthly magazine, entitled *GATFWORLD,* as a service to its members. The magazine contains technical articles that offer solutions to problems as well as profiles of emerging technology, reviews of specific products, and reports of activities within the industry. The SPC Newsletter is also published bimonthly. The newsletter serves as a forum for the exchange of statistical process control information as it applies to printing, and chronicles the activities and progress of the GATF SPC Users Group. The Users Group is dedicated to the promotion and implementation of statistical process control as a means for printers to improve quality and productivity.

The Foundation is staffed by researchers, educators, and technical specialists, all of whom are professionally trained and bring to the Foundation a wide range of experience in their respective fields, along with a strong awareness of the needs of the graphic communications industries.

GATF staff administrate the National Scholarship Trust Fund of the Graphic Arts, Inc., an organization that receives contributions from associations, companies, and individuals for disbursement of scholarships and fellowships to outstanding students who are enrolled in graphic communications programs in accredited colleges, universities, and technical schools. NSTF staff recruit and screen applicants annually.

The Foundation's boards and committees comprise some 300 representatives of member companies. It is these industry representatives who develop and, in large measure, direct the programs of GATF.

These members represent every facet of graphic communications: printers and packagers of every size, product, and process; book, magazine, and newspaper publishers with or without printing facilities; suppliers of ink, paper, chemicals, plates, and press and prepress equipment. Also, there are typographers, binderies, advertising and design houses, trade shops and photoengravers, research and development centers, colleges and universities, and students and teachers of graphic arts at every level of education. Over the years, the Foundation has changed remarkably to meet the needs of these members, but it has never swerved from its original purpose of advancing the industry through research and education.

Chapter 3

The Lithographic Process

The Stages of Printing

A number of basic steps are common to all printing processes. Whatever the means of graphic reproduction, the process starts with **original material** to be gathered, manipulated, and reproduced.

This original material consists of two different kinds: text and illustration/decoration. The first step in any graphic reproduction process is to render the material into printable form. For example, text must be typeset, and illustrations may have to be enlarged, reduced, or cropped.

The next step is to arrange the converted materials as they will appear in the printed piece. This arrangement is used to make an **image carrier,** a device that will transfer ink images to paper or other **substrate** (the material being printed on).

The final steps are printing—the transfer of the ink images to the substrate—and finishing operations—trimming, folding, binding, or other operations required to produce the final printed piece. But while these basic functions are part of all printing processes, the details of how the operations are executed may vary with each particular printing process. For example, in the original letterpress (or typographic) system, typesetting was accomplished by arranging individual metal types by hand into the proper sequence of words, lines, and columns set in metal trays called **galleys.** Type pages were made from these galleys, and often the pages were arranged into multipage forms. Locking up these forms completed the making of the image carrier. As later innovations were made in the letterpress process, the basic operations merged into one another, since the original types arranged in typesetting remained in the **image carrier.**

Following the completion of the image carrier, all processes then go through the printing impression stage, and most go through some finishing operations. The details again vary in the printing impression stage, but little, if at all, in the finishing operations.

The Nature of Lithography

Printing processes are most basically distinguished by their method of image carrying. Letterpress images are carried on the ink-holding faces of projections from the image carrier body. Gravure images are carried in the ink-holding indentations cut into the body of the carrier. Screen printing images are carried as the porous parts of the carrier, through which ink is pressed. Lithographic images are carried as a chemical distinction between the image areas and the nonimage areas on an essentially even surface. (The image areas hold ink; the dampened nonimage areas do not.) Lithographic image carriers were originally stones given a flat and polished surface. The surface repelled ink when wet, except where drawn upon with a material that repelled water but held on to ink.

Letterpress and stone lithography were in almost exactly opposite positions. Letterpress was badly limited in picture reproduction, but excellent in the printing of the written word. Stone lithography excelled in picture reproduction, but stone lithography was badly limited in its ability to duplicate the written word. Many books were produced by combining the two printing processes—the verbal message was printed by letterpress and the pictures by

engraving or lithography. The term "plate" was used to describe full-page illustrations put into books in this manner.

Stone lithography was originally and, for many decades, primarily a picture-printing process. It enriched the graphic arts, but did not change the existing division between printing processes used to reproduce textual and pictorial matter.

The Challenge of Photography

The printing industry remained virtually unchanged until the advent of photography. Photography brought a revolution to the graphic arts and created a demand for an entirely new kind of picture—one tied to the fleeting moment and impossible to reproduce by any printing process.

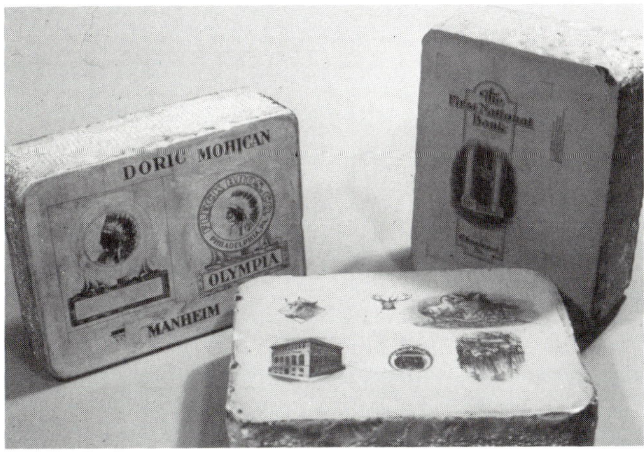

Lithographic stones made from Bavarian limestone.

But photography was not only a challenge to printing, it was also its great benefactor. Photography eventually achieved what had seemed impossible for centuries: the combining of pictures—including photographs—with reading matter into a single printing plate. And photography achieved this result not only for one or another graphic arts process but for all of them. The revolution that started more than a century ago is still going strong today, even into the era of electronic devices.

Lithography and photography. The relationship between lithography and photography is a very old one. Lithography actually stood at the cradle of photography. Joseph Nicéphore Niepce, a pioneer of photography, began his experiments in 1813 with lithography. The two arts have been related to each other ever since.

Lithography was the first printing process to make its whole printing plate—pictures and reading matter together—photographically and photomechanically. Today, photography dominates the whole area of prepress operations, although electronic processes are making rapid progress therein.

Modern Lithography

The basic principle of lithography has remained the same while the process has changed in many major ways. This principle is based on oil and water's resistance to being mixed.

The plate. Present-day lithographic plates are most commonly made of aluminum coated with a layer of a photosensitive material. There is a variety of plates with different characteristics affecting the way they are used. Most plates are exposed through imaged films, producing a surface that has been broken photochemically into two kinds of areas: (1) the nonimage areas, which accept water and, when damp, reject grease; and (2) the image areas, which reject water but accept grease.

Thus, when such a plate on a press is successively dampened and rolled with a greasy ink, only the image areas accept the printing ink. This is the basic principle of lithography.

The blanket. The overwhelming majority of contemporary lithographic presses use the *offset* method of indirect printing. For this reason lithographic printing has become widely known as *offset printing*.

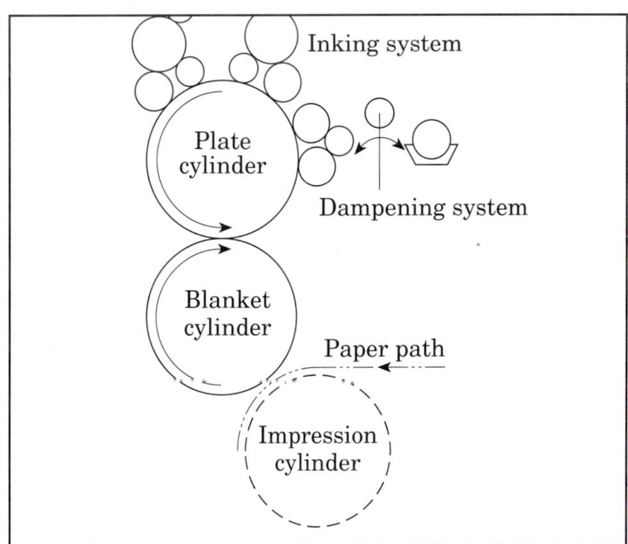

Offset lithographic printing.

In offset, or indirect, lithography, the inked plate image is not directly impressed on the paper or other printing stock but is transferred to an intermediate member, the blanket, which in turn makes the impression on the paper. Offset printing is an essential feature of modern lithography. Old-style lithography was printed directly on the paper, either from stones or from metal plates; modern lithography prints indirectly.

Offset printing has many consequences. One of them is the double-reversal of the plate image by the time it reaches the paper. Offset plates are therefore made *right-reading,* the image appearing just as it will on the paper, as compared to the *wrong-reading,* mirror-image requirement of direct printing image carriers.

A principal result of the offset method is its ability to print finer detail on coarser or structured papers than is possible in direct printing. The blanket is comparatively soft and elastic, enabling it to press ink into the valleys of the paper's surface without unduly squashing it.

Another important reason for offset printing in lithography is that the blanket is gentle on the plate images. The chemically established lithographic images are more fragile than those cut deeply into metal, and they could be abraded by rough paper. But the smooth blanket allows the plates to perform with consistency and endurance during the pressrun.

Rotary printing. The principle of rotary printing is not peculiar to lithography; it is used in many printing processes. But it is very important in contemporary offset printing. All modern lithographic printing is done on rotary presses. Rotary printing, other conditions being equal, is the fastest and most economical type of printing. The speed of offset printing and its comparatively simple makeready are well suited for rotary printing.

The Flow of Lithographic Production

The modern lithographic printing process may be divided into three main stages: prepress, press, and finishing. The progress of automation is merging operations into units within these stages. In some applications, for example, machines are being developed that integrate a number of prepress operations, and some bindery functions tend to be combined into continuous in-line operations. Yet, distinctly different functions continue to exist, however they may be joined.

The remainder of this book treats in detail the operations of lithographic production in their progressive sequence through prepress, press, and finishing. But, of course, the progress is not uniformly straight-line.

The preparation of type and art may proceed simultaneously (we have put typesetting first), some kinds of proofing may precede platemaking and some may follow it (we have put proofing before platemaking, although in past times proofing naturally followed platemaking and often still does), and so on.

And even before prepress operations get under way, there must be overall planning of the job. More detailed planning usually takes place within each operation stage as well. But the first consideration in getting production under way is **planning and control,** the topic of Chapter 4. The production operations, each of which has its individual planning and control aspects, follow.

Lithographic Prepress

Since lithography works with an even-surfaced image carrier, photomechanical platemaking preparation was a natural development. Interestingly, the success of photomechanical preparation in lithography led to the development of photochemical preparation of etched relief plates for letterpress.

Typography and typesetting. Before the development of phototypesetting, lithography relied upon the three-dimensional types of letterpress for its type matter. From these, two-dimensional images of typefaces were made—by pulling a **reproduction proof** or by other means—to enter the type matter into the photomechanical system. The obvious advantage for lithography of having two-dimensional type images to start with provided a powerful impetus to the development of phototypesetting.

Now phototypesetting, along with some occasional use of other two-dimensional type images such as press-on type, is far and away the predominant typesetting method for all printing processes. The development of typography (the science and art of the use of type) and the practice of typesetting are the subjects of Chapter 5.

Art and copy preparation. Besides the preparation of *type* matter, putting *art* into shape for repro-

Producing a printed piece.

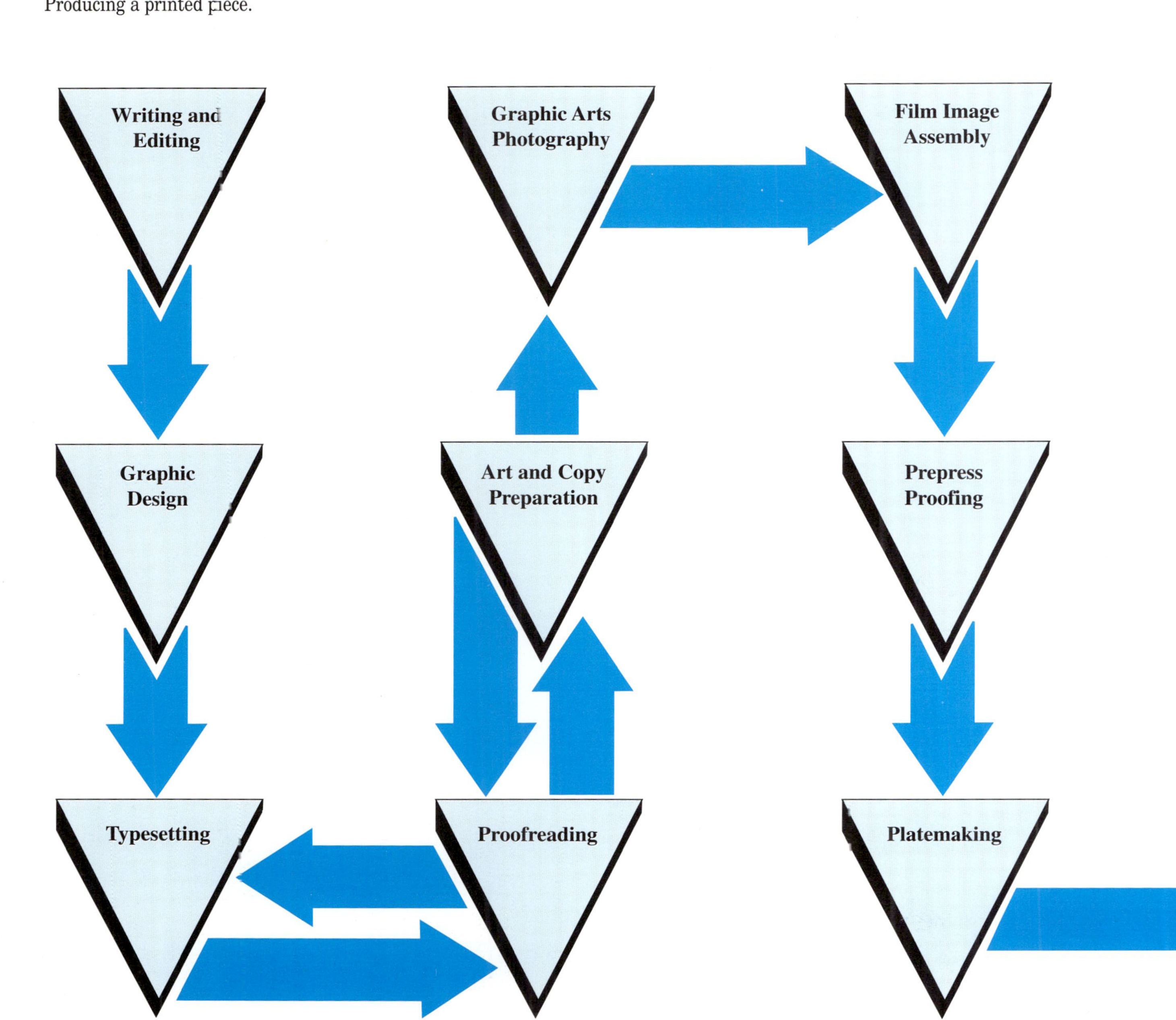

duction is also a necessary preparation. The "raw material" for typesetting is normally some kind of manuscript; but the inputs for art that come to the printer may be anything from suggestions, sometimes with rough sketches, to finished diagrams, drawings, and photographs.

One main part of art and copy preparation is putting this artwork into a form that can be reproduced. Some of the art elements as received may need no further preparation. But rough sketches must be drawn into finished forms. Photographs, both black-and-white and color, as well as other art that has variable tones or colors—such as paintings, which have both—receive special kinds of photographic preparation, discussed below under "Basic Camera Operation."

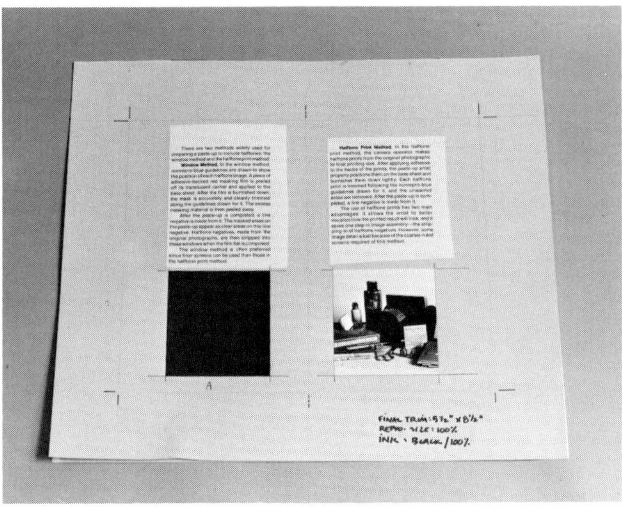

The pasteup, or mechanical.

Another main part of art and copy preparation is called *pasteup*. This operation puts the type matter from the phototypesetter, often in column form, into page form by attaching it, along with artwork, to a strong base sheet. The purpose of pasteup is to provide copy from which a photographic film reproduction is made for platemaking. Art and copy preparation is the subject of Chapter 6.

Basic camera operation. Some photographic operations are done by contact photography; but when reflection copy is used (as with a pasteup), or when a change of size is required, a *graphic arts camera* is necessary. This is a camera with a *flat field* lens system—one that receives light from a plane image copy and projects it as a light image accurately in focus at all points on a plane inside the camera.

Such a camera is used for several purposes besides making a film image of the pasteup. Original drawings are often made larger than the size at which they are to be printed; the camera can be used to reduce them to the reproduction size (or to enlarge any that are smaller). Photographs and other art that have variable tones must be converted into a form that can be reproduced by lithographic printing. A camera process called *screening* can be used for this purpose. Use of the graphic arts camera for such conversions is treated in Chapter 7.

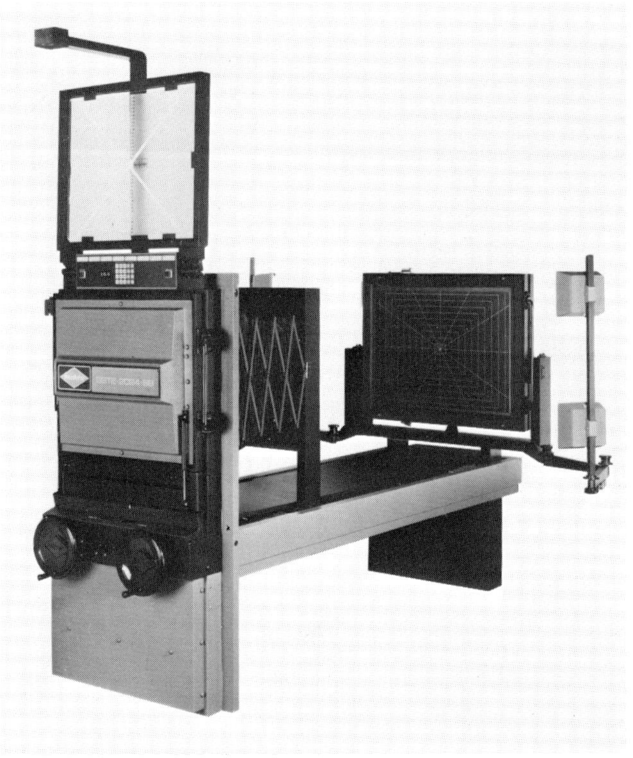

Courtesy nuArc Company

A horizontal graphic arts camera.

Color separation and correction. Full-color illustrations require an even more complicated treatment to prepare them for reproduction. Since a lithographic printing press requires a separate plate for each ink color used, the many color components mixed together in a full-color illustration must be separated by exposing the illustration successively through a series of color filters. This complex subject is treated in Chapter 8.

Film image assembly. A press typically prints several pages of a publication on each side of a press sheet. Therefore, all the photographic page images from which a printing plate is made are

combined on a form called a *flat.* This is used to expose the plate during platemaking. Furthermore, there must be a different plate for each color printed on any side of a press sheet. So for each color to be printed anywhere on a given side of a press sheet, each element to be printed in that color must have its component image in the proper place on the flat for that color. Assembling all these film images (which are usually negative images in the United States) in their exact places on the flats for platemaking is often referred to as *stripping.* Chapter 9 treats this subject of film image assembly, or stripping.

Proofing. There are many reasons for wanting to know how the printed piece is going to look before it is printed: whether the type matter is correct, whether all the intended elements of type, illustration, and decoration are present in their proper places, and what kind of visual effect it makes when it is put together.

The earlier any sources of dissatisfaction are discovered, the less troublesome and costly are the corrections. Typographical errors are best discovered and corrected during the typesetting operation in a process called *proofreading.* The photomechanical nature of modern prepress operations also makes it possible to check most of the other potential errors in the stages before making the plates and running off copies on a press. This is true even of full-color work, for which there are highly developed techniques of off-press color proofing.

That is why Chapter 10, which is concerned with all aspects of proofing except proofreading, precedes the chapter on platemaking. Nevertheless, especially with full-color work, customers may want proofs run on a press for final approval prior to the production pressrun.

Platemaking. After the photomechanical stages have been completed and proofed, platemaking from the flats is usually a relatively straightforward, automated operation. The plates are often purchased precoated with a photosensitive material. They are exposed, often with ultraviolet radiation, through the film image flats, and processed, often with automatic processors.

The resulting plate has a surface with two chemically different areas intermingled: the image areas that reject water and accept ink; and the nonimage areas that accept water and, when wet, reject ink. The various types of lithographic plates and the corresponding platemaking differences are the subjects of Chapter 11.

Electronic prepress. For several decades, most of the changes occurring in graphic communications could be classified as being evolutionary. In the last few years, however, graphic communications has been undergoing revolutionary changes, particularly in the prepress area, where the computer is now the focal point.

Chapters 5–11 of this book discuss what is now termed "conventional prepress." Many of the steps in prepress production can now be accomplished using computer-based systems. This area is now referred to as electronic prepress, which is the topic of chapter 12.

Type is now mostly commonly set using computers and sophisticated page-makeup programs that allow the user to precisely position text and graphic elements; plain-paper intermediate proofs are made using laser printers. Much of the artwork is also created using a computer, scanner, and various drawing packages. Imagesetters can output various image elements—e.g., text, graphics, halftone images, and screen tints—in position on film, photosensitive paper, or even lithographic printing plates. Color separation, film image assembly, and multicolor proofing have also been affected by the computer-based technologies.

Lithographic Press

The press is the point at which ink is applied to the paper from the plate. All the work that has been done on the project to create a printed piece from its conception to this point now resides in the images on the plates. The multiplication of these images is accomplished by the placement of ink on paper by a press.

Satisfactory use of ink and paper depend in good part on actions taken well before the pressrun begins: proper selection, storage, and handling practices.

Ink. Lithographic inks are *paste* inks. A particular ink is chosen for the type of press it will be used on (with respect to the drying system it has) and the requirements of the job (color, optical character recognition, scratch-and-sniff, etc.). Such matters are treated in Chapter 13. Ink control during the pressrun is part of presswork.

Paper. Paper is also selected for the type of press it will run on (e.g., sheetfed or web), for the characteristics of the general type of product (e.g., books, catalogs, maps, newspapers, packaging), and for the particular requirements of the job being run.

Chapter 14 deals with these subjects. Handling paper on press is a part of presswork.

Presswork. Plates are brought to the press from platemaking, paper is brought from paper storage, and ink is brought from ink stores, along with other materials and supplies, to prepare for the printing operation. Plates are mounted, a stack of paper is put into the sheet feeder or a roll (at least) of paper is mounted into the roll stand and threaded through the press, adjustments are made to various units, and the multiplication of printed images gets under way. After start-up adjustments, an OK print is established.

A multiplicity of monitoring, adjustment, and repair tasks are required during the run. Ink/water balance must be maintained, press sheets must be inspected, and web breaks must be repaired. Many variables must be controlled during a lithographic pressrun. But when preparations are good and operation careful, the runs can succeed. The topic of Chapter 15 is how best to achieve favorable results.

Technologically advanced equipment has also entered the pressroom. A new press, for example, may have a remote control console where the press operator can control and adjust various press functions, or it could be equipped with an automatic plate changer. One reproduction technology even enables the direct imaging of printing plates on the press from a computer front end.

Finishing

Finishing operations—cutting, folding, binding, and the like—are little influenced by the type of printing process used. A lithographic printer may use a trade bindery that does work for other types of printers, too. But that can be true for preparatory functions, such as typesetting, as well as finishing functions. And an account of the flow of lithographic production would not be complete without some consideration of the operations that complete the manufacture of the printed product.

These can be quite varied, and sometimes there are none at all, but they usually include at least folding and often gathering (the bringing together of the unit printed piece's parts, such as folded sections), binding, and trimming. These operations, including varieties of binding methods, are the subject of Chapter 16.

Chapter 4

Planning and Control

The quality and efficiency of every printing operation is affected by the structure of the organization, equipment, policies, planning, and systems of control in which it is performed. The environment in which a product is manufactured starts with the plant facilities and workplace equipment. It also includes the organizational structure and procedures by means of which funds, people, equipment, and materials are obtained and managed for productive purposes. Organizational controls for the production processes are often categorized as *production control* and *quality control,* although these are not entirely distinct. Production control consists of the mechanics—forms, devices, and specified procedures—by which the flow of work is guided effectively through its various stages. Job estimating is an adjunct to production control. Quality control consists of the specifications, devices, and inspections by which quality standards are maintained throughout the entire production process.

Plant and Workplace

The subjects of *plant location* and *plant design and layout* do not arise very often in a given company, but they are of great importance when they do. GATF's *Printing Plant Layout and Facility Design Handbook* is a helpful guide when those subjects arise.

Special attention is given here to the principles of plant layout that are generally applicable to most lithographic plants. The options involved in choosing a plant location can be given only cursory treatment by mentioning some major factors: proximity to markets when fast service is necessary, availability of adequate transportation facilities for both receiving and sending shipments, availability of potential employees, wage levels, and rental costs or land and construction costs.

Plant Layout

Regarding plant layout, the first consideration is whether the planning is for a new building or an existing one. The building should be thought of as part of a production machine, and a new structure should be built to fit a predesigned layout planned for the best possible production flow. The lithographer should work with the architect in planning the building. When the building already exists, floor plans and same-scale templates of equipment should be used to develop the best layout for the given structure.

The first principle of plant layout is to provide for **direct product flow** with minimum travel from one operation to the next, without backtracking. The line need not be straight—it can be L- or U-shaped, for example—as long as it proceeds with minimum distance from point to point. Material handling, or the movement of product through a printing plant, is estimated to account for 60% of all direct and indirect labor costs.

Another principle of plant layout is **separation of office and manufacturing** functions. In the earlier days of the printing industry, manufacturing included typesetting, but now all prepress operations are included in the "office" category. The distinction is based on the need for cleanliness and quiet in office areas versus the large, noisy, often

high-ceilinged and heavily trafficked environment of the manufacturing areas.

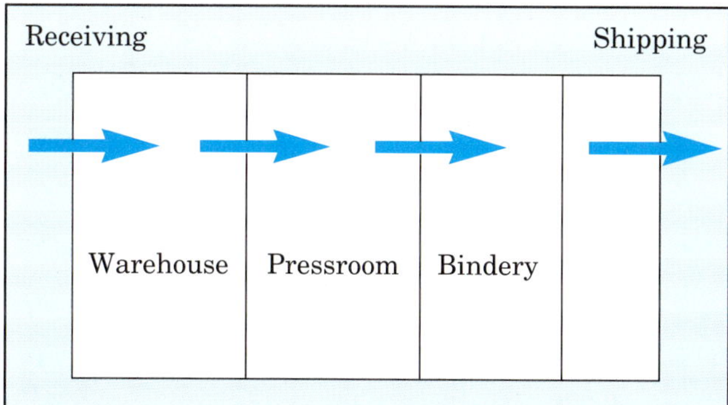

A plant layout showing direct product flow.

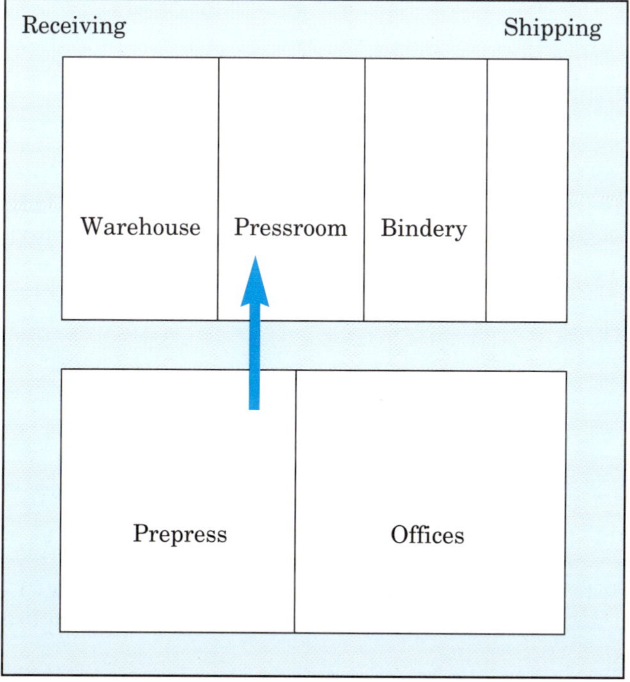

Using two separate buildings to physically separate manufacturing facilities from offices.

Office and prepress areas are designed to promote concentration on particular tasks. The type of environment suited for estimating, accounting, and other traditional office operations has long been understood. However, all prepress operations now require the same environment.

Like business offices, prepress operations ordinarily do not require ceilings more than 10 ft. (3 m) high. There is a natural flow from the business offices into the production management offices—for estimating and production control—and on into the prepress operations.

The press and bindery operations, on the other hand, along with associated receiving/shipping and warehousing functions, can utilize space more effectively in rugged, higher-ceilinged areas so that tall, heavy equipment can be accommodated and skids of paper in sheets, rolls of paper, skids of printed signatures, and bound materials can be stacked vertically, making fullest use of cubic space in a given floor area.

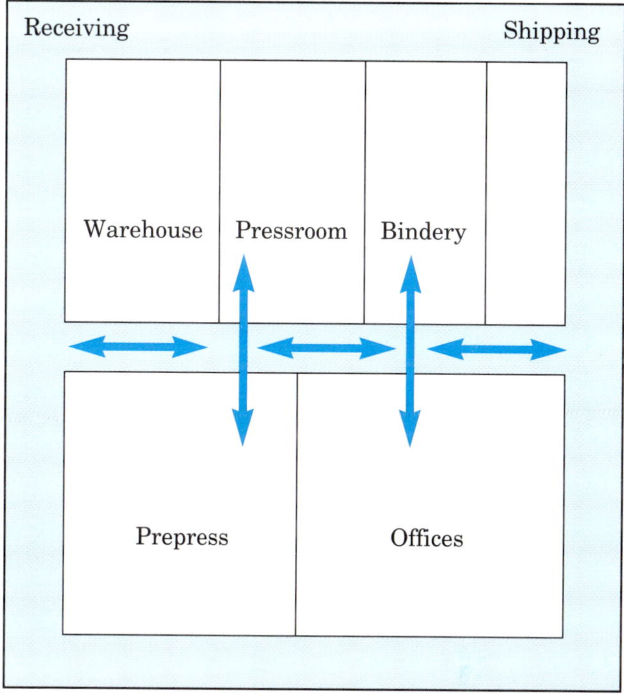

Using a long corridor to physically separate manufacturing facilities from offices.

The physical separation of the manufacturing areas from the office and prepress areas also protects each from the environment of the other. The plateroom atmosphere is kept free of antisetoff powder. The creative areas are kept free of noise and work-in-process traffic. The manufacturing areas should also be kept free of unnecessary visits from customers. The two functions might be housed in separate buildings or have a distinct separation within a building, with a long corridor or hallway between them.

Providing for **expansion** without damaging established layout principles is an important consideration of plant layout. If the office/prepress and the manufacturing functions have been established in a separated but side-by-side direct-flow manner, and space is available for outward expansion of a particular capacity, such as that of the pressroom,

then such expansion can be made without disrupting the overall pattern already in effect in the printing plant.

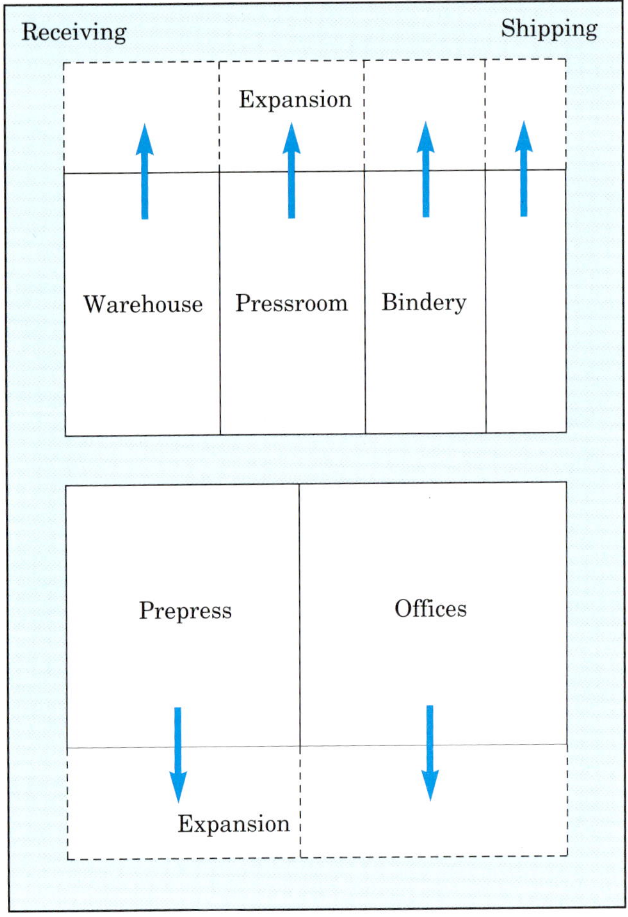

A plant designed with the room to expand without destroying flow and separation.

Equipment and Workplace

Policies and procedures for the acquisition, arrangement, and maintenance of equipment play a vital role in effective operations.

The purchase of equipment is an occasional requirement either to provide for expansion or to replace machinery that has worn out or been made obsolete by new technology. Obsolescence is an important factor in areas of rapid technological advancement. Equipment addition and replacement policies are part of financial planning. At this point, attention is given only to the matters considered in choosing a particular piece of equipment after the decision to add or replace has been made. The first requirement is that the equipment will perform the needed functions *adequately*. "Adequate" should include safety, speed, and quality considerations.

The price of the equipment and the cost of its installation must be evaluated when assessing whether its *cost* lies within available capital resources. The need for additional space, special floors or floor coverings, electrical wiring, acoustical tile, and environmental controls are other possible considerations.

GATF also recommends a skills inventory survey of the work force (see suggested form on page 4:4) for estimating the financial allocation necessary not only for outside installers, but also for hiring or training maintenance and operating personnel for the new equipment.

When new equipment is acquired, or when any new operation is set up, **workplace layout** warrants careful planning. In the case of workplaces that are dominated by large machines, layout planning is a localized part of plant layout, using the same principles.

Maintenance management is another aspect of equipment that needs to be planned. In a large plant, there is usually a maintenance department. It ordinarily has a staff relationship to the production organization; that is, it works through the production manager. But even if a plant is not big enough to have a separate maintenance department, it should have an organized maintenance function. In the face of increased mechanization and complexity, tighter production control and delivery schedules, and stricter quality requirements, good maintenance control becomes increasingly important.

On the theory that it is cheaper to prevent breakdowns than to repair them, the organization of maintenance should be built around **preventive maintenance.**

Plantwide maintenance starts with keeping facilities in good repair and with careful housekeeping. Keeping oil off the floor and trip-causing items out of aisles, for example, are preventive maintenance in the sense that they help prevent accidents.

Preventive maintenance, which is more commonly associated with the maintenance of machinery, consists of scheduled inspection, cleaning, lubrication, and parts adjustment, repair, or replacement. Generally, machinery needs frequent inspection while it is new and when it is very old. Other factors that should affect the inspection schedule include the heaviness of use and the value of the equipment.

A carefully established lubrication schedule for each machine is important. The manufacturer's

Skills Inventory

Name ______________________________ Date ____________

Present position ______________________________ Years ____________

Past positions:

1. ______________________________ Years ____________
2. ______________________________ Years ____________
3. ______________________________ Years ____________

Specific skills:

1. ______________________________
2. ______________________________
3. ______________________________

Training received: ______________________________

____

Education (circle highest grade level reached):

High school 1 2 3 4 College 1 2 3 4 5 6

Specific subjects:

1. ______________________________
2. ______________________________
3. ______________________________

Ability to change: ______________________________

____

Willingness to take responsibility: ______________________________

____

Hobbies and/or interests: ______________________________

____

instructions should be followed regarding type of lubricant and frequency of lubrication. Use of a lubrication chart for routine lubrication is essential. Special lubrication needs are sometimes discovered during inspections, which also help to uncover part repair or replacement needs. Some parts may be replaced on a routine basis, but regular inspections ensure repair or replacement of parts as needed.

People and Organization

If one element could be considered most important among the several essential elements in an organization, that element probably would be people and their management.

The policies that help determine the effectiveness of the work force in a company are wide-ranging. They include employee recruitment, any training of job incumbents, provision of facilities, compensation, supervision, evaluation of job performance, motivation, and advancement.

Recruitment consists of searching for and attracting qualified applicants and, then, selecting those most suitable. Finding suitable candidates is helped by maintaining good relations and holding joint activities with schools and other sources of candidates. Prospective employers can provide guidance in curriculum development and make their own organizations more attractive to prospects by providing informational and cooperative activities with prospect-source organizations.

Selection has two aspects: having accurate job descriptions that stress the pertinent characteristics required for good job performance and having procedures for judging pertinent applicant characteristics. These latter procedures include testing, evaluating past performance, and developing effective interviewing techniques.

Even persons who are already trained and experienced in the type of work they will be doing will need some in-house training concerning the company and its particular equipment and procedures. Others will need more extensive training. Organizations that are not large enough to employ a training director should make sure that new employee instruction is not left to haphazard practices. Management should provide guidelines for training procedures.

Also, in this era of changing technology, employees should attend update training programs, provided by manufacturers and associations. This can be supplemented with **methods analysis** (studying ways to improve procedures); employees may be provided with means for "work simplification" (see sample form on pages 4:6 and 4:7). Policies that recognize employee worth and encourage participation through suggestion systems, work simplification programs, or quality circles can enhance motivation and employee effectiveness.

Estimating

Before a job is entered into production, the printer provides the customer with an estimate of the job's cost, followed by a contractual agreement known as a **quote.**

Estimating is basically a two-step process. The first step is to analyze a job's specifications to determine the best way to produce the printed piece and to determine whether the job should be undertaken. The person estimating or planning a job divides it into its component parts and decides which parts of a job can be completed most efficiently in-house and which ones need to be purchased from an outside source. This person also considers which parts of a job will be done "conventionally" and which ones will be done "electronically" based on factors such as time, cost, and work loads.

The second step is to estimate how much it will cost to produce the job. The estimator assigns costs to each part of the project, based on standard production times and budgeted hourly cost factors. The estimator also assigns costs to materials and outside purchases and then adds a profit margin to the job.

Estimating Systems

Many different estimating systems are in use in printing plants throughout the country. Systems based upon hourly rates, fixed price lists, industry averages, and universal price catalogs may be found. The one feature common to all successful systems is the use of accurate and consistent procedures. An estimating system must also include all production costs and must meet the needs of the particular firm.

Budgeted hourly cost method. The budgeted hourly cost method is used in plants where the cost of individual machine operations can be calculated.

Work Simplification Chart (side 1)

Process Charted; Person, Material, or Product Followed:			Date
			Chart by:
Other Data:			Chart No.
___ Present Method ___ Proposed Method	Department		Page of pages
No.	Symbol	Process Element	Analysis Notes

How to use this form—In the heading for the chart, enter brief description of process charted and person, material, or product followed. If form is used to describe an existing process, check Present Method block. After ideas for process improvement have been developed, use another copy of form to describe new list of elements, and check Proposed Method block.

Date, department, and chart author and number are important items for reference if many charts are developed over time. When more than one sheet is needed for a chart, the total number of sheets in set should be indicated on each sheet. The extreme left-hand column provides space for consecutive numbering of elements. The next column is for symbol of element type. Enter brief description of each process step or element in center column. The right-hand column may be used during analysis for noting possibility of elimination, combination, simplification, or change of sequence, person, or place.

Work Simplification Chart (side 2)

The major steps of methods analysis

1. Select the process to be analyzed
- Where is labor involvement high?
- Where is materials spoilage large?
- Where do production bottlenecks occur?
- Where do safety hazards exist?
- Where is time loss critical?
- Where are operations repetitive?
- Where is space at a premium?

2. Break down the process into its parts
- List the elements of a process, including for each:
  —the action taken
  —the object upon which the action is taken
  —the quantity of items upon which the action is taken at one time
  —the performer of the action
  —the means by which the action is performed
  —the result of the action
- Identify the type of element by symbol.

3. Question every part in detail
- Is the element necessary?
- Why it is performed at its present place in the sequence of elements?
- Why is it performed at the physical place where it is now done?
- Why is it performed by the person(s) now doing it?
- Why is it performed in the way and by the means now used?

4. Develop a new method
- Eliminate unnecessary elements.
- Consider possible reductions of delays, and transportation distances, etc., which could result from rearranged element sequences and places of performance.
- Consider improved utilization of personnel time and skills by having some elements performed by other persons.
- Consider different combinations of elements.
- Consider simplification of element performance by means of:
  —motion study
  —improved workplace layout
  —improved materials, tools, fixtures, guides, stops, and chutes
  —increased mechanization and automation
- Describe the elements of the proposed method on a new process chart.

5. Install the new method
- Get approval where necessary from those concerned with safety, quality, and cost.
- Give necessary instruction and follow up to see that the new method is installed and to evaluate its usefulness.
- Give full credit to all persons who participated in the development and use of the new method.

The elements of a process

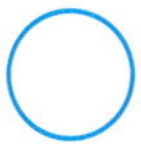

Operations are in the main steps in a process, generally resulting in some modification of a part, material, or product. (Examples: justifying a line, making a flying paster, trimming a lift of paper.)

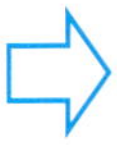

Transportations are movements of persons, parts, materials, or products. In describing a transportation element, it is often useful to include the distance of movement in addition to the other necessary items of information. (Example: hand trucking a load of signatures.)

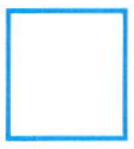

Inspections are the determinations of quantity or quality information by means of visual examination, measurement, counting, weighing, or testing. (Examples: examining print quality, checking for damaged signatures.)

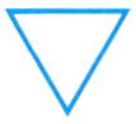

Storages are delays of accumulations of items between the stages of a process. The quantities stored and length of time in storage are helpful items of information when analyzing storage elements. (Example: printed signatures accumulating prior to binding operations.)

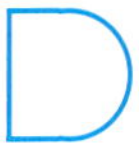

Delays are necessary waits, other than storages, of persons, parts, materials, or products during a process. (Example: load of stock waiting to be moved by a busy freight elevator.)

Sometimes two elements of different types are performed simultaneously, such as an inspection during an operation. The symbols have been so designed that they can be combined without confusion. For example, inspection during an operation is represented by a square within a circle.

A four-step procedure is used to obtain quotations for work:

1. Find the operation costs of each machine, workstation, or printing operation. All factors going into the operation of a given machine are studied and reduced to a dollar charge. Based on square footage, each machine's share of insurance, lighting, heating, maintenance, depreciation, and labor costs is pro-rated and a total operating cost per hour for that machine is developed. This figure is the budgeted hourly cost.

2. Determine the amount of machine time for the particular job. This step involves studying the job to be estimated to find out the number of hours it will take in each department, machine, or operation. The required number of hours in the camera room, stripping area, pressroom, and other departments is calculated and recorded.

3. Estimate outside purchases. Most printing jobs, in addition to work performed in the plant, require some services, materials, or supplies purchased from outside sources or vendors. These materials or services, called **buyouts,** must be included in the cost of the job. These buyouts include subcontracted services such as bindery services and artwork.

4. Establish the sales price. This is done by multiplying the estimated hours of production (step 2) by the budgeted hourly cost (step 1) for each operation. Then buyouts and finally profit and return on investment are added.

Budgeted hourly costs include the total operating costs for a given production operation for one hour. They are constructed for each machine, department, operation, or, in some instances, workstation.

Hourly costs are prepared by the estimator by totaling the annual expenses for each operation or producing unit. The total annual costs for that unit are then divided by the number of productive hours in one year to give the average hourly costs.

Here is a list of major items that the estimator should consider when preparing hourly costs:

- **Rent.** Estimate the annual cost of rental for that producing unit. If you own the building, use the fair market value of comparable space. Base rental on the number of square feet occupied by the producing unit.
- **Utilities.** Estimate the consumption of the utilities (e.g., heat, light, power, and air conditioning) for each unit. Include maintenance costs of air conditioning equipment.
- **Real and personal property tax.** Determine the producing unit's fair share of real property tax and personal property taxes, if this applies in your community. Be sure to include various special assessments that are often included in your tax bill.
- **Insurance.** A distributed portion of all insurance should be charged to each unit. Include fire, theft, liability, and other coverages.
- **Depreciation on equipment.** Calculate the depreciation cost for each unit. This may be done in several different ways, including straight-line and accelerated. Salvage value must also be considered here. Work with an accountant in arriving at a reasonable depreciation cost for each unit.
- **Maintenance of plant.** Determine the producing unit's fair share of physical plant maintenance cost, including painting, plumbing repairs, and reroofing.
- **Maintenance of equipment.** Virtually all plant equipment requires some periodic maintenance. Estimate the cost of maintenance, lubricating, cleaning, and adjusting each machine or piece of equipment associated with each producing unit.
- **Supplies.** Determine the normal supply costs needed for the operation of each producing unit. Such items as paper towels, cleaning towels, solvents, chemicals, adhesives, and tapes should all be considered.
- **Administrative expenses.** Each producing unit incurs an expense to administer. Figure the "front office" cost to keep each unit operating. This will include secretarial time, executive salaries, and cost of key personnel whose attention is required in the department to keep it operating.
- **Direct factory payroll.** Estimate the direct labor cost to operate each unit. Such things as the wages of press operators, strippers, and camera operators should be estimated. Direct factory payroll expenses are incurred by the key, or principal, operators of equipment.
- **Indirect factory payroll.** Often additional labor costs are incurred by helpers, aides, assistants, or supporting operators. These costs should be included. For example, the cost of filing plates or cleaning up after a work shift is an indirect factory payroll cost.
- **Payroll taxes and benefits.** For each dollar of direct and indirect salary paid, the printing company must add a sum for worker's compensation insurance, social security, unemployment insurance, health plan, retirement, and other taxes and benefits. Watch these figures carefully and include a fair share of each for every hour of labor cost.
- **Supervision cost.** Most producing operations require the attention of a foreman or supervisor. For a given number of operators, the plant will incur an additional supervision cost. This figure will vary

with the type of work being done and the skill of the operators. Some portion of supervision cost should be added to labor costs to provide for this important function.

• **Selling expenses.** Each hour of production must ultimately be sold to the customer. This requires the time and expense of "front office" personnel. The estimator should include a portion for costs incurred in selling the work produced.

Markup percentage method. The markup percentage method is sometimes called the "predetermined factory overhead method." Its advantages are simplicity, speed, and elimination of detailed cost accounting studies. It serves the smaller and medium-size plant well, but it may be inadequate for large firms producing complex work and requiring detailed analysis of each cost operation. Using this method, the estimator determines printing prices by using a three-step procedure:

1. Find the markup percentage. Make a study of the previous year's costs and sales figures to determine what percentage of each sales dollar went for overhead, materials, labor, and profit. Using this relationship as a basis, extrapolate your percentages for the coming year. The resulting figures can then be applied to work being estimated for the present period.

2. Find the cost of materials and labor and other direct costs necessary to produce the job. In practice, the job to be estimated is considered item by item, and costs for paper, ink, plates, and other materials are entered on a standard form and a total is drawn. This total includes all costs to produce the job, exclusive of overhead, profit, and return on investment.

3. Establish the sales price. This is done by multiplying the direct costs of the job (step 2) by the markup percentage (step 1). This percentage is added to the costs to ensure that the printing company will recover all overhead costs and depreciation, make a return on investment, and receive a fair profit.

Standard price list method. Another method used by printers is the standard price list. The lists are developed from operating costs over a given period of time. All types of jobs run in the plant are usually listed, identified by number of colors, kind, weight, and size of stock, number of pages, and other significant data. Estimating is easy once the price list has been made up, since the estimator need only look up the particular characteristics of a job on the list.

The difficulty here is that the estimate will be no more accurate than the price list. The method used in calculating prices may not account for all costs. Also, in a sense, each printing job is a custom job and cannot be considered the same as another. Standard price lists do not reflect this factor, so some jobs end up being priced too high and others too low. However, this estimating procedure might prove satisfactory for printers who run a lot of standardized work such as envelopes or forms.

Commercial price catalogs. Many firms use standard catalogs to establish the sales price of their goods and services. These uniform price catalogs are excellent tools for the estimator. However, they should be used with care. Each shop has unique labor, material, and supply costs, as well as production efficiency factors. Your prices should be based upon your own costs and operating expenses. Standard pricing catalogs are most useful as a means of comparison, to show how your prices stack up against national averages.

If your prices differ greatly from the national averages, you should investigate the reasons. For example, if you chronically lose money on halftones, you should analyze your camera department costs to determine the reasons for this.

Estimating Guidelines

Estimating requires a person who has knowledge about the various production steps, capabilities of printing equipment, and the abilities of plant personnel. Experienced estimators have learned to recognize and avoid many pitfalls and problem situations. The guidelines below help in the preparation of accurate and thorough estimates.

• **Know what your customer wants.** Obtain full instructions and job specifications before figuring any work. Know the size, color, weight, and type of stock. Find out if special handling will be necessary. Special color matches, weights, or sizes may markedly affect your costs.

• **Itemize costs.** Do not use gross, unexplained totals when making estimates. Take the time to break costs down into individual details. For example, itemize presswork as pressrun, washup, makeready, and ink.

• **Check copy condition before estimating.** A major element in composition cost is the condition of the copy. Poor copy can cost twice as much to set as does good copy. If necessary, ask the customer to type the copy or, preferably, provide you with the copy on a compatible computer disk.

• **Know what the customer will supply.** Find out if existing artwork or other items can be used for the job. This can save you time and duplication of effort, and the customer money.

• **Always base prices on cost and records, not on guesswork.** Make sure that a profit is included when quoting a printing job. Do not sell loss leaders or give introductory prices hoping that they will lead to profitable jobs later.

• **Never quote printing jobs while the customer waits on the phone or stands over your shoulder.** Estimating must be done carefully. Be sure to have someone else double-check your figures; costly mistakes can be avoided if an assistant or fellow estimator reviews quotations for accuracy and completeness.

• **Write all quotations and figures down.** If an order is taken by phone, summarize it in writing and mail or fax confirmation to your customer.

• **Make sure your supplier price lists and catalogs are up to date.** Ask paper sales representatives, ink vendors, and others to bring price changes to your attention immediately. Enter them promptly in the appropriate price book. Discard outdated price lists.

• **Maintain complete records.** File old job tickets, purchase orders, invoices, and the like in a systematic way. These can be valuable when figuring reruns or revising quotations. Time can be saved by using cost and time calculations from other jobs. Check your figures again, very carefully.

Selecting Optimum Job Design

The estimator should always ask the customer about job specifications, such as whether the customer really requires a specific size, type of stock, or production element. If a small change in a job specification can reduce production costs, it is the estimator's responsibility to bring this to the customer's attention.

When the estimator prepares a worksheet, jobs should be quoted several different ways in order to cost out the most efficient production pattern. This may have the advantage of allowing the customer to choose a less-expensive alternative, while enabling the printer to be more competitive and still net a reasonable profit.

Estimating is as much a science as it is an art, and it is based upon knowledge and experience. It is a good idea to have an assistant prepare another estimate on jobs in the plant. This can often turn up cost-saving ideas or valuable design changes. Sometimes two estimators working together can redesign a job specification to lower cost and still meet the customer's needs.

Following are some specific job design factors that should be examined in estimating virtually every job:

• **Length of run.** Consider increasing or decreasing the required number of copies requested by the customer if this will make a substantial decrease in the customer's per unit cost. Factors that affect length of run economies are paper carton packing schedules, makeready time, and spoilage costs.

• **Question "frills" or other expendable items.** Some jobs include elements that are either unnecessary, arbitrary, or prohibitively expensive. The estimator should question such items as special wrapping, unnecessary folds, difficult diecutting, nonstandard ink colors, unusual sizes, and overly thin or extra heavy stock for the job. By eliminating these frills through the use of bulk packaging and standard stock sizes and ink colors, you may be able to reduce costs significantly.

• **Add extras or other features.** On some jobs it may be possible to add extras that may add little or no additional cost but greatly increase the utility of the finished product. For example, a second color or imprints may be provided at very little extra expense.

• **Gang up the job for press economy.** The estimator should routinely cost out jobs two-, four-, or eight-up to take advantage of press sizes. Job specifications, as well as trim sizes, should be planned to allow for ganging up. Stay with multiples of 8½×11 in. (216×280 mm), 6×9 in. (152×229 mm), 9×12 in. (229×305 mm), or other standard sizes. Gang up line and halftone shots on the camera. In the bindery, gang stitching, trimming, and folding operations.

• **Gang up several different jobs for the same customer.** Estimators may be able to reduce costs substantially by ganging up several different jobs for one customer. Some customers order special stocks, color matches, or typefaces for each job. Point out the savings that can accrue to the customer by ordering several jobs at one time. This will save unnecessary washups and makereadies and may allow you to order larger quantities of stock at a lower price.

• **Consider postage costs.** Printing jobs that are to be mailed should be dummied up and weighed before printing them. Revise printing specifications to reduce postage or to be able to use standard envelope sizes. Standardize inserts or eliminate individual pieces in favor of fan-fold formats or similar measures.

Production Control

Controls of purchasing, materials handling, planning and scheduling, and production records are essential for effective printing production. Some of these controls are plant-wide in scope; others will be treated in more detail in later chapters on various operations.

Purchasing Practices

Consideration will be given here only to controls for purchasing the major printing materials: ink and paper. Buying equipment is discussed above. Further details about specific aspects of choosing the right inks, paper, plates, etc., are given in chapters on those subjects. Here are some general principles of materials purchasing related to ink and paper for lithographic printing.

With respect to ink buying, GATF recommends developing close working relations with about two suppliers. Generally, a backup supplier is needed to provide for emergency situations; while, on the other hand, it is not feasible to give a large number of suppliers enough business to encourage their close attention to a printer's needs. And, the printer should not buy on price alone. Other important factors include service and color strength. One of the simplest ways to cheapen ink is to reduce its color strength. Then, more ink has to be run to bring the ink up to color.

An important factor in paper purchase control is complete and accurate order entry information. A checklist, with all of the necessary information, prevents oversights and permits delivery at the right time and destination.

Materials Handling Controls

Proper materials handling practices provide for the safety of the handler and protection of the materials, economical materials movement, and dispatching that gets the materials to the operation without delay or unnecessary accumulation of work in progress. Paper handling procedures are of major importance in printing.

The first stage of paper handling is inspection of the arriving shipment for damage. GATF recommends making instant-photography pictures of damaged paper to include when filing damage claims.

Damage while handling can be minimized by proper equipment and handling procedures. Paper in rolls needs particular care to prevent costly damage. GATF recommends 1 in. (25 mm) of rubber on lift truck roll clamps and limit switches to prevent excessive squeeze.

Storage procedures should be designed to reduce rehandling of paper before use and to prevent direct contact with damp floors or hot or cold objects. Rolls should not be stored on their sides. Rolls from the same position on the paper manufacturing machine should be stored together to improve press-running efficiency.

The final aspect of materials handling is getting materials to the job at the proper time. This is, in part, a matter of good planning and scheduling.

Planning and Scheduling

Producing a printed piece involves a series of reproduction operations so interdependent and overlapping that the final operations can only be successful to the extent that the beginning operations are planned with those final operations in mind.

Planning and scheduling should be aimed at producing the greatest volume at the lowest cost. The key to achieving this goal is an understanding of the factors that affect throughput. Throughput is the volume of work produced in a given shop in a specified period of time. The greater the throughput, the larger the base over which fixed costs can be distributed. Rent or mortgage payments, heating, lighting, insurance, telephone, sign maintenance, and other such costs become a smaller part of each job as throughput is increased.

Other costs are not affected in this way. Variable costs, such as ink, paper, direct labor, and materials, are generally not affected by throughput. That is, the costs of paper or ink per unit for a given job are usually constant regardless of the overall volume of work produced. The longer the run, of course, the more material will be used, and hence it may be purchased at a lower cost per unit.

Job scheduling involves having materials, supplies, and labor available when needed. It means planning work loads so that help is not standing around idle, nor are they so overburdened that they make mistakes, cut corners, or produce inferior work. Factors that affect the scheduling of a particular job include labor costs, overtime charges, shop loading, equipment capacity, and such production factors as ink drying time. In recent years, the use of computers with the appropriate software programs have made the planning and scheduling of jobs easier.

One important decision that must be made when planning, scheduling, or estimating a job is determining which portions of a job should be done "conventionally" and which portions should be done "electronically." For example, in a printing plant with both conventional and electronic prepress, one decision might be whether to use a camera or desktop scanner to make black-and-white halftones for a particular job. In this example, the decision might depend on the total number of halftones that are needed, whether several photographs can be ganged for halftoning on the camera, how much computer memory will be required, amount of work already scheduled for the camera and scanner, and film assembly considerations (such as complexity of stripping that would be involved if halftones were made on a camera).

Ideally, planning a piece involving complex art and design should be done in consultation with the key people who will work on it. The factors to be considered in this type of work are discussed extensively in Chapter 6, "Art and Copy Preparation," and to some extent in other appropriate chapters, since some of the planning is necessarily done within operating departments.

Some of the techniques that may be used to improve planning and scheduling efficiency are:

• Giving press scheduling precedence, since keeping the presses steadily busy is usually the highest priority.

• Scheduling all similar camera operations, such as line shots, to be done together.

• Scheduling jobs according to color, starting with the lightest color, to reduce washup time and make it easier to run clean colors.

• Scheduling similar kinds of bindery operations together to reduce required adjustments.

• Grouping similar types of jobs to be run on given days of the week to reduce changes in settings and improve runnability in both press and binding machines.

Production Records

Records are an account of what has happened, and their main importance is influencing future happenings. Long term, they are used to determine expectations (which, properly analyzed, can become standards) of production. Short term, they can start corrective action when schedules or standards of performance are not being met, or some failure, such as a lost shipment, needs to be traced. A schedule should indicate the expected time and the actual time of an accomplishment, thereby signaling the need for action if the accomplishment has not happened on time.

Records of time and quantity are necessary for payroll, cost-accounting, and job cost-accounting purposes. (See sample job time sheet on page 4:13.) Some printing jobs are billed on a cost-plus basis, in which case the need for accurate job cost-accounting records is obvious. But a great deal of billing is done from quoted prices (plus any legitimate extra charges incurred during the work). The quoted prices are based on estimates. If a job cost summary shows that actual costs deviate widely from estimated costs, the reason should be determined for corrective action either in operations or in estimating procedures.

Many printers now use computer-based shop-floor data collection systems to keep track of time and costs for each job. Data-collecting devices are linked to the CPU of the company's management information system and information entered on them is added to a database. The devices are usually hand-held or wall-mounted and include a keypad or bar code wand for data entry. The worker inputs job data such as job number, material usage, time started, and time ended, and the system performs various time- and cost-accounting functions and prints out the appropriate forms, such as weekly time sheets or detailed job reports.

Computer Applications in the Printing Plant

Only a few years ago it was rare to find a computer in the printing plant. Now, the computer is used extensively in the prepress, press, bindery, and materials handling areas. These computer applications are discussed in the appropriate chapters of this book.

The computer also assists thousands of printers with estimating, scheduling, production control, billing, and other applications. Some of these major applications programs are described below:

• **Estimating and cost accounting.** The computer prepares costs for producing jobs based upon factory overhead rates, material costs, production standards, or predetermined ratios. It converts job specifications into material requirements and looks up the cost or computes it from standard formulas.

• **Order processing.** The computer prepares job tickets, purchase orders, and material requirements, and handles basic order-processing tasks.

• **Billing, invoicing, and follow-up.** The computer can be programmed to prepare invoices and bills and to track final production costs. It can

Job Time Sheet (Printers)

Job Name ______ Job # ______ Date Entered ______

Operation	**Date**	**Operator**	**Est. Time (E)**	**Act. Time (A)**	**Deviation (E) – (A)**	**Comments**
Layout						
Markup						
Typesetting						
Pasteup						
Negatives						
Stripping						
Platemaking						
Cut Stock						
Press Washup						
Makeready						
Pressrun						
Folding						
Inserting						
Stitch or Staple						
Trim						
Perforate						
Score						
Number						
Collate						

compare actual costs with estimated costs and perform other useful comparisons for the estimator.

• **Paper stock, inventory, and calculations.** The computer can keep a running inventory of all paper warehoused in the plant, according to color, size, quantity, etc. It can be programmed to figure paper costs, based on size and weight, and even to determine spoilage.

• **Reports on shop production capacity.** The computer can be programmed to print out a list of various presses and speeds, together with specifications and operating costs. This report can be used to select the optimum press or production method.

• **Record keeping.** Total sales by month or year may be kept in data storage and printed out by computer. Costs such as paper, ink, and power for a given period may be coded and sorted by computer.

• **Ink inventory and calculations.** The computer can keep an up-to-date inventory of ink on hand by color, quantity, type, etc. It can calculate ink cost based on coverage, length of run, or other criteria.

• **Standardized estimator's worksheet.** The computer can be programmed to print out a standard worksheet from data calculated by the estimator. It can then do routine totaling of costs, add the markup, and print out the selling price.

• **Negative, platemaking, and other price lists.** Basic information can be manually gathered by the estimator and input into the system. The computer can print out a working document for the estimator, which can be easily revised and updated.

• **Job control and scheduling.** The computer can generate reports showing starting and ending dates of various jobs and department schedules.

• **Periodic contract and bidding schedules.** The computer can be used to print out a calendar of items that management, or the estimator, may need to review periodically, such as supplier contracts or bidding dates. This allows sufficient lead time to obtain competitive bids.

• **Depreciation schedules.** Annual depreciation on equipment can be routinely calculated.

Quality Control

Two important aspects to quality control are (1) building quality into a product by the use of good equipment, personnel, and operating procedures and (2) inspection for the removal of unsatisfactory items in the product that result in spite of the attention given to equipment, personnel, and procedures. Both of these are essential.

Building in Quality

The phrase "quality is everybody's business" refers to the idea of building in quality. Not everyone is an inspector who removes bad items from the production output. But, everyone who shares in planning, design, and production affects quality.

The controls for building in quality start with the policies and procedures for the evaluation and purchase of equipment, materials, and supplies. Procurement practices must assure that what the personnel have to work with is adequate for sustaining the desired quality levels of the plant. Furthermore, the maintenance practices must keep the facilities at that level. These points have been discussed above: this is one of the areas in which production control and quality control overlap.

Other overlap areas include all personnel policies for assuring adequately qualified and motivated people—with special reference, here, to the assurance that all employees appreciate management's dedication to the "quality is everybody's business" philosophy.

In printing, special devices especially related to quality control are often used. Some of these are instruments, such as densitometers, for checking work in progress. These are discussed in various chapters with respect to the particular operations in which they may be involved.

A type of control uniquely used in the printing industry is the test image. Such images may be inserted in areas that will be trimmed away from the final product. They are useful for quality monitoring because they are designed to be more sensitive to change and are easier to evaluate than are job images.

Also, test images carry more complete evaluative information. When test images are used from job to job, they provide continuity and consistency of evaluation.

Some test images are designed to provide information about the capability of a process, such as a particular press/paper/ink/plate combination. A process information color chart, for example, shows what colors can be achieved under a given set of conditions.

The purpose of many test images is diagnostic during pressrun. The widely used GATF Star Target, for example, provides visual indication of ink spread, slur, and doubling.

Inspection

Inspection procedures occur throughout the course of production operations. Among the first inspection procedures is proofreading, which is discussed in the next chapter, "Type and Typography." The most important inspection occurs in the pressroom when press operators randomly inspect printed sheets to monitor quality during the pressrun. Other inspections and details of quality control are described in appropriate chapters dealing with the production operations involved.

Total Quality Management

In recent years, many printers have implemented total quality management (TQM) programs to improve quality. Such programs may include the use of statistical process control, self-managed teams, empowerment, and other concepts. Many TQM programs are *customer-driven;* that is, the program is designed to understand a customer's needs and problems.

According to GATF SecondSight 12, *Guidelines for Using Statistically Based Control Charts,* a commitment to total quality includes the following:

- A company-wide system with ample training and resources
- Strong commitment of senior management
- Allocation of resources, particularly time and money
- Translation of customer needs and expectations into operational quality characteristics
- Quality improvement teams
- Authority to act ("empowerment") on the part of process operators and the quality improvement teams
- An effective system for monitoring quality costs
- Standardization of printing variables, including methods, materials, machines, and personnel
- Vendor quality assurance
- SPC tools, including control charts, flowcharts, Pareto analysis, check sheets, cause-and-effect analysis, histograms, and scatter diagrams
- Designed experimentation for process improvement
- Training in basic statistical techniques for all company employees

Statistical Process Control

This section briefly discusses statistical process control, one of the most powerful tools of a total quality management program. In **statistical process control** (SPC), analytical methods and tools are used to interpret data derived from process measurements and to understand process capabilities and variables. The goal of any company is to remove variability from a process and to make it totally consistent. All processes, however, have some variability. The proper use of SPC will indicate trends in a process, identify causes of variability and allow the printer to control the process better. Printers have discovered that SPC can help to make their operations more efficient and reduce waste.

Statistical control charts have a key role in the philosophy and methods associated with SPC. Control charts are used to analyze and control the output of a process by measuring and monitoring key quality characteristics of the product. They enable an operator to use statistically valid principles, rather than more subjective methods, to control a process. (GATF SecondSight 12, *Guidelines for Using Statistically Based Control Charts,* discusses the topic of control charts in more detail.)

Quality characteristics generally take two forms: variables, which can be measured, and attributes, which can be counted. Examples of variable quality characteristics in printing are register and density. Attribute quality characteristics could include hickeys or setoff. Some attributes can be labeled as defects.

When the characteristics are counted or measured, the results are plotted on a chart that contains control limits. The location of the points in relation to these limits indicates whether the process is in a state of statistical control or whether there is a change in that quality characteristic, suggesting that some special, nonrandom cause of variation has been introduced into the process.

Common types of variable control charts include $\bar{x}$ (called X-bar) charts, *R* charts, individuals charts, and moving average and moving range charts. These charts are used when the characteristic can be measured.

Typical kinds of control charts for attribute data include *p* (proportion) charts, *np* (number of affected units) charts, *c* (count) charts, and *u* (count per unit charts). These charts are used to monitor characteristics that are counted.

The limits in a control chart are based on the concepts of average process output, or **mean,** and average process variation, or **standard deviation.**

If the output of a process is varying randomly, indicating the presence of only chance causes of variation, the output tends to follow the bell-shaped pattern of a normal distribution. A normal distribu-

tion is characterized by the mean, which shows where a process is centered, and by the standard deviation, which indicates how much dispersion there is in the process.

Changes in the process could increase the process variation or shift the process average. An adjustment would be necessary to return the process to a state of control.

If the plots on a control chart exhibit no out-of-control signals such as trends, runs, approaches to control limits, or points outside of the limits, the process is assumed to be in a state of statistical control.

If the control chart exhibits out-of-control signals, the first step is identify the causes of this variation, how much each cause contributes to the variation, and what can be done to eliminate each cause. Tools for such an action could include brainstorming sessions using cause-and-effect analysis, Pareto analysis to systematically prioritize the various causes, and rudimentary experimentation to eliminate suspected causes.

Chapter 5

Type and Typography

Introduction

Printed material consists of two essentially different elements: (1) type matter and (2) various kinds of illustration and decoration. This chapter deals with the nature and production of type matter.

For printing, the characters of written language—letters, figures, punctuation marks—are rendered into standardized forms called **type.** While the rendering of each character must have a recognizable basic shape, each particular set of characters (called a **font)** may differ from another set in style, size, or both.

The particular style of a font is called its **face** or **typeface,** named from the flat printing surface on the three-dimensional type of letterpress. The design of a face affects the ease with which it can be read, the mood it establishes, and certain special functions that may be desired in special situations: attracting attention or providing emphasis. The design takes into account both the appearance of the individual characters and how they fit together into an overall effect.

A font has not only a particular style but a particular size. Type size is usually expressed in points. (See the discussion of the point system later in this chapter.) The size of hand-set or machine-set type is equal to the size of the metal body carrying the type image.

The design and selection of the faces and sizes of types and their arrangement and spacing is called **typography.** The actual operation of assembling types into words and lines in accordance with the manuscript and typographic specifications is called **typesetting.**

The technology of typesetting has evolved tremendously in the last two decades as the use of computerized equipment for type preparation has become widespread. As a result of advances in equipment capabilities, what used to be called "typesetters" can now be called "imagesetters," because these newer devices can now output type and graphic images (e.g., logos, line art, halftones) at the same time. This chapter discusses the basics of typesetting as it applies to conventional prepress production, and Chapter 12 discusses typesetting as it relates to electronic prepress production. However, there will be some overlap of information between the two chapters.

The Development of Typefaces

Type designed by the early printers copied the styles of the local scribes. In northern Europe, the boldfaced Gothic letter forms, sometimes called black letter, were predominantly used. Thus, the letter form designed by Gutenberg in Germany for his 42-line Bible, which is said to be the first printing from movable type, is characterized by the heavy Gothic letter form. In southern Europe, the influence of the early Venetian letter forms is responsible for what is known as the roman letter. The Venetian roman letter had minimal contrast between the thin upstrokes and the heavier downstrokes and is characterized by thick, rounded, uneven serifs (short cross-lines at the ends of main strokes) that were similar to those serifs formed by pen strokes or chiseled into stone.

The influence of the roman letter spread northward into France and England, where designers such as Claude Garamond and William Caslon refined the Venetian roman by increasing the contrast between the thin upstrokes and heavier downstrokes and forming serifs that angled out sharply from a rounded bracket where the serif joins the stem.

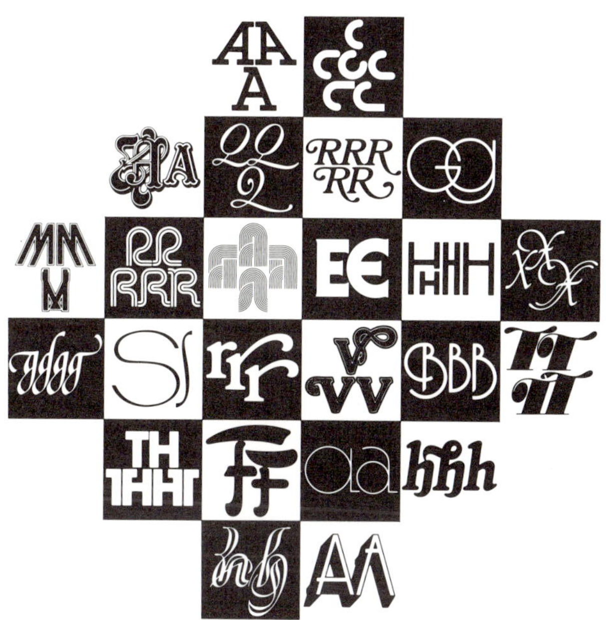

Courtesy International Typeface Corporation

A variety of characters from different typefaces.

The first significant change from the oldstyle roman to what is termed a modern face was brought about by John Baskerville, who used wove paper for the first time in printing. The smoother paper surface made possible the use of finer typefaces. Baskerville's type, a transitional design, refined the thin strokes. Bracketed serifs trailed to a point, and the swells of the round letters, unlike those of oldstyle roman, were vertical except in the "e."

Transitional designs continued until the eighteenth century, when Giambattista Bodoni designed the first truly modern typeface. He made the first complete thrust away from the graceful easy-flowing lines of oldstyle and transitional types. Instead, he designed type with a maximum contrast of thick and thin strokes, terminating the main strokes with straight, thin, and unbracketed serifs. Although he designed in the eighteenth century, the term "modern" still applies to type designs based on Bodoni's principles.

Garamond
Bodoni
Caslon
Baskerville

Four early typefaces discussed in this section.

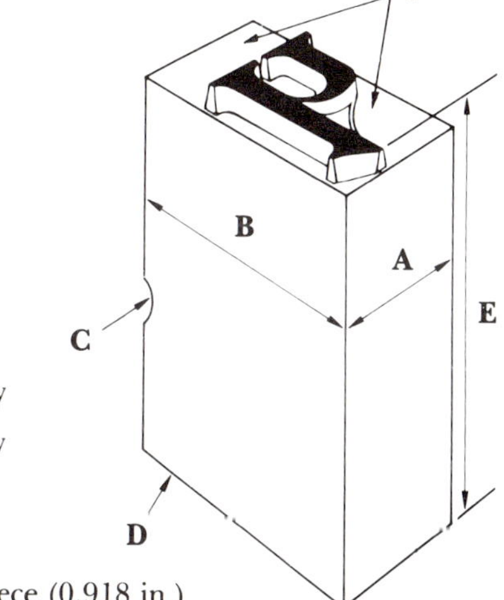

A. Set width of body
B. Point size of body
C. Nick
D. Foot
E. Height of type piece (0.918 in.)
F. Shoulder

Type nomenclature related to a piece of metal type.

Elements of Type Design

The basic unit of type matter is the character, and everything discussed in the preceding segment concerns features of the character: weight of the strokes—thin, thick, or varying; kind of serif and

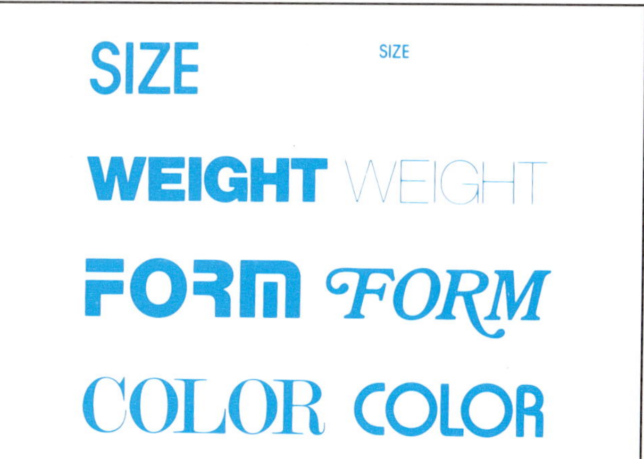

Basic considerations in type designs.

how it is joined to the end of the stroke; slope of the character; shapes of the curved elements; and special features, such as the kind of ear on the small "r." Such design elements affect the suitability of a typeface for specific purposes.

But type designers also have to be concerned with the overall appearance of the type as the characters are fitted together into words and lines. The first requirement for this, of course, is consistency of style, with respect to the features mentioned above, from character to character. Another consideration is how far one character is from the next. For metal or other three-dimensional types set side by side, this space between letters is the difference between the overall width of the character and the width of the **type body** on which the character is carried. Thus basic letterspacing is part of the type design.

One problem is that the visual space between characters is affected by the varying shapes of the adjacent sides of characters. Some combinations of side-by-side letters with normal spacing mesh better than others. The early designers improved many of these problem combinations by designing two or more characters together on one type body, a combination called a **ligature.** A few of these, such as "fl" and "fi" are still present in some fonts.

Sometimes portions of such characters as an italic "*f*" were made to project beyond the type body to permit overlapping an adjacent letter. A projecting part of this kind was called a **kern.** With phototypesetting and imagesetting, the term **kerning** has been extended to the practice of achieving similar results electronically by reducing the normal letterspacing.

AVA AVA

The three letters at the right have been kerned.

The Nomenclature of Type

Although machine-setting has largely replaced hand-setting and two-dimensional type has largely replaced three-dimensional, the traditions, terminology, and principles of typography evolved from the centuries-old system of handset type. For example, the terms "uppercase" and "lowercase" letters originated from the positions occupied by the capitals and small letters in the typecase. The practice of increasing the spacing between type lines by inserting thin strips of lead is called "leading." The term "leading" is also often applied to the control of interline spacing in phototypesetting and imagesetting, although **line spacing,** meaning the distance in points from the baseline of one line of type to the baseline of the next line of type, is the preferred term. Many other standard typographical terms originated in reference to the individual handset types.

Type is available for every letter, numeral, or other symbol that is used in graphic communications, and these letters and symbols appear in a great number of designs and sizes. To describe the characteristic appearance of types, a unique terminology for typography has been developed over several centuries, and since these terms are still used extensively, a student of typography must become familiar with them.

Type Characters

Most fonts include **uppercase** (capital) letters and **lowercase** (small) letters. Although different fonts

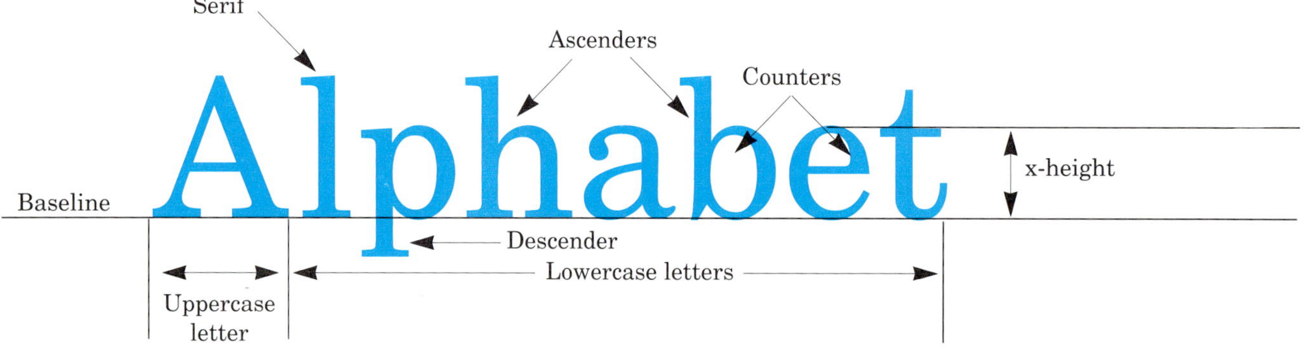

Nomenclature of type.

look different, they have several similarities. The height of the main element of a lowercase letter is called its **x-height.** The lower boundary of the x-height is the **baseline.** All letters rest on this imaginary line. Modern typesetters are designed so that all characters on a line, regardless of their size, rest on the baseline.

Any part of a lowercase character that rises above the upper boundary of the x-height is called an **ascender.** Similarly, any part of a lowercase letter that drops below the baseline (lower boundary) is called a **descender.** The height of a capital letter, or **cap height,** usually extends from the baseline to ascender height.

Some typefaces are designed with short cross-strokes **(serifs)** that project outward from the main strokes **(stems)** at the top and bottom of the letter. Letters without serifs are called **sans serif.** A sans serif typeface appears more streamlined and simple when compared to a typeface with serifs.

Type Family

A typeface whose main strokes are vertical is referred to as a **roman** typeface. If the main strokes of a typeface are slanted to the right of vertical, the typeface is referred to as an **italic** typeface. (With modern digital typesetters and imagesetters, a roman typeface can be electronically angled away from the vertical, producing "pseudo-italic.") Most typefaces are available in roman and italic versions. A roman typeface is more suitable for reading material, while the italic typeface is used to emphasize a word or phrase.

A **type family** consists of all of the variations based upon a particular typeface. Most type families have at least four variations: regular roman, regular italic, bold roman, and bold italic. A **bold** typeface has heavier letter strokes than the regular version. Other variations are also possible. A **light** typeface has thinner letter strokes than the regular version. With a **condensed** or **expanded** typeface, the character width would vary from the regular typeface. Modern digital typesetters and imagesetters are able to electronically condense or expand a regular typeface; however, the effect can be overdone.

Goudy Medium
Goudy Medium Italic
Goudy Bold
Goudy Bold Italic
Goudy Extra Bold

A typical type family.

Helvetica (normal)
Helvetica
Helvetica

Helvetica type *(from top to bottom):* 14-point normal, condensed 2 points, and expanded 4 points.

Type Font

A complete assortment of characters of one size and style of typeface that includes capitals, small capitals, lowercase letters, numerals, ligatures, and punctuation marks is called a **font** of type.

A font of type usually contains a sufficient assortment of characters for setting ordinary composition such as newspapers, magazines, and other nontechnical material. In some cases, a "pi" font must be used in conjunction with a main font to permit the setting of special characters, such as superior and inferior characters, mathematical symbols, and accented characters for certain languages.

Times
ABCDEFGHIJKLMNOPQRSTUVWXYZ
abcdefghijklmnopqrstuvwxyz
1234567890[1234567890]

Optima
ABCDEFGHIJKLMNOPQRSTUVWXYZ
abcdefghijklmnopqrstuvwxyz
1234567890[1234567890]

The character in two different fonts of types.

6 Helvetica
7 Helvetica
8 Helvetica
10 Helvetica
12 Helvetica
14 Helvetica
18 Helvetica
24 Helvetica
36 Helvetica
48 Helvetica
60 Helvetica
72 Helvetica

A typical type series.

Type Series

Most typefaces used in metal composition are made in a wide range of sizes known as a **series.** Generally, a type series in metal composition begins at a 6-point size and goes up to 36-point or in some cases as large as 96-point type. A typical series might have the following point sizes: 6, 7, 8, 10, 12, 14, 18, 24, 36, 48, 60, and 72.

In phototypesetting and imagesetting, depending on the machine, the type series could range from 4- to 128-point (or larger) type in ¼-point (or finer) increments.

The Point System

The term "point" is derived from the American point system. This system of measurement is used in most English-speaking countries. The point system has two units of measurement: points and picas. There are 12 points in one pica and approximately 6 picas in 1 in., or approximately 72 points in 1 in. (In the traditional point system, 6 picas are not exactly equal to 1 in.; they measure 0.99576 in. With some page-makeup software programs, the operator can determine whether he or she wants to use the traditional point system or one in which 72 points equals one inch.) Body size of metal types is specified in points, such as 10-point Bodoni. A pica type is 12 points, and agate type—used in newspaper ads—is 5½ points. There are 14 agate lines to a column inch. This is the measurement used to calculate the space occupied by advertisements in newspapers.

Large wood type used for posters is expressed in pica lines. For example, 10-line type would be 10 picas in height. **Line length** is also specified in picas, such as an 18-pica line length.

A ruler called a **line gauge** is commonly used to measure line lengths and line spacing. A typical line gauge has seven or more scales in various increments, such as 6, 7, 8, 9, 10, 11, 12, 13, and 15 points.

Point Size or Body Size

The height of a font of characters in metal composition is called **body size** or **point size** and is expressed in typographic points. The measure of the height is slightly more than the distance from the highest ascender to the lowest descender of the characters in the font. It must be emphasized that, although different type designs may have the same body size, the size of the faces will appear different because of the difference in the x-height and lengths of the ascenders and descenders.

In phototypesetting and imagesetting, it is difficult to measure point size because the characters are no longer carried on the face of metal type. Instead, a printed or typeset sample is compared with type of the same typeface in a specimen book. A **specimen book** consists of alphabets of different typefaces in a variety of point sizes. A less accurate method is to measure the distance from the ascender to the descender of adjacent characters. Depending on type characteristics and size of the type, this measurement might be accurate or it could be off several points, as would happen if a 60-point typeface had extremely short ascenders or descenders.

Modern typesetters and imagesetters allow more than one type style and/or type size on one line (intra-line mixing) or in one job (inter-line mixing).

Set Size or Set Width

All alphabets have characters of different widths; the letter "l," for example, is narrower than the letter "m." The width of a character is called its **set size** or **set width.**

Basic Typographic Forms

Type may appear in various positions on a printed page relative to the left or right margins, the center of a page, or an accompanying illustration.

The type is this column is set **justified,** which means that each line of text aligns with both the left- and right-hand margins of each column. Most newspapers, magazines, and books are typeset in this manner. Justified type is usually, but not always, set with end-of-line hyphens. (**Hyphenation** is the process of using hyphens to divide words that are too long to fit on the remaining line measure. **H&J** is an abbreviation for type that is both hyphenated and justified.) Short lines of type justified without hyphenation usually have excessively large amounts of word spacing and letter spacing. In fact, with any text that is set justified, the word spacing usually varies from one line to the next.

Another popular method of setting type is the **ragged right** format. In this format, copy aligns only at the left margin; the right margin is ragged. Ragged right is also known as **flush left, quad left** (a term carried over from the days of hand-setting metal type), and **flush left, ragged right.** In ragged-right copy, the word spacing is constant from one line to the next. In general, words are not

During the whole of a dull, dark, and soundless day in the autumn of the year, when the clouds hung oppressively in the heavens, and at length found myself, as the shades of the evening drew on, within view of the melancholy House of Usher. During the whole of a dull, dark, and soundless day in the autumn of the year, when the clouds hung oppressively in the heavens, and at length found myself, as the shades of the evening drew on, within view of the melancholy House of Usher.

During the whole of a dull, dark, and soundless day in the autumn of the year, when the clouds hung oppressively in the heavens, and at length found myself, as the shades of the evening drew on, within view of the melancholy House of Usher. During the whole of a dull, dark, and soundless day in the autumn of the year, when the clouds hung oppressively in the heavens, and at length found myself, as the shades of the evening drew on, within view of the melancholy House of Usher.

Two paragraphs set justified. The paragraph on the right was also set with end-of-line hyphenation.

hyphenated in ragged-right composition unless they are extremely long.

Type can be set **flush right,** that is, the copy aligns with the right margin and the left margin is ragged. This format is rarely used. **Centered** copy is centered on the line length. With **runaround** copy, line lengths are adjusted to accommodate the shape of an illustration or photograph.

During the whole of a dull, dark, and soundless day in the autumn of the year, when the clouds hung oppressively in the heavens, and at length found myself, as the shades of the evening drew on, within view of the melancholy House of Usher. During the whole of a dull, dark, and soundless day in the autumn of the year, when the clouds hung oppressively in the heavens, and at length found myself, as the shades of the evening drew on, within view of the melancholy House of Usher.

During the whole of a dull, dark, and soundless day in the autumn of the year, when the clouds hung oppressively in the heavens, and at length found myself, as the shades of the evening drew on, within view of the melancholy House of Usher. During the whole of a dull, dark, and soundless day in the autumn of the year, when the clouds hung oppressively in the heavens, and at length found myself, as the shades of the evening drew on, within view of the melancholy House of Usher.

During the whole of a dull, dark, and soundless day in the autumn of the year, when the clouds hung oppressively in the heavens, and at length found myself, as the shades of the evening drew on, within view of the melancholy House of Usher. During the whole of a dull, dark, and soundless day in the autumn of the year, when the clouds hung oppressively in the heavens, and at length found myself, as the shades of the evening drew on, within view of the melancholy House of Usher.

The top paragraph is set flush left; the middle one is set with each line centered; and the bottom one is set flush right.

Miscellaneous forms (also called contours) are special shapes into which type is set to achieve a desired visual effect. Type may be set in irregular forms, such as this one. As with justified copy, irregular spacing and hyphenation may be required to maintain the borders of the format. A comp or rough sketch should be provided to the typesetter with the manuscript. Include individual line lengths to insure a precise fit. Miscellaneous forms (also called contours) are special shapes into which type is set to achieve a desired visual effect. Type may be set in irregular forms, such as this one. As with justified copy, irregular spacing and hyphenation may be required to maintain the borders of the format. A comp or rough sketch should be provided to the typesetter with the manuscript. Include individual line lengths to insure a precise fit. Miscellaneous forms (also called contours) are special shapes into which type is set to achieve a desired visual effect. Type may be set in in irregular forms, such as this one. As with justified copy, irregular spacing and hyphenation may be required to maintain the borders of the format. A comp or rough sketch should be provided to the typesetter with the manuscript. Include individual line lengths to insure a precise fit. Miscellaneous forms (also called contours) are special shapes into which type is set to achieve a desired visual effect. Type may be set in irregular forms,

Text set in a special shape.

Once upon a midnight dreary, while I pondered, weak and weary, Over many a quaint and curious volume of forgotten lore—While I nodded, nearly napping, suddenly there came a tapping, As of some one gently rapping, rapping at my chamber door—"'Tis some visiter," I muttered, "tapping at my chamber door—Only this and nothing more." Ah, distinctly I remember it was in the bleak December; And each separate dying ember wrought its ghost upon the floor. Eagerly I wished the morrow;— vainly I had sought to borrow From my books surcease of sorrow—sorrow for the lost Lenore—For the rare and radiant maiden whom the angels name Lenore—Nameless *here* for evermore. And the silken, sad, uncertain rustling of each purple curtain Thrilled me—filled me with fantastic terrors never felt before; So that now, to still the beating of my heart, I stood repeating "'Tis some visiter entreating entrance at my chamber door—Some late visiter entreating entrance at my

Text set to run around an illustration.

Spacing

Line spacing. In hot-metal typesetting, strips of thin nonprinting lead were often inserted between lines of type to adjust the spacing. This practice of inserting lead strips was referred to as "leading." In the conventional definition, **leading** is the value, usually expressed in points, of the additional white space between lines of type. For example, 10-pt. type might be set with 2 points of lead.

In phototypesetting and imagesetting, the distance from the baseline of one line of type to the baseline of the next line of type is often referred to as the **line spacing, interline spacing,** or **line depth.** The term "leading" is now often used as a synonym for line spacing.

Word spacing. Word spacing is the space between typeset words. In phototypesetting and imagesetting, the minimum, normal, and maximum amounts of word spacing can be adjusted. In centered and ragged composition, the normal word space is used between all words. In justified composition, where the type must be flush with both the left and right margins, the equipment automatically increases or reduces the word space or hyphenates end-of-line words to fill up the line length. If the equipment is operating in a hyphenless mode (e.g., no end-of-line hyphenation) or if the line measure is extremely short compared to the type size, the space between words may be excessive and unsightly.

Letterspacing. Letterspacing is the placement of additional space between characters in a line. In phototypesetting and imagesetting, the minimum, normal, and maximum amounts of letterspacing can be changed. If a line cannot be justified by expanding word spaces to their maximum value, additional space will be inserted between letters.

Kerning could be considered the opposite of letterspacing. In the conventional definition, **kerning** is the removal of space from between certain letter combinations to improve the appearance of words. With some desktop software programs, the term "kerning" has taken on a slightly different meaning. With these programs, **positive kerning** is the addition of small amounts of space between certain letter combinations, and **negative kerning** is the removal of small amounts of space.

Tracking is a similar concept to kerning. **Tracking** is the addition or removal of small, but equal, amounts of space between all of the letters in a word or group of words, such as a headline, paragraph, or article.

11-point line spacing: The 11-point type in this paragraph is set with 11 points of line spacing; that is, the distance from one baseline of type in this paragraph to the next is 11 points. Using the conventional definition of *leading,* we would say that this paragraph is set with 0 points of leading, because the line spacing and the point size are the same.

13-point line spacing: The 11-point type in this paragraph is set with 13 points of line spacing; that is, the distance from one baseline of type in this paragraph to the next is 13 points. Using the conventional definition of *leading,* we would say that this paragraph is set with 2 points of leading, because the line spacing *exceeds* the point size by 2 points.

15-point line spacing: The 11-point type in this paragraph is set with 15 points of line spacing; that is, the distance from one baseline of type in this paragraph to the next is 15 points. Using the conventional definition of *leading,* we would say that this paragraph is set with 4 points of leading, because the line spacing *exceeds* the point size by 4 points.

Paragraphs set with different amounts of line spacing.

Early Methods of Typesetting

The operation of setting type by hand remained essentially unchanged from the days of Johannes Gutenberg (about 1450) to the invention of the Linotype type-casting machine in 1886, and it is still in limited use today. Even the alloy used in casting the individual metal types had the same basic constituents as modern foundry type: lead, antimony, and tin. In the typesetting operation, individual types residing in a compartmented case are hand-assembled into words and lines in a hand-

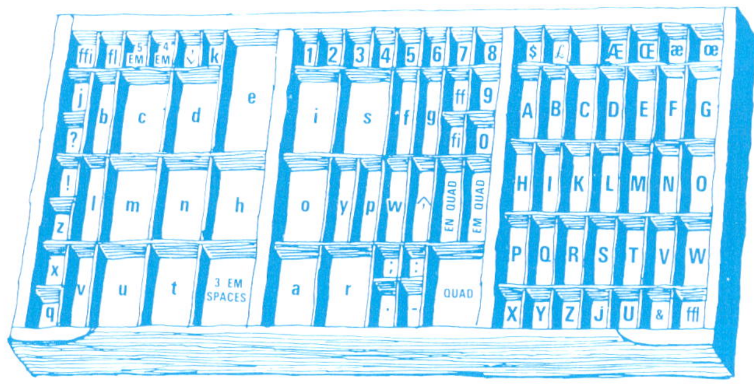

California job case.

held device called a **composing stick.** From there the lines are transferred to a tray called a **galley,** where they are assembled into a printing form for letterpress printing.

The Invention of Linecasting

Many efforts were made in the nineteenth century to mechanize typesetting to meet the demands of the rapidly increasing volume of typesetting required daily by newspapers. These efforts had very little success as long as they attempted to accomplish mechanically the assembly of individual type characters.

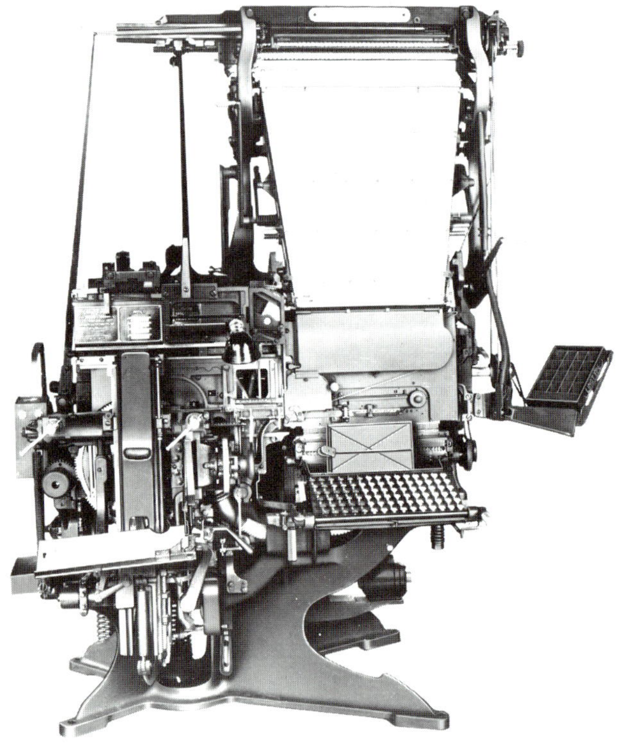

A Linotype, a keyboard-operated linecasting machine.

Ottmar Mergenthaler set off the first revolution in typesetting by inventing the Linotype. His machine, which quickly evolved into a form basically similar to that still in extremely limited use today, had a system in which **matrices** (individual character molds) rather than the type themselves were assembled a line at a time, after which the line of type was cast in lead and the matrices were recirculated.

Fonts of matrices were stored separately in special containers called **magazines.** From one to eight magazines could be held on a machine at one time, depending on the machine model, and they were easily removed to change to a type font not currently on the machine. Extra magazines with additional fonts were stored in magazine racks and labeled according to face and size. A magazine was essentially a flat metal box with channels for each different character of the font. As many as twenty matrices (mats) of identical characters could be stored in each channel. The matrices were released from the bottom of the magazine by means of an escapement mechanism that released only one matrix for each keystroke from the keyboard. Once the line had been cast, the matrices were redistributed into their proper channels.

The keyboard was unlike a typewriter keyboard in that it was composed of ninety keys arranged in three sections—lowercase on the left; figures, punctuation symbols, and spaces in the center; and capital letters on the right.

Each mat had seven teeth on either side of the V-shaped top edge. The teeth corresponded to matching grooves on a distributor bar. Mating of the teeth with the grooves released each mat into its proper channel when the matrices were being distributed back into a magazine.

A reference appeared on each mat enabling the operator to distinguish each letter as it was being assembled. The mold side of a mat contained two characters, which were generally a roman and an italic or a light and a bold. The two faces were in a vertical alignment on the side of the matrix, and the face to be cast was determined when the matrices were being assembled. In the assembly process, matrices were mechanically aligned on one of two horizontal levels, or **rail** positions. The lower rail might be a roman typeface, while the upper rail might be an italic typeface.

When a key was depressed, a mat was released from the magazine and traveled down a conveyor belt into an assembler, where mats and space bands were assembled into a complete line. The line was then transferred to the casting position,

where a justification bar forced the wedge-shaped space bands up, expanding and justifying the line between vise jaws that were set for the line measure and which held the mats during casting.

Once a line was justified, molten metal was forced into a mold and against the mats, forming a slug of type. The bottom and sides were then automatically trimmed, and the slug was ejected into a galley.

While trimming and ejecting of the slug was taking place, the mats and space bands were mechanically separated by a series of arms and elevators. A distributor elevator carried the used mats to a distributor box that transferred them, one at a time, to a series of distributor screws and a distributor bar. The revolving distributor screws transported the mat across the distributor bar until a matching combination of the mat's teeth and the distributor bar teeth released the mat, dropping it into its respective channel for further use.

Most keyboard-driven linecasting machines were limited to a 30-pica line length, although some could set a 42-pica line. Type sizes ranged from 4-point to 14-point for text composition. For special applications, the machines could set up to 60 point type.

Linecasting machines could carry multiple magazines, as well as auxiliary magazines if equipped with auxiliary keyboards. However, such machines were made for specific applications. A machine with a single distributor and single magazine was generally used only for text composition. When equipped with multiple magazines and keyboards, it had the type-mixing capabilities required for advertising and complex typography.

Tape-Operated Linecasters

Some linecasting machines were able to read a perforated paper tape. These tape-operated linecasting machines differed from manually operated machines in two ways: (1) mats of a tape-operated machine had predetermined unit-value set widths, matched to a tape-perforating keyboard and (2) they were either keyboardless but equipped with a tape reader or had a keyboard and a tape reader.

The prime feature of a tape-operated system was a tape-perforating keyboard that counted characters and spaces, signaling when a justification range had been reached.

The six-level paper tape was read by the linecasting machine tape reader, which mechanically activated the cams just as if an operator had struck keys.

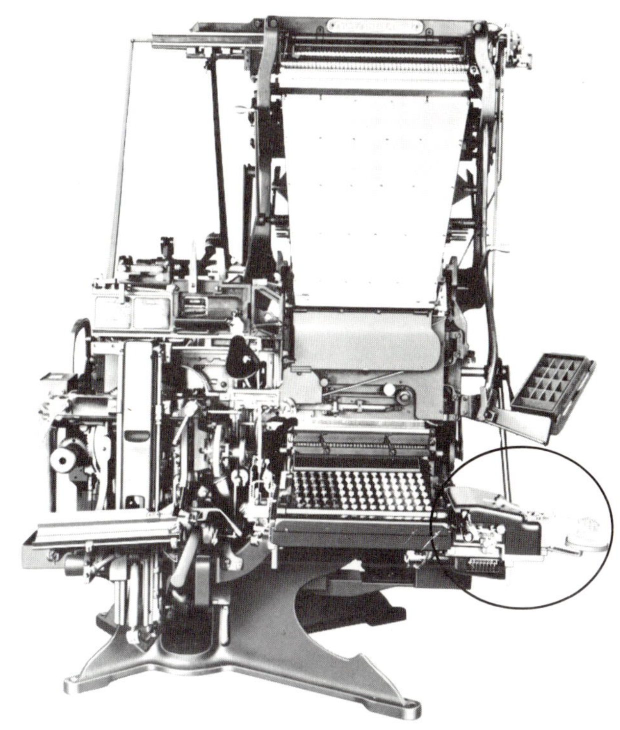

A tape driven Linotype.

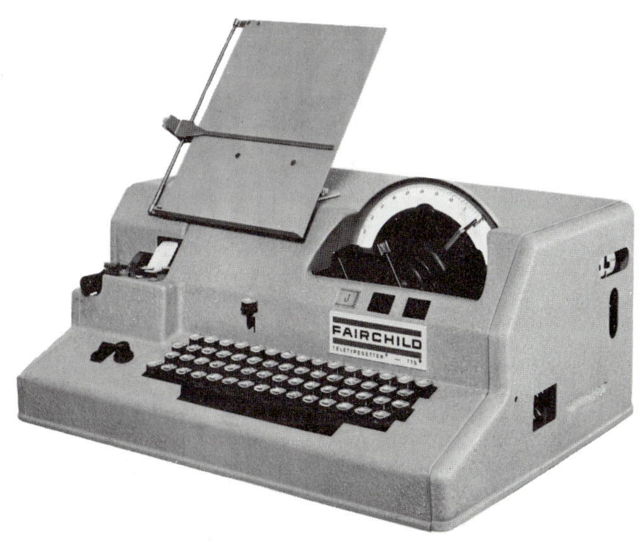

A tape perforator, which generated a paper tape that was used to drive a linecasting machine.

Various input methods were available for tape-operated machines. The original TTS machine of the Teletypesetter System was the first keyboard tape system developed for input to tape-operated machines for *local production* of news or commercial composition. The TTS system was also used for *wire transmission* of composed matter from one

sending station to any number of distant cities to operate linecasting machines.

The first typesetting system that used a numerical control for spacing and justification was not the tape-operated *linecasting* machine, but one that cast *single* characters, the Monotype.

Typesetting by Monotype

The Monotype system was the original tape-operated metal typesetting system. This system cast single characters one at a time and placed them in a line, rather than a solid slug as produced on the previously described linecasting systems. Two machines were used in the Monotype system: a keyboard and a caster. The arrangement of keys on the keyboard was similar to that of a standard typewriter. The operator actuated it to produce a punched paper ribbon, thus encoding the copy. The encoded ribbon included all necessary information to direct the caster in selecting and casting the proper character matrix and such spaces as were needed to produce justified lines of individual type characters.

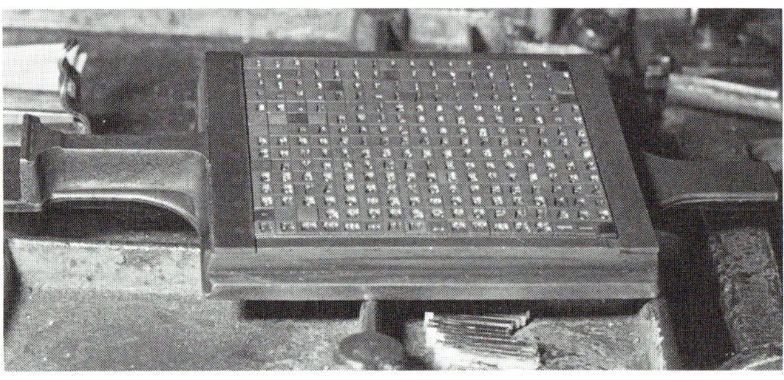

Monotype mat case.

This system used a single matrix for each character. These were stored in a matrix case and were not removed for casting as in a circulating-matrix system, but rather the matrix case was shifted and positioned above a mold for each character that was cast. The positioning of the matrix case was pneumatically controlled through the encoded holes on the perforated paper ribbon. This control of the caster was, in principle, similar to the much older Jacquard loom on which elaborately woven patterns were produced using a punched paper master card.

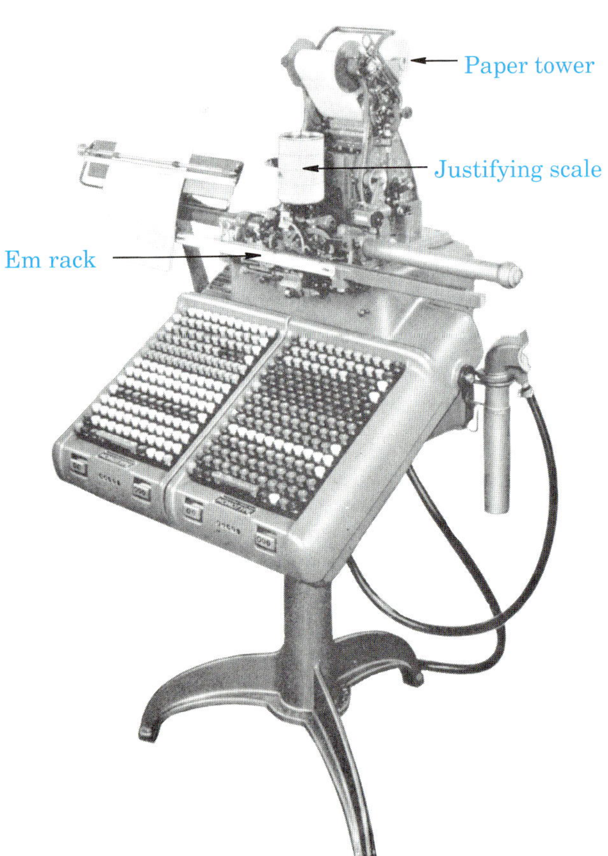

Monotype keyboard.

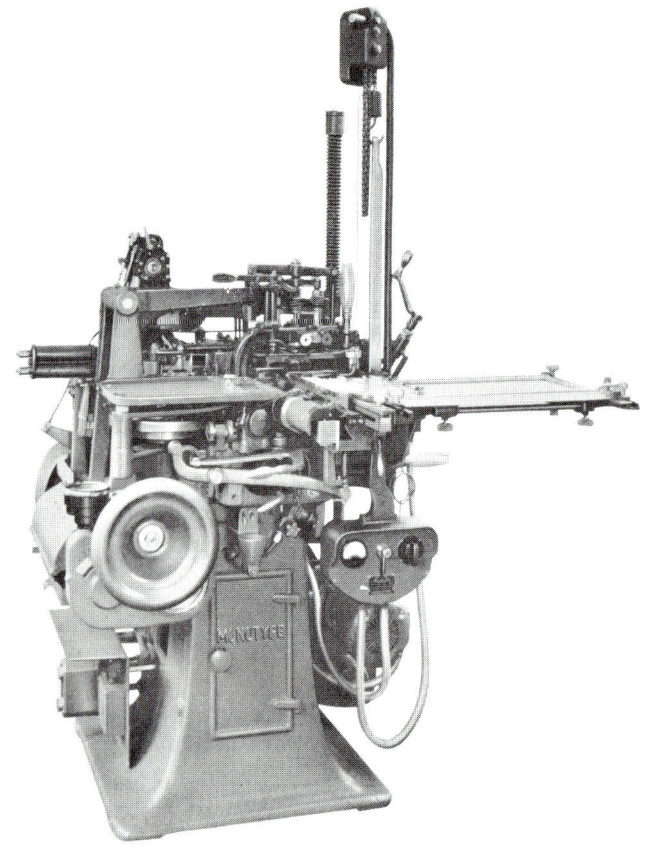

Monotype caster.

Conversion for Lithography

With the rise of lithography and other printing methods having an image carrier produced by photomechanical means, metal type composition had to be converted into two-dimensional type images suitable for photomechanical use.

Several conversion procedures were developed. One method was direct photography of the letterpress form.

Another was a mechanical/chemical method that used a translucent conversion film with pressure-sensitive cellular coatings. The film was placed in contact with the relief image surface and pressure was applied by a large number of tiny metal balls vibrating against the back of the film. This action collapsed the coating cells in the areas of the typefaces. A dye applied to the film darkened it except in the collapsed-cell type areas, which were then transparent. These conversion procedures are now obsolete.

The procedure used most commonly to convert a three-dimensional type form into a two-dimensional image was **reproduction proofing.** A dense black image of the type is produced using a letterpress proof press; the result is a printed **reproduction proof** ("repro") of the type.

Quality in proofing required standards of press settings, ink, paper, bearers, use of a tint bar, etc. Only stiff printing inks that dried readily could be used for reproduction proofing. To accept the ink properly, the printing face had to be free of dirt and oil. The cylinder packing also had to be as hard as practical.

Reproduction proofs could be made on opaque, translucent, or transparent material. The opaque material was generally a stock made especially for letterpress proofing.

Direct Setting of Type Images

The makeshift nature of metal type conversion emphasized the desirability of typesetting systems that produced two-dimensional type images directly. Some of these already existed in forms that had been developed for other purposes. The typewriter, invented in 1868 for correspondence, was modified in special ways to make it more acceptable as a typesetter for printing. Such typewriter-like typesetting is called **strike-on.** Strike-on typesetting systems at first generally required retyping to perform justification of lines. In the Varityper system, the operator set the carriage for a particular line length. He or she typed the line until the internal counting mechanism signaled that a line was within justification range. The operator tabbed over and retyped the line at this time. The variable word space mechanism added space or subtracted space from between words to permit justification.

The IBM Selectric Composer operated in a similar manner; that is, each line was retyped. Both IBM and the Varityper had interchangeable fonts. The IBM had a golf ball-shaped carrier for various fonts while the Varityper had a disk-shaped font.

All strike-on typesetting devices required a nonreusable carbon ribbon to produce a sharp black image on a reproduction grade paper. Paper output was generally mounted on mechanicals with art or other type elements. This system could also be used on paper plates, enabling direct platemaking.

Faster models of strike-on composition machines included the IBM magnetic tape units and the Friden Justowriter system. When the initial typing was done on the IBM unit, a magnetic tape was recorded, containing all line endings and hyphenation decisions. The Justowriter system used paper tape and two typing units.

Evolution of Phototypesetting

The hand-setting of individual types and the machine casting of individual characters or lines of type are now rarely performed. *Phototypesetting,* the second revolution in typesetting methods, and its successor, *imagesetting,* have become so predominant that they have practically superseded all previous methods. In fact, imagesetting has practically superseded even phototypesetting.

Phototypesetting systems have undergone several evolutionary changes. The first generation of phototypesetting devices was patterned after metal and strike-on typesetting machines. Succeeding generations are classified according to the extent of mechanical and electronic sophistication used in the system.

First-Generation Phototypesetters

The first phototypesetting machines, generally referred to as first-generation phototypesetting devices, evolved from two of the metal typesetting machines and one strike-on typesetting device.

The Intertype Fotosetter, first marketed in 1950, incorporated the same mechanical features of the

recirculating matrix system as the Intertype metal linecasting machine (a machine basically similar to the Linotype). One difference is that the Fotosetter matrix, called the Fotomat, contained a single photographic image in the center of the metal matrix rather than a duplex die image on its back edge. Once a line of Fotomats and word spaces was assembled, each Fotomat was positioned one at a time between a lens and a light source to expose the type character onto film or paper. The amount of space each character occupied in a line was de-

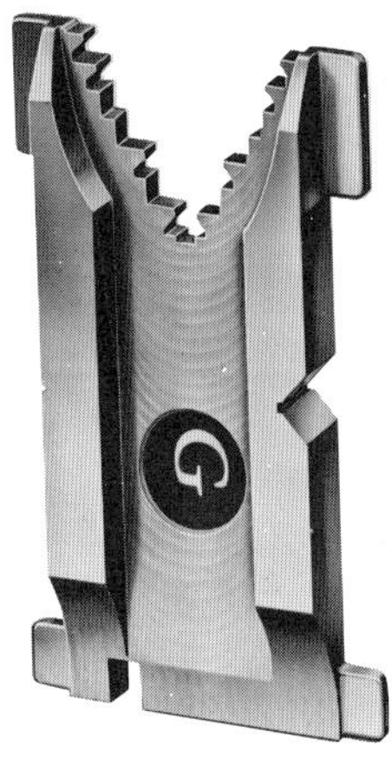

A Fotomat, the matrix used in a Fotosetter.

termined by the width of the brass Fotomat which, by means of a rack and pinion, moved the film cassette the required distance. This was known as the letter escapement.

Justification with the Fotosetter was automatic, but instead of space bands, fixed spaces were used between words. Prior to making the exposure, the

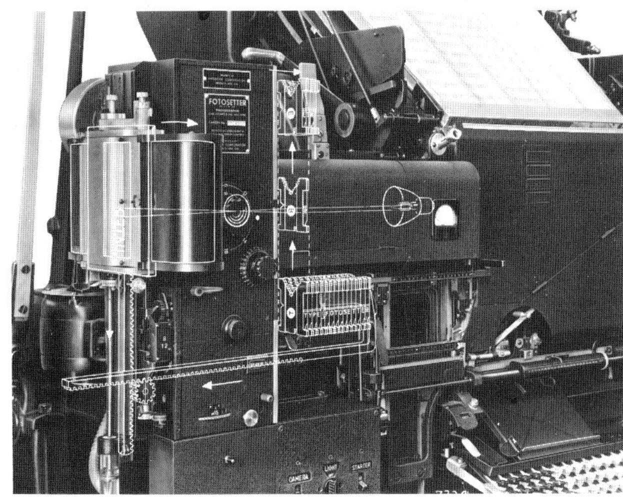

Exposing a character on a Fotosetter.

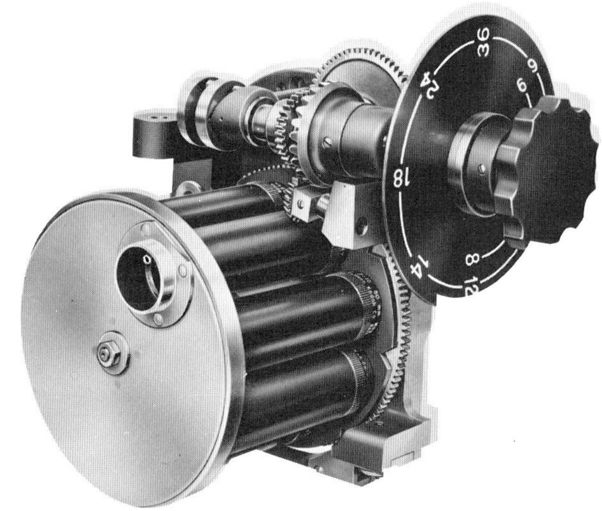

The lens turret of a Fotosetter.

camera measured the entire line length including the fixed spaces, and the deficit needed for justification was automatically distributed between words and, in earlier models of the Fotosetter, between letters.

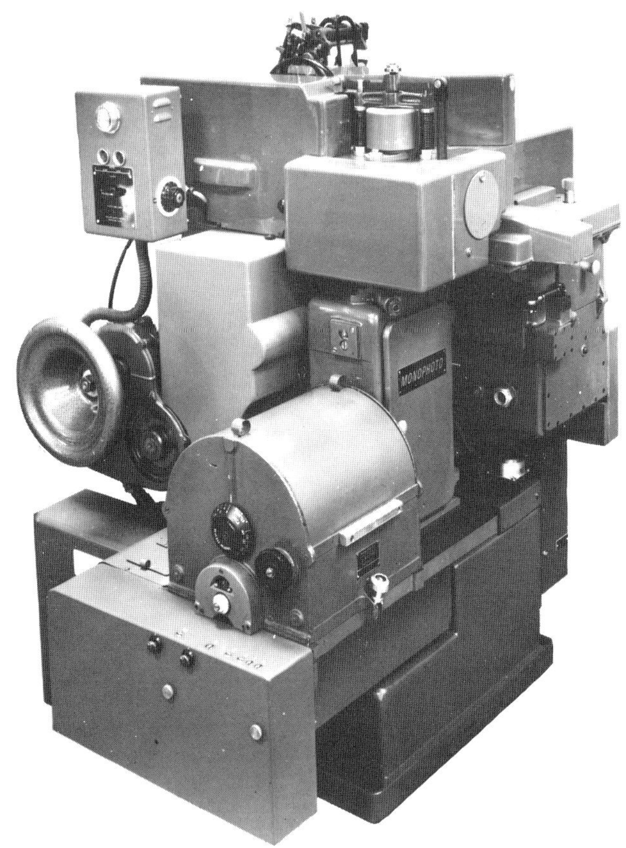

Monophoto typesetter.

The Fotosetter magazines contained 117 channels; a double distributor permitted mixing 228 characters. In addition, a manually operated revolving lens turret with fourteen different lenses made possible reproduction sizes from 3 to 72 points, from matrices of 6, 8, 12, and 18 points.

The Monophoto typesetter was developed to set type photographically rather than by "hot metal" as produced on the Monotype caster. A similar Monotype keyboard for punching the paper ribbon was used.

Justification with the Monophoto was much the same as with metal, and manual adjustment of a single lens reproduced different image sizes. In place of the matrix case with metal matrices, the matrix case was a film assembly of the font.

The Justowriter strike-on typesetting machine, a typewriter-like device, was the forerunner of a first-generation phototypesetting device, the *ATF typesetter*. This phototypesetter was tape-operated and similar to the Justowriter with only one exception, it used a revolving disk containing 168 letter images. The images on the disk were flashed on a photographic film or paper that was carried in a cassette. Escapement, or space required for each image, was determined by a gear mechanism that moved the carriage containing the cassette; the disk did not escape. Size changes could only be accomplished by changing the font disk. For each new font disk, a carriage gear ratio had to be changed manually for the new "unit" of width.

Second-Generation Phototypesetters

Second-generation is the classification of the earliest systems that were designed specifically for setting type photographically; they were not adaptations of earlier typesetters.

Second-generation phototypesetters could be operated directly from a keyboard in which both the keyboard and the photocomposition device were one unit, or from an encoded paper or magnetic tape prepared on a separate keyboard.

Prior to keyboarding a manuscript, format data such as typeface, point size, set width, and spacing between lines had to be entered into the keyboard mechanism. This was done by function switches or operator key commands. Once completed, the operator could then proceed to set the type. A line counter accumulated the width value of each character and space, and when a justification range was reached, the operator made an end-of-line decision that could come at the end of a complete word or, if necessary to fill the line, at a discretionary hyphenation. Each line that was set was held in a buffer until an end-of-line decision was made, then it was released for automatic justification on tape or directly into the phototypesetter.

On some phototypesetters, the character width value or escapement was carried on the encoded paper or magnetic tape, but others required prewired plug boards that were inserted into the phototypesetter for each font used.

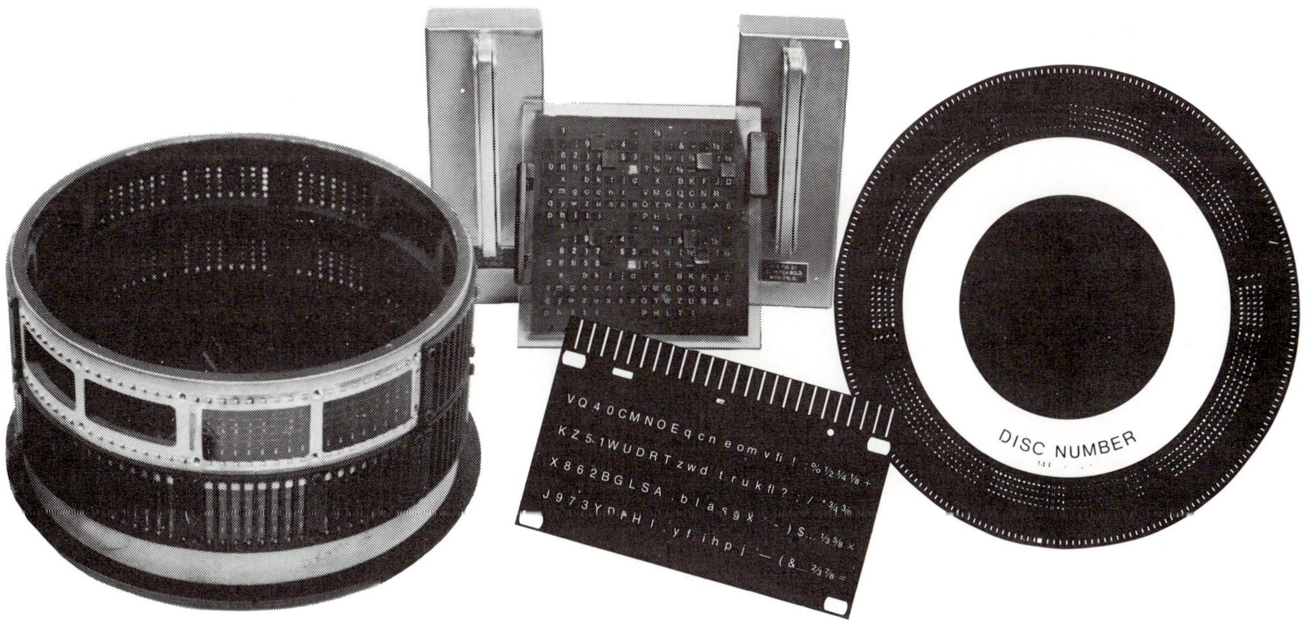

Four common font configurations used in second-generation typesetters: drum, glass matrix, film strip, and disk.

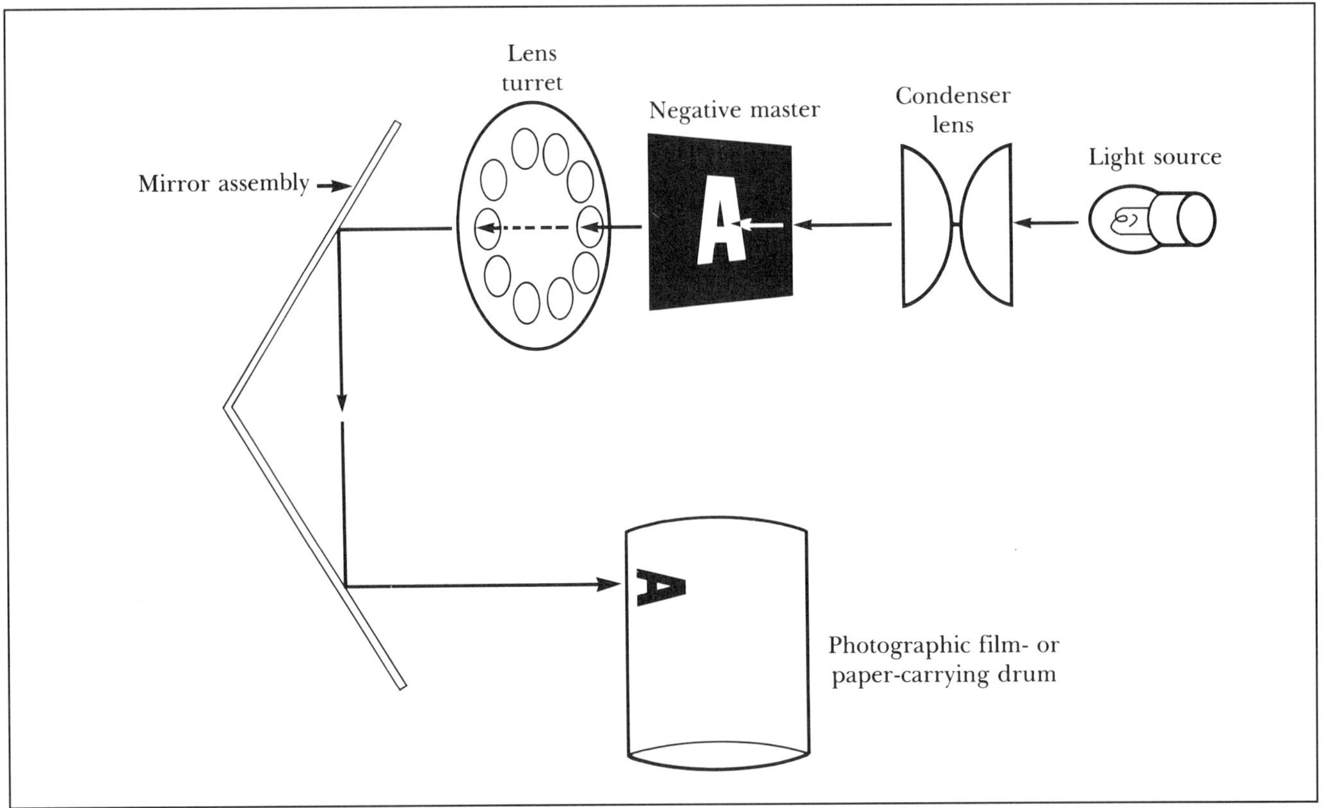

Basic principles of a second-generation machine. The actual mechanics of the system varied from manufacturer to manufacturer.

The output unit. Second-generation phototypesetters used a grid, spinning disk, drum, or similar means to carry negative image matrices that were projected onto photographic film or paper. If the second-generation phototypesetter used a grid, the entire grid was illuminated and the desired character was selected by a series of optical wedges that allowed only the character image to pass through a series of prisms, enlarging lenses, and mirrors until it was finally positioned and exposed on the photographic film or paper.

A stroboscopic light illuminated the negative images carried on spinning disks or drums. Machines using a spinning disk or spinning drum generated characters at a greater speed, since they did not depend upon the mechanical movement of optical wedges. Instead, as each encoded character was spun into position in front of an aperture or shield, a stroboscopic light illuminated and projected it through the optic system to the film or paper.

The horizontal position of each character image was controlled by a traveling lens that escaped the required character width or by a moving carriage that held the film or paper cassette. The film advance mechanism determined the vertical spacing between each line.

When phototypesetting was completed, the film cassette was removed and the film or paper passed through a processor that developed and fixed the photographic images.

Computerized second-generation typesetting. Since perforated tape used for driving typesetting devices was encoded in digitized form, computerized typesetting devices were practical to develop. These devices were made primarily to relieve the keyboard operator of end-of-line decisions, thus increasing machine output. Early models had a controller that contained hard-wired logic to perform hyphenless justification or, in more sophisticated models, hyphenation and justification. Hyphenation in these systems was performed by pure logic only; dictionary and exceptions-to-the-rule hyphenation was not possible.

An input tape—sometimes referred to as an "idiot tape"—was prepared with an encoding scheme that preceded the encoded manuscript. This tape, paper or magnetic, was placed into the controller that produced a second tape containing hyphenation and justification codes. This revised tape was then used to drive the phototypesetter. In cases where hyphenation was not done logically by

the controller, an operator would insert special hyphen codes between syllables in large words that might appear at the end of a line. If hyphenation was possible, the controller would select one of the hyphen codes for the end of the line. All other hyphen codes that were not used were rejected.

The next development was the use of a stored-program computer. A format program (written specifications of typesetting requirements in a language acceptable to the computer) set up the basic criteria from which the computer could arrange or compose the input data. The data was preceded by an encoded format code such as /F1. This code was translated by the stored program, which compiled and executed magnetic tape output that was justified, hyphenated, and paginated.

Hyphenation by computer was done by *logic* and by an *exception dictionary*. (An **exception dictionary** is a computer file listing words that are not logically hyphenated.) A line was set until a word overset the line. The overset word was passed through a hyphenation routine that first checked to see if the word was in the exception dictionary. Failing to find the word in the exception dictionary, the computer then subjected the word to a routine of hyphenation logic. The first breakdown was by prefix and suffix; then the root of the word was broken down according to logic criteria.

Once the hyphenation point was determined, the portion of the word that was to be retained was sent back to the line with a hyphen ending, and justification began. The spaces were counted, and the additional space required to justify was divided equally among the word spaces. The original space between words was the minimal space allowable—approximately one-third of a capital "M." If the "M" was divided into eighteen units, such as in Monotype composition, the minimum word space allowed would be six units.

Through the twenty or so years that second-generation typesetters were manufactured, the mainframe computer was replaced first by the minicomputer and then by the microcomputer, and paper tape was eventually replaced by the floppy disk. Although some second-generation phototypesetters are still being used, most have been replaced by digital typesetters or imagesetters.

Third-Generation Phototypesetters

Computerized photocomposition systems that include a cathode-ray tube (CRT) as part of an image-forming system are termed third-generation phototypesetting devices. Characters are created

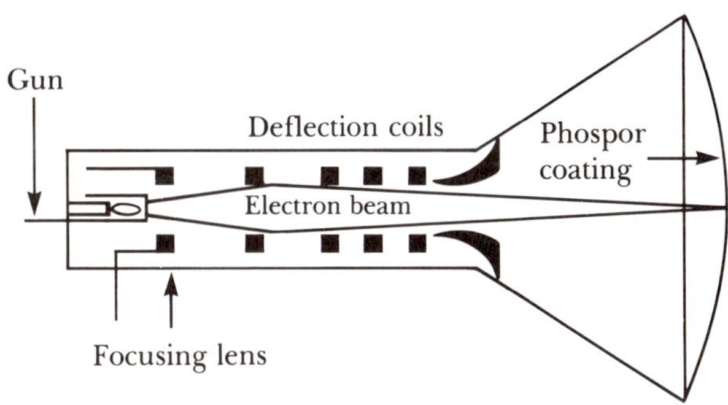

A cathode-ray tube.

through the stroking of an electron beam on the face of a cathode-ray tube.

Early machines stored negative character images similar to second-generation machines. But, instead of strobe lights for illumination, light from an index or blank CRT passed through the matrix to photomultipliers or photoelectric cells, where they were converted to a digital format for stroking on a CRT tube. The strokes on the CRT tube were in vertical patterns, formed by a series of signals.

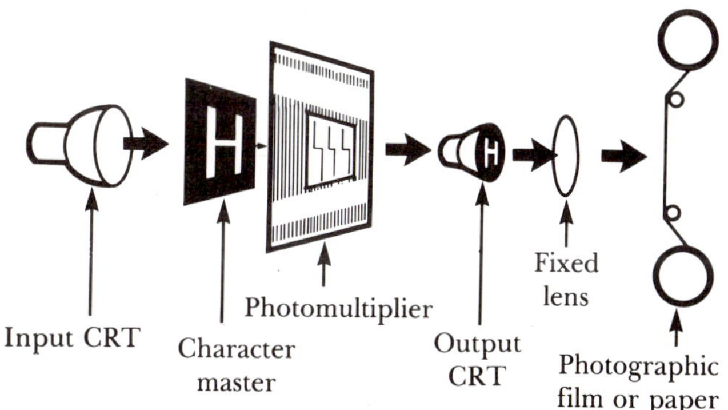

Basic principles of a negative-master CRT phototypesetter. The electron beam of the first CRT produced an area of very fine, closely spaced vertical lines to cover the area of the selected character. The character was housed in either a drum or grid backed by a photomultiplier that converted the vertical lines of the light-projected image into electrical impulses. The character, therefore, was read as a series of vertical lines and fed to a second smaller CRT. This CRT reproduced the pattern of the original character, element by element, as a series of vertical lines. The image then passed through a fixed lens system to expose photographic film or paper.

Each series of signals corresponded to a vertical scan of a narrow portion of the character. As the scan was made, on-off signals indicated the presence or absence of character portions within the

vertical scan. For instance, a narrow vertical scan through the center of a capital "B" would have had six on-off signals. These signals were then transmitted electronically to the face of a CRT. The speed of the scans and the generated signals that appeared on the cathode-ray tube were so rapid that the image appeared as a whole character rather than just vertical signals. The image was picked up from the tube by a traveling lens that projected it onto the film or paper.

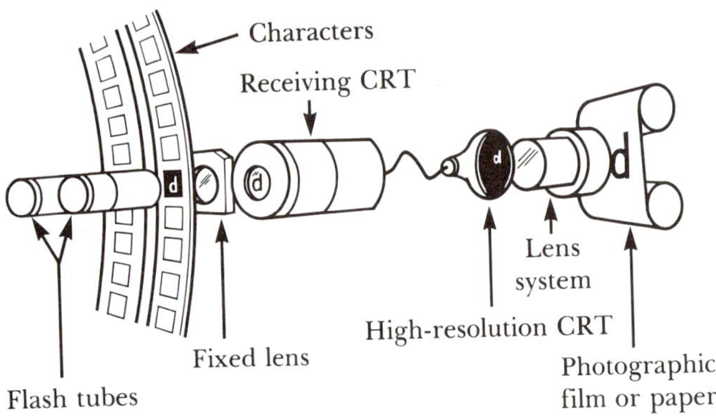

Another early CRT typesetter. Notice that the first CRT is used to receive the character image.

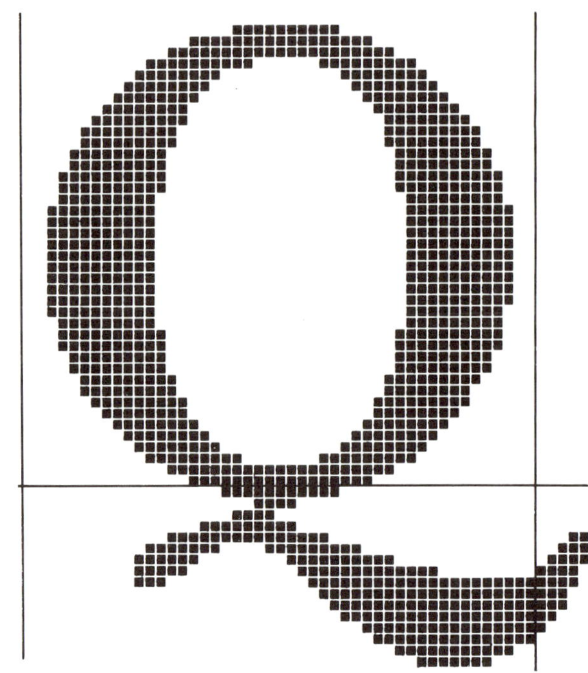

Courtesy Agfa Division, Miles Inc.

A digitized character.

Later versions of CRT typesetters, as well as some of the early ones, use image patterns that are in a digital format stored on either a magnetic tape or disk. When the first character of a font is called for, the entire font is brought over into the machine's electronic memory. Digitization of characters in a binary format is the recording of the starting and stopping points of strokes of an image. Other systems use a matrix of tiny dots for image formation or store the character's outline. Many digitized fonts can be accessed on command at a very high rate of speed. Any typesetter that stores information in a digital format is called a **digital typesetter.**

Two principal systems are used to create the image on photographic film or paper using a CRT. In the first system, a line or character is generated on the face of the CRT and goes through a lens system—stationary lens or moving mirror—to the film. The second system uses fiber optics instead of a lens in which one end of an optical fiber is permanently fused against the face of the CRT and the other end is in intimate contact with the film.

Compared to second-generation phototypesetters, which have a speed of from twenty to sixty lines per minute, CRT typesetters are much faster in terms of characters or lines produced.

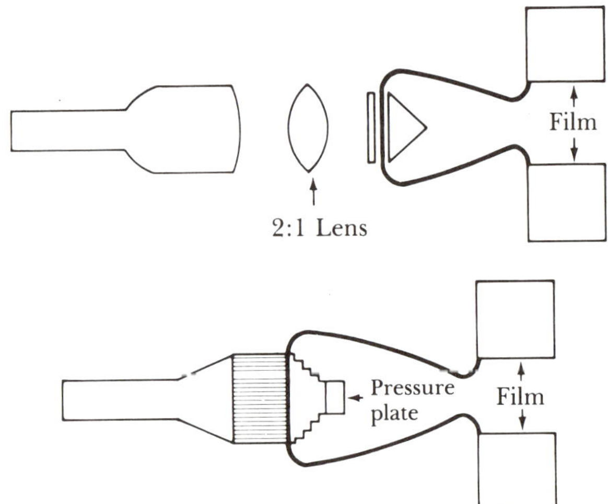

Cathode-ray tube photographic systems used with digitized type: standard system *(top)* and fiber optics system.

Imagesetters

Any typesetter that stores font information digitally is called a digital typesetter. Therefore, the third-generation, or CRT, typesetter is classified as a digital machine. However, several post-third-generation machines are also classified as digital even though they are not CRT machines. In fact, these newer machines are generally referred to as **imagesetters,** because their ability to store infor-

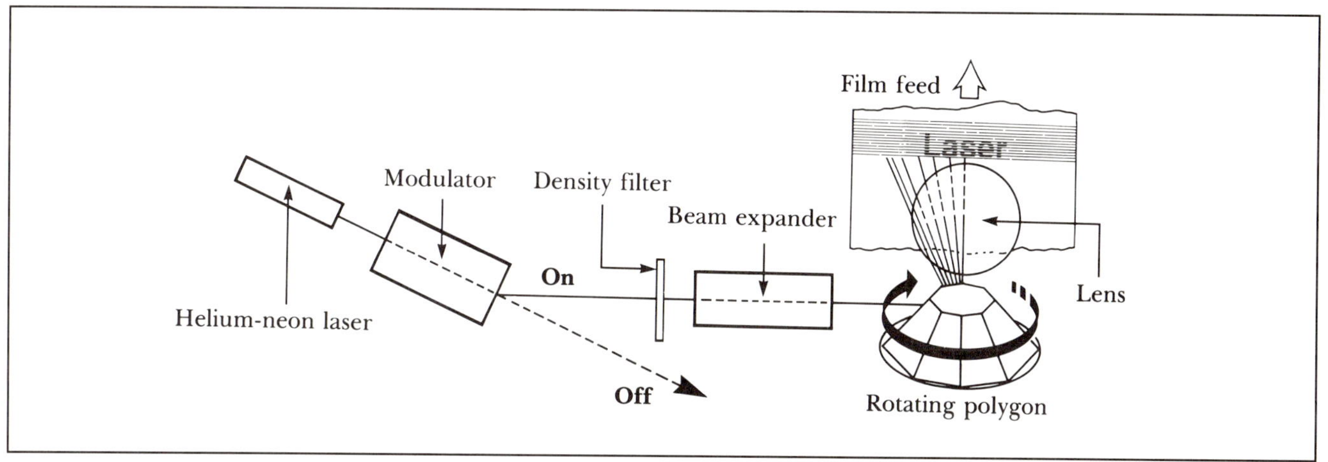

Courtesy Monotype

A laser imagesetter that uses a rotating polygon to position type or graphics on paper, film, or printing plate.

mation in a digital format permits them to output not only type characters but also images, such as logos, line art, and halftones. (Rapid advances in technology have made the concept of "generation" obsolete.)

Imagesetters store characters digitally like third-generation machines but use various methods to produce an image on paper, film, or printing plate.

The laser imagesetter, or fourth-generation phototypesetter, uses digital information to control a laser beam. With these machines, the page to be output is first rasterized and turned into a bitmap. The laser is usually turned on and off rapidly or modulated to produce the desired bitmap on the paper, film, or printing plate as required. The laser beam is deflected across the page using various methods, the most common of which is a spinning polygon-shaped mirror. As the laser sweeps across to form one raster line, it is pulsed on and off to image the bitmap desired. After one raster line is imaged, the output medium (e.g., film) is advanced one raster line and the process repeats itself. High-quality laser imagesetters have a resolution in excess of 1,000 dots/in. (dpi). Most laser printers used in the electronic publishing environment have a resolution of approximately 300 dpi. Laser printers are used to produce illustrated documentation and the first and subsequent typeset proofs before outputting a job on a high-resolution imagesetter.

Although current output devices for imagesetting are typically based on laser technology, other marking engines or output technology is found; for example, ink jet and light-emitting diodes (LEDs). (A **marking engine** is any device that puts dots or other marks on the output medium—the paper, film, or printing plate.)

Regardless of the type of marking engine, current output devices are raster printers and therefore require a means of taking commands for type and graphics and rendering these as bitmaps. This step of rasterizing the data takes place in what is known as a **raster image processor** (RIP). Therefore, most current output systems are made up of a marking engine, a RIP, and an interface between the RIP and the computer used to drive the system.

This is the basic configuration, but many other options are available. One RIP may be connected to several different marking engines, providing bitmaps for different devices with different resolutions. A RIP may be equipped with more than one interface to make it compatible with a variety of computer systems. One marking engine may have more than one RIP connected to it. This may be desirable to improve processing or to support different input command languages. RIPs are controlled by an input command language, also known as a **page description language** (PDL). The most popular PDL today is Adobe PostScript.

Input Units

The primary input device for phototypesetting for years was the video display terminal (VDT). However, with the widespread use of desktop publishing, electronic prepress, and imagesetting, the personal computer has become the primary input device. The use of the personal computer is covered extensively in Chapter 12, "Electronic Prepress Production."

Video Display Terminal

Most video display terminals used in phototypesetting applications were specially designed for the purpose. Those VDTs that could only perform phototypesetting functions were referred to as "dedicated" units.

A VDT consists of a TV-like screen, a keyboard, and, in later versions, a means of storing the keystrokes. A VDT permits typographic material to be input (by keyboard or from a storage medium), displayed, and manipulated by deletion, insertion, and rearrangement; specifications of type size and style as well as line length and spacing to be applied; perhaps a hyphenation-and-justification routine to be performed; and the modified material to be output to a phototypesetter or other device. VDTs specifically designed for typesetting show line endings and word breaks on the screen. If word breaks are incorrect, the operator can correct them on the screen using the discretionary hyphen key, which indicates the point(s) where a word can be broken.

In order to set type using the VDT as an input unit, the operator must input commands into the machine. VDT keyboards have special keys for most of the typographic functions. However, the use of precedence coding allowed the keyboard for many typesetters to be streamlined. **Precedence coding** is the use of special keystrokes to alert the typesetting machine that the character or characters that follow are to be interpreted as instructions (e.g., line length change) or special characters. Some code sequences require an "on command" and an "off command." Most phototypesetters operate on the principle of **mnemonics,** in which simple codes relating to the typographical functions are used as commands. For example, "FT" might be the mnemonic code for font. Special characters, or **pi characters,** not a part of a typical font can be accessed by using precedence coding. Depending on the typesetter, pi characters might include accent marks, asterisks and daggers, degree symbols, mathematical symbols, chemistry symbols, inferior and superior characters, single-piece fractions, bullets, and copyright and trademark symbols.

With a conventional phototypesetting system, the equipment that prepared input for the phototypesetter was sometimes called the **front end.** The term **direct input** was originally applied to a system that combined the input keyboard and the phototypesetter in the same piece of equipment; the keyboarding and typesetting commonly operated simultaneously. Later "direct input" was extended to any small setup in which the same person keyboarded and operated the typesetter; however, keystrokes were recorded on a floppy disk for later rather than simultaneous typesetting; and there might be an additional input/editor keyboard without typesetter. This began to be called a "small integrated system" in contrast to the "large integrated system" consisting of several independent VDT keyboards all feeding the typesetting

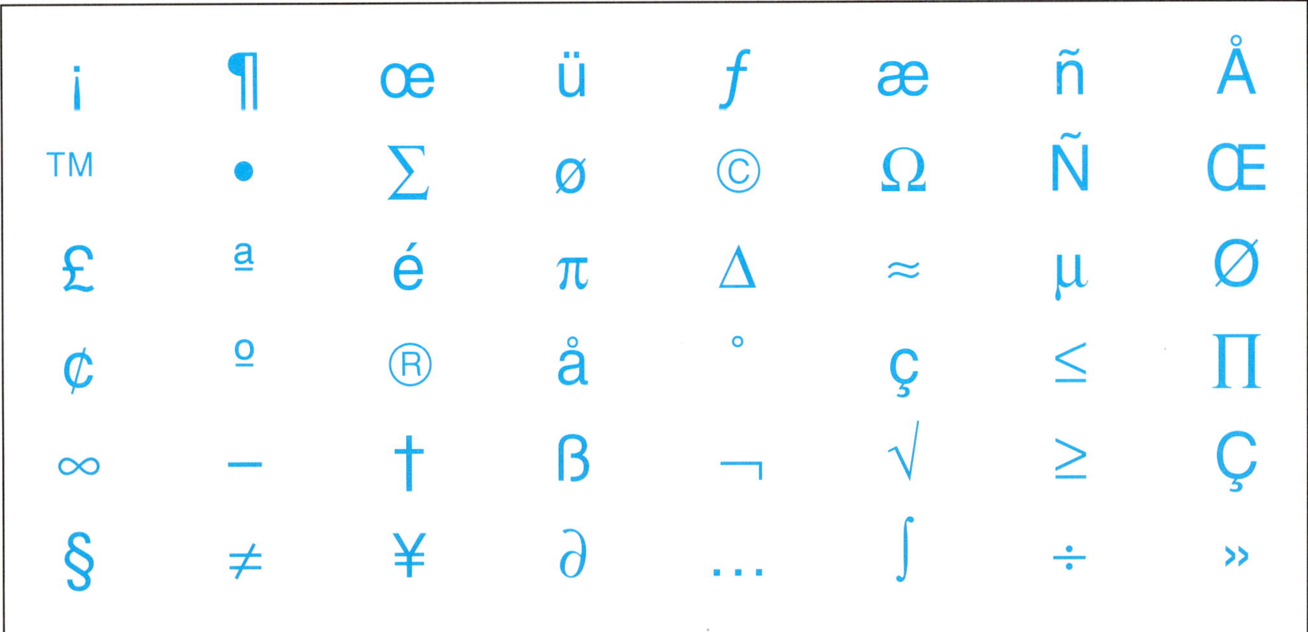

A sample of pi characters, or special characters, that are used in typesetting.

operation. It was to the VDT keyboards of the large integrated system that the term "front end" was most usually applied.

Another common situation with conventional phototypesetting systems was a keyboard with its own video display terminal and computer serving as the input operator's equipment, with the photounit separate. If the VDT is not connected to the output unit, the VDT is said to be "off-line."

Personal Computers

The use of PCs with word-processing programs and/or page-makeup software has become the primary means of typesetter and imagesetter input. These procedures are discussed in depth in Chapter 12, "Electronic Prepress Production."

In brief, however, most customers now capture the keystrokes for a job using a word-processing program and store the information on a floppy disk or other magnetic storage medium. The information is then given to the typesetter or service bureau on disk (or other magnetic storage medium) or the information is transferred via modem, and the typesetter or service bureau puts the information into page format. In another common scenario, the customer will use a page-makeup software program to lay out the pages for a job on his or her personal computer.

In general, with VDTs, typesetting could be classified as a "code-driven" process, because the operator often had to input special codes to access various typographic functions (although special function keys were also available). With personal computers and page-makeup software, the process is better classified as "menu-driven," because the system operator usually selects functions from pull-down menus on the computer screen.

Other Input Devices

In addition to VDTs and microcomputers, several other devices are used as input units. In addition to the devices mentioned below, some systems have a graphics tablet with light pen or mouse to input data and manipulate text and graphics.

Optical character recognition devices. Optical character recognition (OCR) devices, or document readers, recognize typewritten or printed character images and convert them into machine-readable codes that can be stored on a disk for later use. Sophistication of OCR machines vary; some can read only specially stylized typewriter fonts, while others can "learn" to read almost any character image, even previously printed variable-spaced material, such as in a book or magazine.

Illustration scanners. Similar in several respects to OCR devices are black-and-white illustration scanners/digitizers. These devices are specially designed to convert graphic images (e.g., drawings and photographs) into machine-readable codes (digital bits of information that represent picture elements—pixels). The graphic images can be merged with text for full-page composition. Some systems permit the graphic images to be manipulated in a variety of ways.

Several methods have been used to scan images. The use of an array of charge-coupled devices (CCDs) is the most common method today.

With the proper software, many illustration scanners can also perform optical character recognition. Illustration scanners are discussed in detail in Chapter 12, "Electronic Prepress Production."

Image Preview Capabilities

Some VDTs gave the operator a close approximation of how the image would appear when typeset. A VDT with this ability was called a **previewer** and would usually show actual typefaces and sizes. The acronym **WYSIWYG** ("what you see is what you get") was often given to a previewer that gave a representation of the typeset image. Some of these previewers permitted viewing of material in real or simulated typefaces. Some were called interactive previewers, because they enabled the operator to preview a job on a screen and to alter the content or the format without exiting the preview mode.

WYSIWYG is now a standard feature with most word-processing software programs and all page-makeup programs used with computers.

Editing, Markup, and Typesetting Operations

This section discusses "traditional" editing, markup, and typesetting operations. How these operations differ in electronic prepress production will be briefly discussed also.

In traditional typesetting, the typesetter works from a manuscript, or "copy," which is usually typewritten. The copy, as prepared by the author(s), normally undergoes two finishing operations before

it reaches the typesetter: editing and markup. Editing is concerned with the *content* of the written material; markup is concerned with its *format* and *typographical style.*

Editing

In its largest sense, editing deals with the planning, development, and correction of written material in cooperation with the author(s). Much of this editorial function may be performed before a complete typescript is submitted. In this chapter, we are only concerned with the stage of the editorial process that involves the correction of typing and other errors and the marking of head and subhead levels for the information of the designer who does the markup.

A typescript is not a satisfactory manuscript for typesetting if it has many corrections—particularly if there are crowded-in or illegible insertions. The changes should be indicated with standard copy-editing marks. The level of each head, if there are divisions and subdivisions of material, should be identified by writing a letter or number beside each head with a colored pencil, using a code agreed upon by the copy editor and markup designer.

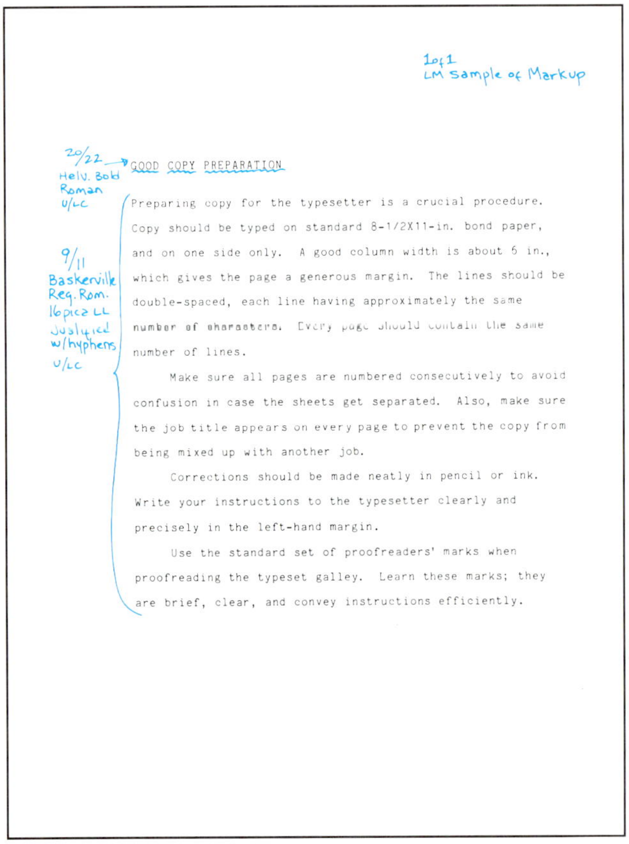

1 of 1
LM Sample of Markup

20/22 Helv. Bold Roman U/LC → GOOD COPY PREPARATION

9/11 Baskerville Reg. Rom. 16 pica LL Justified w/hyphens U/LC

Preparing copy for the typesetter is a crucial procedure. Copy should be typed on standard 8-1/2X11-in. bond paper, and on one side only. A good column width is about 6 in., which gives the page a generous margin. The lines should be double-spaced, each line having approximately the same number of characters. Every page should contain the same number of lines.

Make sure all pages are numbered consecutively to avoid confusion in case the sheets get separated. Also, make sure the job title appears on every page to prevent the copy from being mixed up with another job.

Corrections should be made neatly in pencil or ink. Write your instructions to the typesetter clearly and precisely in the left-hand margin.

Use the standard set of proofreaders' marks when proofreading the typeset galley. Learn these marks; they are brief, clear, and convey instructions efficiently.

Typesetting instructions, the markup, written on the typewritten manuscript.

With the widespread use of computers, changes indicated on an edited printout are made to an existing text file, and a new printout is produced. This is then checked against the previous printout to make sure all corrections have been made. If not, the text file is reopened and the remaining corrections are made. This procedure continues until the printout and the corresponding text file are error-free. The editor then indicates the level of each head on this printout.

Markup

The design function with respect to type matter is to determine the format, typefaces, type sizes, spacing, and other typographic specifications. Marking these specifications on the typesetter's copy is called **markup.**

With metal typesetting, a straightforward and fairly standard procedure of markup evolved. The markup person used standard symbols to convey formatting information and agreed-upon abbreviations to indicate typeface, size, line spacing, and other typographical specifications—for text, for each level of head, etc. The linecaster operator knew how to translate these marks into machine operations (for example, change to upper rail and later back to lower rail), and some of the formatting was done on the makeup table.

With the advent of phototypesetting, the same procedure continued at first. However, as the phototypesetting systems evolved, new complexities were brought to the markup function.

Two general practices resulted, with a variety of gradations between them, depending on the nature of the equipment and capabilities of personnel involved. One practice is to use traditional markup, relying on the operator to translate this information into appropriate machine instructions. The other extreme is to have markup specialists who completely code the copy before it goes to the typesetter.

Typesetting

The phototypesetting keyboard, like the typewriter keyboard, has two kinds of keys: those for the characters, often called the alphanumeric keys, and those for machine functions. The layout of the alphanumeric keys is nearly the same on the phototypesetting keyboard as on the standard typewriter keyboard, with a few important differences. On

most typewriters, the lowercase "l" is used also to represent the figure "1"; in printing, these two characters are different and therefore must have different keys. Typewriter beginning and ending quote marks are the same, the single being on one key and the double on another; in printing the beginning and ending quote marks are different and thus on different keys, while single or double quotes are determined by the number of strokes or by the unshift and shift positions of the same key. There are other differences, but the arrangement of letters is identical.

Function keys are another matter. In addition to the space bar, shift, and return of the typewriter keyboard, the phototypesetter keyboard typically has a super shift or option key to access "pi" characters, keys for en and em spaces, and such formatting keys as "quad left," "quad right," and "quad center." ("Quad left" means to set the copy flush with the left margin. In hand composition, a quad was a spacing piece.) Instead of the typewriter's backspace key, the phototypesetter keyboard has a whole series of editing keys, such as those controlling the movement of the video display cursor (which marks the spot where action occurs), those for character and word cancel, etc.

Although alphanumeric matter may be input without typographic specifications, the keyboard of a phototypesetter typically has provision for these typographic specifications: font selection, point size, line length, and line space. Advanced systems have additional capabilities, especially in formatting, up to pagination.

Thus function keys vary considerably on different equipment. At one time keys proliferated on keyboards because of the inclination to provide a separate key for each new command. But the use of precedence codes—special keys followed by certain combinations of character keys activating the computer to perform certain functions—and other techniques reduced the keyboards to a convenient size. These developments also brought about the variety of special markup procedures previously mentioned. An alternative method to inputting with a phototypesetting keyboard is to put typewritten material into an optical character recognition (OCR) device. With an OCR device, a scanner reads and records the typewritten material on a magnetic carrier device in a form recognizable by a typesetting machine.

The most common method of typesetting today is to use personal computers loaded with the appropriate software that can make up pages electronically and drive output units such as imagesetters and laser printers. The procedures involved are discussed in chapter 12.

Proofreading and Corrections

A system of error detection must be used to make certain typeset output is correct. This inspection system is called **proofreading.** Usually, a typeset proof is read by a proofreader or by two individuals, one called the copyholder, the other a reader. Original copy must be compared word for word to ensure correctness. Each proof is marked with proofreaders' marks, which indicate the nature of the error. Proofreaders' marks are standard and recognized by experienced authors and typesetters. With imagesetting, plain-paper printouts are used for proofreading purposes.

Errors in metal composition are usually erroneous characters or transposition of characters during assembly of a line of mats, transpositions of lines when delivered to the galley, or wrong font characters running in the magazine.

In phototypesetting and imagesetting, additional errors can occur as a result of incorrect keyboarding and incorrect formatting instructions. Error rates for electromechanical and computer-driven phototypesetters and imagesetters are practically nil, but, when they occur, they should be detected during the initial proofreading of computer printouts or galley proofs.

The quality of the copy that is input into any typesetting or imagesetting system must be controlled to ensure rapid and accurate conversion of the material into type for further reproduction. This is important in phototypesetting and imagesetting because corrections are even more costly than they were in metal typesetting systems. A style guide should be available to enable customers to submit copy to which all operators are accustomed. This limits operator decisions and reduces second guesses to a minimum, as well as reduces errors. The style guide should explain and list correct applications of the principles of typography, typesetting, and printing.

Proofreading Procedures

Proofreading is normally carried out in four basic steps:

1. The first reading is to detect mechanical and human errors in the typesetting or imagesetting operation. The first galley proof or laser printout is read to accomplish this.

2. A proofreading of the revised galley or printout is performed to make sure the corrections have been properly made and their position is in correct sequence.

3. Additional revision cycles may be necessary to obtain a correct galley or printout. If completion of the second step results in completely correct galleys, the third proofreading step is eliminated.

4. Composed or made-up pages are proofed for completeness of text including head placement, lines in proper sequence and correctly spaced, pages in proper order, and finally checked to see if all corrections have been made and all special instructions followed. With imagesetting, the placement and size of illustrations are also checked.

A **galley proof** is a proof of type before it is made into pages. The name derives from proofs made from metal type that have just been set with no vertical spacing added. In phototypesetting, the first proof is the phototypesetter output, and in imagesetting, the first proof is plain-paper copy from a laser printer. Computer printouts of word-processed PC manuscripts should be proofed before the job goes to page makeup and imagesetting.

Press sheets should not be checked for accuracy of typesetting, but they should be checked for proper page locations, photo placement, and print quality. Making corrections at this stage is equivalent to redoing the job in its entirety.

Correction

The correction cycle can be more time-consuming and costly than the initial typesetting operation.

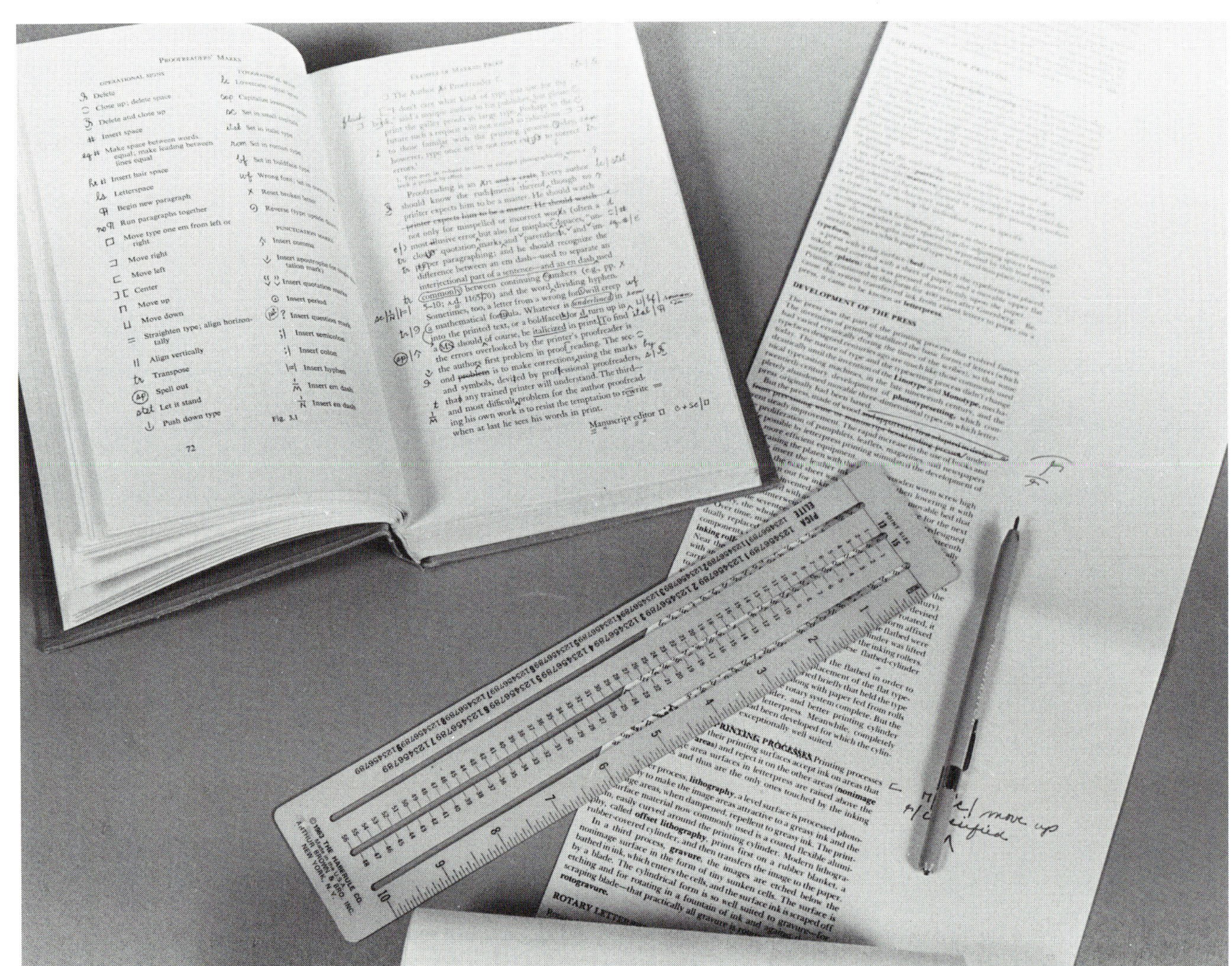

A galley being proofread. Notice the ruler for measuring line lengths and line spacing.

Proofreaders' Marks

Mark	Meaning
⊙	Period or full point
,/	Comma
/=/ or /-/	Hyphen
:/	Colon
;/	Semicolon
’	Apostrophe
!/	Exclamation mark or exclamation point
set ?/	Question mark or interrogation point
1/EN or 1/N	En dash
1/EM or 1/M	One-em dash
2/EM or 2/M	Two-em dash
( ) or (|)	Parentheses
[ ] or [|]	Brackets
“ ”	Quotation marks (double)
‘ ’	Quotation marks (single)
{ or { }	Brace or pair of braces
	Align horizontally
||	Straighten or justify (align vertically)
	Move to the left
	Move to the right
	Bring indented matter to the left
	Bring indented matter to the right
	Move matter up
	Move matter down
⊗	Replace letters that are broken, battered, or otherwise defective
	Set indicated material in boldface type

Mark	Meaning
bf.	Boldface type (margin indication)
	Capitalize indicated material
caps	Capitalization (margin indication)
	Set indicated in small capitals
sm. caps (sc)	Small capitals (margin indication)
	Set indicated material in capitals and small capitals
caps and small caps (c & sc)	Capitals and small capitals (margin indication)
	Set indicated material in italics
ital.	Italics (margin indication)
rom.	Change to roman
∧ or ∨	Caret
#	Insert space
eq. #	Equalize space or space evenly
hr. #	Insert hair space
ls #	Letterspace
	Indent one em or insert one-em quad
	Indent two ems
	Set indicated matter in lowercase (slant through uppercase letter)
lc.	Lowercase (margin indication)
out—see copy	Indicated matter has been omitted and must be set
	Spell out indicated matter

Mark	Meaning
sp.	Spell out (margin indication)
....	Let indicated material remain as is
stet	Let it stand or remain as it is (margin indication)
	Transpose indicated material to the position as shown
tr.	Transpose (margin indication)
	Start new papragraph
¶	Paragraph (margin indication)
	No paragraph—run indicated material together
No ¶	No paragraph (margin indication)
(?)	Query to author
| or —	Delete indicated material (vertical or horizontal line through material)
	Delete or take out (margin indication)
	Take out characters and close up
	Close up
	Transfer encircled matter to the position shown by the arrow
WF	Wrong font or wrong fonts
...	Ellipsis
	Superior character (superscript)
	Inferior characters (subscript)

Good Copy Preparation WF

Preparing copy for the typeseter is a crucial pro- t
cedure. Copy should be typed on standard 8½- x 11
in. bond paper, and on one side of the sheet
only. a good column width is about 6 in., which cap
gives the page a generous margin. The lines
should be double-spaced, each line having
approximately the number of characters. Every same
page should contain the same number of lines.
Make sure all pages are numbered consecutively to avoid confusion in case the sheets get
separated. Also , make sure the job title appears
on every page to prevent the copy from being
mixed up with another job.
Corrections should be made neatly in pencil
or ink. Write your instructions to typesetter the
clearly and precisely in the left-hand margin.
Use the standard set of proofreader's marks tr
when proofreading the typeset galley. Learn
these marks; they are brief, clear, and convey
instructions efficiently.

Good Copy Preparation

Preparing copy for the typesetter is a crucial procedure. Copy should be typed on standard 8½ × 11-in. bond paper, and on one side of the sheet only. A good column width is about 6 in., which gives the page a generous margin. The lines should be double-spaced, each line having approximately the same number of characters. Every page should contain the same number of lines.

Make sure all pages are numbered consecutively to avoid confusion in case the sheets get separated. Also, make sure the job title appears on every page to prevent the copy from being mixed up with another job.

Corrections should be made neatly in pencil or ink. Write your instructions to the typesetter clearly and precisely in the left-hand margin.

Use the standard set of proofreaders' marks when proofreading the typeset galley. Learn these marks; they are brief, clear, and convey instructions efficiently.

Proofread type *(left)* and corrected version *(right)*.

Following are two methods for correcting typesetting errors:

- Make "line corrections," i.e., rekeyboard the lines or paragraphs containing the errors and typeset a "corrections" galley. This method is rarely used today.
- Make corrections to the existing computer file and output a new galley or printout. This is the most common method today.

If line corrections are made, the corrections must be cut from the new galley and positioned over the incorrect lines or, preferably, cut into the original galley or pasteup. Each correction should be at least three lines deep to make it easier to align the correction with the original type. In addition to the awkwardness and high cost of inserting corrections, the density of reset type may not match the surrounding original type. Rigid control of processing procedures minimizes this.

With phototypesetting, making line corrections ultimately saves on the amount of phototypesetting paper used, but it is usually more desirable to correct the entire file and produce a clean galley. (With imagesetting, proofs are made on plain paper, so the issue of saving phototypesetting paper does not apply.) The machine operator opens up the file and uses the keyboard to make the corrections specified by the proofreader on the galley proof or printout. The file is then closed, and a new galley is typeset from the corrected file.

The operator manipulates the text on the screen of the VDT or computer through keyboard controls or a mouse. The keyboard consists of a standard typewriter keyboard, special keys, and cursor movement and scroll controls.

To make corrections, the operator opens up the necessary computer files and the text appears on the screen. A cursor pad and/or mouse allows the operator to position the cursor at a specific place on the screen. Controls permit the operator to scroll through a document one or more lines at a time, either forward or backward.

Deletions are accomplished by various methods on different machines. Most computers or VDTs have a delete character key used in this way: the cursor is positioned at the start of the deletion and the delete key is held down, deleting one character at a time until the deletion is completed. With some software programs, the operator uses the mouse or cursor keys to highlight text to be deleted, and then

the operator simply hits the delete key to remove all highlighted text. Insertions are made by positioning the cursor at the point where the data is to be added, putting the machine into the insert mode (if necessary), and simply typing in the correction.

Blocks of texts, not necessarily definable as a paragraph or sentence, may also be deleted, moved, or written to a new file. Different equipment and software programs have different ways to perform these functions.

Other Methods of Setting Type

Although of limited usefulness in the printing industry, various other methods of laying down letterforms for photomechanical reproduction are used, especially in the preparation of artwork: hand lettering, photolettering, and preprinted art type.

Hand lettering. In hand lettering, the artist uses pens to produce type characters for reproduction. Commercially available stencils can also be used in hand lettering to produce either outlined letters or outlines filled in with pen or brush.

Photolettering. Photolettering is done by assembling individual characters of the alphabet in the form of film positives on a copyboard, carefully spacing them out, and photographing the assemblage. The film characters are redistributed into file boxes for future use. Skilled lettering artists, working on the photo print, then firm up the connectors on scripts, modify special characters, or rearrange them to fit the layout.Photolettering machines are also available. With a photolettering machine, each character is individually exposed through a film negative onto a continuous strip of light-sensitive paper. The machine operator exposes one character, moves the paper, and then exposes the next character. The characters of the alphabet are often stored on a circular disk or a strip of film.

Preprinted art type. Preprinted art type is commercially available in several forms. Each sheet of preprinted art type contains a complete alphabet with capital and lowercase letters as well as figures and punctuation marks. This is an ideal method for setting a limited amount of display type and an inexpensive method for quick, rapid typesetting. However, using small sizes of this material would prove extremely tedious and time-consuming. One form is the **dry transfer** sheet. Here, a character on a preprinted sheet is placed in position and burnished onto the mechanical. The succeeding letters are positioned in proper order until a completed word or line is set.

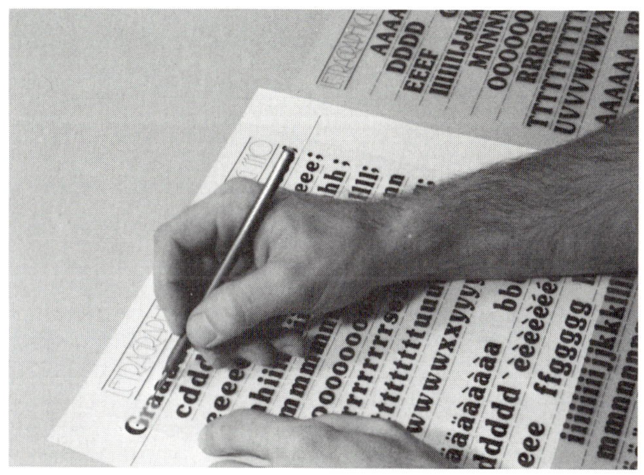

Setting a line with dry transfer type.

Cutout acetate type consists of a preprinted sheet with an adhesive base under the characters. The characters are cut apart and positioned on a mechanical.

Another form of art type consists of characters printed on strips of paper. Each character is selected by hand and placed into a composing stick. After the type is set, a strip of tape is applied across the characters to hold them together, enabling them to be transferred onto the mechanical.

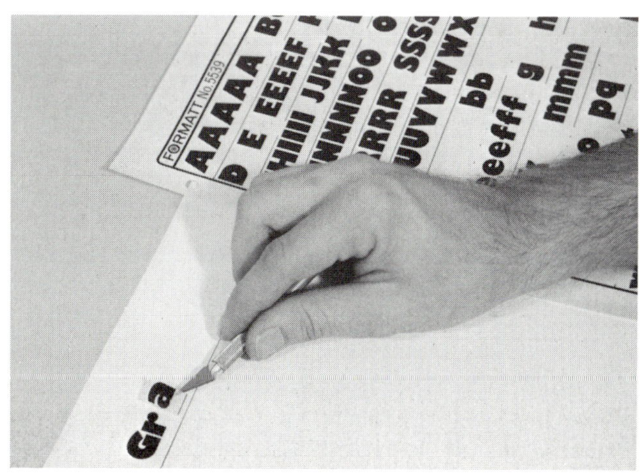

Assembling a line with cutout acetate type.

Chapter 6

Art and Copy Preparation

Planning

Art and copy preparation means transforming the writer's and designer's concepts into a suitable form for reproduction. The person who performs this task may be called a **copy preparation artist, mechanical artist,** or **pasteup artist.** The copy preparation may be done by the customer, the printer, an art studio, or an outside prepress trade shop. Often, all these may be involved in a facet of the art and copy preparation in which a special competency exists. The fact that this happens so often, coupled with the great size and high volume of the graphic communications industry, makes good communications based on technical knowledge so important.

In reality, smooth, well-established standard operating procedures and effective communications are often not the case. A communications gap between designers and artists and printing technologists can cause misunderstanding and misinterpretation of procedures. If designers or pasteup artists are unaware of production problems and technical limitations faced in reproduction, and if printing technologists—graphic arts photographers, film assemblers, platemakers, press operators, and binders and finishers—do not understand the means and techniques that artists must employ to achieve desired aesthetic effects, then high production costs and high tempers due to excessive and unnecessary steps in camera and film assembly (stripping) will result. This chapter is intended to help the graphic designer and artist to prepare art in a way that simplifies reproduction through communication and a knowledge of the most effective procedures for getting the results required without sacrificing the design. This chapter discusses the conventional methods of art and copy preparation, and chapter 12, "Electronic Prepress Production," discusses the computer-based methods of art and copy preparation, among other topics.

The **graphic designer** or **creative artist** may originate the overall design of the printed piece or may design as well as paste up the camera-ready copy or use a computer to create artwork and assemble the pages electronically. As an art specialist—retoucher, calligrapher, illustrator, or the like—he or she may execute only certain elements of the design.

The **pasteup** or **mechanical artist** assembles all the elements of the piece—type, illustrations, etc.—by following an original design or layout, pasting the elements on the board or acetate that serves as the base sheet for the artwork. It is the pasteup artist's complete camera-ready copy that is photographed to make negatives and printing plates.

It is the artist's responsibility to plan his or her work with the goal of minimizing extra production steps in the photomechanical and film assembly operations. The artists must even anticipate printing, finishing, and binding problems that may have been overlooked by the original designer. An understanding of each production operation is necessary if copy is to be prepared for efficient production by the designer or artist.

Importance of Planning

The importance of *planning* cannot be stressed too heavily to the graphic designer, artist, or art director, for they are the ones often responsible for organizing the job, and it is during the conception and design stages that the specifications of the job are detailed for each step through the delivery of the printed piece.

Because too few people take the time to understand properly each stage of production as well as the attitudes, requirements, and customs of the segment of the industry they are working in, printed jobs are often poorly scheduled, incorrectly prepared, and subject to many last-minute corrections. That the same number of printed jobs are not unsuccessfully or poorly produced is a credit to the skill and ingenuity of the employees of the graphic communications industry.

A Planning Checklist

In the chapter “Planning and Control,” which discusses initial planning of a job as it relates to all plant areas that will work on it, stress is given to the importance of consultation among the key people involved. With respect to art and copy preparation, these may include the client (a must), writer, designer, production coordinator, account executive, art director, production manager, scheduler, and printer—in short, whoever must be aware of the details of the job early on in order to perform their tasks efficiently, without causing delays, needless work, or disappointment. Consideration of the limiting aspects of the job are discussed here as they affect art and copy preparation.

Does the client have a format and style in mind for the printed piece? Printed pieces can be produced in a variety of formats and styles involving different design characteristics, different production procedures, and varying costs. A format may be a simple, one-page, one-color mailing piece; the design may call for several parallel and perpendicular folds, or it may be a complex multicolor display with a series of folds and diecuts. Formats can take the shape of folders, booklets, direct-mail pieces, calendars, reply cards, packages, and posters, to name a few. The more complex the format, the more difficult and more expensive it is to produce. The artist should know if the format was determined as a result of a budgetary limitation by the client—he or she should be aware of what the client is trying to accomplish.

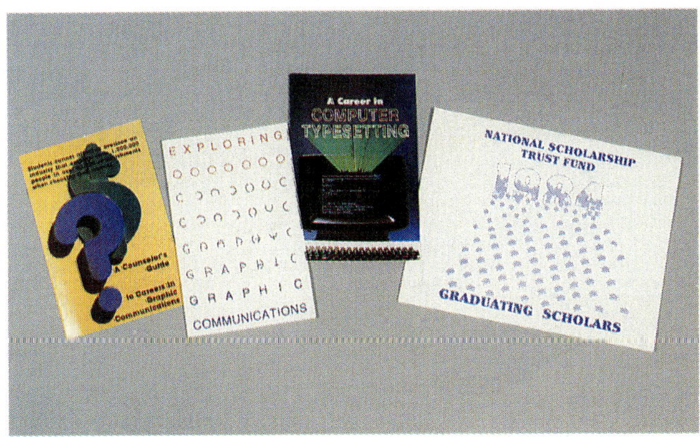

Various design formats include folders, booklets, direct-mail pieces, magazines, greeting cards, and calendars.

Style is the particular aesthetic approach the artist selects to present the client’s message. The message may lend itself to typographic matter only, or it may require a photograph or line drawing with or without type. If illustrations are required, it may be beneficial to produce them in more than one color to achieve maximum impact. In some cases an unusual art treatment may be effective, such as special-effect screens, duotones, caricatures, or calligraphy. Of course, the artist should know the chosen or prospective printer’s capabilities and the customer’s cost limitations before settling on a particular design style.

What is the purpose of the piece? Answers to this question will help determine format, size, shape, and appearance. If it is to be a mailing piece, the postal regulations will have some influence; if an enclosure, the envelope or larger piece in which it is to be enclosed will help determine size, bulk, and weight; if it is intended to be filed, standard file sizes will have influence. If the piece is expected to sell, explain, instruct, or inform in detail, it must be large enough, in dimension or in number of pages, to accomplish its purpose effectively; if it is intended only to remind, announce, introduce, or repeat, brevity may be its virtue.

Who will receive it? How will it get there? What are the delivery requirements? Answers here will further determine quantity, format, and size. The habits of its intended consumers should be known. Shipping addresses, contacts, and the date(s) that the item should be received must be known. The type of packing, transportation, mailing, and handling should be detailed. The method of packing and distributing frequently influences the size of a lithographed piece, but its total bulk also needs to be considered.

Imagine, for example, the plight of a customer accustomed to thinking of 5,000 quantities as small quantities who orders 5,000 12-sheet calendars and 5,000 2×12-in. (51×305-mm) mailing tubes shipped to a small office for inserting, addressing, and mailing. After the job is delivered, the customer is knee-deep in 60,000 calendar pages and 139 cu. ft. (4 m^3) of mailing tubes.

How important is the piece to its overall purpose? The importance of the individual job in relation to the purpose it serves also affects the consideration of format, size, and quantity. Additionally, quality of design, printing, paper, and editorial content are involved. If the piece is but a small part of a large mailing packet, such as a reply card enclosed with information about a product line, then more attention and time should be given to the product literature than to a reply card, questionnaire, or envelope. Discussing the relative importance of each item reveals where money can be saved and where it is better spent. Additionally, after considering the minimum numbers of colors necessary to accomplish the job, the piece may be reviewed again to determine how to derive maximum impact, results, and effectiveness.

How many colors will the job require? When the artist is limited in the use of colors, he or she should know how to gain maximum impact by using tints of colors or by choosing proper color combinations if more than one color can be used. Also, the possibility of making the color of the paper a part of the design should not be overlooked.

If the artist is limited to the use of a single color, a multicolor effect can be achieved by using a solid and one or more tints of the single color; the press requirement of one pass through a single-color press will not change. If the artist is limited to the use of two colors, the design can be produced by using solids and combinations of tints of the particular two colors. The minimum press requirement would then be a single pass through a two-color press or two passes through a single-color press.

The selection of a single color, or a combination of colors, should be determined primarily by the message being presented and the ease with which the message can be read. When combining white stock with text matter, optimum visual appearance and readability are achieved when dark colors such as black, dark gray, dark blue, or dark green are used rather than light colors such as pastels. However, light colors may be entirely appealing for large display type on white paper. A small, crisp spot of a brilliant color attracts as much attention as a larger area of a tint of the color.

What is the budget for the piece? One must not hesitate to ask what consequences will result if the project runs over budget, should unforeseen problems or hidden costs occur (for example, a difficult on-location photograph that requires more than one trip to achieve acceptable results).

Is the designer limited in the type or color of paper or ink he or she can choose? For aesthetic, practical, and cost consideration, attention must be given to paper selection. Paper can represent as much as 50% of the total cost of a printing job. When the artist is able to select the paper, it should be coordinated with the design. When a particular paper is specified by the client, the artist must be certain that the design is compatible with the appearance as well as the print quality characteristics of the paper. The artist should be aware of the wide variety of types, finishes, weights, grades, and colors of paper that are available. There is an easy way to get the "feel" of this abundance. All paper mills furnish swatch books of their products, and paper merchants are usually only too happy to distribute them. Sales representatives from the paper distributor are usually willing and able to help the designer choose a paper that is well suited to the printed piece. Do not hesitate to ask them for advice. Also, many paper merchants will construct the exact format (a dummy) of the piece, from the artist's specifications, in the papers that he or she chooses.

One technical point that a designer or artist must be aware of is that paper has a grain, and that the heavier weights of paper used for covers and portfolios fold more easily and more cleanly with the grain than across it. This is an important point to remember when designing pieces that must be folded. However, if a piece demands a fold across the grain, scoring the paper on press will permit a sharp fold.

When choosing paper, keep in mind that stock with a textured surface may not be suitable for reproducing halftones or line work with fine detail. Rough-surfaced paper finishes and uncoated stock often require a coarser screen ruling for producing

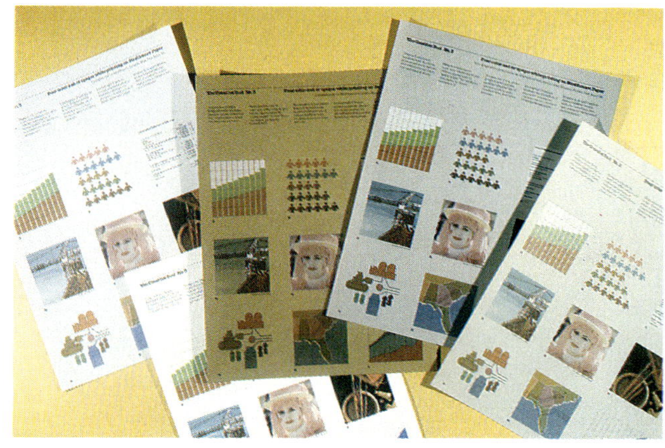

Effect of different colored papers on ink.

halftones than does a coated stock. A smooth, coated stock is best for producing halftone detail because a fine-line screen can be used.

Also, the thickness and bulk of a paper dictate certain limitations. The artist should avoid placing large, heavy, solid images on thin paper having low opacity and, consequently, high show-through. This applies only when the reverse side of a sheet is significant to the overall design of the finished printed product. Generally, it is best to avoid using paper with low opacity for a piece that is to be printed on both sides, no matter how heavy the ink coverage.

The color of paper can play a significant role in the overall appeal of a printed piece. Before beginning initial designs, the artist should know whether he or she is limited to designing for white paper, or whether a colored stock may be selected. If the design must be limited to white paper, the use of color is limited to the number of inks that may be used. If a colored stock may be used and the piece is limited to the use of a single ink, the artist can create a two-color effect by coordinating the single-ink color with the color of the paper. Likewise, if the piece is printing in two ink colors, the artist can use a colored stock as a third color in the design.

It is difficult to coordinate colored ink and a colored stock when the ink must precisely match the color of a product in the design. This difficulty occurs because the appearance of color is affected by the surrounding environment of the color. For example, a solid circle of yellow opaque ink printed on a green background appears different than the same circle of yellow ink printed on a red background. The hue of transparent inks will change completely; for example, cyan transparent ink printed on yellow paper will turn green.

To avoid the pitfall of misjudging how a particular ink will appear on a particular paper, the artist should request samples of the paper and inks to be used. Simple ink drawdown or ink rollout tests that will show the effects of the inks on colored paper can then be made. Some larger art studios and art departments use a small offset duplicator for testing ink on paper. Another option is to send paper samples to ink suppliers for ink rollout tests. Ink swatch books showing the various available colors printed on both coated and uncoated stock are available from most major ink suppliers. Also, paper mills that manufacture colored papers frequently supply brochures of their paper stocks printed with a variety of colored inks. Transparent acetate sheets that are printed with various ink tints are also available. These can be placed over colored stock to help to visualize the combination of ink and paper.

Will the finished piece be handled excessively? Excessive handling of printed pieces coupled with heavy ink coverage usually requires that the piece be varnished on the press. Applying a coat of varnish during a final pass through the press helps to preserve the piece during excessive use and prevents fingerprints that might otherwise appear on solid inked areas.

Further discussion questions should be considered regarding the piece's end use: Will the item be read once and then discarded? Will it hang on a wall like a poster or calendar or will it sit on a shelf to be opened again and again, such as a book? Will it frequently be handled and reused, such as a catalog, cereal box, or bread wrapper? Finally, will it be subjected to extreme temperatures or to chemicals, such as a frozen food box or margarine wrapper; or to bleaching from sunlight, such as posters or calendars?

What type of press will be used to print the piece? The designer or artist should know whether the piece will be reproduced on a web or sheetfed press (the web may limit paper choices) as well as the size of sheet the press accommodates. The press sheet layout required for the press must also be discussed. *Press sheet layout,* or *imposition,* refers to the position of the design (i.e., pages) on the press plate and the direction in which the paper will feed through the press. If no thought is given to press sheet layout when designing a multiple-page piece, *mechanical ghosting,* or *ink starvation,* may result. **Mechanical ghosting** is an uneven inking around the cylinder of the press; that is, ink fails to appear

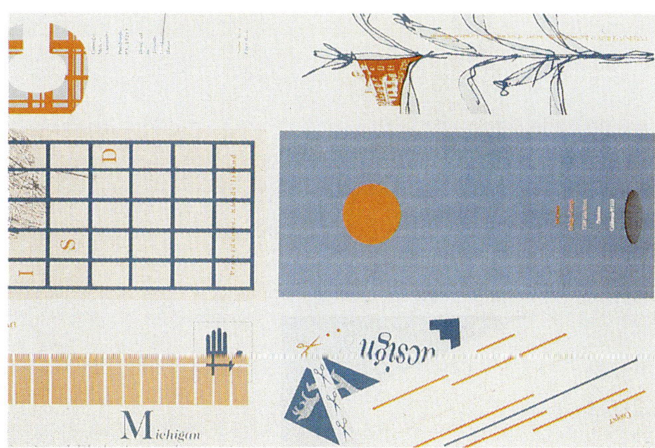

Mechanical ghosting or ink starvation is often caused by the design. Note the light blue lines appearing in the darker blue area.

heavily enough in certain areas and the plate is starved of ink. This is often caused by the design of the piece. Certain designs tend to cause mechanical ghosting; one is the solid-ink T shape—heavy vertical and horizontal solid areas that join. The best safeguard against such mishap is to consult with the printer as early in the design and planning stages as is possible. When mechanical ghosting is anticipated and the design cannot be altered, the artist should consult with the printer to determine how best to lay out the sheet to at least minimize the printing problems that the design may cause.

The three principal types of sheet imposition for a sheetfed press are *sheetwise imposition, work-and-turn imposition,* and *work-and-tumble imposition.* Each type of imposition has its own advantages for planning where to use color in a multiple-page piece. If the artist has a basic knowledge of the types of imposition, then he or she can economically plan, along with the printer, the pages on which color will print. See the chapters "Film Image Assembly" and "Finishing" for more detailed discussion of imposition.

When designing photographs or elements across the fold of a multiple-page piece, keep in mind that bindery machines are not 100% accurate. If image elements must go across the fold of a multiple-page piece, place the elements on center spreads, if at all possible.

What binding and finishing operations may the piece require? It is important that the artist know how a printed piece will be bound and finished. Finishing and binding procedures should be discussed with the bindery before the initial design is determined. Whether a piece will be saddle-stitched, side-wire-stitched, spiral-bound, or merely folded plays an important part in overall layout design.

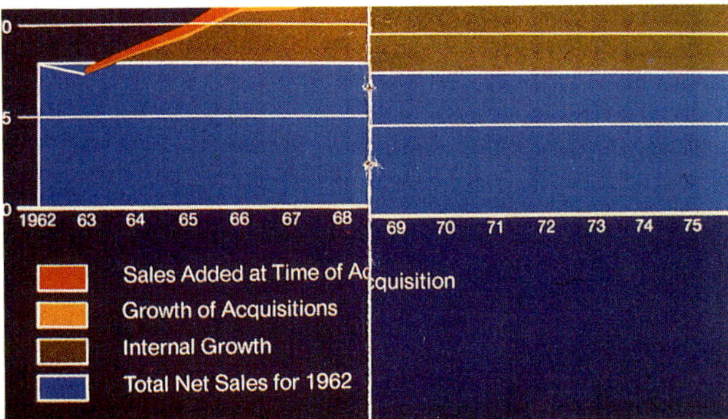

If this chart had been designed to print on a center spread, the misalignment of the art elements would not have occurred.

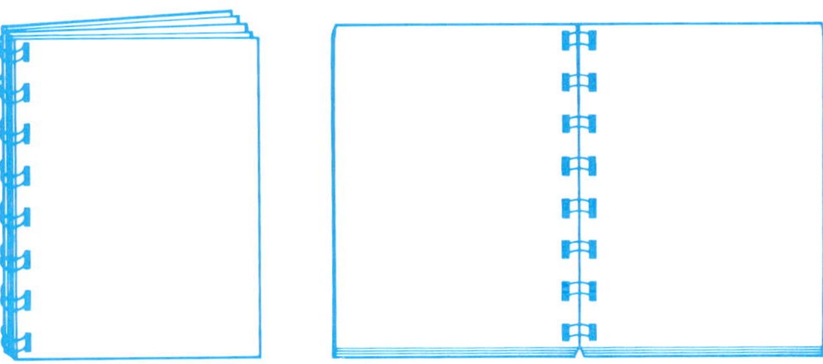

Double-wire-loop bound.

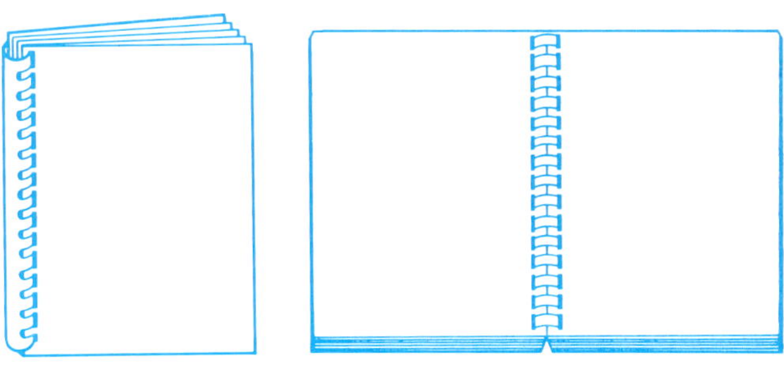

Plastic bound.

Binding that involves folded signatures, especially saddle-stitched binding, may require that the artist compensate in the page layout for the outward *creep,* or *thrust,* of the inner pages unless allowances for this are to be made by the film assembler. Creep results from a buildup of paper thickness at the backbone. The artist can determine the amount of creep that must be compensated for by having the bindery supply a folding dummy of the job, using the same paper on which the job will be printed. By placing a pin through the full thickness of the signature, at both the gutter and outside margins, the artist can see how much creep will occur. To avoid trimming off the image areas that fall in the extended area of the inner pages, the artist must gradually reduce the gutter margins on the layouts and pasteups as they

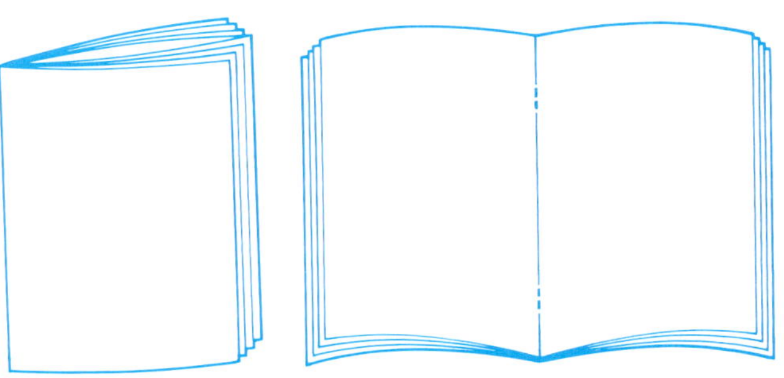

Creep or thrust. Saddle-stitched.

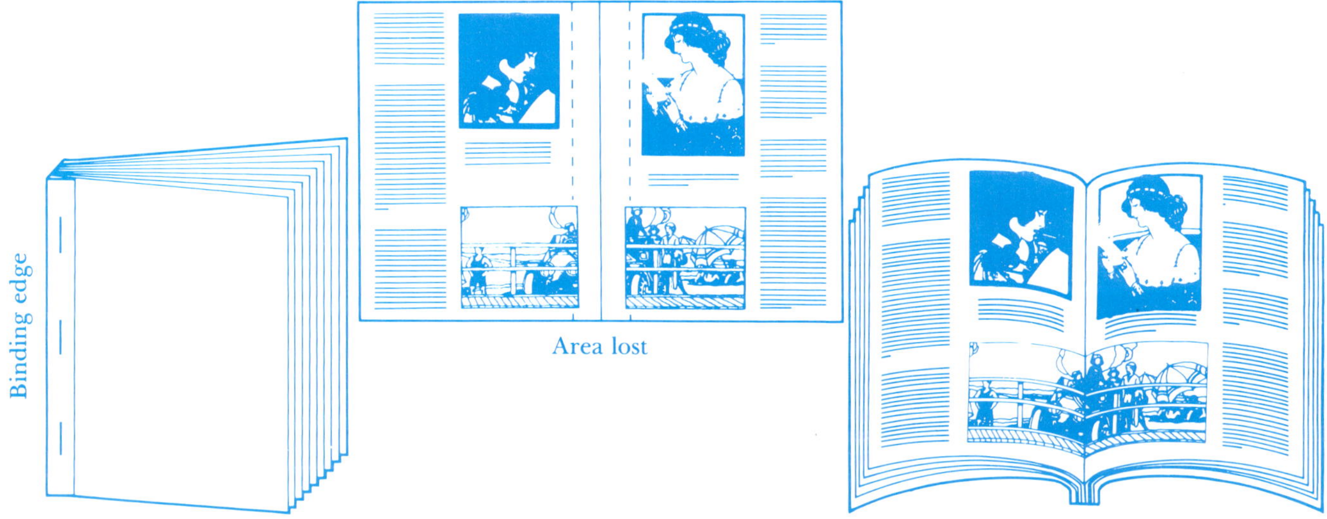

Gutter allowance showing loss of space in a side-stitched booklet.

approach the center of the signature. When bleed images or any art elements are required at the outside edge of the book, the artist must further adapt the design and page content to allow for creep. Keep in mind that bleeds may add costs to the piece, in both paper and cutting time in the bindery.

Likewise, it is important for the artist to know when books are going to be spiral-bound or side-stitched so that the designs can be adapted accordingly. Spiral binding requires the pages to be punched close to the spine; therefore, critical image elements along the punch line should be avoided. Side stitching requires that a portion of the page, sometimes as much as ⅜ in. (9.5 mm) along the binding edge, not have any part of the message printed there.

Another binding concern of the artist is the relationship of paper grain direction to folding. This is important for almost any booklet or book job. When a cover is folded perpendicular to the grain, there is often a tendency for breaking or cracking at the fold. The problem does not occur when the grain direction is parallel to the fold. This breaking is particularly objectionable when a cover is printed with a solid crossing the spine. Generally avoid folding heavy, coated stocks that crack even when folded with the grain. In all cases of design for a multiple-page format, the artist should acquire a folding dummy from the bindery.

Layouts

After the various limitations in planning have been discussed and understood by key people who will work on the job, and a manuscript and visual have been approved, the artist is ready to begin planning the layouts that will lead to art preparation. There are three types of layouts: thumbnail sketches, rough layouts, and comprehensives. Each layout is progressively more precise.

Thumbnail Sketches

The thumbnail sketch, the simplest of all layouts, is drawn much smaller than the final piece will be, hence the name. The thumbnail is drawn quickly, perhaps within minutes. No concern is given to specifications of size, color, type, style, etc., but merely an attempt is made to get original conceptions on paper—to show a visual relationship between the design elements. The text need not be readable nor the illustrations recognizable. Many thumbnail sketches are produced before the artist achieves a rendition worthy of expansion.

Rough Layouts

When a particular thumbnail sketch is chosen for development and enlargement, the artist proceeds with preparation of a rough layout. The purpose of the layout is (1) to further develop the concept visualized in the thumbnail sketch and (2) to serve as a

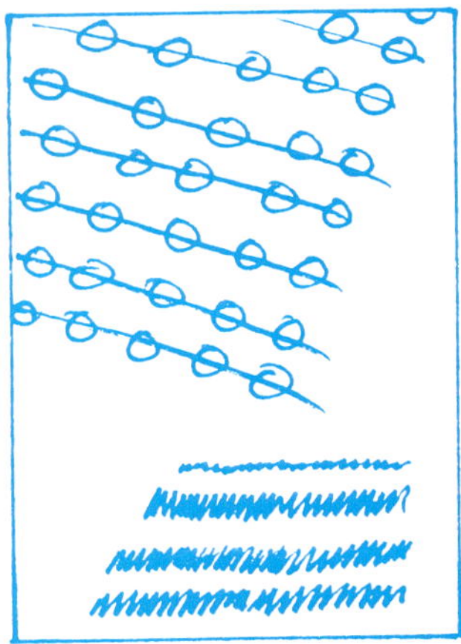

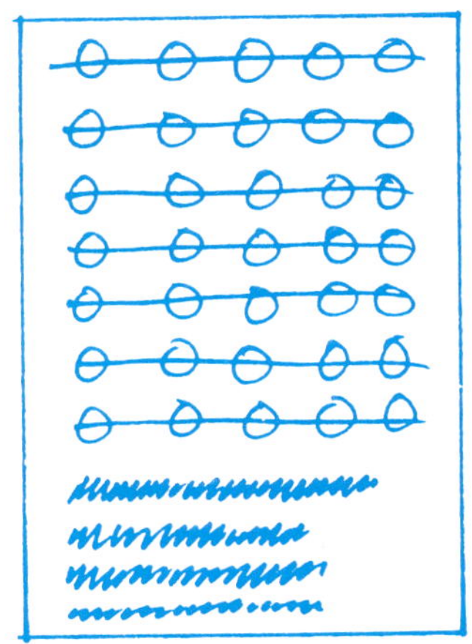

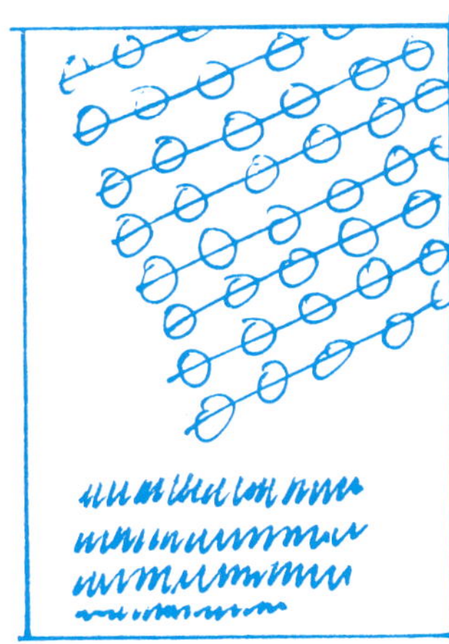

Thumbnail sketches are drawn much smaller than the final piece will print.

means of communicating both ideas and instructions among client, artist, and printer. In producing the rough layout, the artist shows more specific detail than was on the thumbnail sketch by carefully drawing illustrations and indications of type.

Although text type is normally not sketched letter for letter, display and headline type are generally carefully indicated. Illustrations are roughly sketched and recognizable. Company logos are clearly indicated and design characteristics such as reverses, knockouts, and surprints are included. Rough layouts are normally produced to the finished trimmed size, clearly indicating spacing between elements and margins. They may or may not show color breaks.

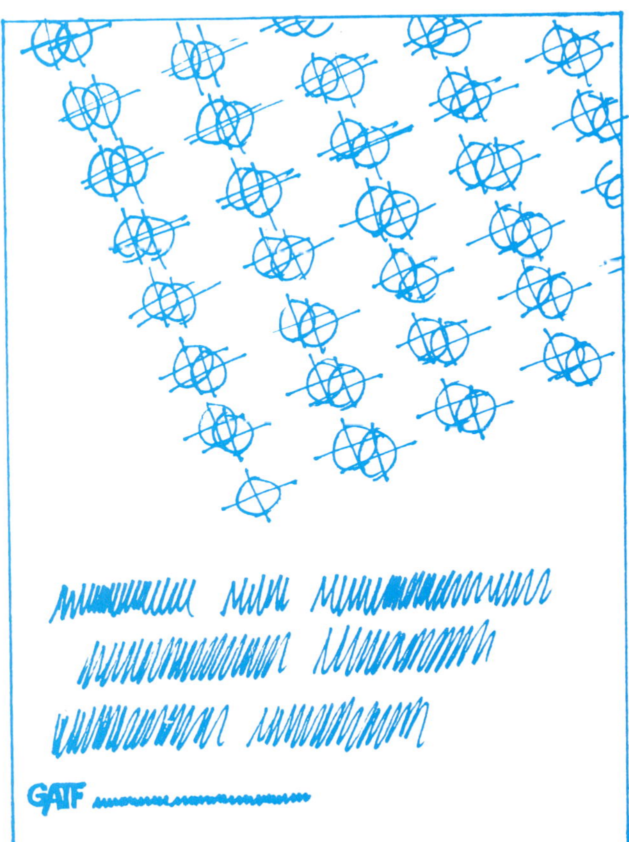

Rough layout.

When deadlines are tight and customer demands are not critical, the rough layout is sometimes used as the final layout for the submission to the client. As a final layout, the rough layout becomes the pasteup artist's guide for preparing the camera-ready copy. Color is then shown on the layout or on a tissue overlay along with type specifications.

Comprehensives

In preparing a comprehensive ("comp"), the artist attempts to come as close as possible to showing what the final printed piece will look like. The artist may go to the expense of hiring specialists in lettering, illustration, or photography. Actual type may be used, or ruled lines showing the precise length, x-height, and placement of the type may be drawn on the comprehensive.

Photographs may also be included in place of sketched illustrations. All color breaks and special effects such as airbrushing, silhouettes, and vignettes are indicated on a finished comprehensive. Instructions and specifications should not be marked directly on a comprehensive layout since the comprehensive is usually an expensive and precise piece of work. All instructions and notations are shown on a tissue overlay that is taped across the top of the comprehensive. Once the comprehensive is approved by the client, it serves as the guide

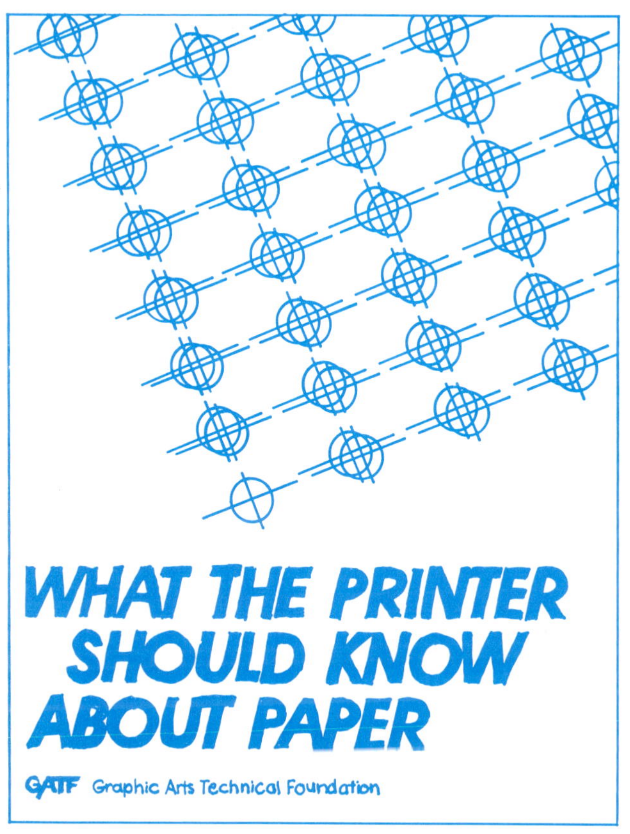

The comprehensive serves as a guide for all art and copy preparation that follows.

or "blueprint" for all art and copy preparation that follows.

Markers are often used to indicate color breaks directly on rough layouts, tissue overlays, or comprehensives. However, for an even more detailed and polished comp, artists can choose from a variety of colored papers and adhesive-backed films, which are placed directly on the comprehensive to show specific color area. These films and papers are color-matched to the litho printing inks that will be used on press. Using these color aids directly on the actual stock intended for printing when preparing the comprehensive helps the client, pasteup artist, and designer to further visualize what the printed piece will look like. In fact, all final comprehensives should be prepared on the stock on which the piece will print.

In addition to the colored papers and films, photosensitive dry transfer materials can be purchased in various colors. This material, along with a negative or positive, is exposed to strong ultraviolet light and then developed. The image that remains can be burnished onto virtually any surface.

Yet another way to produce a colored comprehensive is to create the comprehensive using computer software and to print out the computer file using a color PostScript printer.

When designing for books or multiple-page publications, the artist pastes the final layout or comprehensive to the folding dummy. This practice assists the artist in visualizing the appearance of the finished work. The folding dummy also enables the artist to establish bleeds and margins, and also serves as an example or guide for binding and other finishing operations. In book work, a few specimen pages are set and serve as the comprehensive. A comprehensive can take the exact form of a finished piece such as a display or folding carton, a direct-mail enclosure plus envelope and reply card, or a candy wrapper.

Types of Copy

Once the final layout or comprehensive is approved by the client, the artist is ready to begin assembling the art elements required to prepare camera-ready copy. There are three general types of copy elements: *line copy, continuous-tone copy,* and *full-color copy.* Each type of copy requires a different reproduction technique.

Type, treated in detail in the previous chapter, "Typography and Typesetting," is essentially line art. Full-color copy is a kind of continuous-tone copy. However, because of its special nature and the techniques used in full-color reproduction, full-color copy is further discussed in the later sections of this chapter entitled "Full-Color Copy" and "Color Photography."

Each type of copy may be submitted to the artist in a variety of forms and on a variety of materials. Line copy may come as an original illustration or diagram on various substrates; it may be a photostat; it may be a galley of typeset copy ready to be cut apart and mounted onto the pasteup in accordance with the layout. Sometimes a positive film transparency is furnished. Continuous-tone copy may be a black-and-white or color photograph, a painting, or a color transparency. Most often the artist must handle a wide variety of forms on a single pasteup.

As mentioned earlier, the artist must take the time to plan the overall job. The artist's tasks must also be planned, particularly when a job requires

handling a variety of different types of copy. However, the artist's plan must also take into account the convenience and time of others who will work on the job, as well as the production costs involved.

Line Copy

Line copy is all copy that contains no shades of gray (continuous tones) and prints solid (black or color) on the finished piece without the use of a halftone screen. Pen-and-ink line drawings and type are examples of line copy. Type reversals are also line copy since the background prints as a solid ink with the type appearing as white. Of the three categories of copy, line copy is the simplest copy to reproduce.

Today, a large percentage of line art is computer-generated using a variety of illustration software programs. These programs are discussed in Chapter 12.

Quality requirements of line copy. When submitted for reproduction, line copy must be solid black on a neutral white background. Off-white, cream, or blue backgrounds should be avoided since maximum contrast between image and nonimage areas is the key to good reproduction in the printed piece. The background on which the copy is drawn or mounted should be either smooth, hard-surfaced paper or illustration board. Textured, embossed, or pebble-grain surfaces may be required for creating special design effects, but a smooth, hard surface is important when clean, uniform, straight lines and edges are required. Soft or absorbent surfaces, which often create undesirable bleeding of ink or paint, are not satisfactory for producing the sharply defined lines of original line art.

When drawing the copy—illustrations, diagrams, etc.—it is important that all image segments have uniform density or blackness. If a large solid varies greatly in density, the low density areas may not reproduce as a solid.

Type proofs also should be inspected by the artist (as well as the proofreader) for consistent density. Density variations are usually noticeable when inspecting galleys at normal viewing distance and frequently occur when corrected type is combined with original type—the corrected type appearing lighter or darker. Imperfections such as broken or fuzzy characters must be found and corrected. Normally, a quick scan with a hand-held magnifier will reveal any broken or fuzzy type. Density variations and broken characters are usually sufficient reasons for rejecting type proofs.

With all copy, the artist must keep in mind that imperfections will reproduce if not be magnified in the negatives made from the artwork. Therefore, corrections should be made in the artwork so that extra, costlier photographic and film assembly charges will not be added to the job.

Type surprints and reverses. Type can be used effectively to surprint (overprint) over a background tint of color, or as a reverse, also called a knockout or dropout. When designing a surprint, the artist should avoid placing black type on a dark background. Similarly, reverse type on a light background should be avoided. The artist will be able to combine solids, screens, and reverses in a manner that adds visual appeal and impact to the design.

The following guidelines are helpful in deciding how best to use solid and reverse-type images on screen-tint backgrounds. Keep in mind that (1) the percent tint and (2) the color of ink have considerable influence on how surprints and reverse type appear when reproduced.

- On light-colored, background screen tints of up to 10%, small sizes of medium and bold type work well. However, the monotony of long copy should be avoided.
- Medium-weight typefaces work well on background screen tints of approximately 40%. However, typefaces with fine-line serifs should be avoided, as the serifs will be lost in the screen.
- Typefaces of uniform thickness and strong, thick serifs reproduce well on a 50% screen-tint background.
- Small reversed type of 10 pt. or less may be difficult to read on a tint background of about 50%.
- When printing reverse type on a solid background, provide sufficient line spacing to prevent eye fatigue caused by the illusion of flickering or vibration of the type images.
- When printing reverse type on a solid background, avoid types with fine lines and thin serifs, as they are likely to fill in on the press.

Background screen tints or solids can be used effectively in color, in black, or tints of black, which produce grays. When using colors it is important to consider the overall effect of one ink color printed over another color. For example, if a solid background is printed with transparent yellow ink, and type is surprinted with transparent cyan ink, the effect of the yellow and cyan ink will produce green type. Opaque yellow, however, usually presents an excellent background since most other colors can be printed over opaque yellow without creating readability problems. Opaque inks are preferred when

ABCDEFGHIJKLMNOPQRSTUVWXYZabcdefghijkl
ABCDEFGHIJKLMNOPQRSTUVWXYZabcdefgh
ABCDEFGHIJKLMNOPQRSTUVWXYZa
ABCDEFGHIJKLMNOPQRSTUVWXYZ
ABCDEFGHIJKLMNOPQRSTUV
ABCDEFGHIJKLMNOPQRSTUVWXYZabcdefghij
ABCDEFGHIJKLMNOPQRSTUVWXYZabcdefgh
ABCDEFGHIJKLMNOPQRSTUVWXYZa
ABCDEFGHIJKLMNOPQRSTUVWXYZ
ABCDEFGHIJKLMNOPQRSTUV

20% tint of cyan.

ABCDEFGHIJKLMNOPQRSTUVWXYZabcdefghijkl
ABCDEFGHIJKLMNOPQRSTUVWXYZabcdefgh
ABCDEFGHIJKLMNOPQRSTUVWXYZa
ABCDEFGHIJKLMNOPQRSTUVWXYZ
ABCDEFGHIJKLMNOPQRSTUV
ABCDEFGHIJKLMNOPQRSTUVWXYZabcdefghij
ABCDEFGHIJKLMNOPQRSTUVWXYZabcdefgh
ABCDEFGHIJKLMNOPQRSTUVWXYZa
ABCDEFGHIJKLMNOPQRSTUVWXYZ
ABCDEFGHIJKLMNOPQRSTUV

70% tint of cyan.

ABCDEFGHIJKLMNOPQRSTUVWXYZabcdefghijkl
ABCDEFGHIJKLMNOPQRSTUVWXYZabcdefgh
ABCDEFGHIJKLMNOPQRSTUVWXYZa
ABCDEFGHIJKLMNOPQRSTUVWXYZ
ABCDEFGHIJKLMNOPQRSTUV
ABCDEFGHIJKLMNOPQRSTUVWXYZabcdefghij
ABCDEFGHIJKLMNOPQRSTUVWXYZabcdefgh
ABCDEFGHIJKLMNOPQRSTUVWXYZa
ABCDEFGHIJKLMNOPQRSTUVWXYZ
ABCDEFGHIJKLMNOPQRSTUV

50% tint of cyan.

ABCDEFGHIJKLMNOPQRSTUVWXYZabcdefghijkl
ABCDEFGHIJKLMNOPQRSTUVWXYZabcdefgh
ABCDEFGHIJKLMNOPQRSTUVWXYZa
ABCDEFGHIJKLMNOPQRSTUVWXYZ
ABCDEFGHIJKLMNOPQRSTUV
ABCDEFGHIJKLMNOPQRSTUVWXYZabcdefghij
ABCDEFGHIJKLMNOPQRSTUVWXYZabcdefgh
ABCDEFGHIJKLMNOPQRSTUVWXYZa
ABCDEFGHIJKLMNOPQRSTUVWXYZ
ABCDEFGHIJKLMNOPQRSTUV

100% cyan.

surprinting, unless the apparent color change with transparent inks is desired. The point for the artist to keep in mind, when working with background tints or solids and reverses or surprints, is never to sacrifice readability for visual effect, unless this is called for in the design.

Line Art Techniques

Line art (line drawings) is prepared by a number of techniques, in addition to being computer-generated. Each technique involves the deposit of a uniform black image on a white background. Wherever possible, line art should be prepared larger than its final printed size; a convenient size is usually 25–50% larger. Reducing original copy on camera minimizes imperfections, such as jagged or rough edges, although it does not eliminate them. Conversely, camera enlargements tend to accentuate imperfections in the art.

An exception to this rule is fine-line, detailed line copy. Detailed copy should be prepared in the same size as the printed size because it is difficult to predict how thin the fine lines will become during a camera reduction. Very thin lines may drop out entirely, and very close lines may merge into a mass of solid black.

Some common techniques used to produce line art are pen and ink, charcoal or pencil, brush and ink, patterned shading films, and line conversion or posterizations of continuous-tone subject matter.

Pen and ink. Pen-and-ink illustrations are usually the simplest form of line illustrations to reproduce. A simple line exposure on the process camera usually produces a suitable negative for platemaking, needing little or no stripping hand-work. Most pen-and-ink illustrations are drawn on hard, high-quality, smooth, coated paper or on illustration board, using a ruling pen, technical pen, or crow quill pen.

Brush and ink. Brush-and-ink illustrations are produced in the same way as pen-and-ink illustrations. The brush produces broader strokes with feathered edges. Pen and ink and brush and ink can be combined in the same illustration for a special effect.

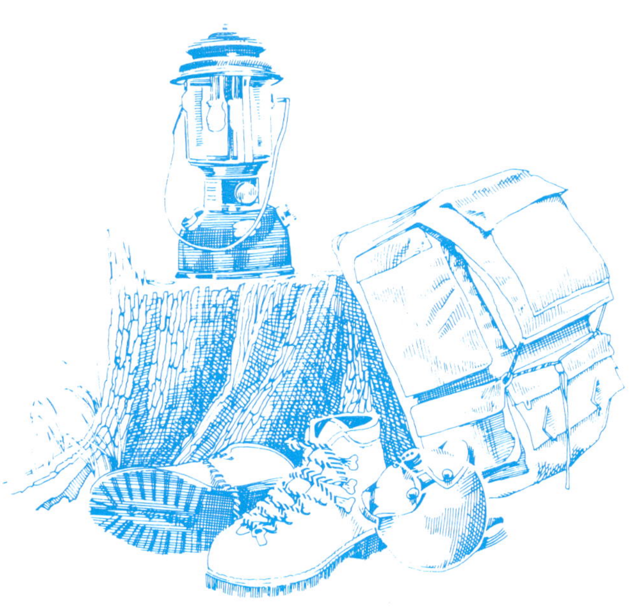

Pen and ink.

Charcoal or pencil. Charcoal or pencil illustrations can create the illusion of continuous-tone copy. As long as the marks are discernible as distinct dark lines or areas varying in size and spacing on the white background, charcoal or pencil illustrations can be reproduced as line art. Pencil work, however, can approach true continuous-tone to an extent that makes it unsuitable for line reproduction and requires halftone screening. (See the section entitled "Continuous-Tone Copy" later in this chapter.)

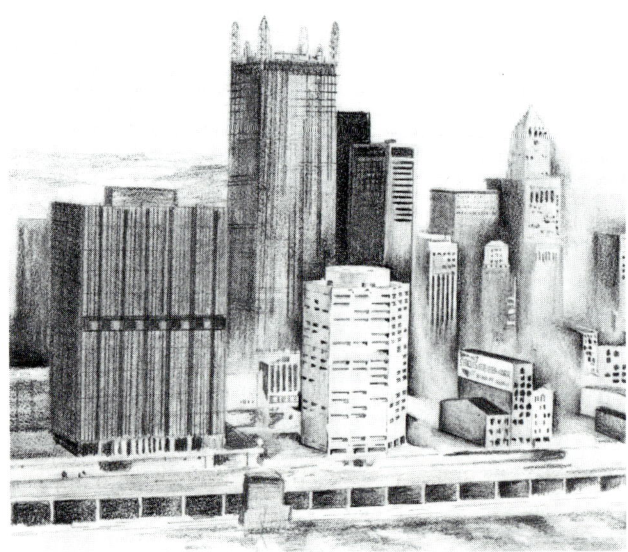

Pencil sketch.

Patterned shading film. Patterned shading film is a pressure-sensitive material on which a screen tint or other pattern is printed. The film adheres to a paper backing that is peeled away before the film is placed on the artwork.

Patterned shading film is printed in black in various patterns and in various percentages of tints. The more popular patterns include the following: conventional round-dot screens in horizontal, vertical, or diagonal directions; straight-line screens in horizontal, vertical, or diagonal directions; circular screens; diamond or square-shaped screens; and mezzotint screens.

A piece of patterned shading film is cut larger than needed and is positioned over the areas of art that will appear as a shade or tone. The image is traced with a sharp knife and the excess patterned shading film is peeled away. The remaining film is then covered with tissue and burnished so that it stays in position.

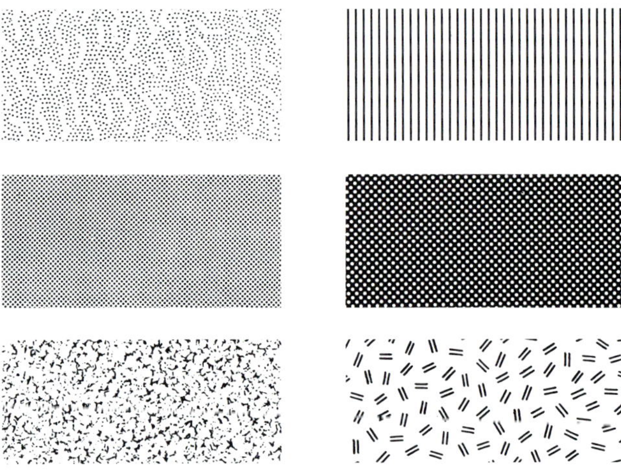

Examples of patterned shading film.

Continuous-tone shading film is discussed in a following section of this chapter entitled "Treating Continuous-Tone Copy.")

Line conversion or posterization. Creating a line conversion or posterization means converting a continuous-tone photograph to line copy. This special effect is achieved by exposing a continuous-tone photograph to high-contrast line film. The resulting negative drops out all highlight and light middletone areas and reproduces all deep middletone and shadow areas as solids.

Line conversions and posterizations can also be computer-generated by scanning in a continuous-tone photograph as a gray-scale image and converting the image into a line conversion or posterization

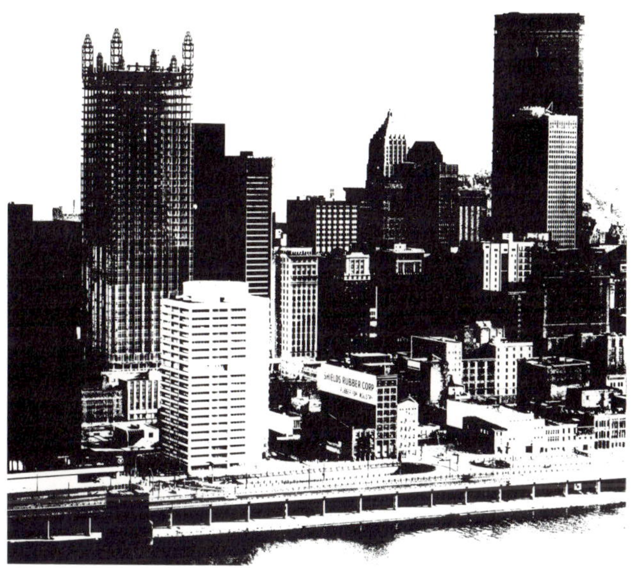

Posterization.

using the appropriate command from within an image-editing software program. The procedure varies depending upon which software program is used.

Continuous-Tone Copy

Continuous-tone copy is copy that contains tones of light and dark areas rather than a solid color only. There is a gradation of tones between the lightest highlight area and the deepest shadow area in continuous-tone copy. The simplest example of continuous-tone copy is a black-and-white photograph. Notice that such a photograph is made up of numerous tones ranging from the pure white of the paper to the deepest black shadow. Other examples of continuous-tone copy are color transparencies and paintings.

Since printing plates print only even layers of ink in the image areas, continuous-tone art must be converted to another form to be printed. A photograph or other continuous-tone illustration must be converted into a **halftone.** With a halftone, the tones of the original image are simulated using different sizes of dots or some other pattern, such as lines. In the conventional halftoning process, the image is rephotographed using a process camera and a special "halftone" screen that breaks up the image into different-size dots. In electronic prepress, the halftone is usually made by scanning the original art as a gray-scale computer image and then using software to convert it into a halftone when the file is output to a laser printer or imagesetter. (This process is discussed in Chapter 12.) When printed, the halftone image resembles the original photograph, with the smaller dots producing light shades of gray, or highlight areas, and the larger dots dark shades of gray, or shadow areas. While the dots vary in size, the center-to-center distance between dots is always uniform with a conventional halftone. These halftone dots are not individually visible at normal viewing distance, creating the illusion of continuous tone. In reproduction, each dot can be considered a piece of line art because it reproduces as a single speck of ink.

Highlight, middletone, and shadow dots. The effect of tonal differences in printed halftones is created by the amount of ink that is seen by the eye in proportion to the amount of white paper that surrounds it. The lightest highlight area will have tiny dots, and much white paper will be showing between the dots. Reproducible highlight dots may range as low as 2%; that is, 2% ink, 98% white paper.

Middletone dots are those dots that make up the midrange of tones in the reproduction. The middletone dot range is usually from a 35% dot to a 70% dot. When magnified, perfect 50% dots produce a checkerboard pattern showing an equal amount of white paper and ink, if a square-dot halftone screen is used.

The shadow dots produce the darkest areas of the print, and normally range from a 70% to 98% dot. In shadow areas, the dots become so large that they merge to produce a nearly solid image. Very little

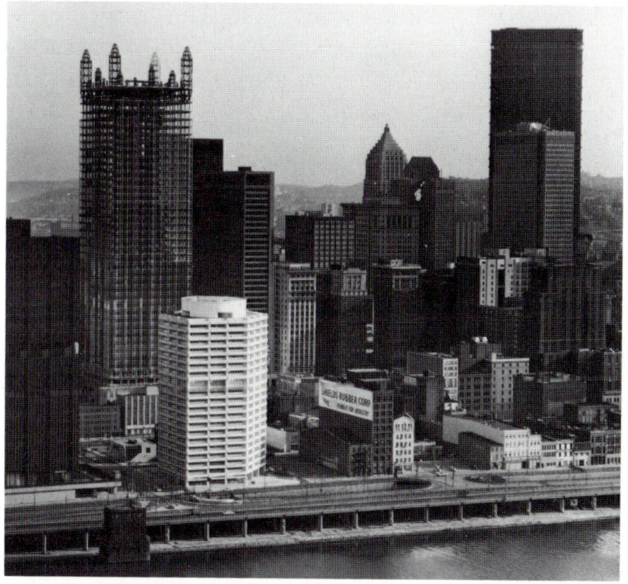

Halftone made from a continuous-tone print.

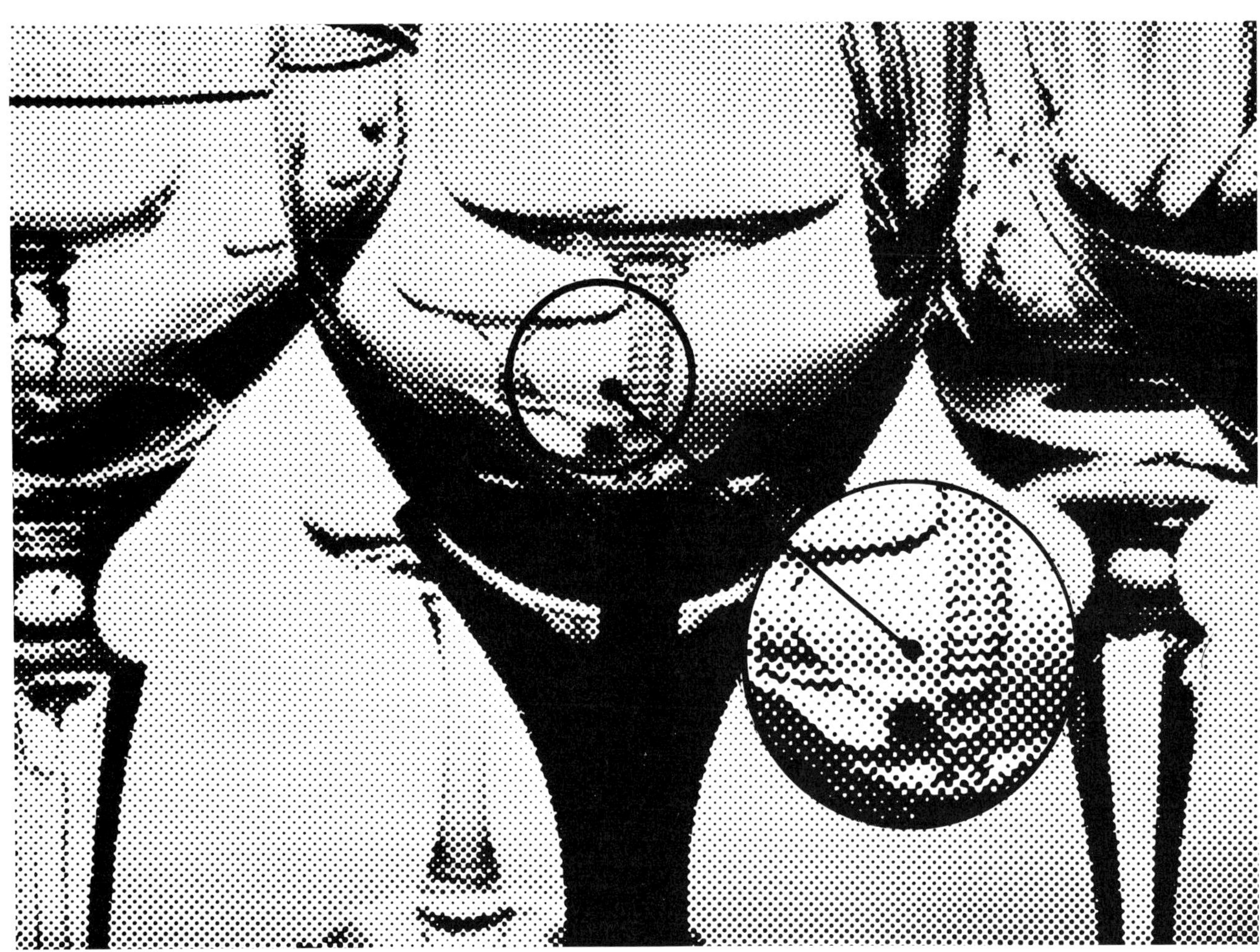

These individual halftone dots create the illusion of continuous tone when viewed at normal viewing distance.

white paper can be seen in a shadow-dot area. The ratio of unprinted to printed area determines the depth of the shadow; a 70% dot (30% unprinted paper) appears as a moderately dark gray while an area printed with a 98% dot appears black.

Halftone screens. The screens used to produce halftones are available in different screen rulings and patterns. Screen ruling pertains to the fineness or coarseness of the screen and is designated in lines (dots) per linear inch or linear centimeter.

The screen ruling specified by the artist depends on the type of paper to be printed and the photographic detail required in the printed piece. As a rule, the finer the screen, the greater the detail of the printed halftone. Coarse, rough paper, such as newsprint, requires a coarser screen for best reproduction; therefore, newspaper halftones are produced with a screen ruling between 65 and 120 lines/in. (26 and 47 lines/cm). A coarse screen allows printing of each dot on the coarse surface of the paper, producing an adequate image. An uncoated stock, smoother than newsprint, usually produces halftones best with screens of 120 or 133 lines/in. (47 or 52 lines/cm). Highly coated, smooth paper stocks are often printed with screen rulings of 133 or 150 lines/in. (52 or 59 lines/cm). Halftone printing requiring the ultimate of detail is occasionally done with screens up to 300 lines/in. (118 lines/cm). However, the successful use of such ultrafine screens requires the utmost control of film processing, platemaking, paper, ink, and press variables.

The most widely used halftone screens are those containing rows of square or elliptical dots. For special effects, the artist can specify screens that have concentric-circular patterns; vertical-, horizontal-, or diagonal-line patterns; random-line patterns, pebble-grain patterns; wavy-line patterns; or mezzotint patterns. These special-effect screens are usually used when detail may be sacrificed for a particular aesthetic effect.

Black-and-white photography. It takes artistry with a camera to illustrate a fact, create an impression, or tell a story photographically. But however skilled the photographer, the genius for staging and taking good pictures suffers if allowances are not made for the changes that inevitably take place in each step—from the original film, to the photographic print, to the lithographer's negative, and finally to dots of ink printed on a sheet of paper. The most successfully printed photograph is one that has reproduced just what was specified for the final printed form. Therefore, vague specifications about a photograph are inappropriate when discussing what is desired in the final print.

Too often, little time is devoted to considering the reproduction qualities of a potential photograph before it is taken. A little extra time and effort spent planning good photography saves later expenditures for costly and perhaps unsatisfactory retouching.

Additionally, photographs for reproduction should be taken by professional photographers. The photographer has a number of things to consider when planning a photograph—for instance, arrangement or composition, lighting, choice of film, exposure, filters, and developing process. The best insurance against photographic headaches is the service of a photographer who understands the requirements of photomechanical production, since the halftone process rarely improves the quality of an original photograph. Black ink cannot match the deep blacks of a photograph, and white printing paper cannot match the whiteness of white photographic paper; therefore, the tonal range from dark to light of an original photograph is compressed in the halftone process. The highlights appear duller and the shadows appear lighter. At the same time, a certain amount of detail is lost.

The term for the tonal difference between highlight and shadow areas of an original or reproduction is **contrast.** A photo with a great range between its deepest black and brightest white has high contrast. Conversely, photos in which the darkest and lightest tones are not greatly separated have low contrast. Because of the apparent increase in contrast when a photo is printed, a moderately low-contrast print is usually preferred over a high-contrast print.

Overall contrast can be increased in the reproduction process, but nothing can be done to provide detail that was never recorded by the camera.

Some compensation for contrast can be made in black-and-white photography during negative-to-positive printing; however, contrast is best controlled by proper lighting of the subject during the photographic session. The artist may benefit by understanding basic types of lighting so that he or she may further specify the desired result.

Flat, front lighting such as common flash-on-camera photography provides may produce high contrast but also may produce large masses of tones that are either very dark or very light. Details are lost. Notice in some newspaper portraits that the subject's face is a white oval with no modeling of the features; flat, front lighting was most likely used.

Side lighting from a single source gives the illusion of depth, but here, too, there are very few middletones. Dark shadow edges of subjects merge with backgrounds and are lost, and the light side is often too bright to show any detail. Many improperly sunlit outdoor snapshots show this.

The alternative to these is a picture with the lighting balanced to show a full range of tones that distribute attention to all the desired details. The photo will have good contrast and detail, which are most often desired in a printed piece. Also, if a photograph is to be outlined, or must otherwise be retouched, the photographer can provide a clear distinction between subject and background by putting strong contrasts in tone between them; for example, placing a light background against dark machinery. Light objects, of course, require dark backgrounds. This practice eliminates guesswork by the artist or retoucher.

Even though it is not always possible for the artist to direct the picture taking, the photographic negative is often available to the artist who is responsible for preparing the copy. A little care in ordering the print goes a long way toward getting better reproduction at no extra cost.

Manufacturers of photographic films produce dozens of different types of photographic papers that vary in contrast, color, texture, and weight. With this selection, the same negative can produce a variety of different prints. Generally, the photographer selects the grade of paper that suits the contrast of the negative and produces a print of normal contrast, unless instructed otherwise. For satisfactory reproduction, the paper the photo is printed on must photograph well since the print is rephotographed in the halftone process.

White fiber-base photographic papers are generally considered to produce the best halftone reproduction. Because of its superior processing speed, resin-coated waterproof paper is commonly used in making photographic prints, but because of its fluorescing properties, this type of print must be handled differently from conventional fiber-base paper

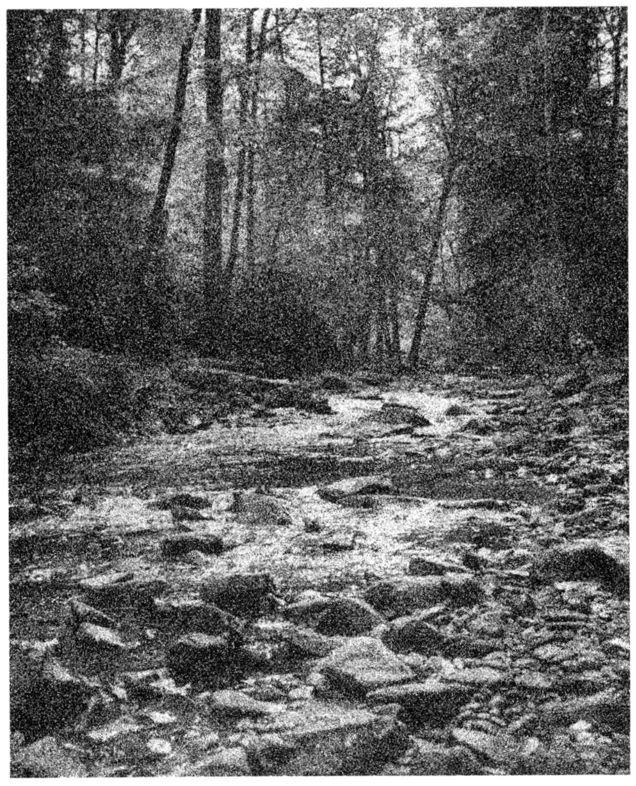

Mezzotint screen.

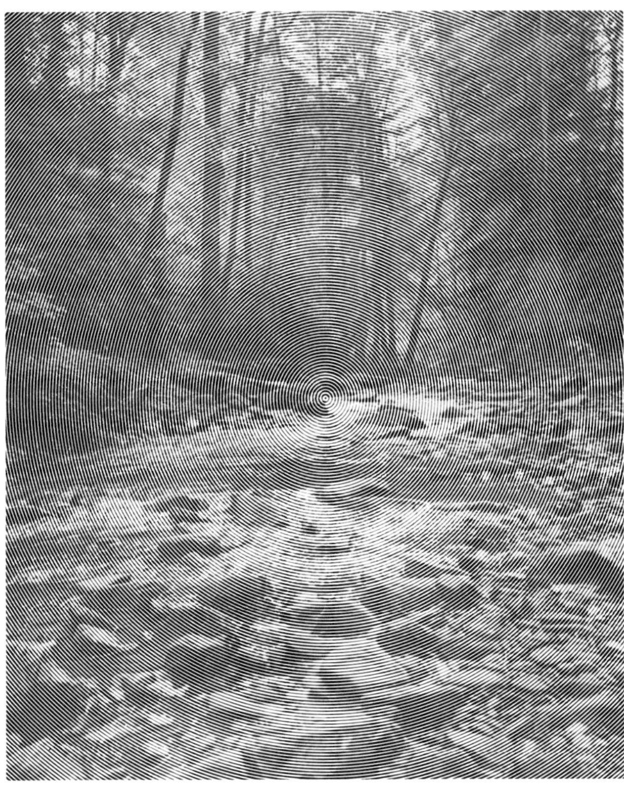

Concentric-circle screen.

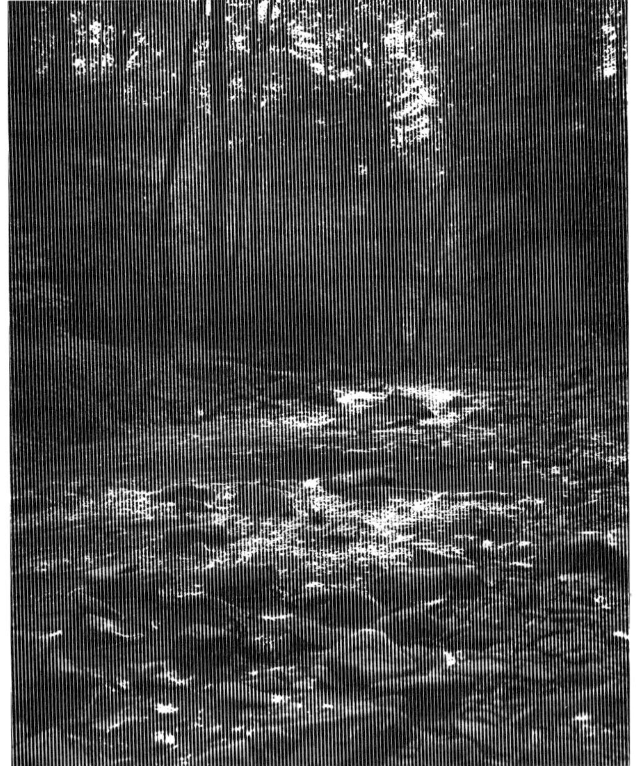

Vertical-line screen.

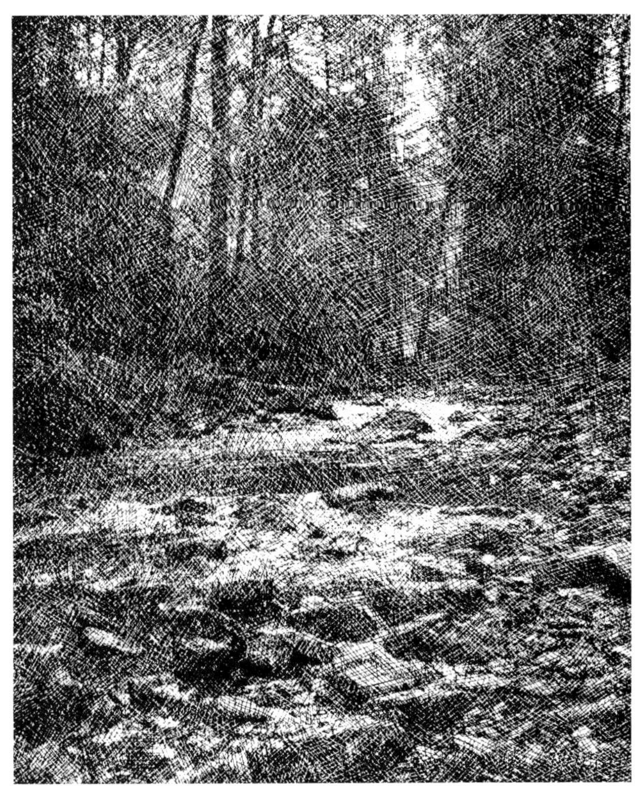

Etched steel-plate screen.

in the process camera. Off-white, ivory, cream, and other colored papers should be avoided because they tend to dull the highlights when photographed in the process camera. Similarly, various photographic papers produce images that differ in color. Those that produce a neutral or blue-black image tone are preferred.

The paper surface influences the amount of detail reproduced from the original negative. A textured paper that is used for halftoning results in less detail, specular highlights, and possibly moiré patterns in the final reproduction. A smooth, glossy surface is the best, especially when the halftones will be printed on coated stock. A glossy surface offers the best separation of tones and good detail. A matte surface is usually specified when photos are to be heavily retouched, or printed in a newspaper, where less contrast but larger tonal steps—from highlight to midtone and midtone to shadow—are present. Generally sepia and hand-colored prints make poor copy for lithographic reproduction.

Care and protection of continuous-tone copy. In order to get the best reproduction from black-and-white continuous-tone copy, it is imperative that the negatives, prints, and original art be stored and handled with care. Spots, stains, cracked emulsion, scratches, blurred images, and discoloration result if the following precautions are not taken:

- Never write heavily on the backs of photographs. Doing so damages the surface of the print. In fact, writing on the backs of photographs should be avoided if possible.
- If photographs must be written on, use a felt-tip marker or grease pencil. Never use a pencil!
- Do not stack photos that have just been written on, particularly when using a felt-tip marker. Permanent marker ink takes a few minutes to dry, especially on resin-coated photographic papers. Stacking photos directly after writing onto them may cause the ink on the back of one photo to offset onto the image (front) of the photo beneath it. Instead, a pressure-sensitive label or piece of masking tape carrying pertinent information can be placed on the back of artwork.
- Do not mail photos in mailing tubes. They should be mailed and stored flat.
- Remember when mailing artwork to address the mailing envelope *before* inserting the artwork. Indentations and scratches may occur if the pen pressure is excessive.
- Always protect continuous-tone art by covering each piece with a tissue overlay that is hinged to the back (top) with masking tape. No artwork should be mailed or sent into production without this protective tissue.
- Refrain from eating, drinking, and smoking when preparing and handling artwork. Coffee, food, and cigarette ash stains ruin artwork, so avoid these possibilities altogether.

Treating Continuous-Tone Copy

Photographs are often treated by the artist to achieve some special effect or to improve reproduction quality. Photographs of machinery frequently are retouched to sharply delineate the subject from the background, to emphasize highlights, or to make certain that small detail is clearly distinguishable. This type of alteration requires special skill and is costly.

Retouching. Much time and expense can be consumed when preparing continuous-tone copy, yet the result is not always what the art director or client had in mind. For example, contrast may be too high or too low, or certain items in the copy may not be detailed or emphasized enough. When such imperfections exist, the artist has two options to improve copy. First, the photograph or artwork can be redone. In the case of a photograph, reshooting may be necessary. When budget and time do not allow reshooting, the artist must resort to the second option, retouching.

Continuous-tone copy can be retouched to improve tone or detail or to de-emphasize certain areas. Tone shading films or an airbrush can be used. Airbrushing is the more effective but more expensive method. Also, the artist can apply special inks or spot dyes with a brush, especially when very small areas must be highlighted or made solid. However, a brush often does not apply a smooth, continuous tone and the retouching may be obvious in the final printed piece. Whatever method is employed, be certain that the materials used are compatible with the artwork. In black-and-white photo retouching, some types of spotting dyes match the print visually but are recorded entirely differently by the process camera. (With color transparencies, extra care must be taken to ensure that the color dyes used are color-matched to the particular type of transparency being retouched.)

Artists no longer retouch as much continuous-tone copy as they once did. Today, it is more common to do the retouching after the image has been scanned into a computer. Many artists now use image-editing programs to enhance computer

images. Electronic airbrushing is one common feature of these programs. This procedure is discussed in Chapter 12.

Tone shading films. Tone shading films are similar to the patterned shading film described in the section on line copy techniques. They are made of thin, pressure-sensitive material. Whereas the shading films applied to line copy have a definite printed pattern (black dots, lines, etc.), the tone shading films have a uniform translucent gray tone. The films are available in a range of tones from light gray to dark gray.

If a key item or area in a photograph must be emphasized, de-emphasizing the photograph's background with an appropriate tone of shading film accomplishes this: the shading film is placed over the entire photograph, the item to be emphasized is traced with a sharp blade, and the shading film is peeled from the outlined image. To protect the photo, a piece of clear acetate can be attached and the shading film placed and burnished onto the clear acetate.

Airbrushing. Airbrushing is one way to alter the emphasis, contrast, and detail of continuous-tone copy, especially photographs. However, airbrushing can be costly and time-consuming and requires a skilled airbrush specialist.

With an airbrush the artist can produce soft, subtle tonal gradations with many ranges from the lightest highlight to a solid opaque covering. Airbrushes are either "single action" or "double action." In the single-action airbrush, the flow of paint or ink is produced by pressing down on the finger trigger. The single-action airbrush has a control valve that regulates the flow for fine or coarse effects, and the width of the spray pattern can be varied during a single stroke, by varying the distance between the nozzle of the airbrush and the surface being sprayed.

The spray of a double-action airbrush is controlled by pressing the finger trigger while pulling back on it. The fineness of the spray can be controlled by various special tips that are used on the airbrush.

An airbrush is operated by an air compressor or a carbon dioxide cylinder. Usually, 25–30 lb. of pressure is sufficient for most airbrush work. The lower the pressure, the coarser the spray.

The airbrush may be used free-hand for painting uniform backgrounds; however, masks or *friskets* are required for isolating specific areas to be sprayed and for precise spot-retouching.

Masking for airbrushing. If a distinct shape must be airbrushed, a blotter or a sheet of acetate is cut to the desired shape and placed in position on the surface of the artwork. The spray is then directed along the edge of the mask. When the mask is removed, the airbrush pattern will be shown. If the mask is slightly above the surface when directing the spray, the sharp edge is softened.

Friskets for airbrushing. If the area to be airbrushed is too complicated or too large for a mask, a sheet of adhesive-backed frisket can be laid over the surface of the art. The frisket is then carefully cut away and removed from the area to be airbrushed. When the desired effect is obtained, the frisket is removed. If necessary, a frisket can be placed over an airbrushed area without doing harm.

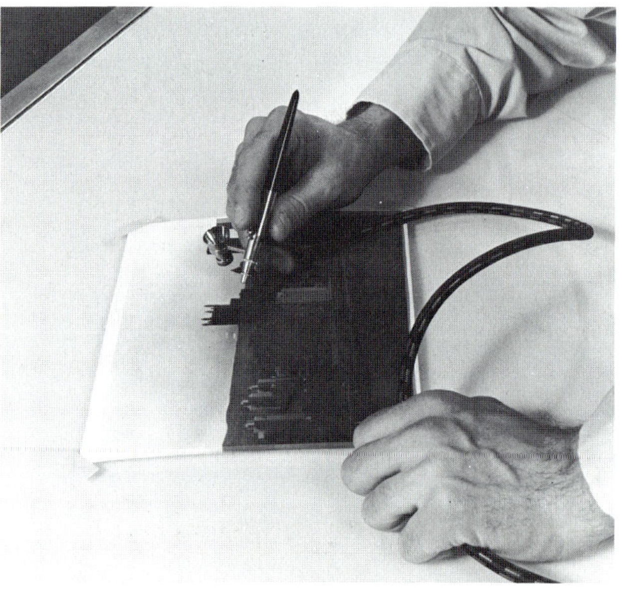

An artist airbrushing the sky in a continuous-tone photograph. Notice the frisket protecting the lower portion of the photograph.

Kinds of Halftones

Square-finish halftone. A square-finish halftone is any halftone where there are four square corners (e.g., the corners are at 90°). It may form either a rectangle or a square. A square-finish halftone is also referred to as a **conventional halftone,** because most printed halftones are rectangular or square.

Combination halftone. The combination halftone combines a line image, such as type, with a halftone image to produce a single printing image. The

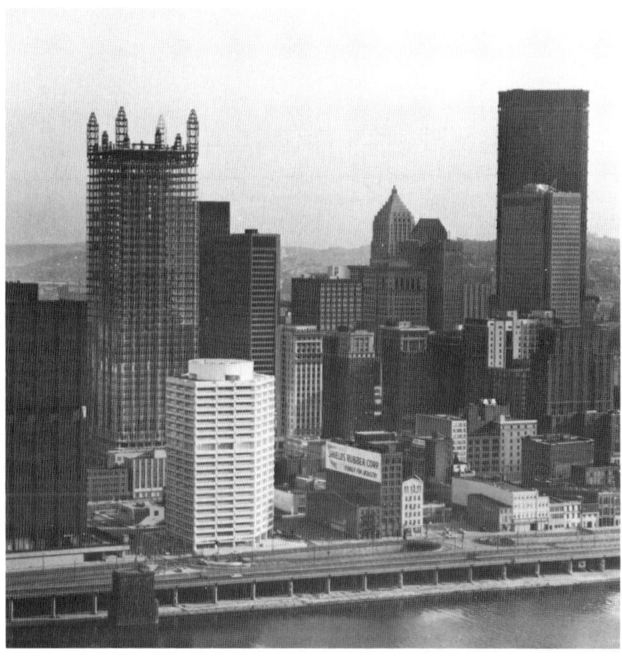

Conventional (150-line screen) square-finish halftone.

continuous-tone original art is prepared in the same manner as for normal halftone reproduction. The line image may be superimposed on the halftone (surprinted); or a film positive of the line image can be attached to the halftone negative to form an open image in the halftone (reverse printed). When preparing this type of halftone, remember that the halftone dots distinguish the type. Place the type so that surprints are within a highlight area and so reverses (or "knockouts") are within a shadow area. Choose a sans serif type, as small, hairline serifs may not reproduce, since the edges of the type will be formed by dots.

Combination halftones can also be computer-generated. In one method, the continuous-tone original is scanned as a gray-scale image. Then, the gray-scale image is adjusted as necessary using image-editing software. Next, the gray-scale image is called into a page-makeup program, positioned on a page, and the type is placed over the gray-scale image so that the type either overprints the image or reverses out of it.

Vignette halftone. Vignetting is the gradual and subtle fade-out of a halftone screen pattern from the background of a halftone. This technique is popular in portrait photography. A properly prepared vignette does not show a sharp demarcation between the printed and nonprinted areas of a photograph but does show a soft, gradual blending of the halftone edge into the paper.

Outline or silhouette halftone. An outline or silhouette halftone emphasizes a particular segment of a halftone image because the background is removed. Unlike the vignette halftone, the outline halftone has an immediate and abrupt transition between the printed and nonprinted areas of the photo. To make a silhouette halftone, the artist should outline the original continuous-tone copy in

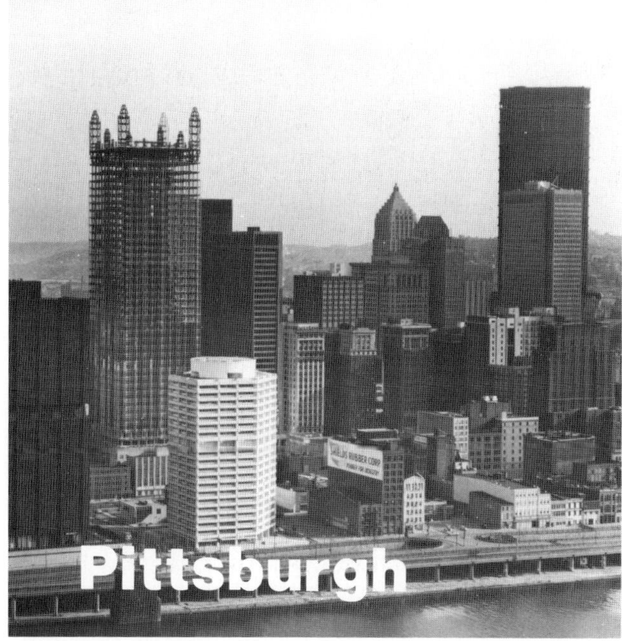

Combination halftone.

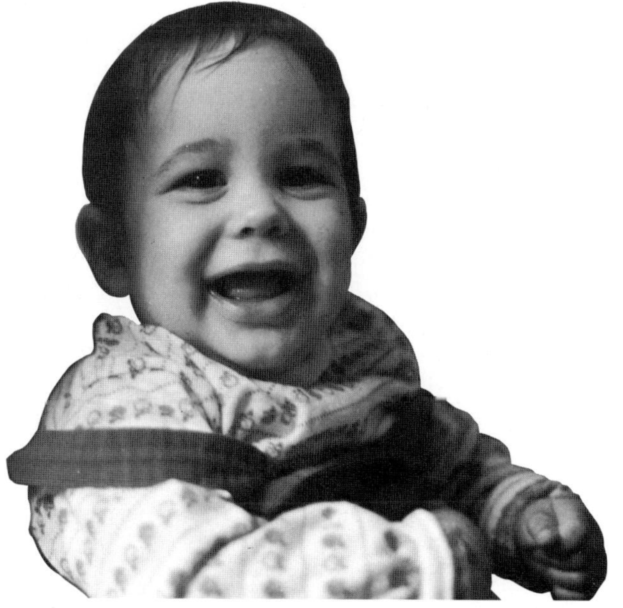

Outline or silhouette halftone.

the desired shape on a tissue overlay and specify the removal of all halftone image from the remaining background area. The film image assembler or camera operator does this by opaquing the halftone negative or by photomechanically making a mask that covers the area that will not appear in the final printed piece.

The artist can also do the silhouetting. A mask can be prepared by opaquing the unwanted area on clear acetate that is taped to the photo. Another method is to place a masking-film overlay over the entire photo and, with a sharp blade, trace the overlay that is to be masked. The masking material is then peeled from the area that will not be seen in the final print. The overlay, by either method, is used as a mask to photomechanically outline or silhouette the halftone image. A third way is to use white paint to silhouette the subject directly on the continuous-tone copy. However, when halftoned, the white paint will reproduce with highlight dots in the final printed piece.

Images can also be silhouetted using computer technology. In one method, a scanned gray-scale image is called into an image-editing program and enlarged to the point that individual pixels are visible. Then the operator uses the eraser tool to delete the unwanted portion of the image, creating a silhouetted image.

Positive halftone prints. Positive halftone prints (also called prescreened halftones) are photographic paper prints made from halftone negatives or by using the diffusion transfer process. Positive halftone prints can be pasted directly on the pasteup and reproduced as line copy because the screened print is made up of dots, and the film will record them as line work. Because they will be photographed as line copy, these halftones have a coarser screen ruling than a typical halftone that is printed on the same grade of paper.

Positive halftone prints are frequently used to minimize the cost of production. It is less expensive for the artist to silhouette and vignette on a screened print than it is for the camera operator or film assembler to do the same retouching on halftone negatives.

The major disadvantage of a screened print is that halftone quality is reduced because of two extra steps in production and the coarser screen ruling of the halftone. When a conventional halftone is being made, continuous-tone copy is exposed and processed to make a halftone negative, and this negative is used for platemaking. When making a screened print from a halftone negative,

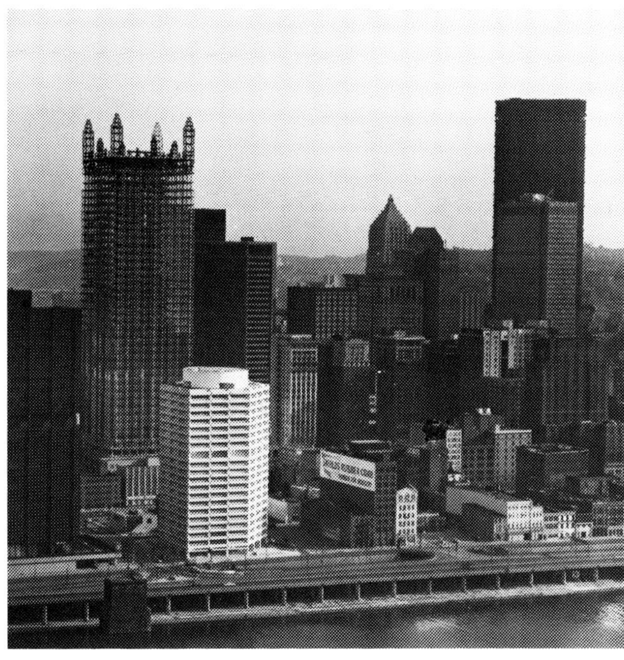

Positive halftone print. Note that the dots are easily seen. This halftone print is comparable to an 85-line-screen halftone.

continuous-tone copy is made into a halftone negative, then into a screened print, and then the already screened copy is shot as a line negative. Each time an image is photographed, quality is lost.

Rescreened halftone. Sometimes, an artist is forced to use a halftone illustration taken directly from a previously printed piece. For best reproduction, it is necessary for the printed halftone to be

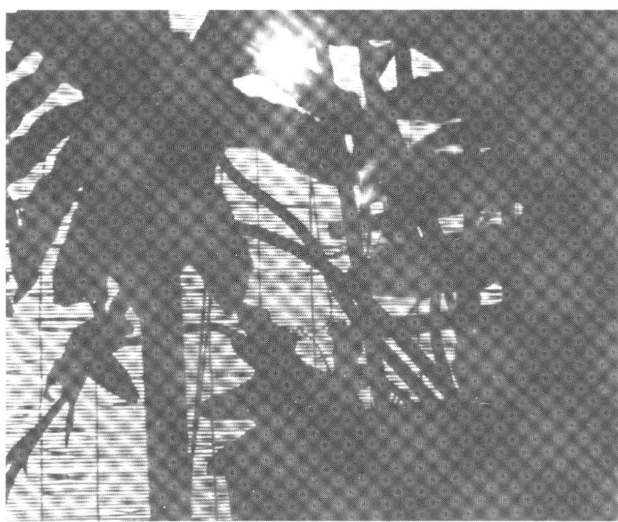

Rescreened halftone with a large moiré caused by rescreening a previously printed halftone without the use of a rescreening or interference filter.

rehalftoned, particularly when the copy must be resized. When rescreening is required, the artist should specify that a rescreening or interference filter be used to an avoid objectionable pattern—called **moiré**—in the final print.

Moiré patterns in a rescreened halftone can be lessened by changing the screen angle or by using a halftone screen with a different pattern or fineness. Sometimes changing the size of the reproduction or diminishing the photograph's sharpness helps.

Scaling Art

All camera copy must be scaled before it can be reproduced. By properly scaling the artwork the artist tells the camera or scanner operator the exact reproduction percentage or that the copy is to be reproduced "same size." Camera/scanner copy is not only scaled to size but must often be cropped by the artist. This tells the film assembler what portion of the image must appear on the negative and plate.

The *diagonal-line method* is a widely used method of cropping and scaling artwork. With this method, a proportional scale or pocket calculator is used to determine the percent reproduction size of the artwork. In the diagonal-line method, crop lines are drawn on tissue that has been placed over the artwork. Never rule these lines directly over pasteups or camera copy without placing a sheet of acetate or Mylar between the pasteup or original artwork and the tissue overlay.

Use as little pressure as possible to avoid creating a depression on the mechanical or across the image area of the original art. Rule crop lines on the tissue with a thin felt-tip marker. Do not use a ball-point pen or pencil.

Diagonal-line method of cropping and scaling artwork. The diagonal-line method is used to change the size of either the original copy or the reproduction-size mask on the pasteup. The dimensions of one remain the same, while the other one is either enlarged or reduced in proportion to it. Usually, the dimensions of the reproduction-size mask on the pasteup remain as they are, and the original copy changes in size. The following sequence of steps, most of which are illustrated, assumes that the size of the reproduction-size mask on the pasteup remains the same.

1. Place an acetate sheet and then a tissue overlay on top of the pasteup. Trace the reproduction-size mask onto the tissue, extending the bottom line to the right and the left vertical line upward.

2. Draw a diagonal line from the lower left corner through the top right corner, and continue the diagonal line beyond the right corner so that it will be longer than the diagonal of the original copy.

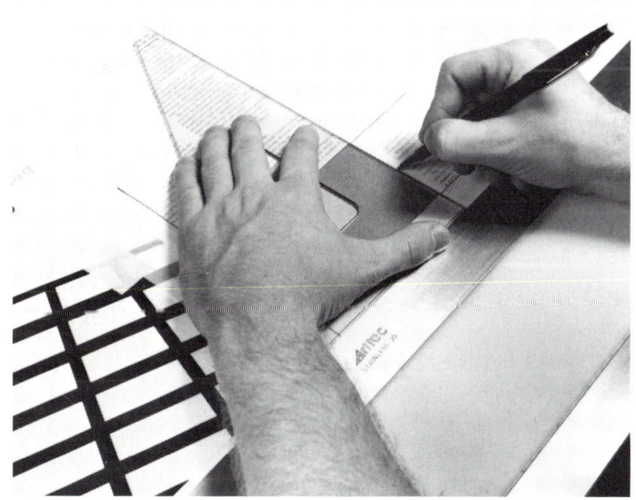

Tracing the reproduction size, extending the bottom line to the right and extending the left vertical line upward.

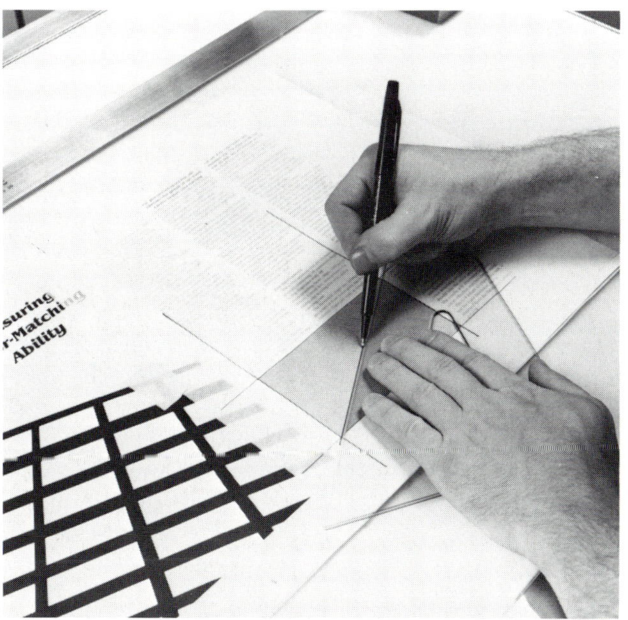

Drawing the diagonal line from the bottom left corner through the top right corner.

3. Remove the tissue overlay and acetate sheet and place them over the copy to be scaled so that the extended horizontal and vertical lines define the bottom and left edges of the desired image area.

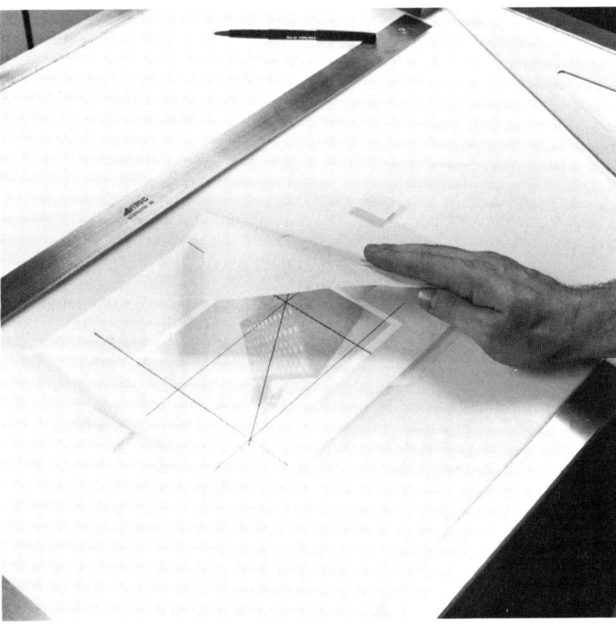

Placing the acetate and tissue over the copy to be scaled. Let the left and bottom lines define the edges of the desired crop area.

4. On the tissue overlay, draw perpendicular lines for the top and right margins of the desired image area, connecting the lines at a point on the diagonal line. These lines show where to place the crop marks.

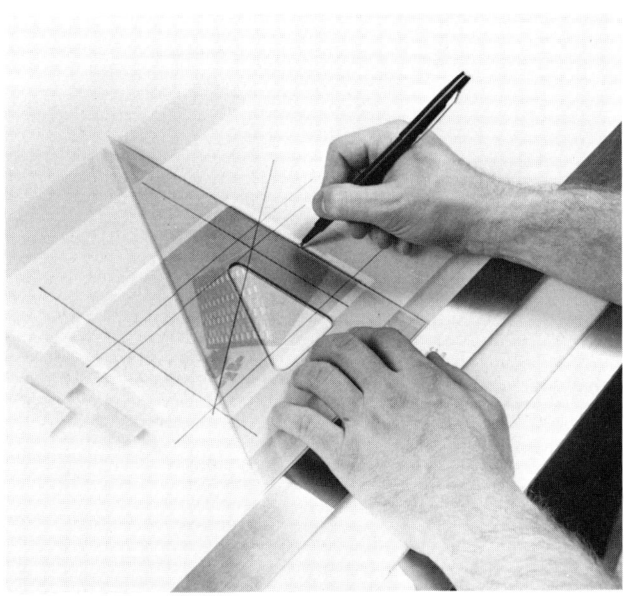

Drawing lines that connect the diagonal to indicate crop area.

5. Place thin crop marks on the borders (non-image area) of the artwork using a grease pencil. This allows the marks to be removed and the artwork to be used again with a different set of crop marks. Only one set of crop marks should be used on each piece of camera copy. More than one set is confusing. Remember, never place crop marks in an area that will be printed. If you are using a full-frame illustration without borders, mount the artwork on a board larger than the artwork, and place crop marks accordingly.

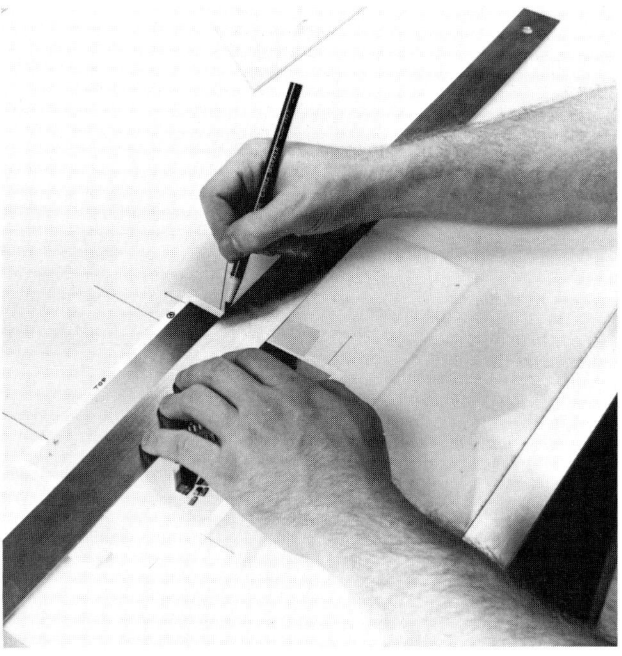

Placing crop marks on the borders (nonimage area) of the artwork using a grease pencil.

6. Indicate the exact dimensions of both the reproduction size (final size) and the area that is cropped to fit the repro size on *the tissue overlay.* These figures will be needed when determining the percent reproduction size.

Next, calculate the reproduction percentage of the artwork using a pocket calculator or proportional scale.

Calculating the reproduction percentage using a calculator. The simplest and most accurate way of determining reproduction percentage is to use an electronic calculator.

1. Divide one dimension of the reproduction size desired (final size) by the corresponding dimension of the cropped original.

2. Multiply this figure by 100. The result is the reproduction percentage that is needed to fit the

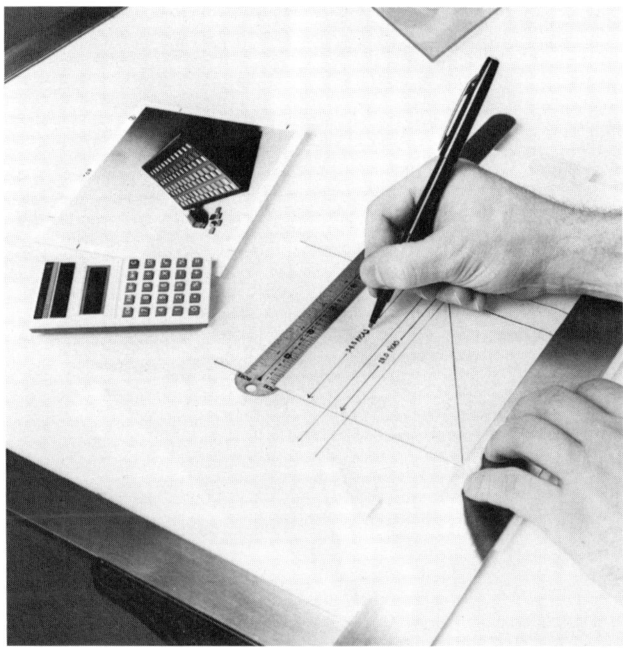

Writing the dimensions of the repro size and the cropped area.

area designated on the pasteup. (A number less than 100 indicates that the original will be reduced on the camera, and a number greater than 100 indicates that it will be enlarged.)

3. Double-check your answer by doing the same calculation using the measurements from the other dimension.

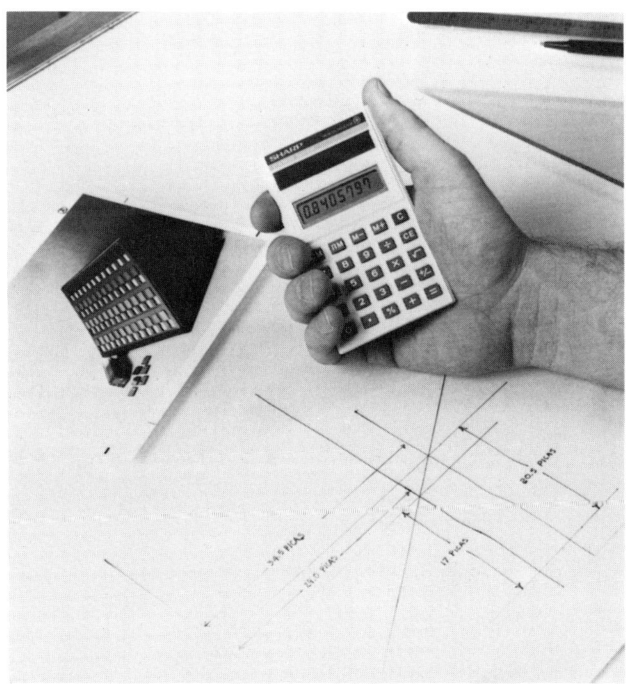

Calculating the percent reproduction size using a calculator.

Determining reproduction percentage with a proportional scale. The most common proportional scale has two round disks, each with a scale marked in fractions of an inch. (There are also metric and pica scales.) The inside scale represents the original size, and the outside scale represents the final or reproduction size.

1. Align one dimensional measurement of the original (inner scale) wth the corresponding dimensional measurement of the reproduction size (outer scale).

2. Look at the scale's window to find the number that the arrow points to. This is the reproduction percentage.

3. While the scale is in place, look for the other dimension on the outer scale. The corresponding original dimension should align directly below the desired reproduction size for that dimension.

If the entire image area of the original is to be used, add one or two percentage points to the final percentage. This is to ensure that the image completely fills the window allowed for it on the film assembler's negative. It is far better to have the negative a percentage point larger than originally figured than to fall short of filling the window completely. This practice eliminates costly remakes.

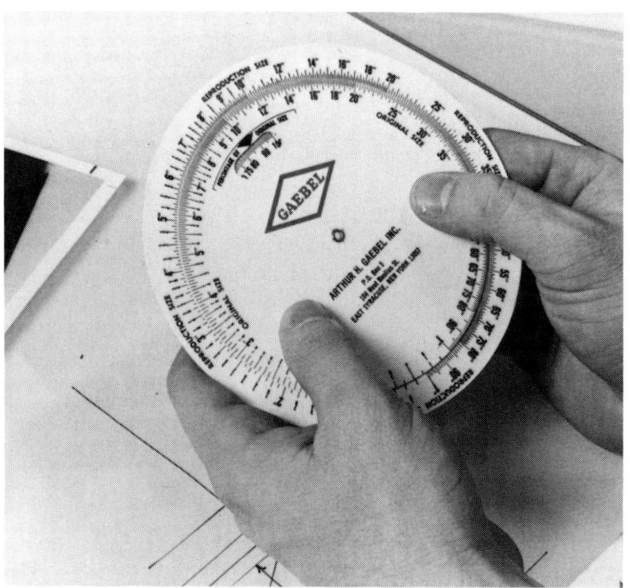

Finding the reproduction size using a proportional scale.

Designating reproduction size. By custom, reproduction size should always be expressed as a percentage of original size. For example, assume the original has a horizontal dimension of 18½ in. that is to be reduced to 14 in.; the reproduction size is 76%. Assume that the original has a horizontal

dimension of 12 in. that is to be enlarged to 18 in.; the reproduction size is 150%. When marking the copy, this reproduction percentage should be marked with grease pencil in the border, margin, or mounting of the artwork. To enhance communication between the artist and the camera operator or commercial lithographer, many artists mark reproduction size as *76% of original,* or *132% of original.* Do not mark within the image area of the copy.

Some artists include the reproduction percentage *and* linear dimensions when marking in the margins of the copy. This is a dangerous and confusing practice. The camera operator wonders which to follow. Therefore, only designate the percentage required.

Finally, since each piece of copy has its specific placement on the pasteup, remember to write the number or letter given to the artwork (check the pasteup) in the border *on the front* of the artwork or on the attached mounting that carries the reproduction percentage.

Minimizing the number of reproduction sizes. When the nature of the art permits, and on jobs containing many pieces of comparably sized artwork, the artist should make slight changes in cropping to reduce the number of different percentages. For example, if a group of similar subjects calls for reproduction at 54%, 54½%, 55½%, and 56%, they should all be cropped and rescaled to 55%, if possible. This often permits several pieces of artwork to be shot in the time it takes to produce one large negative. This simplifies the camera operator's job and reduces the cost of production without harming the design of a piece.

Do's and don'ts when working with photographs:

- Mark "TOP" in the front top margin of every photograph that may be confusing. This greatly helps the film image assembler when stripping the halftone negatives.
- Flop a photograph when, for aesthetic reasons, the design calls for it. However, don't overlook items in the photo that, when flopped, will diminish the quality of the piece. Such things as buttoned clothing (a woman's coat buttons right over left, a man's buttons left over right), hair parts, anything that is printed and would be wrong-reading if flopped (clocks, signs, maps, labels, calendars, license plates, nameplates on equipment), and machinery whose controls would be backwards if flopped should not be overlooked.
- Do not cut photos to the crop lines.

Assembling the Pasteup

To complete a pasteup (also called a mechanical, key art, and camera-ready art), the artist begins by pasting all of the line-copy elements that can be photographed as a unit on a stiff base sheet of paper or acetate, by following the final layout or comprehensive. This is called the **base art** and includes type and line drawings—in short, anything that is not continuous-tone copy.

Continuous-tone copy is not included on the base art because it must be photographed (halftoned) separately. See the previous sections "Types of Copy" and "Scaling Art" for more on preparing continuous-tone art for reproduction. The pasteup often requires an overlay; e.g., when preparing art for surprints, for reverses, or to indicate color breaks. Preparing overlays is detailed in the following section, "Overlays."

Most manual pasteup work has been eliminated by the emergence of page-makeup software programs that allow the artist to assemble pages using a computer system. The electronic makeup of pages is discussed in Chapter 12, "Electronic Prepress Production."

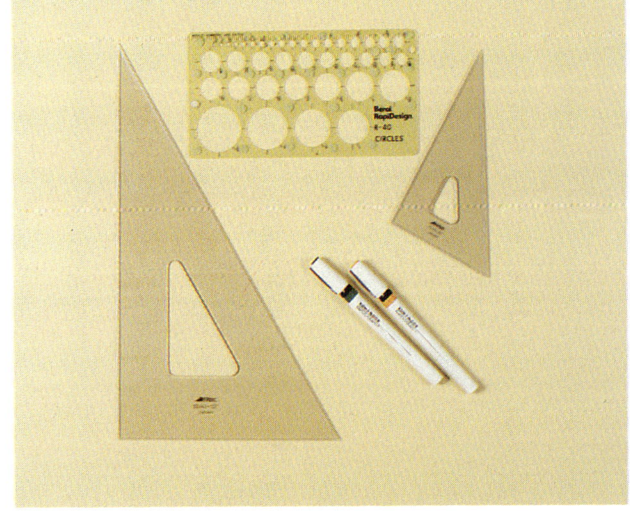

Some tools used for art preparation.

Materials and Equipment

Many kinds of materials, equipment, and tools are available for the artist to use to complete a pasteup.

The choice of materials, the techniques used, and, therefore, the equipment and tools required depend on the complexity of the job as well as the production procedures of the particular printer.

When copy is being prepared to be reproduced on an office duplicator, preprinted stock masters may be all that is needed. The manuscript may be typed directly on a master, and rules and line art can be added to the same master—in effect, the mechanical could be produced using only a typewriter, a ruler, and a pen. At the other extreme, a studio or art department may use a light table; a drafting table with a highly sophisticated drafting machine; a large variety of triangles, templates, and adjustable curves; a compass; a swivel knife; numerous markers, paints, inks, and dyes; and a variety of art boards, paper stocks, and overlay materials, to name a few. To be sure, the materials and techniques used vary from job to job.

Grids. Base sheets preprinted with nonreproducing blue guidelines are often used when assembling a pasteup. Referred to as **grids,** the preprinted, lightweight paper sheets are most often used when assembling a large number of pasteups that follow a similar design and format, such as pages of books, magazines, and newspapers. The same grid format is followed when the designer makes the comprehensive layout.

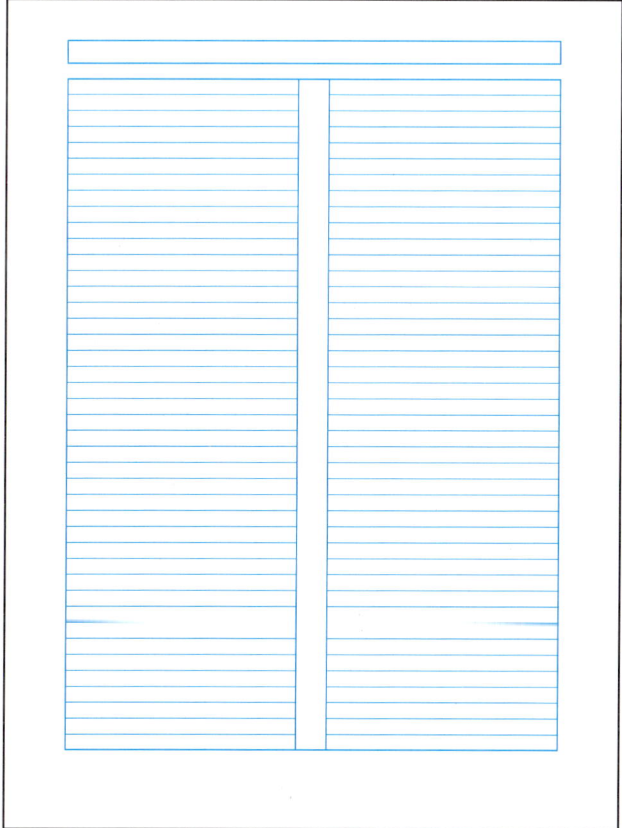

A sample paper grid printed with nonrepro blue guidelines.

Grids are also printed in black on a clear acetate master sheet. This master grid is taped to a light table and either a blank sheet of lightweight translucent paper or clear stable-base plastic (acetate) is pin-registered and/or taped over the grid. The pasteup is then done on the paper or acetate following the guides of the grid.

Guidelines on the Pasteup

Before the artist can paste up the copy elements, certain marks that will be used as guidelines in the production of the printed piece must be ruled on the base sheet. These marks are drawn in the nonimage area of the pasteup.

Crop or trim marks. Crop or trim marks indicate the final dimensions of the printed piece. They are drawn in the corners of the pasteup with black ink so that they reproduce on the negative and guide the film image assembler, as well as indicate to the bindery where to trim the printed sheets. Crop marks should be placed ⅛ in. (3 mm) back from the actual corner of the pasteup; that is, they should not meet to form a right angle, as they may appear on the final printed piece.

Fold marks. Fold marks are drawn as thin dotted or broken lines outside the trim area of the piece to show the printer and binder where the piece will fold.

Center-of-image marks. The center of all pages (vertical and horizontal) must be located and marked as a thin black line outside the trim area. Center-of-image marks help the film image assembler or platemaker.

Each of these marks and other inked lines are drawn with a technical pen. It is best to draw trim, fold, and center marks each as a thin line using a very narrow tip. Ruling pens can also be used, as the thickness of the lines drawn with a ruling pen can be varied by adjusting the vise of the pen. Other marks such as perforation indications and diecutting guidelines are usually drawn in red ink or nonreproducing blue ink.

Any ruled line that is part of the printed image should also be drawn at this stage in the pasteup. Ball-point pens and fine-line markers are sometimes used to draw lines, but the ink flow is not

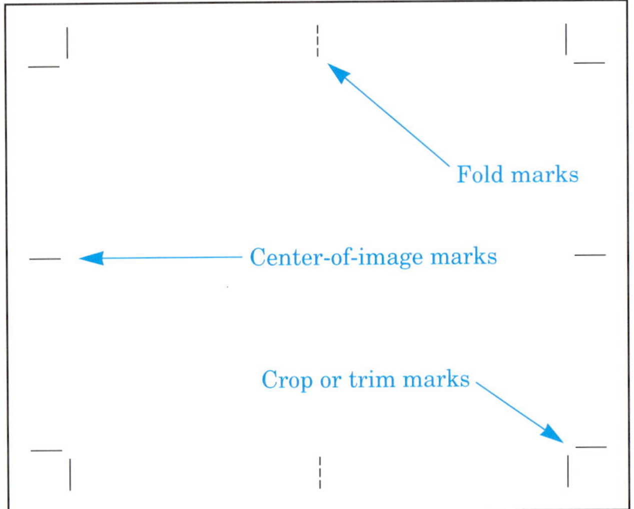

consistent enough and line width is not uniform enough for high-quality work. Rules are often drawn slightly longer than necessary, and the excess is painted over with a brush and opaque white paint. This produces a neat, clean line ending. The white paint can also be used to cover any mistakes that may have been made when using the technical pen. Rules can also be drawn on a separate piece of coated stock, which is trimmed to the desired length and then positioned. Ruled lines can also be made by the phototypesetting machine on the galley along with the typeset copy. The width, length, and spacing of the lines are specified by the artist when the copy is ordered.

Othcr production requirements. It is the rare job where the artist need only be concerned with each page or unit of the piece as if it were the only page. Book or pamphlet work invariably requires pasting up at least two pages on a single base sheet. The artist must then consult with the printer to determine whether he or she should paste up facing pages as units, or folding pages as units. When multiple units are to be pasted up, the printer may require more than just trim, center, and fold marks. The greater the number of units on one board, the more marks that are required. It is important to consult with the binder and finisher and to determine their needs for special guidelines.

Bonding the Art to the Pasteup

After all guidelines have been included, the artist can bond each element in its appropriate position on the mechanical. But first each element, beginning with the type, must be cut from the galley or trimmed before being placed on the pasteup. If possible, the elements to be mounted should be trimmed no closer than ⅛ in. (3 mm) from the image. If the edge of the cut-out copy creates a shadow on the negative when the mechanical is photographed, this margin will allow the shadow to be deleted easily without disturbing the art. It is good practice to use scissors when *first* cutting the copy from the galley. Since scissors give the paper a beveled edge, a shadow is less likely to occur on the negative than if a knife is used.

The two common bonding materials are wax and rubber cement.

Wax. Wax is the most popular adhesive used to bond art to a pasteup. Waxing machines range in sophistication from simple hand-held applicators that allow the artist to roll a coat of wax onto the back of copy to waxing machines that apply the melted wax to copy as it rolls through a series of distributor rollers. Most waxing machines allow the operator to control wax film thickness and melting temperature. Waxing machines are more convenient and easier to use than rubber cement. However, while wax bonds are repositionable, they are

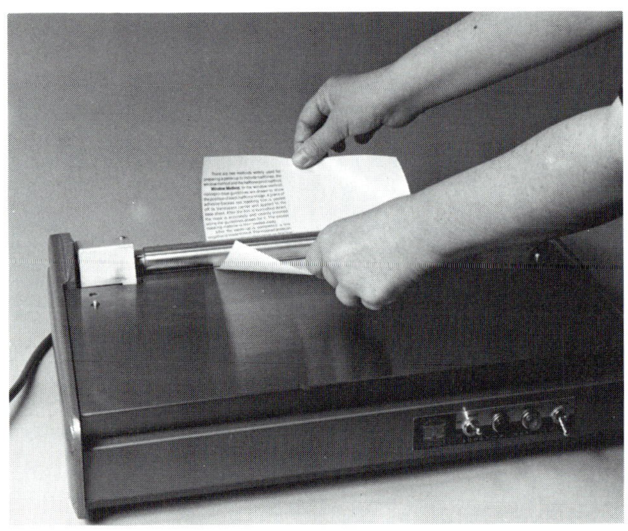

Artist applying wax to the back side of typeset copy.

not as secure as those of rubber cement. If wax is used, it is usually applied before the copy is trimmed.

Rubber cement. Two types of rubber cement are used today: *one-coat* rubber cement and *two-coat* rubber cement.

There are also three ways of using the cement: the dry-to-dry method, the wet-to-wet method, and the wet-to-dry method.

When the dry-to-dry method is used, the rubber cement is brushed onto the back of the trimmed copy and the surface of the pasteup board. Both surfaces must dry completely before the copy is positioned on the pasteup board. Drying may take several minutes, but the resulting bond between the copy and the pasteup board is stronger than when using any other method. With the wet-to-wet method, the cement is brushed onto the copy and surface of the pasteup board, but before the surfaces dry, the copy is positioned on the pasteup. Rubber cement is applied to only one surface using the wet-to-dry method. The cement is still wet when the copy is positioned.

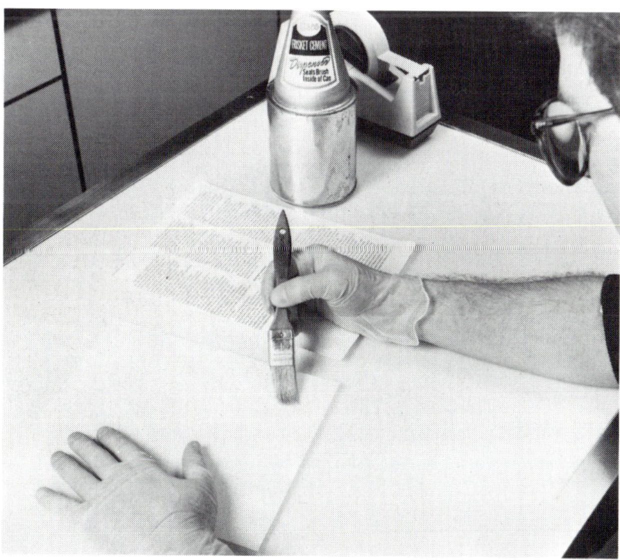

Artist applying rubber cement to the back side of typeset copy.

A very strong bond is achieved with dry-to-dry bonding. However, while the other methods allow the copy to be repositioned, dry-to-dry does not. To remove or reposition copy, a small amount of rubber cement thinner is applied to the edges of the copy to loosen it. The dry-to-dry method must then be repeated in order to adhere the copy to the pasteup board again. In addition to the extra time required to mount art by this method, there are two other disadvantages: dirt tends to accumulate around copy edges, and white copy, particularly phototypesetting paper, may fade over time. The degree of fading is dependent upon the quality of the rubber cement used and the age and type of phototypesetting paper.

Excess rubber cement on the pasteup and along the edges of the copy is as easily removed as wax is. A rubber cement "pickup," a commercially available wedge of resilient rubber, can be rubbed along the pasteup, picking up dirt and excess cement. Excess wax is removed with a paper towel that has been wetted with rubber cement thinner. (Rubber gloves should be worn when handling rubber cement or its thinner.)

Completing the Pasteup

Once the copy is positioned on the pasteup according to the layout, the correct horizontal and vertical alignment of each element is checked with a T square and triangle. The copy is then burnished, or rubbed down, to secure the bond. A piece of tracing paper should be placed over the pasteup to protect the copy while burnishing. Correct positioning is then rechecked, since burnishing may shift the copy.

All art elements that require enlargement or reduction different from the mechanical must be submitted as pieces separate from the mechanical (unattached). Continuous-tone and full-color copy must also be submitted individually, as these art elements require different handling. For ease in handling, most artwork should be mounted on a suitable board or paper and covered with a tracing-paper tissue overlay. The tissue overlay not only protects the art but carries instructions and explanations to the printer. However, writing on the tissue overlay should only be done after a piece of acetate has been slipped between the artwork and tissue. This prevents making indentations into the surface of the artwork.

All line-art elements should be mounted on the pasteup to eliminate costly stripping time. When

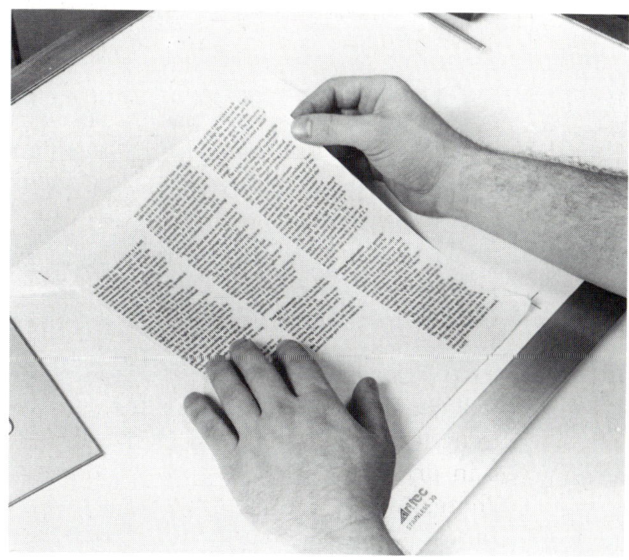

Positioning copy on the pasteup.

these elements are originally drawn, they are likely to be larger than reproduction size. The art can be photographed at final size on high-contrast diffusion transfer paper and mounted directly on the pasteup.

Costly errors are avoided in production when separate art elements are properly keyed and coded so that the graphic arts photographer and film assembler know exactly where each copy element is positioned on the pasteup. A letter or number on each unattached art element should correspond to the pasteup. If a separate art element, such as a photo, is coded as "Copy A," the appropriate area on the pasteup, or tissue overlay, also should be marked "Copy A."

There are four ways of preparing a mechanical to indicate separate (unattached) art elements: (1) keylining, (2) position-only print method, (3) halftone print method, and (4) window method.

Keylining. Using black or red ink, the artist can outline the area on the pasteup where separate art elements are to appear. When photographed, the clear outline on the negative becomes a guide for the film assembler in placing halftones. Keylining is also used to indicate butting of solid colors.

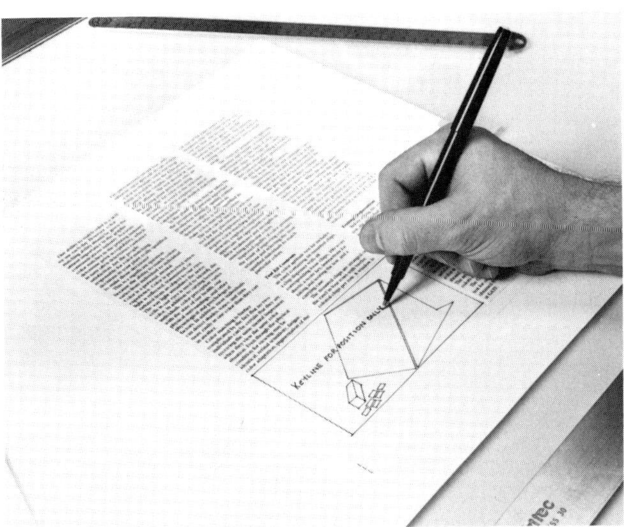

Keylining to show where the halftone will be placed.

Position-only print method. The artist can make diffusion transfer prints (photostats) of the separate art elements to reproduction size and then paste them in proper position directly on the mechanical. Photostats present the advantage of allowing the artist to see the image in its reduced or enlarged state, and they help the film assembler to properly position the halftone negative. They have the disadvantage of sometimes being dimensionally unstable and, therefore, imprecise in their reduced or enlarged form. Once placed on the mechanical, a photostat that is not for final reproduction must be clearly marked in black or red that it is "for position only." This precaution is taken so that the film assembler is not confused between the photostat negative and the negative of the original art. Sometimes it is the most accurate way of indicating placement to the film assembler.

The film assembler will remove the position-only photostat negative and strip in the halftone negative or put the halftone negative on a complementary flat that the platemaker uses to "double burn" the plate.

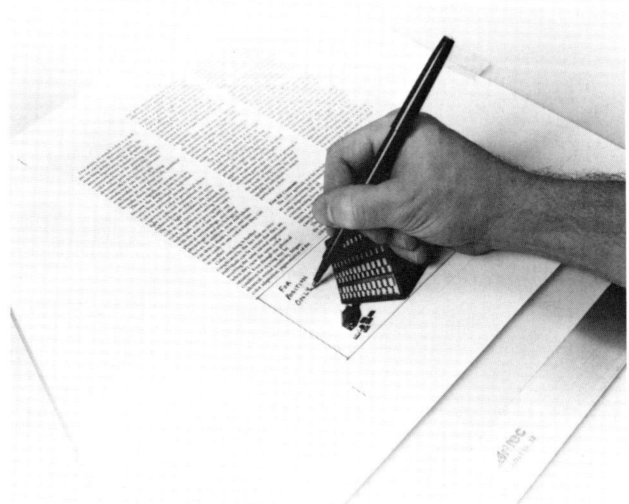

"For position only" is marked over the photostat.

Halftone-print method. Halftone prints are positive photographic paper prints that are made from halftone negatives and are an easy way to reproduce continuous-tone copy. These positive halftone prints are placed directly on the pasteup and reproduced as line copy because the screened positive halftone print is made up of dots and the film records them as line work. However, a major disadvantage of using a positive-halftone print is that halftone quality is reduced. For more on halftone prints see the section "Types of Copy."

Window method. Another method for indicating placement of halftones and screen tints on the pasteup is the window method. Using the window method, the pasteup artist applies an adhesive-backed, red masking material to the mechanical where separate artwork will print. This red mask appears as a clear window on the negative made

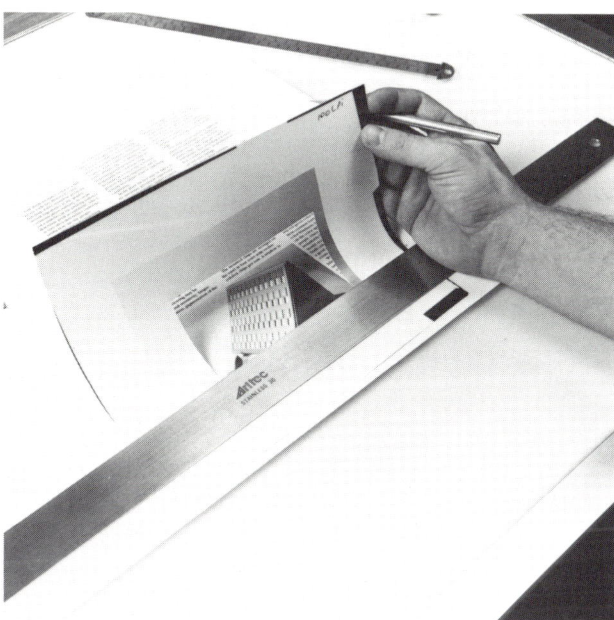

In the halftone-print method, a paper print of the halftone...

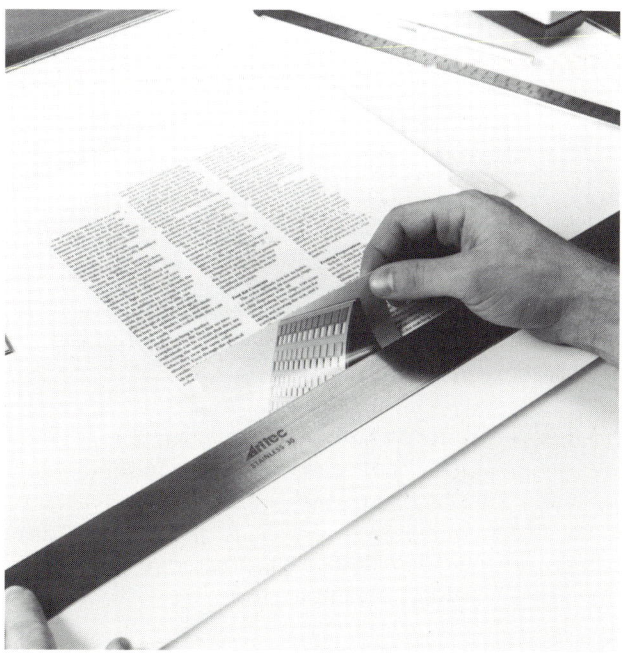

...can be pasted directly on the pasteup.

from the base art. With this method, a halftone negative is made of the original photograph instead of a halftone print. The film assembler positions the halftone negative behind the clear window made for it. The window method is often preferred since finer screens can be used than those used in the halftone-print method. (Some film assemblers use the windows on the line negatives only as a guide; they prefer to create their own windows.)

Sometimes, a positive halftone print, produced at reproduction size but cut smaller than its corresponding window, is mounted on a pasteup over the red window. By referring to the mechanical, the film assembler is less likely to make errors when stripping the negative of the separate art element.

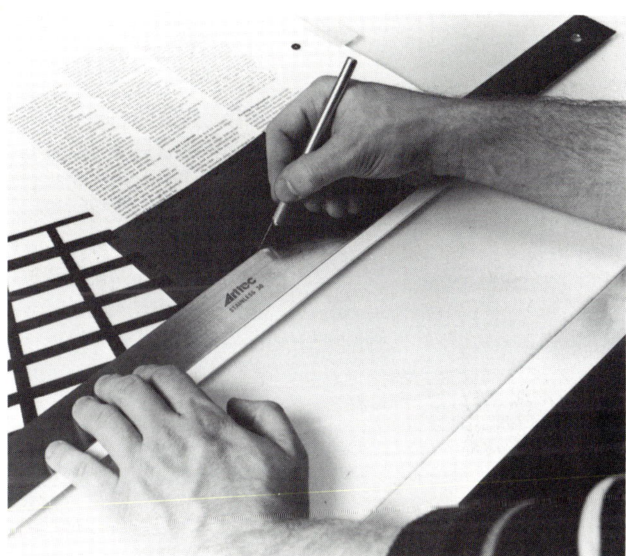

A block of adhesive-backed masking material indicates where separate artwork will print.

Tips and Techniques for Pasteup

- Because cut marks on the pasteup show as clear areas on the negative, corrections within typeset copy must be made carefully. Mortise cutting is an effective way to eliminate outlines around single- or two-word corrections. Place the correction over the original type using a light table. Rub the new type into position. Cut out the correction both through the new and old layers of copy. Remove the old copy and replace with the new. This creates a "jigsaw puzzle" fit leaving no cut marks.
- When entire lines or blocks of copy must be replaced, use a T square to line up type for cutting. Cutting both old and new copy using the T square as a guide allows the edges to butt evenly and therefore be invisible.
- Do not use transparent or masking tapes to adhere art or copy elements to the pasteup. Tapes are not only unreliable for adhesive but also distort the copy when photographed.
- Know the minimum reduction and maximum enlargement capabilities of the process camera used.
- If a design dictates two or more nontouching flat colors, all line art may be pasted onto the base art. The negative will be duplicated and the appropriate

areas marked for each color. But remember to indicate the color breaks correctly on the tissue overlay.

Though the last stages are not the best time to remedy errors in the mechanical, it is better then than not at all. Before sending the pasteup to the next production stage, recheck the following:

- Measure for correct dimensions of the pasteup on all boards.
- Check that all color breaks and instructions are clearly indicated on the tissue overlay.
- Include photos, other separate art elements, swatches, the comprehensive, and folding dummy.

Overlays

When a layout or comprehensive calls for a surprint, a knockout, a silhouetted halftone, overlapping flat colors, or full-color artwork that butts a solid color, it is not practical to place each of the elements on the base art. Examples of such cases include printing black type over black halftones; reversing type out of a background; silhouetting the background of a photo; printing two or more overlapping flat colors, such as a rainbow effect; and tightly framing a four-color photo with a black rule. Under such circumstances, all elements can be made a part of the final camera-ready mechanical by using overlays.

Overlays are usually frosted or clear acetate or polyester. The overlay can be attached to the base art using register pins so that the overlay can be removed when the base art is photographed and accurately repositioned afterward, or the overlay can be hinged at the top with masking tape so that they can be flipped entirely out of the way when the base art or separate art element they are attached to is to be photographed.

Overlays for surprints. The base art includes all elements to be printed in the key color (usually black) shot as line work. A surprint, such as type that overprints a halftone, should be prepared so that the type that will surprint is pasted on an overlay, which is properly positioned over the halftone area of the base art.

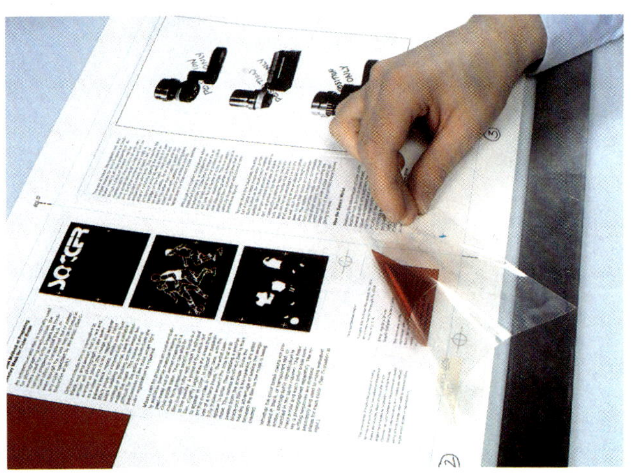

This masked areas (background) will print in a tint of cyan, and the type will print in black. Note the register marks placed on the base art.

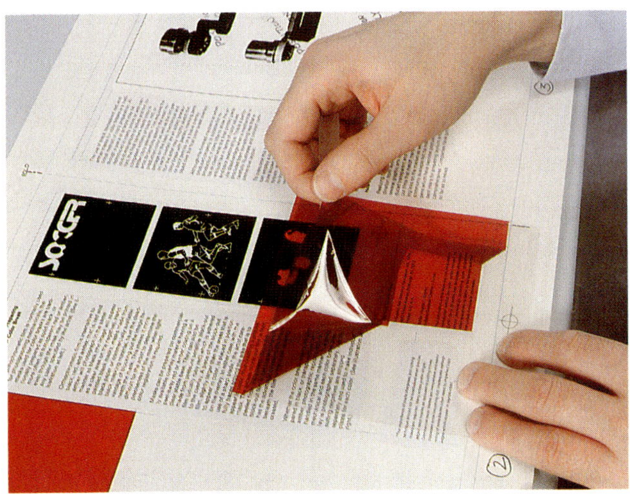

Peeling masking film from its acetate carrier sheet. This becomes the overlay to indicate a tint of ink.

Overlays for knockouts. To produce a knockout, such as type that will reverse out of a solid color, the type should be pasted on an acetate overlay, correctly positioned over the solid area on the base art. Even if the type will appear (print) white, black type can be used and the reverse will be photomechanically produced.

Overlays for silhouetting halftones. Silhouetting for photographs can be done with an overlay of red or amber peelable masking material that is adhered to a transparent acetate carrier sheet. A piece of masking film is cut larger than the size of the desired photograph. The film is hinged at the top over the photo. The outline of the image to be silhouetted is cut into the peelable masking film layer but not into the acetate carrier sheet underneath. A second piece of acetate should be placed under the overlay to protect the photo while the

masking material is being cut. The red or amber mask is then peeled from the unwanted area, such as the background area of the photo. The clear carrier sheet becomes the overlay when the unwanted masking material is trimmed and peeled away. Register marks should be placed next to the photograph, and it should be covered with a protective tissue overlay.

Overlays for overlapping flat colors. Base art that is prepared from a design of flat colors that overlap, such as a square of green and a square of red that touch, require a separate overlay for each color. In other words, two sheets of peelable masking film are hinged to the pasteup. Each film is cut in the square shape (overlapping a hair) and the background film is peeled away, leaving two amber or red squares, to indicate where the color will print.

An alternative to cutting overlays for overlapping flat colors is to draw keylines on the base art in the square shapes and let the masks be made photomechanically. The tissue overlay placed over the pasteup *must* contain an outline of these shapes with color and color identification filled in and include proper instructions to the printer. This type of keyline art is sometimes preferred to overlay art when hairline register is required.

Also, type or other art elements that print in different colors must be pasted on individual overlays if these elements overlap, touch, or come close to touching any base-art element. The overlay is positioned, in register, over the base art. This type of overlay is considered an overlay for color breaks. The base art and each (color-break) overlay are photographed separately. The resulting negatives are stripped separately and used to make individual plates for each color.

Overlays for full-color art that butts a solid color. When a full-color photograph is outlined by a solid rule, the photograph should be prepared as a red or orange overlay mask placed in exact position within the rule. The rule should be placed on the base art.

Complex mechanicals requiring several photomechanical operations may require the preparation of more than a single overlay. Overlays do not always have to be the size of the pasteup but can be cut smaller, just a bit larger than the area to be covered.

Register marks, either commercially available or ruled as very fine cross marks with black ink, should always be placed on the base art when using overlays. Since, in reproduction, the base art and the overlays are photographed separately and the resulting negatives are combined by the film assembler, the register marks make precise positioning possible.

Finally, print the instructions for and identification of each overlay directly on the overlay with black grease pencil. This identification is useful if the overlay becomes separated from the artwork.

The Final Overlay

Once the pasteup is complete, it should be covered with a tissue and burnished. Another tissue overlay should be taped at the top of the pasteup to protect it and carry information to the printer.

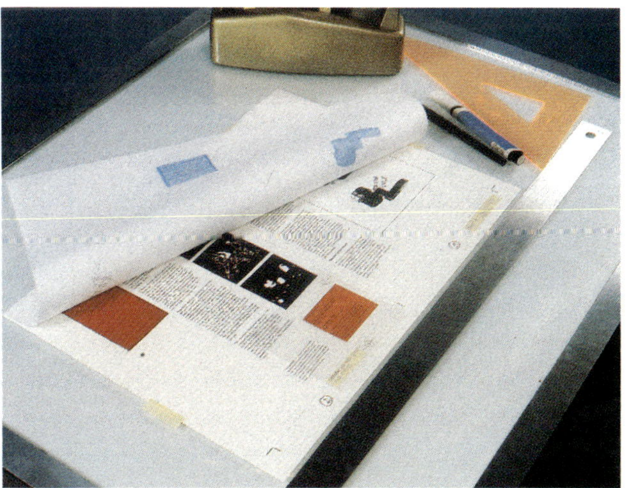

A tissue or tracing paper overlay is hinged on the top of the pasteup.

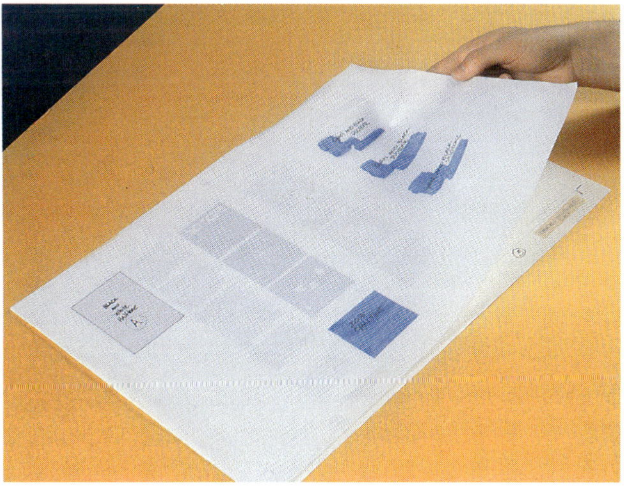

A tissue overlay protects the artwork, carries instructions and tracings of the art elements, and shows the placement of color.

• **Protection:** Tracing paper or tissue overlays protect the camera-ready artwork from dust, fingerprints, and other damage that may affect reproduction quality.
• **Instruction:** Instructions pertaining to color, tint percentages, reverses, knockouts, or any other information of use in the production operations following art and copy preparation should be clearly and neatly written on the tissue overlay.
• **Color breaks:** As a precaution against any misunderstanding, use colored markers to indicate the placement of each color on the tissue overlay.

Type of Register

Register is the accuracy with which images are combined or positioned. A printed, one-color job is in register when the images are correctly located with respect to all edges of the sheet. In other words, when the gripper-edge margins and the side-edge margins are correct throughout the run, the job is in register. A process color job is in register when the first color is correctly placed on the sheet and all other colors are properly placed in relation to the first.

To minimize register difficulties on press, all artwork should be prepared to simplify photography, film image assembly, platemaking, and press makeready. However, certain jobs do occur whose mechanical assembly of the elements is better left to the film assembler, such as butting halftones and tints, making surprints or knockouts, and making type reversals.

The kind of plan that the artist develops in consultation with the photographer and film assembler for handling the preparation of a multicolor job depends on how critical the register is.

Depending upon the complexity of the job, lithographers distinguish four types of register: no register, loose register, lap register, and hairline register. These terms are not standardized throughout the industry; in fact, many printers define these terms somewhat differently or use their own descriptions of register, such as close, butt, and tight.

No register means that several colors are completely independent of one another on the printed sheet. Textbooks often employ this use of color as spot color, printing text type in one color of ink and printing heads and subheads in another color of ink.

Loose register means that minor variations in the relationship of one color to another are inconsequential. Rough shadings or blotches of spot color overprinted on a black line drawing is an example of loose register. It is ideal to cut overlays for color breaks for these kinds of jobs so that each color is on a different "level" or overlay.

Lap register is achieved by overlapping a narrow strip of one color over the second color at the points that they join. This slight color overlap, which is perceptible, prevents the white of the paper from showing. Lap register eases the task of art preparation and minimizes register problems in film assembly, platemaking, and printing. Two black-and-white halftone photographs or screen tint panels separated by a thick red line is considered lap register. Here overlay art is only useful if the desired lap allowance is in excess of 0.015 in. (0.38 mm). It is not good practice to butt colors of similar density, e.g., orange and green, as the lap will print as a dark line.

Hairline register is the joining or butting of two or more colors with no perceptible color overlap. Printing four-color photos side-by-side (touching) or printing solid colors (other than black) that touch is printing hairline register.

It is difficult to achieve precise hairline register, and, in fact, *some* overlap of color *must* occur to eliminate any white paper from showing; however, this overlap is considerably smaller than in lap register and is not perceptible. Hairline register is best obtained from a single piece of base art that is prepared for reproduction with no overlays. The base art is separated photomechanically for precise register.

Two-Color Reproduction

A single-color image can be reproduced using two colors. Producing such a two-color printed reproduction is not merely overprinting two flat colors. The copy for this two-color printed reproduction is always a continuous-tone image such as a photograph. The graphic arts photographer creates two different halftone negatives from that single piece of copy. When these are printed one over the other, the reproduction is called a duotone. Sometimes a halftone is printed over a flat solid or tint of

another color. This results in an imitation or "fake" duotone, which is less costly than a conventional duotone. (Duotones can also be computer-generated using a scanned gray-scale image and the appropriate image-editing software.)

"Conventional" Duotones

A **duotone** is a two-color halftone image made from a single piece of continuous-tone copy with each printed ink emphasizing a different tonal area of the copy. The dominant ink, usually black, often prints the full tonal range, while the less dominant, or second color, prints a smaller range of tones within the halftone.

The photograph or continuous-tone artwork is photographed twice through a halftone screen, with each image recorded at a different screen angle, at a different exposure, and on a different piece of film. The halftone images are printed in register on the press. The dominant image is usually printed in a dark ink while the secondary image is printed in a lighter ink. The differing tonal scales of the two images create an illusion that there is "more" in the reproduction than there was in the original copy, because a properly made duotone extends the tonal range of the reproduction so that it closely approximates both the highlight and shadow areas of the original. This is usually not achievable in single-color halftone printing. For this reason duotones are used to render color, depth, and definition to a subject while hinting at the expensive full-color process.

Artists sometimes specify duotone reproduction of a halftone using a black for both colors (sometimes a black and a gray) to achieve the highlight to shadow tones of the original. The result is a black-and-white reproduction that is superior to a conventional black-and-white halftone. By convention, this two-impression black duotone is called a *true* duotone. Keep in mind that duotones can be printed in almost any ink combination imaginable, including the same ink in varying tints, e.g., a dark blue and a light blue; a dark red and a light red.

In specifying duotone reproductions, the artist is not limited to conventional halftone screens. Special effects can be created by using vertical-, horizontal-, or diagonal-line screens; circular screens; mezzotint screens; and various line screen rulings.

The artist should provide the graphic arts photographer with suitable continuous-tone copy as would be submitted for conventional halftone printing. The copy should not be flat or contrasty but have a smooth and gradual tonal transition from highlight to shadow areas, yet be in sharp focus. Discussing the final duotone result wanted with the printer before the films are made is imperative, and providing the printer with ink swatches is the best method for ensuring that the proper result will be obtained.

As a service to the artist and lithographer, many ink and paper suppliers provide printed guides for duotone reproduction. These guides show the result created when printing various duotone color combinations with various paper colors. These are excellent designing aids, as they present a preview of what a particular ink and paper combination will look like.

Many duotone jobs have failed because clients were displeased with the result of duotone reproductions. On the other hand, carefully made duotones produced from properly processed negatives can simulate full-color reproduction.

"Fake" Duotones

A duotone effect, sometimes known as a "fake" duotone, is created by combining a halftone and a solid or screen tint of a second color. The fake duotone does not produce the wide tonal range and sharp detail of a true duotone but does add visual appeal. Since only one halftone negative is required in producing a fake duotone, the cost of reproduction is less than for producing a true duotone.

Full-Color Copy

Full-color copy may be reproduced with three partially transparent inks, referred to as **process inks,** plus black. When combined and overprinted on white paper, these inks satisfactorily reproduce the color, tonal range, and detail of most types of original full-color copy. Such printing is called **four-color process printing.** The three process colors are cyan, magenta, and yellow. Theoretically, cyan, magenta, and yellow should reproduce a satisfactory full-color copy when printed on a white substrate. However, because of imperfections in inks and papers, black is added to provide the depth and detail of original copy. The process of converting a full-color original into four halftone negatives or positives (to be printed with cyan, magenta, yellow, and black ink) is called **color separation.**

Kinds of Full-Color Copy

Full-color copy is divided into two categories: reflection copy and transmission copy. All copy produced on an opaque material that reflects light, such as paper or board, is reflection copy. Examples include color photographs, paintings, and drawings. All copy that allows light to pass through it is called transmission (or "transparent") copy. A color transparency is the best example of transmission copy.

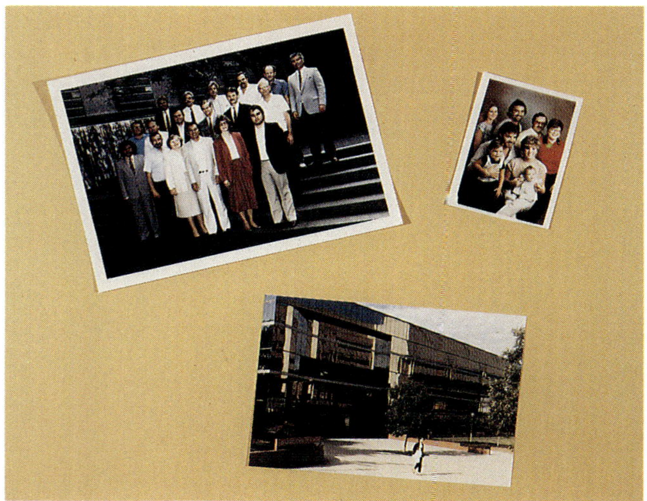

Reflection copy.

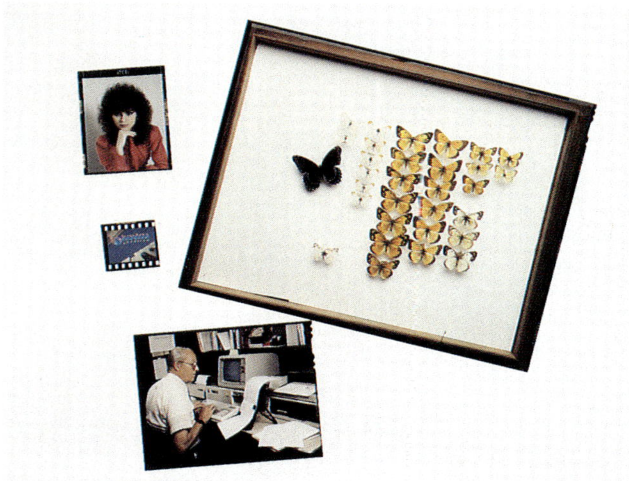

Transmission copy.

Viewing color reflection copy and transmission copy. The way that color is seen is affected by its environment, and surrounding illumination is the most important factor. Misunderstandings occur when a client or art director views a piece of color art under one type of illumination and surround, and the printing production manager, proofer, or press operator views the copy under a different illumination and surround. Fluorescent office lighting gives copy a "cool" effect, and tungsten light results in a "warm" effect. The reflected color of the surround also affects color evaluation.

To overcome ambiguities caused by variations in illumination, the American National Standards Institute (ANSI) established color viewing standards for the graphic arts industry. The standard calls for an illumination temperature of 5,000 K for viewing transparencies and reflection color copy, and for comparing such copy to proofs and production press sheets.

Preparing Full-Color Copy for Reproduction

Compared to those of black-and-white copy, the problems in preparing full-color copy are multiplied. Here, the artist is not concerned with the control of one color, but with many colors. Color copy normally presents considerable expense; therefore, the artist must take all possible precautions to protect it.

The artist should try to specify color copy that will require little or no retouching. When producing photographs or transparencies, it is the commercial photographer's responsibility to "build in" good color balance, proper tonal range, and desirable detail. The less handwork required on color copy, the less chance there is for the art to become marred or even ruined, and the better the final print reproduction will be. However, when necessary, the skilled retoucher can perform miraculous retouching and image manipulation feats on color prints and, to a limited extent, on transparencies. Likewise, the electronic color scanner can color-correct and manipulate color electronically, but this luxury does not remove the need for submitting or choosing quality copy.

Density of color copy. Tonal density range is as significant for faithful reproduction of color copy as it is for black-and-white copy. Extremely light highlight areas and extremely dark shadow areas cause time-consuming and costly retouching and color correcting or result in reproduction difficulties on press.

The tonal reproduction of full-color copy can be predicted with a densitometer. Normally, detail will be reproducible within an optical density range of

0.2 in highlight areas to 3.6 in the shadow areas. Highlight areas of less than 0.2 in density and a shadow density of above 3.6 tend to flatten detail. These measurements should be made in neutral highlight and shadow areas representing each color in the film.

Retouching full-color copy. Retouching and manipulating flexibilities are inherent in reflection color copy; very little can be done by hand to transparencies. Hand retouching can be performed on transparencies by using dyes and bleaches, but such work requires the skills of specialists who provide a unique transparency retouching service. Airbrushing directly on transparencies can be effective but only on the larger transparencies, such as the 8½×11-in. (216×280-mm) size. Transparency retouching is expensive. If time permits, the artist may find that having new transparencies made is the more practical approach. A retouched transparency is subject to damage and loss. It is good policy to retouch a duplicate transparency, not the original.

Retouching reflection color copy can be risky and time-consuming. However, reflection copy does provide the artist with flexibilities that are not available when working with transparencies. Airbrushing, for instance, is a realistic and often practical means of modifying or correcting reflection color copy. The artist can use paints, inks, or dyes. Care should be taken to minimize fluorescence caused by the use of certain pigments and dyes. Fluorescence in retouched areas will "burn" or cause "hot spots" in the color separation films. There are retouching dyes on the market that are color-correct for use when color copy is to be color-separated.

Artists no longer retouch as much continuous-tone color copy as they once did. Today, it is more common to do the retouching after the image has been scanned into a computer. Many artists now use image-editing programs to enhance computer images. This procedure is discussed in Chapter 12.

Handling Full-Color Copy

When handling or submitting full-color copy to be color-separated, keep these guidelines in mind:

- Don't mount color prints on rigid boards that cannot be mounted around a color scanner cylinder, if a rotary-drum scanner will be used to make the color separation.
- Consult with the color separator on the maximum artwork size the scanner or camera will accommodate. Likewise, know the maximum-size color-separation negative the separator can make.
- Mark "TOP" on the front top margin of color prints that may be confusing.
- Likewise scratch "TOP" in the emulsion of transparencies that may be confusing.
- It is a good idea to identify each transparency by scratching a job number in the nonimage area emulsion. Write a job number on the front margin (nonimage area) of color prints too. A pressure-sensitive label or a piece of masking tape containing this information can be attached to the back of color photos only if the prints will *not* be color-separated by an electronic scanner. Scanners often pick up writing on the back of prints and record it in the separation negatives.
- Submit all transparencies unmounted but protected in a plastic sleeve or plastic sheet with pockets. This also makes the transparencies easier to handle.
- Scratch the reproduction percentage into the emulsion of each transparency. Additionally, write this percentage with a grease pencil on the plastic sleeve protecting the transparency.
- Mounted transparencies present more trouble for the color separator than protection for the copy. Cardboard 35-mm mounts must be slit open, and plastic 35-mm mounts must be pried open, usually with a knife or blade, before the transparency can be separated. Don't take the chance of accidentally scratching or cutting the emulsion of the transparency. Submit 35-mm transparencies unmounted.
- Glass mounts are no better protection than cardboard or plastic mounts. They can crack and splinter when opened or during shipping. Therefore, never mail fragile transparencies in even more fragile glass mounts.
- Scratch the crop marks into the emulsion of transparencies. Crop marks on tissue overlays or on the protective plastic that covers the transparencies will not help the film image assembler because the marks will not appear on the color-separation negatives.
- Include all pertinent information, e.g., reproduction size and instructions, with the color copy to be separated. Don't forget to include client comments. For example, if a client is generally happy with a transparency but comments that the overall green cast must be eliminated, and this comment is not written as an instruction to the color separator, the separator will most likely match the original in the separation negatives, and the separations will have to be remade.

Note: It must be stressed that scratching information or crop marks on a transparency must be done with the client's approval, can be dangerous, and could result in the inadvertent scratching of the image. The intentional scratches can also cause confusion if the transparency is used for another job. "Position-only" prints at the final reproduction sizes can simplify the handling of transparencies.

Color Photography

Advancements in lithographic presses and inks and the refinement of electronic scanners, densitometers, and prepress proofing systems have made it possible to predict more accurately the color reproduction result of various ink, paper, press, and full-color copy combinations and to make more precisely the color-separation negatives and color-correction adjustments. This ability, coupled with the advances in color photography, makes it possible for the designer or artist to evaluate the reproduction suitability of full-color copy and to specify what is desired in the transparency, color print, or color duplicate so that quality reproduction is achieved. To do this the artist must know the basics of color photography.

Color Quality of Illumination

Though virtually unimportant in black-and-white photography, the color quality of the light source used is an extremely important aspect in color photography. Essentially, there are two types of color film with particular sensitivities (or "color balances") built into them. The first type is **daylight film,** or film that accurately records color under daylight sources—a combination of sunlight and skylight. This film is said to be color-balanced for daylight. The second type of film is **tungsten film,** which accurately reproduces color under most types of incandescent light. Tungsten film is often used under the hot quartz lights of studios or when photographing work on a copystand.

Furthermore, color film does not "see" or record colors as human beings see them under varying light. For example, a book cover that appears green to a human in daylight also appears green under incandescent light. In reality, the type of light source illuminating the book *does* affect the color reaching the eye, but the brain automatically compensates for the change. Color film has no such automatic compensation; therefore, inaccurate recording of color results if the film is not matched to the light source. If tungsten film is used to photograph a scene outside, the resulting color print or transparency contains an overall blue cast. Similarly, if daylight film is used indoors, such as to photograph inside a home where conventional incandescent light bulbs are used, the resulting print or transparency has an overall yellow cast.

When a photographer views a scene that is illuminated by two different light sources—daylight and incandescent—his or her eye will adapt to see an intermediate color quality, reducing the color effects of the two sources. The film, however, does not adapt. If daylight film is used, the portion of the subject illuminated by incandescent light records off-color. If tungsten film is used, the portion of the subject illuminated by the daylight records off-color. In this case the photographer may choose to substitute electronic flash for the tungsten light since electronic flash units are made to be compatible and therefore "balanced" for daylight film.

Color temperature in Kelvin (K) is used to measure the overall color balance or illumination temperature of a light source. The yellower the illumination, the higher the color temperature. For example, "typical" sunlight can be expressed as 5,000 K. Normal studio photoflood lights are rated as 3,200 K, and quartz studio lights, which are a bit bluer than photofloods, are rated at 3,400 K.

The photographer can, by placing special colored filters over the camera lens, compensate for or correct color imbalances between light source and film. Except when producing special-effects photography, a properly balanced photograph, especially in portraiture and critical color catalog work, can be the most critical aspect of quality color reproduction.

Subject Contrast

At first glance, subject contrast might be considered only a property of the subject before the camera lens, but it is more. Suppose that a woman wearing a white shirt and a dark suit is being photographed. If the shirt reflects eight times as much light as the suit, and these are the lightest and darkest objects in which detail must be reproduced, one might assume that the subject contrast ratio is eight to one. Actually, eight to one is the **reflectance ratio.** From the point of view of the film, subject contrast involves an additional and very important factor, the *lighting contrast.*

Main lights and fill-in lights. The ratio between the highest and lowest amounts of illumination falling on the principal subject in a photograph is called the **lighting contrast.** This is measured with a light meter. Continuing with the previous example, suppose the portrait of the woman will be shot using the simplest portrait lighting—only two lamps. One lamp would be placed at the same distance from the subject as the camera, but at a 45° angle from the camera axis. This light would be the **main light** and would cast shadows that, seen through the camera, would define the contours of the subject's face. But the shadows cast by this single light would be dark enough to obscure some of the important detail of the face. Another light placed close to the camera would soften them. This is the **fill-in light,** because it partially fills in with light the shadows caused by the main light.

With this particular lighting arrangement (two lamps of equal strength used at the same distance from the subject) the areas illuminated by both lamps would receive two units of illumination, while the areas illuminated by the fill-in light alone would receive one unit. Thus the lighting ratio would be two to one. If the main light were replaced by another light twice as strong as the fill-in light, the areas illuminated by the fill-in light would still receive only one unit of illumination, but the areas illuminated by both lamps would now receive three units, and the lighting ratio would be three to one.

Soft lighting. Even in black-and-white work, the skilled photographer knows that lighting requires special care if detail in both the shadow and highlight areas are to be reproduced in the same picture. But since color transparencies are processed as positives by standardized techniques that do not allow the control possible in printing black-and-white negatives, softer basic lighting is mandatory. Light-colored and dark-colored objects cannot be reproduced successfully in the same transparency unless the lighting is adjusted to offset the more extreme differences in tone. If the lighting is not adjusted, dark areas will be much too dark and off-color, while light areas will be "burnt out" and lacking in color and detail. In general, the lighting ratio should not be greater than three to one. The use of higher lighting ratios for special effects should be undertaken only after considerable experience with relatively soft lighting.

Because of the short exposure latitude of color transparency film, it is imperative to determine lens settings properly, to bracket exposures when possible, and to process the film with the utmost

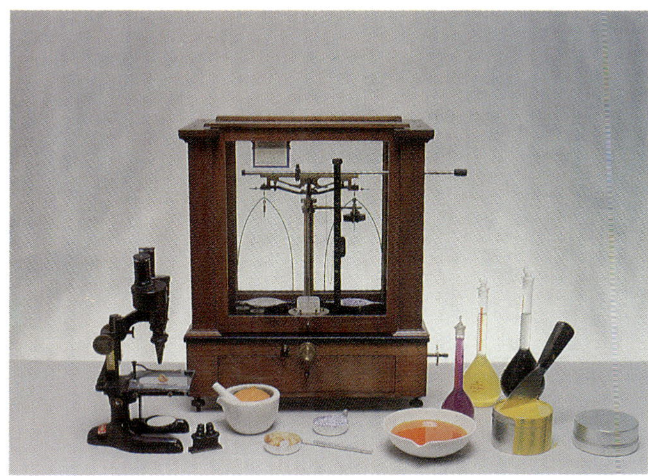

Changes in lighting direction alter highlights and color values—overhead lighting.

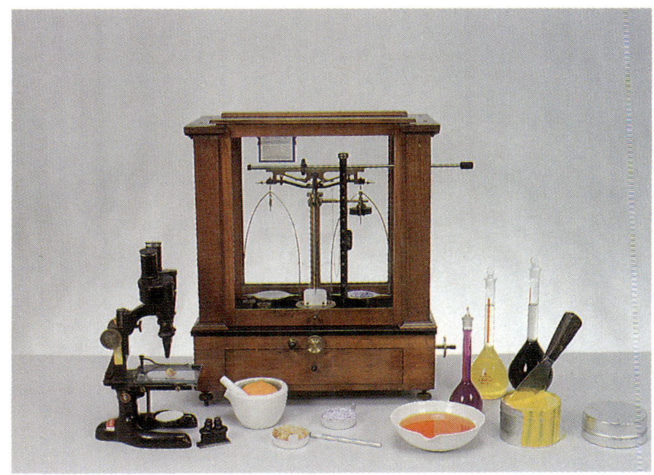

Normal placement of lighting.

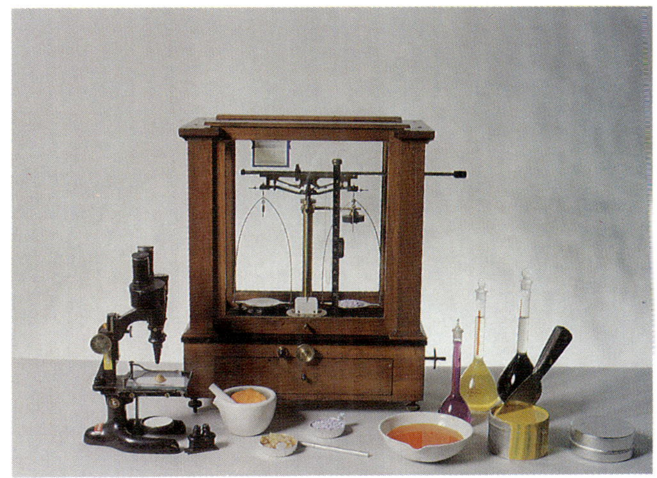

Lighting from the side.

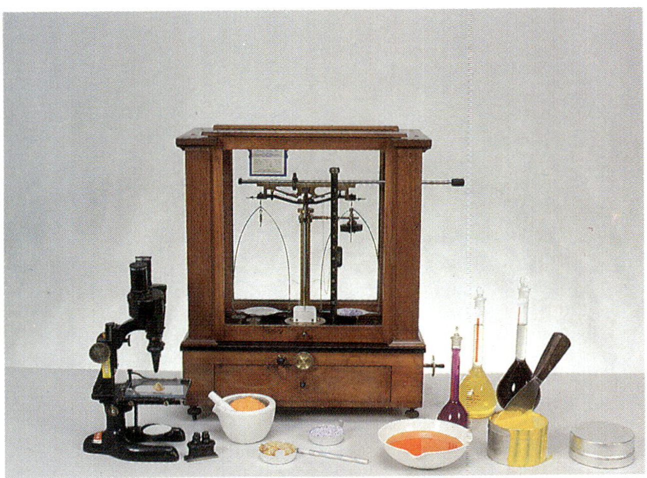

Low-contrast lighting produces soft shadows and highlights.

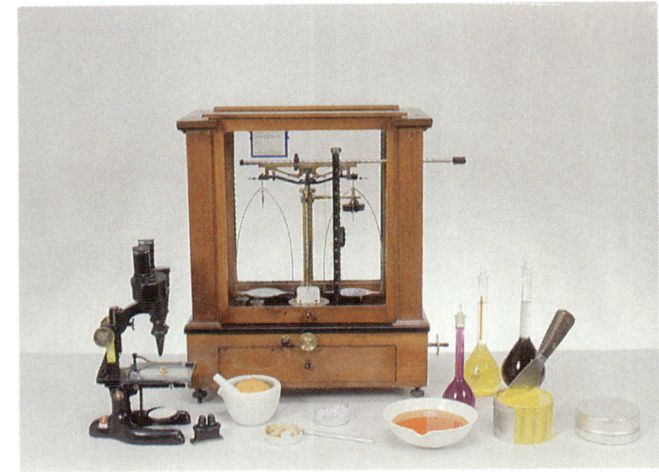

The short exposure latitude of color film narrows the margin for error—overexposure.

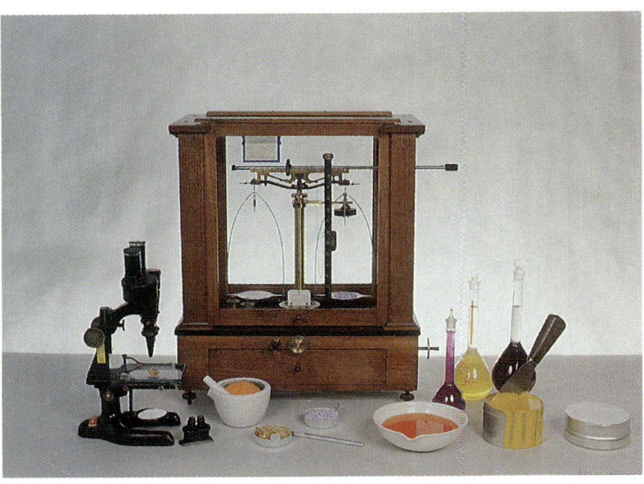

Normal-contrast lighting.

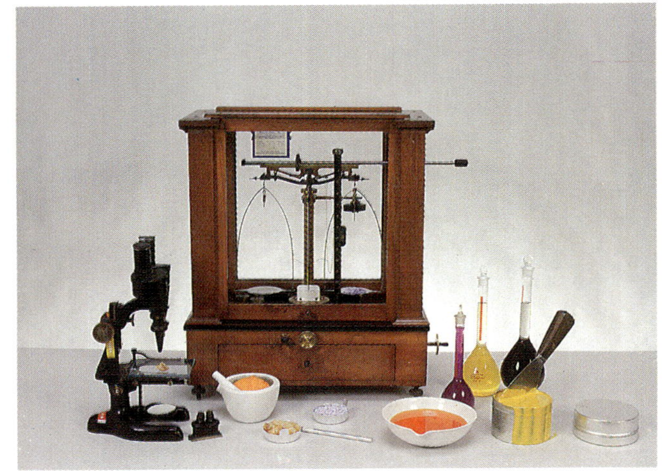

Normal exposure.

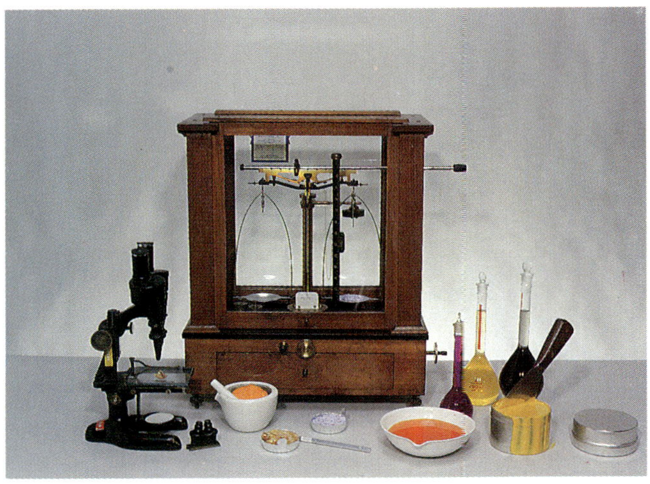

High-contrast lighting produces hard shadows, sharp highlights.

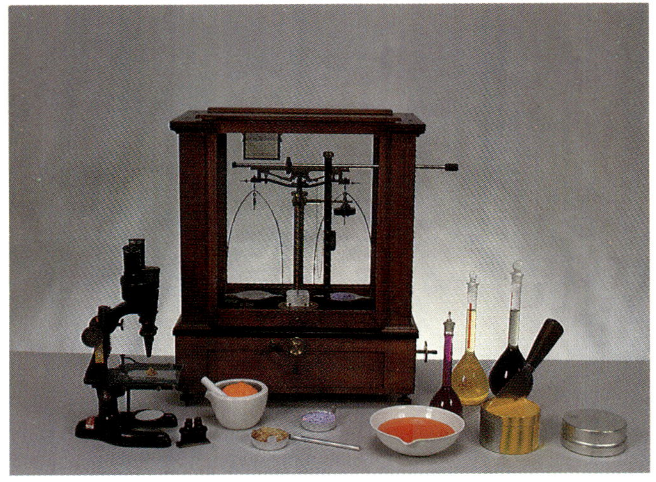

Underexposure.

attention to accuracy. Extra care must be exercised when working with color transparencies because the film that is exposed in the camera is the original used to make color-separation negatives. There is no separate printing stage as with negative-to-positive prints, in which compensation for over- or underexposure in the camera can be made. However, original transparencies are sometimes used to make duplicate transparencies that may be retouched to improve the overall quality of the reproduction.

Color negative materials have somewhat more latitude than transparency films, because minor exposure or color-balance errors can be corrected when printing the photograph. For best results, however, they must be exposed with considerably more care than black-and-white films.

The use of exposure meters. When determining camera settings, a photoelectric exposure meter is a must. Unusual lighting conditions and complex studio lighting arrangements particularly make accuracy impossible without one. However, the meter must be properly calibrated and should be used in accordance with instructions. Furthermore, the photographer must be fully aware of the characteristics and limitations of the meter if he or she is to obtain consistently reliable exposure indications. For the most critical work, an actual photographic exposure test is recommended.

Daylight lighting conditions such as clear sun, hazy sun, etc., are constant enough so that it is practical to use fixed exposure recommendations found in tables, guides, and built-in camera computers. These recommendations give excellent results under the specified conditions. Similar exposure aids are supplied for use with simple arrangements of artificial lights.

Choosing Formats

The basic formats of cameras are the 35-mm, the 2¼×2¼-in., the 4×5-in., and the 8×10-in. These sizes represent the size of the film used. It is a good rule of thumb to choose the camera/film size that will produce a print or transparency that will require the least amount of enlarging. For example, if the photographer is producing photos that will be printed in a brochure cropped to 3×4 in., then the sharpest detail and best resolution will be achieved using a 2¼×2¼-in. camera. In general, the bigger the original format the better. Likewise, the least amount of enlarging necessary, the better the result. Usually the determining factor when deciding which format to use is the subject itself. For example, the size, weight, and flexibility of the 35-mm format is ideal when photographing moving subjects. When the subject is static, as in still-life photography, a large-format view camera, such as the 8×10-in., is the best choice. The large ground-glass viewing screen of an 8×10-in. camera allows the photographer to focus and compose the subject more accurately than a smaller camera does.

Moiré in Full-Color Work

Moiré is an undesirable pattern that occurs on the printed full-color halftone caused by a conflict between the screen angles and the lines or pattern of the original. Moiré is also caused by incorrect screen angles or misregister of the color impressions during printing. (Moiré can also occur in black-and-white photography.) Photographers can help reduce the chance of a disturbing moiré pattern in the final printed piece by knowing what subjects most often produce this effect. Closely spaced parallel lines and small checked patterns in photographic subjects have a high incidence of producing a moiré. For these reasons, avoid or watch for these possibilities in clothing and furniture fabrics, window screens, brick structures, slate roofs, patterned carpeting, wallpaper, drapery, and television screens.

Of course, it is difficult to predict definitely what will cause a moiré—some patterns that are thought to moiré may not—but an awareness of the potential problems will save time and money early in the reproduction stages.

Color Perception and Color Harmony

Color photographs occasionally show colors that appear faulty or false, but were actually present, though unnoticed, in the original scene.

In judging results, photographers are frequently unable to compare the picture with the subject directly, but rely on a mental image of how the subject appeared when photographed. If photographers do not learn to observe color (that is, recognize subtle tints, mixtures, and reflections) when they take photographs, they may find colors in the transparency or print that were not noticed in the original subject.

Unnoticed Colors

Unnoticed colors are largely due to the effects of lighting conditions and surroundings. An example is a snow scene photographed in bright sunlight under clear blue sky. Although the shadows on white should be colorless, the picture shows bluish shadows. Actually, the shadows are blue, and appear so in the picture, because whatever light reaches the shadows comes largely from the blue of the sky.

Influence of Time of Day

A color photo taken outside early in the morning or late in the afternoon may be too orange because the color of sunlight during these hours is orange. Although the warmth of color and shadow effects obtained early or late in the day may be desirable with architectural and scenic subjects, they seldom result in satisfactory rendering of skin tones.

Influence of Reflecting Surfaces

A third example is a portrait posed near a strongly colored reflecting surface, such as a red automobile, painted or wallpapered wall, or large building. The face and arms of the subject may look perfectly natural at the time the picture is taken, but the colored light reflected on them from the nearby object may produce an unnatural effect in the finished picture. If colored surroundings are actually included in the scene area, the resulting picture will seem more natural because the reason for the unexpected color in the subject is evident.

The Difficulty of Anticipating How Colors Will Appear

There are two reasons why such color effects are more difficult to recognize in viewing the original scene than in viewing a reproduction of the scene in the form of a color photograph. First, the color of a real subject is commonly thought of as characteristic of it under all circumstances, and therefore no change is expected. Second, in viewing the original scene, the eye tends to reduce disturbing illumination color by adapting to it in a way beyond the powers of the film. The photographer can be trained to detect color effects in the original scene and take steps to prevent their appearance in the color picture. By doing this, the photographer attains a better appreciation of color and improves his or her ability to remember colors and predict results in color photography. The experienced photographer avoids unnatural effects and achieves realistic colors by exposing film in the most favorable lighting and surroundings.

Color Differences between Objects and Photographs

The foregoing should not be interpreted as indicating that color films provide a perfect reproduction of the colors of the light reflected from a subject into the camera lens. If critical measurements on the very best color photographs are made, considerable differences between their colors and those of the original subjects are found. Actually, there is no available process of color photography that can give entirely accurate and repeatable reproduction of color. Color films when properly used, however, do give "satisfactory" color rendering for their intended purposes, but present technical knowledge does not permit color materials to record precisely what the eye sees. Further, since the reproduction of a physical subject by means of a color transparency or print involves psychological factors in the response of the observer, it can never be "perfect" in any objective sense. It is often the designer's or artist's responsibility to educate the customer to the limitations of the reproduction process, and color photography is no exception.

Color Harmony

Color harmony is the systematic arrangement of colors to give a pleasing effect. The subject of color harmony is complex and very largely a matter of personal taste; nevertheless, a few general suggestions can be offered as a starting point.

Effect of mind on color harmony. Most outdoor scenes display good color harmony, probably because the mind has grown to accept the color combinations of nature as pleasing. Indoors, the colors of the background, clothing, and other properties are usually within the control of the photographer, and therein lies the danger that it is easy for the beginner in color work to become obsessed with the fact that a wide gamut of colors is at his or her disposal. However, the most pleasing photographs are generally those in which only a limited range of colors is used. The use of relatively unsaturated colors frequently adds to the naturalness of the color picture. In any case, care in selection of those colors that are subject to control pays dividends in more pleasing results.

Harmony in color portraiture. In portraiture, the face of the subject before the camera should be the center of interest in the picture. Since conspicuous patterns or contrasting brilliant colors in either clothing or background tend to distract attention from the face, they should be avoided. Clothing colors should harmonize with the complexion and hair color of the subject. Medium or light colors are usually more effective than dark colors or black, and they do not require too much care in lighting to ensure satisfactory detail in the shadow areas. Large areas of solid, brilliant colors should be avoided because they are seldom pleasing, either in the original scene or in a color photograph.

Background treatment in color photographs. Unlike black-and-white photographs, color photographs do not require the use of a background lighter or darker than the subject, because color differences help separate the planes of the scene.

In general the background color in a portrait should be *related to* the dominant color of the clothing; that is, one that lies near it on a color wheel. Touches of color complementary to the clothing color (i.e., opposite it on the color wheel) are suitable for small areas or accessories. While these suggestions refer to hue, the photographer should never lose sight of the possibility, indeed desirability, of variations in brightness and saturation as well. All three characteristics of color play their parts in the success of the picture as a color composition.

Use of complementary colors. In commercial and illustrative work, where the principal subject often dominates the picture simply because of its size or shape regardless of the color scheme, more dramatic effects can be obtained by surrounding the subject with complementary color. Small touches of related colors soften the severity of the bolder contrasts.

Photographer's originality and personality. Color photography allows full scope to originality and individual taste. An observant eye can find endless ideas for effective color schemes in paintings, printed and woven fabrics, interior decoration, and in the purely accidental combinations that occur in everyday life. The effectiveness of a given color scheme depends not only upon the colors themselves but also upon their comparative areas and their distribution in the scene area. The textures of the colored surfaces are also important, because they lead to different color rendering under different lighting arrangements. Ease in composing with color is the result of photographer's experience and observation, but no color scheme can be entirely preconceived. There is always some adjustment and some shifting of the elements, until the scene "looks right" to the photographer.

Chapter 7

Basic Camera Operation

In **reproduction photography,** the camera operator converts original photographic materials into enlarged or reduced intermediate images that are used in producing printing plates or other image carriers. The most important result of this procedure is that it enables the printing processes to approximate the tonal gradations of continuous-tone originals on printed substrates. Alone, few printing processes can produce true variable-tone images because ink films of uniform thickness are applied to all image areas. To compensate, camera operators create "screened," or **halftone**, images in which the tonal gradations of a continuous-tone original are represented by a pattern of fine marks, usually dots equally spaced center to center, but varying size. Because the pattern is so fine a halftone presents the illusion of a continuous-tone image when viewed at a normal distance.

The images created by reproduction photography are referred to as **positives** or **negatives**. A positive reproduction has the same tonal values as those in the original scene while a negative reproduction reverses the tonal values of the original, representing darker areas with lighter tones and vice versa. A positive transmission image on film is called a **film positive** and a negative transmission image on film is called a **film negative.** These reproductions are also distinguished as right-reading or wrong-reading images. In Western countries, **right-reading** images are viewed from left to right (top to bottom). **Wrong-reading** images are represented by an image that is printed backwards from its normal orientation. These terms are used even in cases where no type matter included.

Line copy, type matter and drawings, are reproduced separate from continuous-tone images and without the use of halftone screens. The film used maintains the contrast between image areas and the background, resulting in a **high-contrast** negative or positive film intermediate. Line images appear clear on negatives and dense black on positives. The line and halftone images are combined later during film assembly, which takes place just prior to platemaking.

Light and Illumination

Light is the key to the photographic process: it illuminates copy and affects the development of light-sensitive materials. A form of radiant energy, light emitted from or reflected by an object enters the eye, permitting that object to be seen. Light can be thought of as traveling in a straight line in a uniform medium known as a **ray**. A shaft of light with nearly parallel rays is called a **beam**.

Light sources. There are many sources of light—natural and artificial. The most important source of natural light is the sun, while an electric lightbulb or tube is the most common artificial source. In an electric light bulb, the wire filament radiates light when heated. Light can also be created indirectly through the use of certain chemical substances. For example, the inside of the glass tube of a fluorescent lamp is coated with chemicals (phosphors) that fluoresce (glow) when struck by the invisible ultraviolet rays generated within the tube.

Light may pass through or be stopped by an object. If all the light hitting an object is kept from

passing through it, the object is **opaque.** When some light passes through an object in such a way that it is difficult to see other objects through it, the original object is **translucent.** An example of translucent material is ordinary waxed paper. A **transparent** object, however, allows light to pass through it in such a way that it is easy to see other objects. A window pane is a good example of a transparent object.

Intensity of illumination. The amount of light that strikes a surface is called the **intensity.** The absolute brightness, or luminous intensity, of a light source is expressed in terms of **candlepower**. Originally, a special candle made of a certain oil that burned at a given rate was used as a standard. Two such candles would produce a candlepower of two. Candlepower is abbreviated "c.p."

The intensity of light illuminating a surface is measured in **footcandles.** A footcandle is defined as the amount of light falling on a surface that is one foot away from the standard candle described previously. The candlepower of the original source and the distance from the source to the object both factor in the intensity of light that falls on an object. As it travels from illumination source to object, light obeys a rule known as the **Law of Inverse Squares.** This law states: "The intensity of light of a given source falling on a surface varies inversely as the square of the distance from the source to the object." In other words, light intensity decreases as the distance from the light source increases, in proportion to the square of distance. This law, which is strictly true for a point source and approximately true for any source that is small in relation to its distance from the surface, can also be written as a ratio:

$$\text{Intensity} = \frac{\text{Candlepower of Source}}{\text{Square of Distance}} = \frac{\text{C.P.}}{(D_1)^2}$$

Intensity is measured in footcandles and distance is measured in feet.

Footcandle meter. The footcandle meter measures the intensity of illumination falling on it from any and all sources of light. This meter uses a photoelectric cell connected to a light indicator calibrated in footcandles. When light strikes the sensitive cell, it generates a current that registers directly on the indicator, giving a reading in footcandles.

Exposure meters. The photoelectric exposure meter is used to determine the correct exposure for negatives, positives, and color transparencies. It is essentially a footcandle meter but has a number of scales on it. One scale is set for the speed of the emulsion used and another is set to the meter reading. On a third scale, the correct exposure (in seconds or fractions of a second) is read opposite the various apertures (lens openings) that can be used.

Light integrators. Light integrators are combination light meters and timers. The light falling on a photoelectric cell generates the current that registers units on a timing device. When the preset time is reached, the instrument turns off the shutter and exposure lights. Light integrators are discussed further later in the chapter.

Reflection

The **Law of Reflection** states: "The angle of incidence is equal to the angle of reflection, and the incident ray, the reflected ray, and the normal all lie in the same plane." The angle of incidence (i) is the angle that the incident ray makes with the normal.

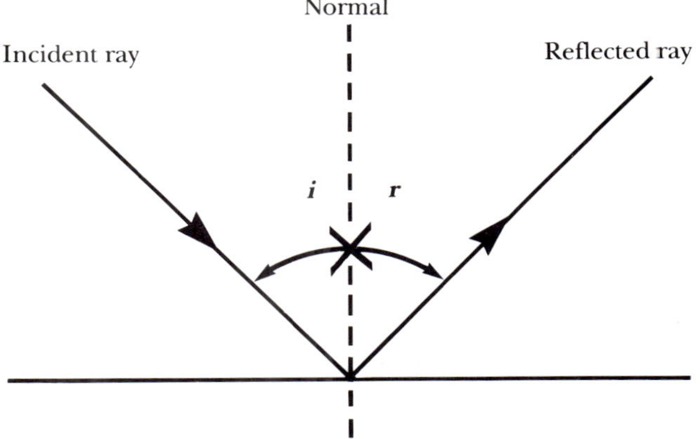

Angles of incidence and reflection.

Specular reflection. When a ray of light is reflected from a smooth surface, the reflection is known as specular. An ordinary mirror produces a specular reflection.

Diffuse reflection. When a beam of incident light strikes a rough surface, such as a sheet of uncoated paper, each light ray strikes a surface that has a slightly different angle. For this reason, the beam of incident light becomes a group of rays that are reflected at many different angles, or scattered to produce a diffuse reflection. This scattering of light

is what makes objects visible because some of the scattered light reaches the eye regardless of the direction of the source. Coated paper with a great degree of specular reflectance looks glossy.

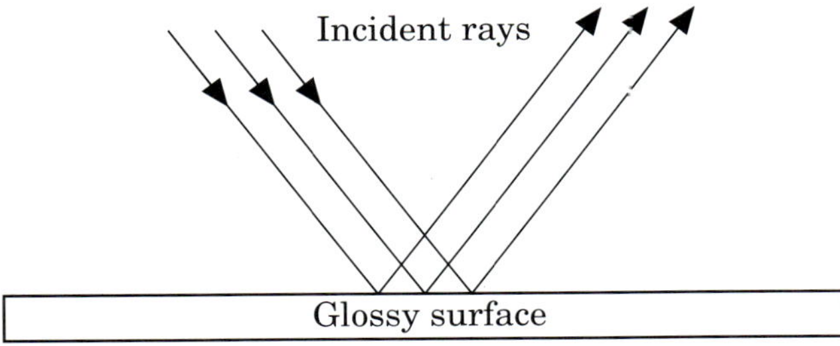

Specular reflection.

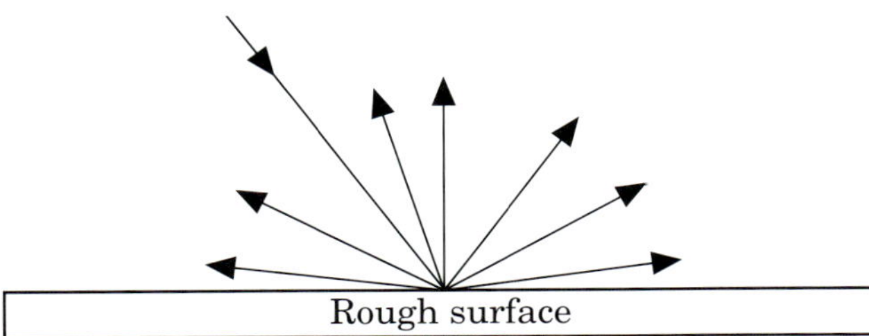

Diffuse reflection.

Reflection and the copyboard. The camera operator arranges the lamps to minimize glare from the copyboard glass. Since the glass surface of a copyboard produces a regular reflection, the glare level will be the lowest when lights are at a 45° angle to the board. As this angle decreases, there is a greater chance of unwanted reflections shining into the lens, especially if the area of the copyboard covered by the lens is large. In other words, the lens must not see a direct reflection of light.

The 45° angle can be varied according to the size and nature of the copy. For example, it may be necessary to retain or accentuate the appearance of a textured original by placing one or two camera lamps at unusual angles. In black-and-white photography, the pencil lines in some large drawings may reflect light at the 45° angle. Changing the angle of the lights eliminates the glare.

The evenness of the light coverage at the copyboard should and can be checked by reading the light falling upon each corner of the copyboard with an exposure meter. However, it is more important to measure the evenness of illumination on the ground glass of the camera back. Light positions and angles should be adjusted to provide maximum evenness of illumination at the film plane.

Refraction and Lenses

Refraction occurs when a ray of light is bent as it passes at an angle from one medium to another. It is sometimes difficult to pick up a piece of soap that has fallen into a bathtub because it is not where it seems to be. This illusion is caused by the refraction of light as it passes from the medium of water to the medium of air. A prism refracts a light ray twice but because the entering and exiting sides of the prism are not parallel, the displacement is greater than usual.

The law of refraction. All light rays obey the **Law of Refraction,** which states: "A ray entering a less dense medium at an angle other than perpendicular will bend away from the normal. A ray entering a denser medium at an angle other than perpendicular will bend toward the normal. In addition, a ray passing from one medium to another parallel to the normal (perpendicular to the surface) will not be bent or refracted at all."

The index of refraction. Light travels at different speeds in different mediums. The index of refraction (n) is the ratio of the speed of light in the medium it is leaving to the speed of light in the medium it is entering.

Critical angle. The illustration of the critical angle shows four light rays striking the water's surface at different angles. Rays 1 and 2 are refracted

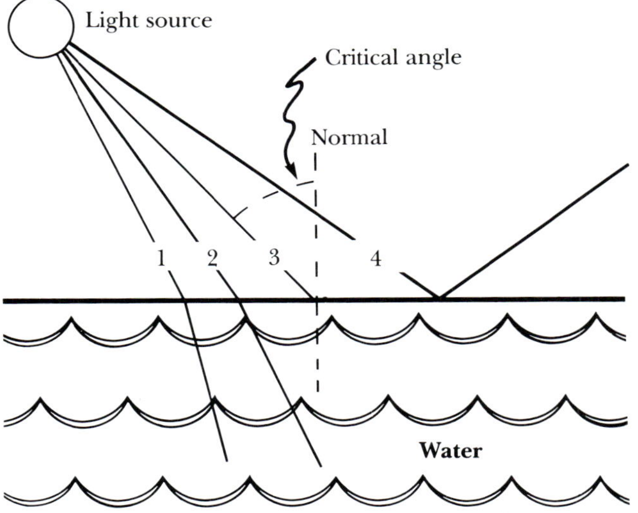

Critical angle.

into the water. At a certain angle, ray 3, after striking the water, continues along its surface. Ray 4 is totally reflected after striking the water surface. The angle that ray 3 makes with the normal is called the **critical angle.** Light striking a surface at an angle larger than a critical angle will be reflected, while light striking at smaller angles will be refracted.

In the case of two different materials bonded together, the angle of the incidence of light in the first medium, at the time it strikes the surface between the two mediums, is greater than the critical angle of the first medium, and the ray becomes internally reflected within the first medium. This fact is used in the design of many optical instruments such as the prism binocular or the prism periscope, where the prism is used to change the direction of light.

The Lens

A **lens** consists of one or more pieces of curved glass with polished surfaces that are mounted for ease in handling. The two basic types of lenses are converging and diverging. The **converging lens** has a center that is thicker than its edges. It is

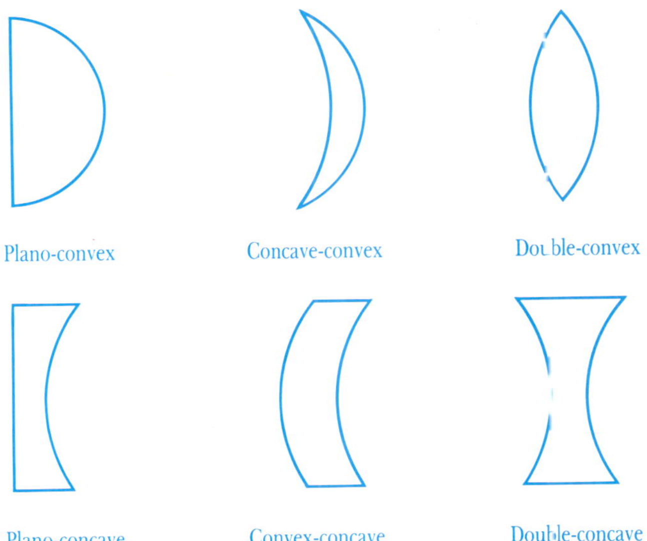

Various lens shapes.

commonly convex on both sides. If parallel light rays shine directly on a converging lens, the emerging rays will come together at a point known as the real focus.

The **diverging lens** is often concave on both sides with edges thicker than its center. Parallel rays falling on its surface diverge. However, as these rays extend backward, they will seem to come from one point identified as the focus of this lens. This focal point is virtual rather than real because the rays do not actually meet there.

The imaginary line drawn through the focus and the center of the lens is called the **axis.** The distance from the focus to the center of the lens is called the **focal length** of the lens.

Both sides of a lens do not always curve in the same way. Thus, the name of the lens depends upon the curvature of its sides. The following diagram shows examples of various lenses.

Images and ray tracing. Ray tracing is a method of learning what will happen to the image of an object as it passes through the lens system. The outcome is based the following two laws:

- Light rays entering the lens parallel to the axis will emerge and pass through the focus of the lens.
- Light rays passing through the center of the lens (the point within the lens on the axis and halfway between both surfaces) and parallel to its axis will continue in a straight line.

These two laws can be used regardless of which side of the lens is facing the light source as each lens has two foci (focal points), one on each side.

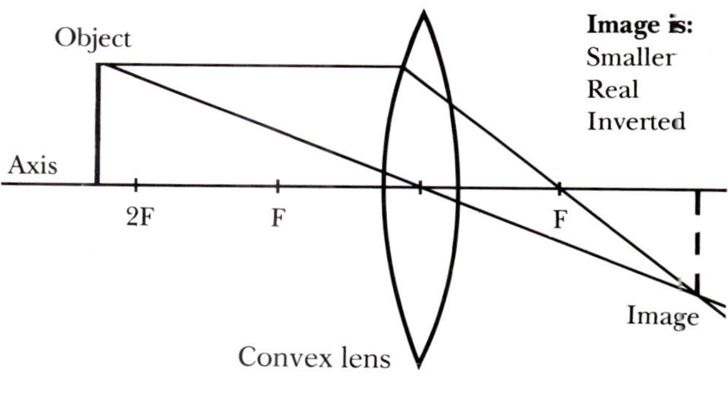

Object at twice the focal length of a convex lens.

Image formation by convex lenses. With a convex lens, the object distance can be greater than twice the focal length of the lens, less than the focal length of the lens, or at the focus. When the object is at a distance greater than twice the focal length of the lens, the image created appears smaller than the object, real, and inverted. As it nears the point

that is twice the focal length of the lens, the image grows in size until it becomes the same size as the object, while remaining real and inverted.

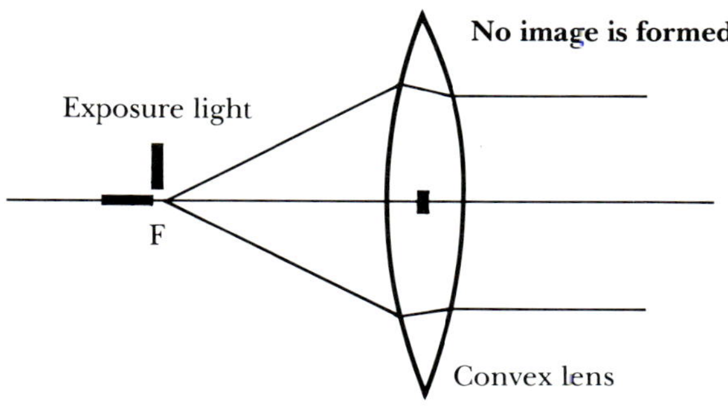

Object at the focal point of convex lens.

Between the distance of one and two focal lengths, the image size becomes larger than the object and still remains real and inverted. Finally, at the focal point, no image is formed. As the object moves between the focus and the lens, the image becomes larger, changing from real to virtual and erect.

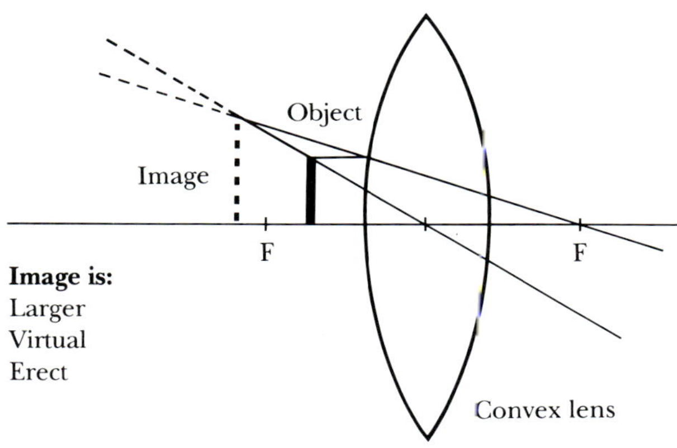

Object at a distance less than the focal length of convex lens.

Image formation by concave lenses. Because light rays diverge after striking a concave lens, virtual images result. In all cases, these images are smaller than the object and erect.

Image formation by concave lenses also follows the rules of ray tracing mentioned previously. However, the emerging ray formed by the parallel ray will seem to come from the front focus of the lens rather than actually pass through the back focus.

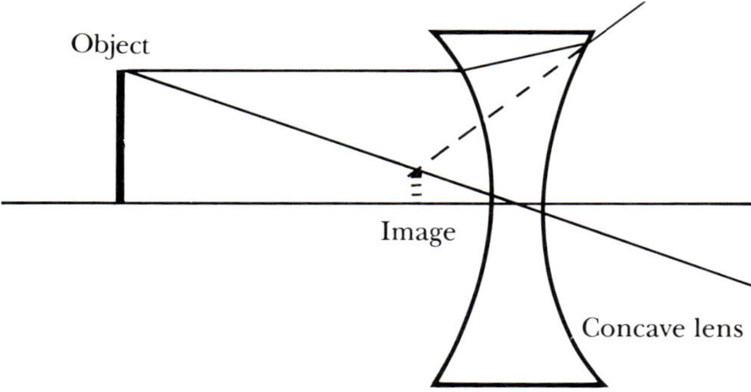

Image formation by concave lens.

Lighting Copy for Reproduction

To reproduce black-and-white or color originals, the light source used should emit a steady intensity of light, have a reliable color temperature, and provide consistent, even coverage of the copy.

The illumination sources used in the graphic arts include pulsed-xenon, tungsten filament, quartz-iodine, fluorescent, and mercury lamps. To select a source, the camera operator determines the range of light or energy that will be most effective in exposing a certain light-sensitive material under specific operating conditions.

The energy output of each light source is known as its **color temperature.** Color temperature refers to the spectral energy emitted by a perfect radiator ("black body") heated to a specific temperature. Color temperature is most commonly measured in "degrees Kelvin" (K). The color temperature rating of a light source gives an indication of its spectral output. At higher temperatures, the light source is bluer, while red predominates at lower temperatures.

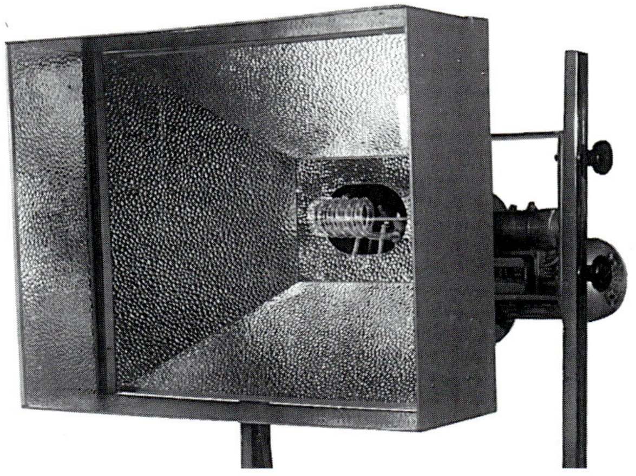

Courtesy Consolidated International, Inc.

Pulsed-xenon lamp.

For black-and-white photography, a light source with a color temperature of at least 3,000K is needed. In color work, the color temperature of the light source should be 5,000K.

Pulsed-xenon lamps are one of the most popular illumination sources for graphic arts photography. These high-pressure discharge lamps, which are made of quartz tubing filled with xenon gas, pulse 60 times per second, but appear to emit light continuously. Pulsed-xenon light sources have a broad spectral output that extends across the visible light region and closely approximates sunlight's color temperature of 5,400K. Although the color temperature and light output of the lamps are very constant, the continuous spectral output has many peaks that can slightly alter photographic response to filters.

Regardless of the light source used, achieving maximum contrast is an important factor in both color and black-and-white reproduction. Tonal contrast may be lost in camera negatives or positives (halftones and continuous tone) because of flare. Flare will affect shadow contrast more than highlight contrast. It can be caused by a dirty optical system, reflection from light-colored or glossy walls in the camera area, or "stray" illumination from a room light left on over the copyboard during exposure. In an ideal setup, flare is alleviated if the room lights automatically switch off whenever the camera lights are activated.

Densitometry

The densitometer is a valuable control device that enables photographers to numerically measure the density of a black-and-white or color tone area on transparent or opaque materials and make a comparison between them. These density measurements can be used as a guide in determining exposure conditions for simple black-and-white photography or for setting up masking procedures in color separation photography. From density values, it is easy to determine the relative speed of the film, the contrast of a particular emulsion, and the correct exposure values.

Optical Density

The value of a tone area—its light stopping ability—is expressed in terms of optical density. Darker tones, such as those found in the shadows of a photographic print, have higher densities than the highlight areas of the same print. On a negative, the same highlights appear dark and therefore will have a high density reading.

Transmission density. Here the term density refers to the light-absorbing ability of the layer of silver found on a photographic film. How well this layer absorbs or conveys light is expressed as its transmission density. The transmission rate of any tone area is the fraction of incident light transmitted through the area without being absorbed or scattered.

$$T = \frac{I_t}{I_i}$$

T is transmission, I_t is intensity of transmitted light, and I_i is the intensity of incident light.

Density is equal to the logarithm of I/t:

$$D = \log \frac{I}{T} = \log \frac{I_i}{I_t}$$

The relationship between density and transmission is illustrated here The light intensity on the first layer is the same for A, B, and C. However, the light intensity leaving the silver layer decreases as the number of layers decreases.

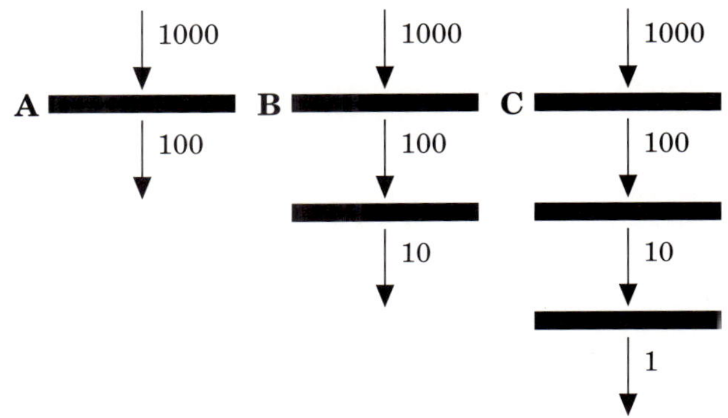

Transmission and density relationship.

The transmission rate has decreased by a factor of 10 for each additional layer, while the density has increased by 1. Combinations of tones are calculated by adding when working with density units. To figure transmission densities, multiply.

Using a logarithmic scale is helpful because the response of the eye is logarithmic. In the example

illustrated, the intensity of the light transmitted through the four different tones (W, X, Y, and Z) on the transparency is indicated by the lower arrows. The numerical values of the light's intensity are shown beside the arrows with the length of each arrow proportional to the light intensity it represents. The values of these tones as the eye sees them are indicated by the solid blocks, and the optical density of each tone is listed beneath each block.

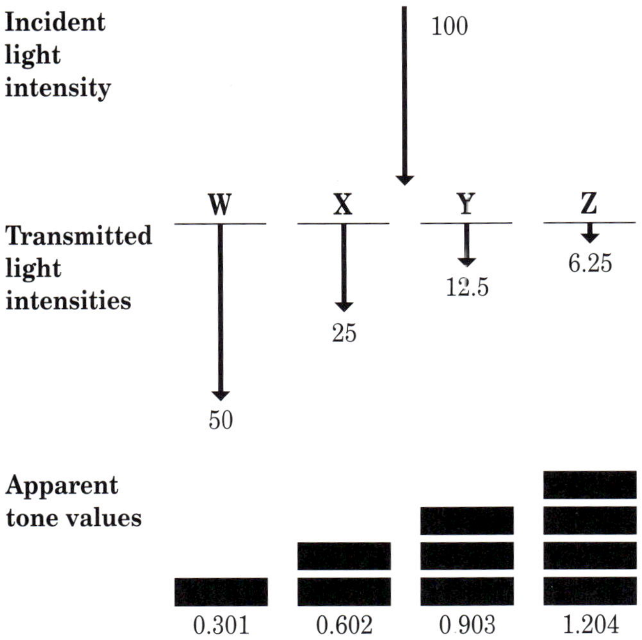

Incident light, transmitted light, and apparent tone values.

The illustration also shows that arrow X is only half as long as W; Y is half as long as X; and Z is half as long as Y. Since the light intensities are cut in half, the apparent tone values increase equally from W to Z, and the measured density increases by steps of 0.3. The eye sees the equal changes of density units as equal tone steps.

Reflection density. When light falls on an image, such as a paper print, part of the light is absorbed, while the remainder is reflected in various directions. How much light is reflected in each direction depends on the tone density and the surface characteristics of the paper. Reflection densities are measured by illuminating the copy at a 45° angle and gauging the amount of light reflected at a 90° angle from the copy.

Unlike transmission density calculations, measuring reflection density does not involve factoring incident light at all. Reflectance is expressed as the ratio between the amount of light reflected from a given tone area and the amount reflected from a white area on the same substrate:

$$R = \frac{I_r}{I_{rw}}$$

R is reflectance, I_r is the intensity of the light reflected from tone, an I_{rw} is intensity of light reflected from white paper.

Reflection density has the same relationship to reflectance that transmission density has to transmittance:

$$D_T = \log \frac{1}{T}, \text{ and } D_R = \log \frac{1}{R}$$

D_T is transmission density and D_R is reflection density.

Reflection density readings express the tone values of a paper print in exactly the same way that transmission density readings express tone values in a transparency. Reflection density values do not express the value of a tone in terms of light intensity. Instead, the darkness of two or more tones is compared. The most extreme highlight on the print—a white area—is chosen as the zero point, and all of the other readings on the print are expressed in relation to this particular value.

Densitometers

The choice of a particular densitometer depends on what it is to be used for and on how much is expected of it. Some densitometers are designed to measure only transmission densities; others will

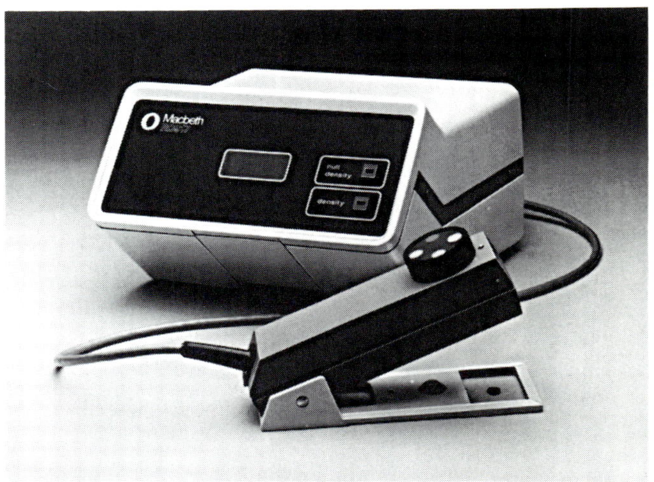

Courtesy Macbeth

Reflection densitometer.

measure only reflection densities; and combination instruments will measure both. If all readings in a given plant are to be made on one densitometer, the instrument should be equipped to measure both reflection and transmission densities. If a plant requires a number of instruments, it might be more economical to supply the pressroom with a reflection densitometer and the prepress area with combination instruments, since they handle transparent negatives and positives as well as opaque originals.

Reflection densitometers should cover a range from 0.0 to 3.0. The range of transmission densitometers should go higher than 3.0. The scale should be calibrated so that it can register a density difference of 0.02 over its entirety. In practical plant operations, an accuracy of 0.02 units will be satisfactory.

A calibrated reflection or transparent gray scale should be set aside as a standard against which the densitometer is checked frequently. When an error of more than ±0.03 is detected, the instrument should be adjusted.

The two categories of densitometers are visual and photoelectric. An arrangement of lenses and mirrors in visual instruments brings together the tone measured and a control tone to make a visual comparison. By adjusting the unit, the operator increases or decreases the density of the control tone until the eye judges a match with tone being measured. Next, the density is read on a calibrated scale and recorded.

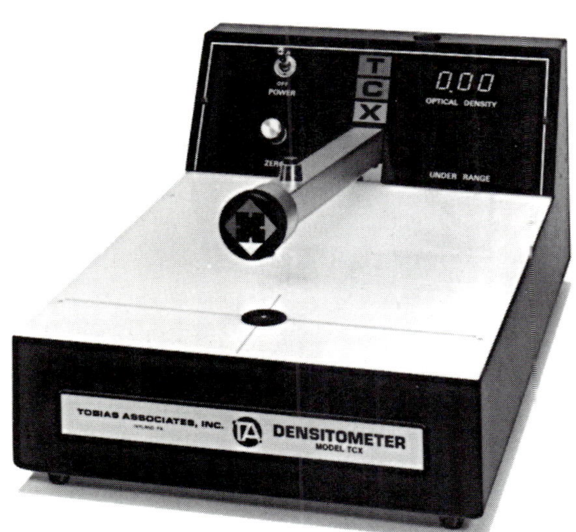

Courtesy Tobias Associates, Inc.

Transmission densitometer.

Photoelectric densitometers are more common than visual ones. One variety uses a cell similar to that employed in photoelectric exposure meters, with a microammeter and a dial, reading directly in density values. This densitometer gives fast readings but the accuracy falls off for densities over 2. Other photoelectric densitometers have solid-state circuitry and provide a digital readout. These units are usually equipped with color filters to measure process-color densities. Some are equipped with printers that provide a record of results.

Visual densitometers are much less expensive than photoelectric units; however, most people feel eyestrain after making 20 or 30 readings. It is also sometimes difficult to make comparisons if there is a slight color difference between the tone being measured and the control tone. Photoelectric units, on the other hand, can be used rapidly and easily. Their measurements are more reproducible and the physical condition of the operator does not affect the results.

The Characteristic Curve

Densitometry can be used to determine the photographic response of a light-sensitive material. The characteristic curve, is a graph that shows how a film or plate performs under certain conditions. It illustrates how much density corresponding to each tone in the original will be recorded on a film exposed for a specific amount of time. Traditionally, the chart has a vertical density (D) scale and a horizontal logarithm-of-exposure scale (log E) scale.

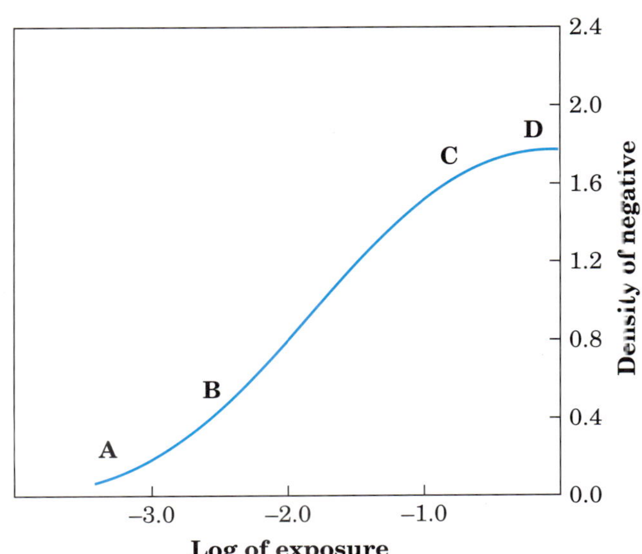

A typical response curve for positive-to-negative films.

The shape of the characteristic curve is the key to the type of image the film will yield. Examining curves is easier than making trial exposures. The tendency of a film to produce high- or low-contrast pictures is best indicated by its characteristic curve. All films commonly used in photomechanical work have characteristic curves furnished by the manufacturers.

Films produce characteristic curves with different shapes when different developers are used. For example, when a continuous-tone emulsion is developed with noninfectious developer, which produces densities in proportion to exposure, it will have a low-gamma value. The same film will have a high-gamma, possibly high-contrast, value if developed with an infectious developer, which has a slow development rate that gradually increases to a maximum at the end of the development cycle.

Plotting the characteristic curve. Film manufacturers use elaborate equipment to expose and develop the test strips used to plot characteristic curves, but the photographer can use a more practical method. Photograph or make a contact print of a stepped gray scale, then plot the density of the contact positive or camera negative against the density of the original.

Because the curve obtained represents a given set of conditions, be sure to indicate the materials and equipment used. Use fresh developer and try to develop the same way every time. After developing the negative or positive, make a table of the scale step numbers, density of the original, and the density of the negative or positive.

Using regular graph paper, set up a scale of density values along the vertical and horizontal axes. The horizontal axis represents density values of the original, while the vertical axis represents density values of the negative or positive. For point no. 1, which corresponds to step no. 1, locate 0.08 along the horizontal (D_0) axis and 2.2 along the vertical (D_n) axis. Where these two values intersect, make a dot. Repeat for the other points. When all the points have been plotted, create the characteristic curve by drawing a smooth curve through the average of these points. (Seldom do all the points line up perfectly to produce such a smooth curve.)

The characteristic curve has three regions: the toe, the straight-line portion, and the shoulder. If the curve is represented as cut by a series of lines at equally spaced horizontal distances, there is an unequal increase in vertical distance for equal horizontal distances in the toe and shoulder regions. In other words, there is an unequal density increase

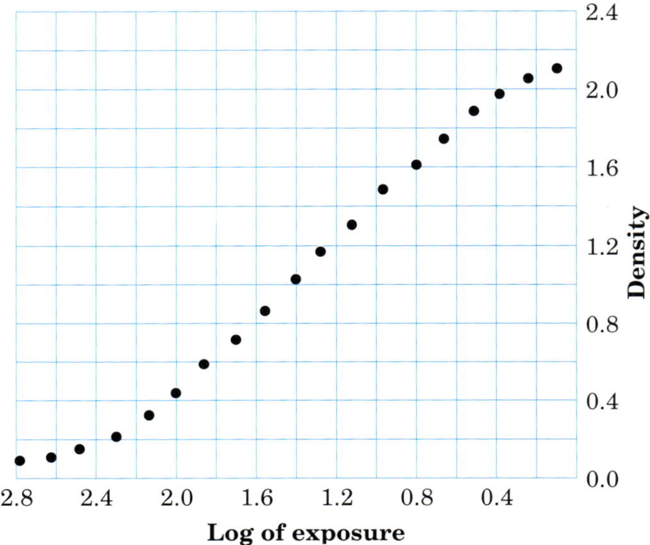

Plotting a characteristic curve.

for equal amounts of exposure. Yet the density rises an equal amount for equal increases in exposure in the straight-line portion of the curve, which is the portion used when working with photographic materials. Using the toe or shoulder regions results in tone distortions.

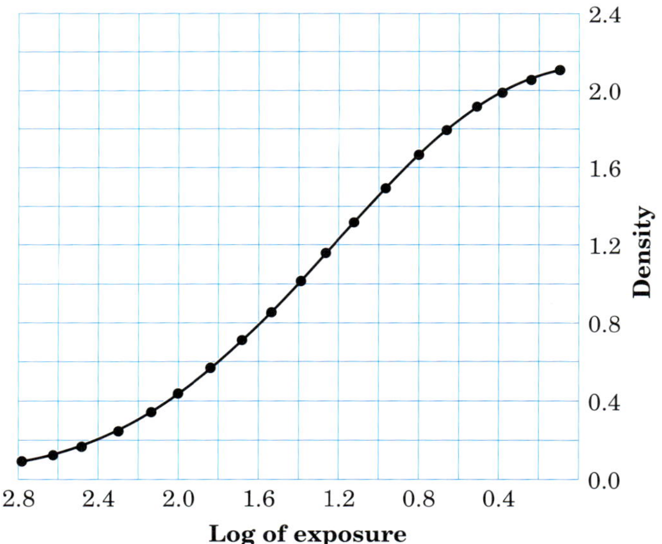

Making the final curve.

From a series of curves a photographer can determine the contrast of an emulsion, filter ratios, and relative speed. While this information is given on the film data sheets, the results obtained under individual shop conditions may differ from those of

the film manufacturers, especially when different combinations of emulsions and developers not specifically suggested by the manufacturer are used to complete the job.

Emulsion contrast and the characteristic curve. Contrast is a photographic term that refers to the distinction among tones on a negative or print. The words soft, hard, and flat may be used in describing contrast, i.e., a reproduction has a higher or lower contrast than the original. When examining a negative or a reproduction, the photographer looks at the contrast in different parts of the tone scale: **shadows, midtones,** and **highlights.**

Gamma. In photography, the Greek letter **gamma** is defined as a numerical designation for the contrast of a photographic material as represented by the slope of the straight-line portion of the characteristic curve. Gamma is numerically equal to the tangent of the angle that the straight-line portion makes with the baseline. The rate of gamma increases with the length of time a film is developed until the gamma finally reaches a limit. With a higher gamma reading, a film negative has greater contrast. Thus a film developed to a high contrast can be represented by a steep characteristic curve and described as having a high-gamma reading. The total contrast present is based on several factors: subject contrast, development contrast, or flare in the optical system of the camera. Gamma refers only to development contrast.

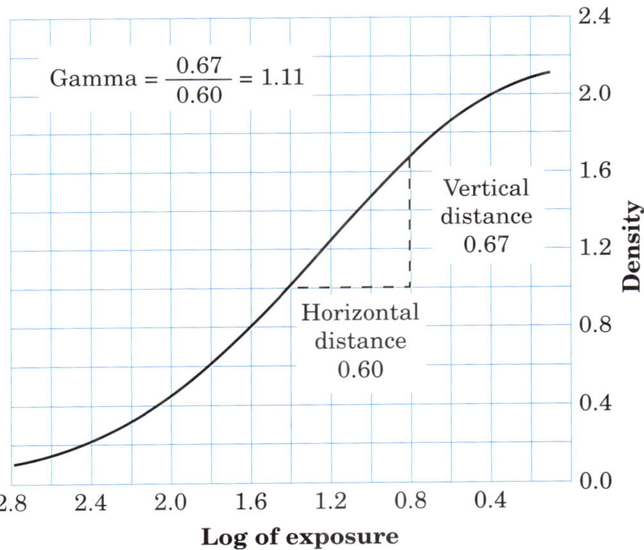

Analyzing a characteristic curve.

The illustration demonstrates how gamma is determined. Vertical and horizontal lines are drawn that intersect each other and the straight-line portion of the curve. The numerical value of gamma is equal to:

$$\gamma = \frac{\text{Vertical distance}}{\text{Horizontal distance}}$$

Characteristic curve of high-contrast film. The characteristic curve of a typical high-contrast material has a steep straight-line portion indicating a sharp jump from low to high density as a result of a slight increase in exposure. This sharp jump in density provides clean edges on lines and halftone dots. When high-contrast film is used behind a halftone screen, little or no density is recorded in the areas shielded by the opaque sections of the screen. A maximum density is recorded behind the almost- clear areas if the critical amount of light passes through. More light passing through the screen causes the jump in density to take place farther in all directions from the almost-clear center, resulting in a larger halftone dot. The size of each halftone dot depends on the amount of light passing through the screen. Dots of varying sizes form the pattern on the film.

Other Uses of the Densitometer

At the camera. The photoelectric cell of some densitometers can be detached and placed on the ground glass of the graphic arts camera where it can serve as a very sensitive light meter, measuring the amount of light coming through the lens. Once a test negative has been made and the proper exposure determined, the ground glass reading is used to determine the correct exposure for other camera positions.

Densitometers with detachable heads also permit a simple and accurate method of positioning the exposure lamps for proper illumination. "Proper illumination" refers to even illumination across the ground glass of the camera. Many process photographers make the mistake of thinking that the exposure of the emulsion will be even if the copy is illuminated evenly.

This assumption is incorrect because light rays from the outer edges of the copy have to travel farther than those that are on or closer to the optical axis of the lens. These same light rays also strike the emulsion at an angle, and since they cover a greater area than those close to or on the axis, their

intensity is diminished further. In addition, lenses tend to cause the light rays to fade away at the edges of the copy because of the barrel length, lens thickness, or both.

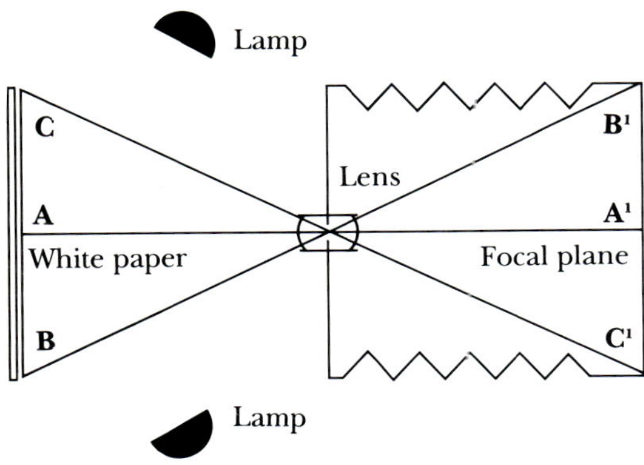

If the intensity of the light from A striking emulsion at A^1 is taken as 100%, the intensity of the light striking the emulsion at C^1 from C and at B^1 from B (25° off the axis) is only about 67%.

If the illumination at the focal plane (ground glass) is to be even, the edges of the copy must receive more light than the center of the copy. The procedure for checking illumination using a densitometer with a detachable head is listed above.

1. Adjust camera and lens for same-size reproduction.
2. Replace ground glass in camera with a pane of clear glass.
3. Cover the copyboard with a sheet of white paper.
4. Cover the window of the photometer search head.
5. Open the shutter of the camera, turn on the lamps, and then slide the search head over the clear glass, noting the variations in light intensity on the readout.
6. Move the exposure lights to different positions until the meter readings show that the intensity of the light at the film plane is as uniform as possible.
7. Record these final exposure light positions and use whenever shooting at the same size.

This same procedure should be followed to determine the best positions of the exposure lamps at other camera settings. Once the positions have been determined for each of the most commonly used camera settings, they should be recorded for reference on future jobs.

If two lamps illuminate the copyboard, it is probably possible to get fairly even illumination in a band across the focal plane, but not vertically. In such cases, oblong copy should be placed on the copyboard with its longest dimension horizontal.

The Chemistry of Photography

Understanding the basic points of chemistry is helpful for an insight into process photography. The chapter discusses photographic emulsion, developer solutions, fixation, and reducers.

Photographic Emulsion

The silver emulsion used on sensitized photographic materials consists of a colloid, such as gelatin, silver halides, and additives that produce certain effects.

Gelatin. Gelatin is a protein obtained from the tissues, hides, cartilage, and bones of animals. Because of its animal origins, gelatin's composition is extremely varied, although it usually includes components of iron, lead, copper, and alumina, with limits of ash and sulfur dioxide.

Silver halides. The salts of silver chloride, silver bromide, and silver iodide, known collectively as the silver halides, are formed by precipitation in the emulsion.

Silver bromide ($AgBr$) is the most widely used silver salt found in paper and film products. It is characterized by its high speed and low fog action on the emulsion. **Silver iodide** (AgI) is used in combination with other halides. In speed, it is approximately one-third that of silver bromide. **Silver chloride** ($AgCl$), a pure white powder, is used primarily on paper emulsions. Its speed is approximately one-eighth that of silver bromide. Silver fluoride is not used because it fogs in combination with other halides. However, silver oxalates, nitrates, tartrates, and citrates may be used.

Emulsion additives. Since silver salts are only sensitive to the blue portions of the spectrum, color dyes that increase the emulsion's sensitivity to red and green are added and absorbed by the silver halides. The resulting increase in color sensitivity is referred to as optical sensitization. Still other

additives are used to increase speed, prevent fog, and control gamma in all emulsions.

Developer Solutions

Light affects the photographic emulsion by forming a latent image that is converted to a visible image by using a developer to reduce the silver halide to black metallic silver. An infectious developer, which is used for line and halftone photography, has slow development rate that gradually increases to a maximum at the end of the cycle. Noninfectious developers are used for continuous-tone photographs.

Developing solutions consist of a solvent (water); a developing or reducing agent (metol or hydroquinone); a preservative (sodium sulfite); a restrainer (potassium bromide); an accelerator or alkali (sodium hydroxide); and miscellaneous additives that do not affect development.

Solvents. Almost all developers use water as a solvent, although some color-coupling developers use other solvents in combination with water. The water used for developers is fairly high in purity and does not contain large amounts of calcium or chloride salts.

Developing agents. The organic chemicals widely used as developing agents are strong reducers that contain the hydroxyl (-OH) and amino ($-NH_2$) groups in varying proportions. The most important of this group is paradihydroxybenzene (hydroquinone) and monomethyl paraminophenol (metol).

Hydroquinone is a powerful developer that reveals a visible image on the film slowly but gains in density rapidly over a prolonged period of time. Metol is a much more energetic agent, showing an image rapidly but building density slowly. Metol and hydroquinone are combined in developers because each chemical helps correct the shortcomings of the other. Most paper and film developers contain varying combinations of these two agents.

Preservatives. Preservatives prevent or control developer oxidation. Sodium sulfite is the most common chemical used as an antioxidant. The sulfite prevents staining, acts as a silver solvent, and, in some cases, serves as a weak alkali, which increases the rate of development.

Accelerators. To increase the pH of the developing solution and the ionization of the developing agent, an alkali, or accelerator, is added. The alkali also absorbs the bromine ions formed by the action of the developing agent in the silver salts. The more important alkalis include the carbonates and hydroxides of sodium and potassium.

Restrainer. The potassium bromide found in a developing solution reduces the ionization of the silver salt, regulating image development.

Miscellaneous additives. The most common additives are listed below:

- Wetting agents permit the developer to penetrate the gelatin rapidly.
- Desensitizers reduce the color sensitivity of the emulsion without affecting its speed. Phenosafranine and the pinakryptols belong in this group of chemicals.
- Silver solvents, including sodium thiocyanite and ammonium chloride, reduce grain size.
- Other chemicals are used to increase gamma, control water impurities, and permit the use of developers in environments characterized by extremes of temperature.

Action of development. The action of a hydroquinone developer on a photographic emulsion is described in the following steps:

1. The alkali dissociates the hydroquinone, liberating the ions of the developing agent in solution.
2. The hydroquinone ion reacts with the silver bromide, yielding quinone and ions of silver and bromine.
3. The quinone then reacts with sodium sulfite to form sodium hydroquinone monosulfonate and sodium hydroxide.
4. The sodium hydroquinone monosulfonate is oxidized to quinone monosulfonate, which, in turn, reacts with sulfite to form sodium hydroquinone disulfonate. The latter is inert as a developer.
5. As the development proceeds, hydroquinone ionizes; hydrogen ions are formed; and bromine ions are released into the solution, which is equivalent to adding potassium bromide to the developer.

In summary, the developing agent forms complex salts that act on the image as the agent is gradually depleted. After the developing agent is completely exhausted, the bromine ions formed by the silver bromide restrain development to the point that sufficient density is no longer produced in a film negative or positive.

Effect of development, temperature, and agitation on contrast. The contrast present in a photographic reproduction increases as development time and temperature are increased, up to the point

where fogging begins to obscure the image, particularly in the low-density areas of a negative. Agitation also increases contrast because it increases the rate of development.

The development characteristics of litho materials are rather different from those of continuous-tone products. Litho materials are nearly always developed to the maximum contrast. The increase in effective emulsion speed coupled with increased development time can often be used to compensate for minor errors in exposure. This factor is referred to as development latitude. Beyond a development time of about 2½ min., however, there is less change in effective speed, a helpful characteristic when several line negatives are processed together or whenever exact timing of is difficult.

Rapid-access developers. Rapid-access developers are high-temperature, single-solution (continuous-tone) developers for standard camera-speed lith (line and halftone), contact, and duplicating (direct positive) films. Offering excellent process control, rapid-access developers can be used in either an automatic processor or in tray developing.

Diffusion transfer materials. Diffusion transfer is a process used to produce positive screened (copydot) images and line prints with the process camera or contact frame. In this process, an exposed photographic emulsion is developed by a developer containing silver halide solvent. The developer dissolves a sufficient amount of silver halides (a positive image) as a negative image is formed in exposed portions of emulsion. The dissolved silver halide particles are transferred to the receiver sheet, creating a positive image on its surface. Some printers use diffusion transfer material to make proofs from film positives. Contact paper prints and diffusion transfer lithographic plates can also be produced.

Fixation

When development is completed, those areas not affected by exposure or development are removed with a fixing bath to make the image on the film permanent. The fixing bath contains a number of chemicals that act on the silver image. The formulation of a typical bath used on lith films consists of:

- Solvent, such as water.
- Silver halide solvent, such as sodium thiosulfate (hypo), which is used to dissolve the silver halides.
- Stabilizer, such as sodium sulfite, that prevents a sulfur precipitate from forming.
- Acid, such as acetic acid, to bring the bath to the pH necessary to neutralize alkalinity caused during development.
- Buffer, such as boric acid, to limit the change in the pH of the fixing bath.
- Hardener, such as potassium alum, that toughens the emulsion against washing or normal handling when the film is dry.

In addition to dissolving the unexposed and undeveloped silver salts, the fixing bath also neutralizes developer alkali, which stops developer action.

Reducers

A reducer is oxidizing the metallic silver on a film to form a soluble silver salt. In some cases, the silver salt is insoluble in water, and the solution must contain another chemical that can convert the silver salt into a soluble silver compound.

Farmer's, a common reducer, is a mixture of potassium ferricyanide and sodium thiosulfate. The silver reacts with the potassium salt to form silver ferrocyanide. At the same time, the iron in the ferricyanide ion is reduced to form ferrocyanide ions. Lastly, the sodium thiosulfate reacts with the insoluble silver ferrocyanide, converting it into soluble complex ions that work in reducing silver on film.

Selecting Photographic Materials

Silver-Based Films and Paper

Film and papers are both silver-based, light-sensitive materials. The basic difference between the two is that films are transparent when processed and papers are opaque. All of the other characteristics are very similar.

Silver-based photographic materials are composed of an emulsion and a base. Films also have an antihalation backing. The **emulsion** is a loose mixture of light-sensitive silver compounds and the **base** is a flat sheet of plastic or a special grade of photo paper that forms the support layer.

A cross section of silver-based photographic film shows a protective overcoat, emulsion, binding agents, base, and antihalation backing. Photographic papers have a similar cross section without the antihalation backing.

The film's **protective overcoat** is a thin layer of gelatin and hardeners applied over the emulsion to

protect it. A **binding agent** holds the emulsion to the base during coating and later during developing, fixing, and washing. Because the base supports the light-sensitive emulsion it must have a uniform thickness without surface irregularities. An additional binding agent applied to the back of the base counteracts curl. The **antihalation coating** on the back side of the film prevents light from scattering and inhibits internal reflection or flare, which causes indistinct images and lack of sharpness.

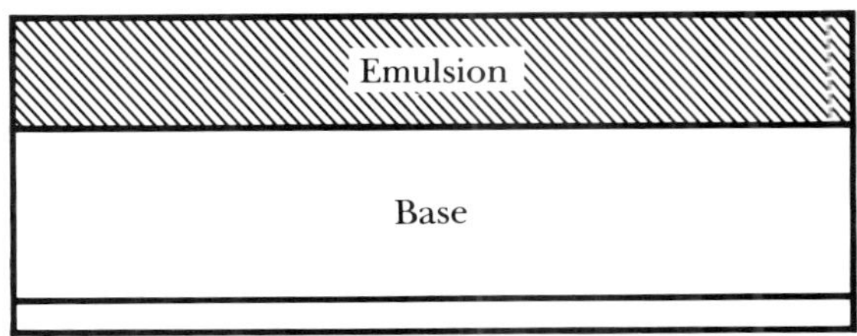

Cross section of camera film.

A dye incorporated into the antihalation coating absorbs this light.

The fundamental requirement in a film for line and halftone work is high contrast. On line negatives, dark areas are rendered clear and background areas as extremely dense, even if the original copy has light or weak lines. In halftone work, the high contrast of the emulsion will produce sharp, crisp halftone dots. Using a fine-grain emulsion keeps the edges of lines and dots from becoming ragged.

Camera film. Lith, or camera film, a high-contrast graphic arts silver-based material, is used to produce line and halftone negatives with a graphic arts camera. Its thick antihalation backing and light-sensitive properties makes it less suitable for contact printing.

Camera film is developed in a lith, or infectious, developer designed to produce high contrast. It has the narrowest exposure latitude of all the photographic products used for photomechanical work. Because of this, control of exposure and processing is very important. Even the smallest exposure errors may interfere with results. Fortunately, today's automatic film processing methods offer excellent and reproducible control of photographic development.

Contact film. Blue-sensitive continuous-tone contact films are used to produce contact positives from negatives or negatives from film positives. When processed in an infectious developer, this film takes on the appearance of lith material, but with the wide exposure latitude and relatively high maximum density afforded by its continuous-tone emulsion. This emulsion also has an excellent resolution that is greater than that of camera films. A special antihalation backing allows exposures through the base of the film without a loss in quality. The base support, 0.004–0.007-in. (0.1–0.2 mm) thick, is made of polyester or similar materials to provide dimensional stability, which ensures exact registration when working from several duplicate images. Unlike camera films, contact films are not affected by slight variations in processing.

Duplicating film. Duplicating film is a direct-positive photographic material that produces a duplicate image from a line or halftone original in one step. Camera and contact films produce the opposite result from an original—a positive from a negative or a negative from a positive. With duplicating film, a number of multiple-negative and step-and-repeat operations are possible.

Unlike other films that produce more density with more exposure, a duplicating film produces less because it was preexposed to maximum density during manufacture through a process called solarization. Blue-sensitive and relatively high in contrast, this continuous-tone film is processed in lith or rapid-access developers. It has a good exposure latitude and high resolving power. A thin antihalation dye backing permits exposure through the base for proper image orientation.

Regular, high-, and super-speed duplicating films are available for photomechanical work. All three differ in light sensitivity. Regular duplicating film, which is not very light-sensitive, is used often in stripping. High-speed duplicating film, which is more sensitive to light, can be used in contact printing and exposed by point light sources. Even with its increased speed, this film still requires longer exposures than any other product used in photographic contacting. Super-speed duplicating film has the highest light sensitivity of the three duplicating films. In addition to providing shorter exposures during contact duplicating, it can be used to produce a line positive from line copy on a process camera in one step. This film also increases the practicality of duplicating in the contact darkroom with a point light source.

Room-light handling film. Room-light handling films are designed to produce contacts with the low-

level incandescent or fluorescent lights found in the stripping and platemaking departments. Because these films are not very sensitive to light, they should not be used with point light sources. Room-light films are used only for emulsion-to-emulsion contacting. Base-to-emulsion contacting produces poor results.

Rapid-access film. Blue- or green-sensitive rapid-access (non-lith) film is used to produce line negatives, contact negatives, and film positives. It has a high-density continuous-tone conventional emulsion. Processing this film in the proper chemicals gives it a high degree of exposure latitude. Special rapid-access processors also produce the contact in 90 seconds dry-to-dry—the fastest means of creating film intermediates.

Storage and Care of Film

To ensure consistent processing results, all photographic materials should be stored under fairly stable conditions. Temperatures between 70° and 80°F (21° and 27°C) and relative humidities between 40% and 50% are recommended.

Heat and humidity. The packages in which graphic arts films are supplied provide adequate protection against the relative humidities commonly encountered in temperate climates. However, they are not intended to withstand long periods of high relative humidities and, because the packages are not heat-proof, they should not be placed near sources of heat.

Static elimination systems, which create a cloud of positive and negative ions that neutralize static charges, are recommended for areas where low humidity is a problem and extreme increases in humidity could damage equipment. Often installed on the ceiling in the camera area, these units generally rely on variable speed fans and air flow diffusers to keep the workplace static free.

Refrigerated storage. During the summer in temperate or tropical zones, unopened packages of film, particularly infrared and very fast films, should be stored in refrigerators. Place refrigerated packages in a warmer location for 24 hours before opening them. Opened packages of film should not be returned to the refrigerator because the high humidity will cause damage.

Storing processed films. Processed films are best stored in dry, dust-free places away from harmful gases and chemicals. Processed films should never be stored for long periods at humidities in excess of 60%. Film negatives should be filed in plainly marked, durable envelopes, in case they will be used again.

Film aging and shrinkage. After processing, all films shrink at a rate that gradually decreases with time regardless of the storage method used. Shrinkage prompted by aging is of little importance when negatives are used within a week or two after processing; however, storing the film in an area with an excess of humidity (low or high) can cause the problem to accelerate. Over longer periods of time, the composition of a particular film (i.e., the residual solvent content of the base) dictates the amount of shrinkage that occurs.

Film Bases

Polyester. Most lithographic films have a polyester base that is 0.004–0.007-in. (0.102–0.178 mm) thick. These film bases are used for applications in which the atmospheric conditions prevent the use of flexible bases. Polyester film bases have excellent long-term storage characteristics and, since they contain no solvents or plasticizers, aging changes are negligible. Under normal operations, no particular handling precautions are necessary, but when extremely accurate film registration is required, the following suggestions are helpful:

- Maintain storage, stripping, and plate exposure areas at approximately the same relative humidity and temperature.
- Break the seal on fresh boxes of film 24-to-48 hours before use and store the film in the work area to allow it to reach equilibrium with the room's relative humidity.
- Condition individual sheets in the darkroom for at least 20 minutes before exposure.
- Handle all films in a set together.
- Quickly squeegee wet film surfaces and dry the processed films at 100° to 125°F (38° to 52°C) in warm circulating air to achieve accurate register.
- Condition processed films at room temperature for at least two hours before further use.
- Store processed film sets together.

Acetate. An acetate base is made of cellulose acetate butyrate or cellulose triacetate, which are cellulose esters. It is cast from solutions of these materials in a solvent, a small amount of which remains in the base. As the film ages, the solvent gradually escapes, causing shrinkage. Humidity

more so than temperature causes reversible size changes in acetate film bases. Acetate films are 0.0035–0.0055 in. (0.089–0.140 mm) thick.

Long storage periods at high relative humidities can result in 1% shrinkage. Lith films with acetate bases exhibit a 0.5% to 0.7% shrinkage rate when stored for a year or more at relative humidities above 60%.

Polystyrene. Because polystyrene films do not contain solvents or plasticizers size changes during photographic processing occur more frequently as a result of the effects of humidity on the photographic gelatin coating. When the room air is constant and the relative humidity is low, the film may swell by 0.03% during processing.

At higher relative humidities, the film may shrink by the same percentage. Shrinkage becomes excessive at temperatures exceeding 120°F (49°C), although the actual softening temperature of polystryrene film is around 200°F (93°C). When the lab temperature is kept at 70°F (21°C) and the relative humidity at 50% shrinkage during processing is virtually eliminated.

Film Speeds and Exposure Indexes

Photographic films that require very little exposure are referred to as "fast," while those requiring more exposure are said to be "slow." All films are assigned an exposure index, a number related to speed, that aids the operator in exposure calculations. Films with higher exposure index numbers are "faster" and require less of an exposure.

Color Sensitivity of Films

All photographic emulsions are sensitive to blue, violet, and invisible ultraviolet light rays, but this sensitivity is not sufficient for many graphic arts applications. The film emulsions used in photomechanical color reproduction, for example, must be capable of recording densities for the broader range of colors that the human eye can see, including greens, yellows, oranges, and reds. During manufacture, dyes are added that make the emulsions sensitive to these other colors.

Blue-sensitive photographic materials. Blue-sensitive photographic materials record high negative densities for the blue areas of the original and, in the final reproduction, render these blues very light, and reds, yellows, and greens very dark. Because the film is only sensitive to blue light, it can be handled under either a red or yellow safelight. Blue-sensitive materials are very useful in specialized work since the nature of its emulsion and processing chemistry offers considerable exposure and processing latitude when making film contacts.

Orthochromatic films. Orthochromatic films have shorter exposure times than blue-sensitive materials and are sensitive to a wider range of colors in the blue and green regions of the spectrum. They can be handled under red safelights.

Panchromatic films. Panchromatic films are sensitive to all visible colors, as well as ultraviolet light. They must be handled in total darkness.

The Darkroom

The layout of a darkroom for commercial photography is determined primarily by the size of the materials handled and the required work flow. Keeping the center of the room free of materials is also an important goal. The physical requirements of most darkrooms include "safe" and white-light illumination; trays, tanks, and a film processing machine; hot-and-cold running water; a thermometer and timer or clock; a bench-top or wall viewing light; storage space for photographic materials and supplementary equipment; and an automatic film dryer, drying rack, or cabinet.

Naturally, all darkrooms must be light-proof, although it is no longer necessary to paint the room jet black. Light gray or white are more popular and increase the effectiveness of darkroom illumination.

Size of Darkrooms

The size of the darkroom is directly dependent on how the room will be used. It is often better to have two specialized darkrooms rather than one large universal room. Extra rooms are helpful if contact printing and masking are done frequently.

The minimum size for any photomechanical darkroom is 6×8 ft. (1.8×2.4 m). If the room will include a graphic arts camera, this minimum size must increase to about 8×10 ft. (2.4×3 m). For darkrooms in which contact printing and large film handling will take place the minimum room size is approximately 10×20 ft. (3×6 m). In every instance, adequate ventilation must be maintained. Without adequate ventilation workers may become ill.

Darkroom Entrances

It is important to be able to enter and leave the darkroom without admitting light. Entrance walls and passageways should be painted with a dark, matte finish to prevent light from reflecting. Baffle, double-door light lock, and rotary door entrances are three popular darkroom entrances.

Baffle entrance. The baffle, or open-passage, entrance provides good ventilation and easy access. The latter is especially important when workers are carrying large films.

Double-door light lock. When floor space is at a premium, the double-door light lock entrance is often used. With this arrangement, one or both of the conventional doors are replaced by heavy single or double curtains. If two solid doors are used, a light-trapping vent placed in the wall of the passageway relieves the changes in air pressure caused by opening and closing the doors. If several persons will use a darkroom with a double-door light lock entrance, it is best to install a warning light or buzzer that will operate when either door is open, thus reducing the possibility of both doors being opened at once.

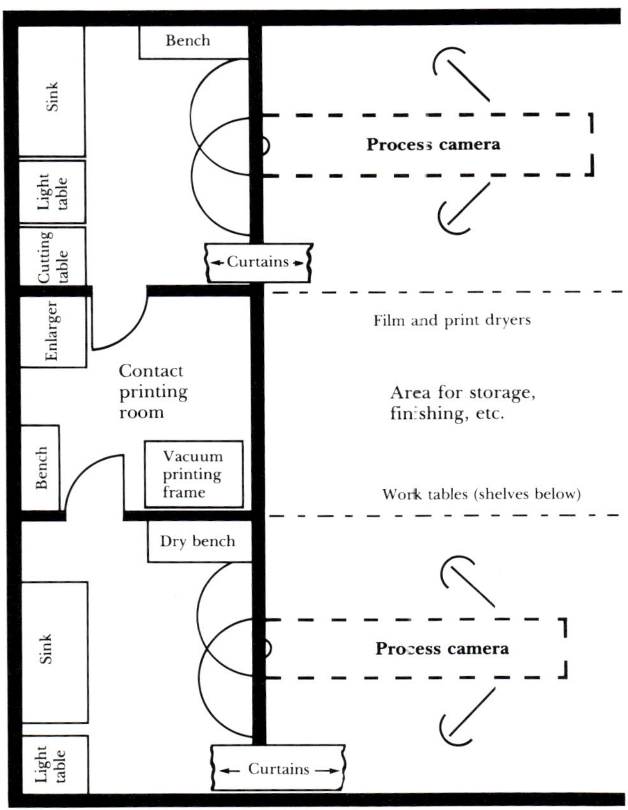

Darkroom layout.

Rotary door. The rotary door is actually a set of upright cylinders nestled one inside the other. Each cylinder has one missing panel to serve as a doorway. A person passes through this door by stepping into the inner cylinder and rotating it to align with the opening of the outer cylinder. The rotary door system works well because so little space is used. However, very bulky items cannot be transported through it, and only one person at a time can use it even in case of emergency. A rotary door may admit some light into the darkroom, but this light is mainly confined to the inner cylinder of the door. To minimize light leaks the inner cylinder should be rotated so that its opening is opposite the darkroom. If the interior and exterior of both cylinders are painted black, light leaks are further lessened.

Darkroom Equipment

Sturdy darkroom equipment may seem more costly at first but is a good investment in the long run. As is true in darkroom design, the maximum film size to be handled is one of the most important things to consider before making major equipment purchases. Some of the most common equipment found in darkrooms is described in this section.

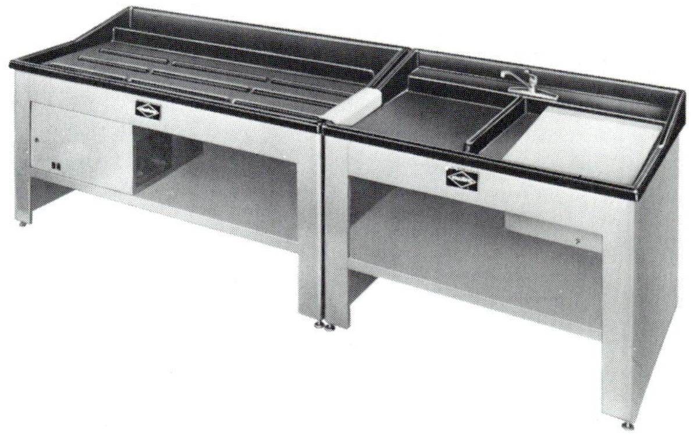

Courtesy nuArc Company

Processing sink.

Processing sinks. Fiberglass and stainless steel are used to construct processing sinks that are mechanically durable and resistant to the corrosive action of the solutions used in film processing. Sinks

constructed of other materials may leak and corrode easily.

Scouring powders can be used to clean stainless steel sinks. A 10% solution of citric acid prepared by dissolving one pound of citric acid crystals in approximately five quarts of water removes a hard scale. Rinse sinks thoroughly with water after cleaning.

Tanks and trays. The best arrangement for trays and tanks is in a straight line along a wall, with aisles at least 3 ft. (1 m) wide. Consider the amount of work done each day and possible future increases in the production load before organizing this area. Storing trays vertically permits easy access while allowing them to drain.

Film processing machines. Film processors take up very little darkroom space, as only the feed portion of the processor is actually located in the darkroom. The delivery end of the processor is situated in a clean, dust-free area just outside the darkroom. Even when automatic processing is used exclusively, a processing sink might be used for specialized processing or as an emergency backup.

Sink-top light table. A light table placed at the end of the sink can be sloped to drain into it. Frosted glass installed below the clear glass on the light table diffuses the light source. A perforated pipe installed at the upper edge of the table can supply washing and flushing water to film.

Water temperature controls. Accurate and consistent control of the temperature of photographic processing solutions is essential. Manual adjustments of water temperature are seldom sufficient in commercial operations. Automatic temperature-control systems eliminate mistakes and delays and save time and materials.

Thermostatically controlled mixing valves provide the most compact and least expensive automatic system available for controlling water temperatures. These valves operate by combining warm and cold water to reach the desired temperature. Artificially cooled water is used in areas where warm summer weather affects the temperature of the regular cold water supply.

Dry bench. Sensitized materials are handled and stored on a dry bench. This bench must be located away from wet areas, such as sinks and chemical mixing benches. It should also include lighttight drawers to store photographic materials. Space for bottled chemicals can be built into a sink unit or wherever it is relatively cool and dry. Remember to keep powders away from open film boxes.

Chemical Precautions

Government legislation codified in the OSHA Hazard Communication Standard now requires that employers develop a written program in hazard communication and that employees working with chemicals receive ongoing safety training and wear protective gear. It is also necessary to compile a list of all chemicals in used in the printing facility, obtain **material safety data sheets** (MSDSs) from the manufacturer or distributor of each chemical on the list, and properly label each container that contains a hazardous chemical. Labeling guidelines are discussed in-depth in the GATF product *Understanding the OSHA Hazard Communication Standard,* which is available in audio visual and video form.

Most of the chemicals used in photography and photo processing are, to some degree, toxic. Photographic developers contain sodium hydroxide or sodium carbonate, both of which are harmful to the eyes. Other mildly or highly toxic chemicals found in the camera area include silver nitrate, hydroquinone, formaldehyde, and hypo. Therefore it is important to wear gloves, goggles, and and an apron when handling these materials.

Silver recovery. Government environmental regulations also require the control of heavy metals once discharged into sewer systems, making it a legal necessity to reclaim silver from photographic

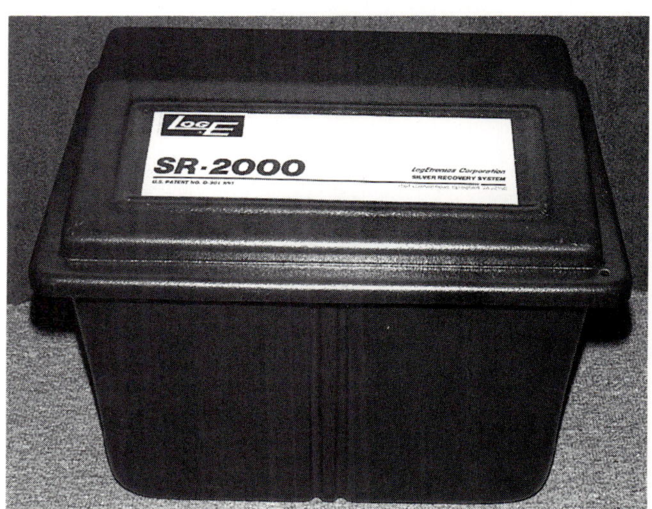

Courtesy LogEtronics Corporation

Silver recovery system.

fixing baths. Silver recovery remains popular as a means of conserving its limited supply while profiting from the sale of the reclaimed metal.

In the electrolytic method of silver recovery, which is widely used today, the fixing bath is transferred to the silver recovery unit containing two electrodes, a carbon anode and a stainless steel cathode. After a low-voltage direct current passes between them, metallic silver is deposited on the cathode. The metallic replacement method features cartridges filled with steel wool. Spent fixing bath is pumped into a cartridge and remains there until an oxidation-reduction reaction takes place. This chemical reaction reduces the silver ions to metallic silve and oxidizes the iron into a ferrous ion.

Camera Darkroom Facilities

A darkroom camera is housed with its back in the darkroom and the rest in the gallery, or outer room. The section of the darkroom devoted to the camera must be large enough to allow the the camera back (filmholder) to swing open and shut. Allow additional room for the at-hand storage of light-sensitive materials, halftone contact screens, and other items used in the photographic process. Some space, such as a shelf, may also be needed for the exposure control units. Place safelights around the camera back to illuminate the area in which the camera operator places materials on the filmholder.

Enclosing the entire the camera within the darkroom is very efficient in terms of the frequency of exposures, but since the camera lights are also in the darkroom, excessive heat is produced. To eliminate any discomfort to the camera operator, provide proper ventilation and air conditioning for this area. In all cases, there must be sufficient space for traffic flow on every side of the camera. Special lighttight storage cabinets must be installed in the darkroom to hold light-sensitive materials when the room lights or the camera lights are operating.

Contact Printing Facilities

The first concern in organizing a contact printing facility is determining where the contact printing frame and the light source should be located. Placing the printing frame in the center of the contact room is ideal, but not always possible because of space limitations. Instead, the frame is located near a wall or in a corner of the room. Painting the walls black and keeping the frame away from reflective objects will lessen most contacting problems. Avoid positioning the frame near air and exhaust ducts, air-conditioning vents, and doorways to keep it clean and dust-free.

Choosing the floor covering for a darkroom presents several unusual problems. The ideal floor covering should be watertight, durable, and resistant to corrosive substances and staining. It is impossible to find all of these qualities in one material, but ceramic or composition tiles come closest to achieving the necessary qualities.

Ceramic tiles. A fully vitreous ceramic tile is a good choice because it will absorb very little moisture and is therefore easy to clean. Most porcelain and natural clay tiles are impervious to dirt and liquids, nonstaining, easily cleaned, and available in nonskid versions. Semivitreous and nonvitreous tiles are not usually satisfactory because of their tendency to absorb photographic solutions and chemicals.

Composition tiles. There are many inexpensive varieties of composition tiles made of plastic, hard-rubber, asphalt, or synthetic resin. These tiles can be laid down over existing flooring, including wood. Asphalt tiles are usually the best choice for most darkrooms because they are stain-resistant and durable. Hard rubber and plastic tiles are usually satisfactory, but some stain easily. Synthetic-resin tiles are undesirable because they tend to absorb chemicals and stain very easily.

Safelights

Efficient darkrooms should have as much illumination as possible without affecting the safety of the materials being processed. For example, an orthochromatic litho film, which is sensitive only to blue and green, can be handled under red safelights without fogging. In fact, the total illumination level of the darkroom can often be high enough for comfortable vision if the proper safelights are chosen. Most darkrooms use red safelights. Red, amber, or yellow safelights work well in contact printing facilities. Combination camera/contact printing darkrooms use red safelights.

Panchromatic materials. Panchromatic materials, which are sensitive to all colors of light, should be handled in complete darkness whenever possible. If a safelight is used, it must be green, the color to which the eye is most sensitive. A dark-green safelight can be used with panchromatic materials if the printed precautions on the film package are followed.

Safelight filters. It is usually necessary to have several safelight filters available when different photographic materials will be used. Safelight filters for different applications are recommended in the manufacturer's directions or data sheets found in each film package.

Safelight lamps are constructed so that the accompanying filters can be changed easily. When the filters are not in use, they can be stored in slotted racks. Safelight filters have been specifically prepared and tested for exacting photographic use. Other materials may appear to be the same color as a tested safelight filter, but using makeshift illumination is one of the surest ways of getting poor dot quality and poor tone rendition.

Kodak Safelight Filters

Filter	Color	For Use With:
OO	Light Yellow	Flashing halftones through magenta contact screens for contrast control
OA	Greenish Yellow	Black-and-white contact and duplicating materials, projection films
OC	Light Amber	Contacting and enlarging papers
1	Red	Blue-sensitive materials
1A	Light Red	Slow orthochromatic materials
2	Dark Red	Faster orthochromatic films and green-sensitive x-ray films
3	Dark Green	Panchromatic materials
6B	Brown	Blue-sensitive x-ray films and other materials
7	Green	Black-and-red infrared materials, except Kodak high-speed infrared films
8	Dark Yellow	Color print and intermediate films
10	Dark Amber	Color negative papers, color slide and print materials, panchromatic papers

To provide direct illumination, install a 15-watt bulb safelight lamp at a distance of no less than 4 ft. (1.2 m) from the work space. A 25-watt bulb placed at the same distance from the work area is used to provide indirect illumination with a safelight lamp.

Safelight precautions. Any photographic material will fog if left under a safelight for a long time. This occurs because even colorblind (blue-sensitive) materials are somewhat sensitive to green, yellow, and red light. The absence of any fog in clear areas of the film does not necessarily indicate that a safelight is safe, since overexposure has an effect on halftone dots that is not readily noticeable.

Any safelight filter used with the proper bulb, at the correct distance, is "safe" for at least 30 seconds with the appropriate dry materials and for a longer time when the material is in the developer.

Since exposure to a safelight can decrease film quality even without producing fog, it is necessary to test the safelights as follows:

1. Make a print from a typical halftone negative on a whole sheet of the film or paper in question, using the printing method commonly employed. Use a border mask to produce an exposed area around the image. No safelight should be used during this part of the test.

2. Now expose parts of the same sheet of film or paper to the safelight by covering successive areas of the film or paper for different lengths of time and keeping one area covered at all times. The test should be made where the material will be handled and developed, and with the safelight located where it is commonly used.

3. Process the film or print and observe the amount of safelight exposure possible without a noticeable change in the quality of the image or highlight dots.

Often a safelight exposure that does not produce any fog in the border area will show veiling in highlight dots and highlight areas in the print.

Drying Facilities

Consider the films used most frequently when planning a drying facility. Films with thin emulsions, such as ortho litho films, dry very quickly under almost any condition while films with thicker emulsions dry more slowly under normal darkroom conditions.

Electric fans. For small-volume plants that process films with thin emulsions, an electric fan is

usually acceptable for drying. To accelerate drying, direct the fan's air flow toward the film or plate. Large-volume plants using all types of photographic materials can easily justify the expense of a film dryer.

Film dryers. A film dryer is an integral part of an automatic film-processing machine, but can also be purchased separately. In one design, the dryer is housed in a sheet-metal cabinet with rods at the top from which the film is suspended as air, warmed by a heating element, circulates around it. These cabinets are designed to dry up to 100 lengths of roll film or several racks of sheet film at one time. The inside temperature is indicated by a thermometer and regulated by a thermostat.

Ventilation

When planning how a darkroom will be ventilated consider how uncovered solutions can increase the room's humidity, processing solutions create slight odors, and drying cabinets give off heat. All of these concerns can affect a camera operator's health and efficiency, and, as discussed previously, excesses of temperature and humidity can alter the physical characteristics of the film.

Exhausting the darkroom air. Darkroom air should turn over six to ten times every hour. Air should be pumped in rather than out and filters that capture dust particles should be installed. The drying cabinet must never exhaust into the processing room. If an air-conditioning system is installed in the building, using the air from the processing room for the drying cabinet may be a poor choice as it might overload the ventilating systems and upset the balance of the pressure and circulation. In such instances, the dryer should have separate ducts not connected with the air-conditioning system. However, with other ventilating systems, the drying cabinet may be used to exhaust air from the room.

Electric Wiring

Although high-voltage circuits do not extend into the darkroom, low-voltage electric outlets and fixtures may present a hazard when water and other processing solutions are present.

The electric wiring and equipment in the darkroom must be inspected periodically to assess conformity to all safety regulations. All exposed metal parts of fixed and portable equipment, such as the metal frame and exterior of each illuminator, safelight lamp, electric timer, and foot switch, must be grounded. Outlets, switches, sockets, and even chain pull-switches must be insulated. Install ground-fault interrupters that detect current leakage between circuits and the ground on floor-based foot-switches that may become damp or wet.

Planning. Place and wire outlets for the convenience of the worker. Locate the switches for all processing-room circuits, white lights, safelight lamps, and outlets near the door outside the processing room. An illuminated safelight switch or a red light over the darkroom entrance will indicate that the darkroom is in use and prevent accidents while films are being processed.

Placement of switches. Place the master switch at the operator's shoulder level and the switch to control the white ceiling light below it. Installing these switches so high on the wall makes it less likely that they can be turned on accidentally. As an additional precaution, the white-light switch should be key-operated. Place the switch the controls the safelight lamps at waist level.

The Graphic Arts Camera

Since so many different kinds of copy are submitted for reproduction, it pays to have a versatile graphic arts camera. It may be small or compact, with a maximum film size of 16×20 in. (406×508 mm), or it may be large, capable of producing film negatives as large as 4×6 ft. (1.2×1.8 m). A camera for ordinary line and halftone work may be simple in design, but fully equipped precision models are required for multiple exposures and other intricate operations. Choose camera equipment based on immediate needs and future needs.

Camera Features

A graphic arts camera can be thought of as two parallel planes (a focal plane and a copy plane) situated at right angles to the optical axis of the lens that lies between them. The focusing screen (ground glass) and the film holder are attached to the housing in which the focal plane is encased. An independent support maintains the alignment of the lens in relation to the copy and focal plane. The camera is mounted on a chassis, or main bed, which

maintains the parallelism between the three essential planes. It also provides the means for adjusting the relationship between the lens, film, and copy for reducing or enlarging the image.

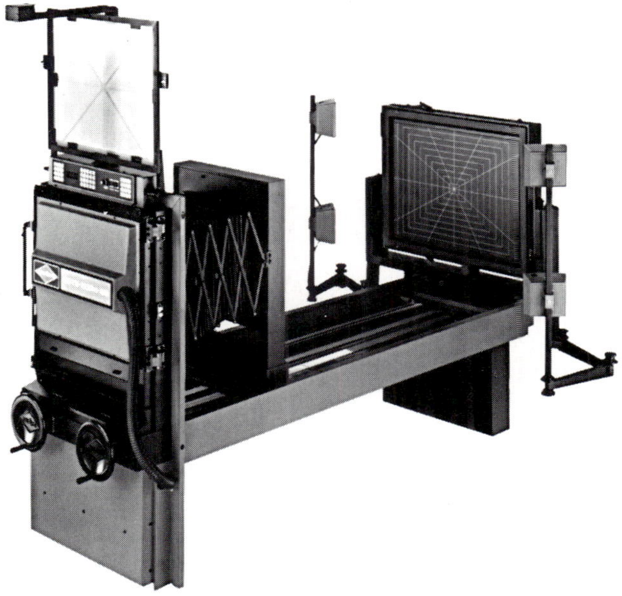

Courtesy nuArc

Horizontal camera.

Gallery and darkroom cameras. A **gallery camera** is not located in a darkroom. Instead, its bulky, lightproof film holder must be transported between the camera and darkroom for loading, exposing, and unloading. **Darkroom cameras,** on the other hand, extend backwards from the gallery into the darkroom where the operator manipulates the controls. Using a darkroom camera makes it possible to expose one negative, while processing another. Even if a gallery camera is installed within the darkroom only one operation—exposing or processing—can be performed at a time. The darkroom camera is available in three different configurations: floor horizontal, overhead horizontal, and vertical.

Horizontal cameras. The main bed of the floor horizontal camera is raised anywhere from 6 in. (152 mm) to 3 ft. (0.9 m) from the floor and can be serviced only from the side. The elevated main bed of the overhead horizontal camera permits easy and unobstructed accessibility to the lens, copy, and lamps.

Vertical cameras. A vertical camera conserves space and can be housed entirely in the darkroom or located in a small, lighttight room directly adjacent to the darkroom. The optical axis of its lens is vertical, with the copyboard and filmholder perpendicular to it.

On some of these units, the camera proper is horizontal and housed in the darkroom with the vertical supporting structure for the copyboard parallel to and closely hugging the outside of the darkroom wall. Since the focal plane and copy plane are at right angles to each other, a reversing mirror or prism must be used. Vertical cameras are more limited in film size and copy capacity than horizontal cameras are.

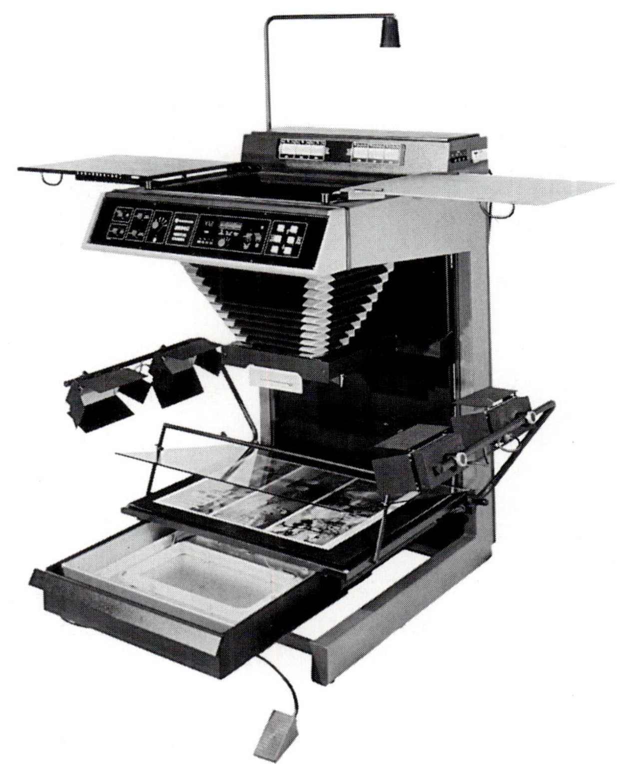

Courtesy Consolidated International, Inc.

Vertical camera.

Lenses and Image Reversal

A process lens consists of several glass elements that are carefully constructed and joined together in the lens barrel, which is attached to the camera on the lensboard. Most lens barrels have iris diaphragms and slots for inserting other lens stops or color filters.

Covering power. The covering power of a process lens is a fixed function dependent upon the inherent image angle and the focal length. The diameter

of the image area, with lenses of the same type and angle, becomes greater as the focal length increases. When the camera is focused for a same-size reproduction, the image area and copy area are equal, as are the distances from the lens to the copy and the lens to the film.

Range of reduction and enlargement. It is not unusual to find a camera that can reduce an image to 25% of the original size or enlarge it to 400% of the original size. The length of the camera bed and the minimum and maximum bellows separation determine the range of enlargements and reductions.

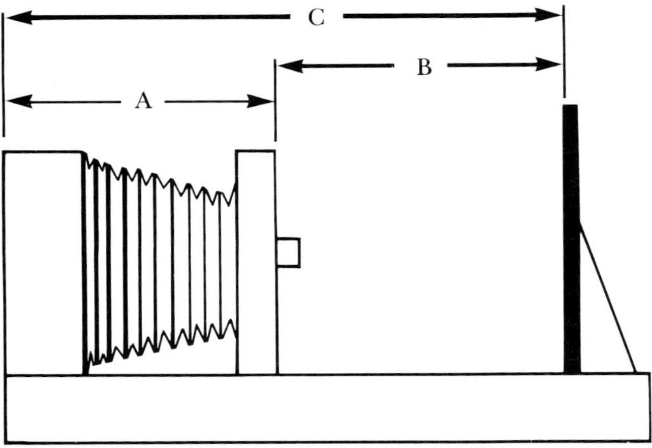

Distances separating lens, film, and copy.

The distances separating the lens, film, and copy are a function of the focal length of the lens and the scale of reproduction. In the illustration, the distance between the lens and the image (B) is directly related to the distance separating the lens and copy (A). The distance between the image and the copy (C) is the total of A and B. Distances A and B are called the conjugate foci and, except when the image and object are the same size, one is always greater than the other. However, the sum of the conjugate foci remains the same whenever the ratio between the image and the copy is the same. The minimum bellows distance limits the range of reduction and the maximum bellows extension governs the range of enlargement.

Auxiliary lenses. To increase the range of enlargement and reduction supplement the standard lens with one that has a shorter focal length. This practice works only when the image-covering power is adequate and there are no mechanical limitations to the process.

An **anamorphic lens** allows the camera operator to create distortion negatives by reducing copy in one dimension while allowing the other to remain unchanged.

Lens requirements. A good process lens must have excellent color correction properties extending from the visible spectrum into the ultraviolet and infrared regions. The lens should also have an antiflare coating and a high image resolution.

Lens aberrations. Lenses can have a number of faults most of which are partially or completely corrected by the lens manufacturer. Spherical aberrations, astigmatism, and chromatic aberrations are three common ones. A lens corrected for these aberrations is called **anastigmat.**

A **spherical aberration** occurs when the rays entering a curved lens near its edges are brought to a focus closer to the lens than the rays entering near the center, producing a blurred image. This problem can be corrected by using a smaller diaphragm opening and longer exposures or using other lenses combined with the faulty one. Compound lenses are specially designed to reduce spherical aberrations.

An **astigmatism** is a defect that causes the horizontal and vertical lines in an object to be brought to a focus on different planes. When the lens is sharply focused on the horizontal lines, the vertical lines are out of focus and vice versa. This fault is also corrected by using a combination of different glasses to form the lens or to create a compound lens.

In **chromatic aberrations** the white light passing through the lens is split into various colors each of which comes to a focus at different points. When this fault exists in a lens, the blue beam of light comes to a focus nearest the lens and the red beam focuses farthest away, again resulting in a blurred image that is corrected when different types of glass are used to form the major lens components.

Single- and double-image reversers. The single-mirror, or prism, that transposes images from right to wrong reading cannot be used on the conventional darkroom camera since the copy must be at right angles to the lens. Instead, multiple-mirror reversers that can handle copy in a straight line are used with darkroom cameras. The multiple-mirror reverser does distort the marginal rays, which limits the usable picture area.

Some double multiple-mirror reversers can create laterally reversed images and "lens only" images.

In this case, two flat mirrors, or one mirror and one prism acting in unison, cancel out the reversals and produce the same image as can be achieved when shooting through a lens alone. Three flat mirrors or one flat and one split mirror create a lateral straight-line reversal. On cameras equipped with double-reversing systems, the changeover from one to the other is usually accomplished electrically. Reversed and regular images are the same size and in register at the focal plane. Some cameras with double-reversing mirror systems can also shoot through a lens directly.

Since mirror systems displace the optical axis, cameras so equipped have special lensboards and copyboards with raised or laterally shifted centers. It is impossible and impractical to install this equipment on a standard camera.

The single-element reverser (mirror to prism) may be used in combination with specially designed darkroom cameras. These cameras have separate beds in which the copyboards are set at right angles to the main camera bed. The two units are controlled from within the darkroom.

Filters

A **filter** is a device that transmits certain colors of light while absorbing others. It never changes the color of light. It just allows certain wavelengths to pass through while stopping others. In the graphic arts, filters are used most often to emphasize or deemphasize tonal areas in black-and-white reproductions produced from colored or damaged originals. Using the proper filter, in the form of thin sheets or disks placed in front of the camera lens or in a slot in the lens mounting, enables camera operators to "filter out," or reduce, the transmission of selected colors of light from a multicolored object. Only the colors transmitted by the filter will be recorded on the photographic reproduction.

Other uses for filters. In addition to emphasizing or deemphasizing selected color tonal areas in originals, filters are often used to provide safelight illumination; modify the output of light sources to more closely match the spectral sensitivity of film; and increase exposure lengths to make them more controllable. At one time, filters were also used to color-separate multicolor originals on the graphic arts camera but this practice is seldom used today.

Filter factors. Each filter is given a number (such as 1.5 or 2), called the filter factor, that indicates the amount of times the exposure must be increased when a filter is used, in comparison to a timed exposure made under the same conditions without a filter.

Camera Rear Assembly

The camera's main operating station is the camera back, or rear case. Devices that hold the photosensitive material and screen mechanisms as well as most of the essential controls are located in this area.

Vacuum filmholders. Metal vacuum filmholders consist of holes or shallow grooves through which a vacuum pump draws air. When film is placed upon the supporting surface it seals the vents, setting up a vacuum. Atmospheric pressure against the face of the film holds it in place.

Masking and valve-cutoff vacuum backs differ in the method used to seal the area not covered by film. On the former, adjustable masks or individual metal shields corresponding to a particular film size seal the area not covered by the film. On the latter, a valve, or a series of valves, confines the vacuum to a specific area determined by the size of the film used.

A vacuum filmholder attaches to the camera housing with hinges on its side or base. With the side attachment, the holder is swung from the inoperative position (where the sensitive material is applied and removed) to the focal plane. This arrangement, in which the holder may be attached to either side, makes it possible to add a ground glass panel on the opposite side. When the base of the holder is hinged to the camera, the holder is lowered (tilted) to a horizontal position to apply or remove the sensitive material. Brackets or chains hold it in place.

Roll-film camera backs. Cameras equipped with backs that can accommodate roll film eliminate the conventional steps involved in loading a camera for each shot. The camera operator can select the width as well as the length of film that is most economical for the shot and load the camera with several different films when size flexibility is not an issue. Roll-film cameras can also hold halftone screens and move them into place mechanically. Some roll-film cameras can even be operated from the gallery, eliminating the need for the camera operator to shuttle back and forth between the gallery and darkroom several times after each shot. Most roll-film backs are also designed to accommodate sheet film.

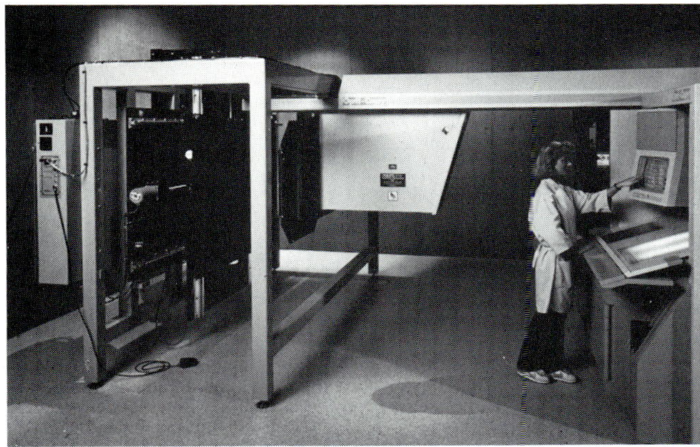

Courtesy Polychrome Systems, Inc.

Opti-Copy Imposer® multiple imaging camera.

Step-and-repeat camera backs. The step-and-repeat camera back has a special mechanism that shifts the film vertically and horizontally in relation to the image axis. A graphic arts camera equipped with a step-and-repeat back is also called a multi-imaging, or imposing, camera because it produces an fully imposed signature on one piece of film from several single-page transmission or reflection originals. In other words, a final-size negative or positive that has all image elements in the proper printing position, effectively combining camera work with film assembly.

Flashing Lamps

A flashing lamp consists of an incandescent light bulb in a housing that produces a uniform and concentrated source of illumination to expose the original copy. This lamp is placed on the copyboard side of the camera lens, inside the bellows of the camera, or on the wall or ceiling of the darkroom.

Darkroom flashing lamps must provide a broad source of illumination. They are simpler in design than those mounted on the camera. Since the film and contact screen are held on the camera back by vacuum, the camera back is opened to the loading position to make the flash exposure. Roll-film cameras must have a flashing lamp that is mounted on the side of the lens or in the bellows.

Camera Capabilities

Today's cameras are microprocessor controlled and may have any or all of the following features:

- Multichannel programmable memory to store exposure information about the various films used
- Built-in exposure computer that calculates exposures for line and halftone negatives or positives
- Pushbutton-operated autofocusing system
- On-line reflection/transmission densitometer used to read the minimum highlight and maximum shadow densities and transfer this information to the camera
- Built-in light integrator to correct exposure regardless of light level and voltage fluctuations
- Error messages that alert the operator to recommended corrective actions
- Calculation of reproduction percentages

Some cameras also have a defocusing device to prevent moire´ patterns on rescreened halftones. Reproduction percentages can be be specified in increments as small as 0.01% on some systems.

Microprocessors are integral components of high-resolution laser scanning devices as well. These devices electronically read photographs and line art and record the image as digital information. They also record the full range of gray levels from the light grays in the highlight areas to the dark grays in the shadows. The images scanned into the camera are recorded on film or paper, or the data is sent to a computer where the image is merged with text. Operators can select negative or positive, right- or wrong-reading, and line or halftone images as output. To produce special effects, such as posterizations, adjust the electronic signals.

Exposure Control Units

To get the best results in photographic reproductions, exposure duration must be controlled and processing techniques made consistent.

Timers. A timer is a clocklike device connected to the shutter and lights of a graphic arts camera or to the light source for a contact printing frame. It is used control exposures. Many cameras have built-in keyboard-operated timers.

Light Integrator. A light integrator is a control device that compensates for voltage fluctuations by measuring the actual amount of light falling on the copy area. The operator sets it for the number of light units required for a given film exposure. A photocell, which is mounted on the copyboard, measures the units of light falling on the copy area. When the set number of light units has fallen on the photoelectric cell, a relay is activated, sending an electronic signal to the timing mechanism. The timing mechanism automatically turns off the light source and closes the shutter on the graphic arts camera. Many light integrators also make calculations based on the density values of the copy.

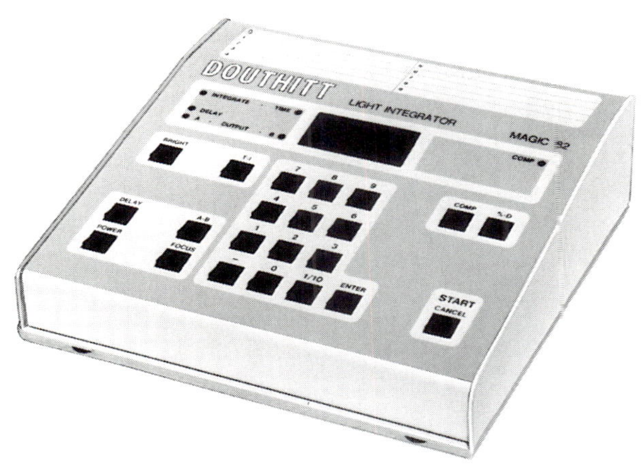

Courtesy Douthitt, Inc.

Light integrator.

A light integrator provides more consistent control of because it counts light not time. With both integrators and timers, the exposure length is determined by making and evaluating exposure tests with the materials to be used.

Electronic exposure control systems use light integrators connected to computers that calculate and monitor the amount of light needed for exposures. Some computers take into account other process variables, including reciprocity failure factors of film, limits of the screen in use, magnification ratio, processor compensation, and camera flare. Systems with memory banks store programs for different films and screens, allowing the camera operator to quickly select the appropriate specifications for the material being used.

Light integrators are also used with point-source lamps on contact printing frames. The photocell is usually mounted on the glass. Contact printing frames without light integrators use voltage regulators to provide exposure control, although tests have shown that integrators are more accurate.

A typical light integrator unit used to measure flash exposures has four low-intensity lamps mounted within the camera bellows near the lens. The unit incorporates a tuning device that allows the computer to be programmed to all conditions, such as flare and reciprocity failure.

Contact Printing

Contact printing is a photomechanical process in which camera-produced films or other forms of transparent or translucent (transmission) originals are exposed in contact with sensitized materials, producing same-size line, halftone, and continuous-tone negatives, positives, and duplicates.

Contact Printing Frames

A **contact printing frame** is the device that holds the imaged and sensitized materials together under pressure. It is also sometimes referred to as a **vacuum frame.** Glass-covered; acetate overlay; or glassless (open-faced) vacuum frames may be used, depending on the size and nature of the contacting requirements.

Glass-covered vacuum frames. The glass-covered contact printing frame is the most common one used in lithography. It consists of a large, heavy, metal base connected to an electrically operated vacuum pump. The frame has a glass cover hinged to the back of the base, which is covered by a rubber blanket. Materials to be contacted are placed on this blanket, the glass cover is closed, and the vacuum is turned on. As air leaves the space between the blanket and the cover, the blanket rises upward and forces the contacting materials together after which an exposure is made.

Drawdown time is the interval required for the air to leave the vacuum frame. The drawdown is somewhat longer with glass-covered frames, but the contact is the closest of all the systems. With any vacuum system, it is important that no air leaks exist. An air leak affects the contact between materials and, in turn, the quality of the reproductions. If possible, locate the vacuum pump outside of the darkroom where it will not stir up dust and cause related problems.

Avoid other problems, such as pinholes, in reproductions by using lint-free tissues and nonstreaking spray cleaner to keep the glass clean. Check the cover before each exposure to make sure no opaque tape residue or dirt particles are present on the underside of the glass. In addition, take care that register pins do not scratch or break the glass.

Acetate overlay vacuum frames. An acetate overlay frame also has a base and a hinged cover and uses vacuum pressure to hold originals in contact with sensitized materials. However, the flexible acetate overlay, which may not require a blanket on the base, greatly reduces the weight of the printing frame. It also has the advantage of

quick drawdown time. When the overlay sheet becomes dirty, it can be replaced quickly and cheaply.

Glassless (open-faced) vacuum frames. A glassless, or open-faced, vacuum frame operates on the same principle as the vacuum printing frames described previously. In this case, the overlay is formed by clear film with a tape hinge and a window cut out for the image area, or the topmost (imaged) film serves as an overlay, providing the vacuum seal.

The window area in the clear overlay is cut slightly smaller than the film and contact materials to ensure a seal around them. It also aids in keeping the materials clean. A drawback to this method is the need to cut windows of different sizes for each film size.

Lamps for Contact Printing

Point light sources, broad, or diffused, sources, and high-intensity sources are the three exposure lamps used in contact printing.

Point light source. The point light source is a clear tubular bulb with a minute filament at the end of the tube. Its modified housing has a small aperture (opening) for light to pass through or may be tubular in shape. Both designs cause the light rays to travel in a parallel path, resulting in less undercutting and improved resolution.

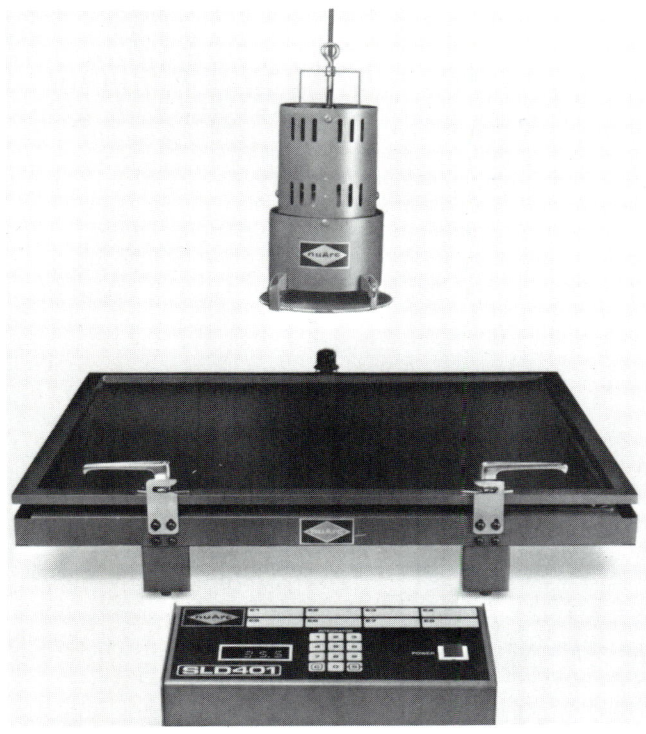

Courtesy nuArc Company

Glass-covered contact printing frame.

The most popular lamps for contacting, point light sources are ideal for ensuring dot-for-dot quality and have been designed not to scatter light. Attaching a filter holder to the lamp housing makes this light source even more versatile. The primary drawback to using point light sources is their tendency to detect dust, dirt, and lint and record these imperfections on the reproduction.

Broad (diffused) light sources. A broad, or diffused, light source undercuts the dust on glass printing frames or acetate overlays to lessen the number of pinholes on a reproduction. Its light scattering capabilities may make it effective in eliminating dust but also prevent it from producing the high-quality emulsion-to-base reproductions created with point light sources. Yet dot-for-dot quality is possible when contacting emulsion-to-emulsion. This light source is often used to alter line widths and dot sizes—spreads and chokes—in the contacting process.

High-intensity light sources. A high-intensity light source exposes special contact materials that are handled in normal room light. A quartz-iodine lamp is an example of a high intensity source. It is mounted so that it swings beneath the point light source when needed.

Basic Contacting Procedures

1. Place the sheet of sensitized material in the center of the vacuum frame with the emulsion side facing the light source.

2. Place the negative, positive, or assembled flat over the sensitized material with the emulsion facing down toward the emulsion of the sensitized material. Be sure to punch the original and sensitized material and place them on register pins to achieve accurate register.

3. Close the frame and turn on the vacuum. Adjust the pressure if needed. The materials must be in uniform contact with no air present before the exposure can be made.

4. Expose the sensitized material with a light source matched to the materials being used. (The correct exposure is determined in advance by making a series of tests.)

5. Turn off the vacuum, and remove and process the exposed material.

6. Examine the results and check the quality.

In most cases, materials are contact-printed emulsion-to-emulsion, as previously described. However, there are times when it is necessary to expose through the base of the sensitized or imaged materials to achieve the proper image orientation on during contacting.

Determining the Correct Exposure

Before production can begin, exposure, or calibration, tests are performed and repeated periodically to determine if contacting conditions have remained constant. The correct exposure reproduces an accurate image with line weights and dot sizes that have not changed.

One method of determining the correct exposure involves bracketing exposures using the camera-produced original as the standard. In the second method, the camera operator brackets exposures on a resolution guide and a step tablet then uses them as a standard with which to compare results. The third method uses a projection exposure indicator as the original copy.

Note: The correct exposure for emulsion-to-emulsion contacting will not necessarily be the correct exposure for contacting emulsion to base, or exposing through an overlay sheet, or with a new bulb when the old printing lamp bulb is replaced. Frequent, careful testing allows more control of the contacting process.

Calibrating with a camera or contact original. Select a good line or halftone negative or positive, or a uniform screen tint as the test copy for this procedure. Use a line image as test copy when the job involves nothing but line work. A large halftone with good highlight and shadow dot structures or a line-and-halftone image is used for tests of line and halftone work.

After selecting the test object, follow these steps:

1. Place the test object over the sensitized material. Be sure to place the materials together in the proper orientation (emulsion-to-emulsion or emulsion-to-base). Turn on and adjust the vacuum and allow time for good drawdown (perfect contact).

2. Select an interval of time to be used for the exposure test and determine the number of intended exposures. As an example, use an interval of 5 sec. and expose the film six times. This results in a calibration test from 5 to 30 sec., with the actual exposures being 5, 10, 15, 20, 25, and 30 sec.

3. Place a large opaque masking sheet (cardboard, black opaque paper, or any opaque material) over most of the contacting materials, leaving a portion uncovered. Try to envison where each exposure will be made, or place tape on the backing sheet or glass to help position the masking sheet. Set the timer or light integrator for the selected exposure interval and make the exposure while holding the mask in place.

4. After the first exposure, move the mask about the same distance and repeat the exposure. Repeat this procedure until the number of desired exposures has been completed. The mask is removed completely for the last exposure.

5. Process the exposed photographic material under controlled conditions. If the processing is not done correctly, the exposure data is not valid.

6. Examine the processed contact and select the step that best duplicates or gives the exact reverse in value of the original test object. The exposure that produced the best stepped-off area on the contact is the correct exposure for the job. If the correct area seems to be between steps, the test must be repeated using a finer increment for the exposure interval.

7. Produce a sample contact using the exposure time selected from the test. Any differences that result from exposing the film for the full duration instead of giving it several "bursts" of illumination will be readily apparent. Check the results by comparing the contact to the original, adjusting the exposure if necessary to eliminate errors.

Variations of the step-off method. The continuous-exposure method and the slotted mask method are two accurate variations of the stop-and-step-off method previously described. The **continuous exposure method** gives each area the full exposure in one burst, not a series of short bursts, because the exposure lamp runs continuously for the length of the longest exposure. After each exposure interval, the mask is moved forward and held in place for the length of the next exposure and so forth It is difficult to move the mask at the exact instant desired since the lamp operates continuously.

The **slotted-mask method** is time-consuming but most exacting. The object is to create a mask that is 2½ times the length of the film and 1½ times its width. Cut a rectagular slot in the center of the mask, making sure the length of the slot is slightly greater than the short dimension of the film and the width is equal to the stepping distance. Next, cut a piece of masking tape, place it on the backing sheet, and mark it with the selected number of stepping distances. The tape helps in positioning the mask.

With this method, each area of the film receives a single exposure. The light-sensitive material and

the original are butted against the masking tape. After the vacuum is turned on and drawdown is complete, the slot is aligned over one end of the original and the exposures are made in the same manner described previously for the step-off method.

Calibrating with a contact control guide. A resolution target, or guide, and a step tablet (also referred to as a step wedge, sensitivity guide, or transparent gray scale) are widely used as quality control devices in the contacting area. Many contact control guides combine the resolution target and step tablet as one single guide.

A **resolution target** consists of groups of adjacent light and dark lines spaced closely together, with the groupings becoming progressively smaller in size. The resolution target can be purchased as a film negative or film positive.

A **step tablet** is a scale of varying densities, with each step numbered. Some step tablets have a 0.15 density change between each step to make the scale a more convenient tool for exposure tests. The step tablet is sensitive to small changes in exposure and processing conditions and provides a quick indication of the quality of contacts. The step tablet results are compared with the test contact and, if the exposure is correct, the same step on the scale will be dropped out, meaning that it will be solid density while the next step is only slightly dense.

There are also many contact control guides designed with line and halftone dots of varying sizes and widths. These devices feature negative and positive images on the same film guide to help the contact operator make an accurate judgment.

The resolution target or contact control guide can be used in several ways to determine correct exposures. One method uses the control guide to refine the calibration exposure after the approximate exposure has been determined from an earlier step-off test. A second method uses the resolution target or contact guide as the original copy. The steps are the same for both methods:

1. Strip a control guide and step tablet into the center of a long sheet of opaque masking material. The masking sheet should be twice the length of the photographic material.

2. Position the stripped-up control guide over one end of the photographic material. Check the emulsion orientation between materials. Decide where the control guide will be placed for each exposure and mark the stepping distance on tape placed on the backing sheet. The sensitized material should be pin-registered. With the materials in position, turn on the vacuum and allow time for good drawdown.

3. Select a series of exposure times for the calibration test. A different exposure time is used at each location on the photographic material. Make the first exposure.

4. After the first exposure is complete, turn off the vacuum and move the mask to the next position. Be sure not to overlap images. Turn on the vacuum and make the second exposure.

5. Turn off the vacuum and move the mask to the next position. Apply the vacuum and make the next exposure. This step is repeated until all exposure have been made.

Note: Place extra strips of masking paper over any areas of the sensitized film that cannot be covered by the stripped-up mask.

6. Process the exposed photographic material.

7. Examine the processed contact and select the image that gives the exact reverse in value of the contact control guide. Check line images, halftone images, and the resolution target and compare them to the original. The image with the best resolution received the correct exposure.

8. If the correct exposure falls between two exposed images, a second test using smaller exposure increments may be necessary.

Production can begin after the correct exposure has been selected from the test results. The control guide can now be used as a standard to maintain quality control in the contact process. Place the guide alongside the original during contacting if there is room, or strip it into a flat with the other originals to be contacted. The quality of each contact can now be determined by checking the control guide on the contacts.

Calibration using a projection exposure indicator. A projection exposure indicator is a device widely used in making exposure determinations for continuous-tone prints. A description for this procedure follows.

Place the light-sensitive material, a uniform tint negative that has about a 20% or 30% dot value, and the exposure indicator into the vacuum frame. Close the frame and apply the vacuum. Use a single exposure of a standard time interval, such as 60 sec., then process the film. The developer, developing time, and conditions recommended on the instruction sheet furnished with the film are used for processing.

After processing, examine the film with a magnifier. The segment that produces the best-developed image is indicated by a number that states the

correct exposure time in seconds when a 60-sec. exposure is used for the test. If a different exposure is used, divide that exposure by 60 and multiply by the number of the indicator to obtain the time.

Making Spreads and Chokes

Often it is necessary to **spread** (expand) or **choke** (shrink) an a line image without changing its overall dimensions on film. A spread is thicker than the original and a choke is thinner. Image thickness may be changed to permit a small amount of color overlap on the press or to create a reverse or other special effects. In planning for this process, remember that only a negative can make a spread and only a positive can make a choke. At the same time, it is possible to produce, either directly or indirectly, a choked negative, a choked positive, a spread negative, or a spread positive.

Spacer/diffusion sheeting method. This procedure for creating spreads or chokes uses a sheet of clear or matte film or thin white (tracing) paper as spacer material and opalized glass or plastic, drafting film, or translucent plastic as diffusion sheeting. All of these materials effectively scatter light.

Spacers or diffusion sheeting may be used separately or in combination. Large spreads and chokes are created by using the materials together; smaller ones by using diffusion sheeting alone, although exposure times will increase. The amount of spread or choke is also dependent on the number of spacer sheets used, their thickness, and whether or not the material is clear or matte.

A step-by-step procedure for the spacer/diffusion sheeting method follows:

1. Clean the film original.

2. Turn out the room lights and then activate the darkroom safelights.

3. Place a piece of unexposed film in the contact printing frame, emulsion side up.

4. Cover this film with the spacer.

5. Place the film original, base down, over the spacer(s) in the contact frame.

6. Close the contact frame.

7. Place a diffusion filter in the filter holder on the light source or a piece of diffusion sheeting over the frame. The spread or choke will appear more "even" when the light is more diffuse.

8. Make the exposure.

9. Develop, stop, fix, and dry.

Specially designed **image modification systems** can make spreads and chokes with more predictability and uniformity. One system uses controlled orbital motion, or the circular vibration of the filmholder. The distance that the filmholder moves determines the amount of spread or choke. No diffusing materials are used, and the exposure is kept constant by a light integrator.

Controls used in making spreads and chokes. Consider these factors when evaluating how much of a spread or choke is necessary.

- Printing inks. The printing image can overlap more when there is a greater tonal difference among printing inks.
- Characteristics of type. A thicker letter, e g. boldface type, can usually be given more of a spread or choke. Script and ornate serif typefaces tolerate very little in terms of spreads and chokes. Large amounts tend to change the shape of these type characters.
- Press register. Press register is the most important of these factors to consider. The amount of overlap is determined by how consistent the press is in maintaining image register. Less overlap corresponds to high register accuracy.

Compare the degree of spread or choke indicated by these factors with a calibrated plant standard, such as a **spread-and-choke guide.** This guide specifies the amount of spread or choke needed and indicates the actual amount produced.

Line Photography

Line photography is used to reproduce black-and-white copy that does not require the use of a halftone screen. The steps for completing this procedure are:

1. Inspect the copy and scale it if necessary.

2. Place it on the camera copyboard.

3. Set the camera.

4. Load the film.

5. Expose it.

6. Remove the exposed film from the camera.

7. Process it.

8. Inspect the processed film to make sure the results are accurate.

Scaling Copy

If the copy has not been scaled during design, the camera operator will have to scale it to the proper

reproduction size before any additional work can be completed. Use a **proportion scale** to calculate enlargement or reduction percentages or determine the reproduction percentage by dividing the original copy size into the reproduction (or negative) size and multiplying by 100. (For detailed procedures on scaling see Chapter 6, "Art and Copy Preparation.") After scaling, organize the copy according to quality.

Examine the color, background, and line quality of an original before reproduction. Some colored copy and copy with a poor range of contrast requires the use of filters. In the latter case, using contrast filters improves the background density on the finished negative.

Placing Copy on the Copyboard

Most copyboards are marked in some manner to help the camera operator position copy. The three most common markings are rectangles (corresponding to the standard film sizes), diagonals, and centerlines. The diagonals and centerlines are usually subdivided into inch or half-inch increments.

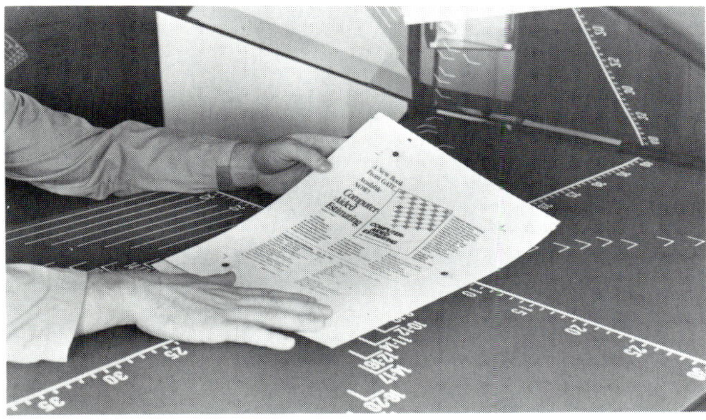

Placing copy on the camera's copyboard.

Setting the Camera

Setting the camera involves choosing the correct lens aperture, lighting angles, filters, and proper reproduction size. For line work, the most common lens openings (f-stops) used for same size reproductions (100%) are f/16 and f/22. A process lens has a **diaphragm chart** mounted on its lensboard. It contains reproduction scales for all of the f-stops and allows the camera operator to select the appropriate aperture for the job.

Filters. Filters used for black-and-white line photography increase the contrast of the original and render certain colors monochromatic, thus holding or dropping them on the finished negative. Contrast filters are used extensively on pencil drawings and originals with grayed or yellowed backgrounds. Comprising the yellow and light orange series, these filters increase absorption of the blue range of the spectrum, thereby increasing contrast on orthochromatic or panchromatic film.

Filters for Black-and-White Work

To Photograph	Use Pan Filter	Use Ortho Filter
Blue as black	Red or orange	Blue
Blue as white	Blue	Blue
Blue-green as white	Blue or green	Blue or green
Blue-green as black	Red	-------
Green as black	Red	-------
Orange as black	Blue	Blue
Orange as white	Red or orange	-------
Violet as white	Blue	Blue
Violet as black	Green	Deep yellow
Yellow as black	Blue	Blue
Yellow as white	Red or orange	Yellow or orange
Yellow-green as white	Green	Green or yellow
Yellow-green as black	Blue	Blue

Film/filter chart.

Lighting angle. A lighting angle of 45° at a distance of 3 ft. (1 m) from the copyboard is considered normal. Reducing the angle lessens the light intensity on the copyboard. Less intense, or "flatter," lighting is used to increase the coverage of larger copy and to eliminate "hot spots" or glare on the copyboard when making extreme enlargements. Increasing the light angle gives much greater intensity on the copyboard but is seldom advisable.

Determining the Basic Exposure

Determining basic exposure for a line negative is important because the high gamma, or the steep slope, of the characteristic curve limits the range of exposures that will faithfully reproduce the light areas of the copy with maximum density and the black areas with minimum density. This is caused by the high contrast emulsions of standard ortho films. The best exposure in line photography, the one that produces a quality reproduction, is determined by using a step-off or test strip exposure test similar to those described under the section about contact printing or by using the gray scale method.

Step-off/test strip method. The step-off or test strip method is used to determine basic exposure time by making a series of exposures on film and then choosing the exposure that provides the best results. Here are the procedures:

1. Set the camera for same-size (100%) reproduction with the lens wide open. Place a piece of sharp line copy (8- or 10-point type matter) on the copyboard and arrange the lights at a 45° angle (standard distance), with even illumination across the film plane.

2. Focus the image on the ground glass, with the lens set at two f-stops from wide open. Cut a strip of film to approximately 3×10 in. (75×250 mm). Place it horizontally on the camera's vacuum filmholder, with the emulsion facing the lens.

3. Make the first in a series of test exposures on this film by using a piece of 6×12 in. (150×300 mm) cardboard to cover up all but a narrow band on the right-hand section of the film. Expose this film for 32 seconds.

4. Move the cardboard to the left to uncover an additional area of film and expose the uncovered film for 16 seconds. Make the remaining test exposures by moving the cardboard mask to the left for each successive exposure. The result is a stepped strip recording exposures from 64 sec. to 1 sec.

5. After the exposed film is processed, inspect the negative with a magnifier and select the step (time) that produced a clear imageand maximum (black) background density. If the best exposure appears to be between steps, make a second series of exposures.

The procedure described above assumes constant developing conditions and continuous illumination. However, the intensity and color of the copyboard lights does not always remain constant. Using a light integrator ensures a constant exposure based upon light "units" rather than time.

Gray scale method. Including a reflection gray scale with the copy also allows the camera operator to determine the exposure time that will produce quality negatives. Place the gray scale in a nonimage area—in the center, between columns of type matter, or at the edge of the copy. (The negative gray scale can be masked out during image assembly.) After positioning the gray scale, follow these steps used to determine exposure time:

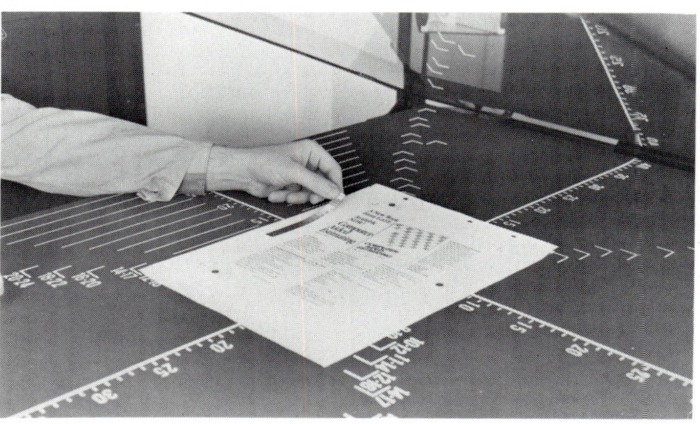

The gray scale method.

1. Set the camera for same-size (100%) reproduction and make several trial exposures on separate pieces of film, with each exposure for a different length of time.

2. Make five exposures: two for less, two for more, and one for the same basic exposure time determined by the test strip method. If a base time is not known, then make a series of exposures as was done with the test strip method. Note that it may be necessary to repeat these trial procedures using additional exposure times.

3. Process the test negative for the time and temperature recommended by the film manufacturer, keeping processing consistent.

4. Examine the gray scale image on each of the negatives. Select as the best the negative in which step 4 (on a 12-step gray scale) is developed to a dense black, with step 5 only slightly dense. Step 4 will be the aim point for normal copy.

Processing Exposed Film

During processing, the latent image is converted into a permanent visible image through the reduction process in a solution called a developer. The developing agent reduces the exposed silver halides to black metallic silver, and the fixer dissolves those unexposed and underdeveloped areas of the film, making the image permanent.

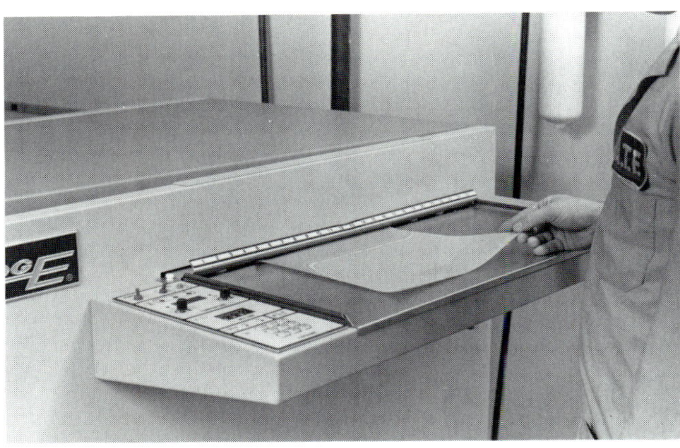

Processing film automatically.

Examining the Negatives

After development for about two minutes in an automatic processor, the film negative is inspected. The camera operator looks to see if it is under or overexposed. An underexposed continuous-tone negative, which is lower in contrast and density than a fully exposed negative, lacks shadow detail. Overexposed negatives are also lower than normal in contrast, but high in density and lacking highlight detail. High-contrast line negatives lose sharpness and detail when overexposed. If underexposed, the backgrounds of line negatives are not sufficiently opaque. Image sharpness is lost and print quality suffers.

Halftones with the Contact Screen

Halftone photography is the process by which continuous-tone copy is converted into a printable image. Most printing processes transfer a uniform color and density of ink to the substrate. However, continuous-tone copy consists of a gradation of tones; therefore, a single ink density appears as several shades.

Photographing continuous-tone copy through a contact halftone screen transforms the original into a printable image on film. The screen breaks up the continuous tones into tiny halftone dots that are equally spaced, center to center. The dot size varies according to the different amounts of light reflected by the tones of the original.

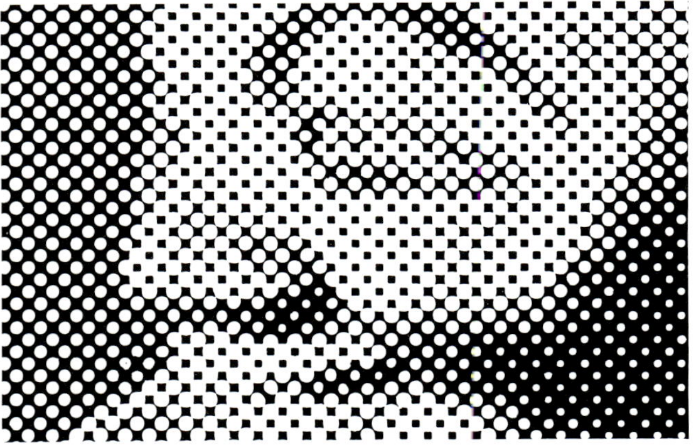

Enlarged halftone reproduction.

The printed image is composed of dots and the white space in between those dots. Dot of various sizes create the illusion of continuous tones. The unaided eye does not distinguish individual dots at a normal viewing distance. Wherever the dots are small and the area of white paper relatively large, the tones appear light. Large dots surrounded by small areas of white paper appear as darker tones.

The light grays in a black-and-white photograph are referred to as the **highlights;** the areas between the light and dark grays as the **midtones;** and the darker areas as the **shadows.** The halftone dots that imitate these tones are referred to by the same names.

The Contact Screen

The **contact screen** is a flexible piece of processed film designed for use in contact with unexposed film. Tiny vignetted dots on the screen gradually vary in density from center to edge. The varying density, or light-blocking strength, of each dot is responsible for the dot formation on film.

Shadow areas of photographs reflect a small amount of light, which penetrates the least dense areas of the vignetted dots on the contact screen. Very small dots appear on the negative. Highlight areas of photographs reflect a great amount of light, which penetrates all but the most dense areas of the vignetted dots. Large black dots appear on the negative. Midtone areas reflect a moderate amount of light, creating dots that vary in size on the negative.

Contact halftone screens are easy to use with any camera, enlarger, or contact frame equipped with a vacuum back. A wide variety is available for specific applications, such as obtaining a certain tone reproduction or dot structure.

Nevertheless, the density range and exposure factor may vary from screen to screen and manufacturer to manufacturer. With age, the density of the dot-forming pattern may also change and alter the screen's reproduction capabilities.

Keep contact screens free of dust and away from extreme humidity. Handle them very carefully because they are easily scratched and stained.

With a contact screen, dots are produced on film by light passing through insufficiently dense areas of the vignetted dot pattern. The vignette blocks the transmission of some low-intensity illumination, but will not block high-intensity illumination.

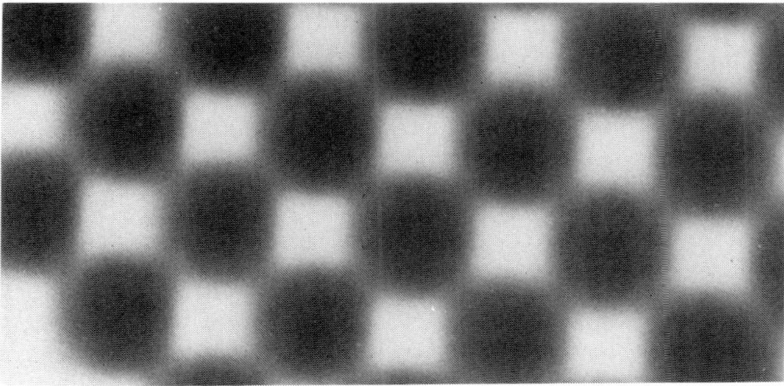

Enlarged halftone screen showing vignetted dots.

The film material receives up to three exposures—main (detail), flash (shadow), bump (highlight, or no-screen)—based on the contact screen's response to light. By combining two or more of these exposures, the camera operator can adjust dot sizes to produce a more accurate reproduction.

Main exposure. The **main exposure** is the light reflected/transmitted from continuous-tone copy through the screen. It reproduces most of the image detail as dots of various sizes. The length of this exposure is determined by examining the minimum highlight density that still contains image detail on the continuous-tone original.

The three halftone gray scales and the corresponding negatives printed in the next column show the effect of different main exposure times on tonal reproduction, i.e., the positioning of dots of various sizes on the reproduction. For gray scale A, the exposure time was equated with the minimum highlight density to produce a 5% dot in the 0.05 density step. In successive density steps, the dot sizes increase until a solid density (no dot pattern) is achieved. Gray scale B has had a shorter exposure, with a 20% dot in the 0.05 density step. In this case, insufficient amounts of light passed through the openings in the vignetted dot pattern, resulting in dots that were too large on the printed reproduction. Gray scale C has had a very long exposure, and the 0.05 density step is totally clear, with the 5% dot lying in the 0.35 density step. Because too much light penetrated the vignetted dot pattern, it produced a solid density on the negative in the 0.05 density step.

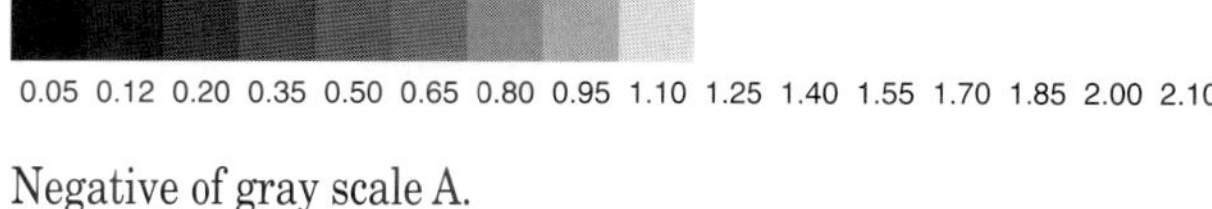

Negative of gray scale A.

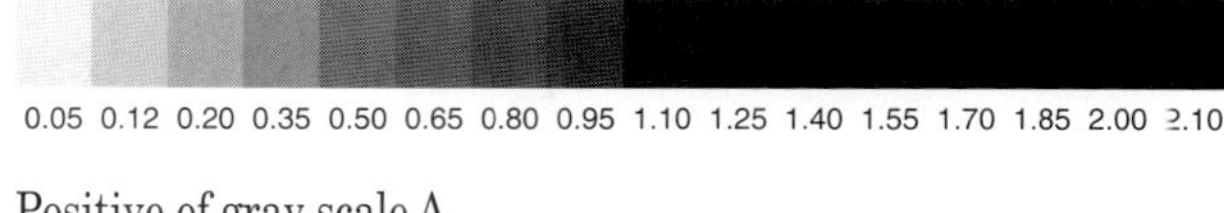

Positive of gray scale A.

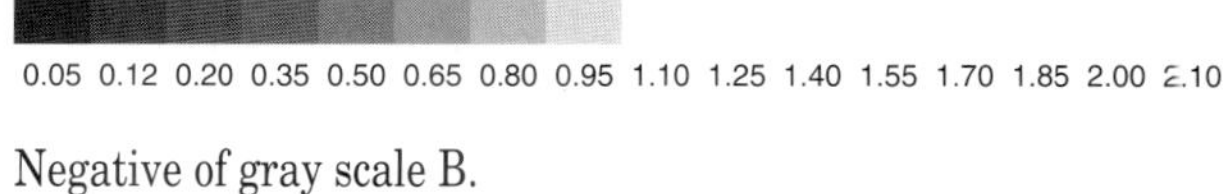

Negative of gray scale B.

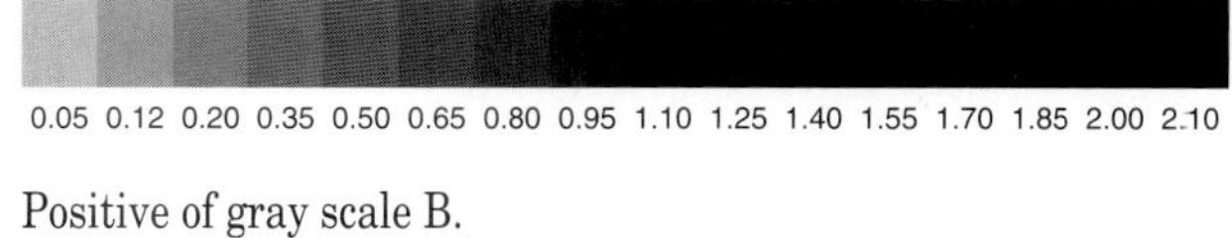

Positive of gray scale B.

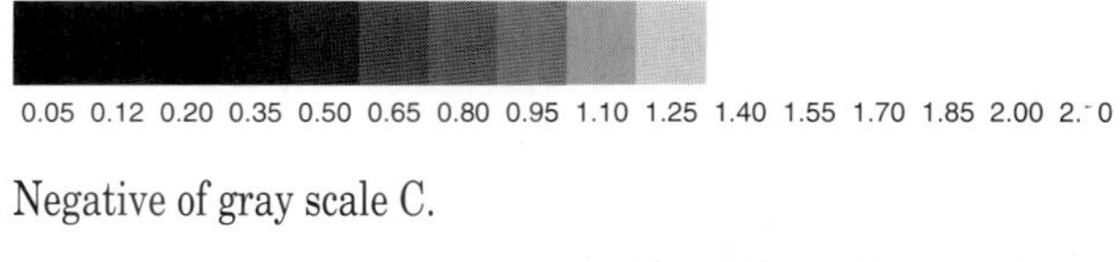

Negative of gray scale C.

0.05 0.12 0.20 0.35 0.50 0.65 0.80 0.95 1.10 1.25 1.40 1.55 1.70 1.85 2.00 2.10

Positive of gray scale C.

Gray scale reproductions.

Note: A perfect reproduction of the gray scale does not guarantee the optimum reproduction of the continuous-tone image. Sometimes certain portions of the tonal scale must be accentuated in order to produce a more pleasing reproduction. In such cases, certain tonal regions of the gray scale may not print, may print as a solid, or may print with dot sizes larger or smaller than normal.

Screen range. The **screen range** is the density range that a particular screen can reproduce. In other words, it is the density difference between the maximum and minimum tones that are reproduced.

Basic density range. The screen's **basic density range,** or **BDR,** is expressed as the difference between the density of the tone producing the smallest printable dot and the tone producing the largest nonsolid dot. These density values are obtained by comparing the critical halftone dot sizes on the print and the film with the corresponding tonal values on the original.

In most printing plants, it is not possible or practical to make a press test to find the BDR of each and every screen. Instead, the camera operator uses a shortcut method based on generally acceptable dot sizes for a given printing process/substrate combination. The press department supplies the camera operator with these specifications.

Here is a simple method for determining the BDR of the screen using these dot sizes:

1. Place a reflection stepped gray scale, preferably calibrated with density values for each step, on the camera copyboard. The camera should be set for 100%, or a same-size, reproduction. **Note:** Use a transmission stepped gray scale to find the BDR when making halftones from transmission copy on an enlarger, contact frame, or camera.

Read all noncalibrated as well as precalibrated stepped gray scales with a densitometer. Write the density values next to the corresponding gray scale step. This calibration procedure makes it possible to read density values directly from the gray scale. Recalibrate the gray scale frequently, especially when a new densitometer is used.

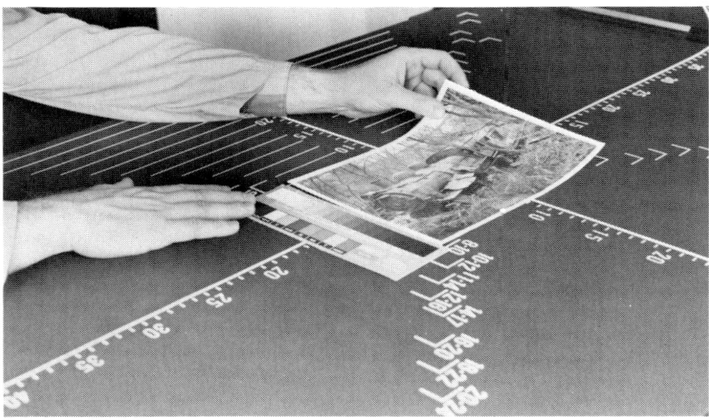

Placing the gray scale on the camera copyboard.

2. Place a sheet of high-contrast lith film on the filmholder, emulsion toward the copy and activate the vacuum.

3. Cover the film with a selected halftone contact screen; contact must be emulsion-to-emulsion.

4. Smooth the entire surface of the contact screen with a roller squeegee or chamois.

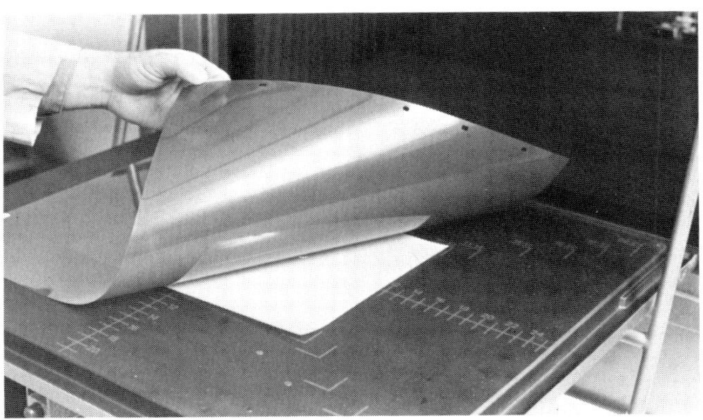

Covering the film, emulsion-to-emulsion with the contact screen.

5. Expose the film to the copy. The exposure time will have to be selected arbitrarily or from past exposure tests. Record the time as the "basic main exposure time" for future reference.

6. Process the film.

7. Locate the smallest highlight dot that is still printable, based on the printing variables. Use established standards for dot size.

8. Determine the original image density responsible for this dot size and then record the highlight density found.

9. Next, using standards for dot size, locate the largest shadow dot that will print as a dot and not as a solid mass. Determine the original shadow density corresponding to the shadow dot and record the shadow density value.

10. To find the BDR, subtract the highlight density from the shadow density.

Flash exposure. If the screen and the original photograph have approximately equal density ranges, varying by no more than 0.10 density units, it should be possible to satisfactorily reproduce the photograph in halftone form (carrying the desired highlight and shadow dots) with just a main exposure. The only requirement is that the exposure time is appropriate for the minimum highlight density that contains image detail.

It is much more common for the copy and screen to vary considerably in density range. In such cases, a simple main exposure will not carry all the detail of the original. The most common copy/screen density relationship is one in which the copy has a greater density range than the screen can produce with the main exposure.

With excess copy density, the screen's tonal reproduction range must be lengthened by the use of the **flash,** or **"shadow flash," exposure.** This nonimage exposure through the contact screen

creates nonsolid printing dots in the shadow area of the negative. (The contact screen must not be moved between the main and flash exposures and the flash exposure should immediately precede or follow the main.)

The usual flashing mechanism is a safelight lamp housing fitted with a light yellow 00 safelight filter and a 15-watt light bulb. Use an exposure timer and a controlled voltage line regulator, separate from the camera, to ensure the accuracy of the results. Mount the flashing mechanism on a darkroom wall or ceiling, 4–6 ft. (1–1.9 m) from the open camera back, or on the inside of the bellows.

When the screen's BDR is determined, the largest nonsolid printing halftone dot corresponds to an original image density (e.g., 1.50). Suppose that the maximum image density of the original was 2.00 instead and the largest nonsolid printing dot should be located there. The screen's range must be extended by 0.50 (2.00 – 1.50) density units to reproduce the maximum image density with any detail; that is, with a dot pattern.

The flash produces this dot in the 2.00 density step by shining a uniform light through the halftone screen. High-density areas of reflection copy reflect very little light. Thus, when the film is given a main exposure, insufficient amounts of light strike the screen, too little to produce small dots in the extreme shadows on the negative. The main exposure could be lengthened to produce these dots but the lightest highlight areas would receive too much light and appear as solid densities on the negative, with no detail produced.

A flash exposure added to a main exposure produces satisfactory highlight and shadow dots. The main exposure produces satisfactory highlights and density on the negative in the lower shadows. By using a flash exposure on the film/halftone screen combination, the additional density range is covered. The flash exposure penetrates the areas of lightest density on the vignetted halftone screen and produces small dots in the shadow areas of the negative. Only the shadows and upper midtone areas of the negative are affected by the flash exposure. Highlight dots change very little because they receive a lot of light.

To determine the average flash exposure required for specific equipment, proceed as follows:

1. Place an unexposed sheet of lith film on the camera back and cover it with a contact screen.

2. Make a series of "stepped" exposures with the flash lamp. Usually, a series of 3-sec. steps covering a range from 3 to 30 sec. will be sufficient to find the optimum exposure time. If the optimum exposure time is less than 10 sec., reduce the light intensity level and run another set of test exposures.

3. Process the test sheet.

4. Inspect this test to determine the exposure time that produced the smallest negative shadow dot that will print.

With average copy and camera conditions, 50–60% of the basic shadow flash exposure is required to put a 10% dot in the shadow area.

Bump (no-screen) exposure. On occasion, the screen's BDR exceeds the copy's density range, meaning that the screen range must be compressed. One way to do this is to add a brief bump, or no-screen, exposure to the main exposure. The bump, which mainly affects the highlights, compresses the screen range in a much different way from that of a shorter main exposure, and, since the halftone screen is not used, it produces no dots.

Shortening the main exposure would reduce the apparent density range of the screen, but the dots in the highlights would be much too large; that is, flat with very little detail. A **bump exposure** briefly allows the full intensity of light reflected from highlights to produce density on a halftone. The technique selectively superimposes most of the light from the exposure on the negative highlight dots (a latent image already heavily exposed). Relatively large (70%) highlight dots spread and become even larger, approaching solid density on the negative. Less light falls on the midtones, so only a small change in dot size takes place and almost no light falls on the shadow dot. A bump exposure thus produces a full range of halftone dots from copy with a short density range. A highlight bump of 5–10% of the main exposure is about average for most camera/copy conditions. A proper highlight bump will hardly change the size of shadow dots.

Find the "percent-bump/density compression" by making a series of bump exposures as follows:

1. If using a camera, place a calibrated stepped reflection gray scale on the copyboard. (To produce halftones by contact printing or with an enlarger, change these directions to suit the equipment.)

2. Position the film and contact screen on the camera back.

3. Make a main exposure that places a 70% negative dot in the first step of the gray scale.

4. Open the camera back, carefully remove the contact screen while leaving the film in its exact position, then close the camera back.

5. Give the copy an unscreened exposure that is 2% the length of the main exposure.

6. Remove the film and process it.

7. Repeat the procedure four times using the same main exposure but with a different percent bump: 5%, 10%, 15%, 20%.

8. Evaluate the density compression corresponding to each bump exposure by determining the exact integrated dot density in the first gray scale step of the halftone made with only a main exposure; establishing the exact integrated dot density in the first step of all halftones made with combined bump and main exposures; and finding the density differences between the dots in the halftone made with only a main exposure and those made with a bump and a main combined.

9. Plot a graph of percent bump versus density range compression. Read values, other than those determined in the test, directly from the graph as long as the percent bump is between 2% and 20%.

Classification of Contact Screens

Contact screens should be selected to suit specific applications. They are available in gray and magenta. A gray contact screen may be used for black-and-white work as well as to photograph color originals. Magenta contact screens cannot be used for color work because the magenta dye absorbs certain colors of the spectrum.

Dot shape. Dot shape is very important in reference to tonal reproduction. Dots may be square, round, and elliptical, among other special shapes.

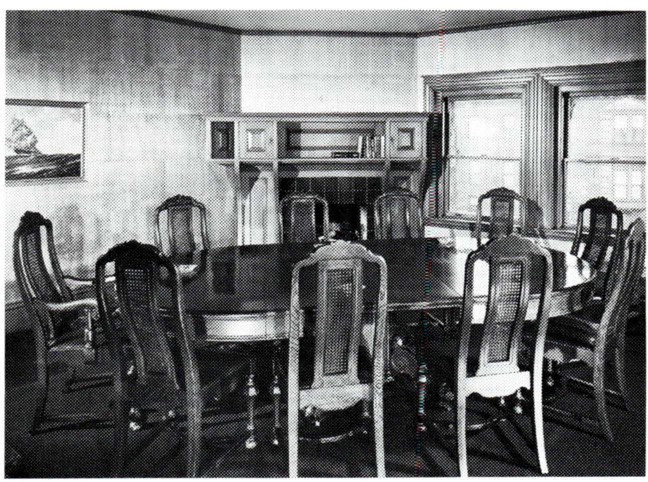

Halftone made with an 85-line screen.

A dot's shape is most easily recognized when its size percentage is 50%. At 50%, a square-dot screen has the appearance of a checkerboard; round-dot screens produce a pin-cushion effect; and elliptical dots have a "chained" appearance. Multiple-dot screens are available in double- and triple-dot patterns and special effects screens are available in straight-line, wavy-line, concentric-circle, and mezzotint patterns. In every case, a test must be performed to find the optimum exposure conditions.

Screen angle. The **screen angle** is the gradient measured from the base of the screen to an imaginary line connecting a row of dots in a direction following the shortest distance between the dots. For black-and-white and other single-color reproductions, the screen angle should be 45°.

When multicolor halftones are printed, the screen angle must be different for each color. A moiré pattern results when the dots of one halftone overlap those of another. The screen angle dictates how objectionable this pattern is. Separating screen angles by 30° minimizes moiré. For example, place the dominant color, usually black, at the 45° angle, with the second color at 75°. If there is a third color, place it at 105°.

Screen ruling. Screen ruling describes the fineness of a screen as denoted by the number of halftone parts per unit length. It is measured along a line connecting the halftone parts in a direction following the shortest distance between them. Contact screens are available in a wide range of rulings extending from 40 lines/in. (16 lines/cm) to 300 lines/in. (117 lines/cm).

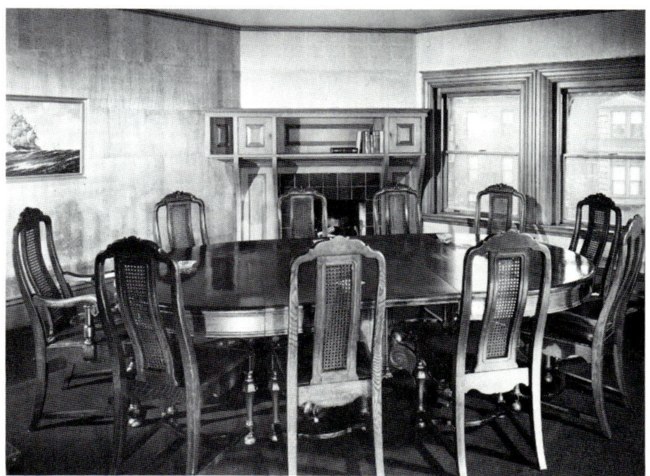

Halftone made with a 150-line screen.

Many special effects screens can only be assigned a relative description, such as fine, medium, and coarse, in terms of screen ruling. This classification is based on the density in a given area.

Consider the production variables, namely printing process, press speed, and substrate when selecting a screen ruling. The gravure process uses the finest screens; lithography and flexography use fine screens; and screen printing, coarse ones. Keep in mind that faster press speeds require the use of a somewhat coarser screen and that coarse- and medium-ruled screens are used with newsprint and other uncoated papers. Coated papers require fine-ruled screens. In addition, screen rulings should be fine enough that the unaided eye cannot distinguish individual dots at the intended viewing distance. For example, halftones for billboards are made with very coarse screens; posters, less coarse screens; newspapers, medium screens; and magazines, fine screens.

Making a Halftone with a Contact Screen

The following steps illustrate a typical procedure used to produce a halftone. Exposure times are determined using the BDR, flash, and bump data previously calculated and manual or electronic exposure calculators.

Note: Assume that the copy is a black-and-white photograph to be reproduced as a same-size halftone on a camera.

1. Clean the copyboard glass.

2. Center the copy on the copyboard. Place a gray scale alongside the copy. Copy should be surrounded by a black or neutral gray background to lessen flare.

3. Prepare the processor.

4. Set the camera for the reproduction percentage. Check the sharpness of the image on the ground glass.

There is no need to compensate for a change in the optical path of the light through the screen Adjust the camera light for even illumination whenever necessary.

5. Turn off the white room light in the darkroom, and turn on the safelight. Place the film on the vacuum back, emulsion out. Hold it in position, and turn on the vacuum.

6. Remove the contact screen from its box. Place it emulsion-to-emulsion over the piece of film lying on the vacuum back. The screen should be placed so that the resulting screen pattern is at a 45° angle.

7. Smooth the entire surface of the contact screen with a roller squeegee or chamois.

8. Swing the vacuum back, film, and screen into a position at a right angle to the flash lamp, then make the flash exposure.

9. After the flash exposure, swing the vacuum back into the closed position to receive the image exposure through the lens. Do not touch the flashed film or contact screen.

10. Make the main image exposure. The lens diaphragm should be set to the proper f-stop, and the exposure control unit (timer, light integrator) should be set to the calculated (or estimated) image exposure length.

11. Open the vacuum back and carefully remove the contact screen, placing it in its box. The vacuum must remain on during this procedure.

12. Close the vacuum back, and give the film a bump (no-screen) exposure to the original.

13. Open the vacuum back, turn off the vacuum, and remove the film.

14. Check and correct developer variables, then process the film.

If the first results are unsatisfactory, repeat the preceeding steps with new film, adjusting exposure and development.

Electronic Exposure Control

Electronic exposure calculators compute exposure times for specific screen range/copy density combinations, by considering factors, such as f-stop setting and reproduction size. Many can be programmed to compute main, flash, and bump exposures, and some have memory banks for different screens and processing conditions.

Handling Problem Copy

Copy with poor highlight detail, dark originals lacking in contrast, and gray originals with poor contrast and low maximum density are some examples of problem copy.

Copy lacking highlight detail has no printing dots in the extreme highlights. Printing dots and image detail will appear in these areas only if the main

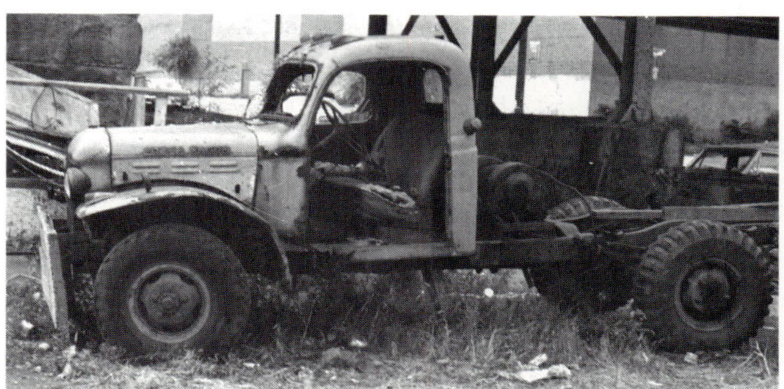

Copy lacking highlight detail.

exposure length is calculated according to the density of the white paper. The main exposure is usually shorter than the basic exposure , and a shorter exposure will keep the highlight dots open on the negative. Conversely, a film halftone with no dots in the highlights indicates overexposure.

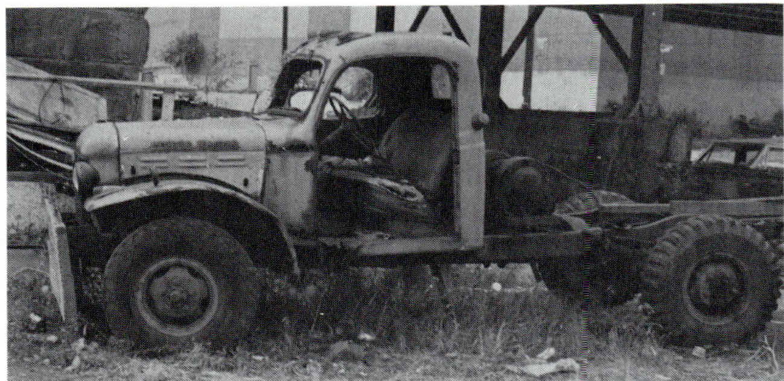

Copy lacking contrast.

Dark originals lacking contrast exhibit very little tonal separation and the equivalent of a 30% or 40% dot in the extreme highlights. Adjusting the exposures produces much smaller highlight dots. To accomplish this increase the main exposure according to the density of lightest highlight area, add a bump exposure, or combine the two.

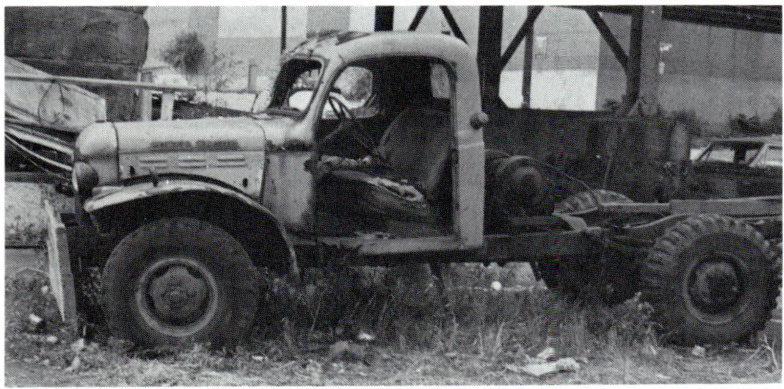

Gray copy with poor contrast and low maximum density.

If the photograph is gray, the shadows can be darkened by decreasing the main exposure. However, since shorter main exposures produce larger highlight dots on the print the film will require a long bump exposure. This no-screen exposure produces lighter highlights and compensates for the fact that the screen's density range exceeds that of the copy.

Dot Gain

The dots on a halftone image may increase in size when printed because of variations in presswork or dot fringe on the negative. Dot fringe is the area of minute density surrounding the edge of each dot on the halftone screen. As reproduced on a negative, the edge does not contain as much metallic silver as the core because it receives only a portion of the light that creates the core.

The width of this dot fringe is based on how the dot itself was made. Halftones shot directly in the camera have the most fringe in the shadow areas of negatives and the highlight areas of the positives. Dots created through contact printing will have very little fringe.

When a printing plate is created from halftone films with wide areas of dot fringe, a minor change in the exposure time can produce a substantial change in the dot size on the plate. The dots may look correct; however, considerable dot gain will be present when the plate is run on the press. This occurs as the fringe begins to take on ink, filling in the shadow detail.

Evaluating the Halftone Negative

In normal halftone work, development time for a particular emulsion and a given developer remains relatively constant. The dot size and the dot structure of the halftone image vary most with changes in exposure. Once the negative has been processed, the photographer must evaluate its highlight, midtone, and shadow areas to assess how well the desired image will reproduce on the printed page.

The highlight area. The highlight areas of the halftone negative contain the darkest tones that will produce positive dots in the 8–10% range. Smaller dots have poor structures that do not stand up well in platemaking. In addition, printed dots varying in size from the barest pinpoint to about a 5% value do not offer sufficient contrast with the blank paper stock.

The midtone area. The midtone segment of a halftone negative is an extremely critical area, because minor changes in exposure and development can create a considerable visual difference in the reproduction. The midtone area consists of dots that range from 30–70% in size. It is important to remember that the midtone area covers a fairly wide tonal range beyond the 50% dot.

The 50% dot marks the approximate dividing line between connected and unconnected dots, and this distinction or the lack thereof is an important visual factor. In the highlight area, a dot can vary a few percent in size and the difference is barely

noticed. However, when the percent change includes the range from an unconnected to a connected dot, the visual change is considerable.

The dots produced within this halftone range should cover all the tone values from 30–70% with a smooth, graduated change. A halftone negative should produce a positive with slightly smaller dots in the midtone area.

The shadow area. The shadow area on the halftone negative should show a series of dots ranging from the barest pinpoint to approximately a 30% dot. These dots, when converted to the final positive image, should reproduce a range from about 70% to almost 90%. Unfortunately, dot size on a negative or positive rarely reproduces as desired. The camera operator should produce a negative with an 8–10% dot in the dark shadow area. A dot smaller than this in the negative can create problems on press. This arrangement provides the best contrast and visual appearance on the final product. Evaluate the halftone carefully.

Special Effects Photography

Special-effects photography refers to the line conversion, tone-line technique, posterization, and duotone as well as other procedures that alter a normal continuous-tone black-and-white photographic print.

Used properly, these techniques present a different, often more aesthetically pleasing, interpretation of the original. Some of the techniques, like posterization, produce strongly graphic images, while techniques such as the duotone process can be used to stimulate new interest in an otherwise dull subject or to provide a reproduction that will more closely resemble the original.

Special photographic effects are not difficult to produce, but their mastery requires skill, creativity, and some artistic ability. Unlike the use of other photomechanical processes, merely executing the techniques correctly with little concern for suitability of the subject or aesthetic content will not produce a pleasing result.

Using the special-effect techniques requires some precautions. Do not overdo the effect. Overemphasizing the image to make it “more graphic” will only destroy the effectiveness of the technique. If the camera operator must try so hard to make the image work, evidently the photograph was a poor choice.

Choosing the proper art is one of the major problems in using special-effect techniques. The most common error is to use a photographic image that cannot stand on its own. Special effects are not meant to help save a poor photograph. To achieve good results, the camera operator must start with a decent photographic image.

Line Conversion Technique

The **line conversion technique** is a method used to convert a continuous-tone photograph into a form resembling a line illustration. It is sometimes referred to as a two-tone posterization. However, printers prefer to use the term line conversion.

This high-contrast reproduction, usually a black-on-white image with no intermediate tones of gray, maintains the essential shapes of the original image. The photographer can isolate an image element in a cluttered composition; create a number of different images from the same piece of copy; combine several images to produce a unique reproduction; or produce multiple images of the same subject. A line conversion can be made from a black-and-white continuous-tone print, a continuous-tone negative, or a color transparency.

Selecting the original. A normal-contrast (normal-key) photograph is a better choice for a line conversion than a photograph that is high in contrast because the normal-contrast print has a greater number of tonal areas. A print with a higher degree of contrast has fewer tones in the original and therefore limits image manipulation.

Another factor affecting the results of a line conversion is the sharpness of detail in the photograph. Large areas containing no distinguishable detail will produce large black or white areas on the line conversion.

Use caution when choosing portraits for the line conversion technique. Portraits are very difficult to control for good results, yet the printer is frequently expected to work from this copy. Lighting, the angle of the head, and the facial features will determine the effectiveness of portrait line conversion results. Portraits that do work well have been planned in advance so that they lend themselves to the line conversion technique.

The line conversion process. High-contrast lith film, processed in an infectious developer (i.e., A

and B developer), produces the line effect in this conversion technique. Exposing a continuous-tone photograph to lith film is equivalent to making a line negative, which has only two tones—density and no density. Consequently, the intermediate tones of gray in the photograph are eliminated.

Altering the length of exposure or development changes the dividing line between solid density and transparent image on the film. The object in the technique is to select the proper exposure that will produce the desired tone breaks. Shorter exposures break between light tones, and longer exposures break between darker tones on the original. Although the location of the break is affected by the length of development, do not use it as a control.

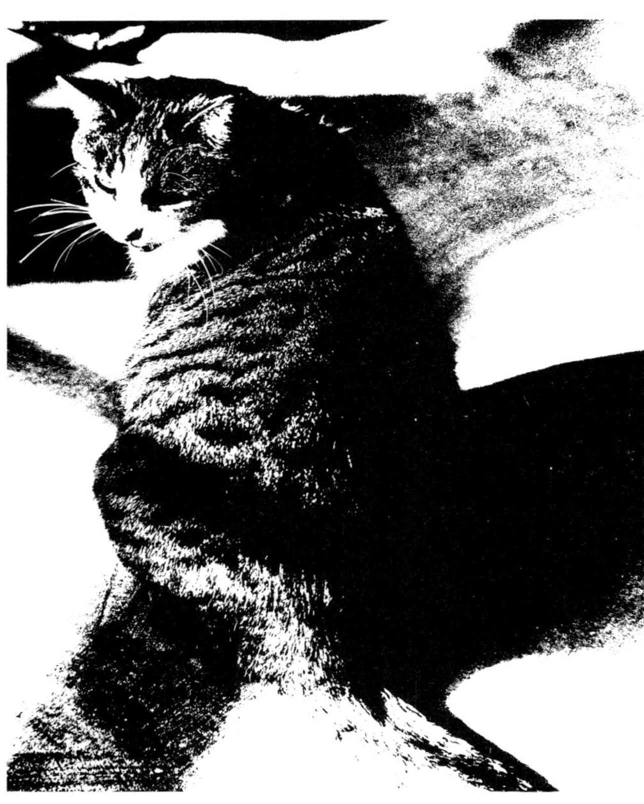

Line conversion, or two-tone posterization.

Since there is no single correct exposure for making a line conversion, a special calibration procedure must be followed:

1. Center a stepped gray scale on a continuous-tone photograph and expose it to high-contrast lith film. The exposure time is not critical; the standard exposure for making line negatives can be used.

2. After the film is processed, determine which step on the gray scale was the last one to photograph as solid density. There may not be a sharply distinct separation (solid density followed by no density), as the next step may have some density.

3. If it is difficult to make a determination from the negative, make a contact print on photographic paper. To locate the last step on the negative that produced solid density; find the last step to produce a white area on the photographic print.

4. After locating the correct step, use a reflection densitometer to measure the reflection density of this step on the gray scale. The relationship of the density reading on the gray scale and the exposure time used to produce the test negative is now the established calibration data for making line conversions. The following example shows the data required for the calibration procedure:

- F-stop: f/22
- Reproduction size: 100%
- Basic exposure: 20 sec.
- Gray scale: step 4
- Reflection density: 0.50

5. Enter calibration data on the computer.

6. Examine the original and visualize the break between tones. Use the reflection densitometer to measure the desired tone on the photograph or gray scale. The tone will appear as a solid density on the negative, with the next darker tone on the original leaving the area clear on the film. This reflection density reading establishes the exact exposure.

7. Use the exposure computer set to the calibration data and read the correct exposure time opposite the selected copy reflection density.

8. After exposure and processing, examine the negative to determine if the break has been achieved near the selected point. Make a contact print with photographic paper to check the final result. If the break did not occur in the selected area, make a fine adjustment in the calibration data and reset the computer. If the line effect on the conversion is not pleasing, select a new breaking point on the copy and repeat the previous steps. The main point to remember is that the change in exposure is found opposite the reflection density of the tone selected as the breaking point.

Using negatives. Continuous-tone negatives can be used instead of photographic prints to achieve a line conversion. Working from negatives gives more control of the process while the procedure used for calibrating the line conversion remains the same. A transparent step tablet or step wedge is used in place of a reflection gray scale. Readings of the step tablet and negative are taken with a transmission densitometer. Exposures are determined using the procedures described above. Producing positive line

images is the most important feature of working from negatives. The positive image helps the camera operator visualize the line effect easily because the results of each exposure can be related directly to the positive image produced.

Using diffusion transfer. Diffusion transfer material does not duplicate the exact results obtained with lith film, but it is high enough in contrast to produce good results. A diffusion transfer print can be produced in a short period of time, allowing the camera operator to see the results of the line effect very quickly.

Posterization

Posterization renders continuous-tone copy into an image represented by a few broad, flat, dark middletones and shadow areas. All highlight and light middletone areas are eliminated. This technique is an extension of the line conversion method, because high-contrast lith film is exposed to continuous-tone copy and processed in an infectious (A and B) developer.

In the posterizing process, the copy is separated into several tone areas, each representing a distinct portion of the copy that will be produced as a flat tone of gray or color. Posterizations contain three or four tone gradations to illustrate the fundamental elements of the copy. It is classified by the number of tones representing the original copy. Thus, a **three-tone posterization** consists of three distinct tonal areas: a dark area, an intermediate area, and a highlight area represented by the paper upon which the posterization is printed. A line conversion is actually a **two-tone posterization**: the line image ink and the paper used to print it.

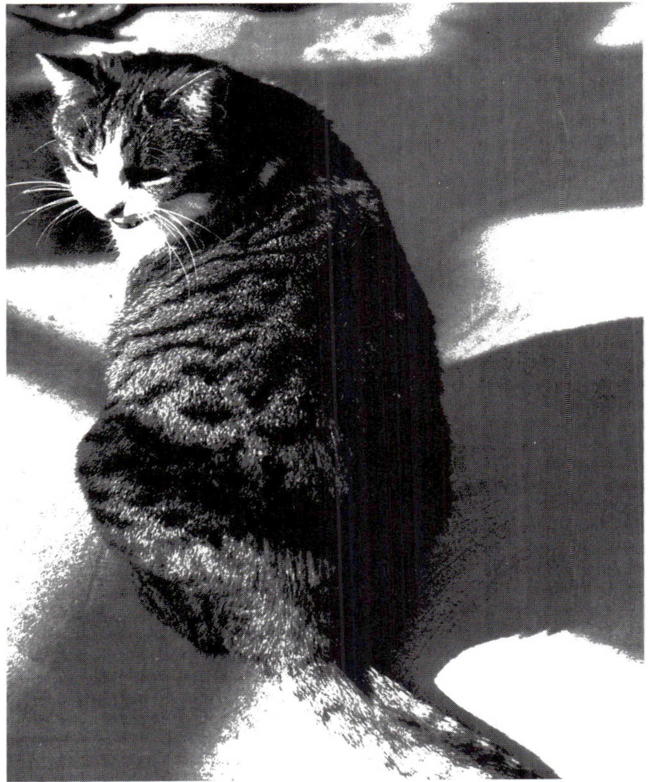

Three-tone posterization.

Copy requirements. The ideal photographic copy for posterization has strong patterns or designs in the image, sharp detail in the main image area, and a slightly lower-than-normal contrast. Large unsharp areas with varying tones of gray actually permit greater flexibility in the technique and help give the posterization its unique character.

Portraits work well as posterizations because the final image is represented by several tones. Posterizations can be made from black-and-white reflection copy, color reflection copy, continuous-tone negatives, and color transparencies. The black-and-white reflection print is the most common copy.

Multinegative posterization. The multinegative posterization technique uses a separate negative for each of the tones. The special effect is produced when all of the images are printed in register using different colors.

A posterization requires several tone separation negatives to be made from the copy, each representing a portion of the original image. The number of separations used is determined by the image and the final effect the camera operator wishes to achieve. Although more separations can be made in this process, the posterization should be limited to no more than four separations, or five tones. More tones would defeat the purpose of this effect because the posterization's appearance would approach continuous-tone.

The procedure for calibrating the camera for the posterization technique is the same as that used in the line conversion technique. Examine the original, try to visualize the posterized effect from the copy, and determine if it is to be a three-, four-, or five-tone posterization. If a three-tone posterization is planned, think of the highlight area as white, the midtones as gray, and the shadow area as black in the finished reproduction. The four- and five-tone techniques are used if there is important detail in the highlights. In addition, the five-tone technique is used if there is a range of tones in the midtone

area. Four- or five-tone posterizations record the highlight or shadow areas as small light or dark areas in the reproduction.

Once the type of posterization is selected, use a reflection densitometer to take readings of the areas on the photographic prints where the breaks are wanted. These reflection densities will now determine the two, three, or four exposures needed to make the posterization. Further instructions follow.

- **Highlight negative**. The highlight negative records the highlight densities of the copy, up to a density of about 0.25. Lesser densities, such as 0.10, are difficult to produce accurately because they require very short exposures. Excessive exposure causes the lower midtones to print as highlights, a common fault in poor posterizations.
- **Midtone negatives.** These negatives record detail in the midtone area of the original. The exposure lengths depend on the tone break that is desired. If the exposure computer is not used, the exposure for the lower midtone negative should be approximately twice the length of that given to the highlight negative. The exposure for the upper midtone negative should be about three times the length. When only a single negative is used to represent the midtones, as in three- and four-tone posterizations, the exposure is approximately 2½ times the exposure for the highlight negative.
- **Shadow negative.** The shadow negative records a very dark tone with detail. For accuracy, it is recommended that a pin register system is used to punch each film before the stripping process. The results on the scale can serve as an exposure guide if changes or corrections must be made in the negative.

The separations can be proofed onto continuous-tone photographic paper, with different exposures used to produce the separate tones of gray. They can also be proofed on color photographic paper using filters to produce the various colors.

Three-tone posterization. Single-film posterizations involve exposing the film through contact screen tints to produce several tones of gray. Three- and four-tone posterizations use the single-film technique.

The three-tone posterization is a two-exposure process. The tones for this effect are a solid shadow, a nonprinting highlight tone, and a single midtone with a density somewhere between the shadow and the nonprinting highlight.

Pure white, the highlights are produced by a no-screen or bump exposure to the original photograph. To produce the midtones, a screen tint (hard-dot, texture, or pattern), placed in contact with the film, covers the entire image except the shadows. Printing density is determined by the screen tint value, not by the exposure. Those areas on the film that have not received enough exposure to produce an image comprise the shadow tone, or the clear area on the film negative.

Here are instructions for creating a three-tone posterization.

1. Place the copy and gray scale on the copyboard. Set camera to the selected reproduction size and aperture and lay high-contrast film on the camera back.

2. Make a highlight (no-screen) exposure that will record only the highlight detail of the copy. (If a specific tone break is desired, use the reflection density of that area to determine the exposure.)

3. Without moving the film, place a 30% or 40% hard-dot (or patterned) screen tint against the film, emulsion-to-emulsion. Give the film a second exposure that is four times the highlight exposure.

4. Process the film according to the manufacturer's directions.

5. Make a contact print from the negative to judge the effect of the posterization.

- Too little screen exposure results in too much black on the posterized print. If the print is too dark, lengthen one or both of the exposures. Start by lengthening the screen exposure.
- Too much of a highlight exposure produces excessively large white areas with no detail. Since the print will be too light, shorten the highlight exposure and, if necessary, also the screen exposure.

Four-tone posterization. The four-tone posterization is a three-exposure process creating a solid shadow, a nonprinting highlight tone, and two midtones with densities somewhere between the shadow and the nonprinting highlight. Four-tone posterization highlights and midtones are produced exactly as they are made in the three-tone posterization process. However, in this case, one screen is placed in contact with the film at a 75° angle and a screen pattern is placed over the lower midtones in the subsequent exposure. Another contact screen is placed against the film, but at a 45° angle, positioning a screen pattern in the upper midtones. The screen tint percentage, screen ruling, and the exposures can be modified to achieve a specific effect.

Using continuous-tone negatives. Single-film and multi-film posterizations can be made from continuous-tone negatives; however, the negative and the film must be pin-registered.

Posterizations are usually film positives or paper prints, although posterized negatives can be made with duplicating film. Negative development can be varied to compensate for exposure.

Creating a posterization from continuous-tone negatives follows the same calibrating procedure as using negatives for line conversions. Exposure is determined with the procedures for reflection copy.

When working with a negative, remember that the no-screen exposure produces density in the shadows. If the shadow area is too small or light, increase the no-screen exposure to produce a shadow tonal break at a lower density. When the shadow area is too large or dark, reduce the no-screen exposure accordingly. The highlight break point is controlled by the midtone "screen time" exposure(s): longer midtone exposures leave less of the highlighted area white or clear. By adjusting the midtone exposure, the highlight-to-midtone break is altered.

Tone-Line Technique

The **tone-line technique** converts a continuous-tone original into a line image that resembles a pen-and-ink sketch or fine-line drawing. A tone-line conversion really has no tones at all but is a detailed outline of the original. Using the tone-line technique to make a line illustration from a continuous-tone original results in a considerable savings in the preparation art.

The tone-line effect is made with a continuous-tone film negative and a continuous-tone positive mask of an almost equal density range. The tones of the positive and negative cancel out each other except at the edges of the image. When the negative and positive are contact-printed in register (base-to-base) to produce a line positive, some light undercuts the edges of the images and produces a clean, distinct line. (Any of the methods for making spreads and chokes can be used for this process.)

When using reflection copy as the original, the first step is to make a continuous-tone negative and then create a continuous-tone positive from this negative by contact printing. The maximum and minimum densities of the positive should be equal to those of the negative in order to produce a "pure" tone-line effect. The creative aspect of this process lies in the proper selection of contrast for each film and the manipulation of the exposure.

The continuous-tone negative. In this special-effects procedure, reflection copy is not the disadvantage it is in the other processes. In fact, it is better to make a negative from reflection copy specifically for the tone-line technique. In this way, the camera operator can be sure the right characteristics are built into the negative.

The original photographic print should be of normal contrast, have a tonal range of about 1.80, and contain sharp detail. Examine this image to determine how well it is suited to the tone-line technique.

Place a gray scale alongside the reflection copy when setting up the camera. It is used to take measurements of the negative. The continuous-tone graphic arts film should be 8×10 in. (200×250 mm) or larger. Exposure and development are manipulated to produce a negative with the correct density and tonal range. The exposure determines the maximum density on the negative; development time determines tonal range.

The contrast must be greater in the shadows than in the highlights to produce the wider lines needed in the shadow area. A negative that has been made properly gives the appearance of being overexposed. Its density range should be between 1.50 and 1.60, based on the characteristics of the film required to make the positive. A short development time will lengthen the density range, and a longer development time will shorten it.

The continuous-tone positive. After a continuous-tone negative has been made, a continuous-tone positive is created from it by contact printing. The film used to make this positive should be able to reproduce the original (the continuous-tone negative) tone for tone. Check the film's data sheet, or ask a graphic arts supply dealer for help in selecting the proper film. Exposure and development are again manipulated to achieve the correct density and tonal range. Use of a pin register system at this stage is recommended to help with registering the negative and positive in a later step.

The film positive cancels the densities of the negative. If a "pure" tone-line is required, a 100% positive mask is needed to completely cancel the image when it is superimposed on the negative. The percentage of masking is the density range of the positive divided by the density range of the negative times 100:

$$\text{Percent Mask} = \frac{\text{Density Range of Positive}}{\text{Density Range of Negative}} \times 100$$

The density ranges of the mask and the continuous-tone negative are determined by subtracting the minimum from the maximum density as

obtained by taking readings of the lightest and darkest steps on the gray scale. With a 100% mask, the density range of the positive mask is equal to the density range of the continuous-tone negative.

The minimum density of the film positive should be between 0.50 and 0.70, with the density range adjusted according to the percentage of masking desired. If tones should appear in the finished reproduction, the positive mask should have a little less density range than the continuous-tone negative. Changing the percentage of the mask will provide different results from the original. Experimentation will help the camera operator establish a set of standards to achieve a desired effect.

Additional tone-line effects. If the negative is placed on top of the positive mask as the line positive is made, the image produced will be represented by two lines separated by the width of the line that would have been produced if the positive mask had been on top. High-contrast paper, stabilization paper, or diffusion transfer materials can be used to make a line print.

If it is necessary to change the size of the line positive, line widths will be altered. This change can either make the line too wide or too thin.

The Duotone Technique

The **duotone process** is a special-effects technique that involves making two halftones at different specifications from the same copy. The two halftones are printed in two different colors, one in a color and the other in black, or both in black. Each halftone is referred to as a printer. One is made with the contact screen at a 45° angle; the other is made with the screen at a 75° angle.

Although most duotones are made from black-and-white reflection prints, color transparencies or continuous-tone black-and-white negatives can also be used. The copy should be chosen carefully to be certain that it is suited to the duotone process. The photograph should have normal or slightly lower-than-normal contrast with good separation of tonal areas. Try to avoid photographs that have large highlight or shadow areas because they seem to produce poor results.

Choosing the technique to use in making the duotone and determining the effect desired from the copy are the most difficult tasks in the process. Experience makes such decisions easier. Unlike many of the other special-effect techniques, the duotone technique takes a great deal of time to master. The

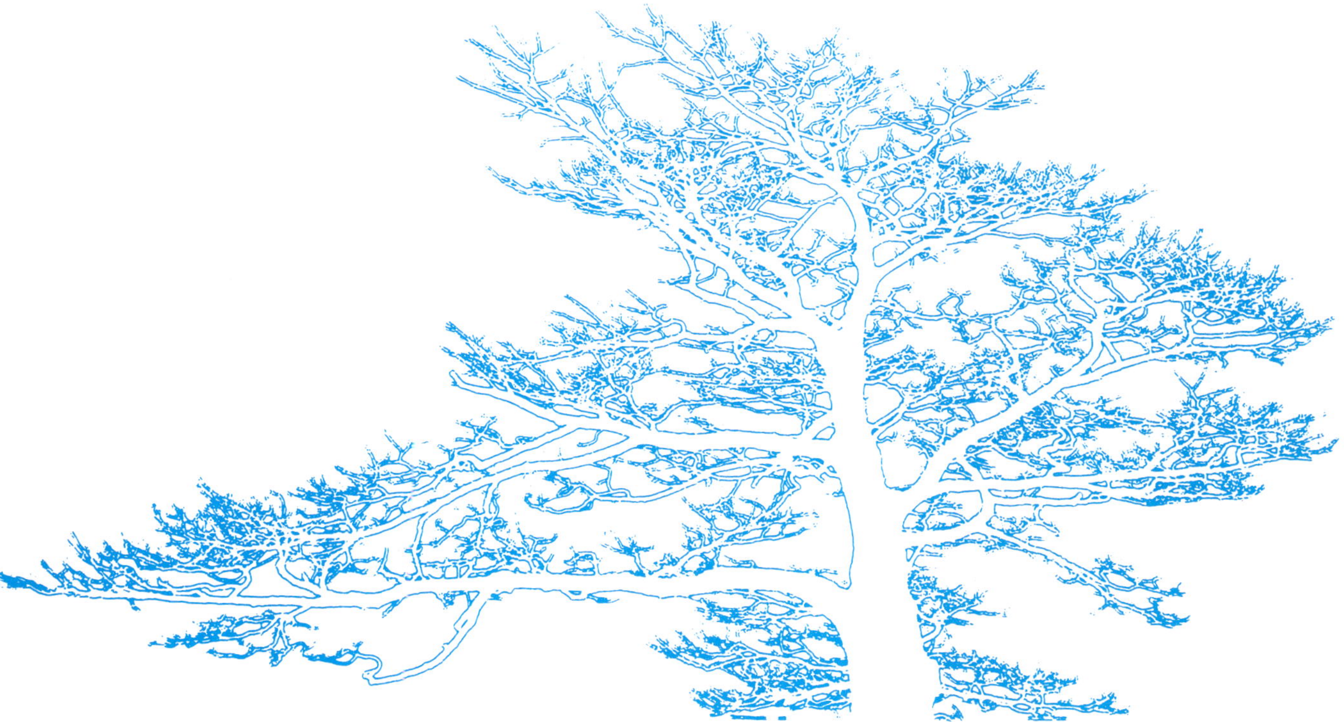

Courtesy Eastman Kodak Co.

A tone-line conversion.

camera operator must have a good understanding of the halftone process plus creative ability and imagination.

To create a duotone, calibrate the graphic arts camera for the halftone process, record the data, and set the exposure computer. Select the halftone procedure that will produce the desired effect. The technique suggested here provides the basic steps for the process and will produce pleasing results from most copy. There are many possible variations, but the camera operator should only experiment after learning the basics.

The duotone process requires a color printer produced as a normal halftone negative and a black printer created to print lighter-than-normal shadows. The shadows will be represented by color to a greater extent than by black.

To make the color printer, determine the highlight and shadow densities of the original, then establish the correct main and flash exposures needed to produce a normal halftone. The negative is made at a 75° screen angle. There must be a 30° difference in the screen angles of the two printers to avoid producing a moire´ pattern. Using register marks and a pin register system also helps in stripping the negatives.

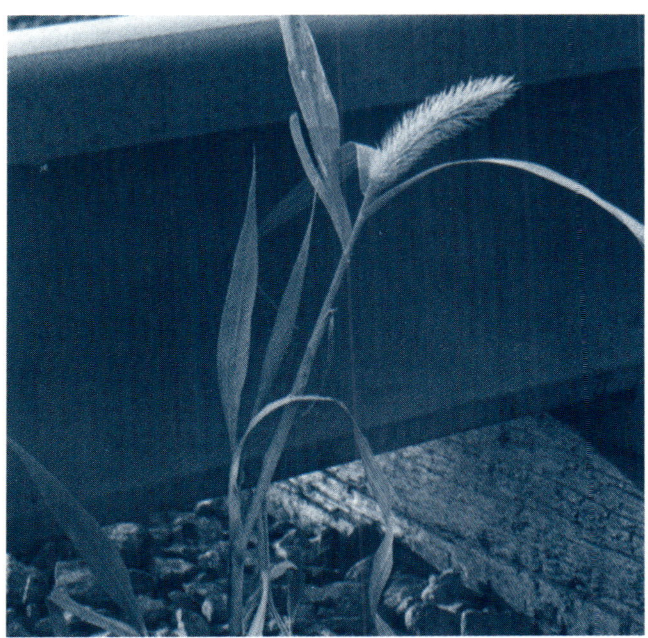

Duotone technique.

The black printer is made at a 45° screen angle. It is a normal halftone, except the shadow dot is larger than it was on the color printer. To make this negative, the main exposure should be the same as it was in the first printer, but the flash exposure can be doubled. The size of the dot and the exposure time required for the flash are based on what the camera operator hopes to accomplish.

It is helpful in the duotone process to place a gray scale along side the copy. The gray scale can be used in interpreting the results and in calculating exact changes in exposure if the camera operator wishes to make additional changes in creating the halftone negatives.

Because of the limitations of the printing process, it is impossible to achieve ideal reproduction. The best reproductions still are not densitometrically or visually identical to the original. This shortcoming can be best understood when the range of the original is compared with the printing capability of the press. The original photograph may have a density range of 2.00, but the press range may only be 1.60. To solve this problem, a duotone black, or double-dot black halftone, can give the reproduction the visual appearance of matching the copy.

A duotone black uses a printer adjusted to cause the highlight areas to drop out, or print as a middletone gray. The exact location is determined by a tone reproduction curve or by what the camera operator wishes to accomplish. In either case, the operator must use caution to prevent the shadow dots from becoming too large when the highlights drop out. The second black printer is made as a normal halftone, using a 45° angle.

To improve the quality of the duotone black, the contrast of each halftone negative can be changed by using a positive-working magenta contact screen to make the first printer and a negative gray screen to make the second printer.

Chapter 8

Color Separation and Correction

Early lithographic color plates were drawn entirely by hand. Ten to fourteen colors were commonly selected to match important areas of the reproduction, and if the pressrun did not meet expectations, additional overprint color stones or plates were added freely.

Creating tone values by hand ended after the introduction of halftone screens. Use of halftone screens opened the color reproduction market to letterpress but, at the same time, photomechanical color lithography became prominent.

While letterpress printers took advantage of the fewer colors needed in process reproduction and soon did credible work with three or four colors, lithographers continued to use at least six colors for many years. Today, four-color printing is standard in lithography, although there is a trend toward five- and six-color printing using special colors.

The four colors commonly used in printed color reproductions are yellow, magenta (process red), cyan (process blue), and black. Each color is applied to the paper by a separate printing plate. To make these printing plates, four film negatives (or, in some systems, positives) are exposed to the original through color filters. The negatives record the proper densities of each of the four colors needed for the printing plates. Making these negatives is called **color separation.** These negatives are often referred to as **printers;** e.g., the magenta printer.

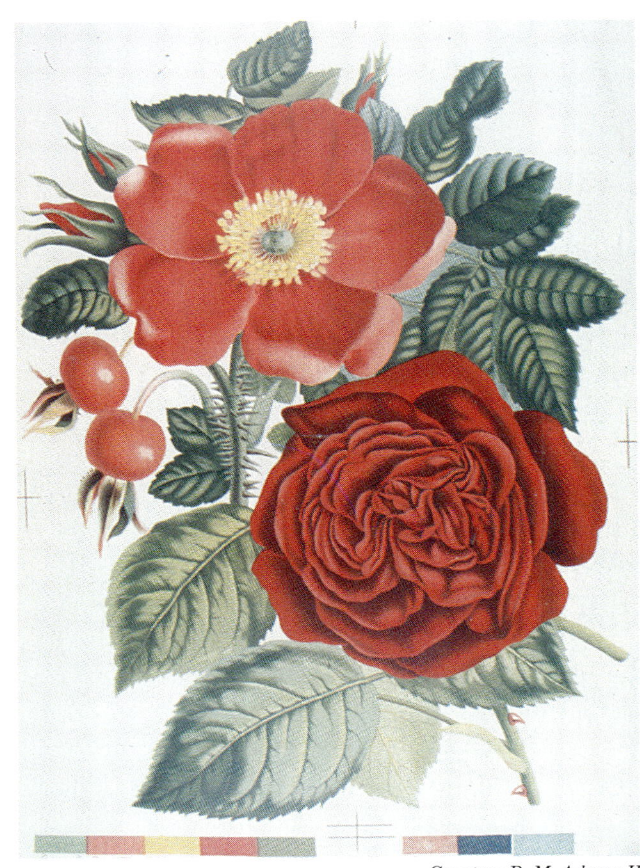

Courtesy R. M. Adams II

Eight-color chromolithography. Note the color bar.

Light and Color

To understand the process of color reproduction, it is necessary to understand the phenomenon of color. To do this, it is necessary to examine the nature of light, without which color would not exist.

Light is radiant energy that is visible to the normal human eye. For the purposes of this discussion it can be assumed that light travels in wave motion, with the color of light varying according to the

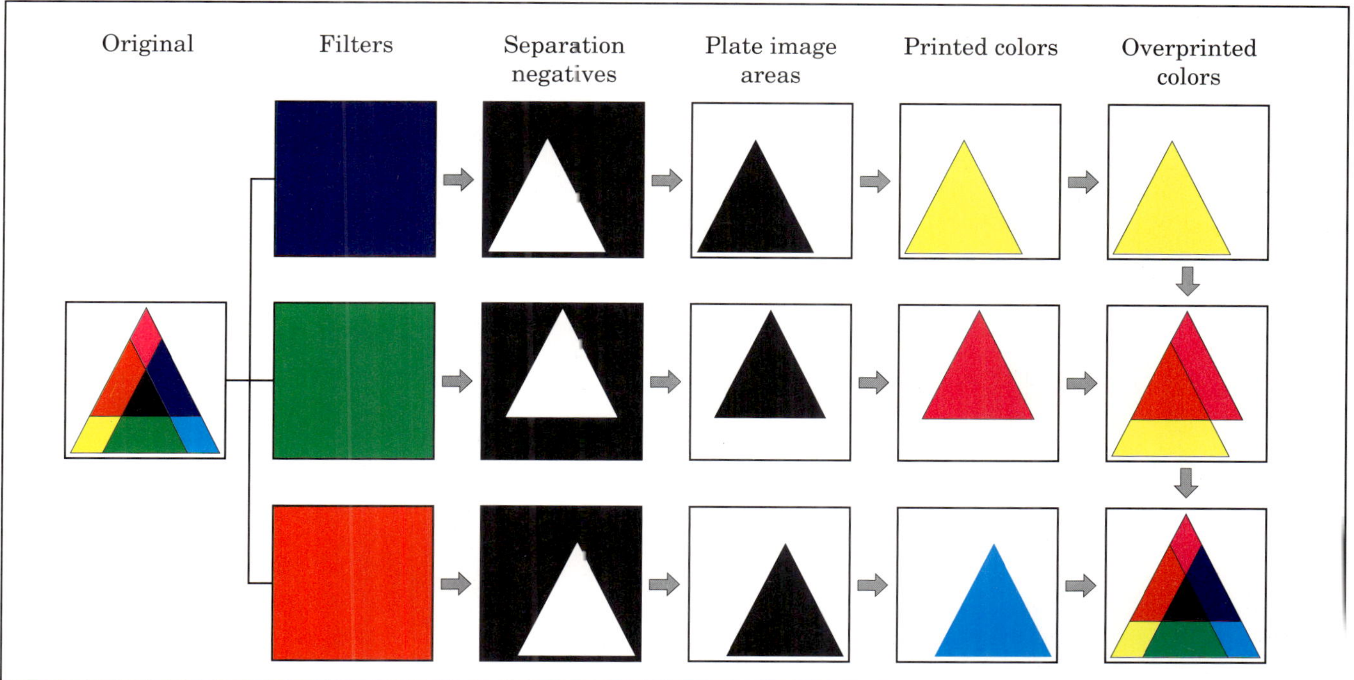

The process of color separation with filters to produce plates that, when inked and applied successively to a substrate, recreate the original *(left)* as a full-color reproduction *(lower right)*. Note the difference in the black of the original and the black produced by overprinting three imperfect process inks.

length of the wave. This wavelength can be measured and classified with other forms of energy on the electromagnetic or energy spectrum.

The scale ranges from the extremely short waves of gamma rays emitted by certain radioactive materials to the radio waves, the longest of which can be miles in length. Light, the visible spectrum, ranges from 400 to 700 nm (millionths of a millimeter) in length. Below 400 nm are the ultraviolet rays, which are important when dealing with fluorescent materials. Some materials absorb ultraviolet radiation, which is invisible, and emit radiation that is part of the visible spectrum. Above 700 nm are the infrared rays, which have significance in certain kinds of photography.

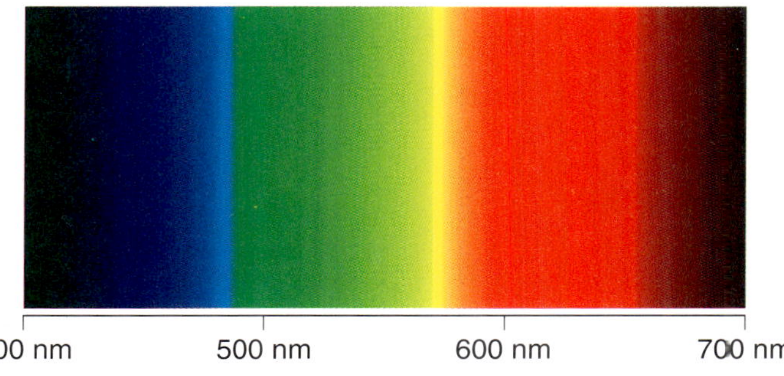

The visible spectrum.

The visible spectrum occurs in nature as a rainbow. It can be duplicated easily in a laboratory or classroom by passing a narrow beam of white light through a glass prism. The spectrum appears to be divided into three broad bands of color—blue, green, and red—but in fact is made up of a large number of colors with infinitesimal variations between 400 and 700 nm. The colors in the spectrum are physically the purest colors possible. Splitting white light into the visible spectrum, and recombining the spectrum to form white light, was first demonstrated and reported by the English scientist Sir Isaac Newton in 1704.

The reason that a spectrum can be formed by passing white light through a prism has to do with the refraction of light as it passes from one medium (air) to another (glass). The prism bends light of the shorter wavelengths more than light of the longer wavelengths, thus spreading the light out into the visible spectrum. Drops of rain act in a manner similar to a prism when a narrow beam of sunlight breaks through the clouds to form a rainbow as the beams are refracted by moisture in the air.

When wavelengths between 400 and 700 nm are combined in nearly equal proportions, we get the sensation of white light. But the human eye is very flexible on this point: we often accept the light from

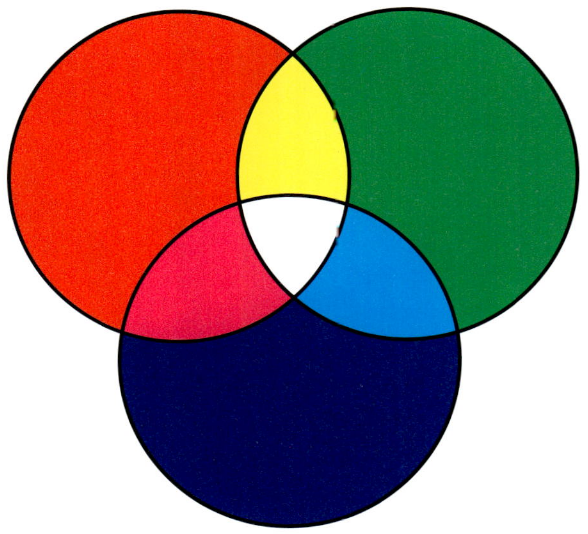

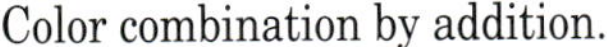
Color combination by addition.

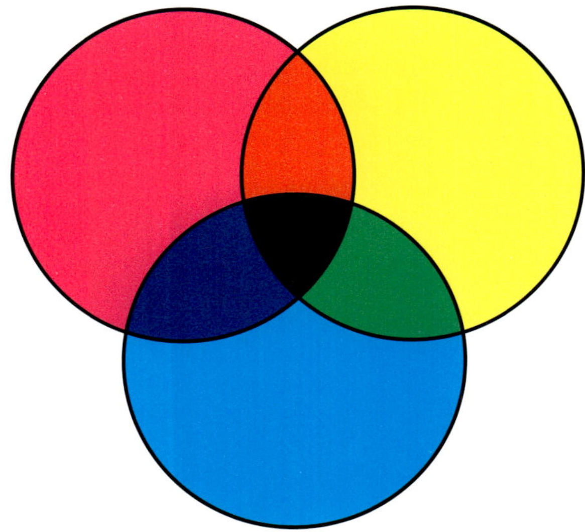

Color combination by subtraction.

a tungsten lamp as white; at other times we accept the light from a cloudless blue sky as white. Clearly, the human eye is very adaptable to different illuminants. For the purposes of graphic arts color reproduction, compromise white light has been defined, a specification that was needed to help minimize color perception and communication problems.

When wavelengths of light are combined in unequal proportions, we perceive new colors. This is the foundation of the **additive color reproduction process** *(above)*. The primary colors of the additive process are red, green, and blue light. In addition to these three colors, secondary colors can be created by adding any two primaries: red and green combine to give yellow; red and blue combine to give magenta; and blue and green combine to give cyan. The presence of all three colors will result in white, and the absence of all three will produce black. Varying the intensity of any or all of the three primaries will produce a continuous shading of color between the limits. This is the principle of color television, which can be readily observed by examining the red, green, and blue mosaic on the screen with a magnifying glass

The drawback with the additive-color reproduction system is that it needs high-intensity illumination in order to produce whites and colors of acceptable lightness. Television systems do not have the problem of low lightness values because self-luminous sources make up each element of the picture. The overall luminosity of these elements can be simply adjusted by the controls for contrast and/or brightness. Also, television is usually viewed in a darkened room, thus creating the illusion of greater luminosity in light tones because of the increase in contrast. Red, green, and blue rotating reflection disks are often used to illustrate the principles of additive-color reproduction, but it is necessary to illuminate the disk with an extremely intense light to achieve satisfactory results.

Color photographs and color printing cannot be produced by the additive process. The limitations of the additive process can be overcome with the **subtractive process** *(above)*. The additive system starts with black (a blank TV screen, for example) and adds red, green, and blue to achieve white. By contrast, the subtractive system starts with white (for example, white paper illuminated by white light) and subtracts red, green, and blue to achieve black.

The subtraction of red, green, and blue is achieved by using colorants that are their opposites. For red, this is a color that is made up of blue and green (i.e., minus red), which is called cyan. For green, this is a color that is made up of red and blue (i.e., minus green), which is called magenta. For blue, this is a color that is made up of green and red (i.e., minus blue), which is called yellow.

Colors are achieved by subtracting light away from the white paper (which reflects red, green, and blue). For example, a combination of yellow (minus blue) and cyan (minus red) results in green.

Any color in between the limit, or gamut, colors may be obtained by varying the proportion of any or all of the colorants. The subtractive color principle is used for most modern color photography and all color printing processes.

Both color television and printing make use of a regular pattern of image elements to create the points in a given reproduction. For color television, this consists of uniform-size elements of red, green, and blue that vary in intensity. At a proper viewing distance the eye does not resolve the individual elements and essentially mixes the red, green, and blue to form a composite color.

In color printing, the process is more complex. For most color printing, the area covered by the yellow, magenta, and cyan ink varies, but the thickness of ink remains constant. Unlike television, these colors overlap each other, producing secondary colors of red, green, and blue. Where all three primaries overlap we have black, and where no ink is present we have the white paper. Thus we have as many as eight separate image elements—white, yellow, magenta, cyan, red, green, blue, and black. Again, at a proper viewing distance the eye does not resolve the individual elements but essentially mixes them to form a composite color.

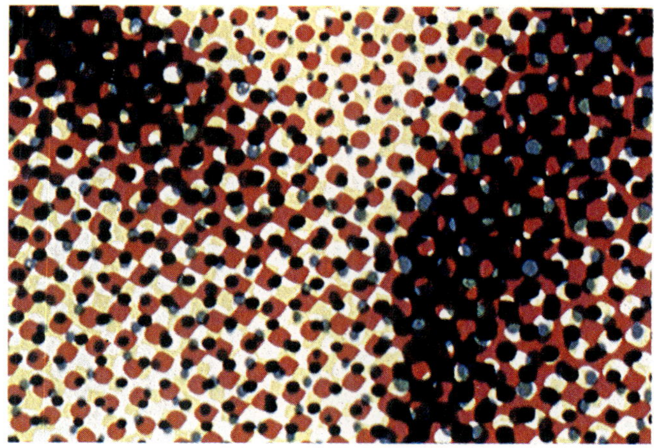

Enlargement of a four-color reproduction.

Describing and Analyzing Color

Color Notation Systems

The physical properties of color are defined in terms of hue, saturation, and brightness.

• *Hue.* Hue refers to the name of the color. Defining a color by hue places it in its correct position in the spectrum. For example, a color said to have a blue hue is distinguished from yellow, red, orange, etc.

• *Saturation.* Saturation is the quality that enables an observer to state how strongly colored something is, or how much the color differs from a neutral gray. To describe an object as a dull green or a brilliant green shows a distinction in saturation. A color that is low in saturation is said to be dirtied with gray.

• *Brightness.* Brightness describes the difference in the intensity of light reflected from or transmitted by the colored image. A shirt may be described as dark blue or light blue. The hue of the shirt's color may be blue, but the terms "dark" or "light" distinguish its brightness.

Hue, brightness, and saturation describe color in general terms. However, a paint or dye manufacturer could not match a color described only in this fashion. To meet the demand for more specific descriptions of colors, color notation systems have been developed.

The Munsell Color System is the most widely used color notation system. It contains opaque colored samples of stable pigments. These samples are combinations of 100 different hues, values (brightness), and chromas (saturation). The Munsell Color Tree contains ten different hues spaced horizontally around the sphere. Each hue is given a number. The Color Tree shows the three-dimensional relationship of hue, value, and chroma.

Radiating out from the center of the sphere are a series of samples of the same hue and value with increasing degrees of saturation. Progressive steps are numbered from 0 at the center, which is a neutral gray, up to 14 or 16, whatever is the purest color possible with the given pigments. Some hues may have only 5 or 6 steps.

By matching a color with one of the samples, a numerical value can be given to hue, value, and chroma. This numerical assignment will enable other viewers to identify the color correctly.

The Ostwald System, which was developed by Wilhelm Ostwald and improved by the Container Corporation of America, is another frequently used color notation system. Like the Munsell System, Ostwald's *Color Harmony Manual* also has a central vertical gray tone scale that is surrounded by a color circle or sphere with complementary hues opposite each other.

Instead of arranging the interior colors in horizontal and vertical rows, Ostwald places them in angled rows. All colors between the basic hues, as well as white and light grays, are arranged as tints made by the addition of white. Shades are made by the addition of black, and tones by the addition of gray.

Color Diagrams

For any study or analysis of color, plotting data on a diagram is essential for visualizing and evaluating the color. One of the best known color-diagram systems is the CIE Chromaticity Diagram. This was developed by the Commission Internationale l'Eclairage. It takes the shape of a horseshoe within right-angle axes. Color values are plotted on it in terms of "x" and "y." The diagram uses ideal red, green, and blue primaries—primaries that are purer and brighter than any in the spectrum. However, it does show the properties of additive mixtures of different colors of light and the color differences as they appear to the eye.

The Maxwell Triangle, although related to the CIE diagram, is based on the use of real primaries. Plots are determined from densitometer readings made through red, green, and blue filters. This diagram is also good to show the properties of additive mixtures of colors of light.

One disadvantage of the CIE and Maxwell diagrams is that they require inconvenient calculations and plottings. Data for the CIE diagram, for example, has to be taken from spectrophotometric curves. Data for use on the Maxwell Triangle is based on percentage-reflectance densitometer readings. Some densitometers read this directly. However, it is much more common for the instruments to read in terms of density. The density readings must then be converted to percentage-reflectance values using tables.

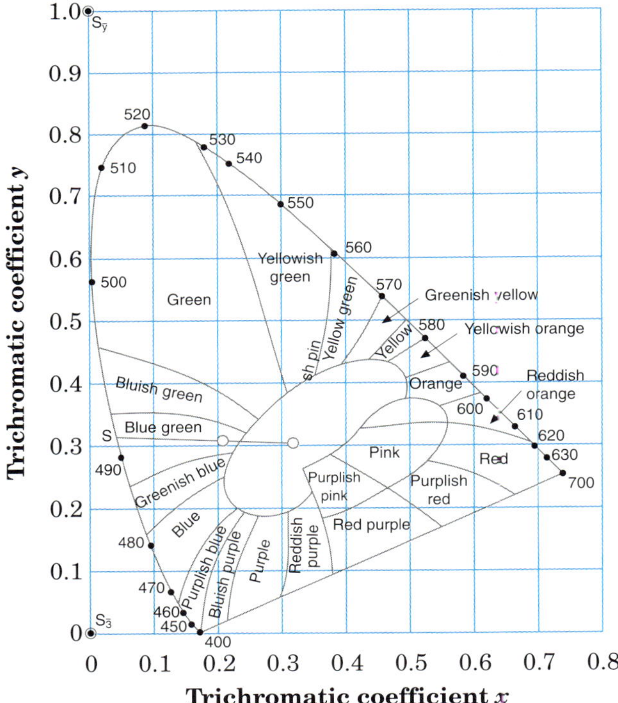

The CIE Chromaticity Diagram.

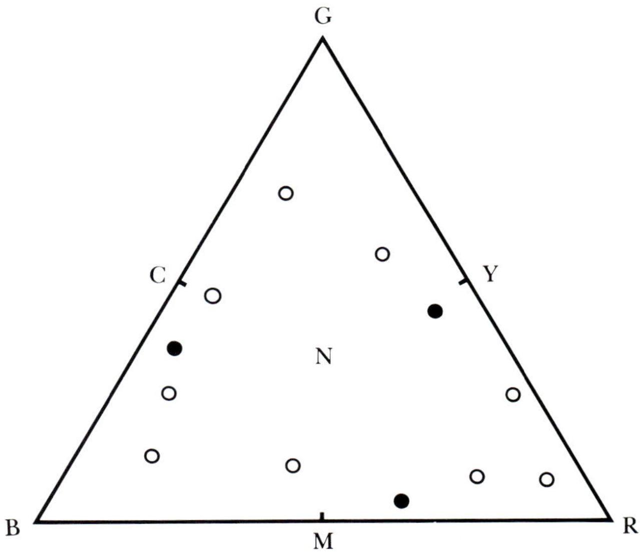

The Maxwell Additive Triangle.

Important disadvantages are also inherent in any color diagram. None of the diagrams show all of the possible characteristics of a color because diagrams are limited to two dimensions. Since the simplest description of any color requires three terms (hue, saturation, and brightness), conventional diagrams always omit at least one of the important qualities.

Still another disadvantage is that no single diagram is suitable for use with all color problems. When color is studied in different fields, different relationships of color properties become important. To best show these relationships, different diagrams are often required.

Before the introduction of the GATF Color Circle, diagrams were based on the primary colors of light and were mainly concerned with showing the effects of additive mixtures of different colors of light.

In graphic arts color reproduction, the conditions and needs are different, since subtractive color effects are used. For example, yellow ink on paper looks yellow because it has subtracted or absorbed the blue from white light. The remaining red and green components of the white light are reflected from the paper and, together, appear as yellow.

GATF Color Circle. The GATF Color Circle, an ink hue and purity chart, was the first of GATF's color diagrams. The Color Circle permits the plotting of a number of different pairs of factors.

In its most common use, the hue difference of inks are plotted around the circle, and the graynesses of the inks are plotted toward the center. The same diagram is also useful to plot hue and printed strength, or hue and another factor that is similar to saturation or chroma.

The two coordinates most commonly used to position a color on the color circle are called hue error and grayness. They are derived from red-, green-, and blue-filter densitometer readings by use of the hue error and grayness equations explained later in this chapter.

The closer a plot is to the "ideal" yellow, magenta, or cyan shown on the outer rim of the circle, the greater the purity of its hue, or the less its "hue error" in process color printing. The farther a plot is away from the center of the circle, the less its grayness or contamination with the third primary.

To plot the color's attributes, take the hue error number (a percentage between 1 and 100) and position it somewhere around the edge of the circle. There are, however, six pie-shaped sectors around the circle where this color could be plotted. Comparing the red-, green-, and blue-filter density readings will indicate the proper sector. A color is plotted across from the color of the filter giving the highest density reading and then shifted away from 0% hue error toward the color of the filter with the lowest density reading.

For example, if the ink's highest density reading is given with a blue filter, the color is basically a yellow. Therefore start counting 2% hue error lines from the 0% yellow position (upper right on the circle diagram). To know whether to count toward 100% green or 100% red, again compare the red-, green-, and blue-filter density readings. For a typical yellow process ink, the red-filter density reading is the lowest of the three. If so, count the hue line by going around the edge of the circle toward red.

The special features of the GATF Color Circle important in a study of process color reproduction are as follows: the coordinate values of a color have a significant and understandable meaning in themselves (they quantitatively specify such factors as hue error or grayness, rather than relatively specifying them in terms such as "more of *x* and *y*"); changes in the location of a plot for a color are easily interpreted to show what change is needed in the color system; equal graynesses are symmetrical; subtractive color mixtures are shown and related more logically between the primary colors; and subtractive complementary colors (not additive colors) are shown directly opposite one another across a neutral center.

A special form developed for use with the circle organizes the data used to locate plots and to record mask factors. This form also provides information on hue shift, additivity, trapping, and other factors.

GATF Color Triangle. Despite the many advantages of the GATF Color Circle, it does not show two other desirable properties: the direct prediction of the color that can be produced by a two-color overprint and the possible gamut of differents set of the three process inks.

The GATF Color Triangle originated as a variation of the Maxwell Triangle. The Maxwell Triangle is not useful for the problems of color reproduction because it describes additive mixtures of colored light, having red, green, and blue primaries. GATF adapted the Maxwell Triangle to the graphic arts industry by substituting the subtractive primaries at the corners of the triangle and inverting it.

The GATF Color Triangle uses the same data as the Color Circle but presents additional color dimensions graphically. For example, predicted secondary colors formed by overprinting the primaries should fall on a straight line drawn between the plots of two primaries. The displacement of the secondary color—above, below, or along the connecting line—is readily interpreted for a particular set of process inks. The Color Circle is suitable for evaluating several sets of process inks by inkmakers or printers, while the Color Triangle serves to characterize a particular set of process inks for press operators and color separators.

The Color Triangle uses hue-error and grayness coordinates, which are calculated and plotted by the same techniques as for the Color Circle. (GATF Research Project Report 6081, *The GATF Color Diagrams,* includes information on how to plot information on all three of the GATF diagrams.) A straight line connecting plots of two of the subtractive primaries will locate the ideal color that can be produced by overprinting those colors. The masking scales printed on the perimeter of the Color Triangle aid in determining color correction (for photographic color separation).

When all three subtractive primaries are connected to form a triangle, the area enclosed is the gamut of color that can be produced with the inks plotted. Colors falling outside the lines can be matched in hue, but not in purity. The total area enclosed in the triangle is not always the most important factor when considering the gamut of a set of inks. The requirements of a particular job determine the suitable characteristics of the secondary colors.

Almost any set of process inks can produce the desired hues for secondary colors if the strengths are adjusted properly. But different sets of inks yield different shades of gray. Grayness of a secondary color can be predicted by observing where the line connecting the two primaries crosses the 100% hue error line. Subtracting this percentage grayness from 100 gives the predicted efficiency of the secondary color.

To predict overprint colors, add the densitometer readings for the primary colors involved. To check the trapping of cyan on yellow, add the blue-filter densitometer readings for cyan and yellow; do the same for the green- and red-filter readings for each color. The resulting sums are used to determine the hue-error and grayness coordinates of the two-color overprints. The plot of the overprint should fall on the line connecting the primaries producing the overprint. Assuming that yellow is printed first, the position of the actual overprint relative to the ideal prediction (X) will give the following information:

- If the actual plot is the same as the ideal prediction, the printing conditions are ideal. This doesn't happen very often.
- If the actual plot falls on the line, but is closer to yellow than the ideal X, the cyan is undertrapping.
- If the actual plot falls on the line but is closer to cyan than the ideal X, the cyan is either overtrapping or the cyan ink is acting as though it is not fully transparent.
- If the actual plot falls outside the line (away from the center), it indicates an increase in the gloss of the overprinted inks.
- If the actual plot falls inside the line (toward the center), it indicates a loss of gloss due to possible excess drainage of ink vehicle or other causes.

It is possible to "predict" an overprint color only if transparent inks that are trapping properly are being used. However, the diagram is still useful to show the trapping of opaque inks. In this case, the original plotting would be made from the OK press sheet. Later plottings during the pressrun will show differences from the original. Opaque inks plot toward the top color in (similar to an overtrapping condition with transparent inks).

GATF Color Hexagon. This chart offers a simple way chart color variations during a pressrun. To plot the printed strength of the separate primary inks (yellow, magenta, and cyan), only one number from a single densitometer reading is required. In process color reproduction, the accuracy or consistency of the overprint colors (red, green, and blue) are important, because most of the colors in a reproduction are created by more than one ink. Changes in trapping or other press conditions could seriously shift the hues of the overprint colors even if the separate inks are still printing without change.

Although shifts in the hue of overprint colors can be detected with two filter readings, the best information about changes is available from three filter readings. These readings are easy to take with modern densitometers that have push-button, prezeroed filters. The problem becomes one of how to chart hue and strength differences from these readings quickly.

In reviewing the literature on color research, it was found that such a system was already in existence. It had been used successfully in studies of Kodachrome film but had not been publicized to the graphic arts. It is a simple charting system in the form of a hexagon and is described in the book *Principles of Color Photography,* by Evans, Hanson, and Brewer. They called it a "trilinear plot." This chart was adapted to graphic arts by modifying its range and working out the simplest alternative chartings.

The GATF Color Hexagon has separate lines that correspond to 0.02 increments of density. The single ideal primary inks—yellow, magenta, and cyan—plot along their radial lines from the center. The stronger the ink color, the farther away from the center it falls.

In using this diagram, no calculations or equations are needed. Color points are positioned directly on the hexagon according to the red-, green-, and blue-filter density readings. To position a color, always start from the center of the diagram. First, use the red-filter density and count toward cyan (away from red) the number of lines equal to this density. Now count downward the number of lines equal to the green-filter density and then upward to the right toward yellow the number of lines equal to the blue-filter density.

In an easier charting method, the lowest density reading is subtracted from the other two readings. In making the plot with the remaining two readings, again start from the center and count in the directions that are away from the remaining two filter colors. For example, suppose the three filter readings of the magenta are red, 0.10; green, 1.22; and blue, 0.46. Since red is the lowest, subtract its value (0.10) from green, which leaves 1.12, and from blue, leaving 0.36. To make the plot, start in the center of the diagram and count down (away from green) to the 1.12 position and then upward to the right (away from blue) to the 0.36 position.

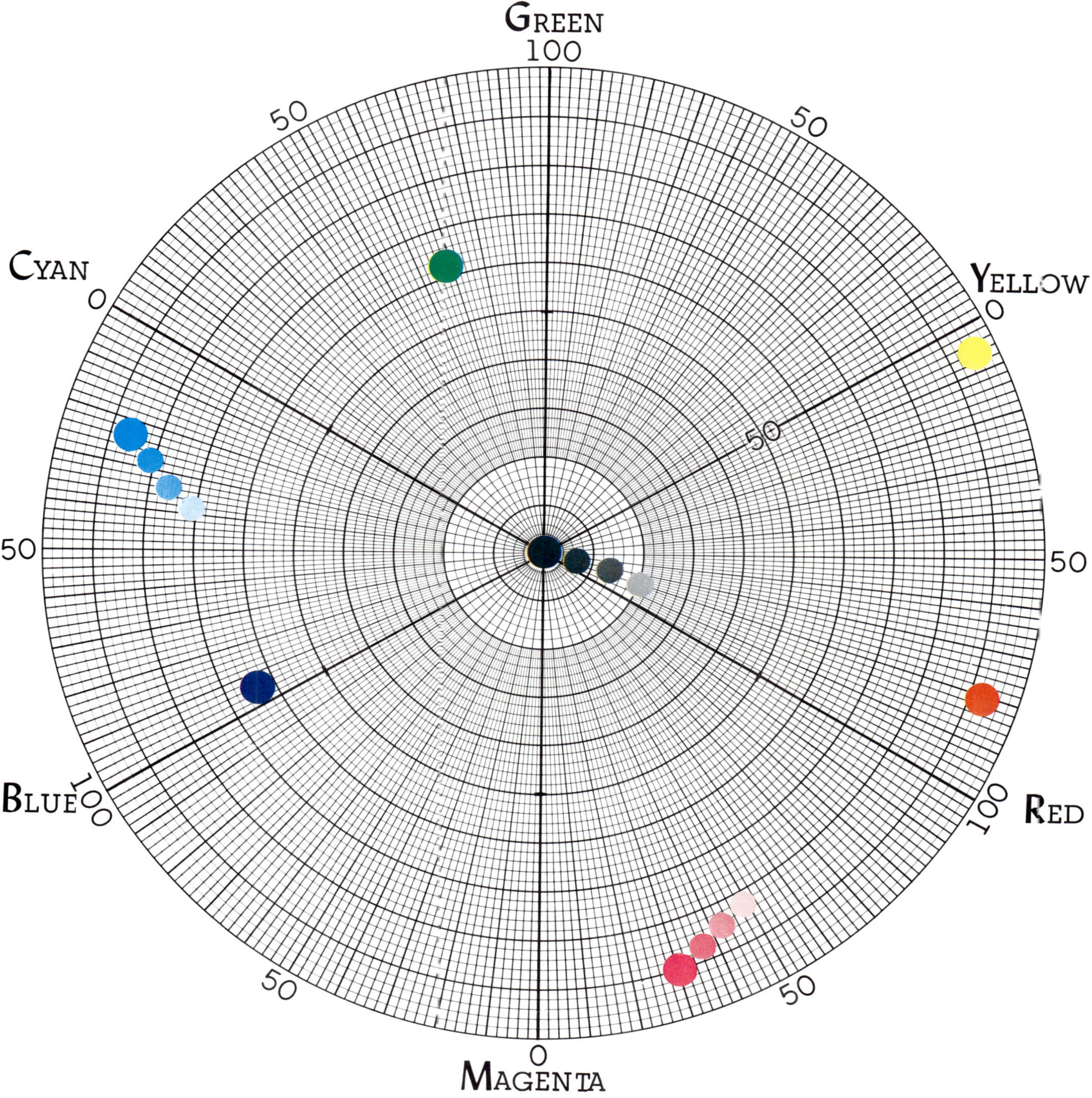

Note: Density measurements and plots are examples of the method of plotting ink on the GATF Color Circle, and they will only approximate the inks on this page.

The GATF Color Circle offers an easy way to visualize the hue error and grayness of a number of process inks. Plots are shown for solid yellows, solids and tints of magenta and cyan, solid two-color overprints of the primaries, and three-color overprints of tints of equal dot sizes (center).

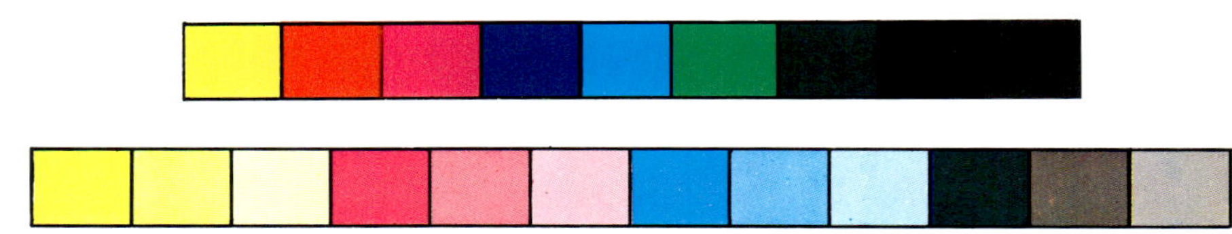

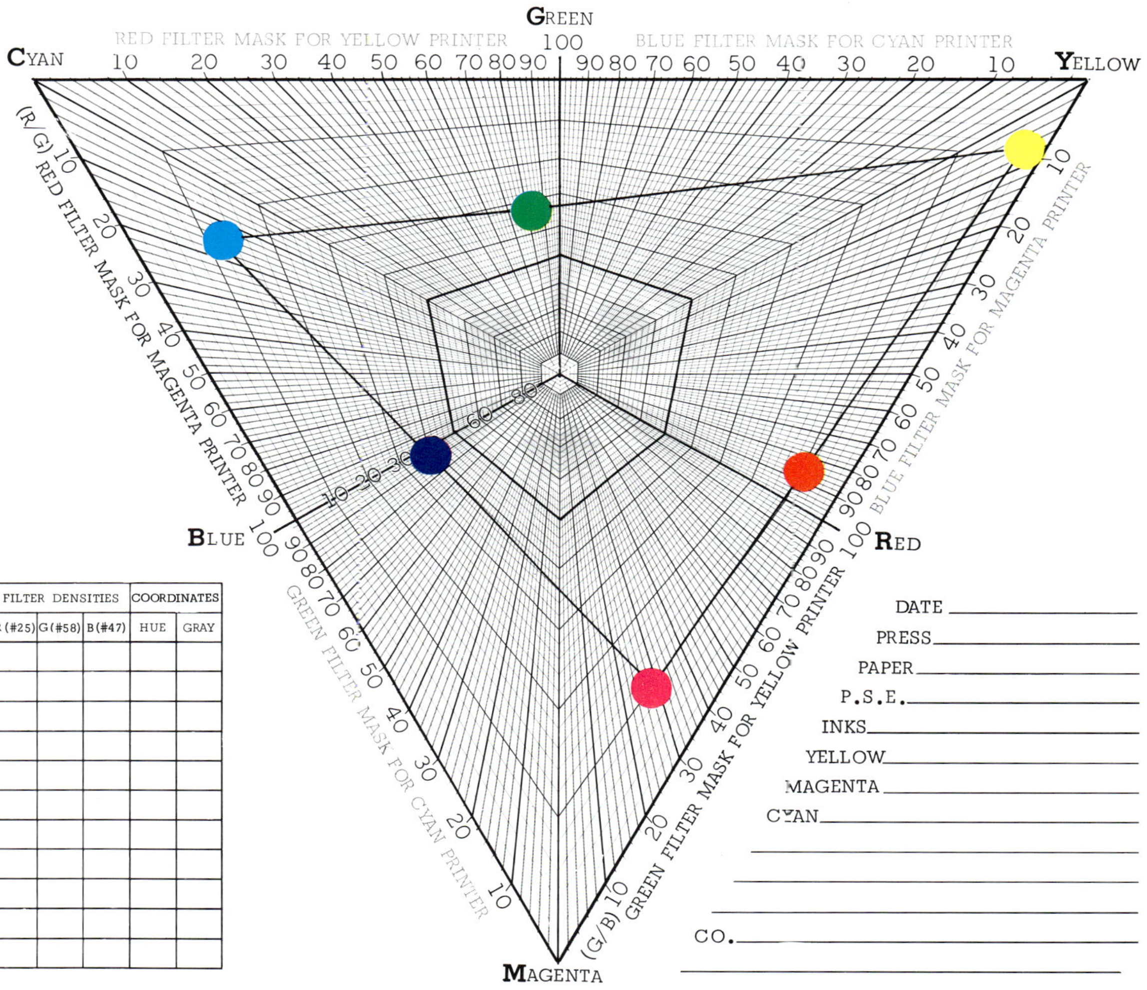

GREEN

RED FILTER MASK FOR YELLOW PRINTER

BLUE FILTER MASK FOR CYAN PRINTER

CYAN 10 20 30 40 50 60 70 80 90 100 90 80 70 60 50 40 30 20 10 YELLOW

(R/G) 10 20 30 40 50 60 70 80 90 100 RED FILTER MASK FOR MAGENTA PRINTER

10 20 30 40 50 60 70 80 90 100 BLUE FILTER MASK FOR MAGENTA PRINTER

BLUE RED

100 90 80 70 60 50 40 30 20 10 GREEN FILTER MASK FOR CYAN PRINTER

(G/B) 10 20 30 40 50 60 70 80 90 100 GREEN FILTER MASK FOR YELLOW PRINTER

10 20 30 60 80

MAGENTA

	FILTER DENSITIES			COORDINATES	
	R (#25)	G (#58)	B (#47)	HUE	GRAY
Y					
M					
C					
R					
G					
B					
3C					
Y + M					
Y + C					
M + C					
Y+M+C					

DATE __________

PRESS __________

PAPER __________

P.S.E. __________

INKS __________

YELLOW __________

MAGENTA __________

CYAN __________

CO. __________

Note: Density measurements and plots are examples of the method of plotting ink on the GATF Color Triangle, and they will only approximate the inks on the page.

For a given set of process inks, the GATF Color Triangle can be used to show the possible color gamut, undertrapping or overtrapping, changes in gloss, predictions of ideal overprint colors, and masking requirements.

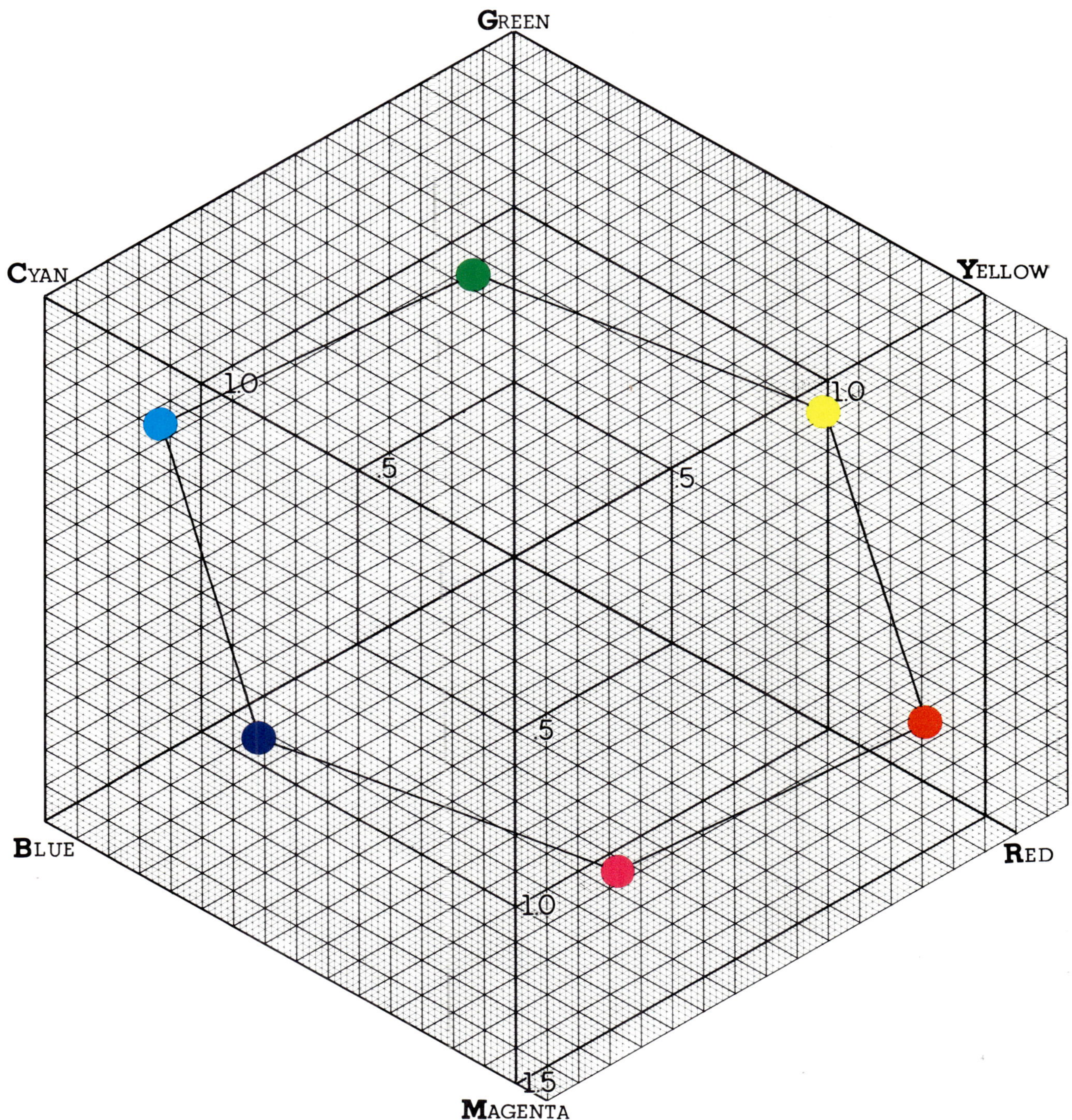

Note: Density measurements and plots are examples of the method of plotting ink on the GATF Color Hexagon, and they will only approximate the inks on this page.

The GATF Hexagon is the only diagram that requires no mathematical formulas or computations to plot color strength and hue differences. It is easy and quick to use and best suited for quality control of the separate primaries and overprint hues.

This diagram is particularly useful to check trapping and the strength of the color being run. To do this, make the initial plot from the OK sheet. Make plots of the solid primary inks and the overprinted pairs of the primary inks that produce red, green, and blue. Then, as the run progresses, make additional plots on the same diagram. Where these plots fall in relation to the original plots tells how close the printing is to the OK sheet.

If the plot for a primary color shifts outward, it indicates that the printed strength or density of the color has increased. A shift inward toward the center tells that the strength or density of the color is less than it was on the OK sheet. In either case, the press ink feed or cylinder packing should be adjusted.

If the densities of the primaries have not changed, but the plots for the overprint colors (red, green, and blue) have shifted toward one of the primaries, overtrapping or undertrapping is occurring.

A change in the printed strength of a primary color will shift the hue of an overprint color produced with this primary. There may also be changes in trapping. This cannot be determined until the primary ink strength has been adjusted back to match the original plot from the OK sheet.

Color Separation Objectives

The task of the color separator is to produce color separation films that convey the essence of the original within the confines of the printing system, which requires extensive knowledge about originals *and* the printing process.

The goal is not always the closest match to the original. It is more important to reproduce a scene the way the client *wants* it to look. For example, it is often preferable to increase the saturation of a blue sky in a reproduction rather than match the original.

The first task is to evaluate the characteristics of the photograph. This should be done under standard viewing conditions as defined by the American National Standards Institute in ANSI 2.30-1989, which specifies viewing standards for transparencies and reflection prints. Questions that need to be addressed during the evaluation of originals include the following:

- Is it a transparency or a reflection print?
- What type of photographic material is it, and who manufactured it?
- Has the photograph been retouched? (It is vital that color retouching be performed with the same dyes that make up the color photograph; otherwise, the scanner will read the two dyes as different colors even though they look the same to an observer.)
- Is it a first-generation original or a duplicate?
- Is it well exposed?
- Does it have a color cast?
- Does it contain neutrals?
- How grainy is the original?
- Is it high or low contrast?
- Should any local colors be corrected?
- Are there memory colors (e.g., blue sky, green grass, or flesh tones) in the original that need to be considered?
- Is the original sharply focused?
- What are the original and reproduction sizes?
- Are there patterns in the original that may cause moiré in the reproduction?
- Is detail enhancement necessary?
- Would the image benefit from gray component replacement?
- What is the area of central interest to the client?

A highly skilled color separator is needed to analyze the characteristics of the original and adjust the scanner to optimize the reproduction quality for that original. The settings for tone reproduction, gray balance, highlight value, shadow density, detail enhancement, local and global color correction, gray component replacement, screen ruling, and dot shape are crucial for high-quality separations.

However, knowledge of the characteristics of the original is not sufficient for making top-quality color separations. It must be accompanied by a thorough knowledge of the printing system that will make the color reproduction. Newspapers, magazines, and annual reports are produced by operations with distinct reproduction characteristics.

Three general limitations of the printing process are tone range, color gamut, and resolution. The **tone range** is indicative of the number of lightness values that are portrayed from the brightest highlight to the darkest discernible shadow detail. Lithographic processes differ with respect to tone range. Sheetfed printing has a tone range of approximately 2.0; heatset web offset is 1.8, and nonheatset printing is limited to a 1.0 tone range. Color transparencies, the most commonly used originals for offset lithography, have tone ranges of approximately 3.5. The color scanner provides tremendous flexibility in compressing the tone range of the original to fit the printing system, but the operator

must determine what areas of the tone scale to compress or exaggerate for a given picture.

Color gamut is the range of colors that can be created with a set of primary colors and is dependent on their purity and saturation. Photographic dyes are colorimetrically more pure than printing ink pigments. Therefore, photographs have a larger color gamut than lithographic prints; they contain colors that are not reproducible by the printing system. More expensive, "cleaner" inks can increase the color gamut of the system, but pigments are not available that would equal photographic dyes.

Photographic resolution is over 600 lines/in. Halftone screen rulings vary with the type of printing and range from 85 to 300 lines/in. Detail is lost as the screen ruling becomes coarser.

Important questions that relate to the printing system include the following:

- What printing process will be used for the job?
- What type of paper, ink, and plates will be used?
- What screen ruling will be used for the job?
- What dot shape is desired?
- What are the dot gain curves for the system?
- What are the gray balance requirements of the printing system?
- What are the minimum and maximum dot sizes reproducible with the printing system?
- Is gray component replacement desired?
- Will the color separation films be composited before plates are made?
- Will other images be printed in-line with this image?
- Will a varnish be used over the image?

Other press variables affect the printing conditions of the system, such as compressible or conventional blankets on the press and alcohol substitutes in the dampening solution. The scanner operator has no way of predicting the individual effects of these factors on printed appearance.

To achieve the highest quality color reproduction from a printing system, the stages of color reproduction must be considered as an interrelated system rather than a disjointed series of operations. The overall color reproduction characteristics of the printing system should be measured and optimized, and it is assumed that no significant changes will be made. Optimization consists of several phases: diagnostic testing, capability testing, variability testing, and color characterization. A test form like the GATF Sheetfed Test Form is useful in performing this testing and analysis. If the color separator does not know the exact characteristics of the system, separations are made to reflect the average conditions of the printing process.

Color Reproduction Requirements

Color reproduction requirements are criteria for evaluating and adjusting color separations for accuracy and consistency. These requirements are tone reproduction, gray balance, and color correction. They are the same for any color reproduction system, whether a graphic arts camera with color filters, a high-end color scanner, or a desktop scanner and computer system. To set up a color reproduction system to make good separations on the first attempt, these requirements must be addressed in order, because they represent a sequence from coarse- to fine-tuning.

Tone Reproduction

A reproduction should match (or improve upon) the original photograph in brightness, darkness, and contrast. Printers face the problem, however, that ink on paper is usually not as dark as silver in photographic prints. Therefore, a printed halftone compromises the density of the shadows and of every gray level throughout a photograph. This phenomenon is known as **tone compression.** For good tone reproduction, the highlight, shadow, and midtone settings must be set to optimize the reproduction's lightness, darkness, and contrast and to reproduce all important detail in the original within the printable density range.

The first step in controlling tone reproduction is to produce a **tone reproduction curve,** which is a graph that plots percentage dot area of the reproduction as a function of the density of the original. Photographing (or scanning) a gray scale with the original provides all the data needed to construct the curve. Reading and plotting the measured reflection densities of the steps of the continuous-tone gray scale in the original versus the dot areas of the halftone gray scale in the reproduction builds the tone reproduction curve.

Including a gray scale outside of the image has several advantages when making a scan. The highlight, shadow, and midtone controls can be set to spots in the photograph, but it is sometimes difficult to find image spots large enough to measure

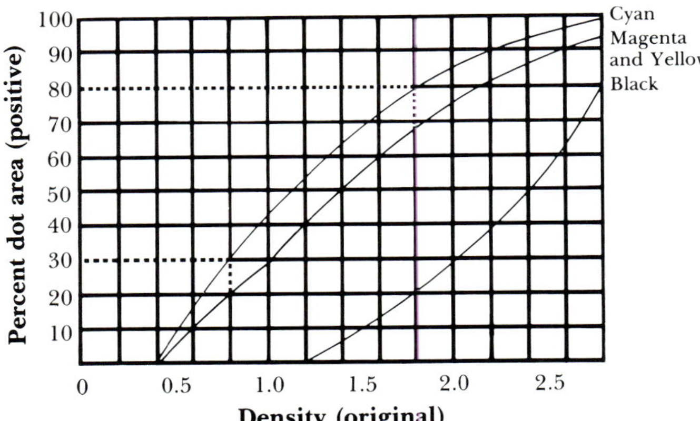

Cyan, magenta, and yellow tone-scale relationship for a specific ink, paper, and printing combination. Here, magenta and yellow share the same curve.

with a densitometer. A calibrated gray scale provides a series of gray levels of known density that are large enough to measure and are arranged in order from lowest to highest density. It offers a method of accurately setting the highlight-to-midtone ratio to provide contrast in areas of greatest interest and to compensate for dot gain on press.

The tone reproduction curve varies with ink, paper, and press conditions. The curve must be adjusted accordingly until it becomes the standard for these conditions. A curve acceptable for black-and-white reproduction can also be used for color reproduction, which simplifies the task of establishing a standard.

It is desirable to establish two different curves, one for normal-key and another for high-key originals. Several halftone negatives (or positives) are made, each having the same basic density range (BDR), but with the midtones varying in density. Results are printed under plant conditions and evaluated visually. The most satisfactory print from each copy is selected, with the reproduction curve of each plotted. These curves then become the standard for quality control for normal-key and high-key copy. However, suitable tolerances should be set to allow for variations in each copy. A third curve for low-key originals could be included, but it is not really necessary.

Once the reproduction curves are established, they must be adapted to the separation negatives.

Tone reproduction can be controlled both by conventional photographic means and by electronic means on a color scanner. To control the brightness and contrast of a halftone, camera operators can make up to three exposures on the same piece of film, obtaining considerable control over the appearance of the halftone. Tone reproduction curves help camera operators determine the optimum exposure times.

With the development of electronic scanners in the 1970s, the tone reproduction curve and the concept of highlight, shadow, and midtone control were applied to the scanner setup procedure. Instead of calculating and making three exposures on the camera, the operator adjusts separate controls with respect to a gray scale for the picture's highlight, shadow, and midtone regions, collectively called **aimpoints.**

Gray Balance

Gray balance is the second of three fundamental requirements for good color reproduction. It refers to the ability to reproduce a neutral gray in the original as neutral with yellow, magenta, and cyan process inks.

The need for gray balance arises from the characteristics of yellow, magenta, and cyan process-color printing inks, which are based on subtractive color theory. Each ink should ideally absorb one-third of the spectrum and reflect two-thirds. Unfortunately, real process color inks have spectral impurities. As a result, a three-color overprint of equal halftone dot percentages (e.g., 50% yellow, 50% magenta, and 50% cyan) of process color inks does not produce a neutral gray, but rather a brownish color.

In lithography, gray balance is influenced by many materials and press variables:

- Hues of process color inks
- Quality and color of paper surface
- Ink film thickness printed on paper
- Ink trapping
- Printing ink sequence
- Press printing characteristics
- Dot gain

By finding out what percentages of cyan, magenta, and yellow are required to produce a neutral gray, the color separator can reproduce all colors in the original accurately. The GATF Gray Balance Chart is a quality control device used to determine the three-color dot requirements for the cyan, magenta, and yellow films to reproduce a neutral scale at four different tone values. Each tone level of the gray balance chart consists of a field of tint patches of gradually changing magenta values along the vertical axis and gradually changing yellow values along the horizontal axis. The cyan dot size is constant for all squares in a given matrix.

After the chart is printed with the plant's standard process inks, paper, and plates on a press op-

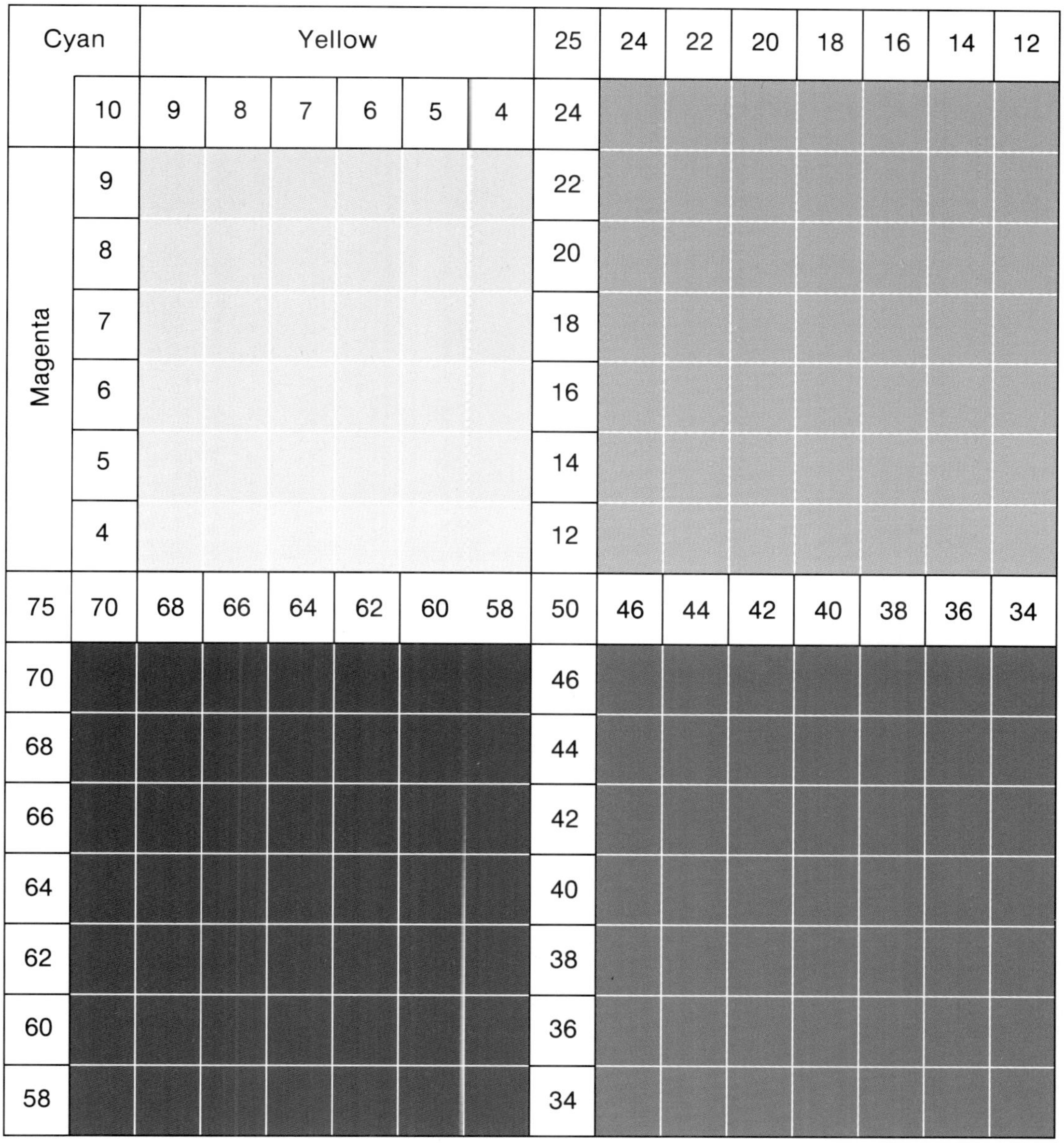

Cyan		Yellow						25	24	22	20	18	16	14	12
	10	9	8	7	6	5	4	24							
Magenta	9							22							
	8							20							
	7							18							
	6							16							
	5							14							
	4							12							
75	70	68	66	64	62	60	58	50	46	44	42	40	38	36	34
70								46							
68								44							
66								42							
64								40							
62								38							
60								36							
58								34							

The GATF Gray Balance Chart.

erating within normal production control limits, the most neutral patch in each matrix of squares is located. For visual evaluation, a photographic or printed halftone gray scale can be used as a reference for comparison under standard viewing conditions. Sometimes holes are punched in the gray scale, and the opening is placed over one printed gray patch at a time to isolate it for evaluation. The patch that comes closest to matching the gray standard under standard conditions is selected. The film dot values that printed the square are determined by looking at the numbers on the chart.

If a gray scale or standard viewing conditions are not available, the target can be evaluated with a color reflection densitometer to find the patch in each matrix with equal red, green, and blue filter densities.

Gray-balanced aimpoints and tone reproduction curves. A gray balance test reveals the aimpoints, or density and dot area coordinates, that will produce neutral gray along the entire tone reproduction curve. When gray-balanced aimpoints are plotted, unequal curves generally result for the

yellow, magenta, and cyan printers. To find the aimpoints, the evaluator records the YMC dot percentages from each gray balance patch that appears to be or measures closest to the paper in neutrality. These gray-balanced aimpoints can then be used to set up the exposures on a camera separation system, to set aimpoints for each color on a high-end electronic scanner, or to calibrate a desktop scanner and software combination.

Color separation textbooks often give generic or "boilerplate" gray balance aimpoints that vary from source to source. Usually such aimpoints specify equal magenta and yellow printers, with cyan dot area slightly higher. Slightly higher dot percentages of cyan compensate for the pinkish-brown color cast resulting fom nonideal spectral reflectance curves of typical process color inks. The cyan generally runs about 2–4% high in the highlights, 10–15% higher in the midtones, and 3–10% higher in the shadows.

While using boilerplate gray balance specifications is better than using none at all, keep in mind that gray balance is influenced by many printing variables. Ideally, a gray balance test should be run for frequently used ink/paper/press combinations.

Color Correction

Original colors can be changed during the separation process. This is useful for three reasons: to print the best reproduction regardless of the substrate and inks used; to optimize the reproduction of different original film emulsions; and to change colors according to customer preference. Color correction is accomplished by adjusting the cyan, magenta, yellow, and black (CMYK) printers with respect to specific colors in the original.

Every method of photomechanical color reproduction loses color accuracy from an original. Even if the separations and printing plates were "perfect," commercially available inks are impure and absorb some of the light that they should transmit. Color correction is necessary because no process ink has the ideal ink characteristic of one-third spectral absorption and two-thirds transmittance.

These spectral impurities are quantified as hue error, a number between zero and 100% (zero is a pure color, and 100% is a totally wrong color). Without color correction, printed reds look orangish and blues look purplish. To counteract ink hue error, color correction can be used to adjust the hue and saturation of printed colors to be more accurate.

Most color correction problems stem from the use of magenta inks that are too red and cyan inks that are too blue. Although yellow inks are the purest process color inks, most adjustments must be made to the yellow printer because of the blue light absorbed by the magenta and cyan inks.

In uncorrected separations, cold colors become warmer or grayer, and warm colors lack strength. Properly correcting separation negatives or positives will make the reproduction colors as close to the original as possible.

Once color correction is set up to compensate for ink hue error, it can be refined to accurately reproduce different dye sets in photographic materials, such as Agfachrome, Ektachrome, Fujichrome, Kodachrome, and other brands.

The third use of color correction is to change the colors in a separation to suit the customer's preference. Customers may want specific colors to appear more or less saturated or to have a different hue. Such changes can be accomplished with selective, or local, color correction.

Evaluating Process Inks for Color Correction

The range of colors that any set of process inks can produce, and the amount of color correction that they will require, can be judged from simple calculations. These calculations are based on reflection densitometer readings of printed ink films of the individual solid colors using filters over the densitometer aperture.

Strength, hue, grayness, and efficiency are four factors that describe the most important characteristics of a set of process inks.

To make an evaluation, first take reflection density measurements of solid yellow, magenta, and cyan. (Color bars feature solid and tint patches of each process color, as well as all overprint combinations.) Measure the density of each ink three times using a red, green, and blue filter over the densitometer aperture. Take readings of colors in the same general area of the sheet. List the readings in a table.

Ink Density Measured with RGB Filters

Inks	Red Filter	Green Filter	Blue Filter
Yellow	0.02	0.06	1.04
Magenta	0.08	1.14	0.45
Cyan	1.02	0.30	0.08

Printed ink strength. To compare the printed strength of different inks of the same hue, merely compare the highest of their three filter density readings. In the example, yellow has a density value or strength of 1.04; magenta, 1.14; and cyan, 1.02.

The strength of an ink is important because it determines the range and depth of colors that can be produced with it. For example, the relative strengths of a yellow and cyan overlap will determine whether a blue-green or a yellow-green will be produced.

It is just as important to control the individual strengths of inks as it is their hues. In multicolor presswork, it is especially important to measure the strength of at least the first color down. Use a densitometer to make sure it is correct for plant standard printing conditions. Strength of the colors that follow can be evaluated visually by checking the colors produced by overprints. For example, if yellow is printed first and has the proper strength, check the strength of the magenta by noting the shade of red produced by a solid overprint patch in the color bar.

Color hue and hue error. The hue of a color is determined by the colors of light that it absorbs and transmits. Perfect process inks would absorb one-third of the spectrum and transmit two-thirds. A perfect magenta would absorb all green wavelengths of white light and transmit all blue and red. A perfect cyan would absorb all red and transmit all green and blue. Likewise, a perfect yellow would absorb all blue and transmit all red and green.

The hue error of an ink is determined by how evenly it transmits red, blue, and green. The ink hue number expresses this error as a percentage. A magenta with zero hue error transmits red and

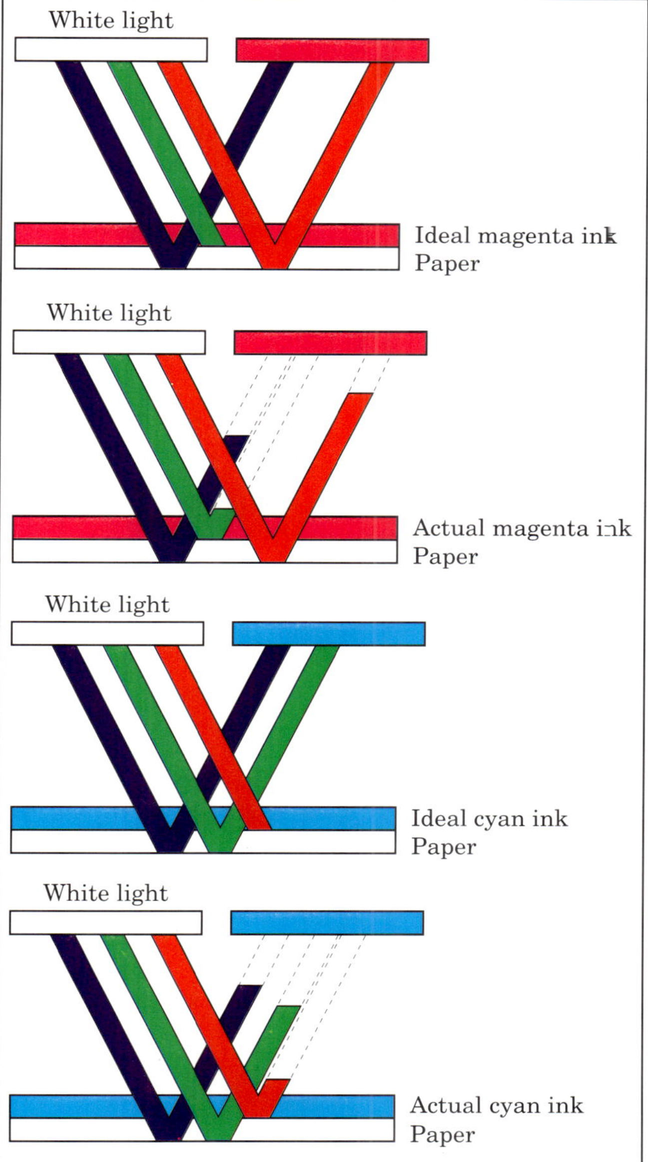

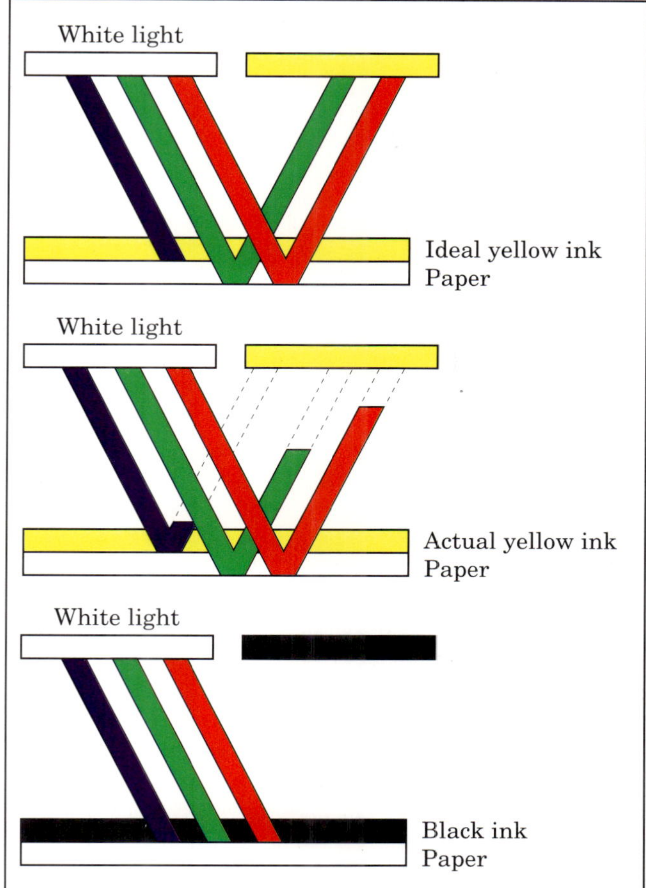

blue equally. If it had a 100% hue error toward red, it would transmit all red and no blue. (Such a color would, in fact, be red and not magenta.)

The hue error of a color can be determined by measuring the amount of red, green, and blue light that it transmits. As an example, consider the magenta in the table above. This magenta has a density of 0.08 with the red filter, 1.14 with the green filter, and 0.45 with the blue filter. The red filter reading is the lowest of the three (L), the green filter reading is the highest of the three (H), and the blue filter reading is in-between or medium (M).

To calculate the hue error, use the following equation:

$$\% \text{ Hue Error} = \frac{\text{M} - \text{L}}{\text{H} - \text{L}} \times 100$$

Using this equation and the figures in the example, this magenta has a 35% hue error:

$$\% \text{ Hue Error} = \frac{0.45 - 0.08}{1.14 - 0.08} \times 100 = 35\%$$

Grayness. The purity of a process color is judged by its freedom from gray. Colors become gray when they transmit less light of their predominant color than the paper that the color is printed on. For example, a magenta should transmit all red and blue. It is considered gray to the extent that it transmits less red than the white paper it is printed on. The grayness of an individual color also affects the grayness of color mixtures in which it is used.

The following equation is used to calculate percent grayness:

$$\% \text{ Grayness} = \frac{\text{L}}{\text{H}} \times 100$$

Using the figures in the table for the cyan ink, the cyan grayness is found to be 20%:

$$\% \text{ Cyan Grayness} = \frac{0.08}{1.02} \times 100 = 7.8\%$$

The lower the percentage grayness of a process color, the higher its purity.

Efficiency. How well a process ink absorbs one-third of the spectrum and transmits two-thirds of it is a measure of the ink's efficiency. A process ink's efficiency decreases in proportion to the amount of light that it should transmit but instead absorbs.

The efficiency of a process color can be rated from the percentage ratio of its incorrect light absorption to its correct light absorption. The equation is:

$$\% \text{ Efficiency} = 1 - \frac{\text{L} + \text{M}}{2\text{H}} \times 100$$

Using the data in the table, the efficiency of the cyan ink is 81.4%:

$$\% \text{ Efficiency} = \left(1 - \frac{0.08 + 0.30}{2 \times 1.02}\right) \times 100$$

$$= (1 - 0.186) \times 100 = 81.4\%$$

The higher a process ink's efficiency number, the greater the range of pure colors it will produce with other process inks. Additionally, inks with higher efficiency require less color correction.

Efficiency values are perhaps the best single number to use in evaluating the color quality of a set of process inks. However, two different inks may have the same efficiency, but differ in their grayness and hue.

Additional Color Reproduction Considerations

The three color reproduction requirements of tone reproduction, gray balance, and color correction are solely involved with the appearance of the printed image. Additional manipulation of the color separations is sometimes necessary to enable the press operators to have more control over press variables such as trapping and dot gain. **Undercolor removal** (UCR) and its variant, **gray component replacement** (GCR), are two procedures used in the color separation process to reduce or remove a gray component made up of yellow, magenta, and cyan inks and replace it with a corresponding amount of black ink. UCR affects predominantly the shadow and neutral areas of a reproduction, while GCR affects predominantly the color areas of a reproduction. Originals can also sometimes be improved by using **unsharp masking** (USM) to enhance detail areas of the copy.

Undercolor Removal

The purpose of undercolor removal (UCR) is to reduce the amount of yellow, magenta, and cyan printed in dark neutral gray areas and replace it

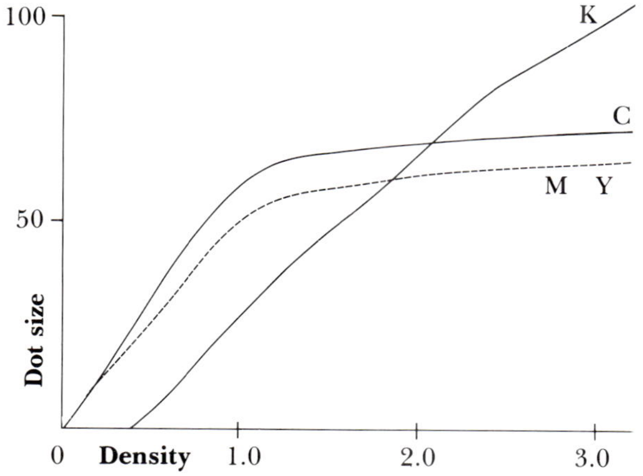

Tone reproduction curves for set of separations made using UCR.

with a longer range black printer that can carry more detail. UCR lowers the total percentage of ink coverage in these areas, suggesting that the percentage of apparent ink trap can be increased and the dot gain can be reduced.

The term *undercolor removal* is derived from the historically used color sequence of yellow, magenta, cyan, and black, whereby a three-color gray component under the black is removed and replaced with black ink.

UCR can be defined by the maximum total printing dot percentage of the four colors in the darkest shadow area of a color reproduction. Examples of different percentages of UCR and typical corresponding YMCK percentages appear in the table.

Sample Percentages of UCR

	260% UCR	280% UCR	300% UCR	No UCR
Yellow	52	60	70	90
Magenta	52	60	70	90
Cyan	61	70	80	95
Black	95	90	80	70
Max. total dot %	260	280	300	345

In summary, the more UCR used, the lower the maximum total dot coverage in the shadow areas of the reproduction. In the table, for example, 260% UCR is actually a greater amount of undercolor removal than 280%.

Limitations with UCR. Extreme amounts of UCR are not possible. For example, in a shadow area consisting of 80% yellow, 80% magenta, 90% cyan, and 80% black, the black can only be increased to 100%. A good rule of thumb for UCR is to replace the three-color gray component with the same percentage of black. Therefore, the three colors could only be reduced by approximately 20% each. If so much of the three-color gray component is removed that the black cannot compensate for it, detail and density will be sacrificed. In an extreme case, a reversal may appear.

In a reversal, the density decreases from midtones to shadows rather than increases. Reversals cannot be corrected, but to prevent them either use a smaller degree of UCR or move the starting point of the UCR closer to the highlight area.

The major drawback with UCR is that as UCR increases, the maximum density of the printed sheet decreases. Reduced maximum density means reduced contrast and reduced quality. Therefore, avoid using excessive UCR whenever possible, as excessive undercolor removal also tends to affect colors. When good-quality materials are available, and the press has been set to minimize dot gain and to maximize trapping, UCR should not be needed. For high-speed magazine production and similar work, however, some UCR may be desirable. The SWOP-recommended UCR amount is 300%.

Advantages with UCR. By reducing three colors (yellow, magenta, and cyan) and increasing one color (black), total ink coverage is reduced significantly, creating several advantages. Perhaps the biggest advantage in using UCR is that it can improve trapping conditions on high-speed wet-on-wet multicolor offset lithographic printing. Other advantages in using this process include:

- Improved color saturation and purity
- Reduced dot gain
- Reduced ink setoff
- Reduced consumption of the more expensive yellow, magenta, and cyan process inks
- More black printing in the dark shadow and neutral areas, making gray balance less critical

Gray Component Replacement

Originally, the limitations of camera and film technology restricted UCR to only the dark shadow and neutral areas. It was not practical to produce a full-range corrected black separation on the camera. Not until recent software was developed for digital electronic scanners could a full-range corrected black be produced practically. Gray component replacement (GCR) substitutes black for gray compo-

nents throughout a reproduction, including colored areas.

GCR is sometimes referred to by other names, including achromatic color removal, achromatics, bichromatic color reproduction, binary primary, binary primary plus black, complementary color removal, full-scale UCR, integrated color removal, polychromatic color removal, programmed ink reduction, tertiary color removal, or two-color and black.

GCR theory. In color reproduction, one or two inks determine the hue and value, while the third ink desaturates the printed color and is referred to as the tertiary color. For example, a color composed of 90% yellow, 80% magenta, and 20% cyan has a dominant red hue, and the cyan makes the red appear slightly "dirty." Cyan is the tertiary color.

In a theoretical GCR separation where ideal inks and substrates with no unwanted absorptions are being used, the tertiary color is reduced or removed completely, along with proportional amounts of the other two colors to define a gray component, which is replaced with black ink.

The gray component of the example color is made up of 20% yellow, 20% magenta, and 20% cyan as determined by the amount of the tertiary color, cyan. A 20% black performs the same function and can replace this three-color gray component, reducing the yellow from 90% to 70%, the magenta from 80% to 60%, and completely removing the cyan. The total dot coverage is changed from 190% to 150% using GCR.

GCR is defined by the percentage of the tertiary color removed, and cannot exceed 100%. Applying 50% GCR to the ink percentages in the example color would reduce each color by only 10% dot size instead of the full 20%. Then only a 10% black would be needed to replace this 50% three-color gray component.

Applied GCR. In reality, GCR is not that simple because real inks and substrates have unwanted absorptions. Applying GCR to the example color of 90% yellow, 80% magenta, and 20% cyan would result in removing only the tertiary color, cyan, which would be replaced with 15% black. Yellow and magenta would not be reduced at all. A 15% black performs the same function as the 20% cyan. Here the total dot coverage is reduced from 190% to 185%. Depending on the color, only one or two of the inks are affected by GCR. In this example, only the cyan was affected. In a colored area, the two predominant inks (in this case yellow and magenta) have to be mostly retained to maintain the hue and value of the color.

Black printer considerations. In a GCR separation, the black printer is not a skeleton black printing only from the midtones to the shadows. It prints wherever there is a gray component. This includes highlights, quarter tones, midtones, three-quarter tones, and shadows.

Thus, the black printer is a full-scale printer and needs to be considered as such. A black tone reproduction curve must be evaluated in addition to the yellow, magenta, and cyan tone reproduction curves. Also, because the black is a full-scale printer and will print in the 40–60% range where dot gain is highest, its dot gain characteristics must be considered.

Since UCR and GCR black printers are different from a typical skeleton black printer, it may be necessary when using high degrees of either UCR or GCR to consult the ink supplier to determine if a different black ink is needed.

Another consideration is color sequence. The color sequence that is normally used for a conventional separation may not be ideal for a GCR separation. Since the black is no longer a skeleton but a full-scale black printer carrying heavy amounts of ink, it may be necessary to run a different color sequence when using plates that are made from GCR separations.

Limitations of GCR. Some potential limitations are associated with this process:

- Film inspection can be confusing, especially for those who are accustomed to inspecting conventional separations. Extreme amounts of GCR produce a black printer quite different than a conventional skeleton black printer.
- GCR software varies among scanner manufacturers. For example, specifying 50% GCR may result in separation films with 50% GCR from one scanner and something different from another scanner.
- When using less than 40% GCR, the advantage of consistent color reproduction on long pressruns is lost.
- Using more than 70% GCR results in abrupt tone gradations.
- Maximum or 100% GCR coupled with misregister may result in white lines around the subjects.
- Increasing the amount of black ink to enhance the contrast and legibility of text may adversely affect the tone reproduction of the pictorial matter.
- GCR can decrease gloss and saturation in some subjects.

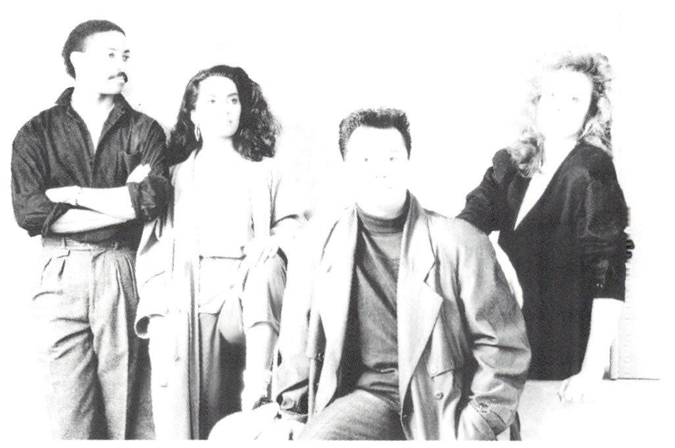

Conventional black printer.

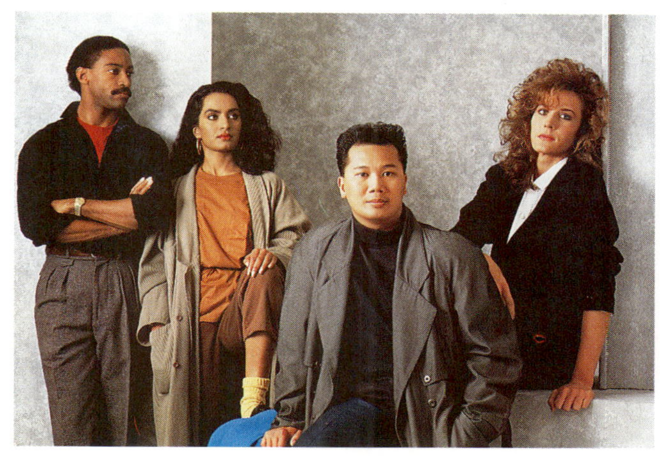

Conventional three-color overprint.

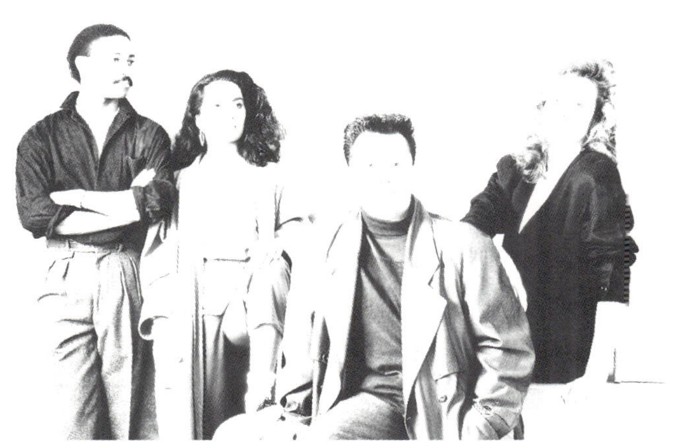

Black printer made with 220% UCR.

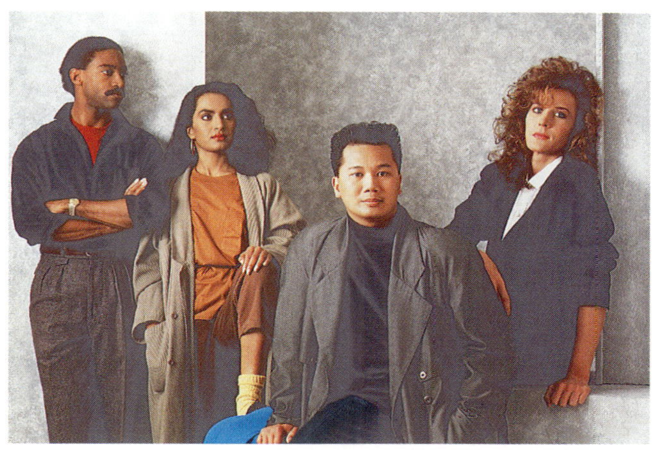

Three-color overprint of separations made with 220% UCR.

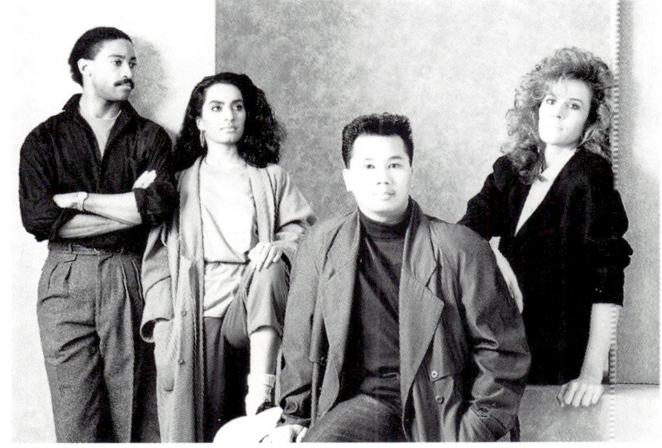

Black printer made with 70% GCR.

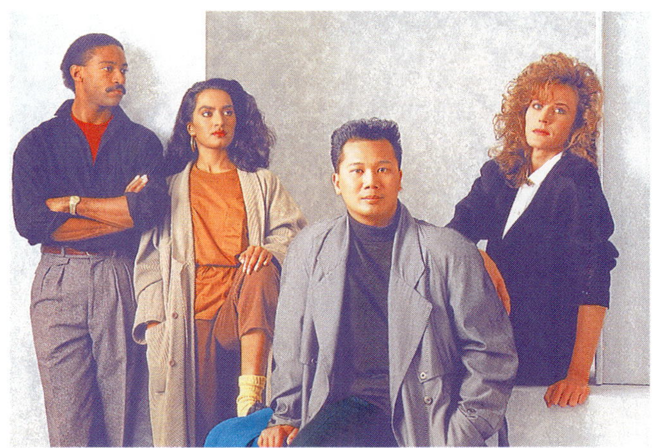

Three-color overprint of separations made with 70% GCR.

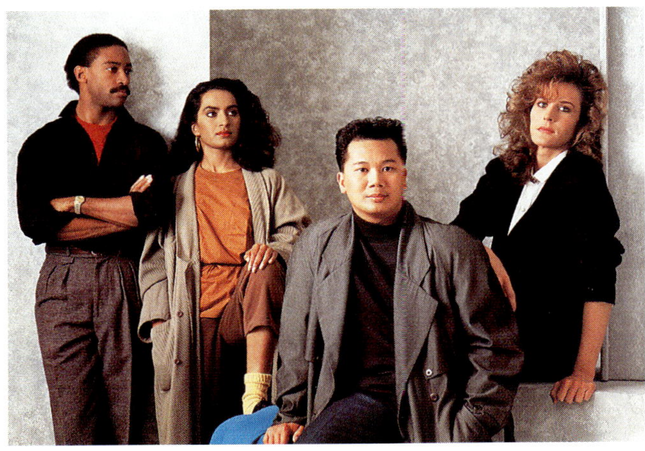

A four-color reproduction made from conventional separations. Reproductions made from UCR and GCR separations should appear identical, even though the individual separations and the three-color images may look drastically different.

Advantages with GCR. When appropriate percentages of GCR are used, advantages associated with this process may include:

- More consistent color reproduction on long pressruns. For 100% GCR separations, any area in the reproduction is composed mostly of only two colors plus black; therefore, any density shift in the tertiary color, black, results in a value shift rather than a hue shift. For conventional separations, however, the tertiary color is a process color and any density shift produces a hue *and* value shift.
- Better trapping because there is less ink on the paper. This is the biggest advantage associated with UCR and is a similar advantage with GCR.
- More saturated colors. Some colors may appear to be less contaminated when using GCR.
- Reduced ink setoff.
- Reduced use of the more expensive process color inks and more of a less expensive black ink.
- Faster press makeready with less waste.

Undercolor Addition

High degrees of UCR or GCR reduce the density of darker colors. For many jobs, this is not a big problem, but for others it may be. To compensate for excessive color reduction, the process of **undercolor addition** can be used. This process is the exact opposite of UCR and makes it possible to add color back into dark tonal areas so they appear richer.

Unsharp Masking

Unsharp masking (USM) is used to make the details of the original copy appear sharper. When done properly, unsharp masking can emphasize selected areas in the original to create an illusion of a sharper image. Unsharp masking works by increas-

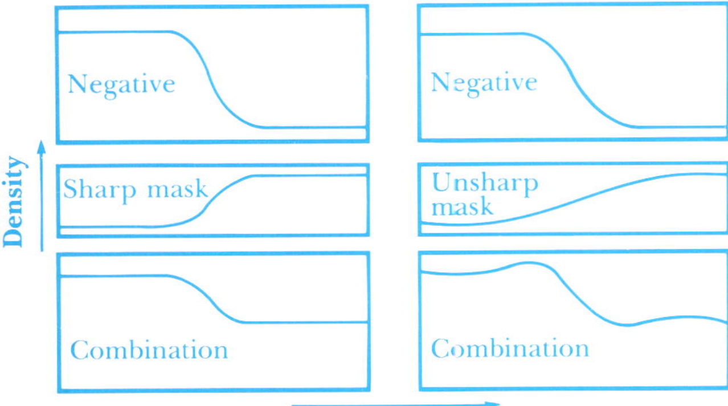

Action of unsharp masking in improving edge sharpness.

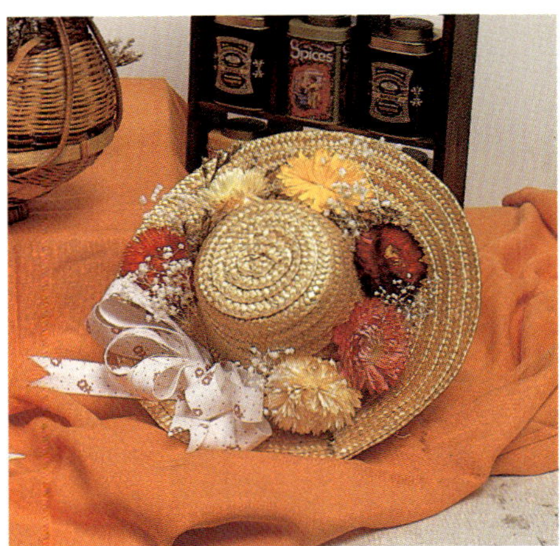

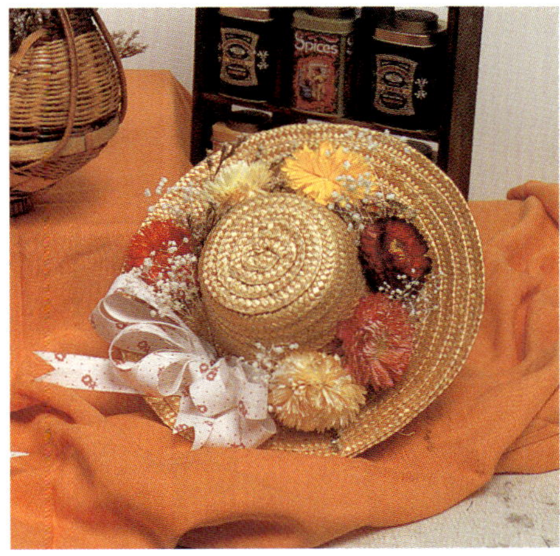

A straight scan *(above)* compared to an image that was separated with unsharp masking applied *(below)*.

ing the density differences at tonal edges (where lighter tones touch darker tones) of the original copy. The light areas become less dense and the adjacent dark areas become more dense. Unsharp masking can be done with conventional photographic color separation by exposing an original through an unsharp mask specially made for that original, and on electronic color scanners by modifying the electronic signals. The color separator must carefully control the amount of unsharp masking; too much can produce objectionable white and black outlines around subjects and increase graininess. In addition, unsharp masking can exaggerate scratches in the emulsion of an original.

Electronic Scanning

Electronic color scanning is the most popular method of creating color separations today; about 95% of all color separations in the U.S. are made by scanners.

Scanners are machines that separate color copy into its components so that it can be reproduced on a printing press. Although the scanners of different manufacturers vary, all use RGB filters to separate color originals into the three subtractive primaries plus a preprogrammed black printer correctly balanced with the color separations.

Scanners can produce continuous-tone intermediate films or screened (halftone) films. Continuous-tone intermediates can be converted into halftones on a standard graphic arts camera or in a contact printing frame for lithography. If the scanning is done properly, these intermediates or halftones will be completely color-corrected and properly masked and will have the proper amount of undercolor removal and gray component replacement.

One important advantage of electronic color scanning is the consistency of reproduction. The scanned separations of matched originals will always match each other, provided the same information is input into the scanner for each original. These sets of separations will match in optical density range, the degree of color correction, and sharpness, which means that separations can be made on the scanner uniformly day after day.

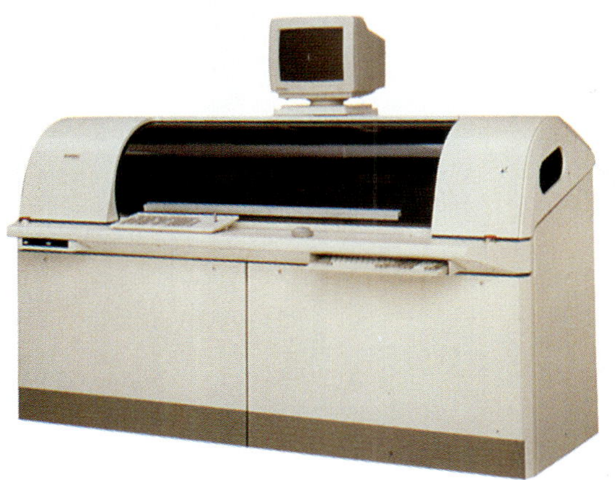

Courtesy of Screen (USA)

The SG–7060P Direct Color Scanner.

Scanner Development

The concept of electronic scanning for producing corrected color separations originated in 1937. At that time, Hans Neugebauer presented a standardized approach in the form of a set of equations that related the tristimulus values of original copy to the density of ink in a three- or four-color halftone reproduction.

At the same time, A. C. Hardy and F. L. Wurzburg published a paper that dealt with the corrections that would be needed if idealized inks could be used. They constructed an experimental scanning machine to substantiate their theories. Eventually, the computer part of this scanner was designed to provide corrections according to the Neugebauer equations. Development continued in cooperation with RCA, which later took over research on the project. At first, the scanner accepted a set of uncorrected camera separation negatives made with standard filters and scanned them using a cathode-ray tube. The corrected signal was projected by a second cathode-ray tube, which exposed the film and provided continuous-tone negatives, one at a time. Research continued for several years, but it was eventually found that the purely theoretical approach of the Neugebauer equations did not yield acceptable separations. The project was suspended in the mid-1950s.

Others also became interested in the concept of electronic color separation. During the '40s and '50s, at least a dozen different scanners appeared. The first and most important of these was developed in the laboratories of Time-Life, Inc., based on research by the Eastman Kodak Co. This scanner was designed on empirical rather than theoretical data and proved to be more successful. It also introduced the principle of color scanning on a rotating drum, with glow lamps traveling across the width.

Rudolf Hell and Crosfield developed scanners that employed cathode-ray tubes to scan uncorrected negatives, producing corrected continuous-tone separation positives. Both of these companies eventually switched to rotary-drum scanners. Hell also produced the Vario-Klischograph, a device that for many years successfully engraved letterpress plates directly on metal and produced halftone positives on plastic foil coated with a nonactinic dye layer that could be converted to silver negatives for lithography. This machine scanned from a flat surface and engraved the plate or foil with a stylus. Several screen rulings could be used, and color and tone reproduction were quite good. Another advantage with letterpress plates was that the camera and conventional platemaking were bypassed completely. After the plates were coated with a resist, they could be re-etched to make corrections in the conventional manner.

Other scanners developed during the 1940s and '50s included the Fairchild, Hunter-Penrose, Belin, and Miehle. The Miehle never got beyond the experimental stage, while the others were more or less successful for some time. These scanners were beset by many problems and therefore had difficulty in competing with conventional photographic methods—although scanners had certain advantages. The output of all of them, except the Vario-Klischograph, consisted of continuous-tone negatives or positives, which still had to be screened by conventional methods. Enlargement was difficult, scans took a long time, and the scanners were expensive. On the other hand, they were capable of producing black printers that could not be matched by conventional photography. Their color correction capabilities were also better in many respects.

The introduction of solid-state electronic circuitry, better light sources, and more suitable film materials led to considerable progress. Direct screening and a wide range of reduction and enlargement, as well as special color correction features, became available. Scanning speed also increased considerably, which helped to justify the high equipment cost. Currently, the rotary-drum scanner is used most often.

Rotary-drum scanners have digital or analog computer sections that assist in making the separations. Digital scanners look up the tristimulus values of the original in a stored color chart, then print out the dot values that were used to generate the appropriate patch on the color chart. Analog scanners read the tristimulus values from the original and process each through the analog computer section for every point on the original. The output values are individually computed and exposed onto film. The output values are individually computed and exposed onto film.

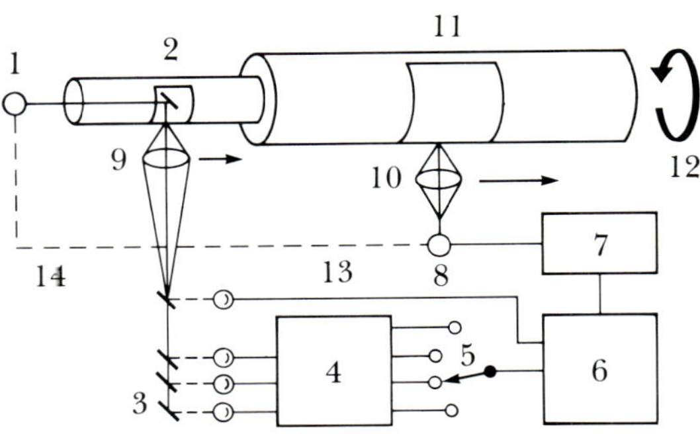

1. Lamp for analysis and exposure
2. Original
3. Color separation mirrors, photomultipliers
4. Color computer
5. Four-color selector switch
6. Tone, UCR, and GCR computer
7. Digital storage for vertical enlargement
8. Light modulator
9. Analyzing lamp advance
10. Exposing lamp advance for horizontal enlargement
11. Enlarged separation
12. Drum rotation (both drums)
13. Unsharp masking channel
14. Fiber optic guide

Simplified block diagram of a rotary-drum scanner.

How a Rotary-Drum Scanner Works

The term "scanner" describes the manner in which copy is viewed (analyzed) and the way the light-sensitive material is exposed.

Mounting the copy. Original transparency or reflection copy is mounted on a transparent analyzing cylinder, or drum, while one or more sheets of unexposed film are mounted either manually or automatically on the exposure cylinder. With scanners that feature one cylinder for scanning and another for exposure, both cylinders rotate at the same speed.

Most of the rotary-drum scanners on the market can scan either color transparencies or flexible reflection copy. Flexibility is necessary because the copy is attached to a rotary cylinder. Positive transparencies are more common, but negative transparencies can also be used on some scanners. Transparencies are far more popular than reflection copy and are usually easier to handle on rotary-drum scanners.

Originals are usually mounted with clear tape. A special powder or oil is applied to the back of the transparency to eliminate or minimize Newton's rings, which are small concentric circles that can

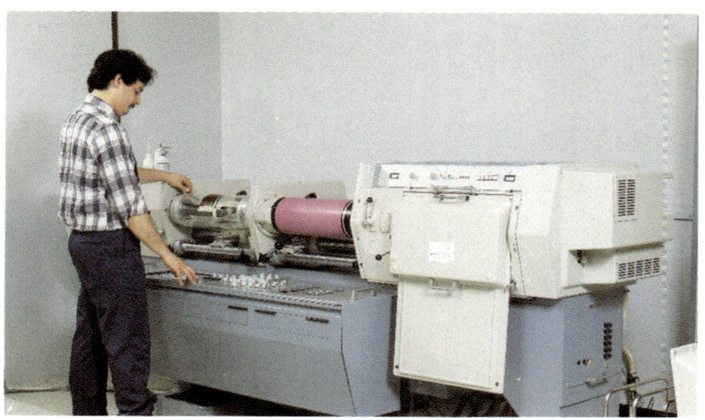

Operator mounts copy and sets reproduction percentage on a Hell rotary-drum scanner.

appear on film when two surfaces are close together but not in perfect contact. In some cases, special holders or drums are used for small transparencies, such as 35-mm transparencies, which are otherwise difficult to hold in position.

Many scanners are equipped with a pin register system to hold the light-sensitive material in place. Such a pin register system ensures that all separations are in register with each other.

Scanning the original. A very small spot of intense white light is projected through or reflected from the original copy. As the analyzing drum rotates, the original copy is scanned by the exposing light source, which travels along the axis of the drum. With each revolution, the light spot advances the width of one scan line. Although this light beam is extremely narrow, the mechanical design provides for slightly overlapping scan lines. These scans are spaced close enough and the exposing beam is wide enough to give the effect of a continuous exposure.

Generally, the number of lines to the inch (or millimeter) is varied to reproduce as much image detail as is desired. Obviously, with more scans per inch or millimeter, more detail can be recorded from the original copy. These scanning lines may vary from a relatively coarse 250 scans/in. (10 scans/mm) to a very fine 2,000 scans/in. (80 scans/mm). It should be stressed that these rates do not refer to halftone screen rulings. These scanning rates determine the **resolution,** or amount of detail, that can be picked up from the original and reproduced on the unexposed film.

Converting the optical signal to an electronic signal. Each spot on the copy is analyzed as light passes from the copy through a small aperture to the scanner's optical system. The exact design of the optical system varies somewhat between manufacturers, but it usually consists of some array of lenses, prisms, mirrors, and interference filters. The net effect of this system is to split the light into four optical signals, each of which passes through either a red, green, or blue separation filter or an aperture for unsharp masking. Each optical signal that passes through a color separation filter is focused on a photomultiplier tube that converts the optical signal into an electronic signal proportional to the amount of each color of light present in the scanned spot on the copy. (As shown above, scanners involve not only photography but also several forms of energy: light, electrical, and mechanical.)

Modifying the electronic signals. These three electronic signals, which correspond to the magenta, yellow, and cyan printing inks, are directed into the **color computer** where they are modified to suit specific inks and are corrected for unwanted colors. Next, the signals go to the **tone reproduction and undercolor removal computer,** which introduces the desired range compression, tone reproduction, and neutral gray balance and, at the same time, computes a signal for the black printer (which can be programmed to be either a full-tone black or a skeleton black).

The fourth optical signal, the one generated by passing light through the aperture for unsharp masking, is activated at this stage. **Unsharp masking** (USM), or **detail enhancement,** is the increase of tonal contrast where light and dark tones come together at the edges of the images. Increased contrast gives the reproduction increased apparent sharpness known as "peaking." This term describes the sudden signal fluctuations at tonal edges. With electronic unsharp masking, the intensity of the peaking signal can be controlled easily.

In the electronic scanning process, the original copy is analyzed from light striking the photomultiplier tube (PMT) through a small aperture. The unsharp masking aperture is normally larger in diameter than the main scanning aperture. As a result, it senses a density change sooner and generates a signal that is much more gradual than the signal generated by the main scanning aperture. The difference between the main scanning aperture signal and the unsharp masking aperture signal is added to the main scanning aperture signal to create the peaking signal. This signal reduces density in the lighter areas, and increases density in the darker areas of the original, creating the illusion of a sharper picture.

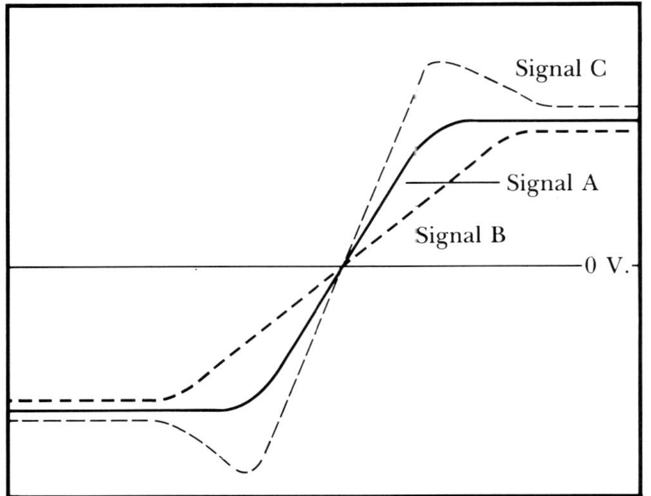

Electronic unsharp masking principle: signal A (from normal scanning aperture), signal B (from unsharp-masking aperture), and signal C (a composite of signal A plus the voltage differential between signal A and signal B).

Where there is no tonal change, both apertures read the same signals and there is no modification to the original signal. The amount of unsharp masking can be controlled by the operator to suit the copy.

Different scanners use slightly different unsharp masking programs to achieve the same result. In this book, *unsharp masking program* refers to the manner in which the unsharp masking signal is generated, controlled, and manipulated.

Controlling reproduction size. The electronically generated and computer-modified signals are sent to a digital **scale computer** that controls reproduction size. Reproduction size in the circumferential direction of the exposing drum is altered electronically. The signals normally produced by the scanning head are converted into digital data using core memory and then played out at a faster or slower speed. Reproduction size in the axial direction is altered mechanically. The scanning head moves at a slower rate than the exposing head for enlargements and a faster rate for reductions.

Reproduction size capabilities of different scanners vary greatly. Scanners with a limited range of reproduction percentages can output a continuous-tone intermediate, which is screened and sized photographically, or a resized duplicate transparency can be used as the original.

Continuous-tone separations made at 500 scans/in. (20 scans/mm) can be enlarged up to three times. Those made at 2,000 scans/in. (80 scans/mm) can be enlarged up to twelve times, when shooting the final printers. These restrictions on the degree of enlargement are necessary because of the lack of detail at the coarser scans. Obviously, if the copy has been scanned at 2,000 lines/in. it has considerably more detail than copy scanned at 500 lines/in. This extra detail in the continuous-tone separations allows greater enlargement.

Exposing the film. With the signals electronically modified, the next step—exposure—is performed. The method of exposure varies somewhat depending upon the sophistication of the scanner. Unlike a separation made on the camera, where the entire light-sensitive material is exposed simultaneously, a separation made on a scanner is exposed in one minute area at a time as the electronic signals are converted into light signals. This exposure occurs as quickly as the corresponding point of the original is scanned and analyzed. The exposure intensity varies according to the relative image density of the scanned original.

Color scanners using contact screens have been available since the 1960s. Newer scanners do not require contact screens for making screened separations. Instead, they use a laser and fiber optics to generate an electronic dot pattern. Such scanners are able to electronically generate halftone patterns

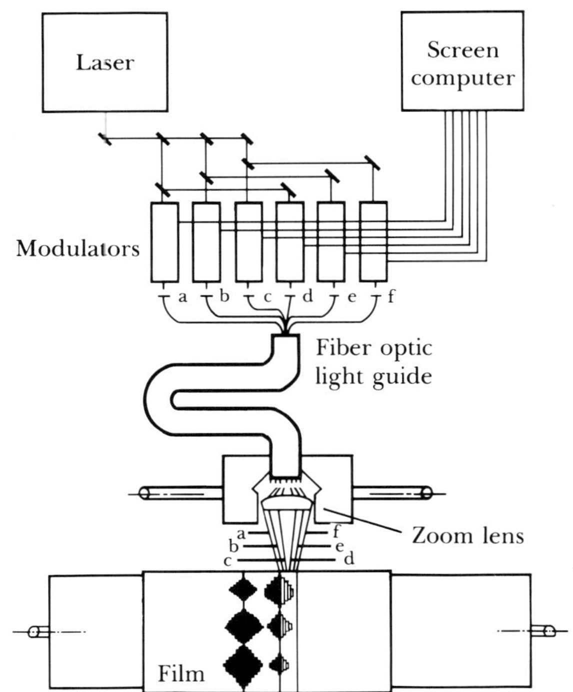

Electronic dot generation.

because separate digital computers store all the necessary information about halftone screens, rulings, and angles. Various screen rulings are available, all of which are switch-selected.

The nature of the dots generated varies with the scanner used. Electronic dot generation (EDG) typically produces hard dots because of the expose/no-expose nature of modulated laser light. Some electronic dot generators produce soft dots; i.e., whole dots with a controlled fall-off, or fringe, around their edges.

A typical EDG system consists of a laser and a bundle of optical fibers or beam splitters. The film is exposed by minute beams of light, which are turned on and off electronically. The elements created by beams of light are referred to as recording spots. Each halftone dot is a grouping of spots; the number of *spots* determines the size of the *dot*. More beams are switched on when a higher dot percentage is required, less for lower dot percentages. The spots overlap somewhat in order to achieve sufficient tonal values.

At first, it was difficult to use laser/fiber optics to generate dots electronically, but today's scanners with EDG capabilities have many advantages. Dots are sharper, picture quality is nearly perfect, and processing is simpler and quicker.

Film and Film Processing

In most cases, continuous-tone or high-contrast orthochromatic film is used, since sensitivity to all colors is not required. Dimensionally stable polyester-based film is the best. When continuous-tone film is used, the emulsion should have straight-line tone reproduction—from approximately 0.30 to 1.80 density—to avoid tonal distortions. Since contact with the exposure drum is essential, a slightly matte surface aids in providing good adhesion.

Typically, the separation film is loaded into cassettes in the darkroom, or the scanner is located entirely within a darkroom. A lighttight cassette is locked into position on the scanner. Its contents are then automatically attached to the exposure drum. After exposure, the contents are unloaded and removed to the darkroom for processing. To ensure the greatest consistency, all four separations should be processed at the same time. Rapid-access films and processors are widely used with scanners. Automatic film processing ensures quick, standardized, quality production.

Before the film can be exposed, however, the scanner must be calibrated to the film and film processing method. The calibration procedure is fairly simple. Four gray scales, each one corresponding to a particular printer, are scanned or electronically generated and exposed to the film. After processing, the exposed steps are measured on a densitometer and the resulting densities or dot percentages are fed back into the scanner. For normal daily calibration, it is only necessary to reset the highlight, midtone, and shadow density steps of the gray scale.

Even if the separations are exposed properly and uniformly, how the film is processed can drastically affect the final results. Therefore, uniformity in developing the film is essential. A properly operating processor ensures that all separations are developed equally and are balanced with each other. Tray development requires time and temperature controls, as well as uniform and constant agitation—and the latter is not easy to do. Thus, the consistency and development control offered by rapid-access films and processors makes the use of automatic processing a necessity.

On the other hand, most automatic lith film processors must be closely controlled to prevent the liquid chemistry from getting out of balance; getting a developer bath back to standard is difficult and time-consuming. Pre-exposed gray scales should be run through the automatic lith film processor and measured densitometrically. These results are then used for controlling developer replenishment. Many newer automatic lith processors have rapid access capabilities. This procedure of calibrating the exposing device with the film and chemistry is known as linearization.

Scanner Output

Most scanners are designed to produce negative color separations. Reversing from negative to positive is simply a matter of adjusting the circuitry, as is changing the image orientation from right- to

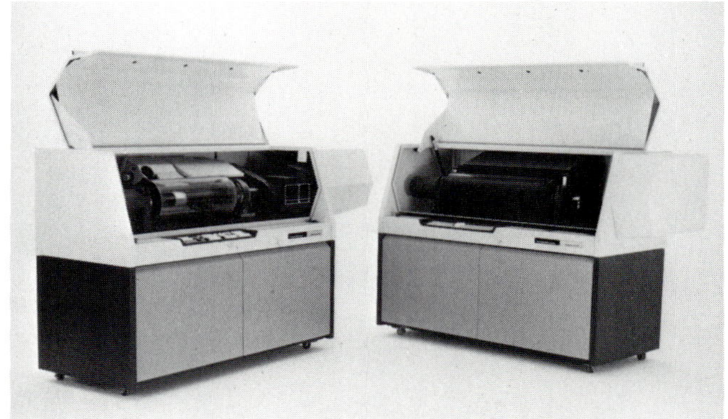

Courtesy Crosfield Electronics, Inc.

Color scanner input unit *(left)* and output unit.

wrong-reading. To those familiar with characteristic curves such as the D log E plot, it is obvious that different response curves are necessary for negatives and positives. This capability is built into the computer portion of a scanner, making the changeover fairly easy.

Halftoned separations are made either by using contact screens and high-contrast films (on older models) or by electronic dot generation. Special filmholders, exposing methods, and electronic circuitry are needed for this purpose. One disadvantage of screened separations is that if they require further enlargement, they cannot be used. However, most scanners have a more-than-adequate enlargement range. In many cases in commercial four-color printing, the same copy has to be reproduced to several different sizes. In such cases, it would be more practical to prepare continuous-tone separations and then enlarge or reduce them as required for the final screened printers.

Scanners produce either one, two, or four separations at a time, depending upon the particular machine and the size of the intermediate needed. Producing four separations at once obviously saves time. However, one-at-a-time separations have the advantage of lower machine cost, since duplicate exposure units are not required.

Many light sources are used to expose film, from glow lamps to lasers. It should be noted that the laser is used only to expose the film (using fiber optics), not to scan or analyze the original. Several manufacturers offer laser-equipped machines or can add the laser attachment to some of their existing machines.

A laser is merely a different exposing light source. Certainly, it has many advantages over conventional light sources: high intensity, resulting in high exposing speeds and the use of less-expensive ortho lith films; more reliable operation; longer operating life; and greater consistency. The laser can be controlled far more effectively, even regarding the shape of the dot it produces. The two most common types of lasers used for exposure are the argon-ion (bluish green light) and the helium-neon (reddish light).

Today's scanners incorporate digital computers. Capturing information in digital form makes it possible to record and store digital data on magnetic tape or disk for later use; to transmit it from one device or location to another; to control graphic placement of data by assigning *x-y* coordinates; to better modulate or control other devices, such as light sources; and to merge with other digitally stored data.

Scanners that can generate their own halftones without a contact screen are the result of linking the laser with digital technology. A laser scanner is able to electronically generate a halftone pattern, because a separate digital computer stores information about the halftone screen, its rulings, and screen angles. Various screen rulings are available, all of which are switch-selected.

Scanner Programming

When a scanner is installed, it is programmed to accommodate the kind of work done in that plant. The program includes the following:

- Range compression
- Tone reproduction
- Gray balance
- Black printer characteristics
- Ink and paper densities
- Platemaking losses
- Screen and photographic emulsion characteristics

Once the programs have been established and recorded, operation becomes standard for the majority of copy. As with any computer, however, these instruments can work only with the information that has been programmed into them. This constraint demands a high level of operator competence. Operators have to know how to evaluate the original and what the computer can do with the information. Operators have many controls at their disposal but must know how to handle them in order to produce excellent results.

Operators who have had no previous experience with scanners are trained for a period of two to four weeks. This training usually takes place during the programming period so that the operator can understand the various functions and learn how to program the scanner, and so that any deviations from the norm can be introduced, if necessary. The training usually includes a period in the scanner manufacturer's training center, in addition to working under production conditions after a scanner has been installed in a plant.

Using the Scanner

Once the scanner has been programmed and tested, a color separation can be made.

First, the original is mounted on the scanning drum. With a scanner that has a removable scanning drum, one original can be scanned while another is being mounted on an extra drum. Next, the required enlargement or reduction percentage is set on the scanner.

Before a separation is made, the copy is first evaluated by using the densitometer built into the scanner. Highlight and shadow densities are analyzed on an optical viewer and entered into the machine. Required densities or dot percentages are entered into the scanner. The computer takes over the calculation of range compression, cast removal, setting midtone, highlight, and shadow densities, gray balance, and color values.

The scanner operator decides how much color correction is needed, which colors to boost, whether shadow expansion is necessary, the amount of undercolor removal, the percentage of gray component replacement, and the amount of unsharp masking to use to emphasize details.

The operator has many controls available to make special corrections or deviations from copy. It is possible to increase or decrease unwanted colors in each separation. Overprint colors of red, green, and blue can be adjusted separately, and flesh tones can be altered on some scanners to favor detail rendition in any part of the scale. Undercolor removal and the black printer can also be varied. Many of these corrections cannot be made with photographic color separation.

At this stage, the machine is ready to run, except for the loading of the unexposed film. If a contact screen is required to make a screened separation, it is loaded with the film. The emulsion side of the film is up, toward the light source.

Once the film is loaded, the scanner can be started. Depending upon the capabilities of the scanner and the reproduction size, one, two, or all four separations can be made simultaneously. At this point, since the scanner is already programmed, it is simply a matter of flipping the right switches or depressing the right pushbutton.

Flatbed Color Scanners

Tabletop and large flatbed color scanners are becoming more popular because of the mechanical simplicity of their design and their ability to accept rigid original copy.

Typical flatbed color scanners accept transparent and reflection copy. Most flatbed scanners are monochromatic or color, not both. The size limits of acceptable copy vary from scanner to scanner. Some scanners accommodate originals as small as 35 mm; many accommodate originals larger than 8½×11 in. (216×279 mm). Enlargement capabilities exist on flatbed color scanners.

The way the original image is mounted on the flatbed color scanner also varies from model to model. On one model, the operator mounts the original copy on a special carrier, which is then put into the machine. On other models, the original is placed directly on the flatbed.

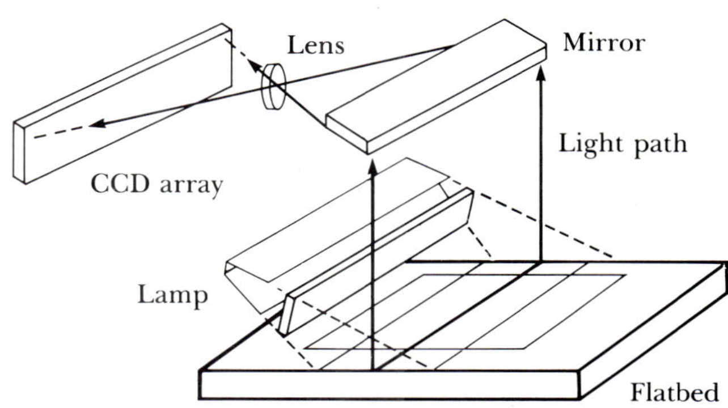

Schematic of a flatbed color scanner.

Once the original has been mounted, the operator can view the prescanned image on the screen of a color image previewer. Almost all flatbed color scanners have options for an image previewer. This previewer allows the operator to rotate the image, crop and size it, mark the highlight and shadow areas, and usually input color corrections. Like the computer of a rotary drum scanner, the computer of a flatbed scanner is programmed to include such things as tone reproduction, gray balance, and ink-on-paper densities. The operator need only press a few keys to initiate the scanning process.

The flat platen moves under a high-intensity quartz-halogen or pulsed-xenon fixed light source and a mirror. The mirror directs the light reflected from (or transmitted through) the original through a lens and then to the **charge-coupled device (CCD array),** a semiconductor device that scans the image in blue, green, and red colored light signals. The flat platen may move back and forth three times to allow these three additive primary color signals to be recorded. Some flatbed scanners make two passes of the image, recording one half of the image with each pass of the platen. This captures a high-resolution image. Separate motors are used to drive the platen in forward and reverse directions. There is less chance of misregister if the CCD arrays read all three colors at once. However, not all flatbed scanners have triple CCD arrays, so it is very important to maintain even illumination of the strip being scanned on the flatbed color scanner. This requirement is especially important if the CCD is going to make two or more side-by-side passes of the image. Uneven illumination could cause misregister and inaccurate recording of color.

Evaluation of Scanned Separations

After development and drying, scanned separations can be treated in much the same way as separations made in a process camera. Dot etching on soft-dot halftones can be performed if necessary; however, one of the objectives of using scanners is to minimize or even eliminate the need for handwork on the separations. If handwork is excessive, then the operator techniques should be modified; either the original evaluation of the color copy is incorrect, or the machine settings are not appropriate. Both should be reassessed, and experiments should be conducted until a higher degree of quality is attained.

Prescan Analysis Systems

Prescan analysis computer-aided systems assist the scanner operator in controlling the numerous variables encountered daily in the color separation process. These systems help the scanner operator identify the variables and program output instructions and set the scanner controls for optimum quality and consistent results. The program automatically calculates the optimum scanner setup based on copy analysis, specific printing requirements, and scanner characteristics.

Prescan analysis systems have four basic functions: they provide for accurate and easily accessible documentation of printing specifications; allow for consistency between operators and between scanners; decrease copy analysis time during scanner setup, which increases scanner productivity; and assist the scanner operator in tone and color balance manipulation for optimum quality, thus reducing the amount of costly time spent on range compression and color correction during the scanning process.

Prescan analysis systems are only as accurate as the information input by the system's operator. Specific data pertaining to the original copy, such as minimum and maximum densities and color balance, must be programmed. Incorporating this information with previously stored printing standards and scanner characteristics, the computer calculates proper tone reproduction, gray balance, color correction, and undercolor removal for a particular original. The computer output is a printed sheet documenting these calculations.

Direct-Screen Color Separation on the Process Camera

In plants that are not equipped with a scanner, the process camera is sometimes used to reproduce a color original. In this method, color separations are made by exposing the color original through a halftone contact screen directly onto high-contrast panchromatic lith film. Red, green, and blue filters are used to separate the picture information into cyan, magenta, and yellow. The black printer negative is usually made by a split-filter exposure. One intermediate step involves making one to four photographic masks, based on the amount of color correction needed. The photographic masks are placed in contact with either the original or the contact screen, depending upon whether the original is transparent or reflective. Five to eight films may be needed for the direct-screen color separation. Using this method, an experienced operator can produce a color separation in approximately one hour.

Preparing the Camera for Direct-Screen Separations

The quality of a color separation depends upon choosing proper filters, film, and chemistry, which should be precisely monitored. Quality control instruments and targets such as a gray scale, color control guide (color patches), and register marks are essential to achieve accurate analysis and repeatable results. Film manufacturers should be consulted to determine which filters and procedures are recommended.

Color separation filters. Color separation filters are dyed gelatin sheets sometimes mounted in glass. Filters for process color work are specific shades of blue, green, and red that divide the spectrum into approximate thirds. The specific color transmission characteristics of the filters are identified by numerical designators. For example, Kodak designates its filters with Wratten numbers; other manufacturers use similar systems. The blue Kodak filter used for making the yellow printer separation is Wratten 47 or 47B; the green filter for making the magenta printer is Wratten 58 or 61; and the red filter for making the cyan printer is Wratten 29, 25, or 23A, depending on the particular color separation/correction method used. An amber filter, Wratten 85B, is sometimes used to make the

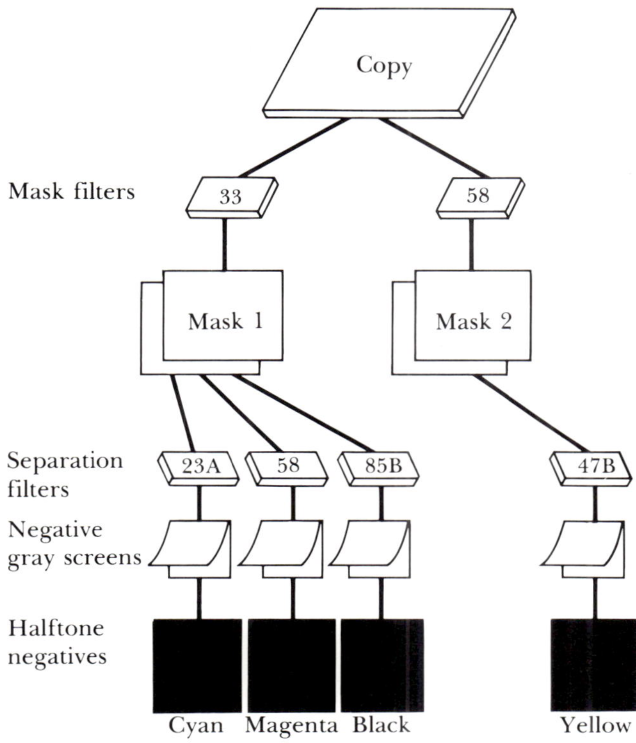

Flow diagram for direct-screen color separation. The filters used may vary depending on characteristics of the photosensitive material used.

black printer or the mask in the single-mask method of color correction.

The gray scale. A photographic gray scale should be mounted along the edge of the original copy to be photographed so that its series of reflection densities, ranging from white to black, will receive the same amount of light as the subject and so that there is no direct reflection from its semiglossy surface into the camera lens. Examining the gray scale reproduced on each separation negative gives a visual indication of the tone separation in highlight, midtone, and shadow areas of each negative.

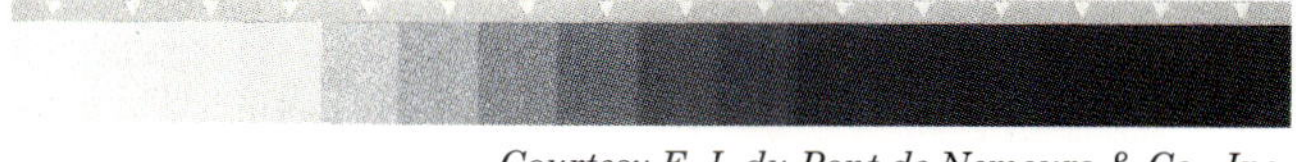

Courtesy E. I. du Pont de Nemours & Co., Inc.

Gray scale.

Color control patches. These patches are supplied as part of the color separation guides and kits available from graphic arts supply houses. The images of these patches on the negatives and positives provide measurable densities that indicate the effectiveness of the separation and color-correction methods being used. If the patches are correctly separated, the copy will be also.

If the inks to be used do not closely match the inks of the color control patches in hue, purity, and saturation, sample patches of the actual inks to be used should be substituted. If the reproduction is to be printed on paper that isn't glossy, these new ink patches should be printed on the paper being used. The GATF Color Reproduction Guide II *(below)* is one quality control device that permits the camera operator to make color separations that compensate for the individual plant's ink, paper, plate, and press variables. The guide is printed in-house under normal production conditions using standard process inks on the most commonly used paper stocks run on as many presses as possible. A four-color patch consisting of a three-color solid plus a 50% tint of black is also desirable. A more complete color chart will give additional information.

Pin register system and overlay mask. A pin register system is mandatory for precisely aligning the four separation films. The film, contact screen, and mask are the important items that must be in register during a color separation exposure. For cameras equipped with a built-in pin system on the

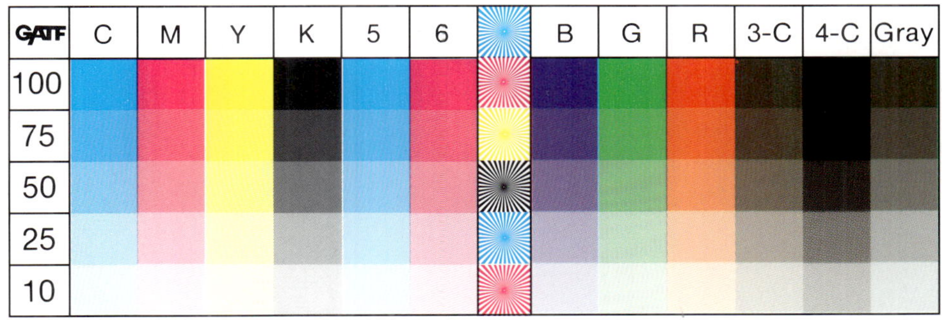

GATF Color Reproduction Guide II.

camera back, a matching punch is needed to punch the film, contact screens, and masks. If a camera is not equipped with a built-in pin system, a separate pin bar is needed.

A set of overlay masks is needed for proper drawdown of films on the camera back. The overlay mask should be about 4 in. (100 mm) longer and wider than the film. A window must be cut out of the mask and overlap the film at least ¼ in. (25 mm) on three sides and ¾ in. (75 mm) on the side with the pins. The overlay mask must be black (fully exposed and processed) to eliminate possible reflections from the camera back. The key to the overlay mask's performance is precise alignment.

Photographic Masking

A **mask** is a weak image recorded on continuous-tone photographic film. **Masking** is the principal means for correcting and adjusting the inherent deficiencies of ink, paper, and press conditions. Several types of masks and masking systems are used in the photographic color separation process, but all are designed to provide three functions: (1) tone compression, (2) color correction, and (3) detail enhancement.

Because originals usually have a basic density range greater than the lithographic process can reproduce with paper and inks, tone compression is necessary. A mask having a density range of 0.80 used with a transparency having a density range of 2.70 reduces the density range of the original to 1.90—within the reproduction capability of the press. Reflection copy has a density range closer to the reproduction range than a transparency has. In addition to tone compression, the tone reproduction curve can be adjusted for a particular original by adjusting the placement of the midtone dot in relation to the highlight and shadow dots. In photographic masking, this is achieved by changing the mask number (see the section on calculating and evaluating masks).

Another function of a photographic mask is to correct for the unwanted light absorptions of inks and paper. To correct for the magenta ink, the yellow separation negative is made to print less yellow wherever the yellow and magenta print together. Similarly, to correct for the cyan ink, the magenta separation negative is made to print less magenta wherever cyan and magenta print together. The yellow is usually not corrected.

The third function of a photographic mask, detail enhancement, is achieved by deliberately making the masks unsharp. In this book, detail enhancement refers to the visual improvement of original copy by increasing the apparent sharpness in the reproduction.

Color correction masks. When the photographic color separation method is used, color correction is accomplished by producing a color-correction mask. The mask is a continuous-tone black-and-white film, which the color separator produces by exposing the original to the masking film though the appropriate red, blue, or green separation filters. The mask is then placed over the contact screen and the panchromatic film during the color separation process. The mask acts as a neutral density filter and reduces the exposure, or amount of light penetrating the contact screen, which reduces the size of the halftone dot produced on the film.

For example, by properly adjusting the density of the mask before exposing the yellow separation, the amount of yellow (or the size of the halftone dots) in the yellow printer can be reduced only where magenta and yellow will overprint. The magenta-yellow overprint will reproduce as red instead of orangish red in the final reproduction.

The amount of density needed for each mask is determined by taking densitometric readings through the complementary red, green, and blue filters of each solid primary color from an ink and paper sample supplied by the printer. These densitometric readings are used to calculate the hue and grayness of the cyan, magenta, and yellow inks. The hue and grayness values of the primary inks can be used to plot the GATF Color Triangle (see p. 8:9).

Straight lines are drawn from each apex of the GATF Triangle through each plotted primary, extending to the edge of the GATF Triangle. Around the outside edge of the GATF Triangle are percent masking numbers that indicate the amount of density needed in the mask to reduce the amount of light striking the separation film during the exposure, which will reduce the size of the halftone dot and color-correct for the corresponding secondary color.

Since each ink has two unwanted absorptions, six lines can be drawn, suggesting that six color-correction masks are needed to completely color-correct for a given ink and paper combination.

However, due to the amount of time and materials needed, it is not practical in a production environment to completely color-correct for a given ink set when making separations photographically. Normally, only two masks are made to correct for the most unwanted absorptions, and the color-

correction process is completed by dot etching the halftone separation films.

With two masks, a considerable amount of color correction for unwanted ink absorptions is possible, in addition to range adjustment and tone reproduction control. One mask is made with a magenta filter, and it is used in exposing the cyan and magenta printer negatives. The other is made with a green filter, and it is used in exposing the yellow separation negative. Most direct-screen separations are made by this two-mask system.

Highlight masks. If color correction masks are made properly, highlight detail reproduces correctly, normally meaning no highlight masking is needed. However, it is sometimes desirable to enhance detail in a high-key subject or to improve poor copy. Highlight masks are made in several ways. For color transparencies, a premask is exposed by contact on a panchromatic lith film and developed in continuous-tone chemistry to a maximum density of between 0.25 and 0.50, with a range between 0.15 and 0.40, disregarding catchlights. Control patches are covered while exposing the premask. The mask is reregistered to the transparency, and the color correction masks are made normally from this combination. When separation negatives are made, the premask is discarded. If the highlights in the copy are colored, rather than neutral, it is better to make three premasks, one through each of the separation filters. The red-filter premask is used to make the cyan mask, the green-filter premask for the magenta mask, and the blue-filter premask for the yellow mask. When making continuous-tone negatives from reflection copy, a highlight premask is made on panchromatic lith film in the same manner and to similar densities, with the premask registered at the camera back when making the color correction masks.

Another method to make highlight masks for continuous-tone negatives is to expose rapid-reversal duplicating film to one or more of the three color negatives and develop in continuous-tone chemistry to the desired maximum densities. The mask made in this way is registered with the negative. This highlight mask is useful if the separations have been made and the copy has been removed from the camera or enlarger.

Unsharp masking. Detail enhancement is achieved by deliberately making the masks unsharp. A certain amount of unsharpness is built into most masking films; however, if a greater amount of unsharpness is desired, a spacer can be used between the masking film and transparency during exposure. Combining the unsharp mask with the sharp original from which the mask is made enhances the apparent sharpness of subsequent images.

The apparent sharpness is a result of the increased density differences at tonal edges. The light areas become less dense and the adjacent dark areas become more dense, thus increasing the density differences at the tonal edges. A comparison between a photographic sharp mask versus an unsharp mask and how each affects the tonal edges of subsequent images is shown on p. 8:21. The "humps" in the unsharp mask combination indicate that the density difference between the light tone and the adjacent dark tone has been exaggerated.

Masking Procedures for the Direct-Screen Method

Because of the wide availability of different films, chemistry, and filters, the procedures may vary slightly. Following are general procedures for masking in the direct-screen method.

1. Load the original in the copyboard, along with a color separation gray scale with three-aimpoint control (highlight, midtone, and shadow representation). Include register marks and a color control guide with primary and overprint colors.

2. Set up the pin registration system and overlay mask.

3. Punch, expose, and process a piece of pan film (0.004 in. thick). This film (spacer number one) represents the actual size and thickness of the pan film used during the separation. Punch, expose, and process a piece of pan masking film (0.007 in.) thick. This film (spacer number two) simulates the contact screen used during the separation. (Note: Both spacer films must be completely black in order to eliminate reflections from the camera back.)

4. Place spacer number one on the camera back, emulsion up. Place spacer number two on top of spacer number one, emulsion up. These films position the mask for exposure at a specific distance from the lens. The mask will be in the same position during the separation-negative stage.

5. Place a magenta filter in the filter holder for mask number one. Photomechanical filters are controlled for thickness and uniformity. This prevents distortion of the image, which would give the false impression of a lens aberration.

6. Punch a piece of pan masking film and place it, emulsion down, on the camera back. Expose and develop the film according to the instruction sheet

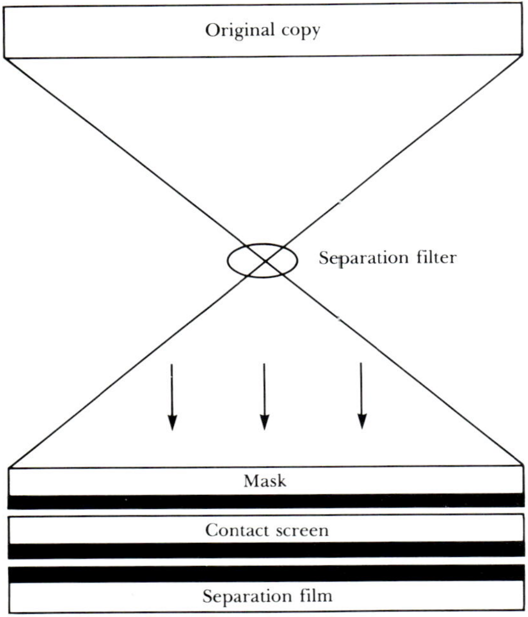

Camera-back masking.

in the film package. (**Note:** This exposure and development information is a good starting point; adjustments may be necessary because of diverse conditions.)

7. To produce mask number two, place a green filter in the filter holder. Expose and develop according to film specifications.

Calculation and evaluation of masks. The mask number is calculated from the transmission densities of the three control patches on the mask, which are expressed as A (highlight), M (midtone), and B (shadow). (The base-plus-fog density must be zeroed on the densitometer before reading the gray scale.) AB is the mask range, which should be between 0.6 and 0.7; a value of at least 0.50 is generally acceptable. AM is the highlight-to-midtone range, and MB is the midtone-to-shadow range. The A density can exceed 1.00, but be careful to avoid mask penetration problems. The B density should not exceed 0.40.

The **mask number** is obtained by subtracting the AM range from the MB range. For example, if the A patch in the mask has a density of 0.95, the M patch 0.65, and the B patch 0.30, then:

Mask range: 0.95 – 0.30 = 0.65
AM range: 0.95 – 0.65 = 0.30
MB range: 0.65 – 0.30 = 0.35
Mask #: 0.35 – 0.30 = 0.05

A mask number of 0 is suitable for separations from average reflection copy. A mask number of 0 indicates a straight-line tone reproduction curve, which means that the midtone density is midway between highlight and shadow. A sagging curve is indicated by a negative mask number, and a bulging curve by a positive mask number.

The above examples are recommended figures; they may vary under certain conditions. For example, mask numbers are highest for separations made by contact printing, and lowest for separations made by camera. The reason for this relationship is that light scattering, which occurs in all optical equipment, causes the gradation curve of the separations to sag more than in contact separations. These differences are small, but they are nevertheless important and should be considered. Some varieties of pan masking film are designed so that mask number and range are adjusted by exposure and development manipulation. A mask calculator is also available, which makes more precise adjustments in exposure and development possible.

In the case of transparencies, a higher mask number is used because the transparency's range usually must be compressed more. A tolerance of ±0.05 is permissible in the mask number and range. The information below is also helpful:

- The greater the AB range, the more color correction and tone compression obtained.
- Longer development time increases the AB range.
- Higher mask numbers produce more highlight/midtone contrast.
- More exposure raises the mask number.

A slight change of AB range will have little or no effect on the mask number. A large change in the AB will affect the mask number; in other words, a change in mask number or AB range would be needed to maintain the original value.

The majority of the time, balanced masks (meaning the same AB range and mask number for both masks) are required for proper tone reproduction. There are instances when unbalanced masks are required due to additional color correction; however, caution must be used in order to acquire proper tone reproduction and gray balance.

Once both masks are exposed and developed with correct aimpoints (AB range and mask number), clean the masks properly with antistatic film cleaner or some other appropriate cleaner.

Exposing the Separation Negatives

Three exposures will be necessary—a main, flash, and bump exposure. The cyan negative should be

made first to acquire the proper tonal scale. Use this filter and mask data chart to determine the correct conditions to expose each printer. (Normally, the screen angles are black 45°, cyan 105°, magenta 75°, and yellow 90° but other combinations are sometimes used. For example, to minimize moiré patterns, the predominant color is often screened at 45°. If a skeleton black is used, as is often done in direct screen color separation, the magenta or cyan is often made at 45° and the black at 75° or 105°.) The steps for exposing negatives follow the chart. (Filter numbers are Kodak Wratten numbers.)

Filter and Mask Data Chart

Printer	Filter	Mask	Screen Angle
Cyan	29*	1	45
Magenta	58†	1	75
Yellow	47B‡	2	90
Black	85B§	2	105

*The 25 filter absorbs less green than a 29 filter, allowing more cyan to print in reds. A 23A filter absorbs less green than a 25 filter.
†The 61 filter achieves higher color saturation than a 58 filter. The 61 filter is ideal when masking is not done for color correction. Excessive saturation causes trouble when masking methods are used.
‡The 47B filter gives a more complete separation; a 47 filter is used to shorten exposure time.
§No filter, 85B, or a split-filter technique can be used. The split-filter method involves using the three separation filters for cyan, magenta, and yellow.

1. Punch and place an unexposed piece of pan film on the camera back, emulsion side up. Place the 45° preangled contact screen on top of the film, emulsion side down. With a clean chamois, gently apply pressure to the contact screen in one direction to ensure good contact between the film and screen. Apply the overlay mask (not photographic mask). Activate the flash lamp, and expose for the proper shadow dot.

2. Remove the overlay mask. Position the cyan photographic mask on top of the contact screen. Reapply the overlay mask, and close the camera back. Insert the proper filter (refer to the data chart). Activate the integrator for the main exposure.

3. Open the camera back. Remove the overlay mask, photographic mask, and contact screen. Reapply the photographic mask and overlay mask. Close the camera back for the bump exposure.

4. Repeat the above sequence for the magenta, yellow, and black negatives. Make sure that the contact screen, filter, and masks are selected for the appropriate printers. The sequence of the main, flash, and bump exposures is unimportant. The consistent repetition of the sequence is significant.

5. Process the exposed films through an automatic lith or rapid-access processor.

Analyzing Separation Negatives

Read the A, M, and B dot values on the gray scale of the cyan printer. Verify that you have the correct tone reproduction for the particular original. Listed below are examples of tone reproduction values for various types of originals.

Typical Tone Values for Different Types of Originals

	Low-Key	Average	High-Key
Highlight	5%	5%	5%
Midtone	55%	60%	65%
Shadow	90%	95%	95%

(Note: **Low-key copy** is an original primarily consisting of midtone to shadow values. **High-key** copy is an original primarily consisting of highlight to midtone values.)

Check the color control guide for color correction. To verify sufficient color correction, the primary overprint patches must be analyzed. Shown is a conceptual example of a perfectly color-corrected cyan printer.

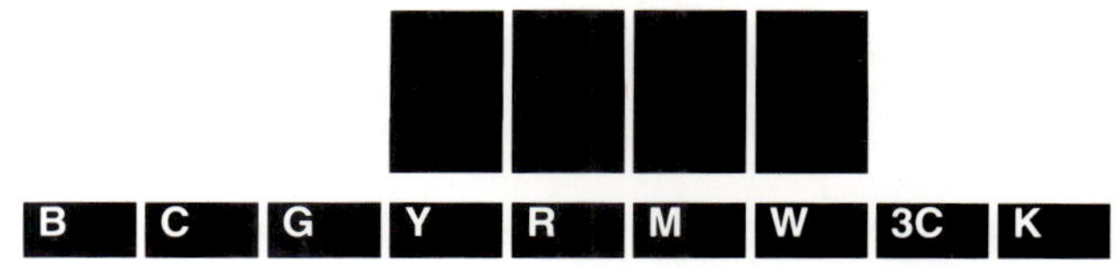

Ideal cyan negative.

If more color correction is necessary, refer to the "Calculation and Evaluation of Masks" section, and adjust the AB range. If adjusting the AB range does not give maximum color correction, a split-filter masking technique may be needed.

Once the cyan printer has the correct tone reproduction and color correction, the magenta, yellow, and black printers must be analyzed for gray bal-

ance and color correction. Listed below are typical gray balance values for average copy. (Note: To achieve the ideal gray balance, the ink and paper combination must be taken into consideration.)

Typical Gray-Balanced Dot Values

	Highlight	Midtone	Shadow
Cyan	5%	60%	95%
Magenta	3%	50%	85%
Yellow	3%	50%	85%
Black	–	1–5%	40–60%

If the gray balance needs to be adjusted, it may be necessary to manipulate the main, flash, and bump exposures. Shown below are conceptual examples of perfectly color-corrected magenta and yellow printers.

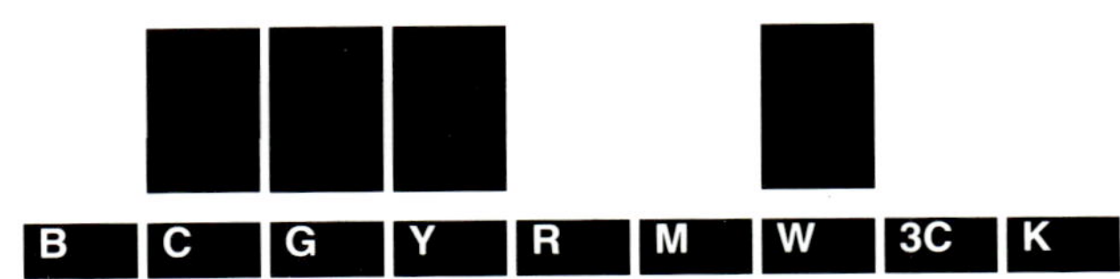

Ideal magenta negative.

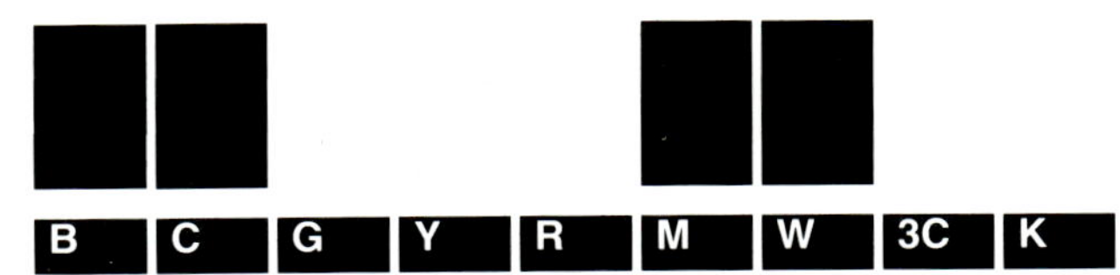

Ideal yellow negative.

Evaluating color separation negatives using control patches. The appearance of the color patches in the masked negatives shows whether the color correction has been properly carried out. For a given color separation, the various patches may be divided into "wanted" and "unwanted" colors. For example, the unwanted colors in the cyan printer are yellow, magenta, and their overprint, red. These require no cyan in their reproduction and, in order to achieve this result, they should match the white patch in density.

Balancing a set of separation negatives. A "balanced" set of negatives is not necessarily one in which all the gray scales match, step for step. Such a set will not print a neutral gray scale with the commonly used process inks, but will result in a series of brown steps unless corrections are made at a later stage. Without further corrections, matched gray scales on the separations would reproduce as neutral gray only with a theoretically perfect set of process inks. *A "balanced" set of negatives is a set that will print a neutral scale of grays with a specific set of inks.* The gray scales on such a set will not match, but the differences between them will be much the same for every color job that is run with these same inks and printing conditions. The operator, then, instead of matching the separation gray scales to each other, matches the red-separation gray scale to other red-separation gray scales that are found correct for the conditions, the blue to other good blues, and the green to other good greens.

Standard Viewing Conditions for Transparencies

Consistency in color viewing becomes complicated because of the number of procedural steps and persons involved in producing a full-color printed piece. If color originals, proofs, and press sheets are not viewed under the same viewing conditions, there will be errors in color evaluation. To reduce these problems, all persons involved in the color reproduction process must view color under the same standard conditions.

In 1989, the accredited American National Standards Institute (ANSI) issued revised specifications for standard conditions for evaluating the color quality of reflection and transparent copy, such as color originals, color proofs, and press sheets. These standards deal specifically with lighting specifications and the visual surround.

Direct Viewing of Transparencies

In the graphic arts, it is frequently necessary to evaluate color transparencies either alone or in comparison to a reflection print. ANSI PH2.30-1989 provides standards for viewing color transparencies either directly or by projection. In both cases, the standards are the same as those for reflection prints with respect to chromaticity, correlated color temperature, spectral power distribution, and color rendering index. (For a fuller discussion of the

ANSI standard with regard to viewing reflection copy, see Chapter 8, "Proofing.")

With regard to transmission surfaces, light intensity is called luminance, and refers to the light emitted by a source. The luminance at the surface of the transparency viewer is specified as 1,400±300 candelas/m^2 (409±88 footlamberts). Departures from uniformity must be gradual, with no area measuring less than 75% of the luminance at the center of the viewer.

ANSI PH2.30-1989 specifies that the diffusion characteristics of the illuminator surface must provide light that can be measured at any angle up to 45° from the surface, and the luminance must be at least 90% of that measured at 90°.

The standard for direct viewing of transparencies has a provision calling for 2-in. white borders on three sides of large transparencies. The border must have a luminance of at least half the value of the luminance behind the transparency. If the size of the border is greater than four times the size of the transparency, then the border should be covered with an opaque gray surface of 60% reflectance.

The environmental conditions for transparency viewing are the same as those for viewing reflection copy, with all surrounding surfaces being a neutral gray of Munsell N8/. If the transparency is being compared with a reflection print, the transparency viewer should be placed in the viewing booth with the print.

Projection Viewing of Transparencies

The projection viewing of transparencies has some unique considerations. As mentioned, many color specifications of the light at the projection plane are the same those as for reflection prints or direct viewing of transparencies. The standard for the luminance at the projection screen is the same as for the surface of a transparency illuminator.

Two specifications relate to the uniformity of screen luminance. Illumination falloff should be uniform and gradual from the center of the screen. The luminance at any point should not be less than 40% of the luminance at the center of the screen.

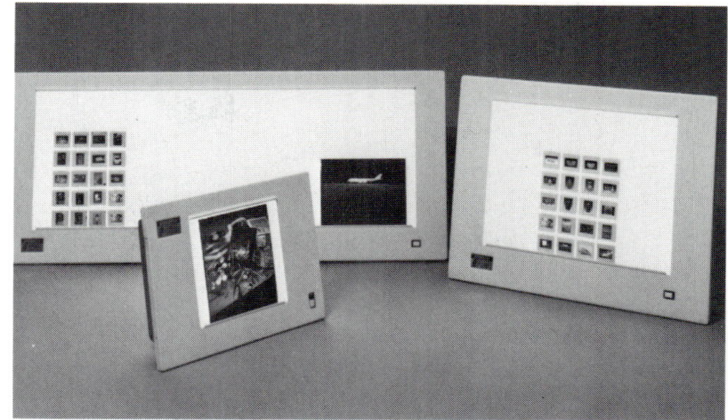

Courtesy GTI Graphic Technology, Inc.

5,000 K standard transparency viewers.

The luminance measured from the center of the screen at any angle up to 25° must not be less than 75% of the luminance measured perpendicular to the center of the screen.

The environmental considerations for projection viewing specify that other sources of illumination must be baffled or extinguished. Furthermore, all exposed surfaces such as walls, ceilings, and floors should be colored neutral gray or blocked by neutral gray surfaces with reflectance factors no greater than 60%.

The ANSI standard contains provisions that shielding should be used to guard against stray light and flare. The inner surfaces of the shielding should be painted flat black. A test procedure is outlined to verify the success of the shielding. A transparency is projected which is entirely clear except for a round opaque spot in the center that has a diameter of one-tenth of the short dimension of the transparency. The luminance of the projected image is measured from 50 cm (about 20 in.) away from the screen. The luminance at the center of the spot must be less than 1% of the maximum luminance from any other area of the screen.

The resolution for the projection system is measured with a standard test target as specified in ANSI PH2.33-1983 (an earlier version of the viewing standard). All patterns with spatial frequencies of 40 cycles/mm (1,016 cycles/in.) must be resolved at any point on the screen. Also, the optical system must not exhibit noticeable spatial distortion.

Chapter 9
Film Image Assembly

Overview of Film Image Assembly

The assembly of film images is still commonly called **stripping,** although the term no longer describes the process. In the past, emulsions were *stripped* from various photographic plates and assembled on a glass plate in position for exposing a press plate. The term "stripping" now refers to the process of assembling imaged films. For convenience, the term "film assembly" will be used instead of "film image assembly." Film assembly is putting films in their proper positions on a carrier called a **flat.** Flats are either **negative** or **positive.**

In recent years, film assembly operations have been aided and/or replaced by computer applications. These applications, which are evolving rapidly, fall into three categories: **imposition systems, masking systems,** and **robotic stripping systems.** To learn how a particular system works, ask vendors for their most recent product literature.

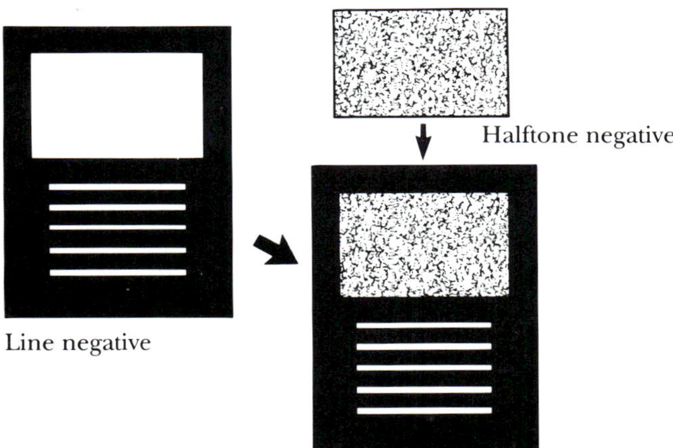

Line negative with clear opening and halftone negative, which is attached to the emulsion side of the line negative *(bottom right).*

Negative Film Flats

Negative film flats are prepared for the production of negative-working plates, on which the areas struck by exposing light become image areas after processing. Such a flat consists of an opaque paper or plastic base onto which film negatives are attached and then, openings are cut. Negative line and halftone images, image control marks, and test

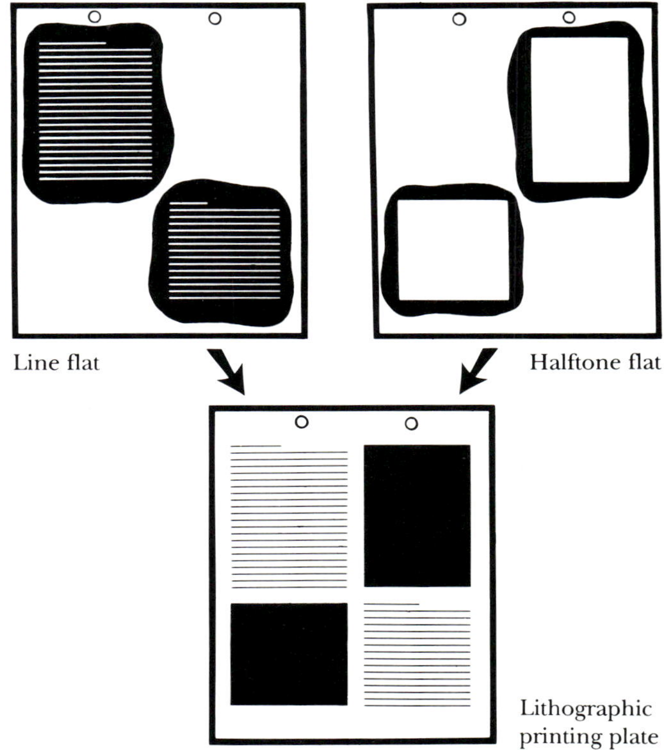

Example of complementary flats.

images may be included. Clear areas on the films transmit plate-exposure light to produce images on a negative-working plate.

Positive Film Flats

Positive film flats are prepared for the production of positive-working plates, on which the areas struck by exposing light become nonimage areas after processing. Such a flat consists of a clear plastic base and the positive films attached to it. Clear areas on the films transmit plate-exposure light to produce nonimage areas on a positive-working plate.

Single-Color Film Assembly

In simple single-color film assembly, all the films to be assembled for one plate can go on one flat. But when some film images would have to be assembled too close to others to permit satisfactory splicing or when one image is to be positioned in register over another on a plate, more than one flat may be made. These flats are called **complementary flats.**

Multicolor Film Assembly

At least one flat is usually required for each printing color since each color requires its own plate. However, if the different colors are to be printed in distinctly separate places, they can be placed on one flat. Each can then be exposed to its plate while the others are covered, or *masked.*

More typically, one key-color flat (often the black) is assembled, and then flats of the other colors are assembled in register with it. The different separation films of process-color work have register marks to permit close registration during film assembly.

Multiple Images

Multiples of a single image can be assembled by making a number of individual images photographically and assembling them on a flat or by contact-printing the image repeatedly onto a single **composite** film. Sometimes multiple images are exposed to a plate from a single film image by a process called **step and repeat.** The film is repeatedly moved (stepped) and exposed by a **step-and-repeat,** or **photocomposing, machine.**

Facilities

Environmental Considerations

Environmental controls are very important in the film assembly (or stripping) area. Cleanliness will prevent spotty films and out-of-contact areas in the vacuum.

Since dust is attracted to film by static electricity, dust reduction can be achieved by temperature and humidity control. Temperature and humidity control also minimize dimensional changes in film and paper.

Space and Layout Considerations

The space required by the department depends on the department's function, the amount of work being done, the equipment used, and the size of the staff. Floor plans should be made to minimize distractions and provide sufficient work space around the equipment.

The arrangement of equipment can vary depending on the flow of operations. One effective arrangement, based on the **carrel concept,** can provide both efficient equipment arrangement and freedom from distraction.

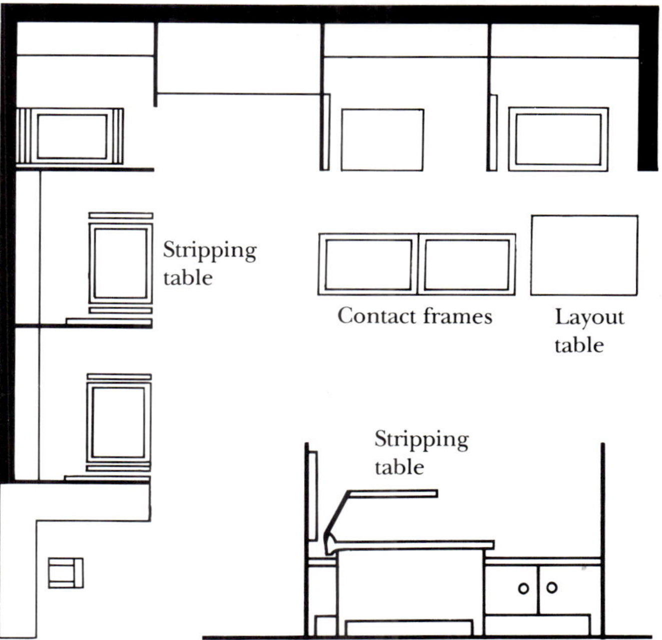

A U-shaped stripping carrel featuring placement of stripping tables, contact frames, and layout tables.

A carrel (or carrell) is a nook, such as that used in a library for private study. When a stripping room uses this principle, work areas with tables are arranged around the walls and separated from each other by partitions. Interior portions of the room are used for layout tables and (if nondarkroom contact printing is done by the strippers) for contact frames.

Construction Considerations

Flooring. True antistatic carpeting (that which is suitable for computer areas), rubber, linoleum, and wood are recommended flooring surfaces for stripping areas. Concrete is undesirable because it is a source of dust and dirt, and tools that are dropped on it are more likely to be damaged.

Ceilings and walls. Ceilings and walls are also a source of dust and dirt unless sealed and painted. Painting the walls a light color is recommended to provide a bright environment for film assembly.

Lighting. Light over each work area should be individually controlled. However, it should be uniformly distributed within the area to minimize shadows. The intensity of the light inside the stripping and layout tables must not differ greatly from that of the room light in order to avoid eye strain, which may occur when inspecting by transmitted light and then changing to reflected light. GATF recommends internal illumination of 60–100 footcandles (5.6–9.3 lux) and room lighting of 25–50 footcandles (2.3–4.6 lux) of a somewhat warm white.

Ventilation. Sealed windows and air conditioning decrease dust and prevent dimensional instability of materials if used with temperature and humidity controls. GATF recommends 50% relative humidity.

Equipment

Stripping Table

The primary function of the stripping table is to provide an illuminated work surface on which films can be positioned and assembled to make a flat. A stripping table has a working surface of plate glass frosted on the underside with uniform lighting beneath it. This glass top should be larger than the largest layout sheet used.

Illumination should be bright enough to permit easy location of pinholes in negatives. White or cool white fluorescent lamps and internal reflectors and diffusers should be used. Two levels of illumination are desirable to permit increasing the light intensity when it is necessary to prepare flats on top of standard layouts or other flats. Hot spots and glare streaks should not be present. High concentrations of light tire the eyes, and hot spots can cause paper or film to change size.

The table should be of satisfactory height and preferably freestanding to permit the stripper access to all sides of the flat. On large tables, the glass should be strong enough to hold some weight as strippers will support their bodies by leaning against the edge of the table when reaching toward the center of it.

Layout Table

If a stripping table is equipped with machined straightedges on two or four sides, it can serve as a layout table for small forms that do not require great precision. However, at least one precision layout, or lineup, table that is never used for stripping or cutting should be in the department. It is almost indispensible for the efficient and accurate preparation of layouts and for checking the accuracy of the completed flat. Besides the top being illuminated from below, a layout table has horizontal and vertical ruling bars—micrometer-adjustable straightedges. These micrometer-adjustable straightedges may also be equipped with scribing, ruling, and other attachments, and digital readouts showing bar position. It is important to keep the table clean and free of bits of tape. If the straightedges are situated on gears, the gear tracks should be clean and unobstructed. The table should be checked for squareness and accuracy each week.

Contact Frame

Contact printing, discussed extensively in Chapter 7, is an integral part of the film assembly process, whether performed by the stripper or a person dedicated solely to making contact prints. A **contact frame,** which is used for contact printing, consists of an ultraviolet light source (quartz light is an example), a vacuum board with hinged cover glass to hold imaged film against the photographic material that receives the image, an electrically, mechanically, or air-operated vacuum pump, and an exposure measurer. The latter may be a timer, but a

light integrator measures exposure more accurately. The vacuum board must be larger than the largest flat made; approximately one-third of its surface should be open to help evacuate air.

Contact printing is an operation in which the presence of dust and dirt can cause problems (i.e., out of-contact areas and spots on the film). Clean the frame weekly or more often as circumstances dictate. Flush the vacuum pump twice a year.

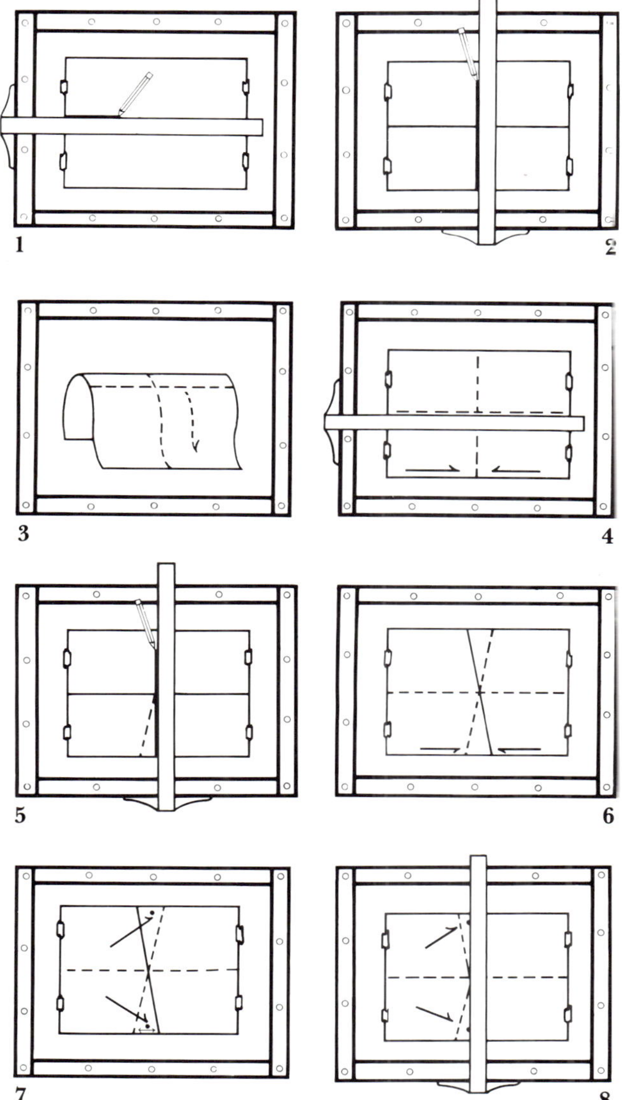

Eight steps for squaring up a stripping table: (1) draw a horizontal centerline, (2) draw a vertical line bisecting the centerline, (3) flop the sheet back-to-front, (4) align the paper using the centerline, (5) draw a vertical line through original point of intersection, (6) measure the distance between the ends of the two vertical lines, (7) mark the halfway points between the vertical lines, (8) Adjust the front edge of the table so that the T square's blade connects the two points.

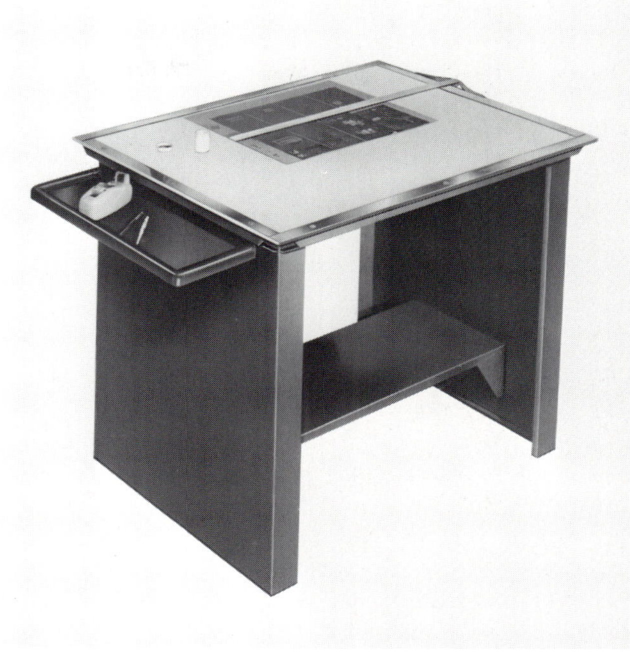

Courtesy nuArc Company, Inc.

A stripping table.

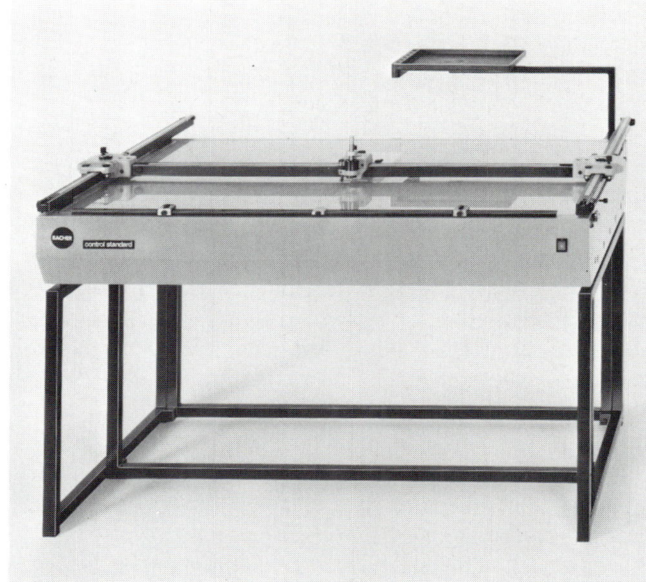

Courtesy Heidelberg USA, Inc.

Layout table.

Other Equipment

A stripping area requires the following equipment:

Work table. A useful adjunct to every stripping table is a work table with large, shallow drawers for flats and flat material, dummy layouts, tint sheets, and masking materials.

Register punch. Register punches for film assembly are extremely accurate for putting round and slotted holes in materials to keep them in register.

Filing cabinet. Flats should be stored in cabinets with shallow drawers to facilitate retrieval and avoid distortion that may be caused by the pressure within high piles and possible tearing when removing a flat. Cabinet storage will protect against scratches and other damage. Vertical storage will also protect against this kind of damage.

A storage room with a fire-resistant vault is recommended if large numbers of flats are retained. It should be insulated to maintain moderate temperature and humidity conditions, which will retard the growth of fungus and keep boards from loosening.

Tools

The following tools are used for film image assembly. Like the equipment discussed previously, the quality of them determines their ease of use and consequently the expense of stripping.

T square. A T-square blade is generally made of stainless steel, with one end attached precisely at right angles to the center of a head to form a "T." Used in connection with a triangle, it provides the most accurate means for establishing right angles. It may also be used for aligning small sections of film and drawing short lines.

Straightedge. Used for drawing long straight lines and scribing negatives, the straightedge is ideally a heavy stainless steel bar, preferably with a beveled edge machined to a true straightness. Nicking the straightedge with a cutting tool or bowing it by dropping it will make it useless.

Ruler, or scale. A ruler is a smooth-edged stainless-steel strip with measurement divisions etched or engraved along its edge. It is used primarily for measuring. A beveled edge permits easy reading without parallax error.

Triangles. Steel triangles for use in conjunction with T squares or straightedges are most commonly of the 45-45-90 and 30-60-90 varieties. Adjustable-angle triangles are also available.

Compass. The compass is used for drawing circles and arcs of circles. (A compass-like device with two sharp metal points called **dividers** is used to transfer measurements from a ruler or to position strips of film before taping.) Metal or plastic templates of fixed sizes can be used to draw circles and ellipses.

French and flexible curves. The drawing of irregular smooth curves is aided by flat devices of fixed, flowing shapes usually called *french curves. Flexible curves* serve the same purpose.

Pencils. Hard-lead pencils (4H to 8H) may be used for drawing layout lines if erasing is needed, but fine-line, long-nibbed **ballpoint pens** are generally preferred.

Markers. Black liquid markers are preferred to crayons where heavy marks, e.g., for identification, are required. These do not smudge vacuum frame glass as crayon marks do.

Brushes. Brushes for opaquing should have fine hairs that form a sharp-point taper. Brush size #00 should be used for repairing small halftone dots. Sizes #2 and #3 are used for general opaquing. Brush sizes range up to #6, which can be used for opaquing large areas, although such areas might be better masked with paper or plastic. A large **camel hair brush** is useful for dusting a film or flat.

Knives and single-edged razor blades. Cutting tools are an integral part of stripping. Knives, and sometimes single-edged razor blades, are used to cut film, peel away material, and cut windows. Knives with replaceable blades are convenient, since blades must be kept sharp. Swivel-bladed knives are often found most convenient for cutting masking films.

Scissors. A lightweight pair of shears or scissors with approximately 10-in. (250-mm) blades is useful for cutting sheeting, especially polyester types.

Lithographic needles. A round lithographic needle with a gradually tapered sharp point is used to mark locations on a film or flat and to transfer locations from one flat to another. It may also be used to prick a small piece of film in order to pick it up or slide it.

Needles with rectangular cross sections can be honed to a sharp edge for scraping off defects in film emulsion, such as broken characters. Sharpened flat needles can sometimes substitute for

stripping knives or for scribers, but tools made specifically for those purposes are better.

Scriber. A scriber can be used to draw lines on a photographic negative by scratching off the emulsion, which results in smooth-edged lines. These lines can be cleaner and smoother than lines drawn on paper, provided that the scriber scrapes away the emulsion completely.

A number of other devices round out the stripper's tool requirements: a **tweezer;** several **magnifiers** including a microscope shaped like a fountain pen to examine halftone dots, a stand-supported low-power magnifier to aid in opaquing out pinholes and printing-area defects, a lower-power magnifier mounted in a sighting tube, or equipped with a GATF T-Kap, to avoid parallax error when registering color work, and a stand-supported higher-powered magnifier for fine detail work; a **screen angle indicator,** such as the GATF Screen Angle Guide, to aid in color stripping; and a **screen tint ruling measurement scale.**

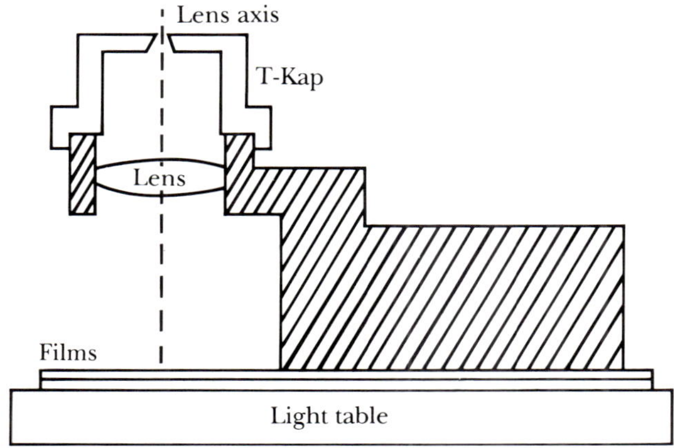

Position of T-Kap relative to magnifier lens.

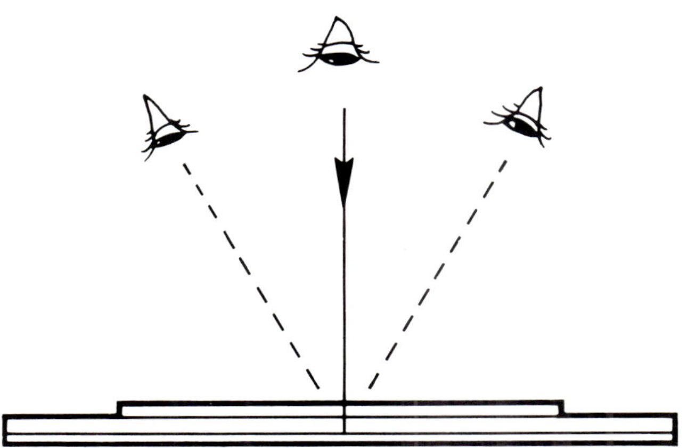

Viewing register marks at 90° to avoid parallax error.

Materials for Flat Assembly and Masking

Flat assembly and masking are the most fundamental tasks of the stripper. Several materials are used in these operations:

Goldenrod. Paper that blocks the passage of actinic (photographic-material-exposing) light is generally referred to as **goldenrod paper,** regardless of whether it is true goldenrod yellow or orange or even red. It is the most popular material for preparing negative flats when register is not critical.

Goldenrod is not suitable for work requiring accurate register because a relative-humidity change of more than 20% will produce an appreciable size change. Another shortcoming of goldenrod is its variable thickness, which can cause gaps between the press plate and the film during exposure in the vacuum frame.

Orange vinyl. Since vinyl is affected only slightly by temperature and humidity changes, it can be used where close register is required. It should never be used when flats are intended for a step-and-repeat machine, since the machine's heat will soften the vinyl. (Although "orange vinyl" is practically a generic term in stripping, some vinyl used for this purpose is red.)

Clear base film. Clear film is necessary for preparing a positive film flat, but it may also be used for a negative assembly when size and register are critical. For this latter purpose, polyester film would be used instead of acetate because polyester can generally be obtained in 0.004-in. and 0.007-in. sizes and is much less affected dimensionally by temperature and humidity changes.

Peelable masking film. A red or orange film bonded with a special adhesive to an acetate or polyester base is often used for masking. The area for a halftone can be cut from the film and peeled away to be used as a window. The remaining film can also be peeled away and attached to the halftone negative as a blockout.

Photographic masking film. Instead of separating by knife-cutting, the separation lines for the mask can be made on photographic masking film by

exposure through a negative or positive, opening the lines by development. The mask and the block-out can then be peeled away.

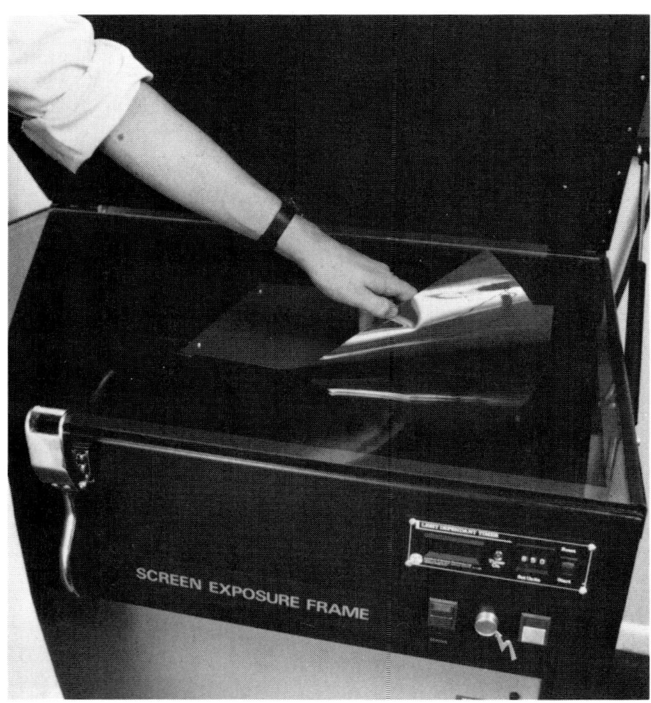

Courtesy Autotype U.S.A.

Place keyline positive against Fotostrip base; expose to UV light.

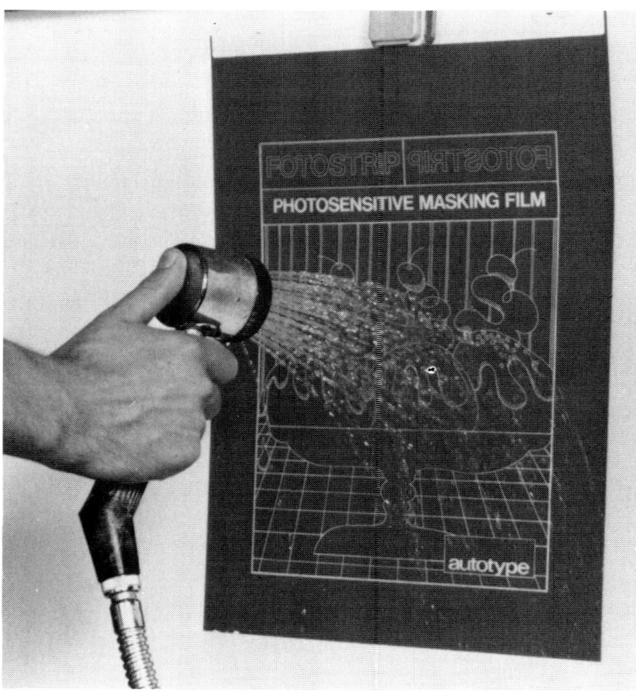

Courtesy Autotype U.S.A.

Wash with water to dissolve all unexposed areas until the image is clear.

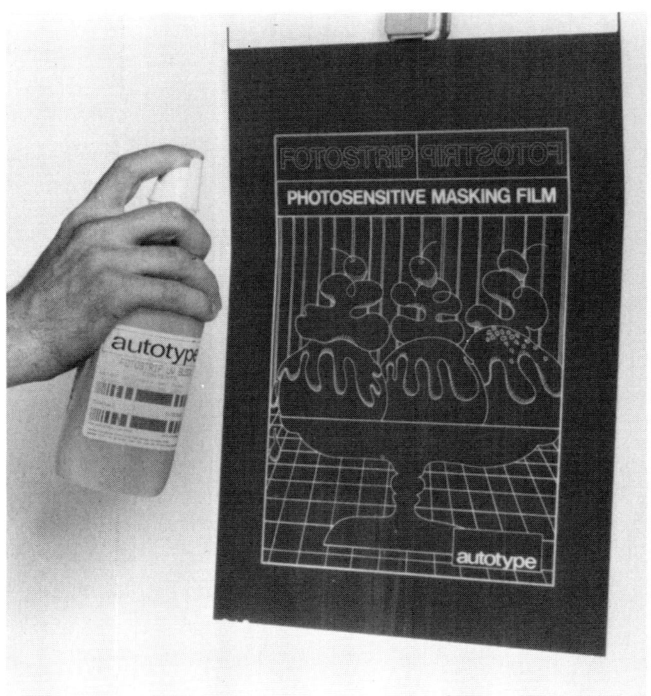

Courtesy Autotype U.S.A.

Spray film surface with Fotostrip UV block to increase density, leave for 1 min. and rinse.

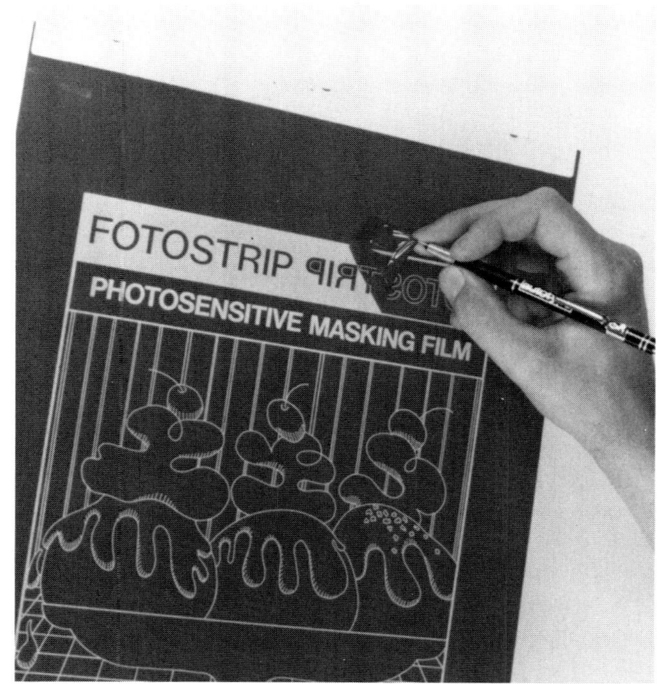

Courtesy Autotype U.S.A.

Then, simply peel the desired areas.

Photographic masking film is widely used in mapmaking and also in intricate color work because it can be used to overlap colors.

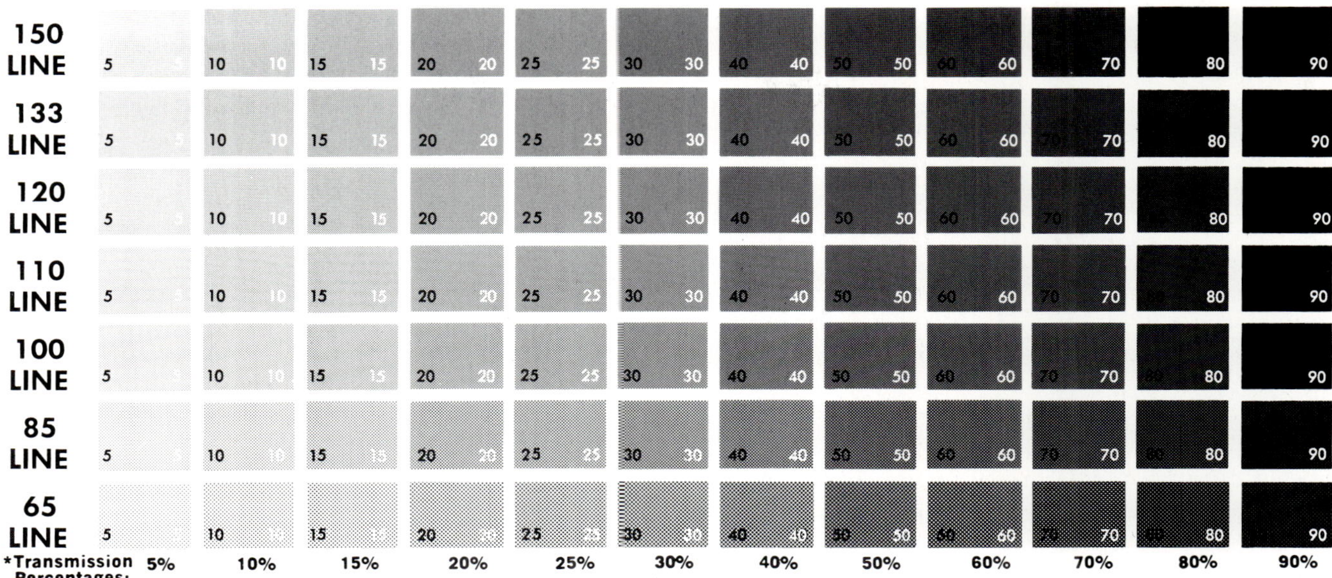

Courtesy ByChrome Company

Percentage-calibrated screen tints.

Photographic Proofing Materials

After a job has been stripped, a proof of some kind is generally supplied to the customer. For more discussion, see the "Proofing" chapter.

Other Stripping Supplies

Opaque. Opaque may be black or red. It is applied to block out defects or unwanted matter from film negatives or to retouch positives. For most kinds of work, opaque is applied to the base of the negative. For very close work, opaque is best applied to the emulsion side.

Film cleaning solution. A film cleaning solution should be nontoxic and evaporate completely, without leaving any residue.

Adhesive. In most cases, rubber cement is the adhesive used by strippers; e.g., for backing up proofs to put them in book form.

Pressure-sensitive tape. Light-blocking tape is useful for securing film sections together and masking the film joint at the same time. Red-colored pressure-sensitive polyester or cellophane tape is used to tape down film. It blocks the ultraviolet light of exposure lamps but is still translucent enough in visible light to permit inspection of sections where the tape has been used to crop printing areas.

Screen tints. Screen tints are films with dots of uniform size, which produce even shades of black or color. They are available in a whole range of screen percentages. Duplicates should be made for production use so that the masters can be preserved.

Register devices. Register devices include register hole tabs, buttons, or dowels, and register pins. They permit fast, accurate positioning of film flats during stripping, proofing, and platemaking. Register devices are discussed later in this chapter under the heading "Systems for Image Register."

GATF control marks. GATF has developed a number of exposable marks designed to control

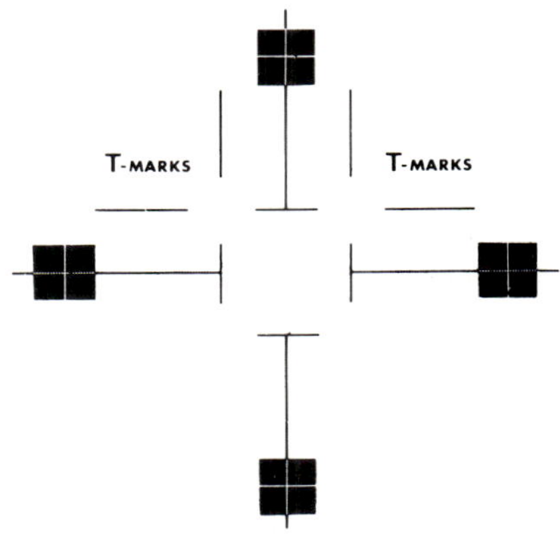

GATF T-Marks.

folds, trims, centers, bleeds, side guides for press-sheet register, and collating.

Quality control devices. An **image alignment grid** indicates image straightness when placed over the completed flat. A **circle center finder** locates the center of images that are to be made into a circular shape. QC devices used in contacting either help establish optimum exposure times or help monitor development after exposure.

Film Assembly Basics

The procedures used for film assembly are not so much determined by whether the job is single- or multicolor. Rather they are determined by whether the film is negative or positive.

A layout sheet must be made before the flat is started. The layout should be planned so that the making of the flat will be as simple as possible. It should also simplify the work to be done in the platemaking area, pressroom, and bindery. The stripper should study all instructions accompanying a job before drawing the layout. If a dummy layout or completely prepared stripping layout is furnished, dimensions must be verified. It must be determined whether the job will fit on the specified paper stock. All film images should be in agreement with the layout dimensions and fit in the designated areas.

Standard press layouts are **one-up, one-side multiple, one-side combination, sheetwise, work-and-turn,** and **work-and-tumble.** These layouts are generally classified as sheetfed layouts, but they are also used on jobs run on webfed presses. Any of the two-sided layouts can be modified to run on perfecting presses. The names of the layouts vary in different parts of the country, but the layouts are actually the same.

One-up layout. Simple one-up one-sided forms are usually prepared for smaller press sizes and usually consist of only one page or subject. Large posters printed on the larger presses also fall into this class.

One-side multiple layout. The one-side multiple layout puts two or more duplicates of the same item on one plate. This layout is sometimes called the **step-and-repeat layout** because the plate is made easily by stepping the image and repeating the exposure. Depending on the size of the job and the size of the press, dozens or even hundreds of duplicates can be printed at the same time.

One-side combination layout. A one-side combination layout combines several different forms on the same plate. This layout is also known as the *gang run layout.* These forms must be arranged so that they can be cut along common lines.

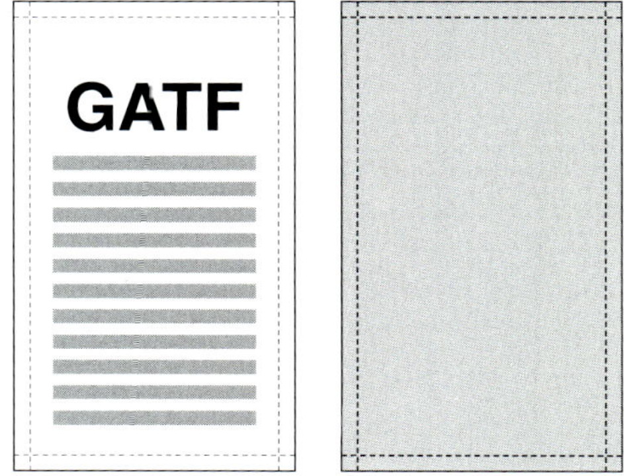

One-up layout.

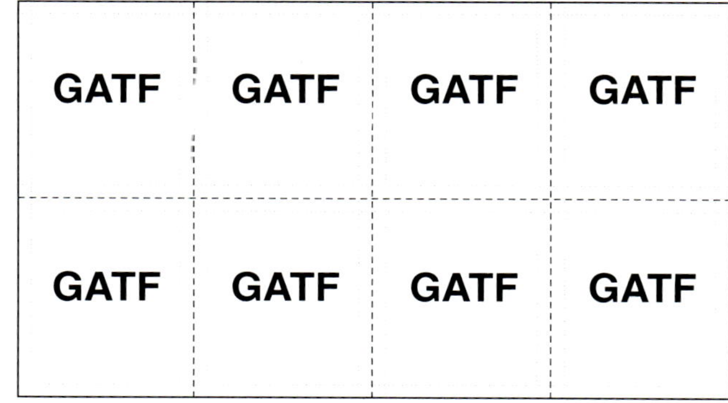

One-side multiple layout.

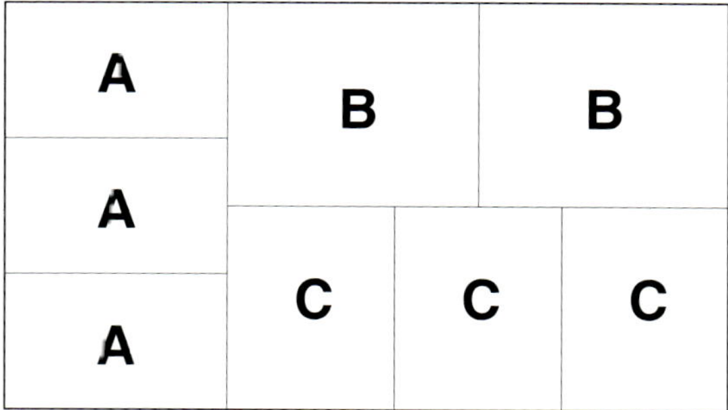

One-side combination layout.

Sheetwise layout. Sheetwise layout is perhaps the most commonly used layout. Different plates are used to print the front and back of the press sheet. Paper is run once through a press that prints one side of the sheet, turned over, and printed on the other side with the second plate. The same sheet edge is used for the lead edge. However, the side-guide edge remains the same. But, because the sheet is turned over, the press itself needs two side-guides. Therefore, this layout can only be used for presses that have two side-guides.

Sheetwise printing can also be done in one pass on a perfecting press. In such cases, layouts are considered sheetwise forms if the images on front and back differ and if two plates are used.

A sheetwise layout is used for signature layouts. A *signature layout* consists of a number of pages laid out so that they fold together as a section of a book.

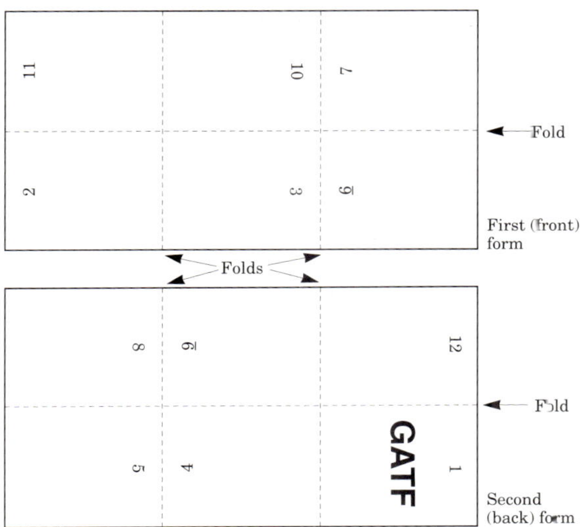

Sheetwise layout.

Work-and-turn layout. With a work-and-turn layout, both sides of the trimmed printed sheet are put on the same plate. Work-and-turn jobs are laid out so that they use the same gripper edge and the same side of the press sheet for positioning to the front and side-guides of the press. This layout method requires the side-guide to be changed to the opposite side of the press when printing the backside in order to guarantee good backup and register.

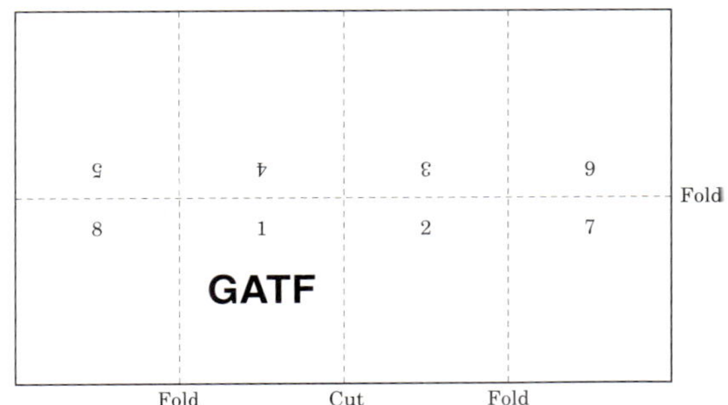

Work-and-turn layout.

Work-and-tumble layout. The work-and-tumble, or *work-and-flop,* layout is also a form in which both front and back pages are on the same plate. In this case, the tail of the sheet becomes the gripper edge (lead edge) for the backup. When a sheet is run in this manner, the paper must be cut squarely before it is printed. Paper that comes from the mill is generally not square enough, and, consequently, it is impossible to get a square backup if this cutting is not done. In other words, the tail edge of the sheet must be parallel with the gripper edge in order to run a work-and-tumble job properly. This layout is used when the format is too long to go on the sheet as a work-and-turn job. Its chief advantage over work-and-turn layouts is that press adjustments are kept to a minimum as the same front and side-guide positions are used. This factor is important on some smaller presses were the press sheet can only be guided on one side of the press.

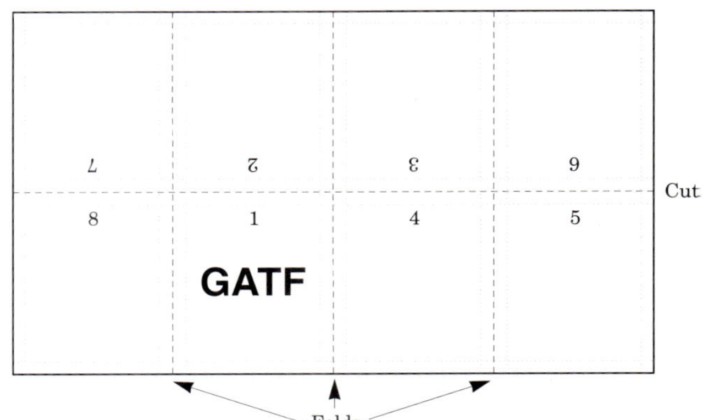

Work-and-tumble layout.

Negative Film Assembly

The *flat material* must be selected first. It should be the least expensive material adequate for the job. Goldenrod is suitable for many single-color jobs. For multicolor jobs, orange vinyl, peelable masking film, or clear polyester with an orange vinyl or goldenrod exposure mask is required. Except for goldenrod, these materials are durable, making them suitable for jobs that will be handled repeatedly.

The *layout material* for a negative assembly is often the goldenrod onto which the negatives will be assembled. For book, magazine, or other production in which the same layout will be used repeatedly, the layout may be drawn on white, coated paper or, preferably, frosted polyester. The negatives may be assembled on clear polyester, with an orange vinyl or goldenrod mask, or on peelable masking film.

A sheet of layout material, somewhat larger than the size of the press plate, is placed on the layout table. The side of the layout sheet that corresponds to the gripper edge of the press sheet is aligned with a T square or the built-in straightedge of the table. If the layout sheet is to be used as the masking material, it should first be punched with the proper holes for pin register. Then, it is carefully placed over register pins and secured to the glass top with pressure-sensitive tape.

All layout lines must be straight and precisely parallel or perpendicular to each other. They must be accurately measured. Measurements should be made in several places, marked with needle points or dots, and rechecked.

The first lines drawn indicate the **plate bend and paper gripper allowances.** The amount of the plate bend allowance is measured backward from the gripper edge of the flat and marked with a sharp pencil or needle. A line is drawn from that mark across the layout sheet parallel to the gripper edge. Another measurement is made from this line

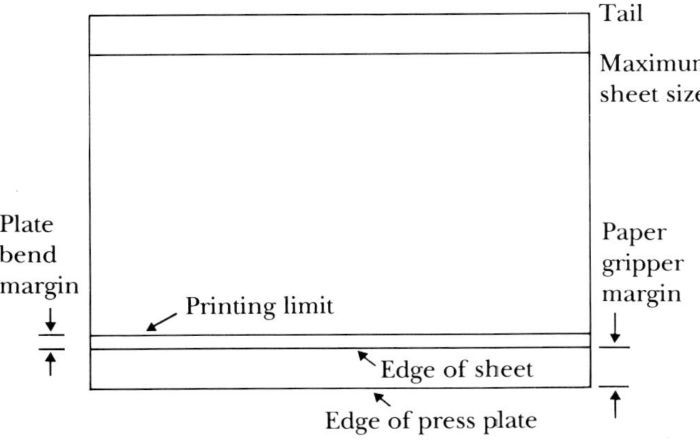

Plate bend and paper gripper allowances.

backward the length of the press sheet and marked. Another horizontal line is drawn. For a web press, these lines show the printing limit. For a sheetfed press, the printing limit is further reduced by another line that provides for the paper gripper. In many cases, the plate bend allowance and the plate gripper are combined, requiring only a single line. In some cases, the printing limit is the same on several or all presses, allowing a standard layout.

Next, horizontal and vertical **centerlines** and **trim, bleed,** and other limit lines are drawn:

1. The horizontal centerline is drawn halfway between the plate bend line and the tail of the sheet.

2. The horizontal outside trim margins are drawn equidistant from the horizontal centerline.

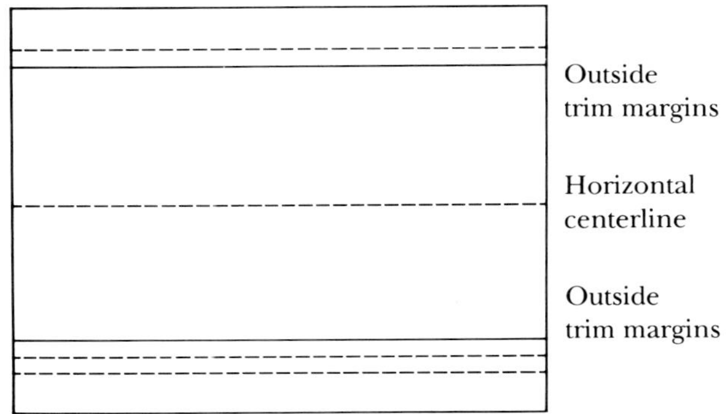

Layout with horizontal centerline and outside trim lines added.

3. The vertical centerline is drawn halfway between the vertical edges of the layout sheet, perpendicular to the paper gripper line.

4. Two vertical lines, equidistant from the vertical centerline, are drawn to indicate the outer dimensions of the printing area across the sheet.

5. Two more vertical lines, each half the width of the press sheet from the vertical centerline, are drawn to indicate the outer edges of the press sheet.

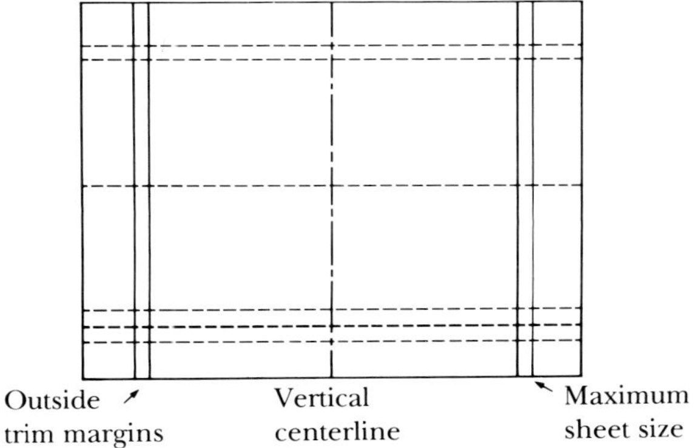

Layout with vertical centerline and outside trim margins.

While film negatives may be positioned on the layout with reference to the trim marks or margins of the type page, GATF recommends using center

marks. The trim-size centers are easily located and marked on the layout. Use the type-page margins only if the negative has no center or trim marks.

Fold, with retrim

Head margin

Back margin

Fold, no retrim

Margins of type being used to position negatives.

Layouts based on film center marks are described here. The centerline for the row of items along the gripper margin is drawn first. The vertical trim size is divided by two and, as required, the gripper margin and trim allowance are added to it. A gripper trim is not required if all the paper on the press sheet is to be used and no printing comes within the paper gripper distance of the gripper edge of the sheet. Otherwise, part or all of the paper gripper distance is added to one-half the vertical trim size of the page.

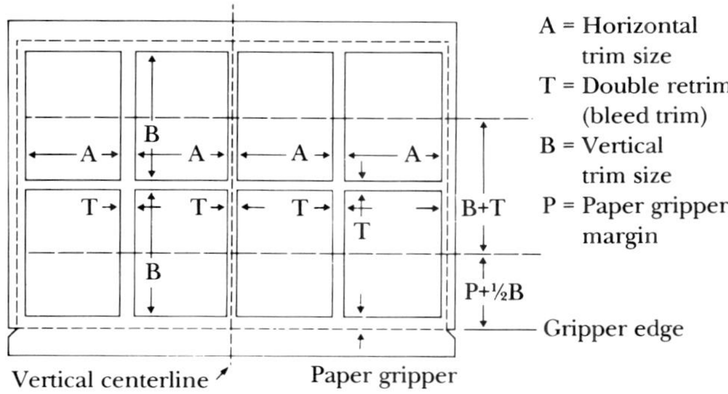

Locating horizontal centerlines of forms.

The distance just calculated is measured up from the gripper edge line and marked. A horizontal centerline for the first row of forms is drawn parallel to the gripper line. Next, the distance from the centerline to the centerline of the second row of forms is calculated, measured, and marked. This distance is the full vertical trim size plus two ⅛-in. (3-mm) trims. A line is drawn through this mark so that it is parallel to the gripper line, and the first line is drawn. Remaining horizontal centerlines are made in the same manner.

Vertical centerlines are located next. If the number of forms located along the gripper edge is odd, the centerline of the sheet is also the centerline of the middle row. The centerlines for succeeding vertical rows on either side are located at a distance equal to the horizontal trim size of the form, plus any required double retrim allowances between forms.

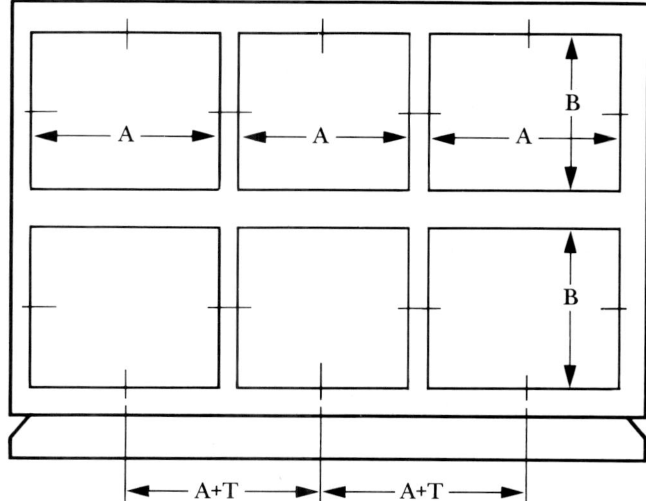

Locating vertical centerlines of odd number of forms across the press sheet.

If the number of forms located along the gripper edge is even, the centerlines for the two central rows are located at a distance equal to one trim allowance plus one-half the horizontal trim size of the forms. The next two vertical rows are located at a distance equal to the horizontal trim size plus a double-trim allowance. Any further vertical centerlines required are drawn by the same procedure.

The locations of various image reference lines are drawn in if they do not appear on the negatives.

Trim, fold, and sheet center marks. Trim and fold marks direct the folding and cutting of the press sheet. Sheet center marks are centered along the edges of all four sides of the press sheet, preferably outside the form trim margins.

Insert locations. When the locations of halftone illustrations or other inserts are not marked by crop lines or windows on the negatives, they are drawn on the layout if there is sufficient space for all of

them on a single flat. Otherwise, they are located on an overlay or complementary flat.

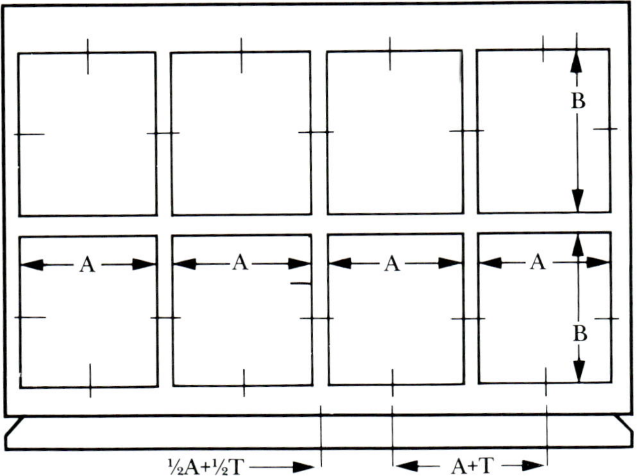

Locating vertical centerlines of even number of forms across the press sheet.

Plate positioning lines. Lines extending to the edge of the layout sheet are drawn at the plate bend line and the vertical centerline of the layout. The flat may be notched at these lines or film tabs registered to them to expose them on the margin of the press plate. If a pin register system continued from stripping to platemaking is in use, the pin holes take care of the position of the flat on the plate.

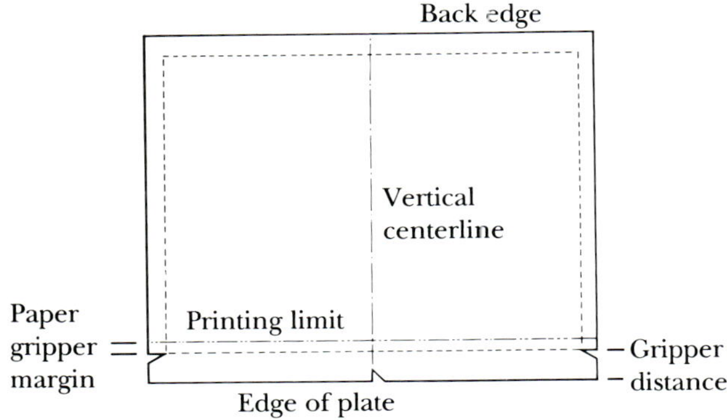

Reference marks used on a flat.

Preparing Negatives for Assembly

Although image assemblers do not produce negatives, they must determine whether they are of acceptable quality before working on them.

The black area of a line negative should have a density reading of at least 3.0. A negative that produces a print with lines thicker than the original copy is called "heavy" (or "fat"). A negative that produces a print with lines thinner than the original copy is called "sharp." Sharp lines require chemical correction with an etchant, such as Farmer's reducer or Farmer's etch. These solutions etch or take away the silver in the emulsion until the image is "opened" to the proper size. They must not be left on too long as to make the image print fat. Small closed areas on the negative can sometimes be scratched open (mechanically etched), even by the stripper, with a needle or knife.

If the halo, or fringe, around the dots of a camera-made halftone negative is extreme, the dots are said to be "blind"—they have too little density. Halftone dots produced by contacting have no halo. Even the best camera-produced halftone dots have some. Therefore, a flat should have all camera-produced or all contact-produced negatives.

A line negative is *trimmed down* to a size slightly less than the space it occupies on the flat to permit taping negatives together without overlapping. If the positioning marks would be cut off by such trimming because of close fit, position the film and tape it along two or three sides. Then, either trim the excess using scissors, or slide a cutting sheet under the film and trim the excess using a knife or razor blade. Do not trim the sides extending into the margins. The marks on the extended sections can serve as the register and trim marks for the flat. To attach negatives to the carrier, place a ruled-up masking sheet wrong-reading on the stripping table. (An alternative is to place a masking sheet over a wrong-reading layout drawn on white paper or frosted polyester.) The negatives are taped to the masking sheet emulsion side up.

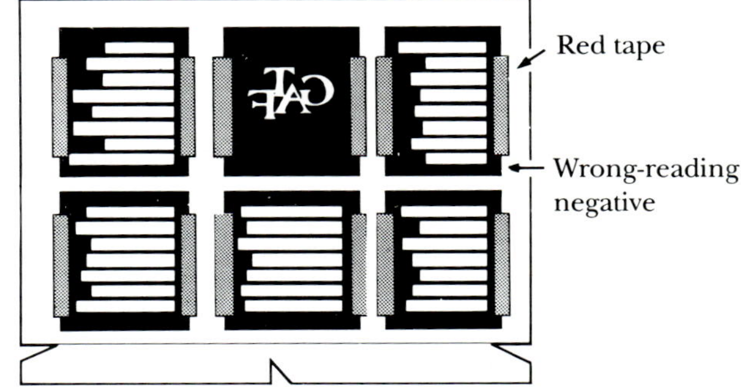

Assembling negatives wrong-reading on masking materials.

The image assembler should start attaching a back-corner negative, with the others approximately in place or moved to one side if an aligning

tool like a T square is to be used. After careful positioning, the negative is taped along two or more sides. Scissors may be used to cut any film edge that needs to be trimmed before that edge is taped down. Tape strips on adjacent films must not overlap. An illustration with a bleed is cut wider along bleed margins.

The flat is checked for necessary positioning marks. Any that are not on the attached negatives must be added by scribing or attaching film tabs. GATF's T-Marks taped on the flat instead of scribing marks provide superior register marks.

If clear polyester is used as the assembly base for dimensional stability and added strength—because openings are not cut in it—a masking sheet with precut openings is overlaid. *Peelable masking film* has a ruby- or amber-colored membrane that may be peeled away from the support base. Peelable masking film generally requires a separate layout.

With goldenrod/orange vinyl flats, the flat is opened (for exposure) by cutting through the masking sheet wherever printing matter or guide marks are located. Correct cutting pressure, which should be tested using waste material, results in a clean cut through the masking material while only lightly scoring the film underneath. Long, narrow strips of masking sheet between opened areas should be replaced with pressure-sensitive red tape. This covers up various light leaks and adds to the strength of the flat.

A peelable masking film flat is placed membrane-side-up to be opened. Using a sharp blade, pressured just enough to cut through the membrane, the stripper cuts within the area of the negative, but keeps close to the printing area. A cut section of the membrane can be pulled away by lifting a corner with a blade and gripping it between thumb and forefinger.

Opaque is applied to negatives to crop illustrations and rules and to spot out pinholes and other defects. It should have the consistency of a light cream for brush application. When used in a pen nib or ruling pen, it should be thinned down a little more to flow easily yet remain opaque.

Positive Film Assembly

Layouts for positive flats are made in the same way as those for negative flats. But the layout is always laterally reversed (wrong-reading) and is prepared on a separate sheet from that used for preparing the flat. The layout is prepared on white, coated paper or rulable plastic. Positive films are stripped, emulsion up, on a clear plastic sheet mounted over the layout. The base material must be immaculate within the printing area because defects in positive flats are much more likely to show up on the press plate.

After the positive is inspected for general quality, minor defects may be corrected by retouching. Just as pinholes in negatives are spotted out, black specks in the clear areas are removed by lightly scraping the emulsion. A crowquill pen or fine brush (#0 or #00 usually) may be used to add broken or missing printing detail.

Next, the positives are trimmed to size. If such trimming would remove portions of reference marks that would make them unusable for positioning, the trimming is not done until after the positives are assembled on the flat.

Whenever possible, the location of trim lines, needle or scriber markings, and tape strips close to or overlapping printing detail should be avoided. This practice reduces the difficulty of the staging out work by the platemaker. Small tabs of red pressure-sensitive tape are used for attaching the positives. The platemaker has to stage out *all* taped areas; the use of red tape calls the platemaker's attention to the areas that require staging out.

To assemble the positives, the stripper squares up and attaches the layout to the stripping table. The clear polyester sheet is placed and smoothed over the layout and carefully taped down. Register and plate location marks are transferred from the layout to the clear sheet by taping positive contacts of the marks in position on the polyester. The film positives are attached emulsion-side-up on this base. With positive flats, there is, of course, no masking material to remove.

Single-Color Film Assembly

Single-color film assembly involves more than just text and/or line illustrations. It also includes procedures on how to handle halftones, screen tints, and double-printed or reversed-out type, which are commonly encountered. The following discussion expands on the basics.

Assembling Negative-Flat Inserts

There are many procedures for assembling halftones and other inserts into negative flats. They depend on preparation of the artwork and the fit between inserts and adjoining printing matter.

Attaching inserts over clear film openings. Red or black masks that were cut to size and attached to the mechanical appear on the negatives as clear areas indicating where the halftones or other illustrations are to be located. When possible, the tape securing the insert should be kept at least ⅜ in. (10 mm) away from the image.

The halftone generally has crop marks for positioning. If these do not match exactly with the sides of the opening, the difference should be split in positioning the film. If the halftone does not have crop marks and is not exactly the same size as the opening (it's usually somewhat larger), take into account vertical and horizontal lines in the image, placement of the principal subject, and distracting edge detail that could be moved out of the window.

One of several techniques can be used to eliminate out-of-contact problems in platemaking when goldenrod or orange vinyl is used for cropping illustrations. The opening could be increased in size and a border could be made on the film with opaque or thin red tape to restore the proper cropping. Or, the platemaker could lay a sheet of thin cellophane across such flats before drawing up the vacuum.

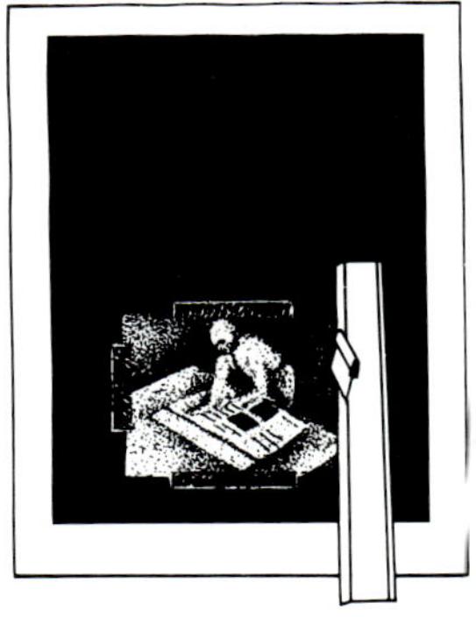

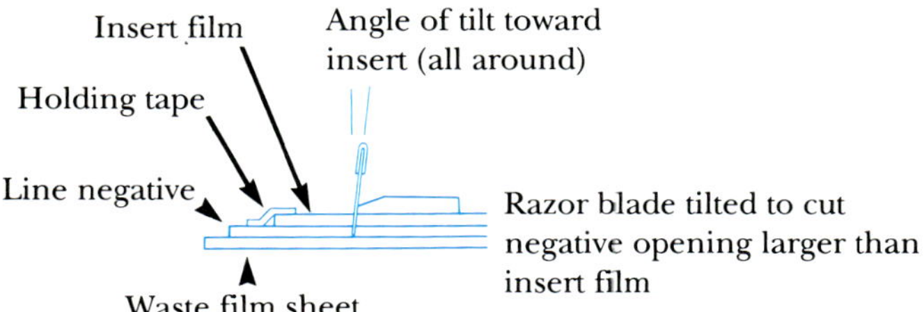

Cutting insert and the negative into which it goes.

Complementary flats. When close fitting between illustrations and other printing detail is necessary, it is sometimes useful to put different material to be exposed to the same plate on **complementary flats.** Combining images on the press plate by means of complementary flats is called **double printing,** and if the images overprint it is called **surprinting.**

When a screened image must touch, or **butt,** any other image—for example, another halftone, screen tint, or rule—complementary flats must be made. Peelable masking film openings are cut so that there is a slight overlapping of images. When only two images butt, it is easy to cut the masks with the necessary overlaps.

Complex layouts are another matter. Although several halftones, tints, and solids may butt or overlap, a stripper may be able to plan it so that only two or three complementary masks are needed. But images on different masks may share a common line. To get an even line on the printing plate, a cropping mask called a **common-line mask,** or **common cropper,** is used. Although it is not a complementary flat, it is punched for pin register the same way. The windows for the images are cut slightly larger on the side where they form the common line and overlap slightly on the side where they butt. The opening of the common-line mask is cut so that an edge falls directly on this common line. The position of the other three sides of the opening mask must be beyond the respective openings in the complementary flats.

A line image void in a solid or tone image is called a **reverse,** or "knockout." To make a reverse in a halftone for negative-working plates, a suitable halftone negative and a line positive film are needed. The two are registered to each other and assembled onto a flat. With positive-working plates, a halftone positive film and a line negative film are assembled into complementary flats.

Illustrations that fit closely to (or butt) other illustrations or text can be assembled on complementary flats and then contacted onto a single film before stripping. This process is called **photocombining,** and the result is called a **composite negative** or **positive.**

Screen tints are screens of a single dot size used to print uniform shades in specified areas. Tints may be used with type by reversing type into a sufficiently dark tint or surprinting the type over a sufficiently light tint.

If tinted type must appear in a solid background of the same color, a screen tint is attached to a negative of the type and a positive is made from the assembly. This positive will be used as a negative when assembling the film. It must be remembered that this use of a positive as a negative requires that the desired dot size be subtracted from 100%

to determine the tint percentage used for making the positive.

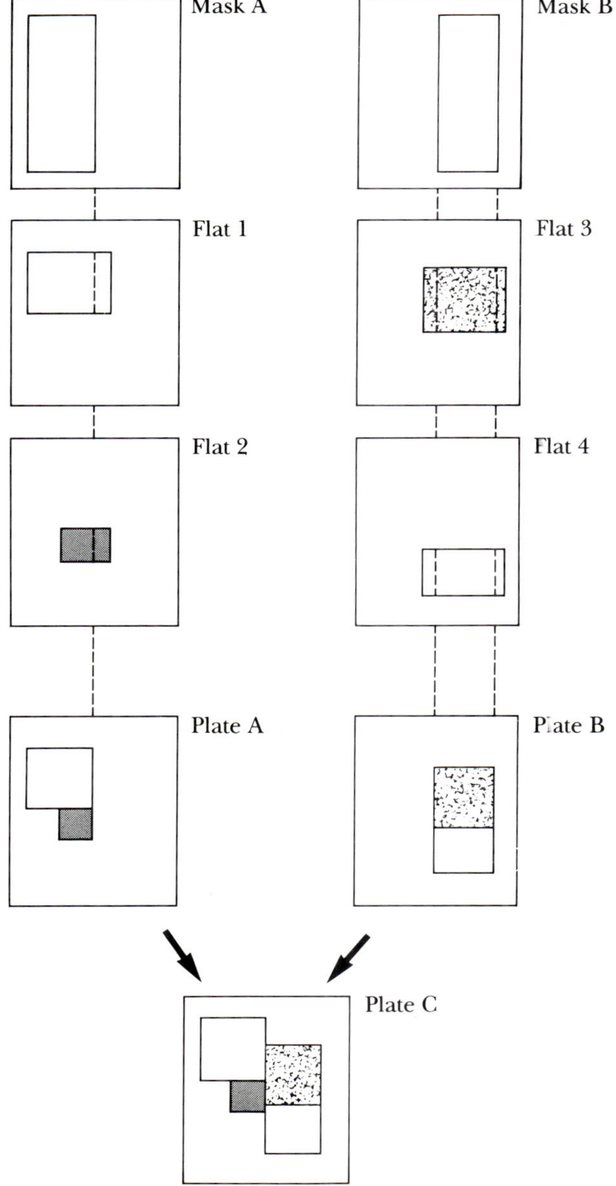

Two common lines that overlap slightly. Common-line mask A is used to crop the windows in flats 1 and 2; common-line mask B is used to crop the windows in flats 3 and 4, which have two lines in common. If mask A, mask B, and the four flats are exposed to the same plate, the result would appear as shown in plate C.

If two different adjacent tint values are required, a line will show between the two values unless a special step is taken to avoid it. **Cross-screening** is one such method. The lighter tint value is positioned over the whole area to be tinted. Then a mask is made for the darker tint area on a complementary flat, and a tint equal to the darker tint area minus the lighter tint area is placed over the area angled at 30° from the first tint. The two tints for the darker area will add together when double-printed on the plate. The film image assembler uses a screen angle indicator to angle the tints.

Systems for Image Register

One purpose of image register systems is making preplate operations more accurate and locating the image on the plate properly to minimize adjustments on press. For high-quality film assembly, the stripping flat is punched with holes along its gripper edge. The hole pattern of many punches is a round center hole with a slotted hole on each side, thus anchoring the center and minimizing the effects of dimensional changes by dividing them. A slotted hole is often centered near the flat's back edge.

Complementary flats are made by punching another sheet of flat material and placing it on the pins, thus avoiding the need for register marks on the complementary flat. In the plate area, matching holes are punched into the plates. Each flat is placed on pins inserted into the plate for exposure.

Tabs and buttons. For work not requiring such hairline precision as that of process color, hole tabs and buttons may be used in place of hole punches and register pins.

Hole tabs, sometimes called "fitters," are small pieces of plastic having prepunched holes usually with centering notches or projections. They are held in place by applying pressure-sensitive tape or adhesive to the tabs.

Buttons, sometimes called "dowels," are plastic disks having pressure-sensitive adhesive for attachment. A button is pressed through a hole in a tab. A system of tabs and buttons can be used for keying complementary flats and for duplicating simple images on film or plates.

Punched-hole method. The punched-hole register method is similar to the tab-and-button register method, however, with the punched-hole method, the film assembler punches matching holes into masking material, clear plastic sheeting, and/or printing plates. Holes are usually punched in all materials before film image assembly begins.

Register pin method. As discussed previously, a register pin, like a button, acts as a post, but it has

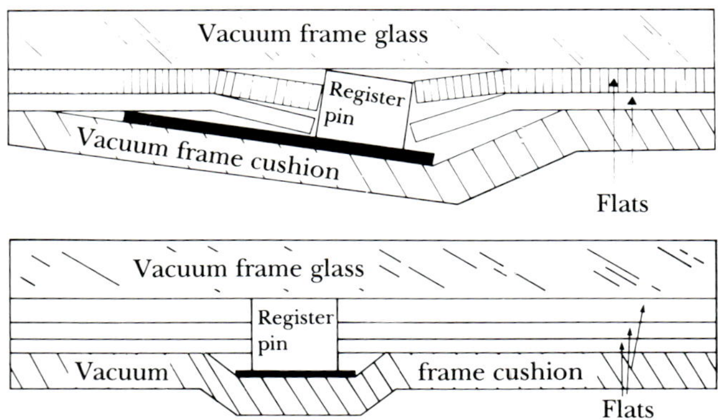

Effect of type of register pin on contact: incorrect *(top)* and correct contact.

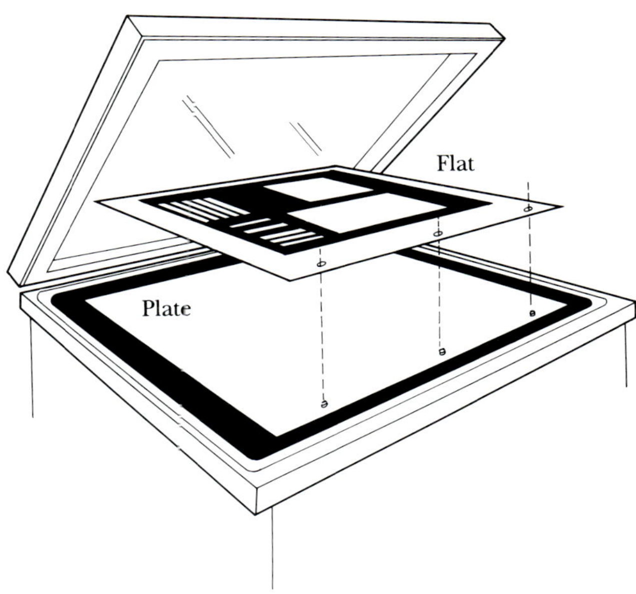

Pin-registering the flat to the printing plate in the contact frame.

a base. The size and shape of the base varies considerably. Low-profile pins are used for contacting, slightly higher ones for ordinary stripping, and high-profile style for multiple flats.

Contact between materials can be affected by the type of register pins used. Single pins mounted off-center on a long base, or shank, are a common cause of distortion because the pin tilts under vacuum conditions and prevents close contact of film images near it. A small-base pin (because of the base's small surface area) or a floating pin does not tilt.

To minimize dimensional changes during film image assembly, allow all film and stripping materials to come into equilibrium with room temperature and humidity for one or two hours before being punched. After exposure and processing, film should be allowed to go through the equilibration period again before image assembly. Critical-register films should be checked before the light table gets too warm.

Multicolor Film Assembly

Printing with more than one color on a given substrate—multicolor printing—falls into three categories: spot color printing, fake color printing, and process-color printing.

Spot color printing is adding nonprocess color ink in selected areas, such as having certain type blocks printed in a color other than black and having backgrounds in color, sometimes by overprinting several colors.

Fake color printing is color printing from a black-and-white original, either a line drawing or a continuous-tone photo. To make a multicolor reproduction from a line illustration, the lines of the illustration are used as outlines for the various color areas. The color and screen tint values are indicated on the original copy or on a translucent overlay sheet. The areas within each outline are stripped as small-size color panels Fake color printing does not require process-color inks, but tries to imitate process-color printing to a limited extent.

Process-color printing is the production of a full variety of colors from the overprinting of three standard-color inks (magenta, yellow, and cyan), in various combinations and proportions, along with a fourth ink, black. The original for process-color printing, a full-color photo or continuous-tone illustration, is color separated before being reproduced.

Register

Two or more colors that are combined to produce multicolor reproduction must have the correct positional relationship with the other colors. This positional correspondence is called **register.** Two different levels of register accuracy are **hairline register,** the accepted standard, with an allowable deviation of 0.003 in. (0.08 mm); and **loose register,** where critical color register is not required: the color images are relatively independent of each other.

Another "register" term requiring definition is **lap register.** This is the overlapping of a narrow strip—the **lap**—of one color over another at their junction to make it easier to fit the colors together on the press. An illustration is the fitting of a line image of one color into a white space reversed into another color, and slightly lapping the edges to avoid having any white space showing. For example, magenta type could be given a cyan background and the slight overlap would be hardly noticeable.

Spreads and Chokes

It is sometimes necessary to move the edge of a line image slightly outward or inward without otherwise changing the image's overall dimensions. This is done to provide lap register. The image whose edges have been moved slightly outward is called a **spread,** or "fatty"; one whose edges have been moved slightly inward is called a **choke,** or "skinny." A spread is made from a negative; a choke is made from a positive.

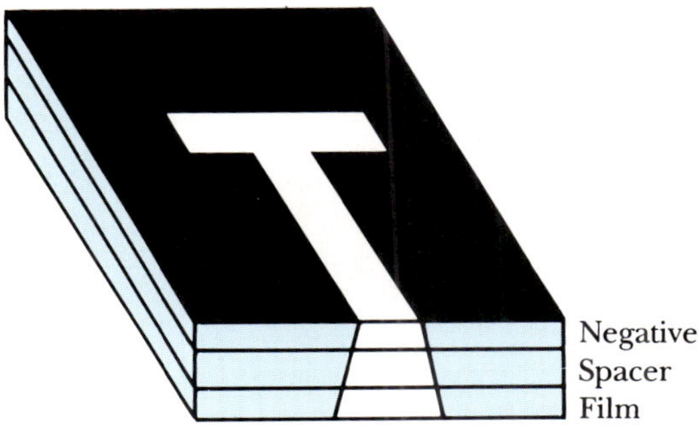

A spread made from a negative. Note how the light undercuts the opaque nonimage areas of the negative, making the image slightly wider.

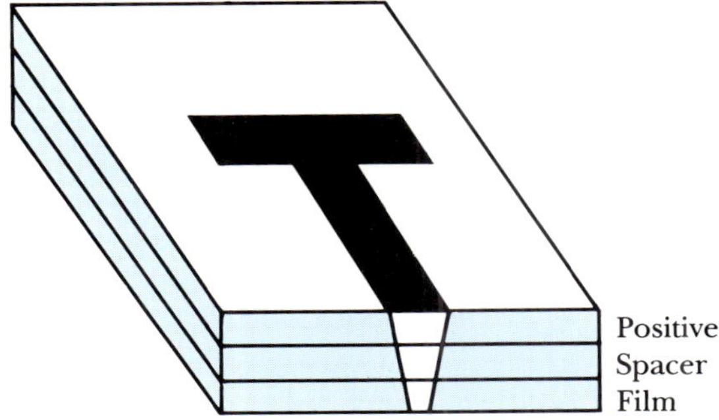

A choke made from a positive. The light undercuts the opaque image areas of the positive, making the image slightly thinner.

Spacer/diffusion sheeting method. Spacer material can be a sheet of clear or matte film. Diffusion sheeting can be opalized glass, opalized plastic, drafting film, or translucent plastic sheeting. Spreads and chokes can be made by using spacers only, diffusion sheeting only, or both.

If the amount of spread or choke is to be less than four points, only diffusion sheeting need be used. However, somewhat more exposure time is required in the absence of a spacer. A calibration guide should be made using varying numbers, thicknesses, and material of spacer sheets with varying exposures.

With spacer and diffusion sheeting, clear film base or matte sheet spacer is placed between the original film and the sensitized material. The diffusion sheeting is placed over the contact frame glass. During exposure, the diffused light passing through the openings in the film is scattered as it passes through the spacer material, slightly enlarging the edges of the images on the sensitized material.

Overexposure method. A small amount of spread can be obtained by simply overexposing to a matte surface film. An improvement of the method is achieved by using an ultraviolet filter on the light source. GATF does not recommend this technique for large amounts of spreads or chokes or with duplicating films.

Process-Color Film Assembly

In process-color film assembly, control marks are handled differently from the way that they are handled in single-color assembly. Layout and film positioning methods are the same as in single-color, but with some additional requirements.

Master marks flat. The marks of the four process-color flats are assembled into a single **master marks flat,** which also includes register marks. Alternative terms for this flat are *master flat, marks flat,* and *key sheet.*

For **negative** assembly, the layout is ruled up on a sheet of orange vinyl with fold, center-of-sheet, and trim lines. Negative marks for trim, center, and fold are aligned with the layout lines and taped base down on the flat. Register marks are also positioned. The flat is turned over and the masking material is cut away from the marks. This flat is labeled "Master Marks."

For *positive* assembly, the layout is drawn on a separate sheet and covered with a sheet of clear polyester. Positive control marks are applied, and

masking material is placed wherever images, carried by other flats, are to print.

Assembly materials. For process color, all color negatives must be in hairline register with each other. Therefore, all components must be assembled on a stable-based material. Polyester sheets are recommended for the assembly of four-color separations, including negative separations. The clear material helps to locate images and place them more accurately. Since openings do not need to be cut for the images, the solid base material remains strong.

For platemaking, a sheet of masking material with exposure openings is placed over the polyester. An alternative is the use of peelable masking film. It remains strong because only the membrane is cut and peeled away for exposure openings; the transparent base remains uncut, and the remaining membrane on the base provides the exposure mask.

Composite negatives. When process-color jobs require several flats with different component parts to make up each color of the set, each color should be contacted into a one-piece composite negative. When this is to be done, it is recommended that the separation negatives be made right-reading as viewed from the emulsion side. The flats are then made with negatives assembled emulsion-down on the top side of the clear polyester material rather than the conventional way. The final negatives are contacted emulsion to emulsion.

Pin register. For the efficient production of high-quality work, pin registration should be used. Every piece of flat material should be punched with register holes correlated to each other with register pins. An additional value of pin register is that any flat of a set can be checked against any other by dropping them over the pins.

Basic Procedures

Color copy is generally assembled in one-page or two-page printer's spread flats. The following descriptions are in terms of single-page flats:

Base negative flat. Black-printing type, ordinarily assembled before process-color image assembly, can be assembled on orange vinyl if nothing else will be on the flat. Clear polyester is generally used if text and black separation negatives will be on the same flat. Type is assembled first; separation negatives are assembled after a stripping key is developed.

Key flat. All units of the key color are fitted to the cropping masks and layout lines. They are attached to the top side of the flat material, which is pin-registered on the stripping table. All other units are registered to this key flat to ensure proper image register.

Stripping key. To aid in registering the other colors, a stripping key can be made as a guide. A stripping key may be simply a contact positive of the key flat. A better method uses a blue key material that is exposed to the key flat through a black light filter. This, also, produces a positive image. Stripping negatives to a positive key image (or any positive image) leaves no clear areas when they are properly superimposed.

The key material, which can be handled under normal room lighting, is punched for the same pin-register used for the other flats. Image-to-image register between the stripping key and the key flat should be checked with a magnifier.

Assembling other colors. The stripping key is placed over the pins with a polyester sheet over the key. The negatives are assembled in this manner:

The top register marks on the negative are registered using a magnifier, and the top edge is taped in place. The bottom edge is checked for register and taped. Then, the top registration is rechecked. Finally, the halftone images themselves are checked for correspondence between negative and key. Accuracy of image alignment is improved by the use of a collimating glass (which permits viewing without parallax) or a magnifier with a GATF T-KAP; either of these forces the eye to look directly through the center of the lens.

Flat identification. After all the negatives have been assembled on the carrier, it is labeled with the name of the printing color and the name of the cropping mask to be used with it.

Great care must be taken in making identifying marks when many complementary flats, masks, screen tints, and knockouts are used to make up a page. When there are a number of mask flats, each should be labeled with a letter. Screen tints and knockouts are identified by their own letters and by the masks that they will be combined with during contacting.

Each color film flat is marked with the color of the plate to be exposed, its exposure sequence number, and the total number of exposures the plate or composite will receive. Example: Yellow, 3 of 5 (Mask B).

Multiple Imaging of Plates

A single image or several different images are often repeated on a printing plate. Multiple imaging of a press plate can be done in one of three ways: (1) assembling several negatives (or positives) of the same image into a single flat to expose the plate; (2) assembling one negative (or positive) of the image in a flat or other carrier and exposing it in a succession of specific positions on the plate manually with the use of pin register; and (3) assembling one negative (or positive) of the image in a flat or other carrier and exposing it in a succession of specific positions using a machine that mechanically moves the image. Multiple exposures can be made on film by the same methods as on plates, since films that can be handled under the same lighting conditions as plates are available.

The second and third methods of making multiple images on a printing plate are collectively called **photoimposition.** (In the past, this was commonly called *photocomposition,* and the term is still used sometimes. However, the term was also used sometimes to describe the system of typesetting by photography.) Within this category, the process of making a plate from a single negative that is exposed, shifted to a new position on the plate, exposed, and shifted (stepped) repeatedly until the plate is finished is called **step-and-repeat,** and the plate thus produced is called a **step-and-repeat,** or **duplicate, plate.** A plate made from several different negatives, usually, but not always, requiring multiple exposures of each, is called a **combination plate** (which was most commonly called a *photocomposed plate*). An example of a combination plate is one resulting from four exposures to one negative, eight exposures to a second, and four exposures to a third. A **step-and-repeat machine** is used for photoimposition.

Photoimposition is used to combine the film assembly operation of accurately locating the film on the press plate and the platemaking operation of exposing the press plate through the film. The accuracy resulting from photoimposition is generally higher than that obtained by film assembly, but its hourly cost is greater. A stripped-up flat can be used to expose an entire press plate in a single exposure. The same press plate may require a number of exposures using photoimposition.

The choice between using photoimposition or film assembly for a job is determined by several factors. A job's run length and complexity are a few considerations. The following factors favor film assembly:

- Combination black-and-white or simple color jobs that are made up of different printing subjects or pages of a publication
- Simple step-and-repeat and average-accuracy jobs, where a maximum of two or three exposures are required in making the press plate
- Large subjects that are too large for the photocomposing machine chase
- Jobs requiring duplicate press plates, either for extremely long runs or for branch plant distribution
- Where minimum press downtime is important, in the event of plate failure on the press

The following factors are more favorable for using photocomposition rather than film assembly:

- Step-and-repeat jobs that require several identical printing forms, such as labels and stamps (some step-and-repeat machines also produce multiple-imaged negatives or positives that can be used to make the plate)
- High accuracy jobs where hairline register or backup is required, including both combination and step-and-repeat subjects

Film assembly and photoimposition operations are combined for many jobs. The stripper prepares a sectional flat consisting of one or several negatives. These sectional flats are then stepped up or combined with each other on the step-and-repeat machine or on register pins.

Step-and-Repeat Machines

Step-and-repeat machines, sometimes called *photocomposing machines,* have six basic units:

- Backboard, or plate bed, on which the press plate is fastened. The plate is always positioned precisely on the backboard so that when plates are made for multicolor printing, the images for each color will be in the same position on their respective plates. If a pin register system is used, the machine should have pins installed on the backboard to correctly locate the plate.
- Chase, a precisely constructed frame upon which the original film (negative or positive) is mounted. It has center marks for the purpose of locating the original, or it can be set up to accommodate a pin register system. The chase is constructed so that the vacuum can hold the negative in contact with the plate. Some step-and-repeat machines are equipped with chases in which the film can be changed automatically: negatives are stacked in proper sequence on register pins in a loading cassette.

- Chase carriage, which supports the chase and is constructed to permit the numerically controlled movement of the chase in both horizontal and vertical directions in increments of thousandths of an inch or hundredths of a millimeter. The carriage is most often screw-driven.
- Vacuum pump or other device to facilitate contact between negative and plate during exposure.
- Exposure source, most usually metal-halide lamps because of their high ultraviolet output. A light integrator is often used to control exposures.
- Numerical control or microprocessor control unit, in which control data is entered through a keyboard, magnetic card or tape, floppy disk, or stored memory. This unit controls the order in which exposures are made; i.e., the stepping pattern.

In operation, the plate is first securely fastened in position on the backboard. The negative is mounted on the chase and properly lined up. The chase is then mounted on the carriage and moved to the correct horizontal and vertical position, as indicated by a prepared layout. The chase is slid into contact with the plate, and the vacuum is applied. After the air has been evacuated and the negative is in good contact with the plate, the exposure is made. Then, the vacuum is released and the chase is moved by the carriage to the next position indicated on the layout. The second exposure is then made. If a combination plate is to be made, it is necessary to remove the chase from the carriage to mount and align the second negative in position after all exposures have been made from the first negative; some machines automatically change negatives. If a pin register system is used on the chase, it is only necessary to remove the first negative from the chase, place the second negative over the register pins, and tape it into position.

Step-and-repeat machines cycle through the different steps automatically or with minimal operator intervention. For example, a fully automated machine will have a special loading cassette in which the negatives—punched for the register pins on the chase—are in sequential order. The machine automatically picks up the first negative and moves it into proper position for exposure. After exposure, the negative is released from the chase, and the next negative is picked up and moved into position for exposure.

Microprocessor-controlled machines. Some machines do not require that each exposure position be given horizontal and vertical coordinates. Microprocessor-controlled machines require only a starting point (with horizontal and vertical—x,y—coordinates) and the horizontal and vertical stepping distances (e.g., 8.500 horizontally, 11.000 vertically). Given this data, the machine—through the use of the microprocessor—automatically calculates the coordinates for each new exposure position. Such machines also determine the order of stepping, or the stepping pattern.

Depending on the machine, only a starting point and stepping distance must be specified, or horizontal and vertical coordinates provided for each exposure position.

Mounting and Masking the Original

The step-and-repeat machine ensures the proper fit of multicolor subjects on the press sheet. However, the final printed result is only as good as the film assembly job. For this reason, center marks and subject matter must be assembled in perfect register with each other.

The stripper must first know the size of the chase to be used. The chase size, such as 16×20 in. (406×508 mm), is the maximum flat size that the chase can accommodate. The flat extends into the frame area so that there is no light leakage into the plate during exposure. Because of this frame, the image area is less than the chase size. The limitations and dimensions of each chase must be fully understood so that the image to be exposed is put on a chase of the right size. Any image that extends under the frame area is not exposed and consequently does not appear on the printing plate.

Film assembly is usually done so that the image or trim size is centered. Centering the image makes it easier and more accurate to calculate the machine readings for the position of each exposure on the machine. If the plate requires many exposures, it is best to make a chase-size, one-piece duplicate negative rather than taping the negative and center marks to orange vinyl. Multiple exposures cause heat buildup on the negative and cause shifting when tape and masking material are used to hold the image in place. Pure vinyl sheets should never be used for step-and-repeat purposes because the heat buildup can exceed the 140°F (60°C) softening point of vinyl. The center marks also function as register marks, but they must be perfectly perpendicular to the work, because crooked marks can cause register problems between colors.

After the negative is assembled into a flat or converted to a chase-size duplicate, it is visually centered on the chase. The chase and negative are placed in a registering device. One such device consists of a light frame that is covered with a glass

into which fine perpendicular lines are etched. Register devices mount the chase in the same manner as the carriage does. The chase and negative are adjusted so that the negative aligns perfectly with the locating marks on the registering device.

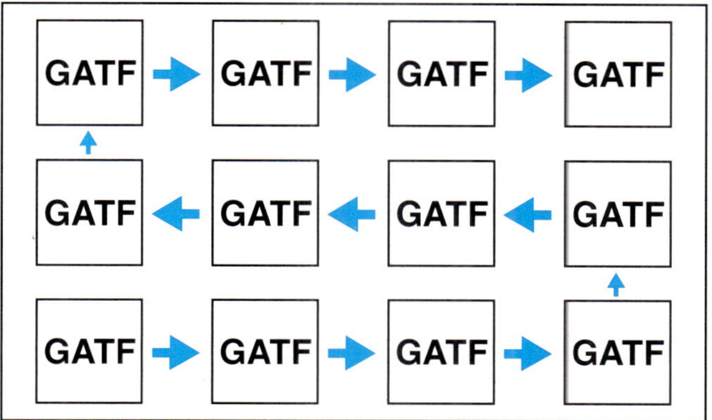

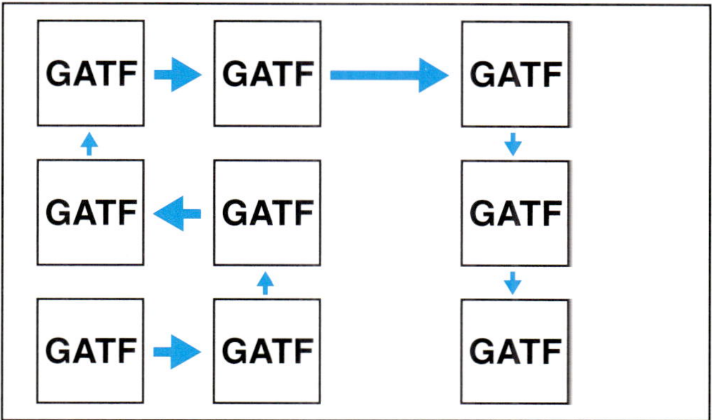

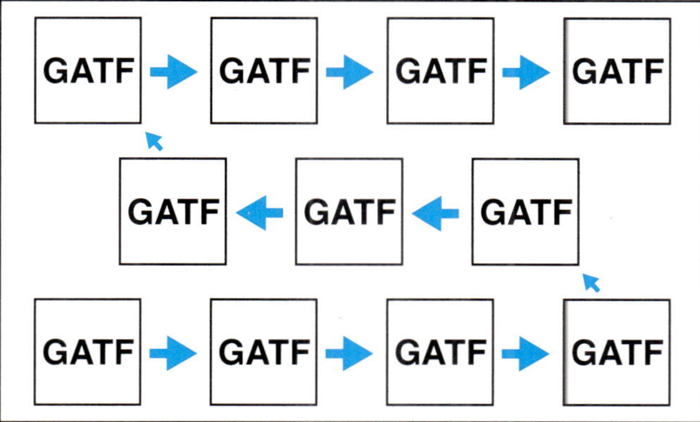

The three basic stepping patterns: equal interval stepping *(top)*, irregular interval stepping *(middle)*, and staggered stepping. The arrows indicate the order in which exposures are made. Each pattern is made of zigzagging movements of the carriage, which minimizes the distance that the carriage travels.

If the chase is equipped with register pins, the image must be positioned in relation to these pins as they determine its location on the chase. In this case, it is essential to have a film punch that has the same configuration as the pins on the chase. All stripping materials must be punched with this punch to coordinate the entire job.

All nonimage areas of negatives are masked. Positives are also masked. The exposure area on a positive should be slightly larger than the trim size requirements; the rest of the positive is masked. By having the exposure area slightly larger than needed, an overlap will result in the trim area between forms. The amount of overlap is usually about 0.60 in. (15 mm) wide, but it can be wider provided it does not interfere with printing detail. The overlap aids the platemaker by reducing the amount of staging-out work required on the exposed press plate.

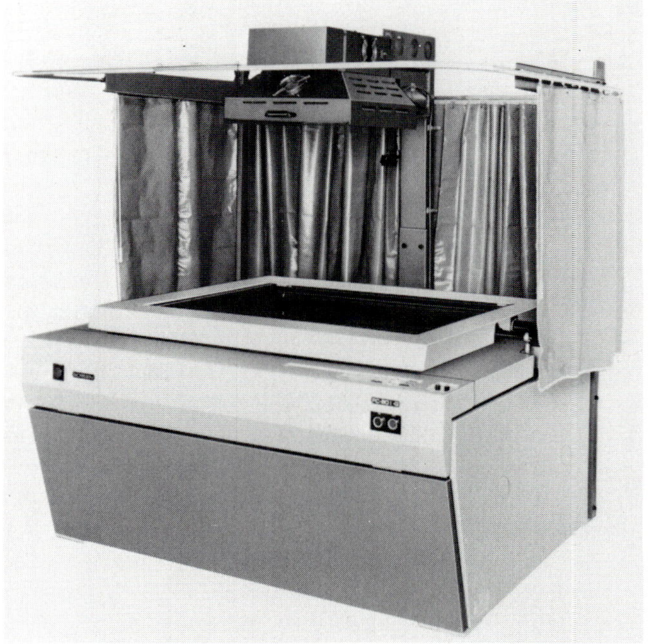

Courtesy Screen (USA)

Step-and-repeat machine with overhead light.

Pin Register Systems

In addition to assembling multiple negatives into a single flat to expose a plate and the mechanical stepping of an image using a step-and-repeat machine, pin register systems can be used to produce multiple images on a plate. There are a variety of pin register systems available for use in photocomposition. Explaining the characteristics of each system and how to use it is beyond the scope of this book. Rather, in this book, the basic step-and-repeat procedure using pin register is discussed. Unlike step

and repeat using a machine—where the stripped-up flat is moved mechanically—the use of pin register requires the manual movement of the film from one exposure position to the next. However, the register punches and stepping aids available commercially increase the accuracy of this method.

Many of the pin register systems are made to control the image from the copy to the press. All of them can be used starting with the stripping operation and be used regardless of whether there are any registration systems on the camera or press. A number of pin register systems and methods are commercially available.

A pin register system provides an accurate method of manually stepping a negative or positive on a plate or film. It also provides a means of positioning a prepunched plate at an exact point to allow for perfect centering and positioning of work for a proper plate clamp and gripper dimension. Exposures are made with the usual platemaking vacuum frame and printing lamp.

A pin register system for photoimposition typically consists of the following elements, although their exact nature varies somewhat depending on the pin register system that is used:

- Register punch, prepunched film tabs, or prepunched film assembly materials that eliminate the need for a register punch. Some register punches are micrometer-controlled so that they can be adjusted to vary the space between holes and the distance that the holes are from the edge of the material being punched.

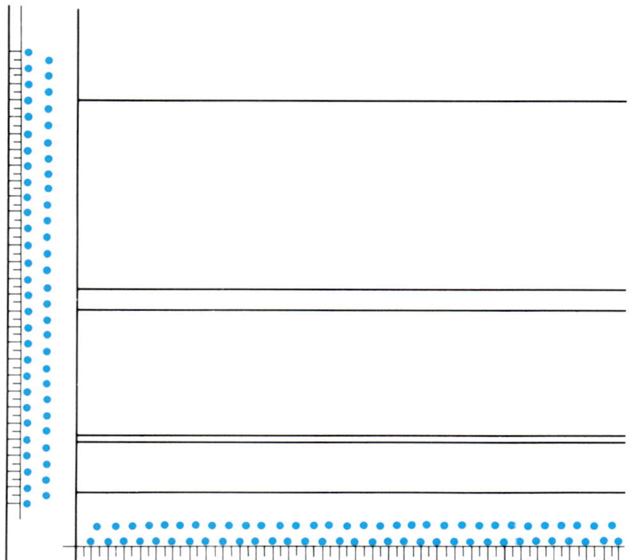

Courtesy Raden C, Inc.

Template with holes for stepping prepunched material around the perimeter.

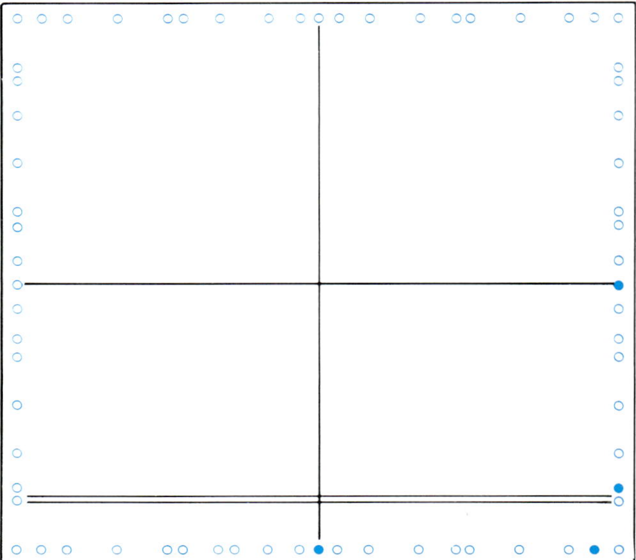

Prepunched template.

Courtesy Raden C, Inc.

Prepunched masking material used to rule up layout.

- Stepping template, or stepboard, with pin register holes properly spaced for the stepping of the film image. The template is placed on the vacuum frame base, and the plate is taped or pin-registered to it. One template prepunched with a double row of holes on all four sides permits step increments of 1/32 in., 1/16 in., 1/10 in., 1/6 in., 1/3 in., or 1 mm. Another prepunched template has a single row of holes along each side. The holes are spaced in inch increments as well as smaller increments to accommodate common fractional-inch trim sizes (e.g., 8½×11

in.). These templates have a horizontal scale that uses the vertical centerline of the template as the zero reference point and a vertical scale that uses the bottom edge as the other zero reference point. Templates are on a heavy-gauge plastic and are about 1–2 in. (25–50 mm) larger than the press plate on each side.

- Master layout sheet, which indicates how the film image is to be stepped. It is ruled up just as any layout sheet would be. Sometimes, the layout sheet also doubles as the stepping template.
- Step sheets, masking material equipped with register holes that permit the film image to be stepped on the plate. The step sheets used with negatives are either orange vinyl or clear polyester, which is easier to work with but requires a separate masking operation. Clear polyester is used with positives. Clear polyester is also used when a second step sheet is needed to permit the stepping of the film image in both the horizontal and vertical directions. The step sheet with the film attached to it is taped to the second step sheet, and both are stepped across the plate. Then, the step sheet with film attached is moved up one exposure position on the second step sheet, retaped, and then stepped across the plate.

This procedure is repeated until the plate is completely exposed. The assembling of multiples of one image on a step sheet often eliminates the need for a second step sheet.

- Control strip, used in place of the second strip sheet. Holes are punched in it to accommodate pins in the template and in the step sheet. Use of a control strip eliminates the taping of the film-carrying step sheet to the second step sheet.
- Masking material to protect areas of the plate not covered by the step sheet.
- Register pins, pegs, or dowels (buttons).

Chapter 10

Proofing

The Purposes of Proofing

Proofing, like proofreading, is one of the inspection operations of printing and can be considered a process control step. The two main purposes of proofing are to check the accuracy and the appearance of the job before it goes to press. Serving as a common reference to the customer, service bureau, and printer, a color proof represents what the finished job will look like.

Color proofs fit into the printing process in the following areas: camera/scanner, image assembly, platemaking, press, and bindery. In the camera/scanner area, a color proof is used to evaluate color balance, color correction, image size, screen angles, register, and overall quality. After image assembly (or stripping), a proof is often made to check sizing, cropping, color bleeds, crossovers, overprints, positioning, register, etc. Dot quality (gain or sharpening) can be determined by comparing the proof to the plate in the platemaking process. When the job finally goes to press, a color proof is used as a guide for print quality; in other words, matching the customer-approved proof is the goal for an OK sheet for the pressrun. Just before being sent out, the final job will pass through the bindery phase of the operation; here the proof will be used as a final check for layout, size, trimming, folding, imprinting, bleeds, and margins. Therefore, although the primary purpose of a proof is to represent as closely as possible what the customer expects to see in the finished job, color proofs are also used for internal quality checking and control throughout the entire color reproduction process.

Traditionally, most lithographic printing jobs had been custom-made from many pieces that must be properly related. Produced under tight deadlines, the risk of error has always been high. Today, however, more and more lithographic jobs are being prepared on desktop production equipment, which enables the graphic designer to position more elements and output them on a single piece of film.

Furthermore, small imperfections can often be very detrimental to a printed product. Thus, proofing provides a specific step for catching errors before they become disastrous.

Accuracy. The proof is checked for completeness, image defects, color breaks, position, imposition, internal fit, and register. Lithographic printing jobs often include many pieces, such as type, scaled and cropped photos, tints, halftones, or other image elements that need to be assembled under tight deadlines. A proof provides a means of making sure all of these elements are present and positioned correctly. (With the increasing use of desktop production systems, however, this will become less of a concern since the imagesetter can output film with many of these elements already in place on the appropriate printer.)

The proof is also checked for broken type, pinholes, or other defects, which generally indicate the presence of dust or scratches on the film (if the proof was generated from film). For spot color jobs, all copy and art must be checked to make sure they will print in the correct color. In addition, various elements of one color must be checked for correct position with reference to other colors.

Imposition is an essential consideration in all jobs that are printed on both sides and folded into their final form. Proofing is the last opportunity for making sure that the job is imposed according to the folding dummy, which should always be the basis of the press sheet layout. The position of each page on the press sheet, its back-up, the inside and outside margins, head and foot trims, and an

allowance for creep are all items with which a printer should be thoroughly familiar.

Internal fit refers to how well all the images register *within* a sheet. On a printed press sheet, fit is affected by the accuracy of the plates in relation to each other and by the dimensional stability of the paper. If a plate has been made incorrectly, or if the paper distorts, and some of the images are out of place in relation to others on sheets printed in register, it is said to have poor fit. Photomechanical proofing provides an excellent check for fit, at least with regard to the plate. Paper shrinkage, of course, cannot be accounted for on a proof.

A distinction should be made between fit and register (sometimes referred to as internal and external register, respectively). Register refers to printing each sheet in the same position relative to the gripper edge and the guide side. If necessary, external register can be adjusted on press by the press crew during makeready operations.

Appearance. One of the most important functions of a proof is to predict the appearance of the printed job. In fact, this purpose is so critical that, once the customer approves and signs a proof, it serves as a contractual agreement between the printer and the customer. The printer agrees to replicate the appearance of the proof when the actual job is printed, and the customer agrees to accept the job. The signed proof is often referred to as an approval proof.

Externally, authors, customers, or advertising agencies may demand proofs for a variety of reasons. For example, ad agencies frequently want to see how the job will look before it goes to press. Customers may need samples for advance distribution, perhaps to salespeople, distributors, or dealers. Or they may need proofs of one job to guide the work of people preparing a related job. In magazine work, regional editions are printed at various sites nationwide, or even around the world. Proofs are critical for each production site so that the different editions have a consistent, high-quality appearance.

Internally, the color separator makes a proof of the separation films to determine whether there are any problems with tone reproduction, gray balance, and color correction. The customer can also indicate changes on these individual proofs (called scatter proofs) of individual photos. Typical examples would be to make the blue sky or green grass appear more saturated.

The press crew uses proofs as a guide for the pressrun. Once the press begins to produce sheets that are an acceptable match to the proof, the customer or customer service representative, as well as the press supervisor, sign off on several press sheets. These OK sheets give the press crew permission to proceed with the pressrun.

Kinds of Proofs

The three main kinds of proofs are press proofs (imaged with ink on paper), photomechanical proofs (exposed through assembled films onto light-sensitive material), and digital proofs (formed directly from digital data and imaged on a substrate in a variety of ways). Photomechanical and digital proofs are also generally referred to as "off-press" proofs.

In lithography, photomechanical proofing is the predominant method. However, digital proofing is gaining acceptance as imaging technology improves, while some customers still prefer press proofs for extremely critical jobs or especially when multiple copies (i.e., 50 or more) are needed.

Off-press color proofs are more economical than press proofs. Secondly, off-press color proofing systems are more compatible with today's production time restraints. The third major reason for the increased acceptance of off-press color proofs is their ability to simulate press results optically. When a standard set of press conditions is defined and an off-press proofing system is calibrated for these conditions, the off-press proof can be a cost-effective aid in achieving quality color reproduction. Correlating the proofing system to the printing system requires the use of a proofing system that is compatible with a particular printing press; it also demands an understanding of the different systems.

There are continuing pressures for improved color fidelity, consistency, and shorter production time for off-press proofing systems. The primary objective is a closer correlation between the off-press proof and the printed product.

Press Proofs

Until the mid-1970s, publishers and agencies would accept only press proofs as verification of the final films to be submitted to the printer. Today, however, press proofing is used on a limited basis in lithographic printing. A notable exception is the area of magazine production.

Producing a press proof. The steps involved in producing a press proof are as follows: exposing the plates from the stripped-up flats, mounting the plates on the press, performing makeready on the press, and, finally, printing a few prints. The customer is given the press proof for approval before the job is run.

Press proofing is very costly, primarily because of the involvement of labor-intensive operations, the need for expensive materials (e.g., plates), and the use of cost-intensive equipment. In an effort to reduce production costs, special, smaller proof presses may be used. This frees valuable time on the printing press, which can then be used more cost-effectively to produce salable products. This does not, however, eliminate the high manpower costs involved in making a press proof.

Advantages and disadvantages of press proofing. Press proofs can have the advantage of being printed on the actual printing substrate using the same printing inks that will be used for the final reproduction. Also, if multiple proofs are required, they can be produced at little or no extra cost.

To accurately predict the final reproduction, the press proof should be produced using similar inks, paper, color sequence, and even a similar press, if possible, to provide similar dot reproduction characteristics. Even if this is done, however, press color proofing can rarely create an exact facsimile of the production print.

Another factor that may affect the reliability of press proofing is that often the printing plates used for proofing the job are not the same plates that will be used in the final production pressrun. In specialized cases such as label work, for example, it is customary to proof these intermediate plates on proof presses before the final press plate is made. Intermediate plates may have been produced using different exposures. Spacers may have been used during exposure to spread the dot in an attempt to simulate the amount of dot gain on the production press. On the other hand, the plates made for the production run may be exposed in such a way as to create a dot-sharpening effect.

Furthermore, press proofs are usually produced in quantities that are relatively small compared to a regular pressrun. While a production press "settles down" after a few thousand impressions and begins to print more consistent sheets, a proof press never reaches this "steady state." Therefore, even if all the materials used to make the proof are the same, it is doubtful that the press sheets would exactly match a press proof.

Ironically, the heaviest demand for press proofs is for magazines, which are usually printed by heatset web offset, while all proof presses are sheetfed. There are many fundamental differences between the two methods:

- Heatset web presses print with heatset inks, which dry by solvent evaporation; sheetfed inks (for both proof presses and production presses) feature drying oils, which generally have better ink holdout and higher gloss.
- Web presses print blanket-to-blanket, which leads to higher dot gain; sheetfed presses print blanket-to-impression cylinder.
- In web printing, the roll of paper feeds through the press grain long, which leads to more fan-out because paper expands more across the grain; sheetfed papers are fed grain short.
- Web presses operate at high speeds, which decreases trap and increases dot gain; sheetfed presses run at much lower speeds.

Special circumstances, such as the need for multicopy proofs, may continue to make press proofing the preferred method for particular cases. But the uses for off-press full-color proofing are continuing to increase.

Off-press proofing technology is continually improving the control of variables to allow more accurate prediction of results.

Photomechanical Proofs

Photomechanical proofs of single-color and spot color work are produced very differently than photomechanical proofs of process color jobs. Proofing for single-color and spot color work is generally done in a contact frame, where the film flats are exposed to photosensitive paper. Several exposures of different lengths may be made if the job features more than one color.

Photomechanical proofs for process color can be made by two methods: overlay or single-sheet. *Overlay* systems consist of transparent films that carry each color image. These films are laid over each other on a base sheet in register in a recommended sequence to produce a composite proof. These films are not bonded together (although the proofing technician may tape them down on all sides). Individual films can be lifted to view the first-down color, the two- and three-color overprints, and the final full-color image.

In contrast to overlay systems are *single-sheet* (surprint) systems, which produce a laminated proof on a single-sheet base using toners or precoated materials for each color.

Photosensitive paper proofs. Single-color and spot color proofs are most often made using photosensitive polymer papers. These proofs are known as dry proofs because they require no processing. Polymer papers are available coated on one side or two. One variety produces an intense blue image (this kind of proof is called a blueline), while another produces a dark gray image.

Polymer papers may be used either as positive-to-negative/negative-to-positive papers, or they may be used as duplication papers (positive-to-positive/negative-to-negative), simply by varying the exposing procedure.

An imaging exposure is made with ultraviolet (UV) radiation, and a deactivation exposure is made with visible light and without the imaging film. For positive-to-negative or negative-to-positive proofing, the imaging exposure is made first, followed by the deactivation step. For a duplication process, the steps are reversed.

The deactivation step is recommended for a permanent proof; otherwise, daylight, which contains UV radiation in addition to visible light, or artificial illumination containing a UV component, produces color formation in nonimage areas.

The imaging exposure should be entirely UV. Any visible light in the imaging exposure tends to deactivate the paper's sensitivity in the image area while the image is being formed. The result would be a lighter image. Since most high-intensity UV exposure sources have some output of visible light, filters are available to remove it. A glass filter of this sort might be put in the lamp holder, or a film filter could be placed over the image film, taped on the outside of the vacuum frame glass, or mounted in a frame that could be placed over the vacuum frame.Similarly, in the deactivation step, special lamps can be used to avoid UV, or the UV can be filtered out with films at the light source, on the contact frame glass, or on top of the proofing paper.

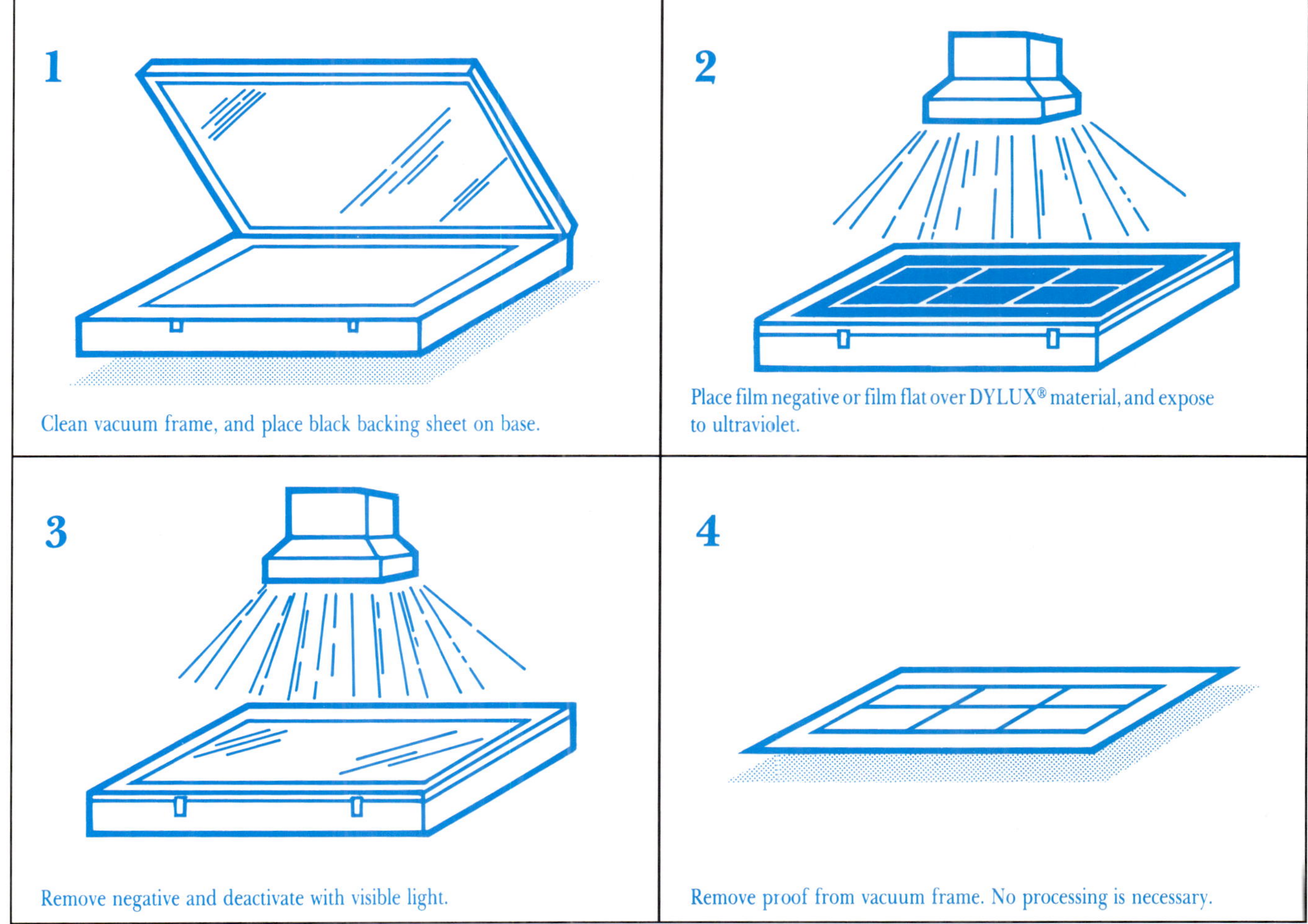

Courtesy E. I. du Pont de Nemours & Co., Inc

The production steps in producing a DYLUX© proof.

Color breaks can be indicated on a single proof by varying the exposure time to indicate different colors with different tones. The longer the exposure, the darker the tone. First establish a series of stepped exposures, increasing each up to the maximum density exposure. Mark the exposure time on each step. This can be used as a guide for selecting the exposures for each spot color.

A two-color job, for example, might be proofed on a single sheet by exposing one of the color printers for about 25% of the exposure needed to form a maximum-density image on the paper. The film for the second color would then be registered to the image on the proof paper and exposed to produce a maximum-density image on the photosensitive paper. For a job with more colors, smaller degrees of difference would be used. This provides a way to check for any missing copy, the accuracy of copy, and color registration and trapping (overlap). This proofing method is also satisfactory for halftone evaluation.

Overlay systems. The first photomechanical overlay proofing system was developed by the U.S. Army Map Service during World War II; however, it dealt with line images only. Other overlay systems followed that used halftone images and process colors.

The first of these to be successful were OSACHROME overlay films, produced by Ozalid Corporation. When these diazo-coated films were exposed and processed with ammonia vapors, they produced dyed images in colors similar to process ink colors. Four-color proofs were obtained by making a photographic print of the black separation on paper, then producing prints of the other three colors on films. The films were then mounted in register and in sequence over the black print to produce the proof.

In 1960, a new overlay system was introduced, which replaced dyes with pigments and used dimensionally stable polyester films. This system became a turning point for off-press process color proofs, which soon began to replace press proofs for internal quality control. Since then, many other overlay systems have appeared.

Today, all overlay proofs, also called multilayer proofs, are made directly from the color separation films, which are used to expose individual, precoated, transparent colored films in a contact frame. The color of the overlay material is preestablished by the manufacturer, and the colors closely match most commercially available process inks. Each colored film is registered to the others, and the complete set is backed by a sheet of white paper. The resulting proof is viewed by reflected light.

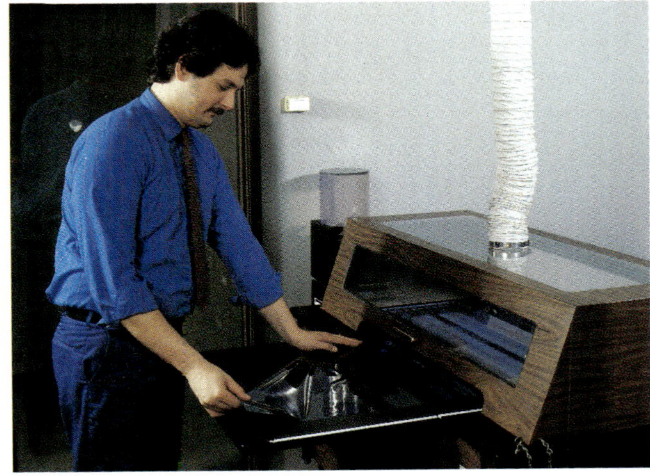

Exposed 3M Color-Key material entering automatic processor.

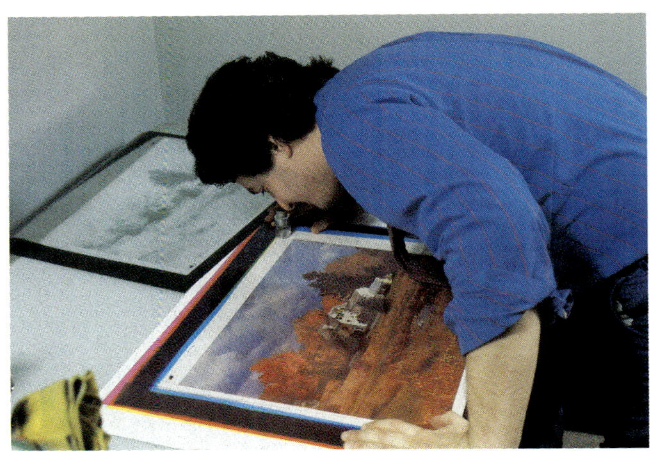

Magenta image being registered to the cyan and yellow Color-Key images. The black image is in the background and will be registered next. A magnifier is being used to register images.

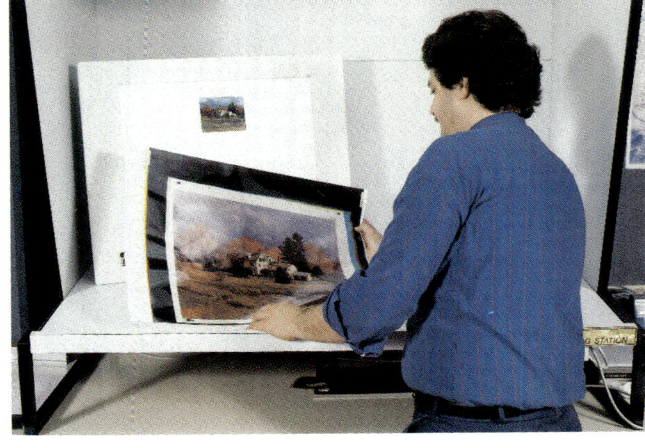

Color-Key overlay proof being compared with the original transparency.

Overlay proofs have several advantages. They are relatively inexpensive and can be made with equipment normally found in a plant's platemaking department. They can be made in 7–20 minutes. A major advantage is that, if necessary, one of the four individual layers could be remade without remaking the others. For example, if a dot etcher retouches one film and wants to see the effect of the change, the old and new films can be alternatively flapped over the other colors in order to judge the effect of the change. One of the major uses of overlay proofs is for internal checking of color separations and color image assembly.

The major drawback to using overlay films is their difference in feel and appearance to the printed result. The surface finish is very glossy, the overlap colors are often different from press results, and the dot gain is perceived as being much higher than it actually is because light scatter between the four transparent films darkens the lighter tones of the proof.

Experienced users of overlay proof materials are adept at "reading" the proof; that is, they are able to adjust their expectations for the job's printed appearance. Overlay proofs should not normally be submitted to those who are novices at buying or judging color printing.

Single-sheet systems. Like overlay proofs, transfer proofs often consist of photosensitive transparent colored films. Other colorants include dry pigmented toners, liquid toners, and silver-halide emulsions that produce a dye image. Depending on the particular proofing system, the base sheet may be either a substrate of the customer's choice (within limits) or a sheet supplied by the vendor. Vendor-supplied sheets often come in several grades, such as publication, commercial, and newsprint. Most single-sheet process color proofing systems are available either as negative- or positive-working.

The order of the steps to make this kind of proof may vary slightly, but all procedures feature laminating, peeling, processing, exposing, and developing. Generally, the proofing technician begins by laminating a precoated, two-ply film of the first-down color (usually yellow) to a sheet of the substrate. The carrier sheet of the film is peeled away, leaving just the yellow photosensitive colorant. The yellow printer is exposed in contact with this colorant, and the substrate/colorant combination is processed. Next, the film of the second-down color (usually magenta) is laminated and peeled. The magenta printer must be registered to the yellow image before it is exposed and processed. These steps are repeated for the cyan and black printers to produce the proof.

In one system, a clear film is laminated to the vendor-supplied base sheet. The combination is exposed to the yellow printer and peeled, leaving a sticky, clear image area on the base. The sheet is fed through the yellow toning cassette of the toner processing unit, and the yellow powdered toner adheres to the sticky image. These steps are repeated for the magenta, cyan, and black printers. This system can be customized to the printing ink color by blending toners to match the hue and by varying the speed at which the sheet goes through the processor to alter the toner density.

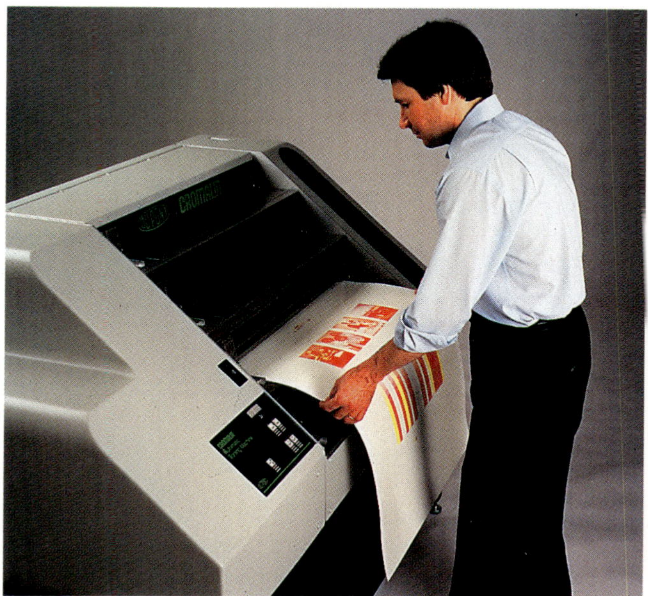

Courtesy E. I. du Pont de Nemours & Co., Inc.

Applying toner to a Cromalin single-sheet proof.

Another system allows all the printers to be exposed to their respective color films simultaneously using the same exposure. The resulting imaged films are registered to each other and laminated to the base sheet.

One of the newest single-sheet proofing systems features a completely water-based processing step. In this negative-working proofing system, precoated films are exposed to their corresponding color separation negatives. The unexposed pigment is rinsed from the precoated film with tap water in the wash-off/drying unit and is safe for ordinary drainage. The resulting positive films are registered to each other and then laminated to the paper stock. This single-sheet proofing system can also produce two-sided proofs, which allows printers to

make multipage prototypes that have been imposed, stitched, and trimmed to resemble the final printed piece.

Dry proofing technology is another new single-sheet proofing method. This system offers development without wet chemistry or toning. For each color, the precoated color film is laminated to the base sheet and exposed. Peeling the transparent carrier develops the image. Dry proofing technology requires only a laminator and exposure unit. It also eliminates the need for chemistry inventory/disposal and processor maintenance.

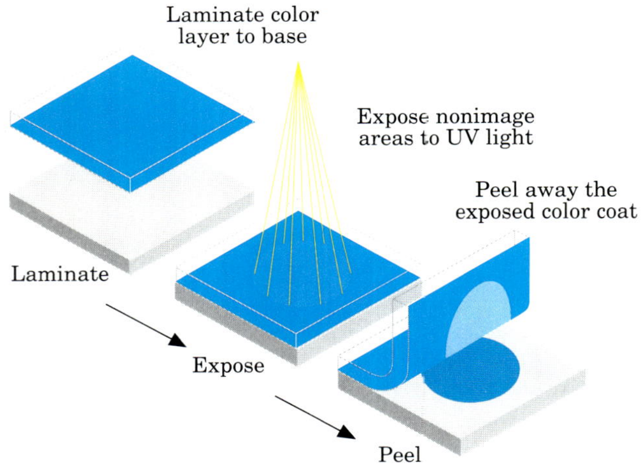

. . . and repeat for the other process colors . . .

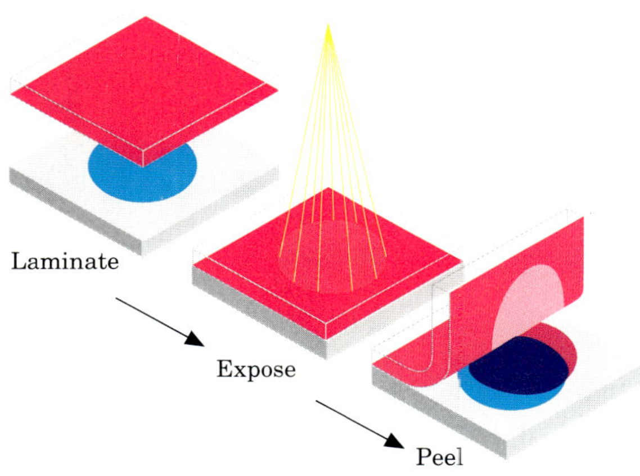

Courtesy Hoechst Celanese

Pressmatch Dry Color Proof.

An advantage to using single-sheet proofs is that they feel and look much more like a printed image than overlay proofs do, and the darkening of highlights from internal light scatter between layers of overlay proofs is virtually eliminated. Also, a reasonable simulation of press dot gain can be achieved

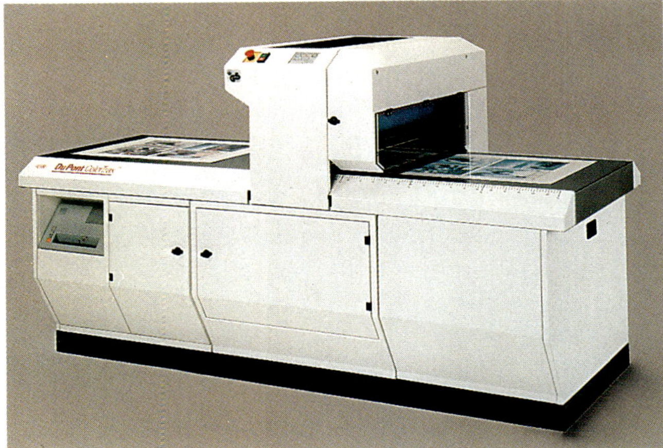

Courtesy E. I. du Pont de Nemours & Co., Inc.

Du Pont ColorTrax, a dry proofing system, that applies colors with precoated ink-carrying foils.

by laminating a clear spacer sheet to the substrate before laminating the colorants or actual images. A key advantage of single-sheet and overlay proofs is their consistency. Exposure is the major variable; therefore, if good vacuum is obtained and light time and intensity are controlled, consistency is almost assured.

The disadvantages with single-sheet proofs include the comparatively lengthy time (about 15–30 min.) to make the proof, the cost of laminating and toning machines, and in some cases, the unrealistically high gloss of the proof. Using a matte finish final lamination on the proof overcomes the high-gloss problem. The cost of materials, like those used for overlay proofing, tends to be high. Another disadvantage for some systems is that a vendor-supplied white plastic material must be used as the base sheet. A final drawback is that these systems cannot simulate four-color press trapping.

In general, single-sheet proofs offer a reasonable alternative to press proofs. If they are made with the proper colorants, substrate, dot gain simulation, and surface finish, they are fair guides for the printer and the customer to judge the expected appearance of the future printed sheet. Their relatively low cost and high levels of consistency will continue to convince more and more people that these proofs are sensible alternatives to press proofs. Unusual or extreme printing conditions, however, will continue to require the flexibility of press proofing.

Digital Proofing

The development and acceptance of digital methods of manipulating and outputting functions like page

layout, typesetting, and illustration are revolutionizing the graphic arts industry. Digital technology allows a proof to be made directly from digital data, *before* color separation films are generated. This ability offers great potential savings in costs associated with rescans (e.g., film, scanner, operator time, and equipment usage).

Digital proofs exist at several levels. Soft proofs are essentially on-screen color displays of the job. Hard-copy digital proofs can be output by a variety of methods, most of which produce a continuous-tone proof. There is a debate within the industry as to whether proofs really need to have halftone dots. Some say that dots are not necessary as long as the tone that is produced accurately simulates what the halftone image would look like. Others say that halftone dots are an integral characteristic of the press sheet and, therefore, a proof cannot accurately predict the press sheet unless it too has dots.

Probably because of this uncertainty, along with the relative newness of digital proofing, digital proofs currently find their greatest acceptance for internal proofing purposes, such as for artists and graphic designers. Most customers rely on more traditional proofs with halftone dot patterns. Some higher-quality digital proofing systems do offer halftoning.

Although most customers won't yet accept a digital proof as a contract proof, some do, depending on the kind of job, and their number is growing. Many trade shops have several kinds of proofing systems, including the more traditional single-sheet systems for contract proofs, and overlay and digital systems for internal use. In this capacity, digital proofs offer fast production time along with a much lower cost per page.

Soft proofing. Soft proofs exist as images on color video monitors. They are called "soft" because they do not exist in a tangible form like all the other kinds of proofs (which can be referred to as "hard").

Soft proofs are mostly used to check overall design and the position of various elements on the page. These images can be generated from completed color separation films or directly from the stored digital image of the original. Soft proofs are also referred to as *real time* proofs because they can be formed almost at the same instant that the original image is scanned into the system.

The major advantages and disadvantages of soft proofs are very distinct. On the advantage side, the ability to generate a color display before separations are exposed is significant. This ability to modify the proof interactively as an aid to tone reproduction, color correction, and retouching has untold implications for film usage and separation costs. In addition, its digital form allows a soft proof to be sent electronically to customers for viewing at remote sites, if they have the necessary equipment.

A key disadvantage of soft proofing is that the monitor images are formed by transmitted light and displayed under ill-defined room light conditions. Soft proof images are formed by the additive (RGB) process like television, whereas the printed image is subtractive (YMCK). Therefore, it is difficult to adjust the lighting for the satisfactory comparison of both images. Obviously, the image quality and the surface characteristics of the press sheet cannot be conveyed. Also, it is doubtful that a soft proof would ever be acceptable as a legal contract. Images are not shown on screen at their actual size. In addition, equipment is expensive, although, as with most new technology, prices are becoming more affordable.

Although the soft proof is unsurpassed as a color separation production aid, it is system dependent. It is not permanent or portable because it exists only as an on-screen image. The growth and success of electronic color imaging systems, however, will ensure that soft color proofing will be commonly used in the future.

Digital hard-copy proofs. Although soft proofs serve a useful function, hard-copy proofs are heavily preferred. Hard-copy digital proofs can be output using thermal transfer printers, ink jet printers, and color laser copiers, as well as dye sublimation and electrophotographic technology. These output methods generally produce a continuous-tone proof.

Some systems may have electronic controls to adjust the appearance of the proof with regard to particular substrate and ink characteristics such as color and reflectance, as well as the production characteristics of the press, such as dot gain, density, hue, and other factors. A few higher-quality, more expensive digital proofing systems are also capable of producing halftone dots, screen rulings, and screen angles.

Dye sublimation is a thermal transfer process in which an image is placed on transfer paper with a special pigment ink called subliminal dye. The transfer is then heated, and the ink turns to a gaseous form and carries the dye with it onto the substrate. Varying the heat changes the amount of dye that is transferred, so a wide range of tones can be reproduced.

Ink jet proofs are imaged with ink droplets forced under pressure through a nozzle. The droplets are controlled by altering the diameter of the nozzle opening and/or by electrostatic charges that determine the path of each droplet and where it will fall on the substrate.

Thermal transfer systems use a colorant known as hot-melt ink, which is carried by a ribbon or sheet. They can use a variety of substrates.

One of the newest systems is a high-end proofer that uses charged liquid proofing ink. Proofs produced on this system are accepted by some customers as contract proofs.

Digital photographic proofs are generated from an electronic database onto photographic color print material. In other words, two images are ultimately generated from the database. One is for the films used to make the plates, and the other is for making the proof that simulates the printed image produced from the films. The image quality and the surface effects of this kind of proof will not be the same as actual ink on paper, but the color accuracy probably outweighs these drawbacks.

The photographic imaging material used in these systems ranges from instant color print material to conventional color print emulsions to electrophotography and toner systems. The image is exposed at high speed through red, green, and blue filters. The time required to make one of these proofs can be as low as 7.5 min.

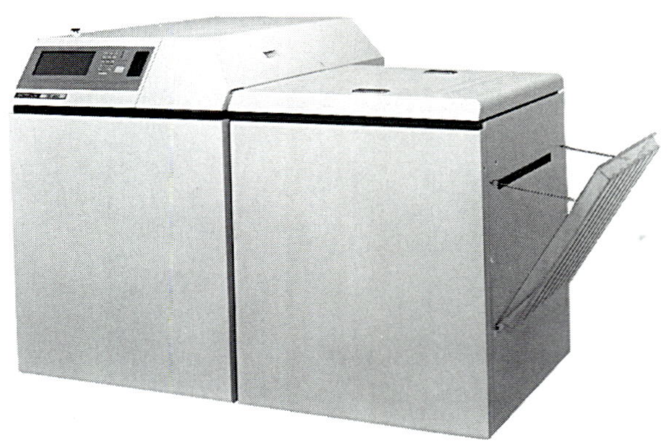

Courtesy Screen (USA), a subsidiary of Dainippon Screen Mfg. Co. Ltd.
DP-460 Direct Digital Color Proofer, which outputs halftoned proofs from scanners or page makeup systems on silver-halide paper.

A disadvantage with digital image proofing apart from those discussed earlier include the high cost of the proof recording unit.

Digital imaging technology is an area of rapid development. As technology improves, digital proofs will come closer to accurately predicting the appearance of the press sheet.

Soft and digital proofs should almost be considered as accessories to what will probably prove to be the dominant graphic imaging technology of the future.

Standard Viewing Conditions

Color Evaluation

The graphic arts industry relies on making color judgments of photographic originals, color proofs, and printed samples. When color separations are made from a photograph, adjustments are made in response to the characteristics of the original, the preferences of the customer, and the characteristics of the printing system.

The color separations are used to image a color proof, which provides the link between the photographic original and the printed reproduction. The proof is submitted for customer approval. The customer views the proof in comparison with the original and specifies any changes that might be required. The changes are accomplished by making new color separation films or by modifying the existing films. A new color proof is made, and the process is repeated until the customer approves and signs the proof.

During press makeready, the signed proof is used in another visual approval procedure. Sample prints are taken from the press and compared with the color proof. Again, changes are specified by the customer. Printing press adjustments are made to accomplish the changes, and another printed sample is taken. This process is repeated until the customer approves a printed sample without further changes. This OK sheet will serve as the guide for the pressrun.

After the job is printed, the customer might also evaluate samples to judge the consistency and overall quality of the job.

Some points of image transfer during the printing process do not require subjective color evaluation. For example, during film compositing or platemaking, the image is transferred from one medium to another, but the fidelity of transfer is monitored by gray scales and other process control targets to ensure that no significant color shift has occurred.

Each of these visual evaluation stages requires standard viewing conditions. Standard viewing conditions are essential because the characteristics of the light source affect what we see. The nature of color perception makes the communication process even more difficult. Fortunately, the American National Standards Institute has developed ANSI PH2.30-1989, which provides a thorough and clearly defined set of viewing conditions for the graphic arts.

The Light Source in Human Perception

Human visual perception has three components. First, vision depends on the existence of light. The hues of color that we see are contained in the light that is illuminating the scene. Second, an object modifies the light by absorbing and reflecting (or transmitting) portions of the light. The object, in the case of graphic arts, is a printed sample, color proof, or photographic original. Third, the modified light is received and interpreted by an observer, the color evaluator.

Light sources have different spectral power distributions, meaning that they contain different combinations of colors in varying intensities. Two lights may look white, and yet be made of different packages of wavelengths. Colored objects viewed under different light sources would not have the same appearance.

The daylight-balanced color film used to photograph the three images in the accompanying figure has a fixed spectral sensitivity. The differences produced by the colors of the light sources are clearly recorded on the film. Human observers, on the other hand, have variable spectral sensitivities. They undergo instantaneous chromatic adaptation when the light illuminating a scene is changed. The dominant light source is seen as white, and our perceptions of colors adjust accordingly. Thus, the incandescent light in the home, the natural sunlight outside, and the fluorescent light at the workplace are all seen as white. Only when the observer sees the three light sources side by side are color differences between the three "whites" apparent.

The instantaneous adaptation process leads to confusion when color fidelity is being judged. The observer feels confident that the light at hand is white light. Two colors may match under this light source, yet look distinctly different under another light. This phenomenon is called metamerism. Thus, to avoid confusion and improve consistency in color judgments, it is imperative that standard lighting conditions be used for all color evaluations.

Specific ANSI Viewing Conditions

Following is a summary of the ANSI standard viewing conditions for reflection copy, such as photographic prints, proofs, and press sheets. (Conditions for viewing transparencies are included in the chapter on color separation.) ANSI Standard PH2.30-1989 addresses the chromaticity, the color temperature, the spectral power distribution of the light source, the color rendering index of the light source, the intensity of illumination, the uniformity of illumination, and the surround conditions. To meet the standard, all of these conditions must be met. An explanation of the meanings of the individual elements of the standard follows.

It is essential to understand that the conditions in the standard apply to the viewing plane. They do not define the characteristics of a light source itself.

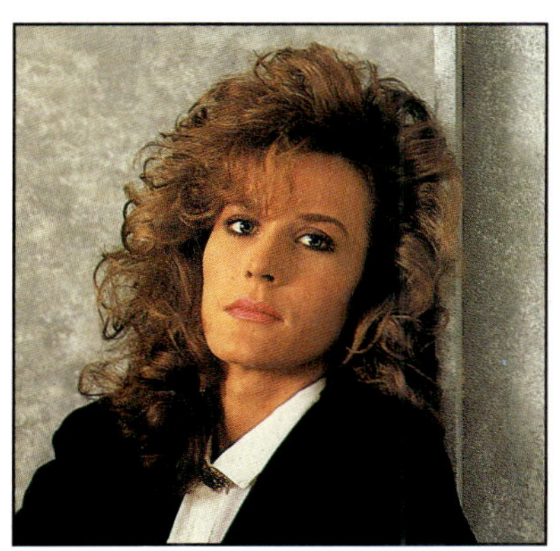

D_{50}

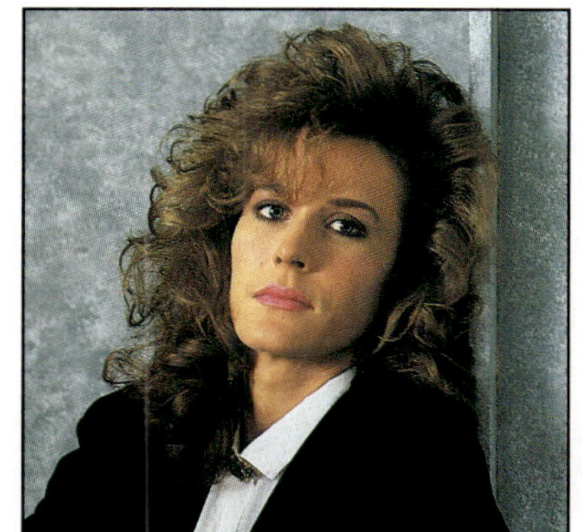

Fluorescent

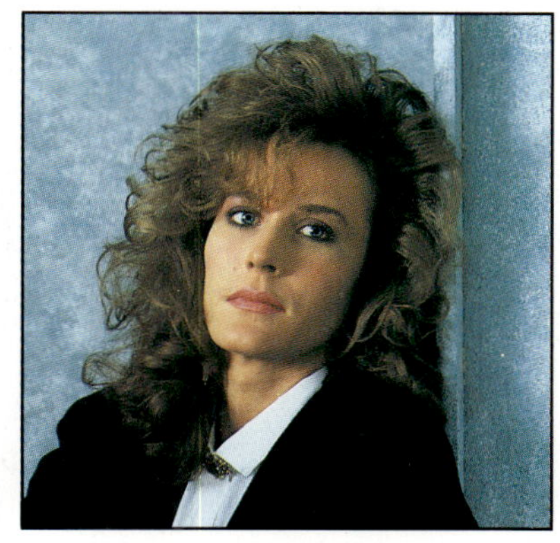

Tungsten

Color appearance under different light sources.

Understanding the ANSI Standard for Reflection Copy

The *chromaticity* of a color is characterized by its dominant wavelength and its purity. ANSI defines chromaticity of the light at the viewing plane using coordinates in the 1931 chromaticity diagram (see chapter on color separation) of the Commission Internationale de l'Éclairage (CIE) and in the CIE 1976 uniform color space (UCS) diagram. Acceptable tolerances of deviation for both coordinate systems appear in ANSI PH2.30-1989. The standard for chromaticity at the viewing plane is based on the chromaticity of CIE Illuminant D_{50}, which represents a phase of natural daylight having a correlated color temperature of 5,000 Kelvin.

The GATF/RHEM Light Indicator quickly and easily determines whether a light source is 5,000 K. If stripes appear on the RHEM Light Indicator, the light source is *not* 5,000 K. The convenience of affixing this device directly to the proof makes it a valuable aid to improving color communication. It is important to note, however, that the light indicator cannot be used to evaluate whether a viewing booth conforms to the ANSI standard.

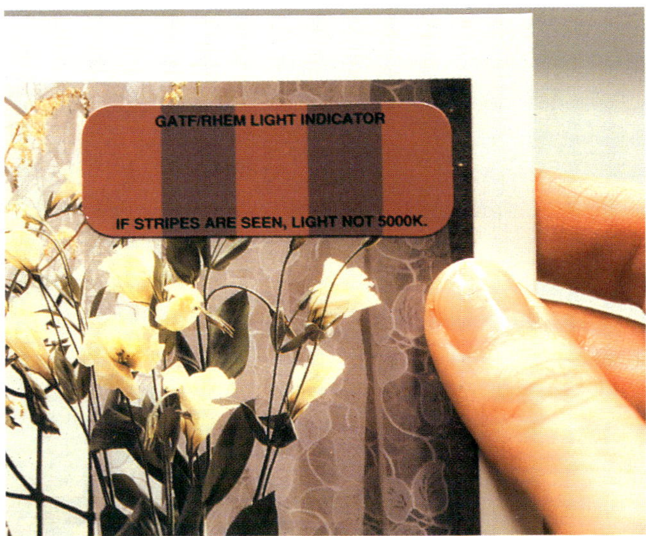

The GATF/RHEM Light Indicator being viewed under nonstandard lighting.

The *color temperature* of a light source is the temperature at which the measured color of a Planckian radiator matches the light source. A Planckian radiator is a blackbody radiator that changes color along a continuous spectrum when heated to high temperatures, as first examined by Max Planck in 1900. Some light sources, such as tungsten, change color with temperature increases in direct proportion to blackbody radiators. These light sources are known as graybodies. Other light sources, such as fluorescent, do not behave as blackbody radiators do; at certain wavelengths, their phosphor coatings produce sudden peaks in the spectral power distribution. The chromaticities of these types of light sources do not lie along the blackbody locus. Their *correlated* color temperature is the color temperature of the blackbody at the point of intersection formed by the isotemperature line passing through the chromaticity point and the blackbody locus. This intersection represents the best perceived color match between the light source and the blackbody. The calculation of the correlated color temperature is defined by the CIE and utilizes either the chromaticity diagram or the UCS diagram.

The *spectral power distribution* of a light source is the relative output of the light source across all the wavelengths of the visible spectrum. ANSI identifies the relative power of the standard illuminant at the viewing plane in 10-nanometer (nm) increments within the range of 360–750 nm, based on CIE illuminant D_{50}.

The *general color rendering index* is described by the CIE as a measure of how well a light source conforms to the color rendering of natural daylight. For example, the spectral power distribution of a light source such as tungsten is deficient in the blue region of the spectrum. Therefore, various hues of blue are not clearly rendered under tungsten lighting. The general color rendering index is derived from the average of the color differences of eight colors measured under the test illuminant and under the reference illuminant (in this case, natural daylight). The spectral reflectance data for these eight colors are specified by the CIE. The ANSI standard requires a general color rendering index on the viewing surface of at least 90.

The light intensity with regard to reflection surfaces is called *illuminance,* and it refers to the light falling on the object. Standard illuminance at the viewing plane is specified as 2,200±470 lux (204±44 footcandles).

The standard further specifies that the illumination at the edges of the viewing plane should be at least 60% of the intensity at the center.

The ANSI standard for the viewing environment specifies that nonstandard light should be eliminated (blocked or baffled) from the viewing surface, and that there be no distracting elements to interfere with the viewing task. Visible surfaces should be colored a neutral matte gray of 60% reflectance, which is equivalent to Munsell N8/.

The standard for the geometry of illumination specifies that the light source, print, and observer's eyes should be positioned to minimize glare from the center of the print.

Installing and Maintaining Standard Lighting

Every color approval in the production of printed products must be made under standard viewing conditions. The viewing conditions in the color separation area, the pressroom, and the customer approval areas have to match. The easiest way to obtain viewing conditions that comply with ANSI PH2.30-1989 is to purchase lighting equipment that has been engineered and manufactured to meet the standard. Viewing stations and transparency viewers are available from several manufacturers.

When standard lighting must be set up in a location unsuitable for available viewing stations, a lighting consultant can help to design a customized viewing system that conforms to the ANSI standard. If the company decides to create a homemade viewing station, extreme care must be taken to comply with the ANSI specifications.

A warm-up time of fifteen minutes to one-half hour is required for the lamps to reach their proper color temperature and color rendering index. Do not evaluate color until after the warm-up period is completed. Fluorescent lamps used in standard viewing stations are rated for a certain number of hours of illumination; however, they do not maintain a 5,000 K color temperature for that full length of time. A color temperature meter and a photographic light meter can be used to monitor changes in illumination. (Color temperature meters should be used to determine the difference between two similar light sources. General commercial color temperature meters are inappropriate for determining absolute or even accurate color temperature of fluorescent sources.)

The most critical point of maintenance is to replace the bulbs in the viewing station regularly. Manufacturers recommend 2,500–5,000 hours of bulb life, or one year, as a good interval between bulb changes. Monitors are available that display the total time that lamps have been used to signal when bulbs need to be changed.

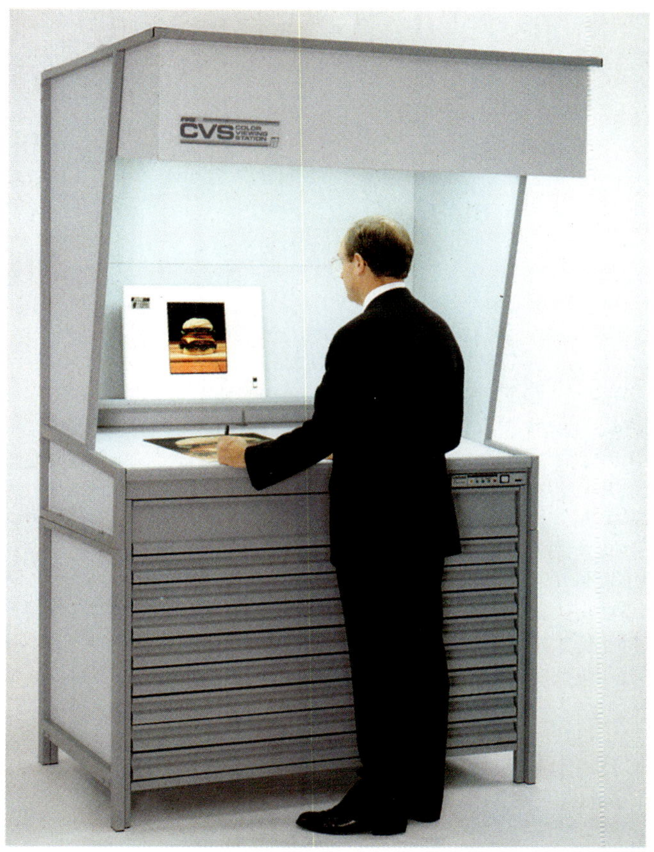

Courtesy GTI Graphic Technology, Inc.

Color viewing booth.

The lamps, lighting fixtures, louvers, and surrounding borders of the viewing stations should be cleaned frequently using a mild detergent (no abrasives) and water. Dirty fixtures and lamps can change the color temperature of the light illuminating the viewing plane.

To prevent extraneous light of different color temperatures from entering the viewing station, install 5,000 K lamps in all light fixtures in the color viewing room. Lamps rated at or near 5,000 K can now be obtained for most lighting fixtures used in pressrooms, offices, and other work areas.

Quality Control of Off-Press Color Proofing

Color prepress proofs are an approximation of what can be expected on press. There is sometimes a tendency to produce beautiful proofs that will please the customer, but which cannot be replicated on press because of their density range or other irreproducible characteristics inherent in the proofing system used. Unrealistic expectations formed at the proof stage inevitably lead to customer dissatisfaction, or even rejection of the job. Quality control of color proofing helps to provide proofs that will

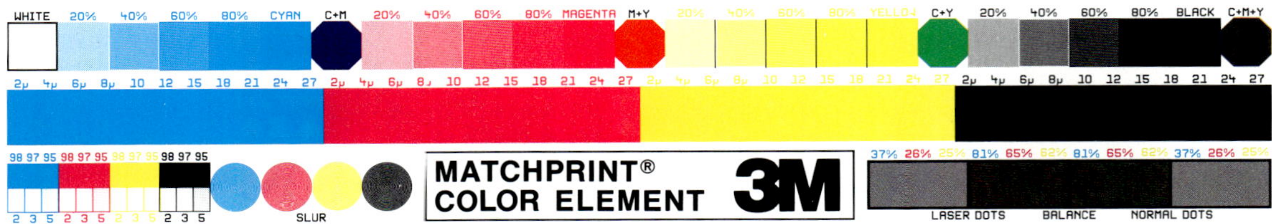

Courtesy 3M

Matchprint® Color Element, which ensures consistency of exposure, dot gain, and tonal reproduction of Matchprint proofs.

match the printed result. Off-press color proofing systems use a variety of image carriers and colorants. It is imperative to process-control these systems in order to produce consistent results. Exposure control guides must accompany each color proof to determine that the correct solid optical densities were achieved, the correct hue was selected, and that there was dot-for-dot transfer from the halftone separations to the off-press color proofs during exposure and processing. In addition, the manufacturer's recommendations must be followed for ambient temperature and humidity, and the appropriate ultraviolet light source must be used for exposure.

Dot Gain

Dot gain is one element that is characteristic of each and every press. A key factor in having an off-press proof match the printed result is taking measurements of dot gain on the production press and compensating for this characteristic in the proof.

Equivalent dot area. In offset lithographic printing, the halftone dot grows in size as it is transferred from the printing plate to the offset blanket to the substrate. This is often referred to as physical or mechanical dot gain. Apparent dot gain is also affected by a phenomenon called optical dot gain; it is caused by light scattering around the halftone dots and within the printing substrate. The total dot gain of an offset lithographic reproduction is the sum of its mechanical and optical dot gain.

An off-press color proofing system exhibits very little mechanical gain, but its optical gain can be adjusted (for example, by adding a spacer sheet to the proof) to simulate the total dot gain found in an offset lithographic reproduction.

Midtone Dot Gain Scale 120/in. 48/cm

1 2 5 10 15 20 30

Copyright © 1983 Graphic Arts Technical Foundation

The GATF Midtone Dot Gain Scale II©, showing the seven individual targets (enlarged 8×).

The total dot gain, which is often referred to as "equivalent dot area" (EDA), can be measured by using a reflection densitometer and the Murray-Davies equation. In various off-press color proofing systems, the largest amount of total dot gain occurs around the 40–50% dot area, and there is a wide variation in the total dot gain characteristics of these systems. However, it is common to find the same range of total dot gain characteristics in the offset lithographic printing process. There can be a significant difference in the total dot gain characteristics for each of the process colors within a given off-press color proofing system, which may or may not be similar to the total dot gain characteristics in the offset lithographic printing process.

GCA/GATF Proof Comparator II

Developed through a cooperative effort by the Graphic Communications Association (GCA) and the Quality Control Division of GATF's Research Department, the Proof Comparator is a visual control guide for advertising agencies, publishers, and printers to check the accuracy of four-color off-press proofs for magazine ad work. It is used as a visual reference tool to indicate whether a single proof is an accurate reproduction of the tonal values in supplied film and whether the proof is an accurate predictor of the color reproduction in a magazine ad. It does *not* provide comparative evaluations between one proofing system and another.

A color proof should show how the separation films for an ad will look on the final reproduction pressrun. It is possible, however, for a proof to introduce variations not found in the film, so it is necessary to know that proofs accurately reflect what the separations will produce on press.

The Proof Comparator can also be used by printers to certify that each generation of films is correct by verifying that contact films furnished for printing are accurate in relation to the original films.

GCA/GATF Digital Proof Comparator

The expanding number of digital proofing and imaging technologies has created a need for a reference digital file to compare digital systems with themselves and with photomechanical technology. Developed as a digital companion for the existing film version of the Proof Comparator, this quality control target is a tool to evaluate how accurately and consistently digital proofing and imaging systems reproduce the picture files that are processed through them. The Digital Proof Comparator can also be used to measure key attributes of an imaging system.

The GCA/GATF Digital Proof Comparator is used to evaluate and compare the output of digital proofing systems. The Encapsulated PostScript (EPS) file of the device is used to make a reference proof with a proofing system. The proofing system manufacturer's recommended procedures and calibration are followed in making the reference proof. Reference proofs are provided to ad agencies and other customers who will later be evaluating production images. These proofs are stored in light-safe conditions for subsequent referral. They should be dated and include the name of the color separation house.

In the production cycle, digital proofs that are submitted to an ad agency include an image of the Digital Proof Comparator along with the production images. The advertising agent or publisher then compares the new Digital Proof Comparator image with the reference proof on file to determine whether the digital proof is consistent with the calibrated reference proof. Evaluation can be both visual and instrumental. If the Comparator image on the production proof matches the reference Comparator, the print buyer can make color judgments with greater confidence.

Furthermore, the films generated from the GCA/GATF Digital Proof Comparator can be used to make plates and print on a press. If the printing press is in good working condition and running in control with materials that are representative of production conditions, then the results will show the relationship between digital proofs and printed results. This approach is also useful with direct imaging presses where PostScript files are sent directly to press without a film generation stage. Whenever the file is printed on a press, the results can be used to adjust the digital proofing system to achieve better visual correlation with the printing system.

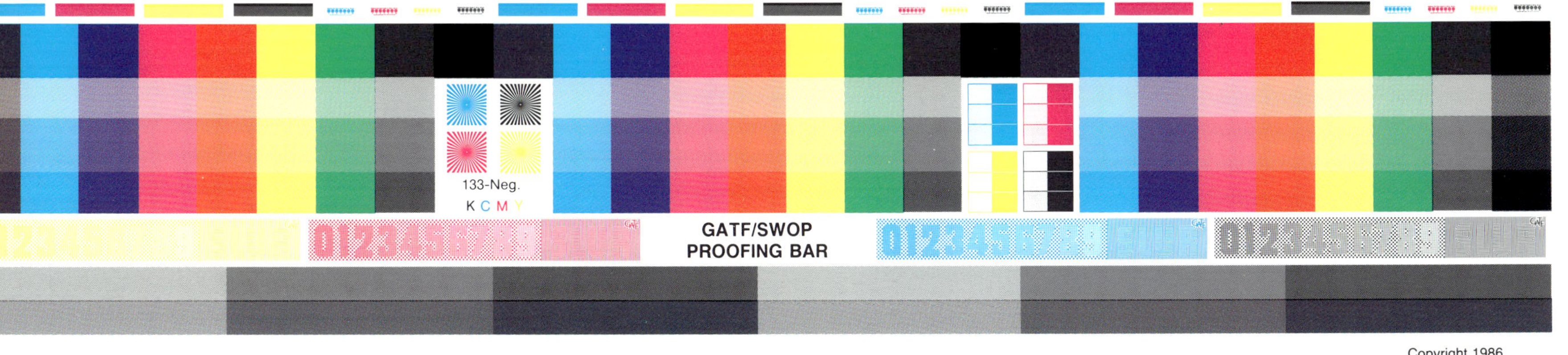

GATF/SWOP Proofing Bar, which is used as a quality control device in web offset proofing.

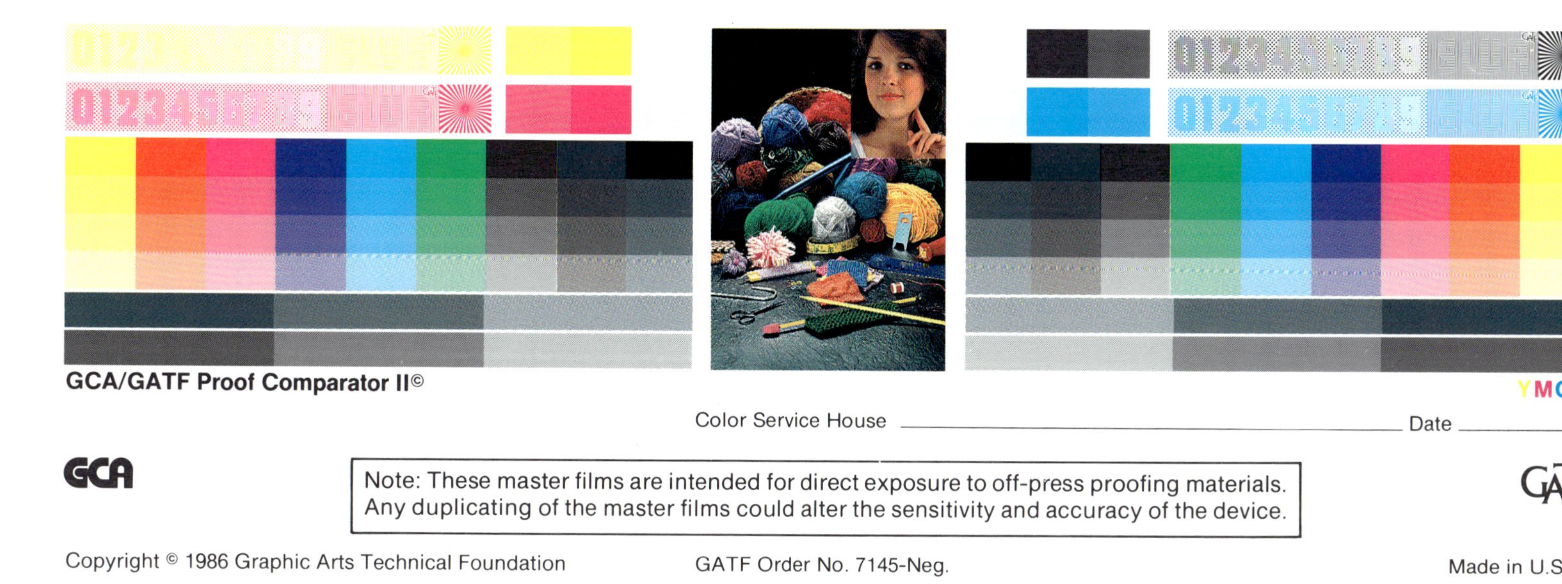

The GCA/GATF Proof Comparator II, which is used to evaluate the accuracy of four-color off-press proofs for magazine ad work.

Chapter 11

Platemaking

Introduction

From the days of Gutenberg in the mid-1400s until the 1960s, letterpress was the dominant printing process. Litho stones were used from the time of Alois Senefelder's invention in the 1790s through World War II. Then, presensitized and wipe-on aluminum litho plates became widely available in the 1950s. Platemaking, however, still required skilled craftsmen until automatic plate processors became available in the 1960s. At the same time, both phototypesetting and high-speed blanket-to-blanket web offset presses became available, and lithographic printing grew rapidly to become the dominant printing method in the United States. For example, most newspapers were printed by the letterpress process as recently as 1980. Today, well over 95% are printed offset. This phenomenal growth could not have occurred without major improvements in litho plates.

There are many excellent plates available in the United States. Over 100 different plates are being produced by at least 10 different plate manufacturers. Today's plates provide exceptional image fidelity. They are also processed quickly and easily, generating little or no pollution. The plates exhibit outstanding durability, latitude, and consistency on press, without excessive cost. On many printing jobs, the film costs more than the plates.

Recent plate advancements include high-speed projection plates and equipment that can produce high-fidelity images from 35- or 70-mm film with short exposures. Nonpolluting water-developable plates are widely used today. New durable camera-speed plates are being produced that can be exposed, without film, directly from computer-controlled lasers. Lithography produces the highest-quality, large-volume printing, faster and at lower costs than any other printing process. The litho industry today is a mature industry with excellent prospects for continued growth in the future.

A lithographic plate must consist of two kinds of areas: the printing areas, which accept ink and repel water; and the nonprinting areas, which accept water and, thus, repel ink. The wider the difference between the ink-receptivity of the image areas and the water-receptivity of the nonimage areas, the better the plate will print and the easier it will run on the press. Many of the earlier plates were difficult to run because only a small difference existed between the ink-receptive areas and the water-receptive areas.

Recent significant developments in lithography have been made, particularly in the area of platemaking. These developments include longer-running plates; easier and faster platemaking; more-consistent, reliable, and durable plates with better readout and contrast; greater latitude on the press; and improved plate processors. Many of these developments have helped to increase the difference between the ink- and water-receptivity of the image and nonimage areas for better latitude on the press. Platemaking has been improved to such an extent that plates are no longer the serious source of trouble that they used to be. Through science, the lithographic craftsman has the materials, techniques, and knowledge to bring about the present state of the art, where there is little excuse for bad plates to go to press.

There are various ways of putting an ink-receptive image onto a lithographic plate. Plates are generally classified according to the method used.

Original plates. Original plates were plates on which the artist drew an image with a greasy crayon or a special ink called tusche. The artist

may also have applied a mechanical dot pattern, or benday, with a greasy ink. This technique provided a method for creating various tone values. Most original plates were on stone. Stones were used for specialty printing well into the 1940s. Some artists use stone as their medium, and stone lithography is still taught in many art schools. The modern "direct-image" plates are so different from lithographic stones that discussion of the direct-image plates is combined with other special contemporary plates in a later section. Direct-image plates are usually paper plates, which are used mostly on duplicators.

Hand-transfer plates. When two or more identical images were to be printed from the same plate, the artist did not draw the same image two or more times. Instead, a single design was drawn from which the required number of ink impressions were duplicated on hand-transfer paper. Hand-transfer paper is coated on one side with a gummy or gelatinous layer. The duplicate transfers were then laid face down in the proper positions on a new plate, and their ink images were pressed against the plate. After soaking in water, the transfer paper was then be peeled, leaving the inked images on the plate. This procedure was used for the first metal lithographic plates.

Contemporary Lithographic Plates

Original and hand-transfer plates are practically obsolete. They have been replaced by photomechanical plates imaged from negative or positive lith film. Direct-image plates (discussed in a later section) are in current use, but only for special uses as in duplicating.

The photomechanical principle. A photolithographic plate is a metal, paper, or plastic plate that is cleaned, treated, and coated with a thin film of light-sensitive, ink-receptive material, and then dried. Litho plates come in two different types: *presensitized plates,* which are coated by the manufacturer, and *wipe-on plates,* which are coated by the printer. Wipe-on plates are discussed later. A photolithographic plate may be exposed through negative (negative-working plate) or positive (positive-working plate) lith film.

A negative-working plate has a coating that is soluble in some solvent, such as water, but becomes insoluble after it is exposed to light. A negative of the image is placed in close contact over the coated plate, usually under vacuum, and then exposed to a controlled light source. The light that goes through transparent areas of the negative polymerizes (hardens) the plate coating and makes it insoluble. Where the coating is covered by the opaque parts of the negative, light is blocked and the unexposed coating remains soluble. After being exposed with light, the plate is developed by rubbing developer over it. Developer removes the unexposed coating from the water-receptive nonimage areas. The exposed coating is ink receptive and provides the printing image.

Positive-working presensitized plates have nonimage areas that are solubilized, or depolymerized, by light. Exposed areas are thus soluble, while unexposed areas remain insoluble in the developer and become the printing image.

The Main Types of Contemporary Plates

For the purpose of this manual, lithographic plates are divided into three groups: surface plates (both presensitized and wipe-on, or consumer-coated); bimetal plates; and direct-image, photo-direct, and electrostatic plates. Each of these is briefly described in this introduction and more fully discussed in following sections. A former plate category called *deep-etch* is now obsolete. Made from positives, deep-etch plates used a light-sensitive coating as a stencil to protect nonimage areas while the printing image was etched into the metal plate. After the image was produced, the stencil was removed.

Surface plates—presensitized and wipe-on. On all surface plates, the light-sensitive coating becomes the printing image. Presensitized plates provide the ultimate in simplicity for platemaking. Presensitized plates are named as such because they are sensitized by the manufacturer. They generally remain sensitive for one year or more. Presensitized plates consist of a thin film of light-sensitive material, usually a diazo compound or photopolymer, that is coated on a specially treated aluminum, plastic, or paper base material. Photopolymer coatings consist of polymers and photosensitizers that react (cross-link) during exposure to light to produce a tough, long-wearing image area. Diazo/polymer coatings also react with light to produce a tough, long-wearing image area. The exposed coatings require special organic or aqueous solvents for processing. Both negative and positive plates are available with diazo or photopolymer coatings.

Wipe-on plates are chemically similar to presensitized plates, but are coated with aqueous diazo coatings in the plate room in a simple roller coater. A specially treated aluminum or anodized aluminum plate is used. Wipe-on coatings are very thin and not durable on press, so special developers are used that contain lacquer or plastic that builds up on the image to greatly increase durability.

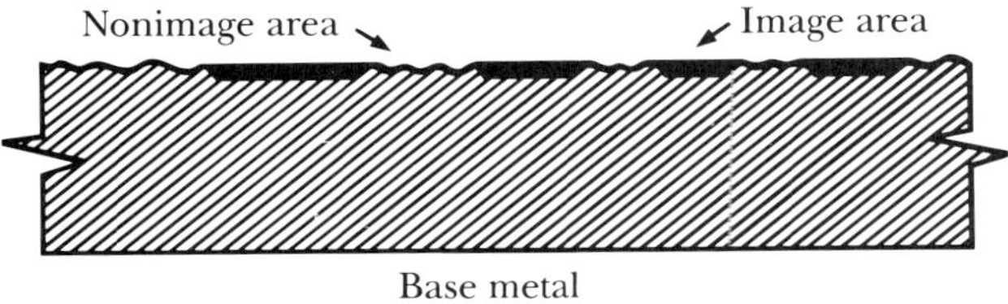

Cross section of a surface plate.

Bimetal plates. Bimetal plates are excellent for exceptionally long runs and for printing with abrasive inks, papers, boards, or metal. Bimetal plates have the widest difference obtainable between the ink- and water-receptivity of image and nonimage areas.

All of the plates described previously have been single-metal plates. Bimetal plates consist of two different metals, one for the image areas and the other for nonimage areas. The metals of bimetal plates are chosen so that the image metal is ink-receptive under the same conditions that render the nonimage metal water-receptive. All bimetal plates, in present use, have copper or brass as the image metal. The usual nonimage metals are aluminum, chromium, or stainless steel. When copper and chromium are used together, they are usually electroplated as layers on a third metal, such as aluminum, mild steel, or stainless steel. Such plates are often called trimetal or multimetal plates, even though the third or base plate metal does not form the printing image.

Most bimetal plates have the image metal electroplated over the nonimage metal, such as copper on stainless steel or copper on aluminum. These plates are presensitized as either positive- or negative-working plates. Bimetal plates resemble relief plates since one metal is above the other. The top layer of metal is so thin, however, that its thickness is usually measured in millionths of an inch. Thus, bimetal plates are true lithographic plates.

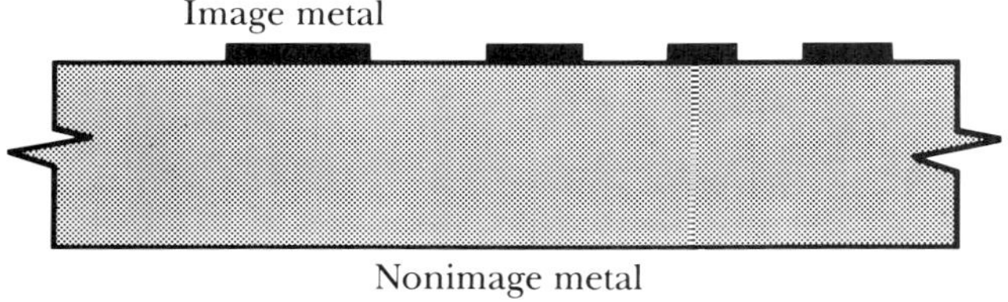

Cross section of a bimetal plate.

There may still be some bimetal plates on which the image metal is under the nonimage metal. Examples of image metals under nonimage metals include copper under chromium or brass under chromium.

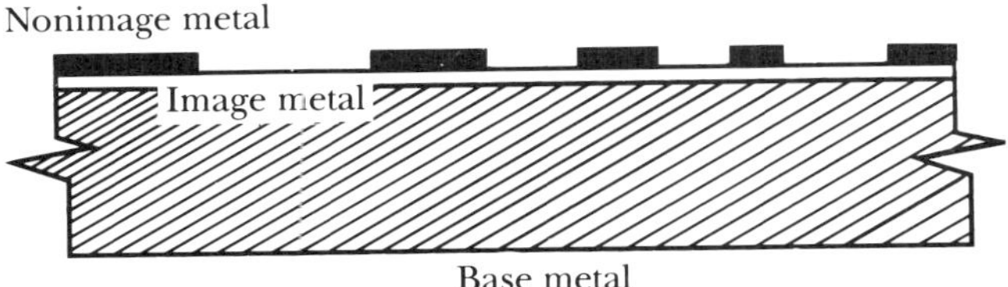

Cross section of a bimetal plate; the image metal is under the nonimage metal.

Bimetal plates are coated and developed much like surface plates. After development, the remaining coating is a resist that protects the top metal when unwanted areas are etched to expose the lower image or nonimage metal.

Direct-image, photo-direct, and electrostatic plates. These plates are generally used for offset duplicating or on small offset presses for short runs. Metal electrostatic plates are being used on larger presses for relatively long runs.

Direct-image plates are made of a specially coated paper that permits direct use of the plate in a typewriter with a special ribbon for applying the greasy printed image. Despite declining popularity, direct-image plates are still used for some printing of personalized checks and duplicator work.

Photo-direct plates can be produced directly in either camera or projection equipment. Projection plates are an easy way of making printing plates directly from a good copy in about one minute. Projection plates eliminate the intermediate step of making a photographic negative. The printing image can be an enlargement or reduction of the original.

Electrostatic plates are made with the Xerographic and Electrofax processes. Most electrostatic plates are on zinc-oxide-coated paper for duplicator work up to 10,000 impressions. Metal plates are usually made by the Xerographic or transfer process using organic photoconductors and are used for newspaper-quality jobs with run lengths in excess of 100,000 impressions.

Equipment for Platemaking

The platemaking room should be air-conditioned and well-ventilated to remove fumes from chemicals and solvents. The room should be large enough to provide ample space for all equipment.

Illumination. Room lighting is also important. Plate coatings are sensitive to ultraviolet and blue light. When coated plates are being handled, they should not be exposed to any stray blue, white, or ultraviolet light. Direct daylight or sunlight should be blocked, or filtered, by fastening yellow or orange plastic sheets over the windows. Yellow incandescent bulbs or yellow fluorescent tubes make suitable safelights for most plate rooms without sacrificing good viewing conditions. Another alternative is to purchase reusable, yellow plastic safelight sleeves that fit over standard fluorescent tubes. The platemaking room should also be wired so that the yellow lights are always lit when the room is in use. Regular white lights should be wired to a separate switch.

Platemaking Sinks

Sinks for platemaking are generally made of stainless steel, plastic, or plastic-covered wood or steel. If stainless-steel sinks are used, the steel should be a good grade of 18-8 stainless steel with a high-gloss finish. Polished surfaces resist corrosion much better than rough surfaces. Wood, plywood, or steel sinks that are covered with fiberglass or polyvinyl chloride materials are also satisfactory.

The sink should be approximately 1 ft. (305 mm) larger in each dimension than the largest plate used. A flat platform to support the plate should cover most of the area inside the sink. The platform should be about 3 in. (76 mm) below the rim of the sink, and should slope toward the sink drain.

Mixing valves. Water should be supplied to the sink through a thermostatically controlled mixing valve. A plastic hose conveniently located for rinsing plates is preferable to a perforated pipe along the front edge of the sink because iron and other minerals can collect in the perforations. The perforations can also cause streaks on the plates.

Developing pads are usually plush-covered plastic, stainless steel, or wooden blocks. The plush covering may be either permanent or disposable. These pads should be kept clean and reasonably dry for best results. They should be large enough to rapidly cover the entire plate with an adequate amount of developer. A clean, flat, smooth table should be provided for finishing and inspecting plates.

Roll Coaters

Simple two-roll coaters, with the coating pan under the lower roller, are used for coating wipe-on plates. The machine consists of two soft synthetic-rubber rollers mounted one over the other, like the wringers on a wringer washing machine. The lower roller rotates partly submerged in a trough or pan containing the coating solution. The plate is passed face down between the rollers, and coating is transferred to the face of the plate. Most of the coating is squeezed off between the rollers. The upper roller is adjusted to maintain just enough pressure between rollers to uniformly squeeze off most of the coating. The coating air-dries very rapidly, but some coaters use heat or circulating air to dry plates. Coaters are very effective, productive, and economical if a large number of plates need coating. However, it is not economical to roll-coat single plates.

Vacuum Frames

The vacuum frame holds the negative and plate in close contact during exposure. The unit consists of two metal frames; the bottom frame holds a corrugated or channeled rubber blanket with a rubber bead or gasket around its edges; the top frame contains a sheet of flawless plate glass. Smaller vacuum frames are usually hinged together on one side. The rubber blanket is connected to a vacuum pump by a flexible rubber tube. Special frames are used with glass on both sides, so plates and films can be put into the top side while exposing plates on the bottom side of the frame.

Photocomposing machines. The photocomposing machine, sometimes called the step-and-repeat machine, is used for exposing lithographic plates or films. The machine produces a series of exposures in register on the same plate or on successive plates. The same precautions as described for conventional vacuum frames hold true for the photocomposing machine. The types of machines and the techniques for using them are described in Chapter 9, "Film Image Assembly."

Exposure Sources

Numerous light systems are available for exposing lithographic plates. The following factors govern the choice of a good light source:

Spectral distribution. Most light-sensitive coatings are only sensitive to blue-violet and ultraviolet light. Diazo coatings are sensitive to blue-violet light of about 420 nm while most photopolymers are sensitive to UV light of about 350–370 nm. The light source used for exposure should have appreciable energy in the near-ultraviolet to blue (350–450 nm) part of the spectrum. Special *water-white glass* should be used on vacuum frames as this glass transmits more ultraviolet light than ordinary plate glass.

Light intensity. The stronger the light is, the shorter the exposure time will be.

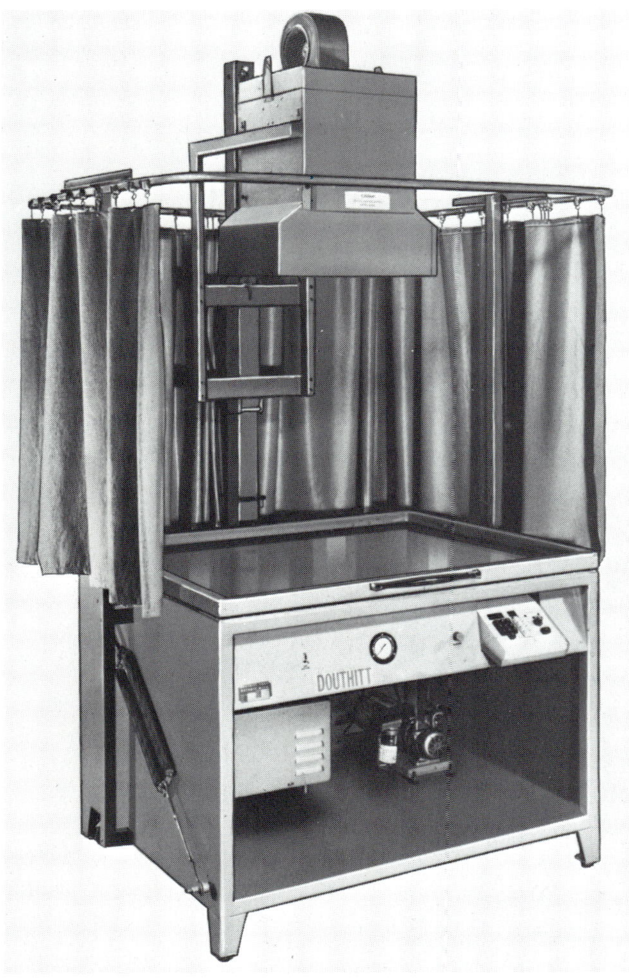

Courtesy Douthitt Corporation

Overhead platemaker.

Point source versus diffuse source. A point source of light produces sharp shadows and reduces undercutting. Diffuse light, or light from a broad source, can cause undercutting, especially when there is insufficient vacuum or poor stripping.

Evenness of illumination over the exposure surface. Light intensity from a point source will vary from the center to the edges of the vacuum frame; this can be corrected somewhat by reflector design. A common rule is to place the light at a distance from the vacuum frame equivalent to the diagonal of the vacuum frame. For high-quality work, continuous-tone gray scales exposed at the four corners of a plate on the vacuum frame must be within one-half step of the same gray scale exposed in the center of the frame. Move the light far enough away to accomplish this. A light meter can also be used to check light uniformity. Greater distances produce more uniform illumination; however, exposure time will be lengthened since light intensity varies inversely with the square of the distance.

Cleanliness. Dirt is a platemaker's worst enemy. A light source should be used that creates a minimal amount of dirt. Carbon arc lights are obsolete and should not be used. Where open-flame carbon arc lamps must be used, they should be vented to exhaust the carbon ash and noxious fumes generated.

Metal-halide lamps. Metal-halide lamps are mercury-vapor lamps with certain metallic compounds added. The diazo metal-halide lamps are particularly efficient for exposing diazo coatings; they also effectively expose photopolymer coatings. Dual-spectrum bulbs may be used to expose both coatings. For exposing plates, a metal-halide lamp gives about twice as much useful light as a conventional mercury-vapor lamp, 2½–3 times as much as a carbon arc lamp, and 4 times as much as a pulsed-xenon lamp, based on equal-wattage.

Integrating light meters. Integrating light meters, or light integrators, for controlling platemaking exposures were used as early as 1940, but they did not come into general use until after World War II. Integrating meters control the exposure in terms of total light units reaching the plate. They integrate or cumulatively measure the light intensity with time, much like a water meter measures water volume in cubic units regardless of its rate of flow. Then, most integrators turn off the light auto-

matically, when the preset amount of light has reached the plate.

Light and power lines. All lights are influenced by line voltage variations. If voltage drops, the integrator will sense the loss of power and increase the exposure to compensate. The integrator, however, will not sense the change in color or spectral distribution of light, which can cause major changes in exposure. In some areas, power companies have separate service lines for light and power. The voltage in the light line is usually more stable than the power line. If possible, the light source should be operated from the light line. The intensity of the light will not vary nearly as much as when the light source is supplied from the power line.

Automatic Plate Processors

Equipment for automatically processing plates has come into almost universal use. Essential in high-volume situations, automatic processors increase productivity, improve consistency, and reduce chemical consumption. Automatic processors are most valuable where speed of production is vital, as in the case of web offset newspapers, which work on edition deadlines. Automatic processors reduce downtime, as well as the number of makeovers from plate failures on press.

Some plate processors are designed for plates of specific manufacturers. Other processors are capable of processing plates from various manufacturers. Some processors are not adjustable; therefore, conditions cannot be changed to accommodate specialized situations.

Most plate processors are automated to the extent that they develop, desensitize, gum, and dry the plate. Chemistry is applied automatically and automatic replenishment is common; it may have continuous filtration and recirculation. A plate processor must be operated and maintained according to its manufacturer's instructions.

Air-Conditioning

An air-conditioning system should have provisions for controlling both temperature and relative humidity. Good conditions are **73°F (23°C)** and 50% RH in the United States and Canada. Air-conditioning is preferred because both plates and films can change size with temperature changes before and during exposure. Dimensional stability of film is extremely important for color separation in the camera, scanning, stripping, and platemaking operations. Therefore, all four areas should be at the same atmospheric conditions for optimum register or fit of images on the plates.

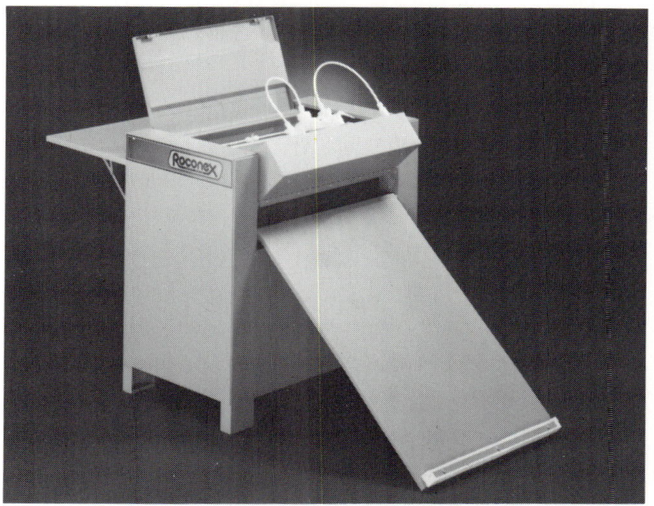

Courtesy Roconex Corporation

Automatic plate processor.

Platemaking Materials

The materials for litho plates consist of the metals used for the plates, the mixture of substances used for coating them, and the chemicals used for processing them.

Unlike letterpress, flexography, or gravure, in which the difference between image and nonimage area is achieved mechanically, lithography maintains this difference chemically. Although litho ink and water partially mix, or emulsify, lithographic ink does not adhere to water. Therefore, nonimage areas of the plate that have been wet with water do not accept ink.

Lithographic Plate Metals

Most lithographic plates are thin metal sheets. Aluminum is the most common metal used. Bimetal and trimetal plates can be aluminum, copper, stainless steel, or mild steel. Plates are usually the full size of the press cylinder and must be thin and flexible enough to wrap snugly around the cylinder. Aluminum thickness varies with press size. Standard thicknesses range from 0.0055–0.020 in. (0.14–0.51 mm), and sizes go up to 59×78 in. (1.5×2.0 m).

Aluminum used for litho plates is a very pure, high-quality alloy that is reduced to final thickness by cold rolling on very smooth rolls. The coils of aluminum are carefully annealed to obtain the proper temper or hardness.

They are then inspected to ensure that (1) they meet the required gauge tolerance; (2) they are flat; and (3) any side to be used for a printing surface is free from dents, scratches, and other surface defects.

Uniform thickness and flatness. Uniform thickness and flatness of plates are extremely important. Plates should not vary in thickness by more than ±0.0005 in. (0.013 mm).

Flatness is important to ensure good register. Buckles or waves in the metal plate prevent it from lying flat on the photocomposing machine, the vacuum frame, or the press cylinder. Any movement of the buckle or wave results in misregister on multicolor work, or misfit where diecutting is involved. Buckles and waves are also a prime causes of metal fatigue and cracking on web presses. Vacuum backs on photocomposing machines are required when making plates for multicolor close-register work.

Graining or Surface Preparation of Metal

Before a metal can be used as a base for a lithographic plate, its surface must be properly prepared. Roughening the surface mechanically, or treating it chemically or electrolytically, helps the plate to coat and perform properly in the lithographic process. The roughening process, whether it is done mechanically or chemically, is called **graining.** The only ungrained plates are either multimetal or chemically treated short-run presensitized plates.

Graining machines. Graining machines produce the grain on lithographic plates either by wet-brushing, dry-brushing, or by electrochemical processes. Grained plates retain water better in the nonimage areas.

Slurry brush graining. Most plates in the United States are grained on a special machine in which a continuous web of aluminum is passed under a series of rotating nylon brushes and the graining is done with a mixture of abrasives and water. To get a good uniform grain, at least three brushes should be used. Otherwise, the grain will be shiny or light with a directional pattern.

A good uniform grain is dark in color. This brush grain is fine and is satisfactory for presensitized and wipe-on plates. Some plate manufacturers use a chemical etch after brush graining the plates to lighten, cleanse, and slightly roughen the grain.

Chemical graining. Several methods of chemically cleaning and graining plates are commercially used. They are used primarily for treating smooth, short-run plates prior to coating in the manufacture of presensitized plates. These plates are usually double-sided plates for use on small presses.

Most bimetal aluminum plates are also chemically grained, but they are much rougher than the presensitized chemically ground plates. Stainless-steel bimetal plates are made of very smooth, ungrained stainless steel.

Rougher-grained plates provide better latitude on press, faster drawdown in the vacuum frame, less trouble with dirt and hickeys, better durability on press, and less tendency to slur. Some premium-long-run presensitized plates are electrochemically grained to produce a uniform, relatively rough grain.

Chemical treatments. In addition to roughening the surface, chemical treatments are also needed for some processes, especially wipe-on and negative-working diazo presensitized plates. The diazo compounds (which are ink-receptive when exposed) react with untreated metals. Therefore, the aluminum is usually treated in a hot sodium silicate solution to create a barrier layer that prevents a reaction between the diazo and the aluminum, desensitizes the plate making it more water- receptive, and bonds the diazo to the aluminum.

When positive-working diazo presensitized plates are made, special surface treatments are not necessary, although cleaning and usually some type of fine graining precede the application of these positive-working diazos. Most premium surface plates (both wipe-on and presensitized) are anodized after graining.

Aluminum anodizing. Aluminum anodizing is a process by which a very thin, uniform layer of extremely hard aluminum oxide is produced electrolytically on the grained aluminum. This anodic layer has many extremely small pores, similar to a honeycomb, that must be sealed before the photosensitive coating is applied. Hot solutions of sodium silicate are used for sealing, which makes the surface hard, inert to most chemicals, abrasive-resistant, and highly water-receptive.

Positive- Versus Negative-Working Plates

Costs. Plates made from negatives are almost always cheaper from the standpoint of labor and materials (especially film).

Dirt. Positive plates, films, and vacuum frames must be kept meticulously clean to keep dirt to a minimum. Positives that have been used over time become marred and dirty, requiring excessive time to inspect plates and remove dirt after development. Dirt is a major problem on positive plates; many printers eliminate dirt by using burnout masks to cover all image areas while reexposing the plate. Negatives can be kept clean by opaquing dirt and pinholes so it is usually unnecessary to inspect and clean up negative-working plates.

Press performance. Most positive plates can be "baked" or thermally cured at high temperatures for longer press life. This cannot be done with most negative plates.

Positive-working plates sharpen while negative plates gain when compared to the film. Thus, positive-working plates have the capacity to carry excess ink and still print reasonably sharp.

Sharpening. Positive plates can be sharpened by increased exposure. This allows more shadows to be open and helps burn out cut lines and dirt specks. Highlight dots, however, can disappear by increasing highlight contrast.

Coating Materials

Gum arabic. Gum arabic with acid bonds strongly to aluminum and is extremely hydrophilic, or water-loving. Capable of holding ten times its weight of water, gum arabic is a major ingredient in most plate etches, finishers, and dampening solutions. Gum arabic is a natural gum from acacia trees that is used extensively in the manufacture of candies, ice cream, and many other food products. It comes either in lumps or as a powder. The type preferred by lithographers is called "Select Gum Arabic Sorts." Gum arabic is no longer used in the United States for light-sensitive coatings, but is widely used in plate finishers as a protective, desensitizing coating. Synthetic gums are often used instead of gum arabic.

Diazo. Diazo sensitizers are used for both presensitized and wipe-on plate coatings. Most of the diazos are condensation products of formaldehyde and diazo diphenylamine stabilized with a compound like zinc chloride. Both water- and solvent-soluble diazos are used. Some diazo oxides or quinone diazides are used for positive plates. Exposure to UV light converts negative coatings directly to insoluble resins that have good ink receptivity and wear characteristics for printing. Positive coatings become soluble upon exposure to light.

Diazo/resin coatings. Plates presensitized with either homogeneous mixtures or separate layers of diazo/resin are very stable, can be stored for long periods, and used for run lengths ranging from short to long. Upon exposure to light, these coatings become insoluble in the special developers used to dissolve the unexposed nonimage areas. Some require a small amount of organic solvent in the developer. These are the most commonly presensitized lithographic plates used today.

Photopolymer coatings. Several reactive polymers can be sensitized with photoinitiators and used as light-sensitive coatings. Photopolymer coatings are either insolubilized by polymerization (cross-linking) during exposure or solubilized in developers by photodegradation after exposure. These coatings are inert and have excellent abrasion resistance. Photopolymer coatings are used for making letterpress, flexographic, and lithographic plates from negatives or positives. They are also used for making printed circuits. There are several photopolymer coatings in use: those that are developed in organic solvents and those that are developed in water or alcohol solutions. The main feature of photopolymer coatings is that they are affected very little by temperature and relative humidity and, therefore, have a very long shelf life as precoated materials. Water-developable photopolymer coatings have recently been introduced.

Developers. Regardless of the coating used, all presensitized plates must use a developer that removes the coating from nonimage areas without damaging coating in the image areas. Aqueous developers contain mostly water and are safe and nonpolluting.

Lacquer emulsion developers. are used extensively on additive presensitized and wipe-on plates. They consist of an emulsion of a lacquer resin, solvent, and a desensitizing gum. They deposit a tough, durable layer on the image to greatly improve press life. Lacquer emulsion developers

can also be used on most subtractive plates to extend the run length if the plates are wearing out on press.

Plate finishers. are usually aqueous gum arabic solutions that are applied to the developed plate. They leave a protective layer of gum over the nonimage areas. Plate finishers are necessary to keep the nonimage areas clean and scum-free on press. If the gum finishers are not properly buffed or squeegeed in plate processors, streaks of gum can adhere to the water-repellent image areas. This condition is known as *gum blinding;* the gum accepts water, and the image will not print solid on press.

Other Platemaking Materials

A number of other materials are used in platemaking. Most of these materials are proprietary or ready-made. In this book, materials are described generically.

Image removers or deletion fluids. Image removers are viscous solvents that can be painted over unwanted image areas to remove unwanted work. They also come in felt tip pens that are convenient and easy to use. When using deletion solutions, great care must be taken to avoid damaging intended image areas.

Abrasive sticks. Abrasive sticks can also be used to remove unwanted image areas from plates. There are two types: snakeslips and scotch stones. Air erasers that use compressed air and pumice are also available.

The problem with most abrasive sticks is that they polish the metal and reduce the ability of the treated area to carry water, thereby possibly causing scum in the polished area.

Chemistry of Platemaking

The lithographic process is based on plate chemistry. Chemical reactions are involved in the production of the image upon exposure to light, resulting in wettability of the image areas by ink, and wettability of the nonimage areas by water.

Control of the Platemaking Variables

Good plates are essential for high-quality printing. With the increasing use of color and ever-increasing quality demands, the successful (profitable) printer must know that plates are good before going to press. If substandard plates are put on the press, it is too late for inexpensive corrective actions. Therefore, good platemaking procedures and accurate test objects are essential for high-quality printing.

Plate sensitivity guide. The first sensitivity guide for platemaking was introduced in the 1940s. The sensitivity guide is a simple photographic measuring device that integrates the effect of many variables: the plate coating, its exposure, and development. As soon as the plate is developed, the guide indicates if the image areas are properly exposed and developed and if the nonprinting areas are likely to cause problems.

A plate sensitivity guide is usually a narrow strip of a transparent continuous-tone stepped gray scale. With one guide, there are twenty-one different density steps. These steps are numbered from 1 to 21, with the low numbers at the clear, or transparent, end of the scale. With many guides, the density difference is about 0.15 between steps, and 0.30 between every other step. This means that the light transmission of every other step is cut in half or doubled, depending on whether the numbers increase or decrease. Step 7 on the scale has about one-half the light transmission of step 5, and step 4 lets through about twice as much light as step 6.

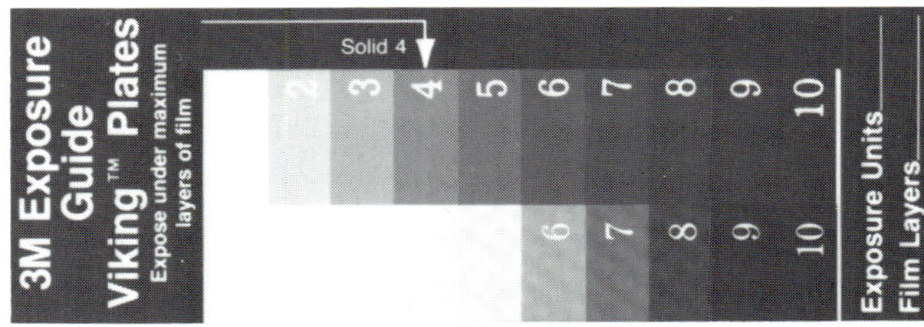

Courtesy 3M Company

Plate sensitivity guide.

The plate sensitivity guide is stripped into the flat or onto the photocomposing machine glass. Any prominent place on the plate is satisfactory as long as all transparent or plastic sheets used over the plate also cover the sensitivity guide.

When surface plates are exposed and developed, a number of different steps of the guide will distinctly show. Ordinarily, on negative-working plates, solid step numbers 1 through 5 or 6 (on a twenty-one-step guide) indicate proper exposure and develop-

ment for maximum run length. If step 5 is the highest-numbered solid step, steps 6, 7, and 8 (and perhaps more) will be scummy or retain decreasing amounts of coating as the numbers increase.

On negative-working plates, the highest-numbered solid step is the critical step. On positive plates, the lowest-numbered clear or clean step is the critical step. With the same exposure, the position of the critical step changes when the sensitivity of the coating changes or when the amount of dark reaction, or development changes. The more sensitive the coating, the higher the number of the critical step with everything else held constant. An increase of two steps from normal means that the coating is twice as sensitive or that the exposure should have been cut in half. Almost all plate manufacturers furnish specific recommendations on the critical step required for best plate performance. On negative-working plates, exposures must be long enough to harden the coating for good image durability even though dot gain increases with higher guide numbers. On positive-working plates, exposure does not influence plate durability so plate images can be sharpened by overexposing the plate.

A plate sensitivity guide is the most important test object the platemaker has. With this device, the platemaker can monitor the entire platemaking process to ensure consistent image fidelity and maximum trouble-free press life. The guide indicates when a change in coating sensitivity, exposure, or processing has occurred and how much of a change has taken place. However, a platemaker must rely on experience to determine the cause of the change.

Control of Tone Values in Platemaking

GATF Star Target. The GATF Star Target is a small wheel-shaped design (⅜-in., or 10-mm, diameter) containing 36 wedge-shaped spokes that radiate from the center of the target. Because of its design, it quickly indicates:

• **Dot gain.** Slight thickening of the image causes the tips of the spokes to join together to produce a solid hub in the target center. Thickening may be caused by poor vacuum frame contact, overexposure of negative-working plates, or overdevelopment of multimetal plates.

• **Dot loss.** Slight sharpening of the image causes the tips of the spokes in the target center to break down, giving a visual impression of a white spot. Image sharpening may be caused by poor vacuum frame contact or overexposure of positive-working plates.

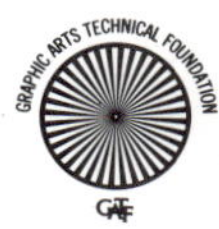

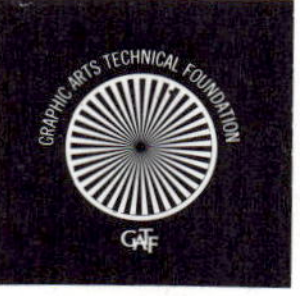

GATF Star Targets: left, positive; right, negative.

The actual amount of spreading or sharpening is magnified 23 times. A magnifying glass or microscope with a calibrated reticle must be used if numerical values are to be obtained. With experience, platemakers and press operators can learn to evaluate dot gain or sharpening from original Star Targets.

The GATF Dot Gain Scale II©. This small target consists of a number of squares and circles or dots. When the edges of the dot expand to touch the squares, the percent midtone dot gain will be shown under that specific image. It can be used to measure dot gains of 1, 2, 5, 10, 15, 20, and 30% on both plates and prints. It can be included in the image area unobtrusively or hidden in a center fold.

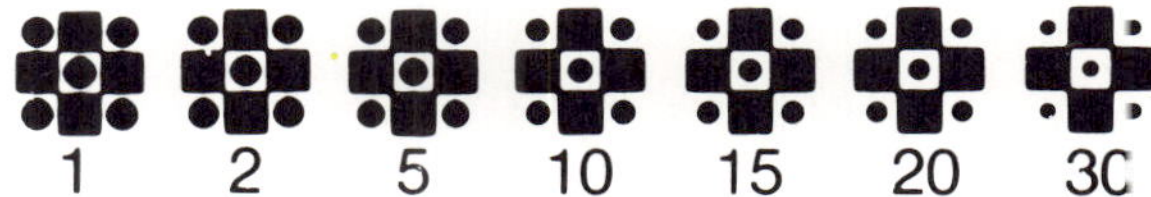

The GATF Dot Gain Scale II© showing seven individual targets (approximately 11 × enlargement).

A printed GATF Dot Gain Scale II© with midtone dot gain of 10% as indicated by the slight connection of the round and square dots of the 10% target.

UGRA Plate Control Wedge. This test object contains a sensitivity guide, positive and negative microlines from 4 to 70 microns, halftone dots from

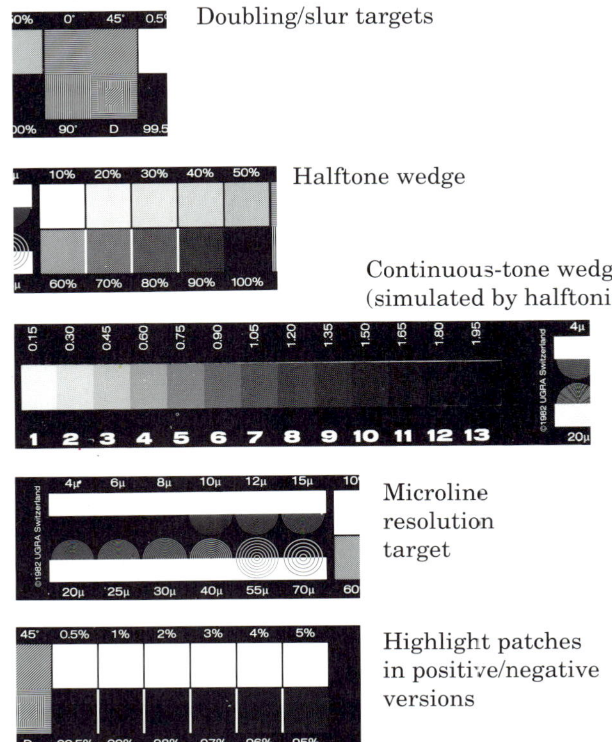

The UGRA Plate Control Wedge (slightly enlarged).

½% to 99½%, and a slur target—all in one $6\frac{7}{16}\times\frac{9}{16}$-in. (175×14-mm) test object. Dot values are extremely accurate in 10% increments from 10–90% so it can be used for plotting plate reproduction curves, determining reproduction characteristics of plates at different exposures, detecting slur or doubling, and determining dot gain or loss on both plates and prints. It is an all-purpose test target that is unexcelled in any area. For optimum results, every printer should use this simple but thorough test object for evaluating lithographic plates, exposure conditions, plate development, and print quality.

The GATF Dot Gain Scale. The GATF Dot Gain Scale contains numbers from 0–9 using 200-line tints with graduated densities against a uniform 65-line tint. On the original film, the number "2" has the same background; therefore, it is invisible to the eye at normal reading distances. With dot gain on the plate (or prints) the fine 200-line screen dots gain more than the coarse 65-line dots, so progressively higher numbers become invisible with increasing dot gain.

On positive-working plates, the number would decrease since these plates sharpen. With good reproduction, the invisible number should never exceed a 3 on negative-working plates or a 1 on positive-working plates. The invisible number on high-fidelity prints will be around 5–7.

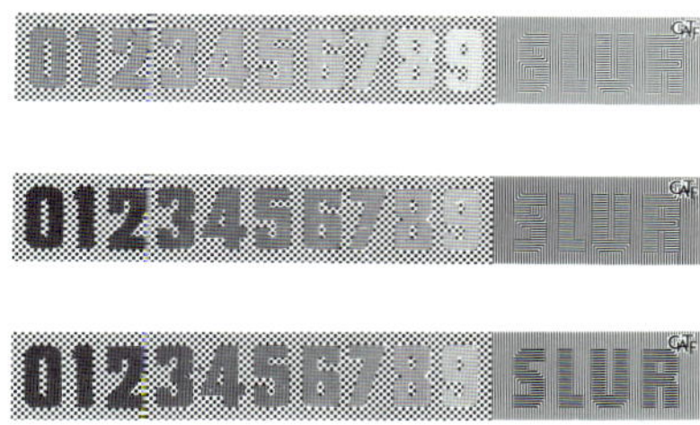

Printed images of Dot Gain Scale: top, sharp; center, dot gain without slur; bottom, dot gain caused by slur.

Since slur will always give higher readings, the Dot Gain Scale contains a section with horizontal and vertical lines that spell "SLUR" if there is slur or doubling on press. Although slur is not a common plate problem, under unusual conditions, the word "SLUR" may show up on the plate. Smooth plates may also contribute to slur on press.

Wettability of Image and Nonimage Areas

Ink and water must intermix on press. A typical lithographic ink should pick up approximately 20% of the dampening solution; however, the ink must never disperse into the water. The process, therefore, works well within certain limits, depending on the compatibility and interaction of the ink and dampening solution. If these limits are too narrow, the process would never work as successfully as it does. Either too much or too little water intermixed in the ink causes problems on press. If the ink mixes in or emulsifies with the water, it is carried to nonimage areas and "tinting" results.

While it is true that a water and ink mixture is necessary for printing on press, in platemaking, any such tendency must be controlled. If the image areas could be wet *only* by ink and not by water, and the nonimage areas *only* by water and not by ink, the ideal lithographic plate would result, and few or no problems would occur on press. Actually, the image areas repel water and thus stay dry. Since the ink adheres only to dry areas on the plate, it adheres only to the image areas. When the image areas are wet by water and not by ink, *blinding* may result. *Scumming* occurs when the nonimage areas are wet by ink instead of water. The wettability of the image and nonimage areas, by ink and water respectively, depends on the physical chemistry of the different surfaces.

Ink Receptivity of Image Areas

Different kinds of image areas are used in lithography depending on the type of plate. Each type of plate has a different kind of image, and each kind of image may have different characteristics with respect to ink receptivity. Most presensitized positive- and negative-working surface plates are the subtractive; the coating is developed away in nonimage areas leaving the coating as the image. There are some presensitized additive plates that use additive developers to deposit resins on the image areas for better durability on press. All wipe-on plates are additive.

Presensitized surface plates. These plates are available for both positive- and negative-working systems. The image areas on many presensitized plates used commercially contain resins (diazo or photopolymer) that either polymerize or become insoluble when exposed to light. In general, these materials have excellent ink receptivity and resistance to wetting by water or gum solutions. Different diazos and/or photopolymer resins are used over aluminum that tend to wet readily with water. The aluminum is usually grained mechanically and anodized for better wear and water receptivity. Press life under average conditions can vary from only 20,000 impressions for thin coatings on relatively smooth aluminum to over a million impressions on rough-grained, anodized plates. Images wear more rapidly on relatively smooth, unanodized plates. Many plates are coated on both sides so they can be turned over and used again after completing the first pressrun. Nonpolluting water- or aqueous-developable plates can use either the photopolymer or diazo coatings. These plates are easy to process and have excellent image fidelity, but they are not yet as durable on press as conventional surface plates.

Wipe-on plates. These relatively inexpensive plates are always negative-working and are widely used by newspaper printers. The coatings on wipe-on plates consist of water-soluble diazos that are applied by the printer. The diazo is stored as a dry powder until shortly before use since it decomposes relatively quickly in water. Thus, the coatings must be used within a few days after mixing with water.

The plates are usually coated in a two-roll nip coater that applies a very thin, uniform layer of the diazo solution to the plate. These plates air-dry rapidly. They have a short shelf life so they must be used within a few days after coating.

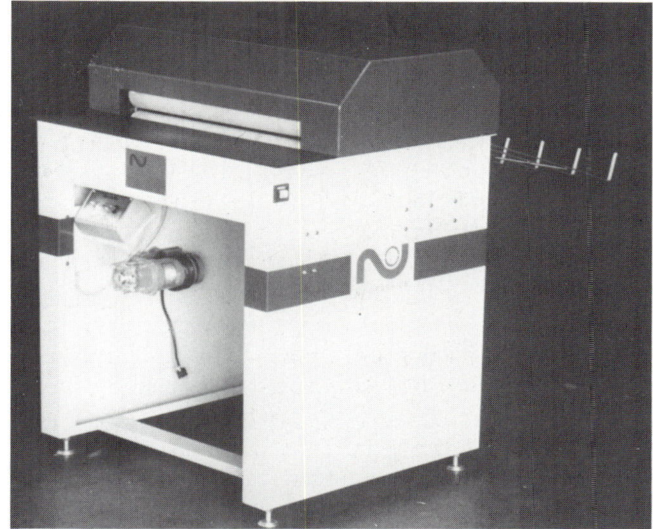

Courtesy Nu-Graphics Mfg., Inc.

Plate coater.

Wipe-on plates are made on grained aluminum (usually anodized) that is silicated by the manufacturer. After coating, these plates are developed with an additive developer composed of both water and organic phases that desensitize the nonimage areas and deposit a lacquer or resin on the image areas. Without the additive developer, these plates would have a relatively short press life. However, reliable press life of 200,000 impressions is common when using a good wipe-on additive developer. These same additive developers can be used to extend the press life of many subtractive plates. Some additive plates are presensitized or coated by the manufacturer. These plates have good shelf life, but otherwise are very similar to wipe-on plates.

Bimetal plates. Bimetal plates are extremely durable and are commonly used on pressruns of several million impressions. Most bimetal plates are made of copper-plated aluminum where copper is the ink-receptive image and aluminum is the water-receptive nonimage area. These plates are presensitized (coated), exposed, and developed much like surface plates. After development, the coating remains over the image areas while the unprotected copper in nonimage areas is etched away completely to uncover the water-receptive aluminum base. These plates are then gummed and run on press like surface plates. The coating over the copper is often removed before going to press since it will print slightly fuller than the copper image.

Bimetal plates are also made of copper-plated stainless steel, which is much tougher than alu-

minum. Thus, stainless steel plates are less susceptible to cracking and can be taken off all types of presses and reused. Chrome-plated brass or copper bimetal plates also offer this advantage, but they are no longer used in the United States. Bimetal plates should run 4–5 million copies under average conditions. Premium long-run surface plates—even with baking or post exposures to extend press life—are generally unreliable for runs in excess of a million impressions.

Driographic (waterless) plates. This planographic plate is unique since it does not require water. The aluminum plate surface has been coated with a silicone material that has such low surface energy that almost nothing will adhere to it. Waterless plates are available as positive- or negative-working, and they are exposed using conventional equipment. Special processors, however, are required to develop the images. Exposure and processing hardens the silicone rubber layer that covers the polymer coating. Processing dissolves the unexposed silicone. Specially formulated inks adhere only to the polymer areas.

These plates require temperature-controlled presses so that they are maintained at a constant, predetermined temperature. Such control stabilizes ink viscosity during the pressrun. Water circulation systems provide heat or cooling as required to control press temperature.

Some newer presses are equipped to accommodate waterless plates; older presses may be retrofitted to operate with such systems. Most newer presses, however, are still equipped to operate with dampening systems, and their heating and cooling capacity can be used to provide temperature-controlled dampening.

Other types of plates. Direct-image plates are made of paper. Image areas of these plates consist of carbon black in wax transferred from a special typewriter ribbon or marking pen. Since these images are easily abraded, these plates are used only for short-run work on small offset presses, or duplicators.

Photo-direct plates can be made of either paper or plastic. Silver halide, diazo/resin, or photopolymers are used for these plates, which are usually supplied in rolls for special platemakers that photograph original copy directly on the plate. Although run lengths are generally low on duplicators, some can be run on larger presses in excess of 50,000 impressions. Some photo-direct plates are satisfactory as projection plates.

In the diffusion transfer process, a negative paper is exposed from the nonemulsion side. The exposed negative is then placed face down on the press plate and fed into the developing unit. After emerging from the developer, the negative is peeled off the plate and discarded. The transferred image remains on the plate and is then dampened with a fixer to make the image permanent while desensitizing nonimage areas. These small, short-run plates are being replaced by photo-direct plates.

The image areas on plates made by the electrostatic processes of Xerography, Electrofax, or organic photoconductors (OPC) consist of toners made with organic resins that are fused or baked on paper plates. These resins can be selected for good ink receptivity and resistance to blinding and abrasion, but runs in excess of 10,000 impressions are usually limited to metal receptor plates where the electrostatic images are transferred from paper and fused to metal. Images with screen rulings up to 100 lines/in. are printed from plates made with dry toners. Plates made with liquid toners are capable of higher resolution.

Computer-to-plate (CTP) systems. After many years of speculation and discussion, printing plates generated directly from personal computers are a reality. Using various desktop publishing software packages, printers and publishers can efficiently and economically transmit digital data, including text, illustrations and halftones, directly from the computer to the plate.

There are several laser printers available that can make paper proofs and plates directly from a personal computer. Furthermore, paper-based and polyester plates can be produced from special desktop printers. Metal plates require a dedicated platemaker.

This capability is eliminating typesetting, keylining, camera work, stripping, and platemaking. CTP technology reduces labor and film costs and helps to improve image fidelity by eliminating the prepress film phase.

Plates used in these systems are based on silver halide, photopolymer, and electrostatic technologies. Silver halide plates may also be used for photo-direct work on cameras by printers who do not possess the direct-to-plate capability, or those who do not produce significant output to make direct-to-plate economically feasible.

Plate sizes for these systems can vary from 8×10 in. to 16×27 in. Plate material may be paper or metal, with run lengths in excess of 100,000 impressions.

Water Receptivity of the Nonprinting Areas

On metal plates, water receptivity of the nonimage area depends on the metal used in the plate and how that metal has been treated. Water receptivity of nonimage areas is also determined by the desensitizing process, the dampening solutions with which the plate is run, and the gumming or finishing operation after developing the plate.

Differences in water wettability of metals. Metals such as aluminum, chromium, and stainless steel are easily wet by water and retain their wettability for a long time. Metals such as zinc or iron, which form loose corrosion products similar to rust, are not wet as readily by water. Since the wettability of these metals changes different stages of corrosion, they are no longer used as lithographic surfaces.

In lithography, the ability of a metal to be wet with water is enhanced or reinforced by the application of a solution of gum—e.g., a gum arabic etch. How well the gum or etch sticks to the metal depends on the composition of the etch and the condition of the metal surface. Metals such as aluminum, chromium, and stainless steel are easily desensitized by the gum and made water-receptive. Residual coating will affect the desensitization of surface plates on aluminum.

Aluminum must be surface-treated before it can be coated with the diazos used for the negative-working presensitized or wipe-on plates. The diazos, which become ink-receptive when exposed to light, react with metal. Therefore, a barrier layer formed from hot solutions of sodium silicate is often used to bond the diazo to the metal while preventing reactions between the diazo and aluminum. Several other treatments have been developed and used for this purpose.

Anodizing is a means of electrolytically producing a film of aluminum oxide of controlled thickness on the plate surface. These anodic films are extremely hard, abrasion resistant, and chemically inert on press. When treated with hot sodium silicate, they will become water-receptive and will not react to diazo coatings. Most presensitized and wipe-on plates are now anodized for longer press life.

Composition of finishing or gumming solutions. The purpose of a plate finisher is to deposit a water-receptive material on the nonimage areas of the plate. A good finisher leaves a film of water-receptive material that protects the plate surface, lasts a long time on the press, and wets with a minimum of water.

Plate finishers usually consist of gum, an acid, and one or more salts or surfactants. The main ingredient of the etch is a good desensitizing gum such as gum arabic.

Researchers are always looking for gum arabic substitutes because the industry is too dependent on a foreign source of supply. Also, since gum is a natural material, it varies widely in composition and purity. Gum arabic is a very unique material because of its low viscosity in water solutions, its good adherence to metal, and its ability to form a highly water-receptive film. Gum arabic is still the major ingredient in many plate finishers or gumming solutions. In acid solutions (below 5.5 pH), gum adheres tightly to metals. It is believed that the reason gum arabic sticks so well to metal is that it contains molecules in the free organic acid (carboxyl) groups. A firm bond is made between the gum and the metal through these carboxyl groups. The gum swells in the presence of water, but the carboxyl bond keeps the gum from dissolving away from the metal.

The acid most commonly used in finishers is phosphoric acid. The purpose of the acid is to convert more of the groups in the gum molecule to carboxyl groups in order to improve the adhesion. There is a limit to the amount of acid that can be used because too much acid can attack the metal and even desensitize image areas. A good plate finisher for aluminum is the 1:32 etch, which consists of 1 oz. of 85% phosphoric acid to 32 oz. of 14° Bé gum arabic. For best results, this should be diluted with water to about 8° Bé.

Plates should be gummed up on press anytime the press will be down for more than 30–45 minutes or whenever the press is to be washed up. This protects the plate for a clean, trouble-free startup. Some plate finishers also contain cleaning agents that remove ink from the image areas and can, also, be used as a plate cleaner. A good plate cleaner usually cleans and desensitizes a scummy plate if the ink has not been on the plate too long.

Automatic plate processors usually do an excellent job of gumming the plate when the recommended finisher is used. When finishing plates by hand, the gum must be buffed dry with clean cheesecloth to produce a good water-receptive layer over nonimage areas. Materials composed of very large molecules, such as gum arabic, cellulose gum, and synthetic gums, undergo a physical change when dried making it difficult to dissolve them on rewetting. Thus, nonprinting areas, on which fin-

ishers have been dried will wet readily with water, but the gum absorbed to the metal will not be easily removed by water.

If the gum is not buffed dry, it may remain on the image and cause gum blinding. Some finishers contain asphaltum or other organic materials in an emulsion that adheres to and protects the image while the gum adheres to the image areas. Only special finishers can be used on plates that are to be baked at high temperatures to harden the image areas for better press life. The high temperatures will char or burn the gum in normal finishers and ruin the plate.

Dampening solutions. Like plate finishers, dampening solutions must desensitize nonimage areas without desensitizing image areas. Since the dampening solution also mixes with ink, it must not emulsify the ink or prevent proper ink drying. The dampening solution also helps keep the plate and blanket cool and washes away much of the dirt and debris on the plate or blanket that might otherwise build up as piling. Dampening solutions are usually sold as concentrates that are diluted with water.

Major ingredients in a good dampening solution are water, gum, acid, buffers, inorganic salts, sequestering or chelating agents, inhibitors to protect the plate, and surfactants. Isopropyl alcohol is frequently used to reduce surface tension and increase viscosity so the plate will stay clean with less water. Neutral and alkaline dampening solutions are often used when printing on uncoated groundwood paper. These solutions have better lubricity and reduce linting and piling tendencies, but overall exhibit less latitude on press.

Despite the numerous advantages provided by isopropyl alcohol, federal and state government agencies are restricting or prohibiting its use by printers. Therefore, alcohol substitutes have been developed to provide benefits similar to isopropyl alcohol while complying with air pollution control requirements. Dampening solutions require much lower concentrations of alcohol substitutes than of alcohol. Some substitutes are intended to completely replace alcohol, while others are formulated to be used with alcohol.

As explained previously, gum arabic binds to aluminum from acid solutions; therefore, pH control between 4.0 and 5.5 is important for acid dampening solutions. Although dampening solutions will desensitize plates at much lower pH values, the higher acid content may desensitize the plate images (blinding) and attack the ink, causing poor ink drying and/or emulsification of the ink in the dampening solution. Thus, pH control is important for proper press performance.

Unfortunately, pH is not a good method of determining if the dampening solution has the correct concentration. The measure of conductivity is often used to be sure the dampening solution has been mixed properly. With neutral dampening solutions, pH has no relation to concentration, so conductivity is the only good way to monitor concentration. Additions of isopropyl alcohol have little effect on pH but significantly reduce conductivity. Therefore, all conductivity measurements should be made before adding alcohol. Alcohol substitutes, however, have little effect on pH or conductivity.

There are many dampening solutions available. However, no single solution works well with all the plates, inks, paper, presses, water, and dampening systems. The printer must select a dampening solution by trial and error. Different solutions should be tried until one or two are found that work well in the operation. Several of the suppliers adjust formulas to meet the specific needs of the large printer. Almost all suppliers have a number of different solutions and are able to recommend a specific one to meet individual needs.

Surface Plates—Presensitized and Wipe-on

On surface plates, the insoluble coating becomes the printing image. These plates include presensitized subtractive and wipe-on or additive plates.

Presensitized Surface Plates

Presensitized surface plates are coated and ready for exposure and processing when purchased. They are used to make one press plate if coated on one side, or two press plates if coated on two sides. These plates can only be used for one image, but they can sometimes be stored and used to reprint the same image on different sheetfed pressruns.

Just prior to World War II, presensitized plastic plates were introduced in Germany by the Kalle Company. The bases of these plates were plastic-coated paper. These early plates were coated with a diazo sensitizer. Although paper plates are available, most presensitized surface plates are on aluminum today.

Presensitized aluminum plates are available with a variety of treatments. The earliest presensitized metal plates were made on aluminum with a chemically produced grain. Presensitized plates are available either with chemically, electrochemically, or mechanically produced grains. For longer runs, presensitized aluminum plates are usually grained and then electrochemically hardened (anodized).

Presensitized plates are sometimes designated as being either additive or subtractive. These terms describe the differences in processing procedures. A presensitized plate is additive when the platemaker adds image-reinforcing materials to the image areas during processing. The coating over nonimage areas must be removed during development. With some additive presensitized plates, image reinforcing is optional. For example, a plate used for a short run may not require the use of an additive developer. A presensitized plate is subtractive if it comes to the platemaker with a durable, long-run coating. During processing, the developer removes the unexposed coating and renders the nonimage area water-receptive.

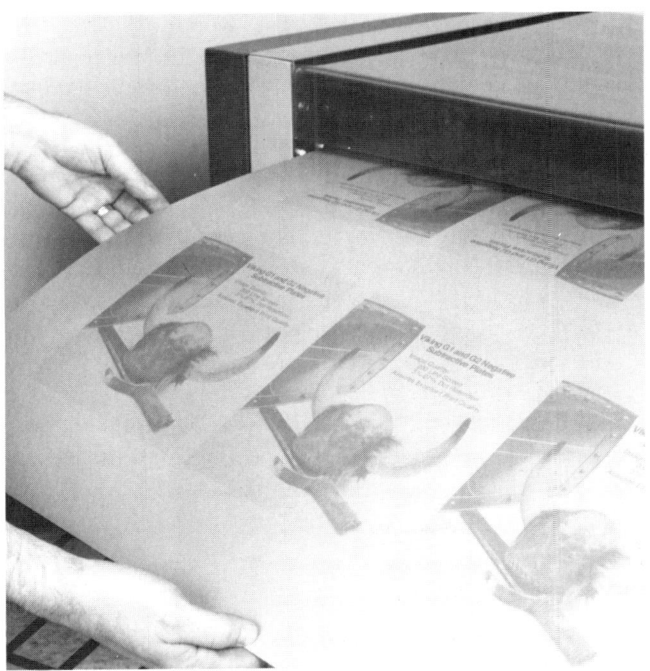

Courtesy 3M Company

Plate exiting processor.

Negative-working additive presensitized plates. These aluminum or anodized aluminum plates are coated by the manufacturer. All additive presensitized plates in the U.S. are negative-working. The steps in making additive presensitized plates follow:

1. Exposing. The plate is exposed through a negative. The exposure required to produce a solid step 5 or 6 on a 21-step sensitivity guide depends on the speed of the coating and the light used.

2. Developing. The plate is developed with a special additive developer that removes the unexposed coating and applies a lacquer or plastic layer to reinforce image areas for good press life. The same type of developer is also used for wipe-on plates.

3. Gumming. Gum or finishing solution is applied to the plate and dried down.

Negative-working subtractive plates. These plates are made by coating aluminum or anodized aluminum with a suitable light-sensitive coating. Diazos, photopolymers, and combinations of both are all used. Although there are many different subtractive negative plates with different characteristics, they are all very similar and are processed using the same general procedures, as follows:

1. Exposing. The plate is exposed through a negative to step 4, 5, or 6 on the 21-step sensitivity guide. On subtractive plates, exposure is somewhat more critical because the coating must be light-hardened sufficiently for good durability on press. Underexposed plates will fail prematurely. The manufacturer's exposure recommendations must be followed to obtain the best possible results. Exposure time required may vary significantly with different plates. Special photopolymers or dual-spectrum bulbs may be slightly faster for photopolymer plates.

2. Developing. The plate is developed with a special solution that removes the unexposed coating applied by the manufacturer. The plate is usually rinsed with water to remove residual chemicals from both the background and image areas, but the manufacturer's instructions should be followed carefully.

3. Finishing. Gum is applied to the plate and rubbed smooth until completely dry. A special inorganic finishing solution must be used if the plate is to be thermally treated for better durability.

Positive-working presensitized plates. All positive-working presensitized surface plates are subtractive where coating remains on the unexposed image areas and the exposed coating is removed during development from the nonimage areas.

The steps in processing the positive-working presensitized plates are as follows:

1. Exposing. Exposure is the same as with negative-working plates except that positive films are

used. Thus, image areas are unexposed and the nonimage areas are degraded or depolymerized by light so they will be soluble in the developer. Plates normally are exposed and developed to a clean step 4 or 5 on a 21-step sensitivity guide.

2. Developing. The plate is developed with a special solution that is wiped over the plate until the exposed coating is removed. Then, the plate is usually washed with water.

3. Fixing. Fixing is seldom needed today, but some plates may be fixed with a special solution that stops the action of the developer or renders the coating insensitive to light. Most positive-working plates should be protected from light for maximum press life, unless they are to be heat-treated for extended press durability. Any deletions on the plate must be made before heat-treating.

4. Gumming. Gumming is done with a gum arabic solution or other type of finisher, such as AGE (asphaltum-gum-etch). Special inorganic finishing solutions must be used instead of gum on any plates that are to be thermally treated.

More information on the various presensitized plates is available from the manufacturers of the individual plates.

Wipe-on Plates

Wipe-on plates are similar to presensitized plates in that specially treated aluminum or anodized aluminum is needed and water-soluble, negative-working diazo coatings are used. They differ in that coatings are applied by the printer by hand or with a special roller coater. Also, the plates used for wipe-on coating all have comparatively fine brush grains. Most wipe-on plates are anodized for better press life. All wipe-on plates are negative-working. A number of wipe-on coatings and processes are available.

Coating. A coating is first prepared by mixing the diazo powder with the water-based solution shortly before use. The coating is applied to a dry aluminum or anodized plate. All aluminum plates sold for diazo wipe-on procedures are pretreated (usually silicated) and sold ready to use. The pretreatment produces the required inert barrier between the metal and the diazo coating. Almost all wipe-on plates are coated with a special nip-roller coater and then air-dried. When coating by hand, a cellulose sponge, cheesecloth, or cotton swab is used to spread the coating with long strokes in both directions to ensure that the entire surface is completely covered. Most wipe-on coatings must be buffed with cheesecloth until dry. Others are dried by a fan after spreading. The manufacturer's instructions must be followed for optimum results with any particular process.

Exposing. The plate is exposed through a negative. Exposure time is about the same as for most presensitized plates. Exposure to steps 5 or 6 on a 21-step sensitivity guide is considered satisfactory.

Developing. Most wipe-on plates are machine-processed. They can also be hand-processed with a lacquer emulsion that removes the unexposed coating from the nonprinting areas and desensitizes the background while the lacquer deposits on the exposed image areas. This operation is followed by the application of a gum finisher or an asphaltum-gum-etch emulsion.

Screenless Lithography

Presensitized surface plates are a result of three developments: the discovery of light-sensitive coatings other than bichromated colloids such as gum, albumin, and casein; improved desensitizing materials and techniques, including plate-surface treatments; and the ability to successfully run lithographic plates with little or no grain.

Through developmental work came the discovery that some grained plates with positive coatings produced a plate capable of holding up to fourteen steps on a 21-step sensitivity guide as compared to two or three steps with conventional surface plates. As a result, researchers thought that screenless lithography could be done if photographic methods could be adapted to platemaking procedures. Some very fine color lithography has been done using continuous-tone plates exposed to suitably produced continuous-tone positives. Although this process has been used sparingly for many years, it is too expensive for general commercial use.

Removing Images from Surface Plates

The best way to remove images from most surface plates is to use image remover or deletion fluid. Image remover is a slightly viscous solvent that can be applied with a small brush or cotton swab to the image areas that are to be removed. These solutions will not work after heat treatments and are to be used on unbaked plates only. In about 30 sec., the solvent will have softened the coating enough to remove the undesired images simply by rinsing with water and rubbing lightly.

Deletion fluids are available in felt tip pens. Great care must be taken when using this technique because these solutions will ruin the plate if they accidentally get on intended image areas. Some of these solutions contain strong acids that slightly etch the metal, so they must be used with extreme care.

Another method of removing small image areas involves using abrasives to erase the image. A snakeslip is a rubber stick, containing abrasives, that can be sharpened to a fine point. Also, a special hone or scotch stone can be used like the snakeslip to carefully rub away all traces of the image. For best results, dip the hone or snakeslip in a plate finisher or dampening solution. An airbrush with abrasives can also be used to erase or abrade the undesired image. After removing the image, the metal underneath should be treated with a good plate cleaner or etch. Then, the entire plate should be washed and regummed with plate finisher.

Adding Images to Plates

For high-quality or long-run plates, or when extensive additions are needed, it is probably better and less expensive to correct the film and make a new plate. Additions to most aluminum and anodized aluminum plates can be made by carefully scratching the surface of the plate with a sharp needle or stylus in the desired shape. A number of short, but relatively deep scratches should be made to fill in the desired area. Then, tusche, press ink, or (for longer runs) a fast-setting epoxy adhesive that hardens quickly with heat from a hair dryer is used. Some plate manufacturers or supply houses furnish special tusches and/or equipment and procedures for making additions.

There is no satisfactory way to add images to finished lithographic plates. Therefore, it is best to carefully inspect the films and correct mistakes before processing the plates.

Bimetal Plates

Good bimetal plates have excellent printing latitude, exceptional image fidelity, and will last for millions of impressions. Stainless steel plates are exceptionally tough and durable on press. Of the two metals that constitute bimetal plates, one forms the image areas and the other forms the nonimage areas. The metal that forms the image areas (copper) is selected for its ability to repel water and accept ink. The metal forming the nonimage areas (usually aluminum or stainless steel) is selected for its (water) wettability and for how well it desensitizes to ink under the same conditions that render copper ink-receptive.

Although other bimetal or trimetal plates (using chromium over copper or brass) are still sometimes used, they are essentially obsolete in the U.S.

Making Bimetal Plates

Bimetal plates are available as either positive- or negative-working presensitized plates of copper on stainless steel or aluminum. These plates can be furnished either grained (aluminum) or ungrained (stainless steel) and are similar to surface plates because their copper image areas are very slightly raised above the nonimage areas. The copper is usually 0.00004–0.00015 in. (0.001–0.004 mm) thick. Presensitized plates have replaced uncoated bimetal plates since toxic dichromated coatings previously used are banned in many locations.

The basic steps for making bimetal plates are given below:

1. Exposing. The plate is exposed either through a positive or negative, depending on the specific light-sensitive coating used. A sensitivity guide should be used.

2. Developing. The plate is developed with a special developer that removes the unhardened coating in the nonimage area. Machine processors are normally used.

3. Staging. Any unwanted light-sensitive coating from film edges, dirt, etc., can be easily removed with deletion fluid prior to etching.

4. Copper etching. The copper is removed from the nonimage areas by swabbing a special etch over the plate. The etch does not significantly attack the stainless steel or aluminum base metal. Again, machine processing is normally used. The expended etch is usually returned to the plate manufacturer for reprocessing, which eliminates serious pollution problems for the printer.

5. Stencil removing. Removing the stencil may not be necessary, as the resist or stencil is ink-receptive. However, the plate will print slightly fuller if the resist is not removed. The resist is easily removed with a suitable solvent or proprietary stencil remover. A special plate processor will remove the stencil, furnish a protective coat for the copper, and apply gum to the nonimage areas.

6. Finishing. Unless the plate is going to press

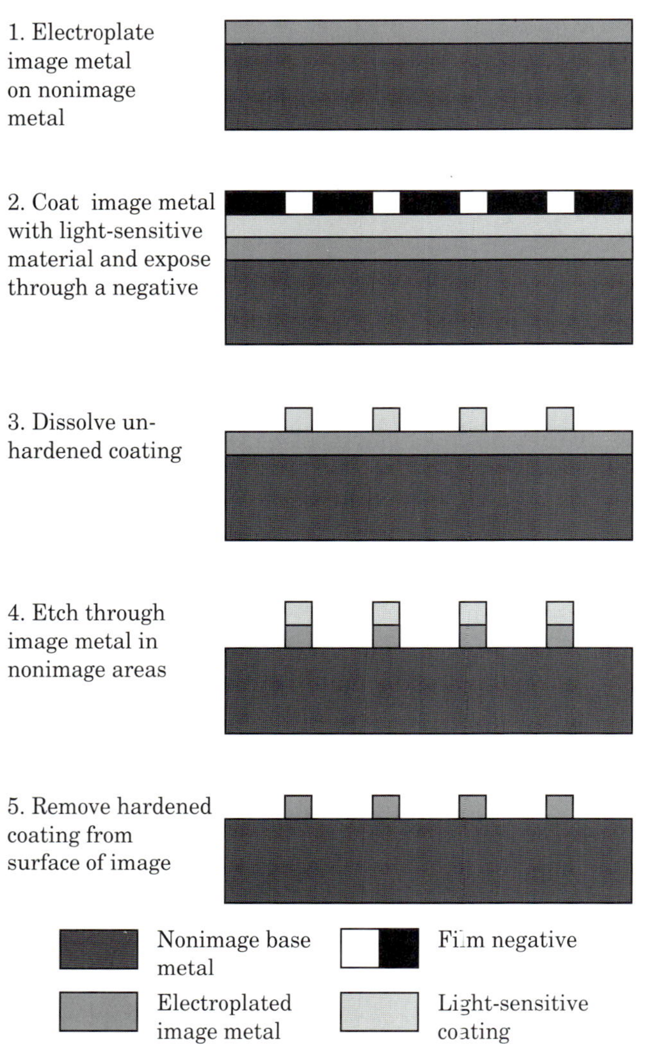

immediately, the copper must be protected so that it will readily accept ink on press. Therefore, if the stencil is removed, the plate must be gummed with AGE (asphaltum-gum-etch) or other finisher that protects both the image and nonimage areas. Alternately, the plates can be gummed with a good gum finisher, wiped dry, and then treated with an asphaltum solution that is wiped down dry over all image areas. A special plate finisher that protects the copper and gums the nonimage areas can be applied by hand or in machine processors.

Obtain detailed instructions and information from the manufacturer before attempting to apply the finisher.

Correcting Bimetal Plates

When removing work from bimetal plates, the photosensitive coating must first be removed with the appropriate stencil remover. Then, the copper can be removed with the appropriate copper etch. Take care to completely remove all undesired copper without etching away any desired image. After the image has been removed, the areas should be desensitized with the plate cleaner or etch. Then, the plate should be washed and regummed.

To add images to aluminum bimetal plates, follow procedures recommended for surface plates. For additions to stainless steel, clean the steel with a hone or snakeslip, scratch the surface with a hard needle, and then carefully apply an epoxy adhesive and cure it with heat. There is no proven method of adding images to finished litho plates. Usually, the best thing to do is to make a new plate.

Direct-Image, Diffusion Transfer, Direct Photographic (Photo-Direct), and Electrostatic Plates

Direct-image, diffusion transfer, photo-direct projection, and electrostatic plates are presently used for duplicating or reprography on smaller presses. Some of these plates are also used on larger presses, but the quality and wear-resistance requirements are not as demanding as they are for plates used on larger presses. It should not be assumed from this, however, that these plates do not represent a large sales market and are not capable of excellent quality or longer runs. The large market for these plates has been remarkably stable despite the increasing use of copiers and electronic printers. Direct-image and diffusion transfer plates have lost most of their market to more modern plates. The market for photographic plates (photo-direct and projection) has grown rapidly and surpassed that of all other duplicating plates combined. Electrostatic printing has also grown and offers unique possibilities for some markets on both duplicators and larger presses.

Direct-Image Plates

The direct-image process is similar to the old *original plates* in that the greasy image is applied manually or mechanically to the printing plate. The plates are called *masters* and are usually made on specially coated paper. The image can be drawn, lettered, painted, ruled, traced, typed, or written on the master by using pencil, crayon, ink, carbon

paper, fabric or carbon ribbon, rubber stamp, or numbering machine. The image can also be printed directly on the plate by offset or letterpress. Only oil-based materials can be used for producing images on these plates. If guidelines and instructions are required, they are often printed on the master with watercolor inks that will not print.

Most direct-image plates are produced directly on the typewriter and are used on offset duplicators. Earlier, these plates were made by transferring images from existing letterpress plates or standing forms. Direct-image plates were used for reprinting books, price lists, and similar products where only minor changes were needed.

Direct-image plates are still used for systems work, since they eliminate the need for preprinted forms. Most of the information that would normally be on the form can be preprinted on the master, and the last-minute data can be typed or drawn on the master. When the master is printed, all of the information prints at the same time. Some MICR (magnetic ink character recognition) printing (used extensively for bank checks) is still done on direct-image plates.

Making direct-image plates. The steps in making direct-image plates follow:

1. The image is transferred to the plate by any of the methods mentioned above. Careful handling of the plate is extremely important. The plate surface must be protected from grease spots, such as fingerprints or grease and oil from the machine, since these spots will print.

2. The plates are mounted on the press, the plate surface is wiped with a special etch, and the press is started. The etch and dampening solution used must be specifically designed for duplicator plates.

Detailed information on individual plates and processes is available from the manufacturers.

Diffusion Transfer Plates

Diffusion transfer plates are made by transferring exposed image areas from a silver sensitized negative paper to either a paper or metal plate. After exposure, the emulsion side of the paper is placed in contact with the correct side of either paper or metal plates. Then, the paper/plate combination is fed into a special diffusion transfer processor where a special activator solution softens the exposed areas of the paper so it will transfer to the plate. Thirty to sixty seconds after the paper/plate combination emerges from the processor, the paper is carefully peeled off the plate and discarded. The plate is then treated with a fixer that hardens the image areas while desensitizing the background. The paper plates are used mostly on short-run duplicator printing. Metal plates are satisfactory for runs up to 40,000 impressions. Diffusion transfer plates have lost a large portion of their market to photo-direct plates.

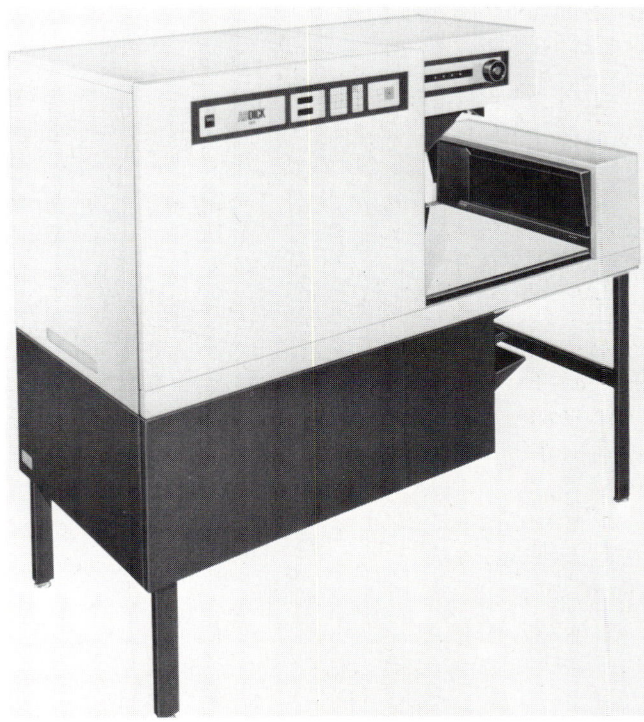

Courtesy A. B. Dick Company

Platemaker.

Photo-direct Plates

Photo-direct plates (or direct photographic plates) can be produced in either projection or camera-type platemakers. These are usually supplied in rolls to fit specific machines that expose, process, and deliver the finished plate cut to the proper size. Automatic platemaking systems allow the user to select roll size, plate length, margins, resizing calculation, and manual or automatic exposure. These systems also provide backlighting, point registration light, multiple exposure options and exposure time.

Photo-direct or camera plates. Photo-direct plates usually have photographic emulsions with speeds high enough for reasonably short exposures in platemakers equipped with light sources of average energy. Photo-direct and camera plates are very fast and easy to make since the original reflec-

tion copy is photographed directly onto the plate. These plates are used on small lithographic presses for short-run work. Both paper and plastic plates are available.

Electrostatic Plates

Three electrostatic processes for making printing plates have been developed—Xerography, Electrofax, and OPC (organic photoconductors). In all three processes, an image is produced by the action of light on a photoconductive surface that has been charged by static electricity. The areas exposed to light become electrically conductive and lose their charge. Unexposed areas remain electrically charged to attract oppositely charged powder or liquid toners that become the image.

In the Xerographic process, a selenium drum is the photoconductor that attracts the toners. The toners are either transferred directly, or from a rubber drum or blanket, to paper or metal plates. The toners are then fused by heat to form the image areas. In the Electrofax process, the photoresponsive surface consists of a zinc oxide photoconductor in a resin binder that is usually coated on paper. OPC plates use organic photoconductors instead of zinc oxide. A corona produces a negative charge on the zinc oxide or OPC coating. Like selenium, the zinc oxide or OPC coating loses its charge upon exposure to light. The image is produced when a positively charged powder or liquid toner is attracted to the charged image areas. The image is then fused at high temperatures to the plate.

Paper electrostatic plates are used on duplicators for printing up to 10,000 copies. Metal plates are used mostly on larger presses for runs over 200,000 impressions. Image fidelity on both plates is adequate for halftones up to 110 lines/in. (4.3 lines/mm).

The photoresponse of electrostatic plates is comparable to that of conventional film. Electrostatic plates have been used in computer-to-plate systems in which exposures are made by computer-controlled lasers. Systems such as these have been used by national newspapers using satellite or wire transmission of complete newspaper pages.

Platemaking Problems

Today, printers are fortunate to have so many excellent plates available. These plates are quickly and easily made and are relatively inexpensive. Most of these plates offer excellent image fidelity with wide exposure latitude, exceptional durability, and consistency on press. When the proper equipment and chemicals are used and the manufacturer's instructions followed, most problems can be avoided. Despite all this, however, problems occur. This section describes some of the most common problems, their probable causes, and suggested remedies.

Presensitized Plates

With presensitized plates, the supplier treats the metal and coats the plate using mass-production procedures, which require excellent quality control. In addition, the manufacturer supplies processing chemicals specifically developed for optimal performance with a particular plate. Automatic plate processors produce high-quality, consistent plates quickly, and reliably.

Despite all this, problems in making and running litho plates still occur too frequently. Some of the common problems that occur with presensitized plates are outlined below.

Scumming. Scumming occurs on press when the nonimage areas accept ink. Several reasons for scum include:

- **Fogging.** Most negative-working plates are easily fogged when exposed for more than a few minutes to daylight or room light. Even yellow plate room lights can fog plates in a short time. Positive-working plates might scum if the plates are not exposed long enough. In both cases, scumming results from residual coating left on the nonimage areas after development. A residual coating problem may be difficult to detect until after the plates have run on press a while. Too often, it is assumed that the scumming is a press problem, because the plates ran clean for as many as 20,000 impressions before the problem appeared. To avoid this problem, always keep plates stored in their original light-tight package in a closed cabinet or drawer until ready to use. Be careful to keep light exposure of the plates to a minimum until after development. Fogging during exposure often occurs when the next plate to be exposed is left face up near the vacuum frame. Always remember that a litho plate is actually a special type of photographic film and should be treated like film.
- **Incomplete development.** Unless the plate is fully developed, very small amounts of coating may

remain and cause scumming on press. This also frequently causes excessive dot gain in halftone areas; so whether processing by hand or machine, overdevelopment is always preferable to underdevelopment. Hand-develop plates carefully and avoid contamination from water, dirty swabs, or dirty sinks. Be sure that the temperature, speed, chemical concentration, and maintenance of plate processors is correct according to the manufacturer's recommendations.

- **Dampening solution.** Scumming may occur on press if the ink is too greasy for the dampening solution. To eliminate scumming, add more dampening solution concentrate and up to one ounce of 14°Bé gum arabic solution per gallon of dampening solution. The pH of acid dampening solutions must be below 5.5 when gum arabic is used as the desensitizing agent. When scumming is a problem, the pH should be considerably lower. Ink dot scumming can result when acids in the dampening solution attack the plate by etching small, deep holes into the plate. Ink dot scumming is relatively rare on anodized aluminum plates, but can occur if excessive dampening solution is left on plates when shutting down the press. Excessive pressure or abrasion on press may also cause scumming.
- **Defective plates.** On very rare occasions, the plate may be defective. Old plates, plates that have been stored at very high temperatures and/or humidities, or plates that were defective when manufactured can cause scumming.
- **Emulsion developer.** On presensitized additive plates, scumming may result if the emulsion developer is bad, if the processor has not been properly maintained, or if the plate is rubbed up until it is too dry. Dirty or contaminated sponges or swabs can also cause problems. On heat-treated plates, the use of an improper finisher before heating can cause scumming.
- **Improper gum application.** Improperly applied gum can cause scumming. Plates should be gummed up on press anytime the press will be down for more than 30 min.

Poor reproduction. Good image fidelity is necessary for all critical jobs. Proper exposure and processing is essential for good reproduction. The images on all negative-working plates gain as exposure is increased, while on all positive-working plates, images sharpen with increasing exposure. Be sure to use only hard-dot or contact film. Camera films with dot fringes cause dot gain on negative-working plates and excessive sharpening on positive-working plates. Most scanner film is hard-dot film. An improperly operating scanner can leave scanner streaks that resemble fogging in halftone areas of negative plates.

Unless development is thorough, plates requiring good mechanical action for complete development may tend to plug in the shadow areas. Incomplete development on some plates may leave a very thin, almost invisible halo around the dots. Although these plates look acceptable in the plate room, they print too full on press. Again, overdevelopment is preferable to underdevelopment. The single exception is additive plates; prolonged development with lacquer-type developers can cause dot gain and plugging.

Image gain or sharpening. Poor contact between the plate and film allows light under opaque areas of the film and causes image gain or sharpening, depending upon whether positive- or negative-working plates are being used. For good contact all plates should be drawn down for over 30 sec. at a minimum of 25 in. (635 mm) of vacuum before starting the exposure. Since the vacuum gauge may not correctly indicate vacuum in the frame, view the surface of the vacuum frame at an oblique angle. The appearance of Newton's Rings, which resemble an oil slick with rainbow colors, indicates good contact.

Photocomposers must also provide proper vacuum, especially when large chases are being used. Overexposure greatly aggravates problems resulting from poor contact. Thus, all exposures should be made with a light integrator to produce the recommended step on the plate sensitivity guide. Placing a sheet of clear plastic between the flat and vacuum frame glass improves contact. Grained or frosted plastic with the frosted side of the sheet toward the film improves contact while diffusing light. The frosted plastic causes some dot gain on negative-working plates and sharpening on positive-working plates.

Premature plate wear. Premature plate wear on press has many causes. The images on underexposed negative-working plates are too weak for good press life and wear out prematurely. Some unbaked positive-working plates fail prematurely due to light degradation caused by excessive exposure to light after development. On some positive-working plates, the developer destroys the light sensitivity of the plate so that this does not happen. Strong solvents, UV inks, or electron-beam (EB) inks can attack some plate coatings and must not be used on those plates. Other causes of excessive

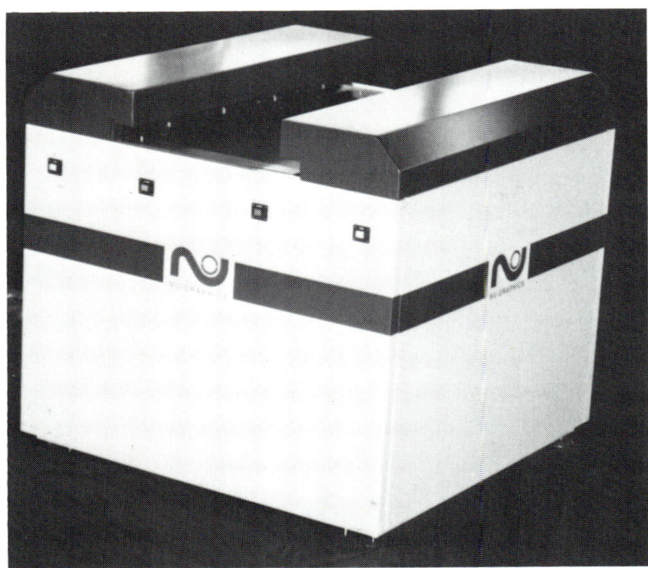

Courtesy Nu-Graphics Mfg., Inc.

Semiautomatic plate bender.

wear include excessive printing pressure, abrasives from ink, paper, or other sources, and excessive relative motion (or slip) between the plate and blanket, Delta rollers, and hickey-picking rollers. An additive developer can be used on press to extend the life of most plates if wear has not progressed too far. Be sure to test the developer on a scrap plate before using it on a live job, since this type of developer will remove the image on some plates.

Blind images. If the image looks strong but doesn't accept ink, the problem is probably blinding instead of wear. Some plates may blind when the pH of the dampening solution is too low or when too much alcohol is used in the fountain. On rare occasions, a whitish salt will deposit over the plate image and cause blinding. The salt can usually be removed temporarily with a good plate cleaner but will return unless the source is found and corrected. On very rare occasions, paper can cause blinding on some plates. Blind plates can usually be brought back with plate cleaner or an additive developer that is compatible with the plate.

Plate cracking. On web presses, plate cracking results when the plate does not conform to the cylinder. It must be bent and mounted properly to conform precisely to the cylinder without flexing.

Wipe-on Plates

Wipe-on plates are very popular with newspapers and some other printers because they are relatively inexpensive. The supplier furnishes a treated (but uncoated) plate along with the chemicals and coating needed to sensitize the plate. Since the printer must apply the coating, these plates are more troublesome than most presensitized plates. The most commonly encountered problems are discussed below.

Scumming. Scumming is a major problem on wipe-on plates. In addition to all of the sources covered under presensitized plates, scumming on wipe-on plates can result from:

- **Wipe-on coatings.** Most wipe-on coatings should be used within a couple of days after mixing. They deteriorate rapidly—especially at elevated temperatures. The dry diazo also deteriorates with age and causes scumming, especially in hot, humid weather. Thus, scumming is much more common in the summer. After coating, the plates should be used within 24 hours.
- **Incomplete development.** Incomplete development may also cause scumming. To test the processed plate, cover a portion of the nonimage area and re-expose the plate. Residual diazo appears as a yellow ink-receptive stain. For best results, this stain should be minimal or absent after redeveloping the plate with an additive plate developer.
- **Quality problems.** Since wipe-on plates are less expensive than presensitized plates, the manufacturer's quality control may not be as good. Problems can result if the quality of the base metal is not consistent. An uncoated plate right from the box that scums when developed with additive developer is more likely to scum on press. A good wipe-on plate should not accept ink when rubbed up with water and press ink or wipe-on developers.
- **Inadequate finishers.** Gum used on newspaper plates is formulated to be removed immediately by the press dampeners, so it may be inferior to gum or finishers used on presensitized plates. Some printers re-expose the finished (gummed) plates to harden the gum and thus reduce or eliminate scum on press.
- **Press and miscellaneous.** When a newspaper press goes down, the plates generally are not gummed. If the plates are left ungummed for more than a few minutes and completely dry, they will probably scum on startup, especially if the residual diazo in nonimage areas is excessive. The neutral or alkaline dampening solutions used by many newspapers can contribute to this scum. Most acid dampening solutions better resist scumming. With some newspaper presses, ink must be applied to the

plates before the dampening solution wets the plate. Most news inks are formulated to pick up a lot of water. If the water pickup is too low, the plates may scum.

Streaked and chalky coating. Streaks and chalkiness result when the coating is too thick. Coating rollers must be kept clean and properly adjusted for best results. Manufacturer's instructions should be closely followed with respect to coating the plate.

Dirt or lint in the dried coating. Dirt or lint from any source can cause problems. A major source of dirt results from using old diazo or reusing diazo coatings that have been drained from the coating pan.

Weak image. A weak or uneven image will result if development is incomplete. Plates must be developed until a strong, uniform image is obtained. Additive developers must be thoroughly mixed before being put in the processor.

Excess water in the developer, a developer that has lost solvent, or a bad plate can cause a weak image or one that refuses to accept lacquer or ink properly during the developing procedure. White spots can result from silicate gels due to poor quality control by the plate manufacturer. Small round spots can be caused by water droplets on the unexposed plate.

Plates that have not been properly pretreated will not work satisfactorily with the diazo coatings used for most wipe-on processes. The pretreatment is required on both anodized and unanodized plates, and it must be compatible with the coating and developing chemicals. Pretreated plates have an indefinite shelf life provided they are stored in a cool, dry location.

Bimetal and Trimetal Plates

Most of the problems encountered with multimetal plates are similar to those encountered with surface plates, so most comments under presensitized plates also apply here.

For diagnosing plate problems, it is necessary to consider whether the plate is negative-working or positive-working. It must be stressed that two different metals are always involved: the image-bearing metal (copper) and the water-carrying metal (chromium, stainless steel, or aluminum).

Copper repelling ink is one of the most common problems. The application of a copper sensitizer, which the plate supplier can furnish, should rectify the problem. The copper should always be protected with asphaltum if the plate is not going to be used immediately. Gum blinding is a common cause of blind copper. Use an asphaltum-gum-emulsion (AGE) finisher when gumming these plates, or apply an asphaltum solution immediately after the gumming operation. A special bimetal plate finisher can also be used to avoid this problem.

Material from the paper rarely causes blinding. A good dampening solution will correct this problem. Sulfur compounds and very strong oxidizers can also cause blinding or premature plate failure.

Computer-to-plate problems. Because of the revolutionary nature of this process, problems may arise from the reassignment or elimination of traditional production duties.

The elimination of the film stage of the prepress process also antiquates many existing proofing systems. Conventional proofing systems need to be replaced by digital systems. Furthermore, financial constraints of implementing the latest technology will limit the number of printers and publishers who initially adopt CTP systems.

Chapter 12

Electronic Prepress Production

Electronic prepress production is a term used to describe the process of creating documents on a computer using special software products that integrate text and graphics. Electronic prepress software enables operators to design and produce books, manuals, brochures, newsletters, annual reports, business forms, flyers, posters, catalogs, pamphlets, presentations, mailing labels, and other publications from the desktop. Its underlying concepts are similar to traditional prepress production except that the images are laid out on a page electronically. Electronic prepress production is often referred to as **desktop publishing (DTP).** Some of its many benefits are stated below:

- A reduction in production costs. By replacing typesetting with desktop publishing, the costs of outputting to film or phototypesetting paper are reduced. Intermediate proofs are usually output using plain-paper laser printers, a procedure that is considerably less expensive than outputting to film or phototypesetting paper.
- A significant decrease in production time from writing the copy to printing the final piece. Because copy is often keyboarded using a word processing program, the text is easily imported into a page layout program where the page and design are created. Rekeyboarding, which was often required in traditional typesetting, and the pasteup step are eliminated.
- Quick verification and revision of information.
- Easier maintenance of security and supervision.

Electronic prepress production encompasses a number of prepress production steps such as art and copy preparation, page makeup, and graphic arts photography. In some instances, electronic prepress production includes electronic stripping and direct-to-plate imagesetting.

Typically, with electronic prepress production, the computer operator performs several functions, unlike with traditional prepress, where one person would prepare the art, another would do the typesetting, a third would paste up the job, and so on. In addition, the customer may perform functions that have historically been performed by the printer. This chapter presents an overview of electronic prepress production and digital halftones, discusses implementing electronic prepress production, and reviews hardware and software in-depth.

Overview of Electronic Prepress Production

Word Processing

During the writing process, the text for a job is keyboarded into a computer. This is done using special software known as a **word processing package.** Inputting data through a word processor is one of the most common ways to enter text into the personal computer. Word processing programs are the most efficient way to enter text for letters and long documents, such as books, magazines, and newspapers.

Word processing files can be converted to work with a wide variety of equipment including traditional typesetting equipment, personal computers, and page layout software. Keyboarding, proofreading, and correcting can all be done efficiently and effectively on a word processor prior to the electronic page layout steps. For this reason, it is important

to provide clean, correct input. Editing is best done in the word processing program since the file should be corrected and finalized before being placed into the page layout application.

Word processing applications offer many features, such as spelling and grammar checkers, search and replace functions, and formatting options. One of the most useful features is the **spelling checker.** This utility "reads" each word in a document and checks it against an internal dictionary. If the word is misspelled or unrecognizable, the program stops and asks the operator to correct it.

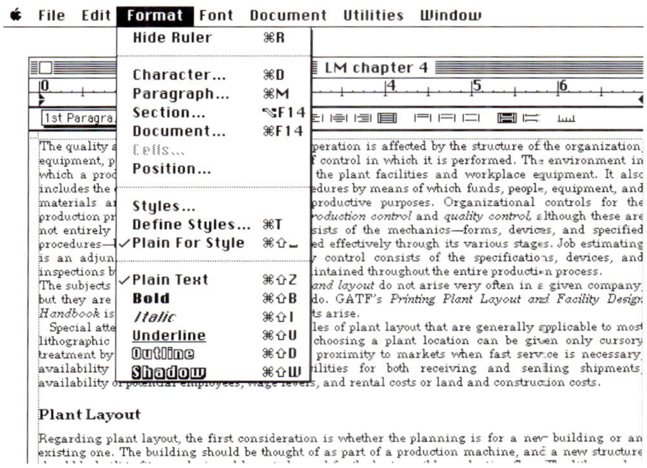

Microsoft Word, a popular word processing program for Macintosh computers.

Another often used utility is called **search and replace** or **find and change.** This option allows the user to globally search a document for repetitive words or symbols and make all of the changes at one time. For example, the user may need to search for an asterisk (*) and replace it with a bullet (•).

Proofreading

Although electronic systems have greatly simplified prepress production, proofreading must never be overlooked. Once the word processed file has been output to paper, either the operator or a trained proofreader must check the copy.

Once the proof has been read and marked for corrections, it is returned to the word processing operator. Within the program, the operator makes the corrections that were indicated by the proofreader. Additional proofs may still be required, but when the text is approved, the file may be saved to disk and submitted for the page layout.

Electronic Design and Computer Illustration

Designing using a computer. In traditional design, the artist typically creates a series of thumbnail sketches, which are miniature drafts of a design. The customer selects one or more designs and each one is recreated in more detail and at actual size—a **rough layout.** A **comprehensive layout,** which closely represents the appearance of the final printed product, may also be created.

Graphic designers may still create thumbnails and comprehensive layouts on paper and then submit them in completed form to an electronic page layout department. The operator will carefully match all colors, type sizes, and type styles to recreate the piece on the computer by positioning each element according to the artist's layout. However, a graphic designer who has access to a desktop publishing system can also create and generate thumbnail concepts directly on the computer screen. Scanned photographs and line illustrations, along with the actual text in the proper typeface and font, can be imported from other software programs and integrated into the page layout template. The designer can resize type, photos, and artwork, and test different page configurations with greater flexibility. The artist may use a graphics or illustration program to create logos, manipulate type, and edit scanned images.

For design purposes, the artist may make typeface selections and place headlines and boxes (or borders) directly on the computer. The actual text or "copy" will be produced in the word processing stage. Photographs or illustrations are often indicated by boxes or shaded areas. The designer's goal is to create a sample layout that can serve as a guide for the final positioning of all elements on the page. Using the computer as a design tool makes it easy to experiment with the appearance, position, and size of any element on the page. It is also ideal for "visualizing" the final printed piece. Designers and their clients can preview several different concepts in near-final form much earlier in the design process.

This type of electronic design enables the artist to experiment with colors, textures, and type sizes and styles independently without incurring the expense of proofs or stats in order to create a traditional hand-drawn comprehensive. Even if the traditional design methods are used, it is important for the designer to be familiar with the features and options, as well as the limitations, of the hardware and software used in electronic prepress production.

Creating illustrations. Illustration programs are often used to create designs, logos, or illustrations directly in the computer. An operator will usually create artwork when a higher-quality graphic is required than that which can be obtained from scanning. Most computer drawing is simply combining the correct geometric shapes to create objects and illustrations. Tracing images is a common practice. A scan of the image can even be used as a template for redrawing or tracing.

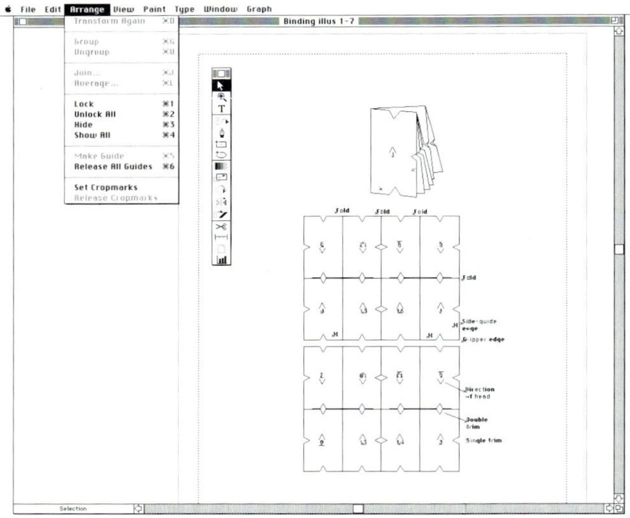

An illustration being created using Adobe Illustrator.

Complete color images and logos can be created in an illustration program. Any image may be resized or reshaped as required by the customer. Because the images were created on the computer, most editing or correcting is also a relatively simple process. Many times, the customer can look at the computer screen and guide the operator through the desired changes.

Draw programs are often referred to as **vector-based** programs. They create images using line descriptions that appear on screen in **bezier curves.** Each line may be manipulated by moving the nodes or control points that appear on it. Illustrations created in these programs will output at the highest resolution of the printer or imagesetter because they utilize the PostScript language. Draw programs are often used for manipulating type by rotating, skewing, stretching, or setting text to a curve. Logos, ads, and detailed graphics can be created easily on these programs. Many designers and illustrators use draw programs to design printed pieces, such as covers, posters, labels, etc.

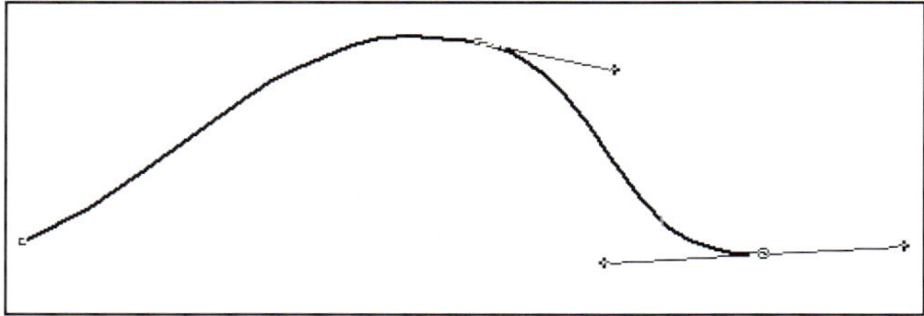

A bezier curve used in vector-based illustration programs. Notice the nodes or control points on the curve.

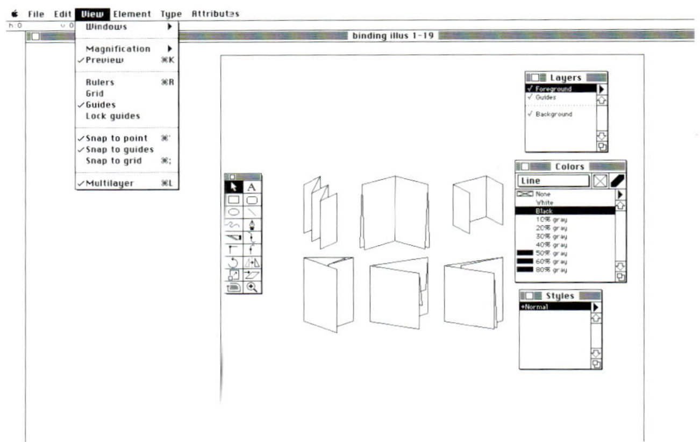

An illustration being created using Aldus Freehand.

Paint programs allow the operator to alter or create images one dot or pixel at a time. The output quality of these images is dependent upon the resolution of the monitor in use. The "jaggies" or stairstep edges on curved lines are often apparent on paint images. These jaggies are less obvious when a high-resolution monitor is used.

Scanning

"Desktop" scanning is an essential part of electronic prepress production since scanners provide many functions. When an image is scanned, it is said to have been "digitized" so that it can be manipulated on the computer. There are several different types of scanners: **hand-held, flatbed,** and **overhead.** An operator uses a **hand-held scanner** by moving it across the image. Hand-held scanners are especially well-suited for scanning small items, such as logos and clip art. They are less expensive than flatbed or overhead scanners. **Flatbed scanners** are used to scan larger documents. They resemble small photocopiers. The bed is covered by a piece of glass and a flexible cover. The operator positions the image to be scanned face down on the glass of the scanner and closes the cover. Each page is scanned separately. Automatic sheet feeding

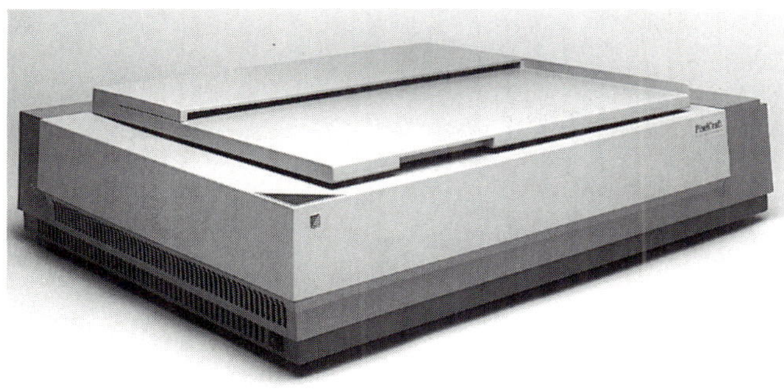

Courtesy PixelCraft, Inc.

7650 Pro Imager, a flatbed scanner.

attachments are also available for these types of scanners. **Overhead scanners** are designed to scan large books and/or three dimensional objects; they resemble enlargers. The operator can place flat sheets or objects on the glass-covered copyboard or position objects on the stand.

The scanner is activated and controlled by a special software program. The operator may choose the lightness, darkness, and the reproduction size needed. Options for scanning line art and/or halftones are also available. If desired, the operator can select the type of halftone dot (round, square, or elliptical) and the screen ruling needed. The screen ruling used is often determined by the limitations of the output device. Finer screen rulings such as 133 lines/in. (lpi), 150 lpi, and 200 lpi require high-resolution imagesetters.

After positioning the image on the scanning surface, the operator often makes a **proof scan** to check the position and quality of the scan. This indicates the rough size and basic appearance of the object before the actual scan occurs. The image can also be "cropped" so that only selected images on the page are scanned. Brightness levels may also be selected to lighten or darken the picture. Once the final scan is made, special painting or editing tools can be used to clean or edit the digitized image in the computer. Each image that is required for the job is scanned and saved to a separate file.

Color scanners are used to digitize color or black-and-white images. Color scanners are similar in appearance to black-and-white scanners. Files of color images, however, are significantly larger than those of black-and-white images.

Electronic Page Layout

A page layout program is used to define the page size, margins, and number of columns to be used on the page. These procedures are typical of the tasks involved in traditional pasteup of pages on artboards.

Once the page has been "defined" as indicated by the designer's layout, the operator may begin to place the elements on the page. The text or body copy that was keyboarded in the word processor is "imported" or placed into the page layout program. When the text is in position, type sizes and styles may be assigned to the text. Headlines, captions, and other special areas of text may also be imported from a word processing file, but these are often created directly on the page by the operator. Next, information that will appear on every page or many pages, such as chapter titles and the title of the book, are added to the document. These are often called **running heads** or **footers.** Elements that must repeat on every page are placed on a "master page." A master page is a concept similar to the traditional overlay sheet used by pasteup artists. The computer automatically places the elements assigned to a master page into every designated page in the document.

The drawing capabilities of most page layout programs are rather limited, although most provide basic line and box tools. The **box tools** are used to apply a border or frame around ads, photos, and illustrations. **Line tools** are used to create straight or diagonal lines. Various styles and line widths as well as colors can also be applied to either lines or boxes. Boxes may be "filled" with solid colors or decorative screened patterns. The computer operator uses these drawing tools to create borders and rules on the page as specified by the designer.

During the electronic page layout process, the computer operator "imports" photographs, logos, or other illustrations into the page layout program. The operator locates each file from the directory

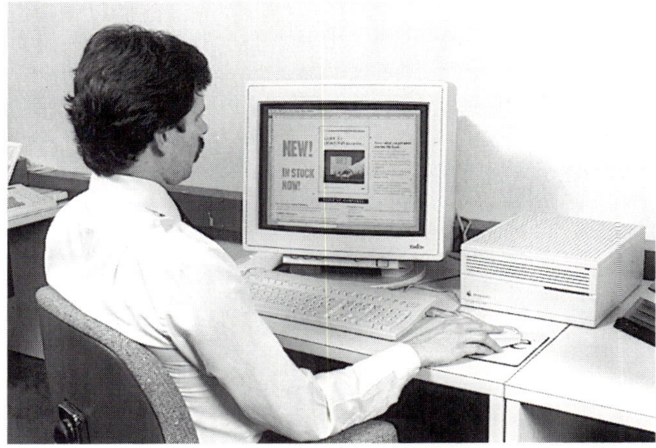

Designer using QuarkXPress to lay out a page.

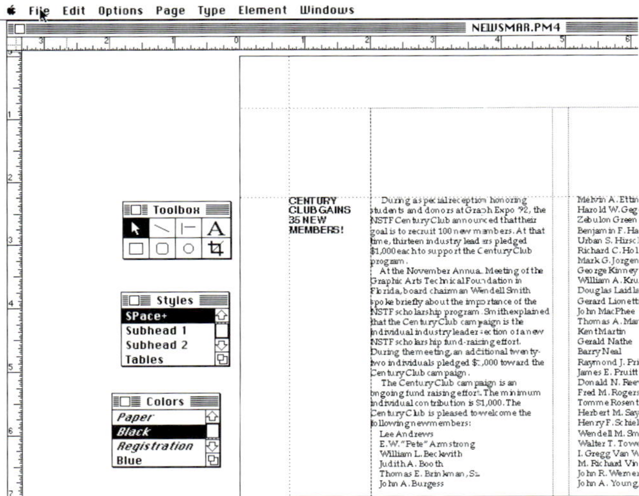

Aldus PageMaker, a page layout program.

and selects the appropriate command to import the file into the document. Once the graphic has been retrieved, many options may still be applied to the image. For instance, each element can be resized, cropped, lightened, darkened, or colored as required by the design directly in the page layout program.

Other adjustments may be made to the page by rearranging text, graphics, or boxes where needed. Once all of the elements are in place, the page is often output to a plain-paper laser printer to create an in-house or customer proof of the job.

The client's proof may indicate changes or corrections. On the computer, the operator opens the previously created document and makes the corrections on the screen.

Upon final approval of the job, the file is generally output to a high-resolution imagesetter. These machines will output a "typeset-quality" version of the document onto either photographic film or paper materials. These photographic films and papers must be processed using special equipment and chemistry. Gray scales, color bars, register marks, and crop marks are usually automatically produced on the film by the software program. If the document includes color photographs, graphics, or text, the imagesetter may *color-separate* the file automatically. This means that the imagesetter prints each color of the document onto a separate film so that it will be ready for the film assembly procedure.

Other Options

Final films produced on an imagesetter are often sent to the stripping or film assembly department for traditional film assembly. Many electronic advancements are also being made in this area. Already, a document of several pages may be imported into another software package that will create "impositions" for the press plate. Depending on the number of pages in the document and the type of binding required, there are many different ways to impose a job. This can be a difficult, time-consuming procedure for the stripper whereas electronic imposition systems will output the pages in the appropriate position automatically.

Imposed pages may also be imaged directly to plate material if desired, which also saves an additional step in the prepress process. Imaging directly to plate material is a significant development for companies using small press formats.

An even greater advancement is the ability to image the cylinders on the press directly from a computer workstation. When properly set up and manipulated, this technology enables printers to virtually eliminate the traditional procedures of pasteup, stripping, and platemaking.

Digital Halftones

A digital halftone is merely a halftone produced by a computer system. Halftones are created to render continuous-tone images into something that can be reproduced on press. In the traditional halftoning process, photographs are reshot through a film-based contact halftone screen. The resultant image is comprised of tiny dots that can be square, round, or oval, but always evenly spaced. The sizes of the dots vary. Dots in light areas of the image are small, and dots in dark areas are larger. This varying dot size is what gives the illusion of continuous tone.

With digital halftoning, the continuous-tone photograph is converted into a digital format when it is scanned into the computer system with a desktop scanner or video digitizer. Only scanners with gray scale capability (the ability to recognize multiple shades of gray in the images it captures) should be used. Many scanners also have a halftone setting. This setting will produce a halftone, but the resulting image will be bitmapped and therefore difficult to manipulate. For example, the screen angle and dot shape are set and cannot be changed, the halftone cannot be freely sized without creating

objectionable patterns, and it cannot easily have its contrast or brightness modified. If adjustments must be made to the halftone, the image must be rescanned at a different set of values. Halftoning may also be accomplished in the image manipulation software.

The preferred method for producing digital halftones on desktop publishing equipment is to scan a picture as a continuous-tone, gray-scale image and let the PostScript imagesetter perform the actual halftoning. This has the advantage that it allows the user to freely edit pictures in appropriate image manipulation software. It also permits them to be sized within page layout programs. This is a significant advantage because the size of a photo is often related to its placement on a page and the cropping desired. Changes to the size of a photo also change the effective resolution of that image. Extreme changes must be taken into account prior to scanning, although minor size adjustments usually do not cause problems with resolution.

Scanning with gray scale allows the operator a great deal of flexibility in manipulating and retouching the image without rescanning. Several image-editing programs are designed specifically for manipulation of gray-scale images produced on a scanner. These programs are similar to paint programs but are geared toward images in which each dot can be one of several shades of gray.

Though image-editing programs vary widely in functionality, some features are common to all, including paint tools, selection tools, image filters, and gray-scale editing functions. Gray-scale editing functions are especially useful in improving the quality of halftones produced on the imagesetter. They typically include brightness and contrast controls. The better image-editing programs can produce photographic effects previously achieved only in a darkroom. An image can be made lighter by lowering the gray value of each pixel. It can be converted into a negative by reversing the gray values. Painting tools enable the operator to remove objects or add new ones. Cloning and texture tools allow reproduction of a portion of an image elsewhere. Selection tools enable the operator to copy an object from one image and paste it into another.

After an image is scanned, it is saved as a graphics file in one of several standard formats. **TIFF,** or **tagged image file format,** is the format most widely used to save gray-scale images. It can be used with both Macintosh and PC-based software. **RIFF,** or **raster image file format,** is a gray-scale file format that allows compression of gray-scale images for reduced consumption of disk space. PICT2, an extension of Apple's PICT format, can save bitmapped images with gray-scale information. **EPSF,** or **encapsulated PostScript format,** is a variant of the PostScript file format that can be used to store halftone images. It does, however, consume even more disk space than uncompressed TIFF files.

Some scanner programs scan an image into the computer's memory, after which it is saved. Problems can result if the computer does not have enough memory to handle the image data. Gray-scale images (files) can be quite large, even several megabytes (MB). Other programs can scan the image directly into a disk file. Once it is saved, it may be imported into an image-editing program designed specifically for manipulation of gray-scale images produced on a scanner.

Digital halftones can be output on laser printers or high-resolution imagesetters. Like a printing press, these output devices are limited by their inability to produce dots with varying intensity. However, unlike a printing press, they cannot print different size dots. To give the effect of variable-sized dots, digital output devices use a technique called **dithering**. Dithering introduces a third kind of dot called a **halftone cell.** When a page layout program sends a dithered image to a laser printer, it groups two or more printer dots into a cluster—the halftone cell—that simulates one halftone dot. To avoid confusion in referring to these different kinds of dots, printer dots are sometimes called "spots."

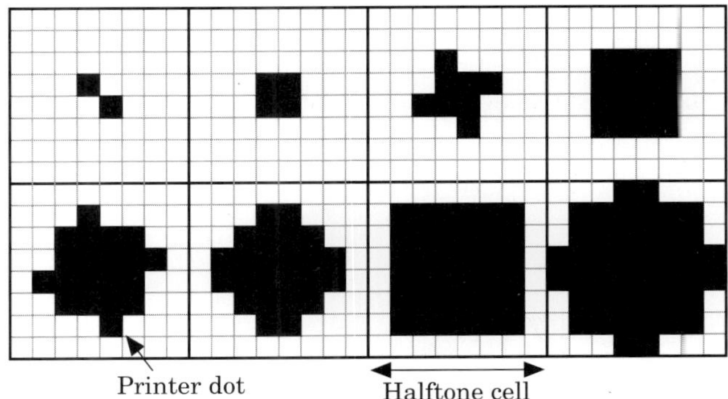

Digital halftone dots in an 8×8 matrix, which produces 64 gray levels.

Dithering can enable the operator to get the appearance of gray scale, but with a loss in resolution. Resolution is the density of dots or pixels on a page or display. It is usually measured in dots per inch. However, halftone resolution—also known as screen

frequency—is measured in lines per inch (lpi). Halftones with a high screen frequency, or high number of lines per inch, have a high density of dots and present a sharper image. For instance, newspaper halftones only have a density of 65 to 100 lpi, while magazine halftones generally offer 120 to 150 lpi, and fine art reproductions require 175 lpi or higher.

Output resolution, halftone screen ruling, and the number of gray levels in an image are all related to one another. The goal of creating a digital halftone should be to print the image at the finest screen ruling that is consistent with the maximum number of gray levels desired, taking into account the resolution of the output device. The interrelationship of these concepts is explained below.

Resolution

Both scanner input resolution and imagesetter output resolution are important in producing digital halftones. Most desktop scanners today have a resolution of 300 dpi. This resolution is necessary for producing a high-quality halftone because scanners give the best results if they oversample the data using approximately double the final output screen ruling desired. An image that has a screen ruling of 150 lines per inch should thus be scanned at 300 dpi. A drawback to oversampling is the large files created; doubling the sampling rate quadruples the file size. Files that are to be output at lower screen rulings may be scanned using a lower input resolution to make the process more efficient. The large files created by the scanning process not only rapidly fill up the computer's disk space but also slow the CPU in processing the image, tie up the network in transferring that image, and lead to excessively long output times.

If the image is to be sized significantly, this should be taken into account in determining the scanning resolution. Images that will be reduced in size gain in resolution and need not be scanned at the highest rate. Images that will be enlarged lose resolution accordingly and must therefore be scanned at appropriately higher resolutions.

The resolution of the output device is significant in determining the number of gray levels obtainable and in selecting the screen ruling for a halftone, as discussed below.

Gray Levels and Screen Ruling

Gray scale is a measure of the different levels of gray that an image can display. A continuous-tone image can show a nearly infinite number of gray values. Halftones simulate these continuous tones by varying the size of halftone dots. The number of possible dot sizes determines how many shades of gray can be shown in a particular image. In an image with 64 levels of gray, a dot can be any one of 64 sizes.

An 8-bit gray-scale scanner can recognize up to 256 shades of gray. Those models rated as 4-bit scanners can capture 16 gray levels, and those rated as 6-bit scanners can capture 64 gray levels. To look acceptable, a halftone needs somewhere between 64 and 256 levels of gray. Images with an insufficient number of gray levels will appear to have distinct bands of gray rather than smoothly blended tones in transitional areas.

Output resolution, however, is also an important factor in determining the available number of gray levels, regardless of what was used during input. The formula to determine the number of gray levels obtainable on an output device is as follows:

$$\text{Gray levels} = \left(\frac{\text{Printer Resolution}}{\text{Screen Ruling}}\right)^2 + 1$$

Given a constant output resolution, to obtain more levels of gray, the screen ruling must go down; higher screen rulings limit the number of gray levels that are reproducible. This is because each halftone dot is made up of individual printer pixels. Since the size of the output spot does not change, smaller halftone dots (which correspond to higher screen rulings) will be made up of fewer pixels. The output device turns the appropriate pixels on or off to simulate different shades of gray. Larger halftone dots, which are spaced further apart, will thus have more pixels, and therefore more levels of gray. For example, a 300-dpi printer can produce a 150-line halftone, but it only has five levels of gray; the results are poor. The same 300-dpi printer can produce 33 tones using a screen ruling of 53 lines per inch. On an imagesetter recording at 1,270 dpi, the 150-line screen has 73 possible levels of gray, while imagesetter output at 2,540 dpi produces a 150-line halftone with over 256 levels of gray.

The scanner's calibration should be checked by scanning a 12-step reflection gray scale and checking the densities using an image manipulation program. Adjustments to the tone reproduction curve may have to be made so that step 1 of the gray scale records as 0%, the middle step as 50%, and the last step as 100%; the quarter tone (step 3) and the three-quarter tone (step 9) can also be adjusted

as necessary. The tone reproduction curve can be adjusted to compensate for specific press requirements. For example, if the printing press requires a 5% highlight dot and 95% shadow dot, the curve can be adjusted so that an input of 0% outputs a 5% dot and an input of 100% outputs a 95% dot.

Implementing Electronic Prepress

Choosing a System

Implementing electronic prepress production involves several distinct tasks, which are described in this section.

Understanding the technology's capabilities and limitations. One of the keys to taking advantage of the opportunities provided by electronic prepress production is to make use of the best parts of the technology, while minimizing those parts that present problems or offer no significant improvements over other methods of production. For example, advantages of electronic prepress production include the relative ease of use of the systems and the ability of many systems to merge text and graphics. New developments in hardware and software have dramatically improved the flexibility and productivity of electronic prepress production systems.

Electronic prepress technology has many benefits to the user. For some, control over typesetting and page layout operations are very important benefits. This technology can also reduce the time it takes to make corrections. In addition, text can be checked and double-checked at the word processing stage until most of the errors have been corrected. This text is then placed directly into the page layout. Changes or corrections at the layout stage are not a problem, since they can be made relatively quickly.

The ability to view pages on a screen as they will appear when printed offers benefits to everyone involved. Page proofs from a laser printer are relatively inexpensive to produce and give a very close approximation of what the typeset version will look like. For some, having this type of control of the production of documents often justifies the expense of the hardware and software. This technology also provides fast turnaround time at a reasonable cost and does not require the coordinated efforts of several specialized technicians for design, typesetting, and pasteup. Installing a system can also have significant cost savings when compared to traditional typesetting and prepress production costs.

Electronic prepress production is a complicated process. Physical problems include software/hardware incompatibility, font management, and output or processing complications. The operators must be knowledgeable about the entire printing process in order to produce readable and visually pleasing printed pages. Procedures such as trapping, imposition, color separation, screen angles, and screen rulings are placing additional pressure on the operator. These issues are critical to producing quality printed products and must be considered from the design stage through to final output of film. Manually trapping colors can be tedious, requiring extra steps that are often error-prone. Imposition is not provided within most applications, although separate programs can impose pages previously created in a page layout program. Scanning black-and-white and full-color images requires a solid knowledge of resolution, file sizes, dot shape, dot gain, screen angles, and screen rulings.

Typical system configuration. Complete systems are more expensive than basic office computers, which are usually configured to handle word processing, spreadsheets, and database applications. These systems should have more memory and faster operating speeds than a standard office computer. The first decision to make before purchasing a system is choosing the hardware platform. There are two primary platforms: Apple's Macintosh and IBM-compatibles that use graphical operating environments such as Microsoft Windows. Using a Windows operating environment on IBM-compatible systems provides many of the user-friendly advantages of the Apple Macintosh machine. Unix-based workstations are also used.

Most businesses that are already using IBM compatibles for office operations tend to lean toward these systems to handle desktop publishing as well. Others prefer the easy learning curve and graphical capabilities of the Macintosh system. Current software programs and hardware provide a quick and easy exchange of information between both of these platforms.

A basic system could be assembled with a minimum of the following components:

- One or more color Macintosh II (or higher) computers for page layout and graphics creation
- One or more IBM or compatible computers with color monitors for text entry, page layout, and

graphics; must include a graphical user interface (GUI) such as Microsoft Windows or the OS/2 operating environment

• Sufficient random access memory (RAM)—8 megabytes (MB) being the minimum; 16–32 MB optimum to efficiently operate most programs
• Appropriate hard disk storage—80 MB is standard, although a hard disk with 150–300 MB or more is highly desirable
• Monochrome (black-and-white), gray-scale, or color monitor
• At least one laser printer with a resolution of 300–600 dots per inch (dpi) or greater
• Software including a word processing program, such as Microsoft Word; illustration software, e.g., Adobe Illustrator or Aldus FreeHand; page layout software, such as Aldus PageMaker, QuarkXPress, or Ventura Publisher; and appropriate support software such as fonts, virus detection programs, and utilities

The total cost for a basic installation such as this would be in the $10,000–20,000 range. This approach would have a few disadvantages: the level of service would be very low; the user would lose the advantages inherent in outputting directly to film negatives for desktop publishing projects; it would limit the output of halftones and screen tints to low screen frequencies; and it would require the assistance of a service bureau for high-resolution output when needed.

Other equipment considerations. To expand the basic system to a higher level of production and output, the following options should be considered:

• An 8-bit gray-scale or color desktop scanner
• A full-page monochrome, gray-scale, or color monitor
• High-resolution video card or accelerator—a 24-bit or higher color card is required for most image editing or color-correction applications; accelerator boards are needed for fast color display
• Image editing software
• A local-area network (LAN) that permits easy file exchange and peripheral sharing among various devices
• A high-resolution PostScript imagesetter with the ability to output 12-in. (305-mm) or wider film or resin-coated (RC) paper
• An appropriate film processor
• Modem and telecommunications software
• Tape backup system

The addition of these options significantly improves the speed of throughput and the final level of quality. All system configurations should be kept modular, so that additional workstations can be added easily as required, making investment a gradual process and keeping the ability to upgrade the system as more powerful hardware or software is introduced. Brief descriptions of each of these options are provided below.

An 8-bit gray-scale scanner can reproduce 256 gray levels, which is consistent with those in traditional halftone photography. However, color/gray-scale scanners are now available for about the same amount of money that a gray-scale-only device cost just a few years ago. Most manufacturers are also offering scanning packages that include image-editing and/or OCR software.

Large, monochrome (black-and-white), gray-scale, or color monitors dramatically increase productivity by allowing the user to see every element on the page at actual size. This reduces the need to zoom in and out to view portions of the page as required on small monitors. Monochrome monitors depict every element in black-and-white. Gray-scale monitors display 256 levels of gray, allowing the user to edit scanned black-and-white images. Color monitors are necessary to scan or edit color images. Color adapter cards expand the number of colors represented on the monitor. A 4-bit card displays 16 colors, an 8-bit card displays 256 colors, and a 24-bit card will display over 16 million colors. To perform quality color correction or editing, the 24-bit card is preferred.

Networking is a justifiable option when managing several workstations. It provides a means to transfer files from one computer (or platform) to another and allows several systems to share peripherals such as printers, plotters, scanners, or imagesetters. Network servers are classified as "distributed" or "dedicated." Dedicated servers are preferred. Distributed servers are recommended for use only in conjunction with a dedicated server.

High-resolution imagesetters are capable of producing monochrome and/or color separation output of complete page layouts including images. A low-cost capstan imagesetter with a repeatability within 2–4 mils provides quality output of text, line art, and spot-color separations. A more expensive capstan device can have a repeatability within 1–2 mils, which is acceptable for color separation work. Drum imagesetters produce the highest quality color separations since they have a repeatability rate of 1 mil or less. Also available are large-format imagesetters that are capable of outputting impositioned pages to larger-than-normal film widths.

Another option would be to dedicate one computer to telecommunications by connecting it to a

modem for 24-hour service. Some form of automatic backup system should also be considered to secure all jobs in production as well as the system configuration and software.

File and system backups are important. Downtime can be crippling when backups are not available. The more time spent on a job, the more valuable it becomes. Every effort should be made to build a system that provides for simple and/or automatic backups. In addition to a backup system, power protection is also a must. Surge protectors and uninterruptible power supplies can cost a mere $20 or as much as $1,000.

These system add-ons provide many benefits; however, the price for such a system could easily exceed $200,000. The cost of such a configuration can be reduced by using a high-resolution plain-paper laser printer (such as a 600- or 1200-dpi machine) for final output, if this level of quality is acceptable to the customer base.

Storage options. Soon after the electronic prepress system is in place, the need for additional means for storing data becomes apparent. Documents created in page layout programs quickly outgrow the storage capacity of floppy diskettes. Scanned gray-scale and color images can have file sizes from 2–20 MB or more. For this reason, many users are now turning to external hard drives, removable-cartridge drives, or even optical disk drives.

Removable-cartridge drives typically hold 44 or 88 MB of data. Optical disk drives can hold 600 MB or more of information. They are great for storing clip art, fonts, color images, or large documents such as books and catalogs.

Justifying the expense. In order to justify the expense of such a system, the user should consider the following:

- The financial impact of the system, including equipment and training of personnel
- Reduced design, typesetting, and layout costs
- Increased revenue from extended deadlines
- Internal control achieved over editing, design, and page preparation
- Reduction in charges for author's alterations

Typical Products

The specific configuration desired will be greatly influenced by the types of services to be offered. It will also be influenced by the types of products to be produced.

The basic system described earlier is well-suited to handling products such as flyers or brochures. Higher productivity can be achieved by adding a large monitor capable of displaying at least one full page at one time. Color work would require the use of a color monitor, a 24-bit or higher color card, and, for even greater productivity, a color PostScript proofing device.

Halftones or full-color images produced on computer systems have several drawbacks. If scanned images are to be included, provisions must be made for large amounts of memory and disk storage, as well as graphics accelerators to speed display processing. To attain reasonable output speeds, purchase the latest and fastest raster image processor (RIP) when selecting the output device.

It is important to produce appropriate products on these systems. Large directories, for example, may be easier or faster to produce on other systems. Projects with a number of color images to be assembled might be handled more efficiently by using the equipment only to output type and geometric shapes or by using a desktop-to-prepress link.

Staffing the Department

Staffing—hiring, training, and ongoing technical support—is one of the most important, yet least emphasized aspects of electronic prepress. Today's systems are sophisticated, requiring knowledgeable users. Problems that are not supposed to come up frequently do, and someone must be able to solve these problems while keeping the system running.

Staffing requirements for these activities will vary based on the type of services offered. Printers or service bureaus offering consulting services to their customers will need highly qualified experts capable of meeting with clients and offering them practical recommendations. In-house users will need less expertise and will not need the ability to communicate well with customers. In-house users are the easiest to train since they will only need to work with the specific combination of hardware and software used in their production environment. Staffing requirements will be more stringent for those companies that offer consulting or training or provide a service bureau. These employees should be conversant in a wide variety of hardware configurations and software applications and have excellent troubleshooting skills.

New equipment installations should be coordinated with the staff involved. Place a great deal of emphasis on immediate training and include plenty of time for practice.

Computer Systems

Personal Computers

Investing in a personal computer for electronic prepress production should be thought of in different terms than investing in other pieces of printing equipment, such as an offset press or saddle stitcher. Such traditional printing equipment has a reasonably long life span and is usually replaced on a predictable schedule. Computer systems have short life spans, largely due to the rapid evolution of these systems. Frequently, a personal computer needs to have its memory upgraded, have coprocessor chips installed, and/or have **input/output** (I/O) boards replaced, as more efficient systems become available.

Personal computers include a monitor, which may be either internal or external; the keyboard, which may be offered in various models; a mouse, which may come standard or may be optional; and firmware, usually in the form of read-only memory (ROM) chips mounted on the system board to provide basic software functions to the computer upon startup.

A basic difference between the various models of personal computers concerns the capabilities and peculiarities of its microprocessor. Two basic families of microprocessors are used in the most popular personal computers: the Intel 8086 family used in the IBM and compatible machines, and the Motorola 68000 family used in the Macintosh.

Macintosh. The Motorola 68000 family used in all Macintosh computers is a 32-bit microprocessor. The models since the Macintosh II use the Motorola 68020, 68030, or 68040 (commonly referred to as the 020, 030, and 040 processors); these microprocessors use a 32-bit data path.

The Macintosh was designed with the system software integrated into the entire product. Much of the system software is built into ROM (firmware). A collection of these routines is commonly known as **QuickDraw.** QuickDraw images the icons, menus, windows, and fonts found on the screen of a Macintosh. QuickDraw's code has been optimized before being stored in ROM chips, which has made its most important graphic routines available to the computer for fast execution. The current operating system used on Macintosh computers is called System 7.

Macintosh computers come in a variety of packages and models, including portables. The high-end models of the Macintosh line, such as the Quadra series, are commonly used for electronic prepress production.

IBM PC and compatibles. The IBM and compatibles use a CPU from the Intel 8086 family, which includes chips such as the 8088, 8086, 80286, 80386SX, 80386DX, 80486SX, 80486DX, P5 (Pentium) or a "compatible" chip from one of several manufacturers. The total number of chips available from Intel and the other companies is probably over 50 because each type of chip is available in varieties that operate at different clock speeds (e.g., 12 MHz, 20 MHz, 25 MHz, and 33 MHz).

The IBM and compatible computers have an open architecture, in that they have expansion slots to accommodate circuit cards for numerous functions, including support for a monitor, serial and parallel printers, modems, and expanded memory, as well as many special-purpose input and output tasks. A number of the compatible models have some of the basic functions built into the machine itself and do not require the purchase of as many expansion cards.

IBM PCs and their compatibles come in a variety of packages, including desktop models, portables, laptops, hand-helds, and towers. Regardless of the packaging or manufacturer, they all share a number of common characteristics. They all are capable of running some version of DOS, although other operating systems may be used on some of them as well, including Unix and OS/2. Their central processor is a member of the Intel 8086 family or a compatible chip, although specific differences exist in terms of size, speed, and other characteristics. They all have expansion slots and a standardized data bus to take advantage of the many add-on products available.

Unix-based workstations. Most Unix workstations have a 32-bit microprocessor, usually a member of the Motorola 68000 family, although Intel and various proprietary processors are in use as well. Most Unix workstations have large, high-resolution, bitmapped displays with approximately 1,000,000 pixels. The system RAM may be as large as 64 MB or more.

Unix workstations come in models with large amounts of hard disk storage or as diskless workstations that rely on a network file server for storing programs and data.

Monitors

The monitor helps determine the resolution and accuracy that is possible with the system. Monitors are measured diagonally in inches. They are also rated by pixel resolution expressed as the width in pixels by the depth in pixels. Different monitors have different aspect ratios between the screen and actual output. For electronic prepress production, it is important to have a 1:1 correspondence between the monitor and output in order to accurately align sample copy and layouts to the screen.

Monochrome monitors. A monochrome monitor is often chosen over color for some electronic prepress applications because it is considerably less expensive and faster to display images than a color monitor.

In selecting a monitor, important considerations include the size, sharpness, degree of flicker, glare, and other visual defects across the entire screen, software enhancements, and support by desired application software. From the user's standpoint, freedom from glare and sharp focus are of primary concern.

Monitors are available in a number of standard resolutions. A monitor using a **color graphics adapter** (CGA) has a resolution of 320×200 pixels, and one with an **enhanced graphics adapter** (EGA) renders up to 16 colors at a resolution of 640×350. The **video graphics array** (VGA) monitor has a resolution of 640×480 (720×200 in DOS text mode). **Super VGA,** or **16-bit VGA,** increases the resolution of VGA to 800×600 (Super VGA) or 1024×768 (sometimes referred to as extended VGA).

One specialized type of monochrome monitor is the gray-scale monitor. These are most useful for dealing with scanned images, especially for image manipulation purposes. Gray-scale monitors are available in large sizes and usually support up to 8 bits per pixel, resulting in 256 levels of gray being displayed on the screen. Standard bitmapped monochrome displays can simulate shades of gray by dithering or creating patterns of black and white pixels to simulate gray, but the results are crude by graphic arts standards. Color or gray-scale monitors can display true shades of gray, making them more desirable for applications such as image retouching and scanning.

Color monitors. Color monitors are described by their size and resolution, by their total color palette available, and by the number of colors they can display at any one time. The 32-bit version of QuickDraw, for example, supports a palette of 16.7 million colors. For many applications, a color palette of 16.7 million colors is not necessary. For example, if equipment is used for occasional spot colors, the color on the monitor does not have to be a photographic reproduction of the color desired on the press sheet. However, many applications require hardware and software that can handle color photographic images at graphic arts quality levels. For these applications, monitors that support a color palette with millions of colors are a necessity.

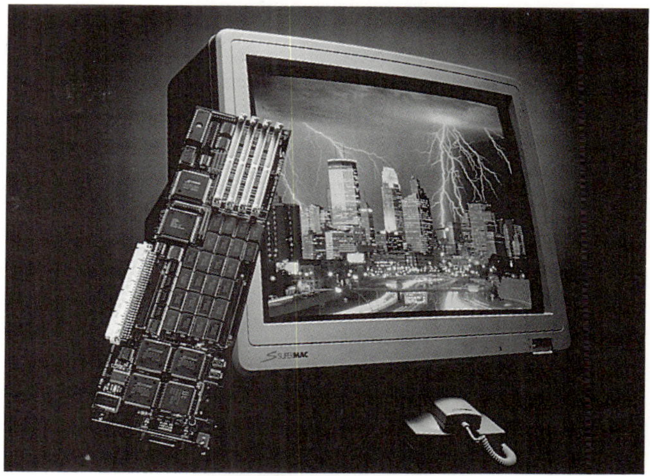

Courtesy SuperMac

A SuperMac color monitor with a 24-bit graphics accelerator card.

Color displays require significantly larger amounts of RAM than monochrome displays. Often some of the additional RAM required for a color monitor is on the video board itself. Color graphics adapters can produce two kinds of output: **composite video,** which mixes red, green, and blue together into a composite signal; and **RGB video,** which keeps each signal distinct. Composite video can be used to control a monochrome display as well as a color one, which RGB video cannot. RGB, however, provides a higher-resolution display.

Full-page monitors. Large monitors are a major productivity improvement for electronic prepress. They permit working on a page at actual or nearly actual size without having to constantly scroll or zoom the image. Monitors oriented in the vertical direction are called **portrait monitors** and easily display an entire page at one time. These are typically about 15 or 16 in. (381 or 406 mm) in size. Monitors in the 19- to 24-in. (483- to 610-mm) size can display up to two pages at once. A virtual screen is available with some large monitors, per-

mitting an even larger image to be worked on by panning the edges of the display when the cursor touches them. Although full-page and two-page displays are expensive, they represent a significant method of speeding up electronic prepress operations by permitting the operator to work at actual size with little scrolling or zooming required.

Memory

Computer memory, or **random-access memory (RAM),** is a key part of computer systems used in electronic prepress. Its speed, cost, size, power requirements, and upgradability are all important factors for consideration.

The speed of RAM is measured in nanoseconds (ns), which are billionths of a second. Smaller numbers represent faster chips. Common speeds used with personal computers are 150 ns, 120 ns, 100 ns, and 80 ns. A 386 or 030 processor running at 20 MHz needs RAM in the speed range of 80–100 ns. Slower chips can be used, but they cause wait states. If the processor is faster than memory, it must wait for memory to catch up.

RAM normally is manufactured on chips with either 256 kilobits (Kb) or 1 megabit (Mb) per chip. Since there are usually 8 bits per byte, either eight 256-kilobit RAM chips or eight 1-megabit RAM chips are used to make a RAM bank of 256 KB or 1 MB, respectively. Some computers, however, need nine chips rather than eight, if they use the ninth bit as a parity bit to verify that there have been no errors in transmission of data in the computer.

Many electronic prepress production applications require large amounts of RAM to work effectively. This usually means a minimum of 2 MB. In most cases, 8 MB or more is recommended, especially if scanning and creating complex graphics are routine operations. Font rendering on the screen typically uses significant amounts of RAM. Graphics programs that use curves and that describe complex shapes typically require large amounts of memory.

Scanners, particularly those designed to scan continuous tone with multiple gray levels, require very large amounts of RAM. A consideration when purchasing a scanner and planning to manipulate scanned images in various software packages must be the amount of RAM required to handle the images without running out of memory.

Mass Storage

Mass storage—the storage and retrieval of information on magnetic floppy disks, rigid disks, magnetic tape, and optical media—is an essential component of any system. Mass storage is used to store and retrieve applications, text, and graphics, for backup purposes to prevent data loss, and for archival purposes.

Floppy disks. Floppy disks are a common, inexpensive, and easily transportable storage medium. They are generally not used for running programs, since they are relatively slow—typically ten times slower than the slowest hard disk. They represent the most common method of distributing software and are useful for backing up smaller hard disks in the range of up to 20 MB. Floppy disks also represent the most common way that customers deliver jobs to commercial printers or service bureaus.

Several disk formats are in common use, although they are not necessarily compatible with one another. Two sizes of floppy disks are used with IBM PCs and compatible computers—5¼ in. and 3½ in.—but not all computers support both sizes. Several standard storage densities also are used. For PCs using 5¼-in. disks, the standard densities are 360 KB and 1.2 MB. For PCs using 3½-in. floppy disks, the densities are 720 KB, 1.44 MB, and 2.88 MB. The Macintosh computers use 3½-in. floppy disks in three standard densities: 400 KB, 800 KB, and 1.4 MB.

Hard disks. Hard disks, or rigid disks, are sealed in a clean environment. They may be written to at a much higher density and accessed at much higher speeds than a floppy disk. The access time of a hard disk is usually measured in milliseconds (ms)—thousandths of a second. Typical speeds vary from 14 to 80 ms. Transfer speeds are also important in evaluating overall disk performance.

Several standards specify how the hard disk is connected to the motherboard of the computer. The following are the three most common interfaces: **enhanced small device interface** (ESDI), **integrated drive electronics** (IDE), or **small computer system interface** (SCSI). With an IDE, the control circuitry is build into the disk and the motherboard. With ESDI and SCSI, a separate adapter is required.

In addition to the standard hard disk system, also available are removable cartridge disks. A cartridge is essentially a cross between a floppy and a hard disk, housed in a sealed rigid plastic case. These cartridges are removable and hold over 40 MB of data. Cartridges represent a good way of securing data, since they may be physically removed to a safe location.

Magnetic tape. Magnetic tape, the least-expensive source of mass storage, is normally used in electronic prepress for backup purposes. Daily backup is inexpensive insurance against loss of data.

Tape cartridges that use ¼-in. (6-mm) tape and that are known as DC2000 are a common backup medium. Normally they have a capacity of 40 MB per tape cartridge, but higher-capacity tapes are available. A cartridge using the DC600 format, a higher-density version, typically holds 150 MB or more. The TEAC format, which is also popular, holds up to 150 MB. Nine-track reel-to-reel tape is useful for exchanging data tapes or reading data tapes from minicomputers and mainframes.

Digital audio tape (DAT) and 8-mm videotape are also used for data backup. DAT cassettes with 4-mm tape hold up to 1.3 Gb. The 8-mm tape holds 2.2 Gb.

Optical disks. Optical disks use lasers for reading and writing information. More data can be stored on an optical disk than on a magnetic disk. Three types of optical disk storage are in general use: CD-ROMs; write-once, read-many [times] (WORM) disks; and erasable optical (EO) disks, sometimes also magneto-optical (MO). Access times are typically two to six times slower than high-quality magnetic disk drives.

CD-ROMs and compact disks come in a standard 120-mm (4.7-in.) size. CD-ROMs are useful for distribution of large amounts of information not requiring frequent updating. Examples would include databases and clip art libraries. Another popular use of CD-ROMs is for the storage of photographic images in a special format known as Photo CD.

With a WORM disk, information can be both read and written to disk, but it cannot be changed once it is written. WORM drives are useful with information that is custom yet rarely changes, and where the cost and inconvenience of mastering a CD-ROM is not warranted. Examples of its use include legal evidence, medical records, and back issues of newsletters. A 5¼-in. (133-mm) WORM disk holds 300–600 MB per side. WORM disks are available in a variety of sizes.

Magneto-optical (MO) disks are currently available with storage capacities in the range of 640 MB. As part of a jukebox system, these disks can provide 30–50 Gb of on-line storage.

Networking

Networking permits the sharing of expensive resources, such as high-resolution output devices, and it provides an easy way to transfer files between different types of computers connected to the network. Networking may involve as few as two computers or as many as hundreds or thousands.

A **local-area network** (LAN) is made up of computers and shared resources that are physically connected, usually in a single building or limited area. A **wide-area network** (WAN) uses computers that are far apart and are connected by telephone, satellite, or microwave links.

LANs are useful for sharing resources, such as printers and imagesetters, modems, fax machines, and software applications. In sharing software on a network, a site-licensed network version of the software is installed on the file server so that a number of users can access it simultaneously. This is less expensive than purchasing a separate copy of the software for each user; however, the design of the network must take into account the amount of usage of the system to ensure adequate performance of the application when run in a networked mode.

Network services can be delivered in a variety of ways, which are characterized by different combinations of hardware and software. All but the peer-to-peer method of networking requires a central or dedicated computer. With a peer-to-peer system, network services can be provided by installing software programs on each computer connected to the network. With a dedicated, or centralized, system, file servers may run on specialized hardware and are designed specifically to accomplish networking tasks efficiently.

A file server is one of the main features of most networked computer systems. File servers allow users to exchange files and applications, to copy and update data to a personal computer from the file server, and to load applications and files on the server as if they were located on their own local hard disk.

A valuable use of a network is to make high-cost resources such as printers and imagesetters available to all users on the network. Output devices with appropriate interfaces may be connected directly to the network and may be shared by the connected computers. One drawback to a network printer or imagesetter is that there may be a significant wait to use the output device. A **print server**—sometimes called a **print spooler**—helps to eliminate this bottleneck in network printing. A dedicated print server or a multiple-service computer running spooling software intercepts all files sent to the output device and stores them on its own hard disk. Then it transmits these files

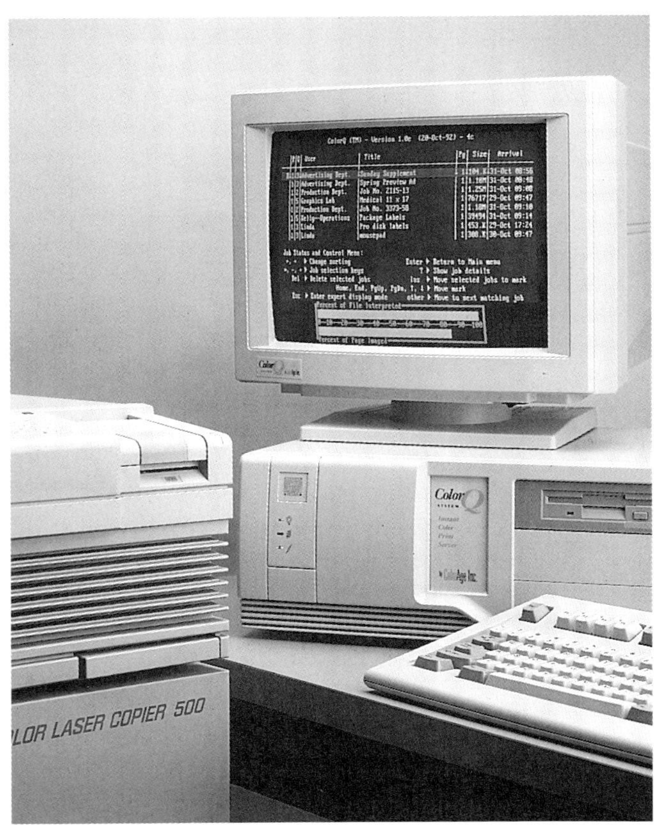

Courtesy ColorAge, Inc.

The ColorQ *(right),* a network color print server, shown connected to a color laser copier.

individually to the output device when it is ready. This system allows the user to regain immediate use of the computer rather than waiting for printing to be completed, and the order of printing spooled documents may be changed by the users as required.

A network is made up of nodes, each representing a computer, workstation, or other network device. Transceivers interface the computers to the network media or wiring system. Other important components of the network include shared printers, servers, and appropriate network software.

The network media—the cabling and wiring that interconnects a network—is the most visible and most expensive part of a network. Different types of media have different characteristics that need to be considered in an installation. The medium used by a network limits the transmission speed possible. Network transmission speeds are measured in bits per second, with ratings usually specified as kilobits per second (Kb/s), megabits per second (Mb/s), or gigabits per second (Gb/s).

The primary network media are twisted-pair wiring, coaxial cable, and optical fiber. **Twisted-pair wiring** is one of the most popular wiring systems for local-area networks because of its low cost and ease of installation. Twisted pair is made up of two separately insulated wires that are twisted together and covered by an insulated casing. **Coaxial cable** (coax) has higher performance than twisted-pair wiring and as a result is the media of choice for higher-speed networking. It is similar in construction to the wire used for cable TV: a central conductor is covered with insulation, a braided wire shield, and finally an insulated cover. **Optical fiber** is known for its fast rate of data transfer, long distances it can cover, and freedom from electrical interference. High-performance networks use fiber optics as the network medium.

The architecture of a network has to do with how the parts are arranged and how information is transferred in an orderly fashion without becoming jumbled with other information traveling on the network simultaneously. Network topology is the physical layout of a computer network. Three popular topologies are (1) the **linear bus** topology, which has two distinct ends with all nodes coming off the central part of the network; (2) the **ring** topology, which has each node connected to its adjacent nodes forming a closed ring; and (3) the **star** topology, which has all nodes radiating out from a central controlling node.

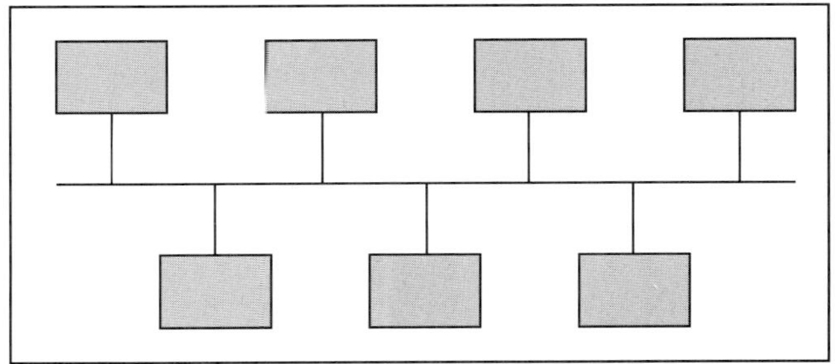

Linear bus topology for a computer network.

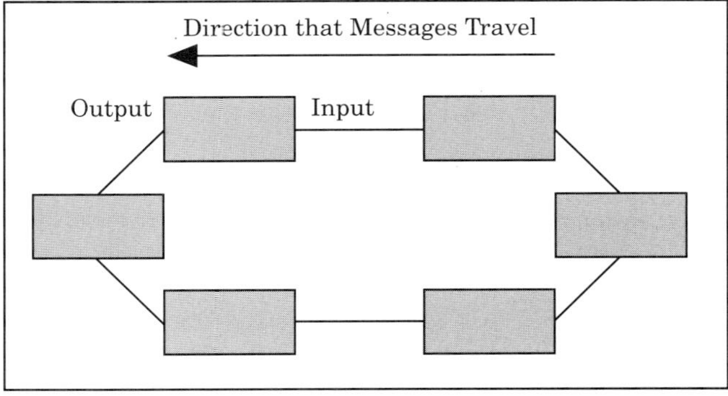

The ring topology for a computer network.

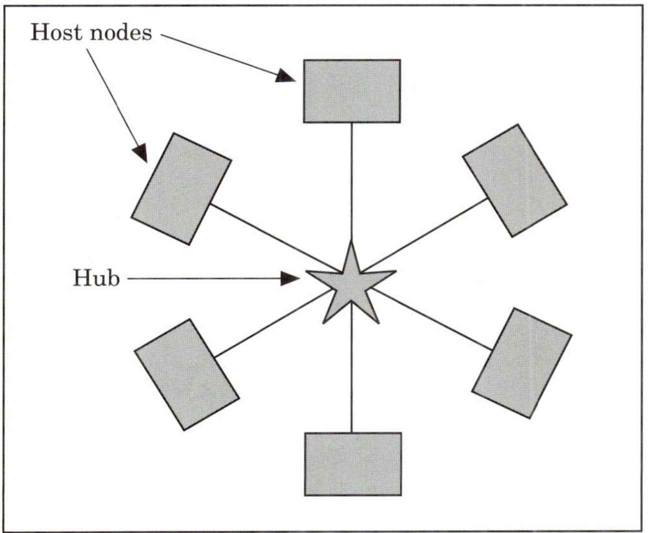

The star topology for a computer network.

Connecting networks together. A repeater may be added to a network to increase the maximum length between nodes or the maximum overall length of a network. Repeaters can also extend the total number of nodes that can be used on a network or connect two smaller networks into one. Repeaters amplify and retransmit signals on the network to prevent them from becoming weakened. One method of improving network performance is to split a large network into smaller ones so that messages do not have to travel through the entire network, increasing the traffic. A **network bridge,** a hardware device, connects two networks in such a way that they appear as one to the network users. A bridge can read the node address on each packet and selectively transmit it to the proper destination. A **router,** a more intelligent bridge, selects the most efficient data path to send information and can automatically provide detours if a connection is broken on a given path. A **gateway,** a sophisticated hardware device, connects different types of networks. The purpose of a gateway is to translate from one network the different addressing, protocol, and message content required to receive the information on a dissimilar network. Ethernet cabling is frequently used as a backbone to interconnect various dissimilar networks.

Modems

Digital information cannot be transferred over phone lines directly. It must first be **modulated,** or converted to an analog signal that can then be sent over the phone. At the receiving end, the modulated signal must in turn be **demodulated,** or converted back to a digital signal. The term "modem" is a contraction of "modulator-demodulator." Modems also handle many telecommunication tasks related to the telephone itself, such as making sure that a dial tone is present, dialing the phone, checking for a computer answering at the other end, looking for busy signals, and hanging up the phone when appropriate.

Several types of modems are on the market. Most are compatible with the Hayes modem command set. This means that if a modem is 100% Hayes compatible it should work with nearly any telecommunication package desired. The Hayes commands—sometimes referred to as the Hayes AT command set—provides a standard method for applications to communicate with and control the functions of a modem. It should also be noted that some modems available today also function as facsimile (fax) machines.

Scanners

Applications

Desktop scanners help to automate and streamline the production of halftones and color separations. Many black-and-white and color scanner halftones are used as low-resolution position-only prints that indicate the actual size, positioning, and cropping desired for a conventionally produced halftone or color separation.

Scanners also offer the means to incorporate line art and logos into printing jobs without the use of conventional cameras. Scanners are commonly used to input templates for creating vector art, especially with PostScript graphics programs. These templates are rough bitmaps that are traced—either automatically or manually—in the PostScript graphics program to create the high-resolution artwork.

Optical character recognition (OCR) is another application of desktop scanning technology. In the past, OCR was a major investment that used proprietary hardware. Today most OCR systems can use standard scanners, which are also used for various other scanning applications. OCR is most commonly sold as a software package that runs on off-the-shelf desktop computers.

Line art and logos. Line art and logos may be incorporated into jobs using conventional cut-and-paste techniques and graphic arts cameras to complete sizing as needed. Desktop scanners, however, offer a relatively inexpensive means of completing this work electronically. This can be especially useful when a job is output on a high-resolution imagesetter using film, as it eliminates extra time and materials spent in camera and image assembly. Output to plate material requires that all graphics be incorporated in a file prior to generating the plates electronically. From the designer's perspective, it is helpful to be able to manipulate a scanned graphic within a page layout program. There it can be positioned and sized as the type is being assembled on the page. The results of this process are better than waiting for photostats to be completed, since the image on the monitor provides instant feedback to the designer.

Desktop scanners usually have an input resolution of approximately 300 dpi. More-expensive desktop scanners are available with resolutions up to 900 dpi or greater. The files created by these higher-resolution scanners can be very large, which tends to cause problems. Sizing the scanned images may also present problems, as this will change the resolution of the image. A better solution for many applications is to use a lower-resolution scanner to create relatively coarse bitmapped scans of line art and logos. These scans may then be used as tracing templates with vector drawing programs to create high-quality artwork that requires little file storage space.

Templates for creating vector art. PostScript graphics programs offer some of the best potential use of scanners. One way of creating illustrations is to trace an existing piece of artwork. This artwork may be clip art, a company logo, or a pencil illustration drawn specifically for this purpose. The existing artwork may then be scanned at a modest resolution in order to create a template that will be used for tracing within a PostScript graphics program. Scanning at a resolution of 72 or 75 dpi will often be adequate to provide the detail needed for tracing. This results in a quicker scan and a much smaller file size. Images that are more detailed may be scanned at appropriately higher resolutions for tracing purposes.

The scanned template is turned into PostScript vector art through the use of the tools provided in the graphics application. Autotracing of the template may speed this process. **Autotracing,** also known as **raster-to-vector conversion,** is available in most of the PostScript graphics programs and as stand-alone applications. These files may then be brought into PostScript graphics applications for editing and enhancements as needed. The resulting PostScript files from this process are compact and device-independent; that is, they contain the PostScript code necessary to image the artwork at the full resolution of any desired PostScript output device. When a file is saved in a PostScript graphics application using the encapsulated PostScript format (EPSF or EPS) option, most programs also generate a low-resolution screen image of the artwork. This screen image is useful when the artwork is placed in a page layout program, as it indicates the exact position of the graphic and provides visual feedback when sizing it as well.

PostScript graphics programs can be used to create high-resolution film masks for use in color image assembly. These films are used to mask conventionally produced color separations, in order to make the image assembly process more efficient. The PostScript programs have the added advantage of being able to incorporate screen tints into the films.

Halftones and color separations. Creating halftones and color separations using desktop scanners has some problems. The major problems involve the large file sizes involved, the importance of color calibration, and the time required to move the digital images through the system, from the scanner, to the disk, to the display, to the CPU for image processing, and to the output device for imaging. In some cases, producing conventional camera halftones and high-end drum scanner color separations is still faster, better, and cheaper than producing their desktop equivalents, although the number and quality of halftones and color separations produced using desktop scanners is increasing.

The quality of desktop halftones or separations is dependent to a great extent on the resolution of the scanner. If not enough data is recorded by the scanner, high-resolution output cannot be produced. A general rule of thumb is to scan the image at a resolution twice the final screen ruling. For example, if the final screen ruling will be 150 lines/in., the resolution of the scanner should be at least 300 dpi, which is twice the screen ruling.

Black-and-white and color position prints. Low-resolution scans used for screen display can be an effective use of desktop scanners. This process allows the customer to see the exact location, cropping, and sizing of each photograph. **Position-only**

prints, also called **"for position only"** (FPO) prints, are popular as a means to ensure clear communication with regard to the location, sizing, and cropping of each photograph. These position-only prints are often made as conventional, low-quality black-and-white halftone prints. Photos scanned on a desktop system effectively function as position-only prints. File sizes can be small, since high resolution is not required—usually only the resolution of the monitor, or about 72 dpi, is needed.

These FPO prints may be used to assist in sizing, cropping, and assembling high-resolution black-and-white halftones and separations conventionally or electronically. They may also function as electronic position prints in linking a high-end **color electronic prepress system** (CEPS) with a desktop publishing system. With this approach a high-resolution scan is completed on a conventional scanner. A screen representation, or low-resolution image, is transferred to the desktop publishing application. There, the screen image is sized, cropped, positioned, and rotated as desired. When the document is completed, including all type, the entire file is transferred to the CEPS equipment. At this stage, the original high-resolution scan is sized, placed, rotated, and cropped to replace the low-resolution screen image. This approach maximizes the potential of each type of equipment.

Optical character recognition. Optical character recognition (OCR) provides a means of inputting copy that is not already in electronic form. OCR has the potential to automatically recognize clean manuscript copy, saving it on disk. Some OCR systems can also scan typeset text, including text positioned in multiple columns on a page. Furthermore, some systems are able to distinguish between text to be recognized and saved, and graphics to be captured and saved, using the appropriate file formats for incorporation into a document. Some problems encountered with OCR systems concern accuracy, setup or training time, and speed of throughput.

Types of Scanners

Different physical formats and imaging formats are available in popular scanner models. Usually Macintosh scanners plug into the built-in SCSI port, while on PCs, an expansion card is required. Most desktop scanners are based on a sensing element known as a **charged-coupled device** (CCD) that has many light-sensitive receptors. When light hits each receptor, it is charged with a voltage proportional to the light striking it. Although most scanners are based on CCDs, they vary significantly in how the CCD is mounted, how the scanner is designed, and how many bits are used to store each sample of the scanned image.

Several physical formats are found in desktop scanners today. The flatbed scanner is perhaps the most popular because of its high-quality and moderate cost. Some scanners accept reflection copy (photographs), others accept transmission copy (slides and transparencies), and still others accept both reflection and transmission copy.

Hand-held scanner. This type of scanner looks like a hand roller connected by wire to the computer. It is rolled across the part of a page or image desired for scanning. This type of scanner is inexpensive, but the quality is generally low. It may be suitable for capturing logos or letterheads for tracing templates. In some cases the aspect ratio of an image may be distorted as the scanner is rolled over the image. Hand-held scanners are poor for images taller than 3–5 in. (76–127 mm) since these need to be scanned in several passes and are difficult to align after scanning. Hand-held models are available in resolutions up to 400 dpi.

Sheetfed scanner. Sheetfed scanners use a system of rollers to guide the original past the CCD. The rollers, however, make accurate alignment difficult, and preclude scanning from books or rigid artwork. Rotating the resulting scans in software is possible, but this has drawbacks as well. The transport system on sheetfed scanners can also mar the original and can make it difficult to scan small pieces of art. Many sheetfed scanners come with an optional **automatic document feeder** (ADF). This is particularly useful with OCR software, since an entire manuscript can be loaded in the ADF for scanning and recognition.

Flatbed scanner. A flatbed scanner consists of a glass-covered box that resembles a photocopy machine. Originals are placed face down while the CCD or a mirror assembly moves past the image. Like sheetfed scanners, an ADF option is available and recommended for OCR applications.

The flatbed scanner design offers an advantage not found with the other models described: an image may first be scanned quickly at a low resolution, followed by a selected area scanned at a high resolution. This is possible because the original stays in its same location on the scanner glass. Most software supports this function, which is useful to keep the size of image files small. The quick

scan is displayed on the screen, where the user can draw a selection box to indicate the area to be included in the final high-resolution scan. Most flatbed scanners have a resolution of at least 300 dpi and provide 256 gray levels.

Overhead scanner. Overhead scanners consist of a platform with a digitizer mounted from above. This permits overhead scanning of images such as books and small three-dimensional objects as well as flat sheets. Some overheads have their own overhead lighting units. Overhead scanners are often expensive models and cannot use an ADF for OCR work. Some offer resolutions as high as 900 dpi.

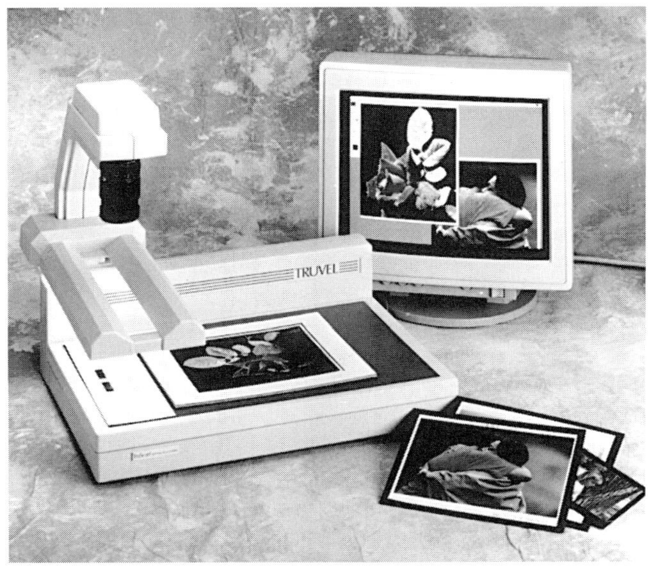

Courtesy Truvel, a division of Vidar Systems Corp.
TruScan 3D overhead color scanner.

Slide scanners. Slide scanners are becoming increasingly popular for color work since transparencies are a common high-quality color image source. These scanners generally use 35-mm slides for input, which is one of the most popular photographic formats. Because of the small size of the original slides, much higher resolutions are often found on these scanners, sometimes exceeding 4,000 dpi.

Drum scanners. Desktop drum scanners are input-only devices that have a high-speed rotating drum and use **photomultiplier tubes** (PMTs) instead of a CCD array to record the image. High-end drum scanners used in traditional prepress production also use PMTs. Typically three photomultiplier tubes are used to record blue-, green-, and red-filter signals. PMT-based drum scanners typically have resolutions of 600 to 4000 dpi, and they can distinguish a wider range of gray levels than a CCD-based scanner.

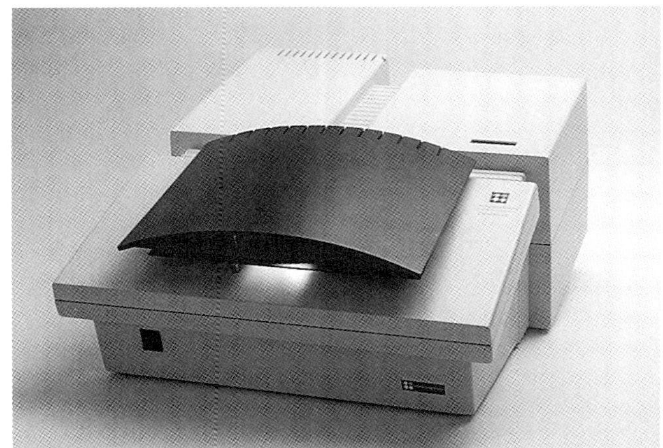

Courtesy PixelCraft, Inc.
4520 RS, a color slide scanner with a resolution of 2000 dpi.

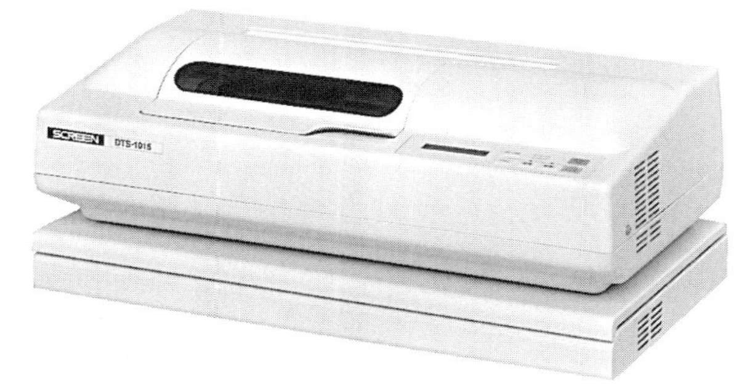

Courtesy Screen (USA)
DT-S1015 color drum scanner.

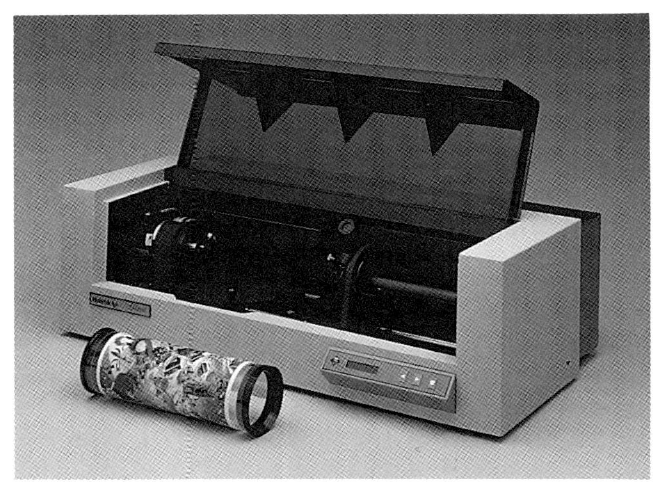

Courtesy Howtek, Inc.
Scanmaster D4000 drum scanner.

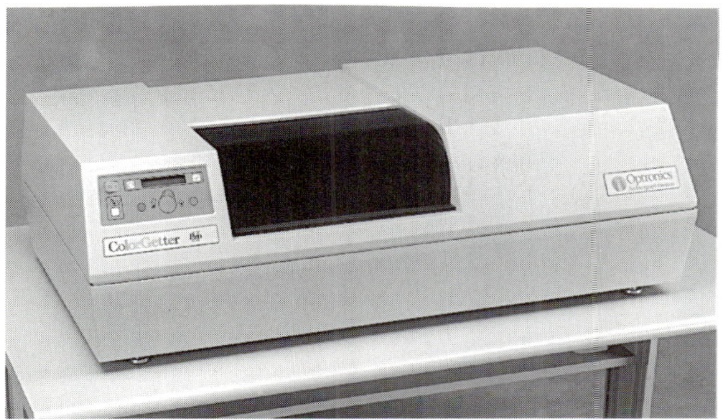

Courtesy Optronics, an Intergraph Division

ColorGetter II Pro color drum scanner.

Imaging Format of Scanners

The different physical formats found in popular scanners are distinct from the data formats of the images captured. Images scanned from the equipment discussed above may be line art, gray scale, or color. Except for low-end products, most scanners support all three types of image capture.

Line art. Line art is an image that is either black or white with no shades of gray. A line art scan is stored as a bitmap of the image. Since each bit representing the image is either black or white, this is often referred to as a **bilevel scan,** or **one-bit scan.** This type of scanning is commonly used for input of tracing templates to be used with PostScript graphics applications. Many scanners, when operating in their line art mode, have software for simulating halftones at the time the image is scanned. This process, known as **dithering,** places pixels in such a way that they simulate shades of gray. The resulting patterns may emulate conventional halftone dots or may be any of a variety of other dither patterns.

Gray scale. Gray scale scanning captures a photograph as a continuous-tone image. Each pixel of the scanned image has a particular level of gray assigned to it, based on the brightness of that spot in the original photograph. The number of levels of gray that may be assigned to each pixel is determined by the design of the scanner. Increasing the bits per pixel allows more gray levels to be stored. Pixel depth is the amount of information that can be stored about each pixel. Increasing the pixel depth provides more information about the original photograph but also increases the size of the resulting file. Scanners that store 4, 6, and 8 bits per pixel are common, but 8-bit scanners are becoming the most popular. This is because 8 bits per pixel results in 256 levels of gray, the amount usually necessary for a quality halftone.

Storing photographs as gray-scale images allows the user considerable freedom in manipulating the images after they have been captured. Gray-scale images may be edited with respect to their brightness, contrast, size, tone reproduction characteristics, and sharpness. In addition, these files may be extensively retouched in appropriate image manipulation software. The final halftones, at the desired screen frequency, are generated by PostScript during the output process.

Color. In considering a desktop color scanner, the entire cost of the system must be evaluated. This includes not only the scanner itself but also a powerful personal computer or workstation with a large amount of RAM installed; possibly a graphics accelerator; an appropriate color monitor; a high-speed network; and a storage system that can handle the huge amount of data to be put through the system.

Most color desktop scanners capture a total of 24 bits of information, with 8 bits for each of the three primary colors (red, green, and blue). A good original may have brightness values that exceed this capability, so tonal compression is necessary. Typically detail is lost from either the picture highlights or shadows. Ideally, the color monitor used to view images thus scanned should be able to image 8 bits per color, for a total palette of over 16 million colors. Less-expensive color monitors can only display a total of 8 bits for all colors, generating a palette of 256 colors. If an image scanned at 24 bits is to be displayed on an 8-bit color monitor, the image must first be converted to 8 bits.

Color scanners usually come with software to control scanning and image manipulation. Some systems provide options for built-in color correction. Most color scanners provide controls for characteristics such as brightness, contrast, color balance, cropping, and tone reproduction curve.

Related Input Devices

Still video. Electronic still-video cameras offer the potential of complete electronic imaging of photographs from the moment of clicking the shutter on a camera to the output of final film or plates on an imagesetter. Still-video cameras, which have been introduced for the consumer and professional market, capture an original scene using a CCD mounted at the film plane on a special camera. The scene is stored on a floppy disk. These images can

be displayed on a TV monitor using a player or still video camera equipped with playback mode. Unwanted images can be erased, and the entire disk can be used an infinite number of times, eliminating the cost of film.

A device known as a **frame grabber,** or **video digitizer,** may be connected to the computer in order to digitize the still-video image. During this stage, the image is converted from its native analog form to digital form. It is also converted during this process to the appropriate file format for importing it into the image manipulation and page layout software.

Video digitizer. A video digitizer, mentioned above with reference to still-video cameras, can also be used to capture any video signal. In addition to working with still-video images, frame grabbers can also digitize images from broadcast TV, video cassette recorders, and video cameras. Images thus captured can be modified and enhanced in appropriate editing software and merged into documents created with page layout programs.

Digitizing tablet. A digitizing tablet is an alternate input device to a mouse. The flat surface of the tablet may vary in size from about 12×12 in. to 40×60 in. (305×305 mm to 1016×1524 mm) or larger. This surface has fine sensing wires embedded in it that work with a puck or stylus. A **puck** is a pointing device that resembles a mouse, and a **stylus** resembles an electronic pen. Unlike a mouse, which usually relies on a rolling ball to indicate the relative position of the cursor, a digitizing tablet senses the exact position of the puck or stylus by its electronic impulse. As a result, a digitizing tablet gives an accurate one-to-one aspect ratio for drawing. These are popular input systems for computer-aided drawing (CAD) applications. They permit accurate same-size tracing of artwork.

Output Devices

Output systems are characterized by a diversity of resolutions, speed, controlling electronics, imaging technologies, and transport mechanisms. Color output devices are also available. They are most commonly used as proofing devices, because they are usually low-resolution devices. Among the technologies used in these color output devices are ink jet, thermal-transfer, and dye-sublimation.

Although most output devices used in electronic prepress are based on lasers, other marking engines

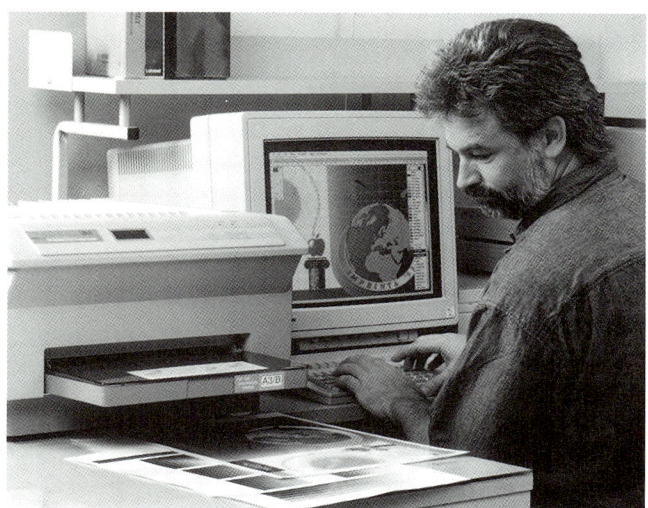

Courtesy 3M

3M Rainbow desktop color proofing system, which includes software and a dye sublimation printer.

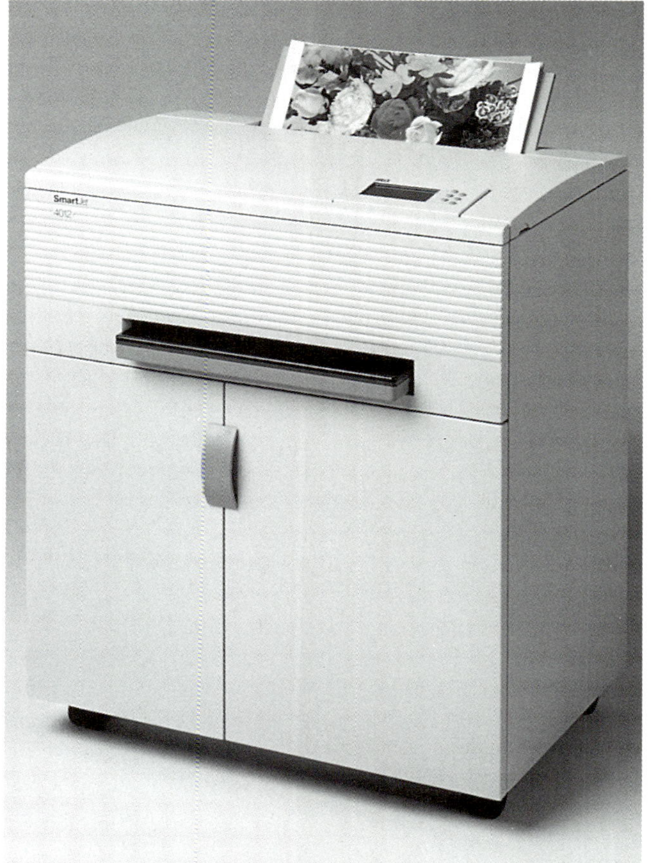

Courtesy IRIS Graphics, Inc.

SmartJet 4012 continuous ink jet color printer.

or output technologies are found; for example, ink jet and light-emitting diodes. Regardless of the type of marking engine, current output devices are raster printers and therefore require a means of taking commands for type and graphics and rendering these as bitmaps. This step of rasterizing the data takes place in what is known as a **raster image processor** (RIP). Therefore, output systems usually include a marking engine, a RIP, and an interface between the RIP and the computer used to drive the system.

This is the basic configuration, but many other options are available. One RIP may be connected to several different marking engines, providing bitmaps for different devices with different resolutions. A RIP may be equipped with more than one interface to make it compatible with a variety of computer systems. One marking engine may have more than one RIP connected to it. This may be desirable to improve processing, or support different input command languages. RIPs are controlled by an input command language, also known as a **page description language** (PDL). The most popular PDL today is Adobe PostScript.

Raster Image Processor

Most raster image processors are PostScript compatible; that is, they are able to interpret the PostScript page description language. PostScript commands are generated by the printer driver on the computer being used. These commands are transferred to the RIP through the printer interface, where they are converted to the bitmaps necessary for printing on a raster printing engine. The RIP itself may be located in a number of places. It may be in the same cabinet as the output device, as with many laser printers; it may be housed in a separate compartment, as with many high-resolution imagesetters; or it may be a software RIP located on the personal computer used for the electronic prepress applications.

PostScript is designed to take advantage of application software such as draw programs and page layout software that generate vector data. Raster files, such as those created with paint programs, keep their original resolution—usually tied to the monitor resolution—and generally do not improve as they pass through the RIP. The RIP is designed to take vector graphics, such as lines, shapes, fills, tints, and text, and convert them into bitmaps at the resolution of the marking engine. RIPs may be capable of rotating type, halftoning, and layering images. A variety of schemes for handling type are used in RIPs. As the image of the page is being built in the memory of the RIP, it is stored in an area known as a frame buffer until it is completed and ready to be sent to the marking engine. Some RIPs are designed to make use of a hard disk to store the entire frame buffer prior to imaging the page. Others use RAM for this purpose and are fast enough to rasterize the data on the fly while pages are being output.

With some output devices, the imaging system stops and starts as it is waiting for the RIP to complete its task. Unless special provisions are made this can result in fine screen tints showing banding effects or stripes.

In addition to PostScript, other PDLs are used. The most popular alternative to PostScript is the Hewlett-Packard Printer Command Language (PCL), used on LaserJet printers and compatibles. PostScript interpreters have become the most popular because they provide a wide range of abilities to image complex text and graphics across a range of output devices and resolutions.

A RIP may be designed to serve a number of separate print engines, and it is also possible to have several RIPs serving one print engine. Some systems consist of several RIPs along with several marking engines networked together. These approaches provide faster output for high-volume production, because the system will not bottleneck if one RIP is tied up with an extremely complex page, or if one output engine is busy imaging a particular page.

In most cases, only one PDL will be used on a given output system, although some products on the market support more than one control language, for example PCL and PostScript. Some systems support the mixing of different PDLs on the same page, which is useful in high-resolution systems that have their own proprietary PDL and RIP. It may be advantageous, for example, to merge files of different types on such systems in order to gain speed or quality improvements in the imaging of screens and halftones.

Marking Engine

Many marking engines are standardized products supplied as **original equipment manufacturer** (OEM) components to be assembled with other essential parts, such as a RIP, fonts, an interface, and a cabinet. With respect to laser printers, many are based on standardized print engines from manufacturers like Canon. The products are therefore usually differentiated by the controlling electronics

such as the RIP, the interfaces, the spot size available, optional paper handling equipment, and the software.

Different output devices with a wide range of resolutions are based on similar technology. Most raster printers use a laser in their marking engine. Other imaging methods are also found, such as ink jet, light-emitting diode (LED), and liquid crystal shutter (LCS). Lasers have become popular for raster printers because they provide an intense, coherent light with a very small spot size that can be accurately positioned and modulated as desired. Both gas lasers and solid-state or laser diodes are found in a variety of output systems having a broad range of resolutions. Laser diodes are less expensive than gas lasers and are generally found in laser printers rather than in high-resolution imagesetters. This trend is changing, however, since many leading manufacturers of high-resolution devices are offering lower-priced models that use laser diodes and higher-priced models based on gas lasers. This is due partly to recent improvements in solid-state lasers and partly to new photographic papers and films that have been developed for use with these devices.

Laser diodes can be instantly switched on and off by the controlling electronics, whereas gas lasers require a warm-up time and therefore need to have a shutter or light modulator added to pulse the light beam. The RIP controls the "on" and "off" pulses of the laser light. While the light is being pulsed, it is also swept across the exposing section of the output engine. The most common means of sweeping the laser beam is a rotating mirror. This mirror is generally made with several facets in order to move it quickly across the exposing section of the machine. After each raster line is swept across the exposing section, the output media is advanced by one scan line until the entire page is imaged.

The output media, along with the type of laser, printer construction, and exposing optics, contribute to the differences among marking engines. A laser printer uses a photoconductive drum or belt. The laser light induces an electrostatic charge in the photoconductive surface. Toner powder or liquid is attracted to the image areas on the photoconductor. The toner is then electrostatically transferred to paper where it is fused to the surface with heat. In a photographic marking engine, the photoconductor is replaced with photographic film, paper, or plate material. The original high-resolution imagesetters used media from a roll, while some of the newer models use a sheetfed drum design for better dimensional stability.

Electrostatic marking engines can be designed to be write-white or write-black. The write-white system uses the laser to erase the background, leaving the image areas properly charged to accept toner. Because of the necessary overlap of laser spots, this can result in images that are somewhat thinner than desired, with ragged edges, particularly at lower resolutions. Write-black technology is designed so that the overlapping spots expose the desired image areas, therefore creating characters that are somewhat fatter than desired, although not as ragged as with write-white systems.

Output Media

The application programs in electronic prepress are capable of providing output to a variety of systems using different media with little need for conversion of files or other inconvenient procedures. This is mainly due to the device- and resolution-independent nature of PostScript.

Plain paper. Plain paper is used in devices that range from 300 dpi to over 1,000 dpi. The "plain paper" used on many desktop printers is usually a specially coated paper designed for optimum results with a laser printer. This provides better blacks and sharper characters than is possible with normal bond or copier paper. However, the term **plain-paper printer** is appropriate to describe machines that do not need to use photographic materials, or the chemicals and processing equipment normally associated with them. This output medium is widely used to proof jobs that will eventually be output using a photographic medium. This medium can also be used as final output at 600–1,000 dpi if the quality difference is not important but cost savings in photographic consumables are significant. It should be noted, however, that even 1,000-dpi plain-paper pages need to be photographed for most printing operations. Outputting these pages to film on a high-resolution device may therefore be justified by the savings in camera time and subsequent retouching of the films during image assembly.

Resin-coated paper. Resin-coated (RC) paper is the standard photographic material used in typesetting systems. It provides a high-resolution image with a solid, dense black, on a bright white base. It is ideal for work that needs subsequent mechanical pasteup; e.g., incorporating type and graphics with prescreened paper halftone prints. When selecting an output device that uses RC paper, film, or plates, consideration must be given to the requirements for

an automatic film processor, including consumables, maintenance, and appropriate handling and disposal of spent chemical solutions.

Film. Film has many inherent advantages as an output medium for a high-resolution imagesetter. If the job will be printed using a printing press, output to film is often cost-effective. The majority of applications support output to film in either positive or negative format, both right-reading and wrong-reading. Additionally, many software applications can automatically generate crop and register marks on the films. The resulting films generally produce pages that are sharper and cleaner than those generated by shooting RC paper on a process camera.

Film is especially desirable for jobs that require screen tints and would otherwise necessitate labor-intensive image assembly and film contacting. The quality of screen tints output to RC paper can be a problem because it is difficult to maintain good dot quality when those pages are photographed using a process camera. Direct film output to an imagesetter also provides the advantage that no time-consuming manual opaquing or retouching is required. Because camera negatives are eliminated, the common problems of overexposure and underexposure are also eliminated.

Plates. Photographic plate material can be imaged on some high-resolution imagesetters. Direct-to-plate technology has the advantage of eliminating not only pasteup, camera, and image assembly tasks, but also platemaking. Short-run applications can benefit from direct-to-plate technology.

Resolution

For the purposes of this book, output resolution is divided into low-end, 300-dpi systems; mid-range, 600-dpi devices; and high-end, with resolutions of 1,000 dpi or greater. Resolution is a major determinant of text quality and screening capability. Also important to overall quality is the spot size itself.

Resolution and addressability are different. **Resolution** is determined by the spot size, but since the spots may overlap, the distance between the center of each spot, or the **addressability,** may be different than the resolution. Two printers with the same rated resolution may produce images of different quality. In addition to these factors, specific optical differences exist between machines with similar resolution ratings, such as the size, shape, and consistency of the imaging spot. Mechanical differences and electrostatic methods used also significantly affect the output quality of different printers.

Low-resolution devices. The low-resolution printers are popular as output devices for final pages of work of a nondemanding nature. They are useful for generating proofs of pages that will be output to compatible high-resolution devices, thereby saving the expense and time involved in proofing on the high-resolution device.

Mid-range devices. Through changing the controlling electronics it is possible to drive some of the 300-dpi print engines in higher-resolution modes. A variety of printers have been designed specifically for resolutions of 600 dpi or more. A printer in this category will typically be useful for many more categories of final output than 300-dpi devices. A major distinction between the output possible from printers in this category and that found on imagesetters, however, is that imagesetters are capable of photographic output on a variety of media.

High-resolution devices. This category includes plain-paper machines with resolutions of 1,000 dpi or greater and photographic imagesetters. The standard industry definition of true typesetting quality is 1,000 dpi or greater. Commercial quality screens and halftones usually require a resolution of 2,000 dpi or greater.

In the area of high-resolution plain-paper output devices, several manufacturers have provided

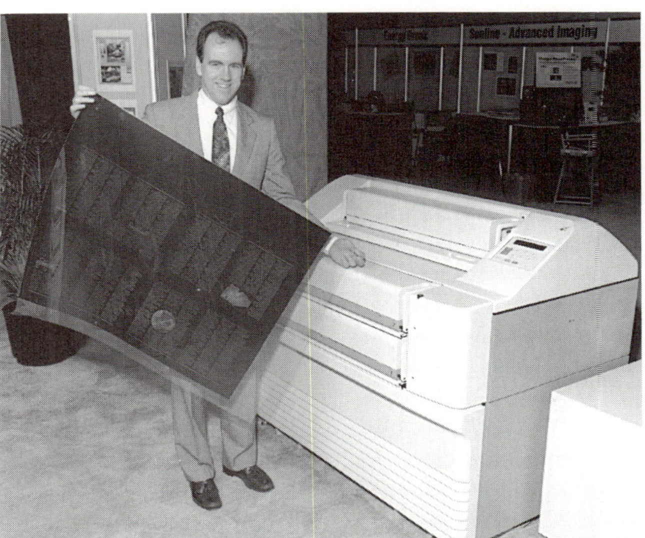

Courtesy Hyphen, Inc.

A plate-ready imposed film that was output on the large-format imagesetter at the right, Hyphen's Spectraset 4800.

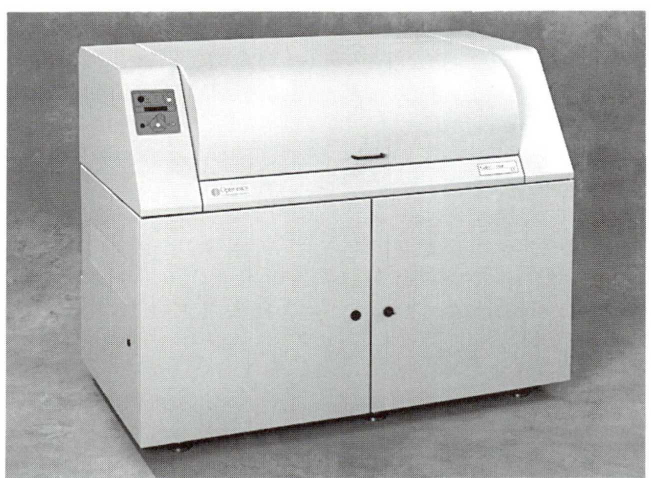

Courtesy Optronics, an Intergraph Division

The ColorSetter XL 4000, a large-format imagesetter.

systems that have a 1,000- to 1,200-dpi resolution across the page by 500–600 dpi down the page. These provide significantly better resolution than the mid-range devices, though at somewhat higher prices. These printers have been used as high-quality proofing devices or final output systems designed to save on photographic consumables.

The high-resolution imagesetters are of three general designs: flatbed (capstan), external drum, or internal drum. With a flatbed imagesetter, the film is feed from a roll of output media (paper, film, or plate) and passes over a flat imaging bed. As the film or paper moves across the imaging bed, a laser images the output media. With an external drum imagesetter, the output media (in sheets) is manually positioned onto the drum, which uses vacuum to hold the film in place. An imaging head scans across the drum as it rotates. With an internal drum imagesetter, the output media is fed from a roll into the stationary drum automatically. An imaging head on a spindle rotates and travels across inside the drum to image the output media.

Resolution and Screen Frequency

Type and illustrations can often be reproduced adequately at modest resolutions, but when selecting an output device for use with screen tints or halftones, higher resolution is desirable. The number of gray levels obtainable on an output device is directly related to the resolution of that device and screen frequency or ruling desired. The number of gray levels determines the number of discrete screen tints printable, whether banding effects will be noticeable on tint gradations, and to what extent tones will appear smooth on printed halftones.

A photo with an insufficient number of gray levels appears too high in contrast. This reproduction can even take on the appearance of a **posterization,** an image in which the tones are grouped into distinct levels rather than blending smoothly together. For example, if a 300-dpi printer outputs a 53-line screen, only 33 different shades of gray result. This makes many photos appear somewhat blotchy, instead of having smooth tonal transitions. Even newspapers typically use screens of 65 lines or better. But by increasing the screen ruling to a 71-line screen and printing it on a 300-dpi printer, the number of shades decreases to 19, far worse than with the 53-line screen.

In a halftone image, there should be at least 100 shades of gray, and preferably 256. A 71-line screen can produce 256 shades of gray if the resolution of the output device is 1136 dpi. A printer with a resolution of 2,400 dpi is needed to generate 256 shades of gray with a screen ruling of 150 lines per inch, which is the level of quality needed for most commercial printing.

PostScript

Adobe PostScript is the most widely used page description language in electronic prepress production. It allows a file to proofed on a 300-dpi laser printer and output to a 2,540-dpi imagesetter without modification of the source file. This is possible because PostScript was designed to be a device- and resolution-independent system.

Both hardware and software components make up the PostScript standard. The hardware component of the standard is the PostScript interpreter. The function of the RIP is to interpret PostScript page descriptions and create a bitmap for imaging by a raster printing engine. PostScript printers range in resolution from 300 to over 3,000 dots per inch; however, the same page data can be imaged on any of them without modification. This is because in normal PostScript page definitions, no device coordinates are specified. It is the job of the RIP to convert the coordinates defined in the page description into the actual device coordinates.

The software component of the PostScript standard is the PostScript page description language. It includes arithmetic, boolean, string, program control, and file operators. These operators are present to complement its powerful graphics capabilities.

In normal circumstances, the application and system software printer drivers automatically generate the PostScript page description, which in turn is interpreted by the RIP. Application programs

that can output PostScript page descriptions are available today on nearly all types of computer systems. The user seldom works with the page description coding at all, since the application and system printer drivers generate this code automatically. It is also possible, however, for a user to write PostScript programs directly that will result in printed pages. This is typically done to achieve graphic effects not available in commercial software or to solve other problems. PostScript programming is a skill that is useful when outputting pages on a high-resolution printer.

The manner in which the PostScript imaging model treats text as a graphic element makes it useful for creating special text effects. Such effects are difficult to achieve on traditional typesetting devices without resorting to labor-intensive manual techniques including pasteup, airbrushing, process camera work, and image assembly manipulation. These text effects include the ability to rotate, slant, stretch, skew, mirror, reverse, curve, shade, shadow, and outline. PostScript's ability to render lines, curves, and shapes makes it an excellent tool for creating detailed illustrations. Programs such as Adobe Illustrator and Aldus FreeHand allow graphic artists to use many of these capabilities.

The PostScript or other codes sent to the printer by most applications can be intercepted and captured on disk. This is one method of submitting a file to a PostScript service bureau. It is particularly useful if the service bureau or commercial printer does not own the application used to print the file. The PostScript code saved on disk can be downloaded to the printer with a downloading utility program. In addition, this captured PostScript code can be edited in a word processor, since PostScript programs are written in plain ASCII text. Various PostScript commands can be thus inserted into files for printing in order to achieve effects not possible with standard applications.

Several important extensions have been added to a second-generation PostScript, called PostScript Level 2. Most significant are new methods for handling screen angling, image compression, and support for device-independent color. Also included are enhancements to printer memory usage, fonts, Display PostScript, image templates, and patterns.

Rendering of Screens

The rendering of screens on output systems used in desktop publishing and electronic prepress production is becoming increasingly important, as users create more of the finished product within the desktop system and save costs traditionally associated with conventional prepress production. This currently is most prevalent in the use of screen-tinted shapes, screened type, color-separated synthetic images created in vector programs, and black-and-white and color halftone reproductions. The important characteristics to screening in these output systems are discussed below.

Screen ruling. Screen ruling (or the number of screen dots per linear inch) and resolution are the determining factors for the number of gray levels that can be imaged with a particular screening system. Each PostScript printer has a predefined default screen ruling. PostScript, however, has a straightforward command to change the screen ruling, and many applications give the user access to this capability. Most of the popular PostScript graphics programs are able to create tonal and color gradations or blends. In order to minimize **banding,** or visible tonal changes, care must be taken in selecting the proper screen ruling and number of steps in the blend.

Dot shapes. PostScript provides considerable flexibility in creating screens that have dots shaped in custom ways. It is possible to write PostScript procedures to define numerous dot shapes.

Screen angles. Monochrome images are traditionally screened with the dots at a 45° angle, an angle at which the dots are least noticeable to the viewer. In conventional color separation, the screen angle of dots in color images are normally placed 30° apart from one another wherever possible to minimize moiré patterns. Because of the way in which digital halftone dots are formed out of smaller pixels, the rough edges of the dots can cause moiré problems even when screens are angled 30° apart. Manufacturers of imagesetters have addressed this problem and have developed several patented techniques to eliminate moiré and to improve screening in general, including stochastic screening.

With conventional and most digital halftones, the dots are usually positioned in the center of a halftone cell, and the illusion of tones is produced by varying the sizes of the dots, not their positions within the cell. With **stochastic screening,** the illusion of tones is produced by increasing the number of micro-sized dots (spots) in a small area, rather than increasing their size. In addition, the position of the spots is random in comparison to a conventional halftone. Stochastic screening is sometimes called **frequency-modulated screening**

because the position of the spots is based on changing the spacing (frequency) of the spots rather than changing the size of the dots.

Image detail. PostScript generates a digital halftone dot made up of individual pixels to represent each tonal value. The tonal value is equal to the average gray level for the corresponding sample of the original continuous-tone image. PostScript, however, does not take into account adjacent samples, nor does it attempt to alter the shape of the dot based on the shape of the image, such as takes place in conventional contact screen halftoning. To illustrate this, suppose that part of a given image has a sharp transition from black to white. If a halftone dot falls right on the edge, its gray level will be 50%. However, the PostScript dot shape—with the center pixels turned on—creates a ragged edge on the image. But if the halftone dot could have 100% of its pixels turned on for the part of the dot covering the dark area of the image, and 100% of its pixels turned off for the part of the dot covering the light area of the image, the results would be far superior.

Software

System software—the operating system and various associated utility programs—is largely determined by the hardware platform selected. Choices, however, can be made regarding the version of software and options to be selected for optimum performance.

A distinction may be made between system software and application software. Most **system software** comes standard with a computer and is required for its basic operation. The operating system is the set of instructions that manages a computer's basic resources: regulating the flow of activity and controlling each of the peripherals, including the disk drives, printers, monitor, etc.

Application software is a program that performs a specific function, or *application,* such as graphics, word processing, database management, or page layout. The application depends upon the system software for many of its functions and must be compatible with the version of the system software on the computer at the current time.

The reader should be aware that features described in various software packages in this section are subject to change with new releases.

System Software

The operating system is functional whenever the computer is in operation. The user does not always interact with the operating system and may not be aware of its presence or the various tasks that it controls. Although it completes most of its functions transparently to the user, the operating system is responsible for operations such as controlling the central processing unit (CPU), disk drives, printers, and other peripherals. The user interaction with the operating system mainly takes the form of file management tasks and launching applications.

An operating system consists of a number of programs or program modules that coordinate the operation of the computer's hardware and software. The operating system controls input and output tasks, manages files, and processes commands issued by the user. Some operating systems provide additional functions such as a security system, time-sharing capabilities, and program development tools. A program may be overlaid on top of the basic operating system to give the computer a particular user interface.

On IBM PCs and compatible machines, the operating system used most often is known as MS-DOS, named after the development company, Microsoft Corporation. DOS is an acronym for **disk operating system.** Most IBM PS/2 computers and compatible computers can also use an operating system known as OS/2, which also functions as a graphical user interface. Macintosh computers have their

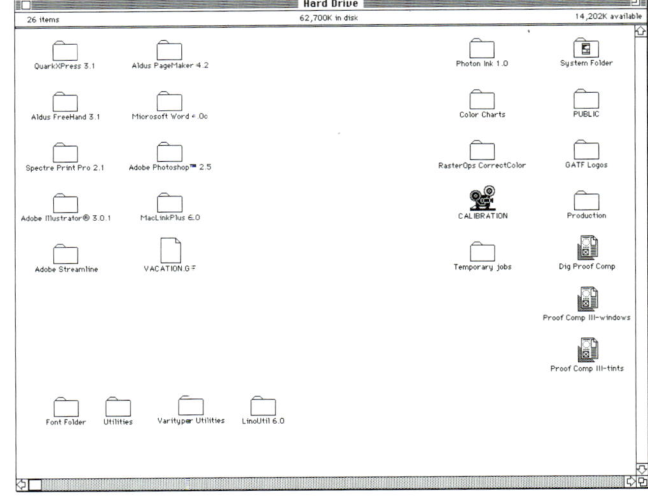

The graphical user interface (GUI) on a Macintosh computer.

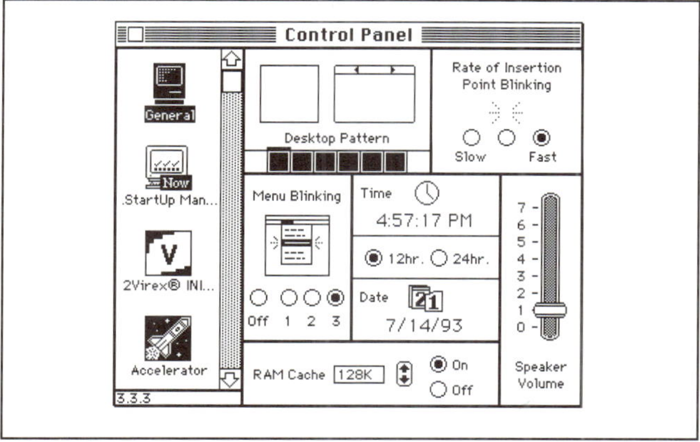

The control panel on a Macintosh computer, where the computer user can control a variety of computer functions, such as setting the clock, adjusting the speed of the cursor, changing the speaker volume, and adjusting memory allocation.

own operating system, called System 7. There are many varieties of the Unix operating system.

A computer system with a graphical user interface (GUI), such as Microsoft Windows in the PC environment, is important. GUIs permit short learning times and easy completion of sophisticated file management tasks. The ability to suspend one task to complete another and then return to the first instantly can make a personal computer highly efficient. While working in a page layout program, for example, the user may notice a graphic that needs to be edited. Context switching allows the page layout operations to be halted, the graphics program to be activated and, after editing, the page layout program to be reactivated. An extension of this principle is **multi-tasking,** wherein several tasks operate concurrently on the same processor. An example is the automatic composition of a document that might take many minutes. While this task is being completed, another document can be worked on simultaneously, or an entirely different program can be launched.

Networking permits multiple users to work together as a group in completing activities. The operating system should support the various network functions such as file sharing, printer sharing, and electronic mail (E-mail).

The basic user interface found with MS-DOS and Unix computers consists of a command line at which appropriate commands are issued. The GUI popularized by the Macintosh uses appropriate menus and icons for each operating system function desired; typically, file names do not need to be typed to execute a command since they are chosen from a list of available file names. It is more difficult to automate sequential procedures with a GUI since icons may be located in a different place on the screen when they are needed in the future. Command-driven operating systems may have a graphical shell placed over them, as is the case with Microsoft Windows for MS-DOS.

Word Processing Software

Word processors have far more features today than they did even a few years ago. Excellent word processors are available for each of the major computer platforms. Some programs work on different computer platforms and may be accessed by users on a network. Word processors are the primary means of entering text for desktop publishing and electronic prepress production. After the text has been entered into the word processor, it may be formatted and assembled using a page layout program. Alternately, simple projects may be output directly from the word processing application.

For the majority of users who work with page layout software for final assembly of documents, it is important to select a word processor that is fully supported by the page layout software that will be used. Nearly all page layout programs will import files saved in a word processor as a text-only document. However, all of the formatting information, such as the fonts, type sizes, and styles are lost with this approach when the file is saved as a text file. The word processor should be able to save files in a manner that retains the formatting information and is supported by the page layout program that will be used to assemble the document.

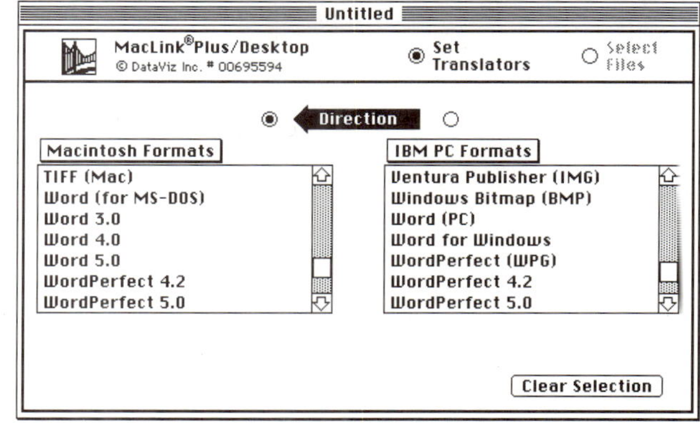

MacLink Plus, from DataViz, Inc., a program that converts various file formats, including popular word processing programs.

Features. Word processing is a highly competitive marketplace, and the list of typical features grows as it becomes hard to differentiate the contending

manufacturers. In the PC environment, most companies market DOS and Windows versions of the same word processing program.

Most support the use of multiple fonts, in various sizes and styles. Many word processors today also permit the incorporation of graphics in some form within the word processor. Some also permit graphics creation, editing, and sizing, although these functions are usually basic compared with full-featured graphics applications. Nearly all word processors on the market offer a spell checker including a user-expandable dictionary.

Virtually all word processors provide the ability to find a text string and to complete search and replace operations. Some of the more sophisticated programs allow the user to search and replace particular fonts or sizes of type and provide the use of wild cards when performing search and replace functions. Formatting can also be automated in a word processor through the use of style sheets. These add a number of user-definable attributes to a paragraph simultaneously without the user having to enter the commands for each attribute separately.

Most word processors have mail-merge capabilities and the ability to automatically create headers, footers, outlines, and indexes.

Features associated in the past only with page layout applications are finding their way into word processors. Examples include kerning, automatic text flow around graphics or other defined areas, multicolumn pages, and the ability to create and edit graphics within the word processor.

Graphics Software

Like word processors, graphics programs have evolved rapidly with additional features introduced with each new release. Excellent graphics applications are available for each of the major hardware platforms.

In general, computer graphics applications are either raster or vector in nature. A **raster graphics program** manipulates and stores images as bitmaps. An application of this type is sometimes referred to as a **paint program.** The resolution available with paint programs is generally tied to the resolution of the monitor on the computer used to create the graphics. Typically what appears on the screen is exactly what prints out, even on high-resolution imagesetters. Because of the bitmapped nature of the graphics they create, curves, diagonal lines, and type will all have jagged edges, defined by the resolution of the screen.

Paint programs, however, are ideal for artistic expression. The user can create shading and textures that are difficult to achieve with other graphics applications. Raster graphics applications allow the user to magnify parts of a painting and edit those parts pixel by pixel. This is known as **pixel editing.** Some painting programs offer extended resolution by allowing the user to create artwork in enlarged views that will eventually be printed out smaller. Using this method, it is possible to have raster images with a resolution of 300 dpi. These higher-resolution images typically take a long time to create and edit and require extensive storage space.

A **draw program,** or **vector graphics program,** manipulates and stores images as objects. These objects are not bitmaps but are geometric descriptions of objects that may be easily edited. These vector descriptions are stored in files that

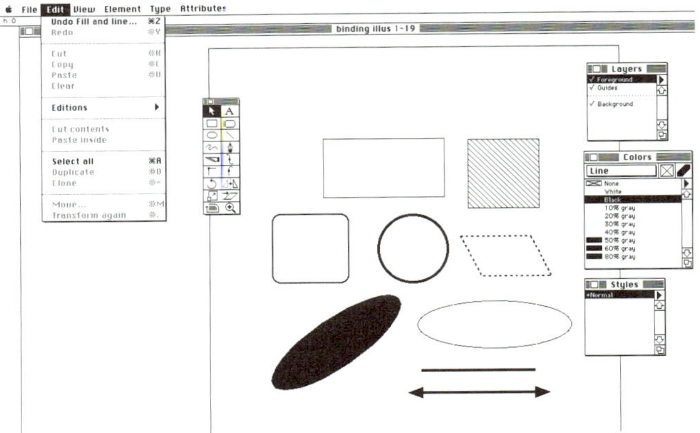

A variety of simple shapes that can be created using the tool palette in Aldus Freehand.

are smaller in size and are resolution-independent. This means that they will take advantage of the maximum resolution available on the output device. Images that look coarse on the screen, including curves, diagonal lines, and type will all print on laser printers and imagesetters significantly better than they appear on the screen.

A specialized type of graphics application is a vector program that is designed to take advantage of special features and characteristics of the PostScript language. These PostScript graphics programs are capable of creating sophisticated graphics, although they are harder to master than standard vector graphics applications. Another type of specialized graphics application is a program that combines vector and raster techniques in the same illustration. This allows vectors to be used for

type, curves, and diagonals, yet allows flexibility in adding shading effects with raster graphics tools.

Features. Most graphics applications provide a toolbox or tool palette with a number of icons representing the different functions available. Graphics programs provide the user with tools to create graphic primitives, such as lines, ovals, rectangles, rounded-corner rectangles, and text. The more sophisticated offerings provide additional special features, such as the creation of both irregular and regular polygons including user control over the number of sides desired on regular polygons. Some programs give the user a choice of creating elements from either corner to corner or from the center of the element out, for maximum flexibility. All such programs provide control over the thickness of line weights, but some programs offer much finer increments than others. Similarly, all programs offer the ability to fill graphic elements with shading or patterns.

All of the graphics applications provide various functions for editing, including the standard cut, copy, paste, and undo functions. Some programs offer such features as the ability to stretch, distort, slant, or create a perspective.

Most programs provide the means to enlarge or reduce all or part of an image; some programs permit this to be done to a specific percentage, and to different degrees in the horizontal and vertical planes. The PostScript programs give the user the option of either scaling or not scaling the line weights when enlarging or reducing elements. Photographic scaling automatically scales line weights proportionately to the scaling applied to the entire drawing. The ability of PostScript drawing programs to scale line weights separately means that a large drawing can be digitally reduced to the point where lines would normally drop out and print poorly or not at all, yet these lines can retain their original weight, thus greatly improving the final quality.

Draw programs have some unique features. Since they are designed to be used in a more structured manner, draw programs normally have rulers for accurate measurements and grids to aid in positioning objects. Some software permits the customization of both the rulers and the grids for various purposes. For example, in business forms work it is useful to have a different grid in the horizontal axis compared with the vertical axis. An automatic alignment feature permits the user to select any number of objects and align them to one another choosing from a variety of useful options. Objects created in most draw programs may be grouped together and ungrouped as desired. Grouping essentially creates a new object out of the composite parts. The new object may be sized, rotated, shaded, or manipulated in various other ways as a single object rather than many component parts.

Most of the graphics programs operate on the principle that an outline or series of paths will be generated to create an illustration. Each path may be stroked with a desired thickness and color of line and filled with a desired screen percentage of any color. The paths or outlines making up the structure of the illustration may be drawn freehand, with the program interpolating rough movements to make them smoother.

Page Layout Software

Page layout, or page makeup, software allows the integration of text and graphics that may come from a variety of other applications. Page layout programs facilitate easy production of multipage documents, including those with unusual page sizes. They are well suited to documents that have a mix of text and graphics, particularly if the interaction between the text and graphics is complex.

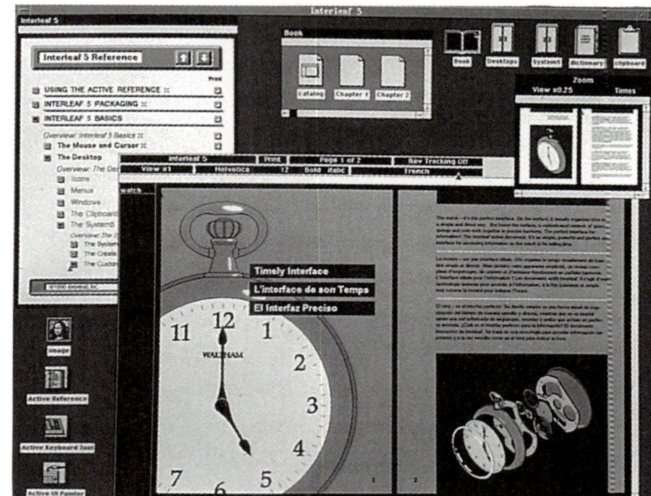

Courtesy Interleaf, Inc.

Interleaf Publisher, a page layout program.

Page layout software provides tools to crop and precisely position graphics on a page. The typographic control offered in this category of software is typically more sophisticated than that offered in word processing or graphics programs. Unlike most word processors, page layout programs permit the user to see various views of a document and to make changes at all views.

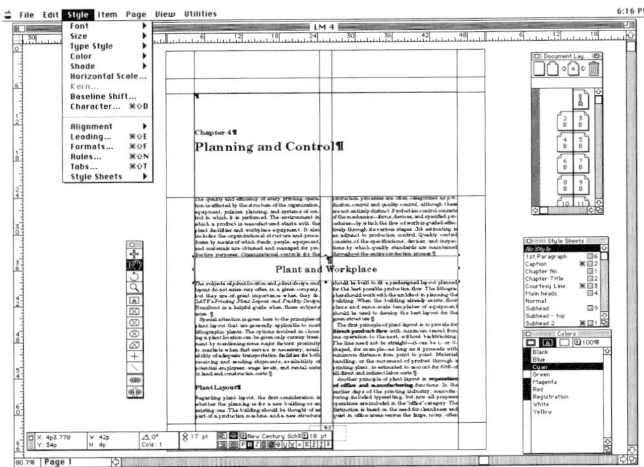

QuarkXPress being used to lay out the pages of the *Lithographers Manual.*

Page layout software also provides more flexibility than do most word processors in regard to the number of columns on a page. This can usually be specified for each page of a document and may even vary in different areas on the same page. Page layout programs are particularly good at combining work that was created in different applications. The user can thereby work with tools that are optimized for each part of the task and subsequently assemble all of the components in the page layout program.

Typical features. Page layout programs have a variety of methods for emulating traditional page layout techniques. They all allow the user to assemble and view the pages in WYSIWYG ("what you see is what you get") form on the screen. This is often done using on-screen rulers, grids, nonprinting guidelines, and/or measurement dialog boxes for precise positioning. A function known as **snap-to** is frequently provided to cause mouse movements that are close to a guide, ruler, or grid line to hit the alignment marks exactly.

The programs allow the user to import text from a variety of word processing programs and to place that text in the document in columns. Like text, graphics may be imported from numerous supported programs, and once positioned on the page, these may be sized, moved, cropped, and in some cases edited as desired.

Most programs use master pages that define repeating elements or formats that apply throughout a publication. Usually these may be created separately for left and right pages. Master pages can be canceled or deleted as needed on a page-by-page basis.

Most page layout programs provide several views of the page. These views may range from displaying a reduced thumbnail-sized page up to as large as 400% of actual size. In some cases, two-page spreads may be viewed at once. Most operations can be completed in all views. Through the use of keyboard shortcuts, an experienced user can quickly switch views to select the best for a given task.

In order to display reduced pages quickly on the screen, **greeking** (the use of horizontal lines to indicate the size, weight, and spacing of the text) appears in place of the actual text. In some programs, text greeking can be specified below a given point size to speed display times or to permit headlines to be readable in reduced views.

The available page layout programs vary with respect to which text editing functions they support. Some merely allow the user to delete or add text. Others are more extensive and include spell checkers and search-and-replace functions such as those found in the better word processors.

Most text handled in a page layout program will be imported from a word processor. Properly importing text means that the formatting as well as the text will be retained. This formatting may include fonts, sizes, type styles, tabbing information, indents, and styles. Virtually all page layout programs import what are known as ASCII text files, but these files include only the text portion of a document; all formatting information is lost and must be reentered in the page layout application.

Page layout software varies considerably with respect to the typographic capabilities offered. All offer a selection of fonts, type sizes and styles, and the capability to hyphenate and justify text. Some offer a wide range of word and letter spacing limits and offer sophisticated controls over hyphenation. Kerning is available in most page layout programs, and some of the programs support tracking (the

Page setup [OK]
Page: [Letter] [Cancel]
Page dimensions: [8.5] by [11] inches [Numbers...]
Orientation: ◉ Tall ○ Wide
Start page #: [1] # of pages: [1]
Options: ☒ Double-sided ☒ Facing pages
☐ Restart page numbering
Margin in inches: Inside [1] Outside [0.75]
Top [0.75] Bottom [0.75]

The page setup menu in Aldus PageMaker.

tightening of character spacing) automatically as the type size increases. Kerning is generally available in both manual and automatic modes.

The graphics capabilities of page layout programs permit the user to import files from graphics programs that are supported. They also allow the user to create basic graphics without leaving the page layout program. The basic graphic functions in most page layout programs include the ability to draw lines, circles, ovals, rectangles, and squares. These objects can be shaded, filled, sized, moved, and have their line thicknesses adjusted.

Automatic text-wrap around graphics (a runaround) is available in most programs. This permits the user to specify the amount of space around a graphic element and to have the text run around that area automatically.

Color support grows more important in today's page layout applications. Programs use some or all of the following color models to create color documents: CMYK (cyan, magenta, yellow, and black), RGB (red, green, and blue), HSB (hue, saturation, and brightness), and one or more proprietary color matching systems. Color page layout can include the ability to apply color to text, graphic fills, and lines. It also takes the form of compatibility with a variety of color file formats and may include links to high-end color prepress systems.

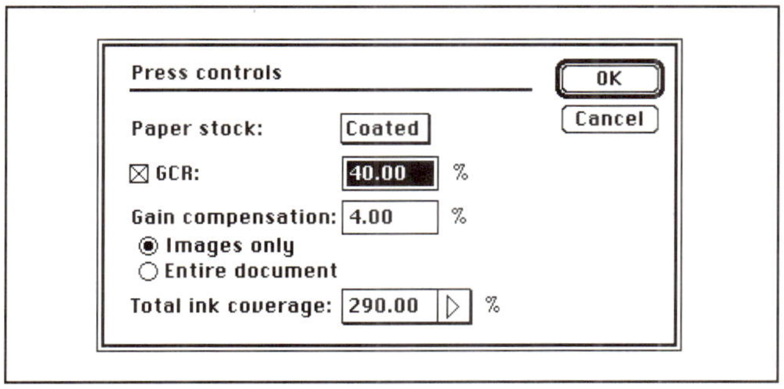

A color separation program such as Aldus Preprint allows the computer operator to produce color separations from page layout files.

Selection. Purchase and support of a particular program may come down to preference for a specific graphic user interface, support for specific file formats that need to be imported, particular features required for a given type of document, program speed, support of color, and customer requirements and preferences.

When selecting a page layout program, it is necessary to determine what the hardware requirements are for that program. Most programs require at least 2 MB of RAM. The software vendor will be able to provide that information, along with detailed lists of a program's capabilities.

Printers and service bureaus can offer output capability for a program that they do not fully support by having customers save their files as PostScript output files. These files can then be directly downloaded to an imagesetter without having the required application.

Scanning Software

Scanners usually come with software to aid in capturing images. Image editing/manipulation software is provided along with some scanners and is also available separately. A desktop scanner can be used as an OCR system with appropriate software. Although the scanning software described in this section is divided into categories, a given application may have capabilities in more than one category. The file format used in a scanning program should be carefully considered, just as with graphics software. These must be compatible with the page layout program used to assemble the final document.

Image capture software. Software to capture images is usually included with the scanner. Separate programs are available for use with line art and gray-scale scans, or both functions may be available in the same application. Most image capture software permits selection of scanning resolution; sometimes this is selected from a list of a few choices, although the better packages allow the user to set resolution in increments of 1 dpi. This is useful in trying to find the proper balance between file size and resolution, especially when sizing the scanned image.

Image capture software should allow the operator to select the area of a page to be scanned, thus saving time and resulting in a smaller file size. With flatbed scanners, this is usually accomplished by making a quick scan and then selecting the portion of the image desired from the low-resolution view on the screen. Some image capture programs allow the user to print images right after scanning them. This can be helpful in checking the quality of the scanned images, since it saves the time required to import the scans into a page layout program for printing. Different image capture programs support different file formats, which should be chosen for compatibility with the page layout program, best quality, and smallest file size. Many programs estimate how much system memory and disk space will

be needed to store a given scan, based on the part of the image desired, percent size, resolution, and number of gray levels selected.

Most programs also provide controls for adjusting the brightness and contrast of a scan. Some image capture programs provide a threshold setting that is designed to easily set this characteristic in one step, without the need to experimentally find the proper setting for both the brightness and contrast. Some image capture programs provide editing tools for use after the scan is completed, but the best results are obtainable in software that has been specifically designed for image manipulation.

Image editing/manipulation software. Some scanner manufacturers bundle image manipulation software from other vendors with their scanners, or they offer special versions of standard software for this purpose. Scanned line art is usually edited in a paint programs.

Gray-scale images can be extensively manipulated using software such as ImageStudio and Digital Darkroom. Some page layout programs such as PageMaker and QuarkXPress have built-in tools for adjusting picture brightness, contrast, and other tone reproduction characteristics. Color images can be retouched in programs like ColorStudio and Photoshop. Use of this software requires an appropriate gray-scale or color monitor. For black-and-white image manipulation, an 8-bit system with 256 gray levels is desired. A color monitor and controller supporting 24- or 32-bit color is usually needed for successful operation of the color image manipulation software.

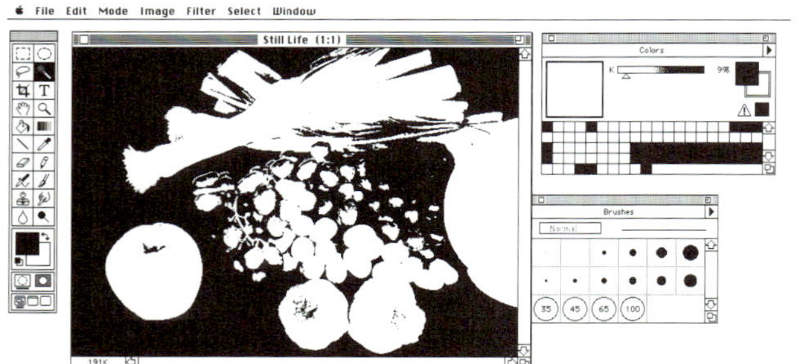

Adobe Photoshop, a color image editing program.

These programs provide appropriate tools to adjust picture contrast and brightness either globally to the entire picture or selectively to masked areas. Masks can be created in a variety of ways, including freehand, through the use of drawing tools, or by sensing contrast or color differences in parts of the picture. A variety of painting and airbrush tools

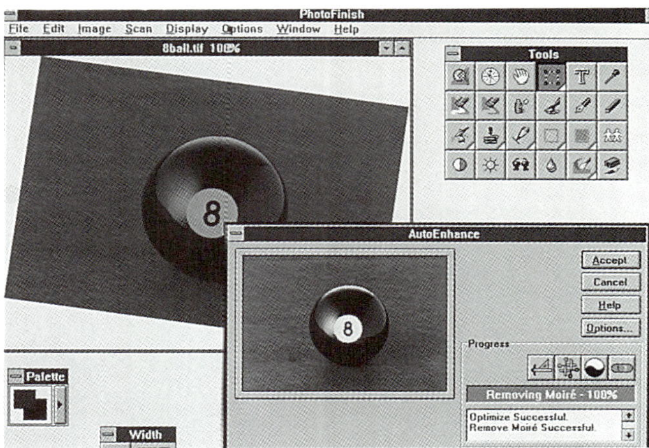

Courtesy ZSoft Corporation

PhotoFinish, a color image editing program for Windows.

are provided for image manipulation. Most of these programs also offer the capability to sharpen or blur image details as desired. Some permit combining images from different pictures and cloning parts of images.

OCR software. Several optical character recognition (OCR) packages are available for use on Macintosh and IBM-compatible computers. These can be used to aid in inputting typed or typeset documents, thereby saving the labor of rekeyboarding the work. Character recognition on many OCR products can be slow and error-prone, depending on the quality of the original copy.

Most of the OCR packages require a fully configured computer, with a large amount of RAM installed. A scanner equipped with an automatic document feeder can help make OCR operations more efficient. Some OCR packages can directly drive the scanner, which is convenient; others require that documents are scanned first, saved, and then run through the OCR program.

Some programs, known as trainable OCR software, require the user to help build type recognition tables for particular typefaces that need to be processed. Once trained, the program can then recognize these fonts in the future. The training process should be factored into any cost justification of this type of OCR software.

Some OCR programs can recognize and properly capture multiple columns of text, and some programs can distinguish between text and graphics.

Other Software

Other categories of software are important besides those covered in this section. Most are significant in

specialty applications. Numerous software packages are specifically designed for newspaper production tasks, including editorial, classified, and display ad production.

A number of software packages have been introduced to aid in the creation, input, and management of business forms. Most business forms can be created in standard vector graphics programs or any of the PostScript graphics packages, but forms software is optimized to do this quickly and efficiently. Some of the forms packages also permit not only the design and output of business forms, but maintain a database system where forms may be entered into the computer and the data may be managed accordingly.

Several utility programs on the market assist in the task of database publishing. They work with page layout programs to convert database files into formatted or tagged information that can then be flowed into appropriate style sheets. This approach can greatly reduce the time required in publishing information contained in a database.

Imposition/stripping programs. Several software applications are designed to provide stripping or image assembly functions on PostScript files. These **imposition/stripping programs** take desktop-published pages and assemble them electronically into proper position for printing, account-

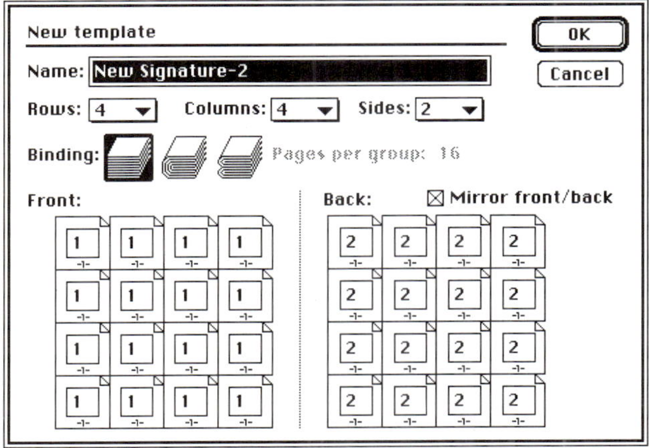

Aldus PressWise, an imposition program.

ing for page rotation, gripper margin, plate bend, shingling, bleeds, bindery lip, and other image assembly requirements. These imposition programs are particularly suited for use with large-format, high-resolution output devices using either film or printing plates. Such programs reduce the amount of manual film assembly required.

File Formats

Throughout this discussion of software, various file formats have been mentioned. A major area of concern is the compatibility, or lack thereof, found in the format used by various applications to store data. Because of the different methods used to store files, it is not usually possible to open up a word processing file or page layout file in a program other than the application that created it. This trend is changing, as some popular programs support the direct opening and saving of documents in other file formats.

A common denominator in word processing programs is the ASCII text file format. In an ASCII file, all formatting information has been removed ("stripped") from the file; only the text content remains. Virtually all word processors and page layout applications can work with files saved as ASCII text. The disadvantage of this method of saving files is that formatting information such as bold face, italic, type size, and font changes are not saved, and formatting information must therefore be redone in the application that needs to use the file saved in the ASCII format.

In addition to applications that save and open files created in different formats, translation programs convert from one word processing or graphics format to another. Some page layout programs can be used to translate between word processing programs, if they have the appropriate export filters available for the desired program.

File formats for graphics include the Macintosh PAINT format for raster data and the PICT format that stores the Macintosh QuickDraw commands used to image the screen. PICT can save bitmaps as well as vector data, but it is most commonly used to export files created from draw programs. Most Macintosh page layout programs expect to see graphics stored in PICT format rather than the native format of a draw program such as MacDraw or SuperPaint. Most Macintosh vector graphics applications provide an option to save files in PICT format.

The encapsulated PostScript format (EPSF) is used to import images from PostScript graphics programs into page layout applications. The EPSF format optionally includes a screen preview or PICT image to display on the monitor, which is useful in positioning and sizing the graphic within the page layout application. EPSF is also used on the PC for PostScript images.

PCX is a common paint format on the PC. The Windows Metafile format and CGM are vector file

formats on the PC, as is the GEM format for graphics applications running within the GEM environment for use with Ventura Publisher or other GEM programs.

Tagged image file format (TIFF) images are used on both the Macintosh and PC and are usually scanned images, which may be continuous-tone images or line art. TIFF files can be of unlimited image size and have the ability to store gray levels and colors for each pixel. TIFF files can also store two images in one—a low-resolution image for screen preview and a high-resolution image for output. It is supported by most page layout programs on Macintosh, PC, and Unix computers. Most page layout programs that use TIFF files do not save the high-resolution images as part of the page layout document. Instead, a low-resolution screen image is saved with the document. Customers who bring these page layout documents to a remote imagesetter for output must also bring the high-resolution TIFF images. This is necessary to ensure that the high-resolution images are output, rather than the low-resolution screen images. TIFF images can be very large, however, and difficult to transport to an output service bureau.

People in desktop publishing and electronic prepress need to pay close attention to the use of file formats. Files stored on the Macintosh in different formats can often be identified by the distinctive pattern of their icons, while on the PC different file types are usually identified by their three-letter file extension. In saving files or accepting files from customers, the appropriate file types must be used. These file types must also be compatible with the desired page layout programs. Support for appropriate file formats should be considered in selecting a page layout program and setting up guidelines for accepting work from customers.

Chapter 13

Ink

Printing Inks

Since lithography uses a planographic plate, separation of the image from the nonimage areas is accomplished by chemical differences on the surface: the image area of the plate is preferentially wet by ink, and the nonimage area is preferentially wet by water. Therefore, unlike other inks, lithographic ink must be formulated to work with water. In offset lithography, the ink on the plate is transferred to a blanket; in direct lithography, the ink is transferred directly from the plate to the paper or other substrate.

During printing, the ink must remain sufficiently fluid to transfer properly, and the printed film must afterwards dry to a solid. How fluid the ink must be and how it dries depends on the printing process, the material being printed, and the press speed.

Ink is a complex mixture of *pigment, varnish* or *vehicle, modifiers* or *additives,* and *drier.* The important properties of ink are *color, color strength, opacity* or *transparency, body* or *working properties,* and *drying properties.* All of these properties must be selected to suit the particular job; most importantly, they must suit the paper or other material being printed.

Drying of sheetfed inks is affected by temperature, moisture, acidity of the fountain solution, and absorbency of the substrate.

Printing problems are often blamed on ink when the real cause lies elsewhere, such as with poor plates, dirty dampeners, or improperly set rollers. Good lithographic reproduction requires good plates, optimum press conditions, and the appropriate paper and ink. Although requesting the ink manufacturer to formulate press-ready inks to meet the specifications of a particular job is the best thing to do, it is sometimes necessary to add compounds to the ink to overcome specific problems. When inks must be altered to overcome some problem, the additives should be recommended by the manufacturer of the specific ink. Homemade remedies should never be applied.

Formulas and compositions of lithographic inks vary to meet the requirements of the press and the printing substrate. Sheetfed and web offset inks require fundamentally different vehicles. Variations are made for printing on uncoated, enamel, and cast-coated papers, film, or foil and for printing on metal-decorating substrates.

A lithographic ink is made from a **pigment** or from a blend of pigments dispersed in a viscous liquid called the **vehicle.** Sheetfed inks consist of a pigment, a modified drying oil, a drier, and additives or modifiers. Web offset inks consist of a pigment, a modified rosin or a hydrocarbon resin, a hydrocarbon solvent, and additives. Inks for metal-decorating consist of a pigment dispersed in a heat-curing resinous vehicle and additives. Most lithographic news inks contain pigments dispersed in a vehicle consisting of a nondrying hydrocarbon oil and a resin.

Additives include such material as **waxes** to provide slip, **surfactants** to improve dispersion of the pigment, and many other ingredients.

Ultraviolet-curing inks include a pigment together with an acrylic varnish, a photoinitiator, and an inhibitor. These inks cure (polymerize) under ultraviolet light. Electron-beam drying inks are similar to ultraviolet-curing inks except that they do not require an initiator.

Properties Required of Lithographic Inks

Many factors influence an ink's printing performance. The ink must remain stable on the press but must dry on paper. It must be suited to the substrate being printed, and it must provide the required end-product characteristics. In addition, the ink must be economical. The color and behavior of the ink on the press and on the print are the most important characteristics. These characteristics are determined by the ink's color, color strength, flow, and ability to dry.

Color

The color properties of an ink, which depend largely on the pigments, are known as *masstone, undertone,* and *tinctorial strength.* Associated with these color properties are *transparency* or *opacity.*

Masstone is the hue, or color, of a thick film of the ink. It is the color of both the bulk ink in the can and the light reflected by the pigment. **Undertone**—the hue, or color, of a thin film of the ink—is the color of light reflected by the paper and transmitted through the ink film. **Tinctorial strength** is coloring power, or the amount that an ink can be reduced or diluted with a white pigment dispersion to produce a tint of a given density or saturation.

Brilliance and hue of pigments. Pigments, which are finely ground solid materials that give color to ink, vary in brilliance and in hue. Few inorganic pigments—pigments not derived from dyestuffs—have acceptable brilliance. Inorganic pigments are generally low in color strength and are therefore often blended with organic pigments to increase their color strength. Organic pigments are very numerous, quite brilliant, and available in a broad range of hues. Because of their many useful properties, organic pigments are widely used in lithographic inks.

All of these properties affect the appearance of a print. No printed ink film is completely opaque or completely transparent. As a result, what one sees on a printed sheet is a combination of light reflected in different ways. Part of the light is reflected by the ink, and part is reflected by the paper through the ink. Therefore, masstone, undertone, and tinctorial strength must all be integrated to obtain an exact ink match. How to observe the masstone, the undertone, and printing strength is discussed in the section on "Color" under "Testing of Litho Inks."

Color and color match. The color of an ink is imparted mostly by the pigment; different pigments give different colors. For example, the rubine pigments are less blue than the rhodamine pigments. These in turn are greatly different from red pigments, such as red lake C or permanent red 2B. It is therefore a mistake to call the magenta pigment "red," although this is commonly done in the printing industry. This error may be due partly to the fact that commercial magenta pigments are typically more red than blue.

Similarly, phthalocyanine pigments give different hues. Even blacks have different colors; specifically, carbon blacks are too brown, and when used in inks, they are made more black by adding a blue toner.

Matching the color of one ink with another ink is a craft that requires a great deal of skill, training, and experience on the part of the ink manufacturer. It is impossible to match certain natural colors with existing pigments. The ink manufacturer and the printer must arrive at the best possible compromise under these circumstances.

Color strength. Because the ink film is split between the plate and the blanket and again between the blanket and the paper, printed litho ink films are very thin. In fact, they are the thinnest films printed by any conventional printing process. To produce adequate color in such a thin film, pigments of high color strength are required.

An ink's color strength is determined partly by the amount of pigment used in its manufacture and partly by the efficiency with which this pigment is dispersed. Since the pigment is usually the most expensive component in the ink, it is easy to reduce the cost of the ink by reducing the amount of pigment used. Grinding on the three-roll mill is another expensive part of ink manufacturing. Reducing or omitting this grind will reduce the cost of the ink. However, both the dispersion of the pigment and the pigment strength will also be reduced.

Flow Properties

The flow characteristics of an ink are determined principally by varnish and pigment. Lithographic ink is a paste ink that is changed into the proper viscosity as it is worked in the inking system. A lithographic ink must be sufficiently fluid to travel from one roller to another as it passes from the ink

fountain to the plate and the blanket and thence to the paper. It must also adhere to the image areas of the plate and not to the nonimage areas, which have first been made wet by the dampening solution. Once the printing ink is on the substrate, it must not set off or strike through, and it must dry satisfactorily.

Body, consistency, or **viscosity** is the resistance of a fluid to flow under a force or shear. For practical purposes, the ink manufacturer and printer often consider body as a combination of ink tack, length, and fluidity or viscosity. In the can, ink becomes quite stiff, but when it is worked with a knife (or on the press rollers), it quickly becomes softer and more fluid. The change in viscosity with working is known as *shear thinning,* or **thixotropy.**

The fact that temperature also greatly affects viscosity has several implications for the printer. To avoid changes in the flow of the ink, the press and pressroom should be up to temperature before attempting to feed paper into the press. If the press is cold, for example, the viscosity of the ink will be high and may cause picking of the paper. Changes in flow cause changes in the color of the print on multicolor presses.

This temperature coefficient of viscosity helps inks to set. Most of the energy fed into a lithographic press is converted into heat on the ink rollers as they distribute and split the ink. Viscosity lessens and the ink flows readily. As the ink cools in going from roller to plate to blanket to paper, its viscosity increases rapidly. This contributes to the goal of every printer, the goal of "printing dry with wet ink." It is this rapid increase in viscosity when temperature decreases that enables the ink to flow readily on the ink rollers and to be stiff, resisting setoff and loss of dot sharpness on the paper.

The precise measurement of viscosity is highly technical. For record keeping, one needs an accurate instrument that gives numerical values. Furthermore, in testing the viscosity of the ink in the laboratory, it is absolutely essential that the measuring device be maintained at a constant temperature. If the temperature of the ink is not known, viscosity measurements become meaningless. Two commonly used instruments are the Laray viscometer for measuring viscosity and the Inkometer for measuring the tack on rollers at printing speeds. The finger tests for flow, tack, and length must always be comparison tests made against inks that are known to work properly.

Tack. Tack is the resistance of a thin film to rapid splitting. It is sometimes estimated by a tap-out test with the finger, usually in comparison with another ink that is to be matched. It can be determined on the tack-measuring instruments. An ink that is not tacky enough may not print clean and sharp. An ink with too much tack will pick and sometimes tear the paper.

On a multicolor press, the tack of the ink on each succeeding press unit should be less than on the previous unit so that the last-down ink actually has considerably less tack than the first-down ink. It is advisable, though, not to go too low because soft inks mix too readily with the dampening solution. For best color, the normal sequence should be cyan, magenta, and yellow with black usually first down. The first-down inks should be strongest with the lowest thickness progressing to the weakest and the highest film thickness down last. This order will give better **trap**—the acceptance of a second-down ink by a first-down ink.

Example of Tack Sequence

	First Down	Second Down	Third Down	Fourth Down
Sheetfed	16	14	12	10
Web Offset	10	9	8	7

However, once the inks are tack and strength rated for best trap, the color sequence can not be changed without changing the inks. It is possible, with the use of quicksetting inks and the right paper, that the first-down ink sets sufficiently between units to trap the next-down ink from the blanket. This setting permits the printer to use inks all of the same tack on the various units of the press. Then the printer can run any color sequence. This represents a considerable convenience to the printer and the ink supplier, but the printer pays for it in poor trap. To get the best trap (and consequently the best color), it is highly desirable that inks of the proper tack and strength sequence be employed.

As web inks have a higher solvent content than sheetfed inks, their tack is less and they are less viscous. Because of the high speed at which web presses operate, inks used in this process would destroy the paper if they were as tacky as those formulated for sheetfed operations.

Length. An ink's length is determined by the length of the string or filament it will form before breaking. Ink can be pulled out with a finger or

spatula to see how long it is. A certain degree of length is necessary for a lithographic ink to feed properly to the fountain roller and transfer without piling. An ink that is too long can fly or mist. Both the apparent tack and length of an ink change when it is worked with a knife or on the ink rollers.

As dampening solution is emulsified in an ink, the tack and the viscosity of the ink go down. The quantity of the dampening solution fed on the press must be controlled so as not to lower tack excessively. The dampening solution affects not only the vehicle but also the pigment used in a lithographic ink.

Lengths and viscosities of familiar materials are illustrated in the accompanying table.

Flow Properties of Familiar Materials

	Short	Long
High Body	Putty	Petroleum Pitch
Low Body	Mayonnaise	Syrup

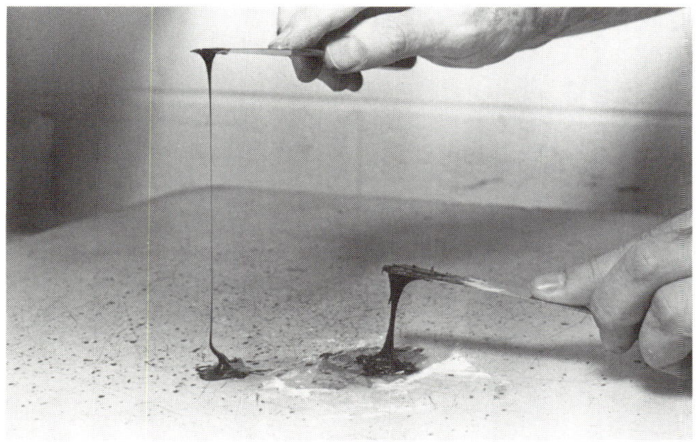

Comparison of long ink *(left)* and short ink.

Drying

The ability to dry is the most important ink characteristic. While it must remain stable on the press, ink must dry suitably after it is on the paper or substrate. There are two widely different ways of achieving such drying in common lithographic inks: oxidation/polymerization and evaporation.

Inks for sheetfed presses dry by a complex chemical process called **oxidation/polymerization.** The reaction occurs in the presence of a catalyst, which is called a **drier.** When properly formulated, sheetfed litho inks should set in 2 to 4 hr. in the pile. If the inks are formulated to set in less than 2 hr., they may dry up on the press, requiring the press operator to clean up the press. Removing dried ink from a press is a tedious, difficult job. If the inks do not dry fast enough—for example, in 4 hr.—work in the pressroom is delayed.

The ease with which an ink dries depends to some extent on the pigment in the ink. Some pigments promote drying, and inks containing them need less drier than inks containing pigments that dry poorly. Ink manufacturers are well aware of this, and they add suitable amounts of drier for the pigment used in the ink.

Inks for web offset presses dry by evaporation. If the inks are formulated with solvents that are too volatile (solvents that evaporate too readily), the inks may dry up on the press. If the solvents are too "slow," the ink is not suitably dried by the dryer at the end of the press. Resins with good *solvent release* are used so that the ink is set reasonably hard as it comes off the press. Use of resins with poor solvent release is a major cause of smudging.

Influence of acidity and moisture on drying. Most uncoated papers are usually acidic because aluminum sulfate (papermaker's alum) is added during papermaking. The alum is an acid, setting the rosin size that provides the water resistance required in lithographic papers.

Lithographic dampening solutions are, for the most part, acidic. Acidity is required to put the gum arabic in the proper form for retention by the plate. At high pH values (that is, when the dampening solution is neutral or alkaline), gum arabic is not retained by the plate, and it does not protect the nonimage area.

With stone and zinc plates, the acid actually etched or ate away the surface of the printing plate, exposing a fresh water-receptive surface to the dampener. The surface of aluminum plates is actually aluminum oxide. It is not etched or eroded by dampening solutions that have pH values between about 2 and 12. Therefore, the name "etch" is incorrect chemically. It is a carryover from the older forms of lithography when stone and zinc plates were used. Unlike zinc, aluminum is a highly reactive metal, and it oxidizes immediately upon exposure to air during the manufacturing process. Aluminum oxide is a form of emery or corundum. The coating of aluminum oxide is transparent and very hard, and it adheres to the aluminum quite unlike iron oxide, or rust, which is opaque, reddish yellow in color, and readily removed from the surface of the iron. (There is a corrosion problem of aluminum lithographic plates that is often called, incorrectly, "oxidation.")

Excess acid (low pH) can cause corrosion on the plate and press, may attack the ink to cause tinting, and will increase drying problems. Therefore, a properly formulated dampening solution is more important than high acidity in keeping aluminum plates running clean.

When large amounts of dampening solution are used, delayed drying or complete failure to dry can occur because, at high relative humidity (RH) in the pile, acid attacks the ink drier. A high RH in the delivery pile indicates either excessive amounts of dampening solution or excessive moisture in the stock. Neither high RH nor high acidity (that is low pH) by itself prevents the drying of properly formulated ink. However, when the dampening solution pH is low and RH is high, drying problems occur frequently in the printing plant. Even in an air-conditioned printing plant, the humidity within the skid may rise to high levels as a result of excessive amounts of dampening solution. Therefore, the best way to avoid ink drying problems is to keep the pH of the dampening solution high enough so that changes in RH do not cause ink drying problems. However, it is vital that the dampening solution desensitize the plate at a minimum level. Thus, it might be better to use a pH of 3.5 with a minimum amount of dampening solution than to run excessive amounts of dampening solution.

Effect of alcohol on drying. The amount of water emulsified in the ink influences its drying. Adding alcohol to the dampening solution reduces the water in the ink, increasing the drying rate of inks that dry by oxidation/polymerization. For years, a concentration of 18–25% isopropanol was used, but this percentage has decreased due to environmental regulations. Several alcohol substitutes have been developed. Many of these depend upon the wetting characteristics of various surfactants. Others depend upon an understanding of the plate chemistry or the function of isopropanol.

Neutral or alkaline dampening solutions. Neutral or alkaline dampening solutions have been used, especially in web offset news, in place of the acidic dampening solutions containing phosphoric acid and gum arabic. These solutions contain no gum because gum would be ineffective at pH values above 6.0. These dampening solutions depend upon the actions of various silicates and/or phosphates on the aluminum plate. Because of a chemical behavior known as *buffering,* the pH of the resulting dampening solution does not vary with the concentration of phosphate, and the pH meter cannot be used to measure the concentration. On the other hand, the pH of the dampening solution is much less critical on the alkaline side than it is on the acid side, where excess acidity retards the drying of the ink. These alkaline dampening solutions have been used little except for web offset news presses, where they speed production by permitting the press to be started up without washing plates and blankets. In addition, there are reports that alkaline dampening solutions reduce the linting of newsprint.

There seems to be little advantage in using neutral or alkaline dampening solutions in commercial and publication web offset printing. Alkaline dampening solutions promote ink emulsification if the inks contain any significant amount of free fatty acid. Acidic dampening solutions generally have better latitude with less scumming.

Other Properties

Gloss. Paper is the most important factor in the printing of gloss inks; best results are obtained with high-grade coated and enamel papers. But inks greatly affect the gloss of the print. The resin component, the oil or solvent, and the pigment all affect gloss. Generally, synthetic resins of high molecular weight that do not penetrate into the paper pores provide good holdout, enhancing the gloss. Inks made from flushed colors often yield a higher gloss than inks made from dry pigment. High-gloss coatings are frequently used over inks to increase image gloss.

Emulsification. The formula for a good working ink may contain 18–22 different ingredients, and it is developed only after many trials and experiments. The principal reason that lithographic inks differ from inks used in other processes is that litho inks must work in contact with water.

The ink manufacturer, therefore, must select materials that are more readily wet by varnish than by water. The pigments in litho inks must not dissolve in water or separate out in the presence of water. Likewise, the varnish must not mix into the water. Furthermore, the combination of pigment and varnish must not emulsify or mix excessively with water. Ink mixing into the dampening water produces a disastrous overall tint on the printed surface.

Bleeding in the dampening solution. Pigments for lithographic inks should not bleed in the dampening solution, although there are some exceptions.

Because isopropanol is still occasionally used in lithographic dampening, lithographic inks must also be resistant to alcohol. Some pigments bleed more at lower pH values. Peacock blue, calcium litho rubine toner, and permanent red 2B tend to bleed when the pH becomes low. A large increase in the acidity of the dampening solution causes even more severe consequences.

Interaction with plates. A litho ink must never contain anything that can react chemically with the plate, or dissolve the image from the plate. Undesirable chemical reactions between ink ingredients and the plate can cause scum, plate discoloration, or plate blinding. Finally, an ink should not contain abrasive particles that will wear the plate. Grit is sometimes detected by a fineness-of-grind test.

Ingredients of Litho Inks

Pigments

The specific gravity, particle size, wettability, opacity or transparency, color and tinting strength, and their effect on drying vary with different pigments. Inks of different colors, therefore, cannot be built on any one standard formula. Each pigment has its own characteristics, and its ink must be formulated to accommodate those characteristics. The nature and amount of pigment that a litho ink contains, as well as the type of vehicle, contribute to the body and working properties of the litho ink. Resistance of the pigment to light, heat, and chemicals is also important.

Pigments are classified as *organic* or *inorganic* depending upon their chemical nature. The **organic pigments** are made from petroleum products: blacks by burning gas or oil, other colors by reacting organic chemicals derived from petroleum. Organic pigments such as the phthalocyanines are prepared by mixing and heating the ingredients in a solvent with a high boiling point. Many **inorganic pigments** are formed by precipitation—that is, by mixing solutions of chemicals that react to form the insoluble pigment, which then precipitates, or settles out. The pigment is separated by filtration, washed to remove soluble salts, and either flushed into a varnish or dried. Some inorganic pigments used to be based on lead, cadmium, and mercury salts. Owing to the high toxicity of these metals, their use in recent years has been severely restricted or eliminated by government environmental regulations.

Ink pigments are often produced by a process called **laking.** The pigment manufacturer adds a precipitating material to the solution of the dye so that an insoluble pigment is formed and precipitates out.

Except for iron blues, inorganic pigments have a higher specific gravity than organic pigments. In addition, inorganic pigments often are opaque while the organic pigments are usually transparent.

Pigments are supplied either as *dry colors* or as *flushes.* Most pigments are made by mixing two or more chemical solutions. These solutions react to form tiny solid particles of pigment, which are then filtered out. The filter cake is collected and pressed to remove as much water as possible. If the filter cake is put into an oven to evaporate the water, the product comes out as **dry color.** If, on the other hand, the filter cake is put into a mixer and mixed with a varnish, the pigment flushes, that is, becomes wet with the varnish and leaves the water. The water is then poured off or evaporated, leaving the pigment well dispersed in an organic varnish. This product is called a **flush.** Flushed pigments are much more easily dispersed in inks than dry pigments are. Inks made from flushes are easier to grind and therefore likely to have higher color strength and to contain less grit. Although flushes cost somewhat more than the corresponding dry color, the ease of dispersion and the superior properties of product make them the preferred way of handling pigments.

The dry pigment process, however, does have a major advantage in that this type of pigment can be dispersed into any vehicle that the ink manufacturer or customer chooses. On the other hand, if pigment has been flushed into an alkyd varnish, it cannot be used to make a urethane ink or a water-based ink and poses some severe restrictions in making a UV ink.

A few familiar ink pigments are listed in the accompanying table.

Ink Pigments

Color	Organic	Inorganic
Yellow-Orange	Diarylide Yellow	Lead Chromate
	Hansa Yellow	Molybdate Orange
Cyan-Blue	Phthalo Blue	Ultramarine
	Peacock Blue	Iron Blue
Magenta-Red	Rubine	Vermilion
	Rhodamine	Cadmium Red

Resinated pigments. Pigments are often treated with resins during manufacture in order to make them more easily dispersible. The resinated pigment is more easily wet by oleoresinous vehicles. Most calcium, barium, or aluminum resinates, used originally, have been replaced with thermoplastic synthetic resin latices and emulsions. The pigment precipitates on the surface of the resin. This precipitation prevents the agglomeration of pigment particles during drying. When the resinated pigment is mixed with an oleoresinous vehicle, the resin of the pigment dissolves and the pigment is rapidly dispersed.

Lightfastness. Most lithographic pigments are affected by light in some manner. This characteristic makes it imperative that the degree of permanency required for each application, as well as the lightfastness rating of each pigment at different pigment concentrations, be known. Among the pigments with excellent light resistance, both indoors and outdoors, are carbon black, lampblack, phthalocyanine blues and greens, and many iron oxides.

Lightfastness is often required of litho inks; the degree of lightfastness depends upon individual end-use application. The effect of light, be it sunlight or fluorescent electric light, depends on the concentration of the pigment in the ink film and the intensity of the light. Tints, whose pigment concentration is low, tend to fade rapidly, whereas inks with high concentration of the same pigment are less affected.

Outdoor exposure. When lithographic inks are exposed outdoors, as on posters, they encounter both light and rain. Laked pigments are unlaked by rain, yielding their original dyestuffs. As these dyestuffs are soluble in water, they are removed by the rain, causing the ink to fade.

Vehicles

Vehicle is the liquid into which the pigment is dispersed. It consists of a *varnish* and *additives*. The **varnish** may be a modified drying oil (in which case, driers must be added), it may be a solution of a resin in a solvent, or it may be a combination of these. Litho inks were first made from heat-treated drying oils, but today, drying oils are chemically modified. These chemically modified oils are sometimes called **100% synthetic.**

Besides carrying the coloring matter from the ink fountain to the paper, the vehicle serves, when dry, to bind the ink film to the substrate. Drying can be accomplished either by oxidation of the modified drying oils, by the evaporation of the solvent, or by both evaporation and oxidation. News inks dry primarily by absorption, while the ultraviolet inks dry solely by polymerization. Vehicles must provide the proper degree of water resistance.

Sheetfed inks are made from varnishes such as linseed oil and alkyds or other resins that dry by oxidation/polymerization. Quicksetting or gloss varnishes may be used. A drier is added to convert the liquid ink to a solid after it has been printed on a sheet.

Vehicles for web inks are frequently prepared from a modified rosin; e.g., a pentaerythritol ester of rosin or a rosin-maleic resin. Hydrocarbon resins, produced by polymerizing low-molecular-weight olefins, are finding increasing acceptance in production of ink vehicles for web offset inks. These materials show somewhat poorer *solvent-release* than do the rosin esters.

Lithographic varnishes. The commonly used materials in lithographic varnishes are linseed, tall (from manufacture of kraft pulp), dehydrated castor, chinawood (tung), or soya oils reacted with an alkyd or other synthetic resin. Modification of the drying oil generally enhances ink holdout and finish and improves setting, drying, and gloss. Because the synthetic resin replaces part of the drying oil, less oxygen is required for drying.

The properties of a dried alkyd film are dependent on the type of oil and the nature of the alcohol and acid from which the alkyd was derived. The oil in combination with polyol (glycerol or pentaerythritol) is heated and the mixture is esterified with an acid, usually phthalic anhydride or isophthalic, to form the alkyd. Formulation of inks with isophthalic alkyd resins gives excellent pigment wetting properties and drying performance.

Modified oils are called *short, medium,* or *long* depending on the amount of oil in the oil-resin mixture. The **short-oil** alkyds have small amounts of drying oil; the **long-oil** alkyds have large amounts of drying oil in the mixture. Generally, the less drying oil, the higher the viscosity, although the type of oil, polyol, and acid are all influencing factors. For best color retention, resins based on soya and dehydrated castor oil are favored. Linseed oils have a tendency to darken.

Tung oil vehicles dry harder, become more insoluble, and are more alkali resistant than linseed oil varnishes. Tung oil tends to form a very hard, impenetrable film that resists dry trapping of subsequently printed inks. Such an ink is said to have

crystallized, or dried so hard that other inks will not adhere to it.

In addition to alkyds, important synthetic resins used in lithographic inks include phenolics, urethanes, maleics, acrylics, and epoxides. Oil-modified phenolic resins impart good drying speeds, film toughness, and excellent gloss and resistance to alkali. Maleic improves adhesion, quicksetting, and hardness during the early life of the film. Acrylics and epoxides provide good chemical resistance to the dried film.

Heatset vehicles. Heatset vehicles are composed of a resin dissolved in a petroleum distillate or heatset oil, such as Magie 470 or Magiesol 47, boiling in the range of 470–515°F (240–270°C). Recent improvements in these vehicles have reduced the energy required for drying, reduced visible emissions from the dryer, reduced the amount of solvent required, and yielded films with higher gloss.

Quickset vehicles. Quickset vehicles are useful in sheetfed printing where high production speeds require fast setting, as with work-and-turn jobs. They are composed of two liquids that are marginally soluble in each other; for example, a high-viscosity oil and a solvent. When the ink is printed on an enamel stock, the low-viscosity solvent is quickly absorbed by the paper coating, leaving the high-viscosity oil on the surface. This means that quickset inks are less effective on uncoated than on coated paper, and they do not set at all when printed on nonabsorbent substrates.

A new class of quickset vehicles, based on new acrylic resins, shows very fast setting properties and good water balance for sheetfed offset inks. Further developments will be required to give good gloss and resistance to rubbing and solvents.

Gloss vehicles. Often called *gloss varnishes,* the high-viscosity gloss vehicles are made by adding a phenolic rosin-ester resin or a phenolic resin to a drying oil such as a linseed alkyd. In addition to gloss, these vehicles provide hard drying, good adhesion, or binding, and good resistance to fountain solution.

Metal-decorating vehicles. Polyesters with excellent adhesion to aluminum, high gloss, resistance to abrasion and chemicals, and the capacity to dry quickly when heated in a dryer (as rapidly as 40 sec. at 375°F or 180°C) are replacing the older metal-decorating vehicles as aluminum cans replace the older three-piece metal cans.

Long-oil alkyds based on linseed, soybean, safflower, or dehydrated castor oil are often modified with other synthetic resins as varnishes for flat-sheet tin.

Ultraviolet (UV) and electron-beam (EB) vehicles. Vehicles for inks that are to be cured with ultraviolet radiation contain acrylic prepolymers (also called oligomers) and a photosensitizer (photoinitiator). Upon exposure to UV, the photosensitizer is activated, the energy is transferred to the prepolymer, and polymerization occurs in a fraction of a second. Photoinitiators are not required for curing with electron beams because electron beams are more energetic than UV. These inks have outstanding rub, scratch, and skinning resistance, but cannot be deinked by conventional methods. With compact curing units installed between the printing units of a press, *dry trap* printing is recommended for UV, but is not needed for EB. This eliminates the major problem with only one UV curing unit where the top ink is dry while overprinted inks are still uncured.

The relatively high cost of the materials used in UV and EB inks has limited their use to specialty areas where the cost is justified: album covers, textbook covers, plastics, foils, and metal decorating.

Infrared vehicles. There are several ways to make inks that will set and/or dry rapidly under infrared (IR) radiation. In the first place, IR warms the print, and heat alone accelerates both drying and setting of conventional inks. Heat also lowers the viscosity of the ink, so excessive or uncontrolled use of IR can cause setoff.

Driers

Driers promote the oxidation/polymerization of inks containing drying oils or drying oil derivatives. They are soaps of such metals as cobalt, manganese, lead, cerium, or zirconium. When metal salts are suspended in a liquid such as a petroleum solvent, they are referred to as **liquid driers.** Octoates, naphthenates, linoleates (derived from linseed oil), and resinates (salts of rosin acids) are the salts that are soluble in petroleum solvents or oils. Since different driers promote drying by different mechanisms, blends of the driers are often used. Because of its toxic properties, use of lead has been virtually discontinued; mixed driers of cobalt and manganese are commonly used. These are sometimes called **two-way driers.** Cobalt is very active and is referred to as a **top drier** because it gives a very hard

surface to the ink. Manganese, on the other hand, is less active and therefore considered a **through drier:** it dries the ink film throughout and does not form a hard surface.

Paste driers are soluble driers containing resins and plasticizers to achieve the desired body or viscosity. Printing ink driers modified with lead linoleate or resinate were once commonly used paste driers. The paste driers in use today are soluble driers cooked with resins, which yield a controlled high viscosity, that can be added to a printing ink without destroying its body.

Perborate or **"Grapho" driers** are oxidizers that furnish oxygen to speed up drying. They are completely different from conventional driers and can only be added to the ink immediately before printing.

Solvents

The most commonly used solvents in the manufacture of lithographic inks are petroleum hydrocarbons called **heatset oils.** When used to make web offset inks, the rate of evaporation must be controlled, and the oils are carefully fractionated to yield a product that boils over a narrow range. The lower the number of the oil, the lower its boiling range, or the temperature required to dry the print. The higher the boiling point, the more stable the ink is on the press. The simplicity and low toxicity of these heatset oils give web offset an advantage over rotogravure, where a wide variety of solvents are used, some of them rather toxic.

Ink manufacturers have a number of heatset oils, differing in their boiling range (rate of evaporation), at their disposal. The heatset oils can be treated to remove smog-forming components.

Heatset ink systems have been specially formulated to reduce or eliminate air pollution. One system uses a dual solvent to reduce the heatset oil content by more than one-third, thereby reducing the amount of solvent vapor discharged to the air. Complete drying occurs at web temperatures of 250–275°F (120–135°C).

Selection of the solvent depends not only on the boiling point, but also on the characteristics of the dryer and the press, press speed, ink coverage, and paper stock. Special heatset rubber rollers are needed to minimize solvent absorption. Also, solvents for offset inks must be compatible with blankets. Solvents that extract plasticizer from the blanket make it extremely smooth. Very smooth blankets have been shown to cause more picking than blankets with a rougher surface.

Ink Additives

Plasticizers. Plasticizers make the ink softer, more flexible, and more adherent to the substrate. Resins are often stiff and brittle. Thus, they adhere poorly to flexible substrates. A plasticizer, by improving the plasticity of the film, improves adhesion. Selection of the plasticizer depends on the printed product and the resin in the ink. Since the boiling points of plasticizers are generally high, they do not evaporate in the dryer, and they become a permanent part of the ink film.

Waxes. Waxes are used in vehicles to impart slipperiness and rub resistance to the dried ink film. Waxes also reduce setoff, improve water resistance, and slow drying. They can reduce tack without appreciably altering other flow properties. Excessive wax softens the ink and reduces viscosity.

Waxes are used in the form of a compound, which is either a micronized, dry powder or a fine dispersion of several waxes in an appropriate oil vehicle. Common classifications of waxes are animal (beeswax, lanolin), vegetable (carnauba, candellila), mineral (paraffin, microcrystalline), and synthetic (polyethylene, polyethylene glycols, Teflon).

Regardless of its initial solubility, the wax will not function properly as a slip agent unless it is partially insoluble in the final dried ink film, migrating to and remaining on the surface. Some drying oils tend to keep the wax in solution after drying, giving an ink with unsatisfactory rub resistance. Waxes are preferred only in the last-down ink since they migrate to the surface of the ink during drying, making it difficult for subsequent inks to trap or adhere. If varnish or coating is to be added, the inks should be wax free.

Wetting agents. Wetting agents promote the dispersion of pigments in ink varnishes. There are many varieties of wetting agents, and the selection of an appropriate one should be left up to the ink manufacturer. Wetting agents for lithographic inks must be carefully selected; otherwise they can cause excessive emulsification of fountain solution into the ink, plate blinding, and other associated problems.

Antisetoff compounds. Various compounds prevent setoff either by protecting the ink surface or by shortening the ink (decreasing its gelling time). Compounds containing wax or grease shorten the ink, thereby speeding up its setting. Antisetoff compounds that contain magnesia prevent setoff also

primarily by shortening the ink; however, addition of such materials may also promote blanket piling.

Spray powder or starch reduces setoff by slightly roughening the surface of the ink film. The starch is blown onto the printed ink; it should never be mixed with the ink. The starch reduces contact between adjacent sheets and allows more time for the ink to set.

Solvents that increase the rate of absorption of an ink vehicle by the paper may reduce setoff, but may also cause chalking on coated stocks. Furthermore, they tend to reduce the gloss of the dried inks. Wax, starch, and magnesia compounds are less objectionable. The wax compounds, if used in excess, can prevent good trapping of succeeding colors if the inks dry between printings.

Shortening compounds. Shortening agents reduce ink flying, or misting. The addition of a wax compound shortens an ink. The printer should not add such materials except on the advice of his ink manufacturer because they can interfere with proper ink flow on press.

Reducers. Oils or other petroleum solvents are occasionally added to soften and reduce the tack of an ink. A light varnish, such as #0000 litho varnish, boiled linseed oil, or a light linseed isophthalic alkyd, will also reduce the tack of an ink. It is much easier to reduce the tack than it is to increase it. The addition of any reducer will increase dot gain.

Stiffening agents. For sheetfed inks, body gum—#8, #9, or #10 linseed varnish—is used to stiffen an ink that is too soupy and fails to print cleanly and sharply. It "pulls the ink together" when the ink tends to cause scumming or tinting, and it can help prevent chalking on coated stocks. Heavy-bodied gloss varnish (binding varnish) or gel varnish can also be used for this purpose.

Antiskinning agents. Antiskinning agents are antioxidants that counteract the drying of sheetfed offset inks so that they will not skin over in the can. If they are used only in the top of the can, they will not greatly retard the drying of the rest of the ink.

Printers sometimes spray antioxidants onto the plate and blanket of a sheetfed press to prevent drying or skinning during lunch time. The ink so treated will not dry properly, but a few sheets run through the press will take most of the treated ink away.

Manufacturing Litho Inks

Formulation and Mixing

The actual process of making an ink is relatively simple, but formulation is a complex problem depending partly on science and partly on skill, craft, and judgment. In the preparation of a **flush,** the varnish and the pigment or pigments are weighed and stirred together in a tub, using high-speed dispersion equipment to mix the pigment with the varnish.

The mixing operation, by wetting the pigment and mixing the ink ingredients thoroughly, saves subsequent milling time. The mixture is then ground on a three-roll mill, where it is sheared as it passes between rollers.

The **dry pigment process** is older and requires more milling time. The dry, crumbly pigment cake is ground into a fine powder and then milled into the vehicle.

Milling

The rollers of the three-roll mill turn at different speeds and thus severely shear the ink film between them. This shearing breaks up the pigment agglomerates into microscopic particles so that each becomes completely surrounded and wet by the varnish.

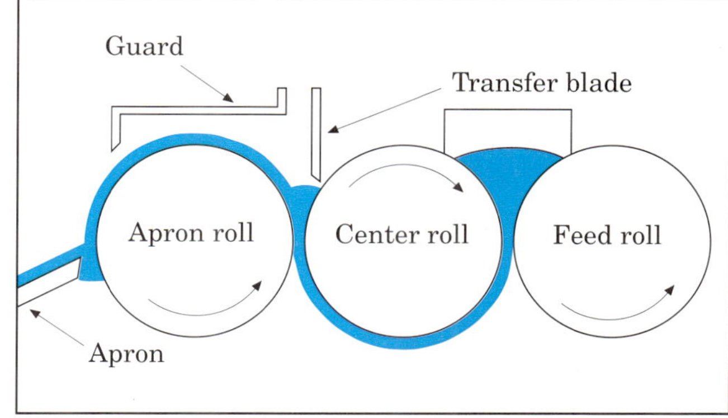

Courtesy Day Mixing Co.

Grinding action of a three-roll dispersion mill.

The mill also *classifies* the pigment, permitting finely dispersed pigment to flow through the mill and retaining or holding back coarser pigment particles. The ground ink is taken off the high-speed roll at the left by a doctor blade. A thorough job of

grinding may require as many as three passes over the mill, depending on whether the pigment is soft or hard and how easily it is wet by the varnish.

Milling is a costly procedure, and inks can be cheapened by reducing the amount of milling. This causes several problems, including lower color strength. Since the pigment is the most expensive part of the ink, the printer naturally wants to receive an ink of full value, which is developed by milling.

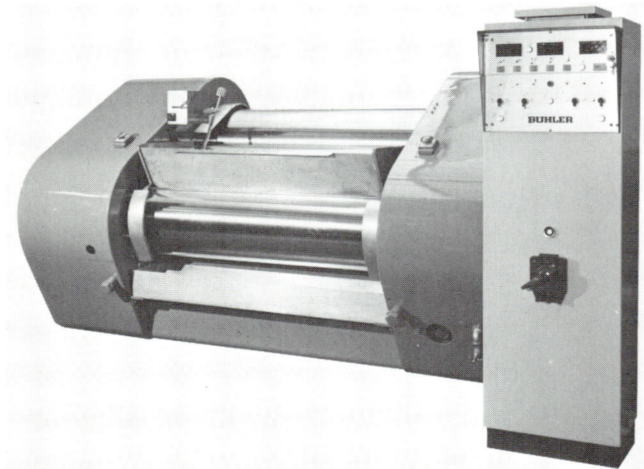

Courtesy Buhler-Miag, Inc.
Programmable three-roll mill.

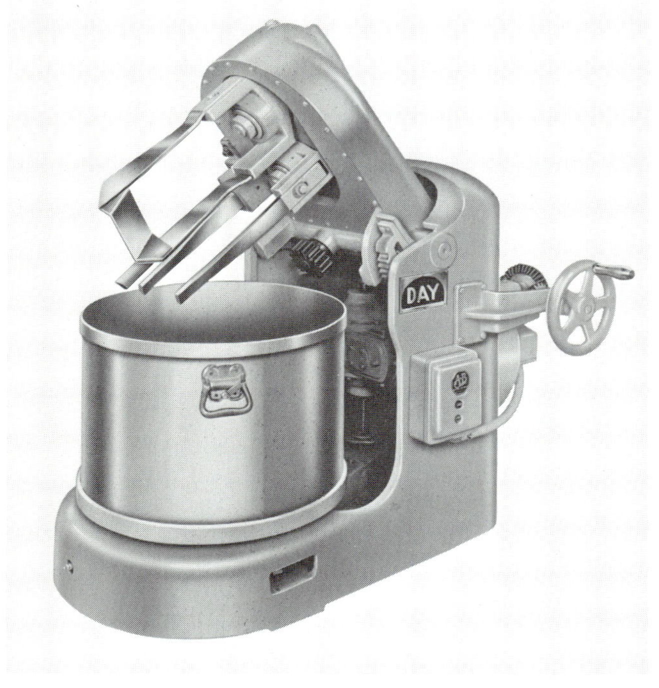

Courtesy J. H. Day Co.
Twin-motion pony mixer.

Stability of Packaged Inks

Progress in recent decades has led to the manufacture of the inks that have good stability in the can. **Livering,** a large increase in body resulting from reaction of pigments with vehicles that have a high fatty acid content, has been virtually eliminated by producing vehicles with very low fatty acid content.

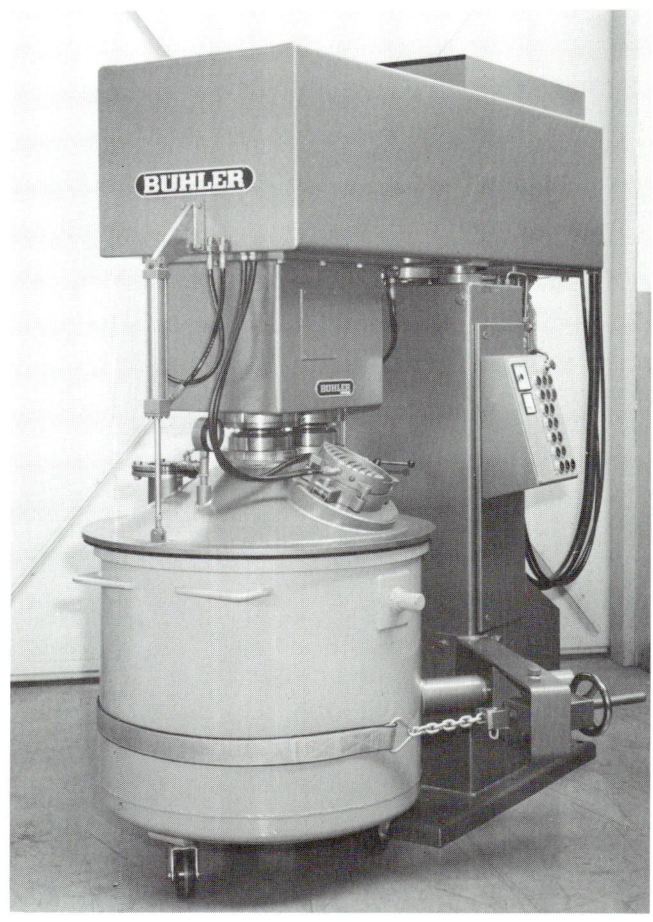

Courtesy Buhler-Miag, Inc.
Disperser with covered container to avoid contamination.

False body, which may look like livering, occurs when inks are stored for a very long time. But if the thickened batches are worked with a spatula or run through a three-roll ink mill, they revert to their original flow and body. Choice of suitably treated pigments together with good wetting techniques reduces the formation of false body.

When inks are stored for a long time, driers often become ineffective. Any ink that has been stored for one year or more should be checked before putting it on the press. If it fails to dry satisfactorily, drier can be added, or sometimes the ink can be returned to the ink manufacturer for reformulation.

How Inks Dry

There are eight different methods by which printing inks dry: *absorption, oxidation / polymerization, radiation polymerization, catalytic polymerization, evaporation, gellation, infrared radiation,* and *precipitation.*

Lithographic inks set and/or dry by all of these methods except precipitation. In practice, several methods may occur with one type of ink. For example, in a web offset ink, drying may result from absorption, evaporation, gellation, and solidification. If an oxidation/polymerization vehicle is included in the formula, a fifth drying method may be introduced.

Although most experts distinguish between setting and drying in the theory, it is very difficult to do so in practice. With sheetfed offset inks, for example, **setting**—the increase in viscosity or body that occurs immediately after the ink is printed—is followed by drying. While setting occurs as a result of thixotropy and the absorption of solvent or low-viscosity components by the printed paper, **drying** is a complicated chemical reaction that normally takes 2–24 hours. However, drying starts immediately after the ink is printed (actually, as soon as the ink is exposed to air). Moreover, experimental measurement of ink drying can determine only the increase in *body* (or rub resistance), which is actually a combination of setting and drying.

Methods by Which Inks Set and Dry

Method	Examples
Absorption	News, Quickset
Oxidation/Polymerization	Sheetfed Offset
Evaporation	Web Offset
Radiation Polymerization	Metal Can Decorating
Catalytic Polymerization	Metal Can or Glass Decorating
Infrared Radiation	Quickset, Web Offset
Solidification	Heatset
Gellation	Quickset
Precipitation	Moisture-set

Absorption

Most news inks dry primarily by **absorption.** The vehicle drains into the sheet, leaving the pigment trapped by the fibers near the surface of the newsprint. There is no true drying in this mechanism, and the black pigment in the news ink comes off on the reader's fingers the next morning or weeks later.

Absorption, however, is also important in the setting of inks that dry by other mechanisms. For example, quickset inks are formulated with a high-viscosity varnish that has been cut with a low-viscosity oil. When the sheet absorbs the oil, the viscosity rises rapidly and the ink sets. Accordingly, quickset inks will not function on nonabsorbent surfaces—an example of *the importance of having litho inks formulated by the ink manufacturer for the job.*

Absorption, like other physical and chemical phenomena, is accelerated with heat. At least one of the means by which infrared radiation speeds the setting of ink is by increasing the rate of absorption of solvent from quickset inks.

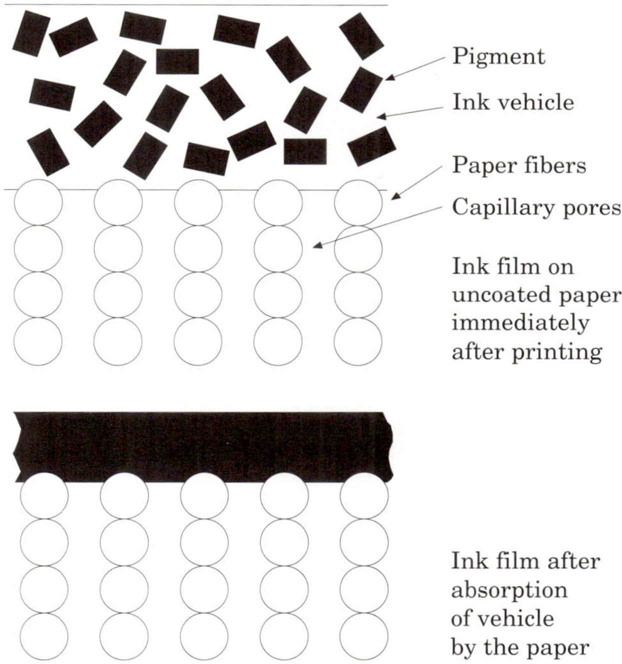

Oxidation/Polymerization

The exact chemical reactions by which oxidation/polymerization inks dry are unknown. There have been a number of mechanisms proposed, but none explain all the facts. The principle of polymerization is illustrated in the accompanying diagram. Those varnishes that are derived from drying oils, such as linseed oil, chinawood oil, or soya oil, react with oxygen in the air to form a chemical called

a *hydroperoxide.* In the presence of a cobalt or manganese salt, called an **initiator** or a **catalyst** (a drier), the hydroperoxide forms a free radical, which reacts with another oil molecule, forming a molecular chain that continues to grow. As the chain gets longer and longer, the ink flows less and less readily until, after 2–24 hours, enough chains have been formed so that the ink no longer flows. It is dry and will not smear when rubbed.

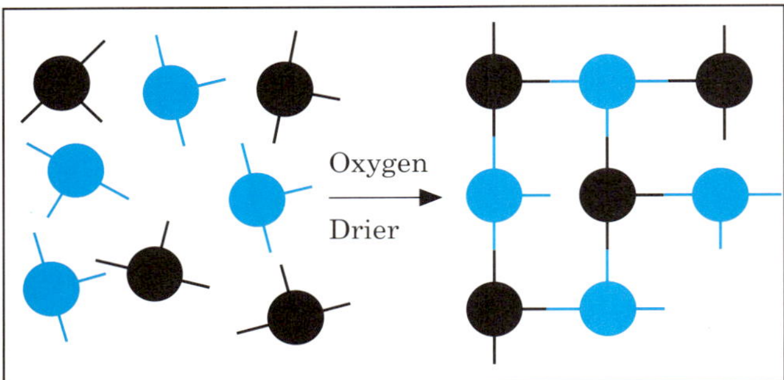

Oxidative drying inks generate an **allylic** free radical, a relatively stable, slowly reacting species. These characteristics of the free radical explain why oxidative drying inks can remain stable on the press for many hours and take hours to dry on the printed stock. In the absence of any drier, the reaction proceeds at a very slow pace, if at all.

Among the factors still not fully understood is why cobalt salts act as *top driers* while manganese salts act as *through driers,* but good lithographic inks must contain at least two types of driers. Lead salts were favored for many years but are no longer used because of the danger that someone might eat the printing and get lead poisoning. Cobalt salts promote rapid skinning of the printed film and manganese salts promote formation of a tough film throughout.

The oxidation/polymerization reaction is affected by many factors: *the kind of pigment, the kind and amount of drier,* and *the type of varnish in the ink; the absorptivity, pH,* and *RH of the paper;* and *the pH of the fountain solution.* Consequently, drying problems often cannot be blamed on one particular material. Ink, paper, and fountain solution must all contribute to good drying performance.

The following precautions are the most important in striving for adequate drying of inks:

- Be sure to select an ink suited to the job.
- Do not alter the ink without consulting the ink manufacturer.
- Keep the pH of the fountain solution between 4 and 5. Low pH inhibits the reaction by which these inks dry.
- Keep water at a minimum. Water likewise inhibits the reaction.

Vehicles based on drying oils are sometimes added to web inks to provide extra hardening after drying. Ordinary web offset inks, for example, after drying can be smeared with greasy fingers. If a drying varnish is used in the ink (sometimes used for cover stock printed by web offset), the drying is hard and permanent.

Radiation Polymerization

During the 1970s, inks containing **acrylates,** especially reactive monomers, were developed. Under the influence of *ultraviolet light* or *electron beam radiation,* these inks react very quickly. Unlike oxidation/polymerization, which requires several hours, this reaction is complete in a fraction of a second. In a matter of a few seconds, prints are ready to be cut or folded. No spray powder is required to prevent setoff, and on folding cartons, the resulting varnished print has a smoothness that cannot be achieved by conventional sheetfed inks.

They are primarily used for metal can decorating, where the quick drying speeds production. They are also used in the printing of folding cartons that command a premium price, such as cosmetic boxes and gift boxes for liquors, and in screen printing, where the speed of the reaction is useful in printing films and plastic containers.

Catalytic Polymerization

When the substrate will withstand the heat, as with metal cans or glass, a slow-reacting polymerization can be used to cure the ink. For example, melamine formaldehyde polymers give a hard, resistant print or varnish on beverage cans and bottles. To achieve the hard coating, melamine formaldehyde prepolymer is mixed with a catalyst. On baking, the catalyst completes the polymerization. Several other catalyzed polymerizations are also used for baking varnishes and inks.

Evaporation

Webs printed by any process usually dry by absorption or evaporation. In heatset web offset printing, the absorption of some of the vehicle by the printed sheet may assist in the setting of the ink, but *evaporation* of solvent is of prime importance. Drying of the ink is accomplished by this evaporation. The resin left behind then bonds the pigment to the paper or film so that it will not rub off.

Evaporation occurs very rapidly. Control of drying is of utmost importance if the print is to be delivered dry without **cooking** (overheating) the paper or plastic and adversely affecting final gloss.

Gellation

Quickset inks set by **gellation**. They contain a gel varnish that has been cut to desirable body with a small amount of solvent. When the solvent is absorbed by the paper, the gel varnish reverts to its original high body, and the ink has **set.**

Infrared Radiation

Although heat reduces the viscosity of the ink, it accelerates absorption of solvent from a quickset ink and accelerates the oxidation/polymerization reaction.

Because infrared radiation accelerates both the setting and drying of inks, it greatly reduces the amount of spray powder required to prevent setoff and blocking in the printed pile.

By taking advantage of some new acrylic resins, ink chemists have made infrared inks that, in effect, set very quickly. By accelerating the separation of solvent from gel or resin, infrared radiation makes these inks set even more quickly.

It is possible to accelerate the setting of inks with infrared radiation, and infrared inks will set quickly without radiation, but by judicious use of both, remarkable results can be achieved: prints are ready to be backed up in a few minutes and are ready for cutting and trimming in less than an hour.

Printing Ink Problems in the Pressroom

The following discussion highlights problems commonly encountered in the lithographic pressroom.

Drying of Sheetfed Inks

The complicated chemical reaction by which sheetfed lithographic inks dry is fraught with many problems, the most common of which is slow drying. Quickset lithographic sheetfed inks should set sufficiently in 2–4 hr. so that the sheets can be rerun or sent to the bindery. When the setting time stretches out in excess of 4 hr., production schedules are interrupted, or it may be necessary to rerun the job. There are two common causes of drying problems: (1) ink not suited to the substrate and (2) excessive use of dampening solution with a low pH. Dampening solutions with pH lower than about 4.0 may contribute to drying problems with some inks.

Ink may be unsuited to the job because it was not formulated properly, the ink may have been ordered for a different job or the printer may not have given the ink manufacturer enough information, or the properties of the ink may have been altered in the pressroom. Variations in absorptivity, relative humidity, and pH of the paper can aggravate drying problems.

Mottle. Irregular and unwanted variation in color or gloss is referred to as **mottle.** There are a number of different types of mottle. **Absorptive mottle** is caused by an imbalance in the ink and the paper. All paper has nonuniform absorptivity, although some textbooks state that handmade paper is uniform. Fibers from which the paper is made cannot be distributed completely uniformly. If the ink is absorbed more by one part of the sheet than by another, nonuniform penetration may yield the visible pattern of mottle. One way to overcome mottle is to select an ink that is either uniformly held out or uniformly absorbed by all areas of the sheet. If the sheet is reasonably uniform, this will not be a difficult task. However, for some types of substrates, especially paperboard, differences in absorptivity may be so great as to make the selection of a suitable ink very difficult.

Mottle is also aggravated by the responses of the eye. Variations in brown, blue, and green solids are more visible than are variations in other colors. Pattern prints show less mottle than do solids. Inks that set and dry quickly probably cause less mottle than those that set and dry slowly. The longer it takes for the ink to set, the more time there is for differences in the absorption to become apparent.

Chalking. When a dried ink pigment does not adhere to the substrate and can be brushed off with the finger, the problem is called **chalking.** If the ink varnish is too thin or is improperly formulated for the paper, the pigment will not be bonded to the sheet. This lack of bonding also occurs when drying is delayed too long. To prevent chalking, the ink can be stiffened with a binding varnish. Before doing this, however, pH of the dampening water and the paper should be checked. If the relative humidity is unusually high, more drier or a stronger

drier may help. Unfortunately, chalking is usually not noticed until the job is off the press, and then the only remedy is overprinting with a transparent size or varnish.

Use of a drying accelerator (a salt of cobalt) in the dampening solution will accelerate drying where drying problems can be anticipated, but they usually are not anticipated and are discovered only after the job is completed. Grapho or perborate type driers may also be used as recommended by the ink supplier.

Chemical ghosting. Chemical ghosting is also known as *gloss ghosting* and gas ghosting. It is the transfer of a printed image (but not by setoff) from the front of one sheet to the back of another, but not through the sheet. It is found most frequently on enamel papers using quickset inks where a high gloss is desired. This type of ghosting results from one printed ink film altering the drying of a printed ink film on the adjacent sheet in the pile. It can be seen on metal that is printed on two sides, but slip-sheeting the pile eliminates it. The ghost image is always the image of the *other* side of the page.

A number of factors work together to cause chemical ghosting. The problem is usually noticed most on an exacting job in which the smallest defect is apparent. Furthermore, small differences in gloss are readily detected on glossy jobs. GATF laboratories showed that a high concentration of drier, required if the job is to be run in a hurry, promotes gloss ghosting. Backing up the prints that have dried less than 24 hr. also promotes gloss ghosting. Gloss ghosts often plague annual reports where prestige, high gloss, and fast turnaround come together.

Most gloss ghosting can be minimized by varnishing or coating the ghosted area with the proper varnish. To determine what varnish will best eliminate the ghost, it is necessary to apply 5 or 6 different varnishes to ghosted areas, let them dry, and then see which is best to use for correcting the problem. UV or aqueous coatings and liquid laminating will usually eliminate the problem.

The best cure is to prevent ghosting by recognizing conditions under which gloss ghosting is likely to occur. The following steps are recommended: (1) Use ink that has been carefully formulated for the job. Printers should not make any changes to the ink in the pressroom. It is especially important not to add drier. (2) Schedule the job so that it is not necessary to rush it. Allow the first side of the print to dry at least 24 hr. before backing it up. (3) Carefully wind the printed skid to eliminate any moisture or vapors that are by-products of the drying of the ink. (4) Stack the printed sheets in small lifts that are easily winded and that will dissipate the heat generated by the oxidation/polymerization reaction. (5) Printers normally like to print the light form first and the heavy solids second. However, if the heavy first-down coverage develops patterns in the light second-down film, they will be invisible. In addition, of course, if the heavy solids are printed first, the first-down side must be thoroughly dried before it is backed up. This in itself helps to eliminate the gloss ghosting. (6) Varnish in line when possible to reduce ghosting tendencies. (7) In severe cases, it may be possible to slip-sheet the printed sheets. Slip-sheeting is a slow, costly means of preventing gloss ghosting. It is completely effective, however, and many printers who have lost jobs because they were not able to correct the gloss ghost would have been economically ahead had they used slip-sheeting.

Drying of Heatset Web Offset Inks

Because heatset inks dry primarily by evaporation, problems are much simpler than with sheetfed inks. In addition, because the inks normally dry while the job is on-press, the press operator can take immediate steps should problems arise.

Temperature control is of prime importance. To make sure the inks are dry, web offset dryers are usually run too hot, often as much as 50°F above requirements. This practice not only wastes expensive gas but deteriorates paper, causing cracking and brittleness. As the web emerges from the dryer, it is still hot and the ink is melted. The web must be cooled by passing it over the **chill rolls,** hollow cylinders cooled with cold water, to solidify the ink. If the chill rolls are not functioning properly, the print will still be wet when it goes to the folder.

Other Problems

Ink contamination. In handling ink, the press operator should take every precaution to avoid its contamination. Special care should be taken to prevent the mixing of dried ink (ink skin) into the fountain ink. In removing the skin from a can or kit, first cut around the edge with an ink knife and remove the oiled paper cover. Then scrape off any ink skin formed around the edges. Use a broad knife to remove ink evenly from the surface rather than digging deeply into the can. When the required amount of ink has been taken out, smooth the surface with a broad knife and either replace

the old oiled paper circle or apply a new one. Press it into uniform contact with the remaining ink so as not to entrap air bubbles.

Be sure that the press is clean before inking up, especially if a light color or tint is to be run. Tints can be markedly altered in hue or cleanliness by traces of a previous ink remaining either on the ink rollers or on the dampening rollers. To avoid this condition, ink up the press with a light-colored ink or a transparent white ink and run it for several minutes. Then, scrape some of the ink off one of the rollers to see how much its color has changed. Wash up the press and repeat until the ink is no longer contaminated.

Hickeys. Small solid areas sharply defined and surrounded by white halos on the print are called **hickeys.** They are caused by dirt: dirt from the ink, dirt from the paper, and dirt from the press or the pressroom. Controlling hickeys means keeping the press and the pressroom scrupulously clean, making sure that the paper and ink are clean, and handling the ink with care. Ink returned to the can by the press operator must be handled with care to keep dirt and air out of the ink.

Dry trapping. Sometimes it is difficult or impossible to trap an ink over a dried print, creating a **dry-trapping** problem. Dry-trapping problems arise from the use of hard-drying varnishes in the ink, such as those involving chinawood oil, from the presence of nondrying oils in the ink, and from the use of hard waxes in the ink. Hard waxes, such as carnauba or teflon, give a hard, rub-resistant finish to the ink, and the printer must specify to his ink supplier the printing sequence so that slip agents and waxes are incorporated only in the last-down ink, especially if the print is to be dried before subsequent inks are printed.

Nondrying components incorporated in the ink or the varnish will bleed to the surface during drying and present a thin surface film that will not accept ink on subsequent printing.

Trapping problems are one of the most serious causes of color variation, one of the major problems with lithography.

Wet trapping. A **wet-trapping** problem occurs when a printed ink film fails to accept a succeeding ink film applied on the press. Wet trapping is accomplished by control of the ink tack and the ink film thickness. It is extremely difficult to trap a thin film over a first-down thick film. To improve wet trapping on relatively nonabsorptive stocks, GATF has always recommended use of a tack sequence of about two tack or Inkometer units between each press unit of a multicolor sheetfed press and about one Inkometer unit between each unit on a web press. Absolute tack values will depend on many variables including the press, the dampening solution, the paper, and the ink.

For best trap, GATF also recommends that inks be printed with the strongest inks first progressing to the weakest inks down last. Emulsification or water pickup should also be lowest on first-down inks progressing to the highest on the last-down inks. This is unnecessary for most uncoated stocks as the ink oils are rapidly absorbed by the paper.

Picking. If the ink tack is too high and the speed of the press is too great for the paper being run, bits of paper may be picked out of the surface, dirtying the ink and spoiling the print. This problem is referred to as **picking.** In extreme situations, the sheet tears. Picking has become increasingly serious as ink coverage and press speeds continue to increase. Picking can be reduced by using stronger paper, slowing down the press, reducing ink tack or using a lower tack ink, reducing back cylinder squeeze on the press, and increasing ink film thickness.

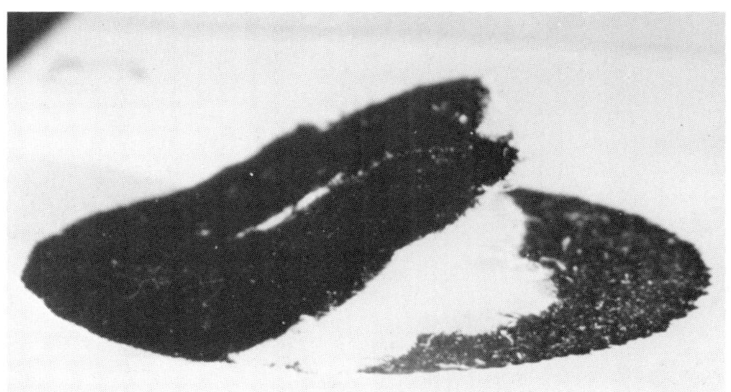

Paper pick-out.

Piling. The accumulation of pigment or coating from the paper onto the blanket or plate is called **piling.** Piling occurs when ink is made short on the press by emulsification with water and by dilution with dust, pigment, or other debris from the paper. As these are worked into the ink, transfer properties change, sometimes enough to prevent adequate ink transfer.

Ink, paper, dampening solution, and blankets are among the causes of this very complex phenomenon. If the surface of the blanket is very smooth, it forms a tight bond with the paper, pulling dust and pigment from the surface. Changing to a rougher

blanket may help, but adding a **nonpiling additive** (a glycol or a wax emulsion) to the dampening solution will also improve blanket release and often solve the piling problem. Dampening solution additives, of course, should be purchased from suppliers.

Ink setoff. When the ink of a printed sheet rubs off onto or marks the next sheet as it is being delivered, **setoff** has occurred. Ink setoff occurs when too much ink is run, when the ink is too soft, or when the ink does not set quickly enough. To avoid setoff, the ink's color can be strengthened and run in a thinner ink film. Also, the height of the delivery pile should be decreased. Setoff is less likely to occur when the ink has been made for the paper or board being printed. Most commonly, however, the printer solves setoff problems by using more spray powder or a coarser powder.

Tinting. Ink emulsifying into the dampening solution, which usually results from a poorly formulated ink or one that has been softened excessively, causes **tinting.** Excess acid in the dampening solution can also cause this problem. The usual remedy is to change inks. It is also possible to stiffen the ink with a binding varnish. Soaps and detergents should be avoided in dampening solutions. If wetting agents are required, the printer should secure an approved compound from a local supplier of lithographic chemicals.

Scumming. When the background area of the plate takes ink instead of remaining clean, **scumming** occurs. The ink adheres to the plate and is not readily wiped off with a cloth. Bad ink formulation, poorly chosen pigment, dirty dampeners, improperly set form rollers, too much pressure between blanket and plate, a poorly desensitized or light-struck plate, unsuitable paper, and improperly prepared lithographic film are among the causes of scumming.

Stripping. A lithographic ink must emulsify dampening solution moderately so that the ink continues to follow the rollers. If dampening solution replaces ink on the rollers, the phenomenon is called **stripping.** Glazed rollers where water-receptive materials have built up on the surface must be deglazed and cleaned with an abrasive pad.

Stripping usually occurs first on the form roller. Some inks can absorb as much as 100% of their weight of dampening solution and still transfer properly from one roller to the next and finally to the plate. Some stripping problems can be corrected by changing the ink-water balance or by changing the ink.

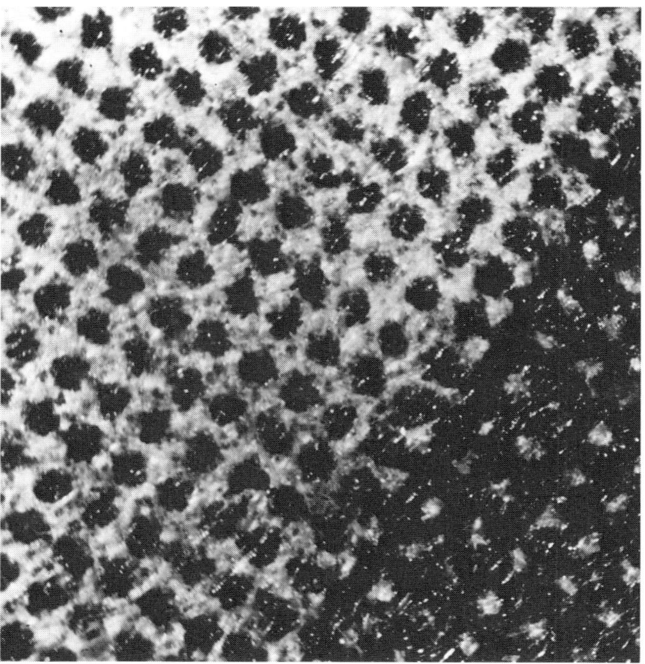

Ink-dot scum.

Mechanical ghosting. The problem known as **mechanical ghosting** occurs when a ghost image appears in the printed image. It results from inadequacies of the inking system, i.e., uneven ink take-off from the form rollers. Thus, the press cannot deliver a uniform ink film on jobs with nonuniform coverage. Ink removed from the ink form roller by the image on the plate is not completely replaced by the ink on the vibrator, which means that the form roller carries insufficient ink to the plate. Since the area that carries insufficient ink exactly corresponds to the image on the plate that removed it on the prior revolution, the image is reproduced and a ghost appears. Mechanical ghosts are always on the same side of the sheet as the image that is ghosted, unlike chemical ghosts that always appear on the opposite side of the sheet. Mechanical ghosts appear in both sheetfed and web lithography. Chemical ghosts occur only in sheetfed lithography.

Increasing the ink film thickness, adding an opaque ink, and reducing the amount of water on the plate help to reduce mechanical ghosting. Some presses cause much less ghosting than others. Special oscillating form rollers can greatly reduce mechanical ghosting. Good design of the form also keeps mechanical ghosting to a minimum.

Testing of Litho Inks

Ink tests are carried out either on the ink itself or on a printed sheet. Although printers normally rely on the ink manufacturer to conduct tests, some testing by the printer is recommended.

Color

A prime consideration of an ink is that it be the correct color for the job. In lithography, the existence of masstone and undertone is more significant than in the thicker gravure or screen inks.

In checking for batch-to-batch color variations, one of the simplest and most useful tests is to **draw the ink down** on a sheet of paper—a soft, white, rag bond—or on the paper that is to be printed. To make a drawdown, place a pea-sized dab of standard ink on the upper right-hand corner of the test sheet and place a similar sized dab of the ink to be tested next to it. Draw a wide, smooth steel blade or spatula across the pair of inks, drawing down in one even motion, first a thick film 1 in. long and then a thin film for the balance of the drawdown. The films should join to facilitate comparison. The drawdown shows the operator the comparison of the masstone and the undertone, the color match, and the comparative color strength of the prints. If the ink is drawn down on the paper to be printed, judgments can be made concerning gloss, mottle, and drying characteristics of the ink on the sheet.

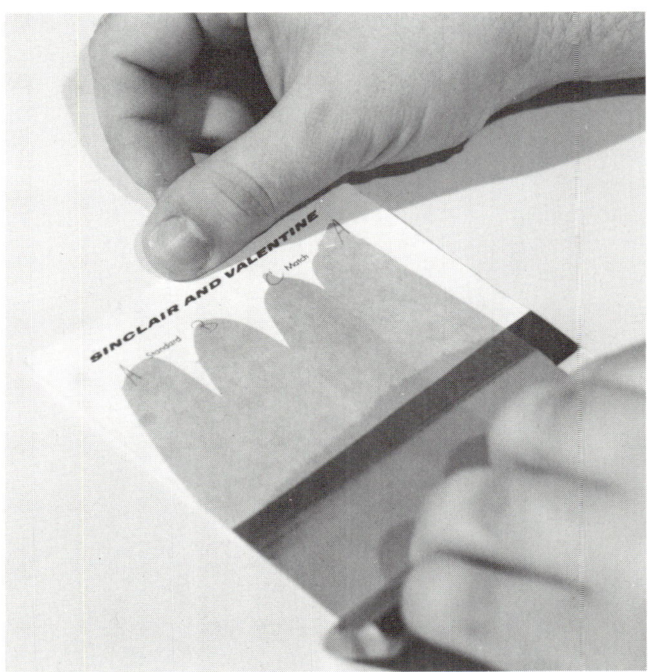

An ink drawdown.

Drawing ink down on a coated sheet is difficult, but the **Thwing-Albert Quickpeek Tester** provides a relatively simple way to apply ink to any sheet. A specific amount of ink is measured onto a stainless steel plate. Once the ink is properly distributed and worked, it is rolled onto the paper sample. As with drawdowns, the Quickpeek test is useful for observing drying time, gloss, mottle, and the color of the print.

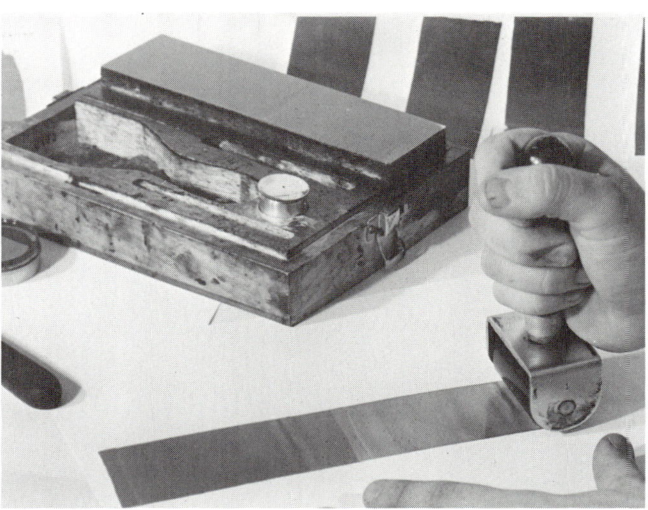

Quickpeek tester.

Ink Drying

A print is not ready for the next operation—cutting, folding, binding, or shipping—until the printed ink film is dry. Thus, it is imperative that the printer test the sheets to be sure that the ink is dry before proceeding with the job. This can be quickly and easily done with the thumb, or by rubbing a piece of paper over the print surface. If the prints are not dry, they must be allowed more time. If they do not dry within a few days, it may be necessary to varnish the sheets with a varnish containing excess drier to be sure that the job is acceptable. Although this is time consuming and will delay rush jobs, it is much better than doing the job over. Aqueous or UV overcoats can also be used. Conditions in the printing plant, as well as many other factors, affect drying time. Although a number of tests will give a good indication of what to expect in the pressroom, none will accurately

predict the time required before a printed pile may be cut, folded, or sent to the bindery.

For complete information on the rate of ink drying, the ink should be tested both on paper and on an impervious surface, such as glass. The time required for ink to dry on paper can vary with the stock and should be tested on the stock to be printed. The drying time on glass or metal is independent of any stock and indicates the tendency of an ink to skin in the can and dry on the press rollers.

In testing the drying time for sheetfed inks, the hand proof press or Quickpeek tester provides the best results, although a simpler method is to make a tap-out of the ink. The ink film should be about normal printed thickness. In either case, the proof or tap-out should be marked with the time it was made and inserted in a book or pile of paper or between glass plates. Then, every half hour, it should be removed and tested for dryness by rubbing with a finger. If the prints are allowed to remain on the workbench, they may dry somewhat faster owing to the ready access of air and lack of moisture.

The instruments designed to test drying time give better precision than rubbing with a finger. However, because so many variables are involved in the drying process, the accuracy with which they can predict the time required for a pile of prints to dry is probably no better.

Drying time for web offset inks can be tested with a **Sinvatrol tester.** In this device, a wet printed sample is passed through the tester on a conveyor. The tester measures conveyor speed and temperature, giving information used to predict specific dryer and web temperatures needed to dry heatset web offset inks on a given press.

Emulsification

There are many simple tests to determine the *tendency* of litho inks to emulsify. Unfortunately, none of them provides results that can be used to predict how an ink will perform on press. Inks that do not emulsify sufficient water and inks that emulsify too much water both perform poorly on the lithographic press.

The tendency of an ink to emulsify is best determined with a Duke tester, which controls the rate at which ink is mixed with water. Ink and water are mixed in the Duke tester for 10 min., and a sample is removed each minute. The water content in the emulsified ink sample is determined and water content is plotted against time on a graph. The accompanying figure illustrates both good and poor lithographic inks. The ink represented in curve A picks up too much water. It will tend to transfer to both image and nonimage areas, causing scumming, emulsification, low print density, and snowflaked solids. The ink on curve A will "gray out." The ink plotted on curve B can probably be run, but it will require constant attention. The ink represented in curve C, however, is an ideal lithographic ink. It will print sharply and be easy to run. Ink D cannot handle the water on press and the dots will tend to sharpen. Ink E cannot dispose of the water applied to the image area and will not print at all.

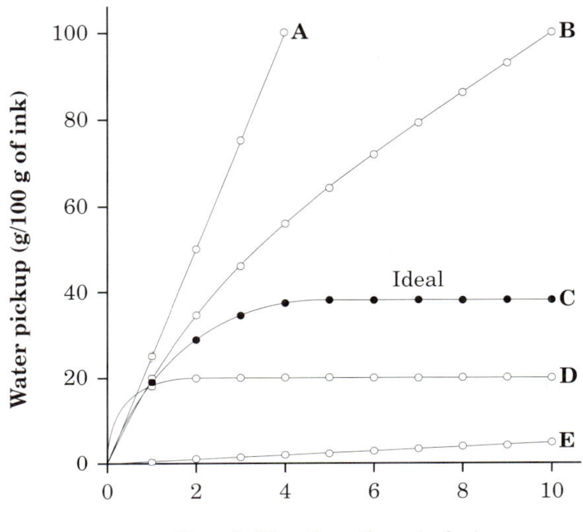

The GATF procedure for the Surland Emulsification Method using the Duke tester is as follows:

1. Place 50.0 g of ink in the bowl of the tester. Record the weight of the bowl, ink, and beaters.

2. Set the Duke tester for 90 rpm.

3. Place 100 ml of distilled water or test dampening solution in a 250-ml beaker and note its pH and conductivity.

4. Add 15.0 ml of the water or test dampening solution to the bowl with the ink, and turn on the tester. It will shut itself off after 90 revolutions. (Note: web offset or news inks may require 30.0 ml of test solution.)

5. Lift the beaters from the bowl, pour the unemulsified water back into the beaker and weigh the bowl, mixing blades, and emulsified ink. The increase in weight is the amount of water emulsified. The amount of water emulsified times two is the percent emulsification.

6. Take another 15.0 ml of water from the beaker, add it to the emulsified ink and run the test for another minute (90 revolutions).

7. Repeat steps 5 and 6 until ten tests have been run (the ink has been emulsified for 10 min.). Note the color, pH, and conductivity of the test solution, and draw a curve to show the amount of water taken up after each test. (The test takes about 45 min. to complete.)

Tinting Power

The test of tinctorial strength is probably the most important ink test for the printer. The value of an ink is directly related to its color strength.

Tinting power is determined by weighing a sample of the ink and diluting it with a large amount (usually fifty times as much) of a white ink or *tint base*. The ink is then thoroughly mixed. A similar amount of a standard ink is also weighed and mixed with the tint base. The two inks are then drawn down side by side, and the color is observed. Additional tint base is now added to the darker sample until the lightness of the two mixtures match. The relative amount of tint base required to give a match is noted.

Viscosity

The viscosity of an ink determines how it flows on the press; viscosity affects the tack, penetration, drying, gloss, rub resistance, and color of the print. Instruments that measure viscosity, called **viscometers,** range from relatively simple viscosity cups to sophisticated electronic instruments.

Because viscosity is affected by changes in temperature, the temperature of the ink must be controlled if the measurement is to be meaningful.

The most common viscometer used for measuring ink viscosity is the **Laray viscometer.** This instrument consists of a rod that drops through a film of ink held in a cuff surrounding the rod. The more viscous the ink, the longer it takes the rod to drop. Various weights are placed on the rod, and the time is measured accurately with an automatic timer. As the weights change, the time changes, and the results are plotted on a suitable graph. The graph gives three values, the viscosity, the yield strength, and a measure of thixotropy of the ink.

Flow

A test for relative flow properties of two or more inks is made with the **Columbian carbon flow plate.** Work the inks to be compared thoroughly on the ink slab. Place exactly 3.0 grams or 3.0 cm^3 of each ink in the upper end of a channel and tilt the bed to the desired angle. Record the length of flow after 15 min. This flow plate is helpful to ink manufacturers in testing the flow characteristics of disperse pigments, especially blacks.

Tack

The ink manufacturer is primarily interested in tack as a quality control measurement, whether the ink under study has the required properties and whether it has the same properties as the last batch. The printer is interested in controlling ink tack to prevent picking of the paper and to ensure proper trapping in multicolor printing.

Tack used to be judged with a finger tap-out, but this outmoded test is highly subjective and nonquantitative. Results are not closely repeatable, even by an experienced observer. The GATF-developed Inkometer (now provided by Thwing-Albert Instrument Co.) and several other instruments give numerical results that are far more useful in measuring or comparing inks.

The **inkometer** is a machine that simulates the rollers on a press. It measures the integrated forces involved in film splitting and the effects of speed, film thickness, temperature, and solvent evaporation on these forces. The electronic models provide digital readouts automatically every 10 sec. Mechanical models are similar except that the readings are taken by manually balancing a scale beam at measured time intervals.

Because there are many variables on a multicolor press—such as the speed of the press, the surface of the paper, and the use of inks in the sequence—different tacks are required depending on the job. The inkometer is useful for determining comparative standards and for determining whether batches of inks delivered from time to time are uniform. It

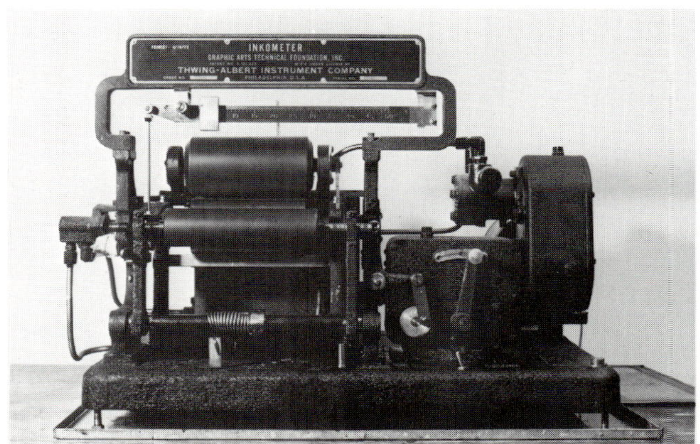

Inkometer.

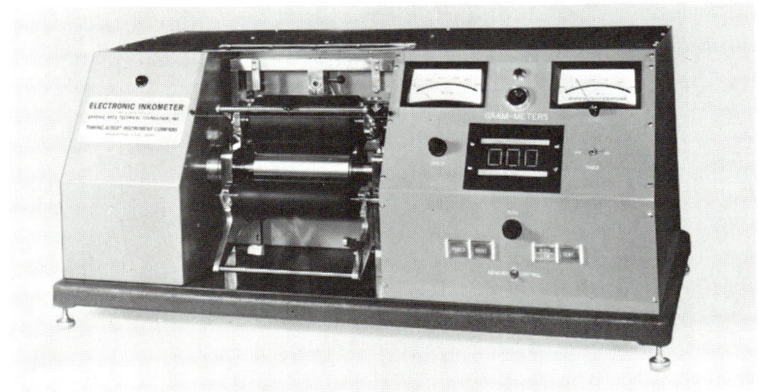

Electronic Inkometer.

can also be used to determine whether or not the process colors have the proper tack sequence. Because of difficulties in standardizing the test, absolute values are often misleading.

Length

Ink that is too short does not transfer properly (from roll to roll or from blanket to paper). Ink that is too long tends to fly or mist. While these are not common, serious problems, it may be useful to check ink length. There is no standard test for this property.

To test for length, place small, equal portions of the standard and test inks on the ink slab and work each ink thoroughly with the spatula to break down any false body. Compare length by lifting a portion of each ink with a spatula or fingertip several times and estimating the distance at which the string breaks.

Fineness of Grind

The test for fineness of grind is one of the most important of all ink tests. It gives a measure of pigment dispersion and indicates the presence or absence of particulate debris in ink.

Inks containing well-dispersed pigments are important to good performance on the press. Poorly ground ink contributes to piling on press rollers, plates, and blankets; weaker colors; streaking; plate fill-in; unnecessary wearing of plates and rollers; and scumming.

A fineness-of-grind gauge is used to measure pigment dispersion. Although the test cannot predict that an ink will pile or cake, when piling or caking occurs it can indicate whether improper pigment dispersion is the cause.

Product Resistance

There are many tests for determining whether the ink used to print a package will be resistant to the product within the package. These products can include substances such as alkali, soap, alcohol, and varnish. The ink manufacturer should be relied upon to conduct the appropriate tests. For further information, contact the Paperboard Packaging Council, 1101 Vermont Avenue, N.W., Suite 411, Washington, DC 20006.

Density and Specific Gravity

Density is the weight/volume ratio and is measured in terms of the number of grams per milliliter. **Specific gravity** is the ratio of the weight of ink to the weight of an equal volume of water.

Inks are most commonly purchased on a weight basis but consumed on a volume basis. Therefore, it is desirable to determine the volume represented by a pound of ink, or the weight of ink per given volume.

Specific gravity of ink is related to ink mileage. In general, higher-gravity inks yield less mileage per pound than lower-gravity inks.

The American Society for Testing and Materials (ASTM) has a number of tests for density and specific gravity.

Chapter 14
Paper

Papermaking

Papermaking is a blend of ancient craft and modern technology. Chemistry and engineering are making major contributions to papermaking. Pulp and papermaking are becoming increasingly automated through greater understanding of the process and through techniques and instruments used to measure and control products and processes.

The word "paper" is derived from "papyrus," the reed that grows along the Nile River. The ancient Egyptians wove papyrus into mats and used it for writing. True paper originated in China, about the first century AD. To make paper, bamboo or mulberry was beaten in water, and the resulting suspension of fibers was formed into a sheet by filtering them through a screen. The invention of paper is generally ascribed to an imperial officer, Ts'ai Lun, in AD 105.

Paper can be made from various plants. The shape of a plant's fibers determines its suitability as a fibrous source. A papermaking fiber must be hollow and tubular or quill-shaped. Other determining factors in the selection of a plant for fibrous raw material are its dependability of supply and the costs of harvesting, transportation, and manufacturing into pulp.

Paper has been made from trees, rags, sugarcane, straw, grasses such as esparto and kenaf, and other vegetable substances. Sugarcane is grown in most tropical and subtropical regions. After the cane is ground to obtain its sugar juices, a fibrous residue called **bagasse** remains. Before chemical pulping, bagasse undergoes a depithing treatment to isolate its fibers. Cereal grain straws are sources of papermaking fiber in some parts of the world. **Esparto** is a grass that grows wild in North Africa and southern Spain, and has long been used as a papermaking fiber in England. **Kenaf** is an annual agricultural plant native to India. It is being researched as a potential fiber source in the southern regions of the United States. **Bamboos,** wood plants of the grass family that grow in tropical regions, are important sources of papermaking fibers in some countries. **Manila hemp** or **sisal hemp** from used ropes and cordage and jute cuttings from burlap are sometimes used in papermaking.

Cotton and linen fibers have long been used. Cotton fibers are derived from cuttings, threads and waste from textile manufacturing, raw cotton, and cotton linters. Cotton **linters** are the short, seed-hair fibers remaining on cotton seeds after the staple, long-fibered cotton, has been removed by ginning. Cotton fibers are excellent for producing high-quality, fine-textured, durable writing papers because their fibers are longer than wood fibers and are flat and twisted. **Flax tow** is the source of linen fibers used to manufacture cigarette, Bible, carbonizing, and other high-quality specialty papers.

Other materials used to make paper include polyethylene and acrylic polymers. However, internationally, 95% of all papermaking fibers are derived from wood. In North America, about 99% of papermaking fibers are derived from wood.

Wood. Trees are divided botanically into two groups: softwoods and hardwoods. The **coniferous,** or cone-bearing, trees are also designated as the softwood group. Examples are redwood, spruce, pine, fir, larch, cedar, and hemlock. Softwoods are called **gymnosperms,** which means "naked seed," by the botanist. From the papermaker's point of view, their most important characteristic is that their relatively long fibers—0.12 to 0.16 in. (3.0 to 4.5 mm)—yield paper of high strength. The **deciduous,** or hardwood, trees include birch, beech,

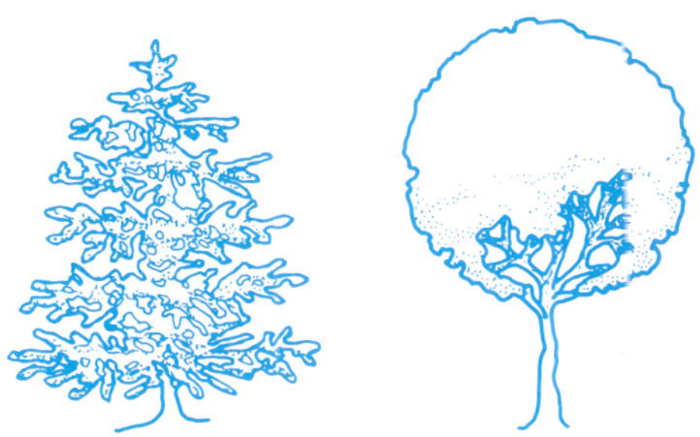

Outlines of a coniferous tree *(left)* and a deciduous tree.

maple, elm, oak, poplar, gum, aspen, and cottonwood. These **angiosperms,** which means "enclosed seed," have fibers that are about one-third as long as those of the coniferous. Their fibers contribute smoothness to the paper.

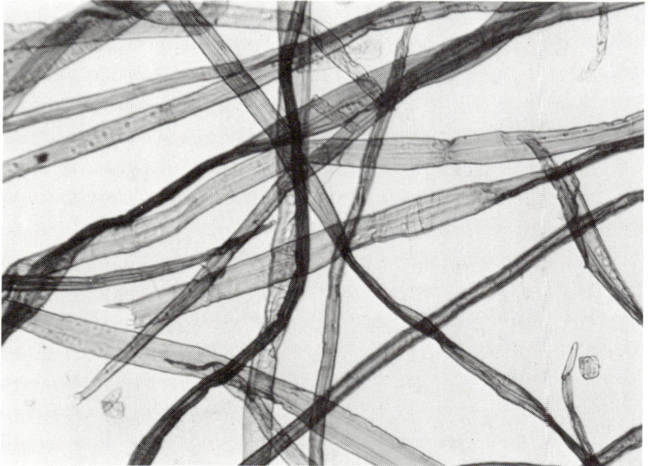

Courtesy Institute of Paper Chemistry
Softwood fibers (jack pine), enlarged (90×).

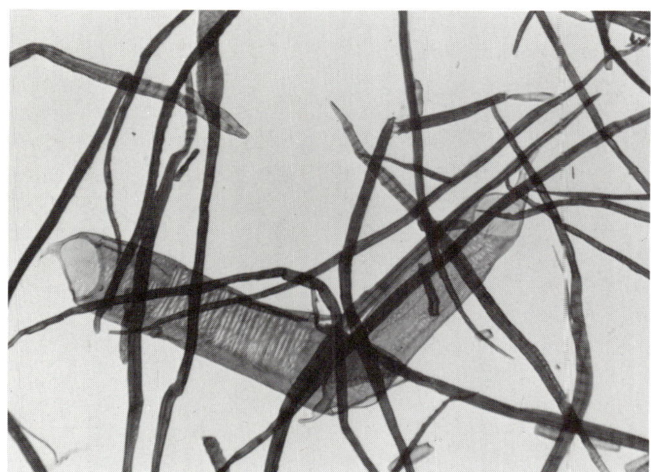

Courtesy Institute of Paper Chemistry
Hardwood fibers (beech), enlarged (90×).

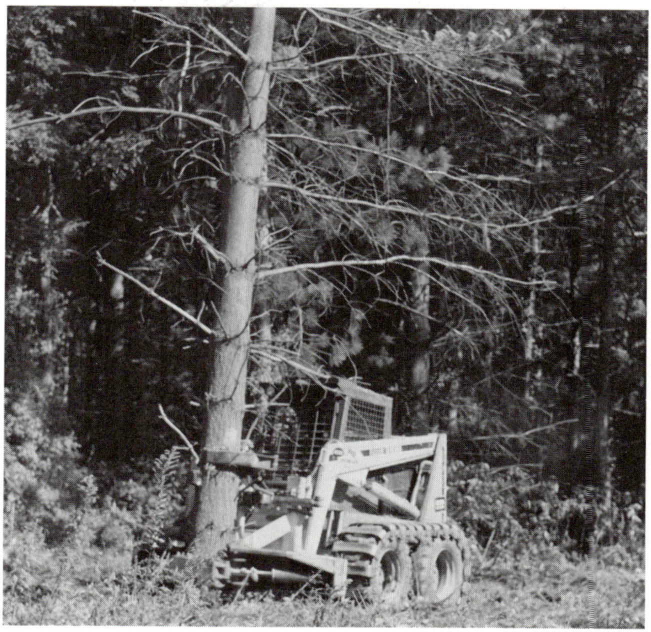

Courtesy Glatfelter Pulpwood Co.
Ground-level hydraulic shear, permitting whole-tree utilization when converting wood into chips at the harvesting site.

Since strength and smoothness are both desired in a printing paper, hardwood and softwood pulps are blended, usually in the ratio of about two parts hardwood to one part softwood.

Wood is composed of cellulose, lignin, and hemicellulose. Approximately one half of the tree is **cellulose,** which are the fibers used for making paper. Cotton fibers are over 98% cellulose. Cellulose is nature's most abundant organic chemical. It

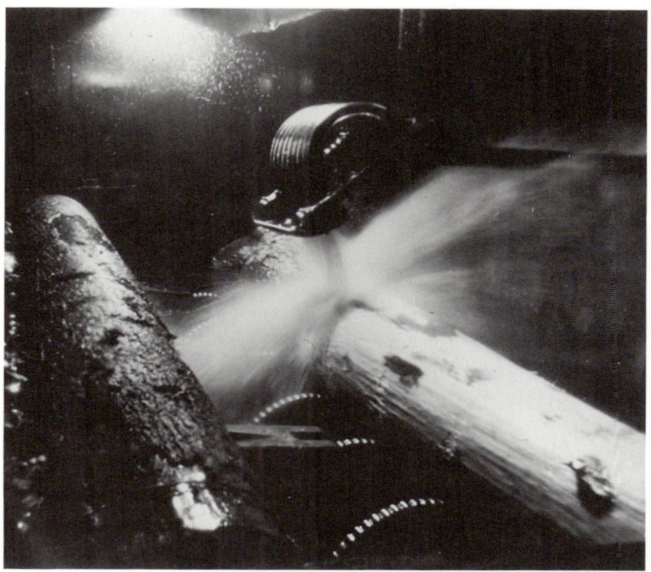

Courtesy Georgia-Pacific Co.
Hydraulic barking with jets of high-pressure water.

is a very complex polymer structured by nature from the chemical elements carbon, hydrogen, and oxygen. Cellulose has many properties that make it useful for papermaking: it is abundant and replenishable; it can be harvested and easily transported to its usage site; and in its fibrous form, it has very high tensile strength and a great affinity for water.

About one quarter of the tree is **lignin,** which is the adhesive that holds the cellulose fibers together. The remaining quarter is **hemicelluloses,** which are by-products of the growth of the cellulose. Hemicellulose contributes to paper strength, but much of the hemicellulose content is lost during pulping by chemical processes.

Throughout most of the world, the supply of pulpwood is constantly being replenished. Furthermore, forest industries are making increasingly complete use of the tree, using large trees for lumber and pulping the sawdust and trim for paper. Waste, bark, and leaves are burned for power at the mill or they are returned to the soil. Better utilization of wood is provided through this whole-tree concept. The tree is cut at its base or ground level and its entire foliage, branches, and trunk are converted into chips at the harvesting site. The pressure on future fiber supply will be relieved as better processing technology for the utilization of wood is developed and whole-tree chipping is increased.

Pulp

The character of fibers in different woods varies considerably, and trees of the same species from different parts of the country have fibers that are different in character. Consequently, it is difficult to describe and classify all of the fiber differences that occur in pulp. However, important classes of pulps commonly used can be grouped as follows: mechanical pulp (groundwood), chemical wood pulp, reclaimed paper pulp, and rag pulp.

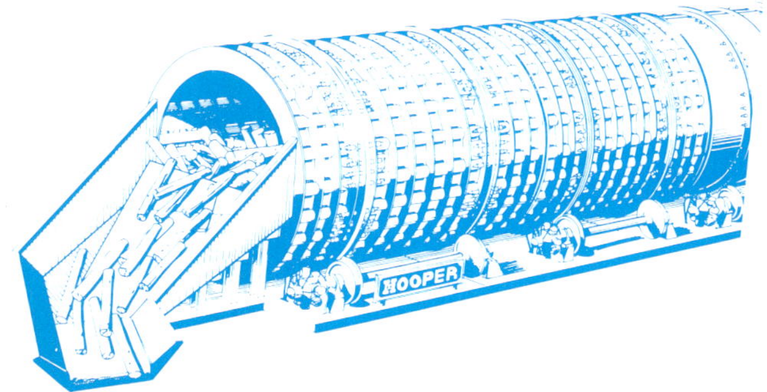

Courtesy S. W. Hooper Corp.

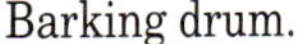

Barking drum.

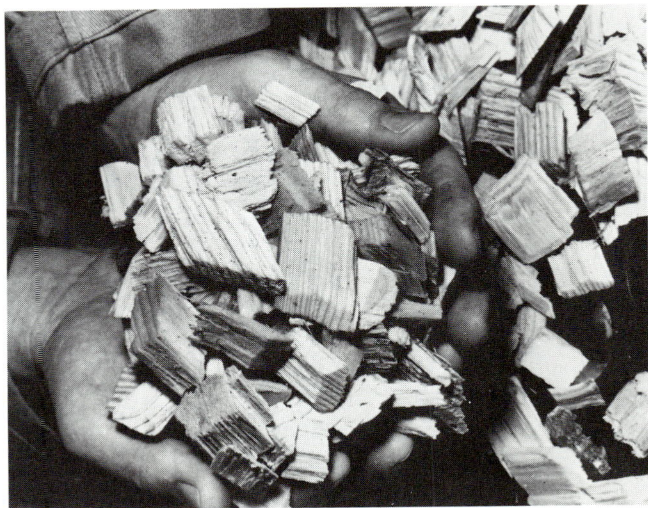

Courtesy P. H. Glatfelter Co.

Chips ready for conversion into chemical pulp.

Pulpwood comes in various forms: roundwood, chips, sawdust, shavings, slabs, and edging. Many pulpmills receive a major portion of their wood in chip form. Bark is often removed from roundwood since it has little or no fiber value, contributes to dirt, consumes wood-digesting chemicals, and lowers pulp quality. (Nevertheless, whole-tree chipping is an important and growing practice.) Bark can be removed from pulpwood logs by processing them in a drum-type barker or by hydraulic means.

Debarked logs are sent directly to the pulp grinders. When it is used with other pulping methods, it is converted into chips or other suitable form for traveling to refiners or digesters.

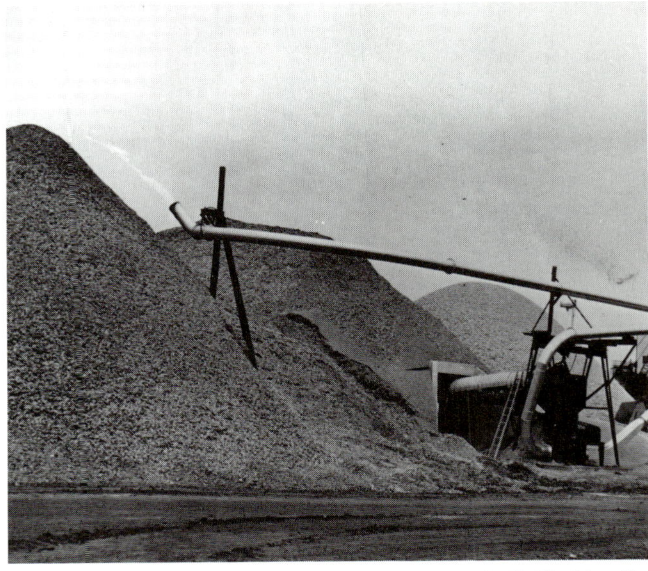

Courtesy P. H. Glatfelter Co.

Piles of chips ready to be taken to the digester.

Mechanical pulp (groundwood). Mechanical pulp, or groundwood, was the first commercial wood pulp. In the conventional method for producing groundwood, a peeled log is placed against a grindstone. The friction generates heat that softens the lignin, and cellulose fibers are pulled out of the log. The fibers are washed away from the grinding stone with water showers, and they begin to travel to the paper machine.

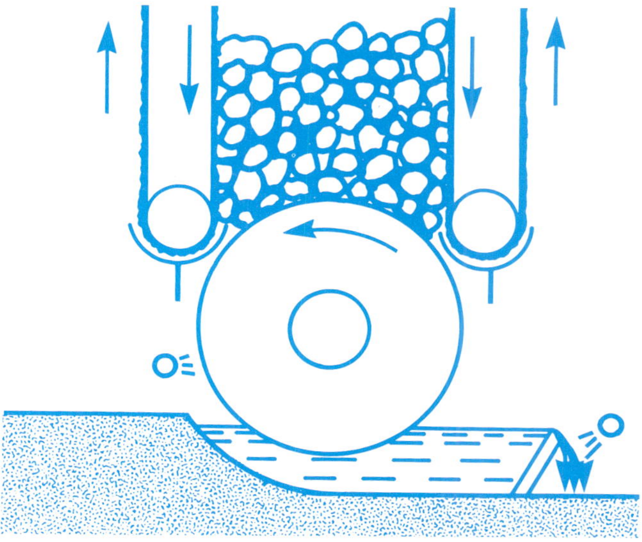

Stone grinder.

The advantages of groundwood pulp are its low cost and high yield. It has high bulk and opacity, and excellent printing cushion and ink absorbency. The disadvantages of groundwood are low strength and brightness, lack of permanency, yellowing with age, and the presence of objectionable shives. **Shives** are undefibered fiber bundles that are torn from the wood during grinding. Papers produced from groundwood pulp yellow with age because all of the lignin of the tree is included in the pulp. Lignin darkens very rapidly when exposed to light, and less rapidly when stored in the dark. Papers with groundwood content are generally unsuitable for printed products such as encyclopedias, dictionaries, ledgers, or other items that must remain useful over the years.

Twenty-five percent or more of the world's wood pulp is derived from groundwood. Its uses include the manufacture of newsprint, coated groundwood printing and publication papers, uncoated groundwood papers for pulp magazines, telephone directories, catalogs, and household papers. The groundwood process is simple and, historically, inexpensive. However, it yields no by-products that can be used as fuel, and the increasing cost of electricity has reduced the economic advantage of producing pulp in this way. Nevertheless, because lignin and hemicelluloses are not dissolved in the pulping process, most of the wood is converted to pulp, and the yields are very high.

Coated groundwood paper has better brightness and better brightness retention than uncoated groundwood. It is used for printing magazines, catalogs, and other low-cost publications.

Refiner mechanical pulp (RMP). Advances in pulping technology have made it possible to overcome some of the undesirable properties of groundwood while retaining its advantages. One advance is refiner mechanical pulp, or RMP. It is produced by passing wood chips through a **disk refiner** instead of grinding wood against stone. The refiner has two disks that rotate in opposite directions at high speeds (or one is rotating and one is fixed). The disks have grooved surfaces, and when chips with water are placed between them, they are subjected to an intensive mechanical action as they contact each other and the refining surfaces. The chips are heated and the lignin is softened with the high frictional resistance, thereby permitting fiber separation with little fiber damage. Refiner mechanical pulp has few shives, and has fibers more individually separated compared to groundwood. It also has fewer fiber fines and longer fibers than groundwood.

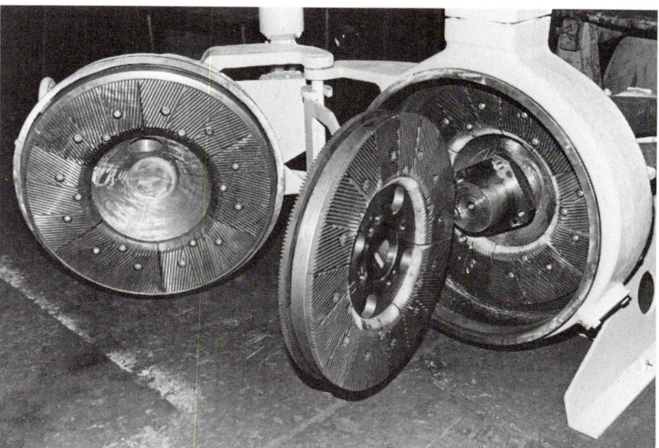

Courtesy Black Clawson Co.

Twin-disk refiner, open.

Thermomechanical pulp (TMP). Another advance in pulping technology is thermomechanical pulp, or TMP. It is produced similarly to RMP except that the wood chips or sawdust is preheated with steam before passing through a disk refiner.

The lignin that binds the cellulose fibers together is softened by preheating. Therefore, fibers are separated more easily, with less splintering and damage, as the softened chips pass through the refiner. It retains the advantages of high opacity and a high-yield pulp, and is virtually free of shives. TMP is used to produce newsprint, magazines, and coated publication papers.

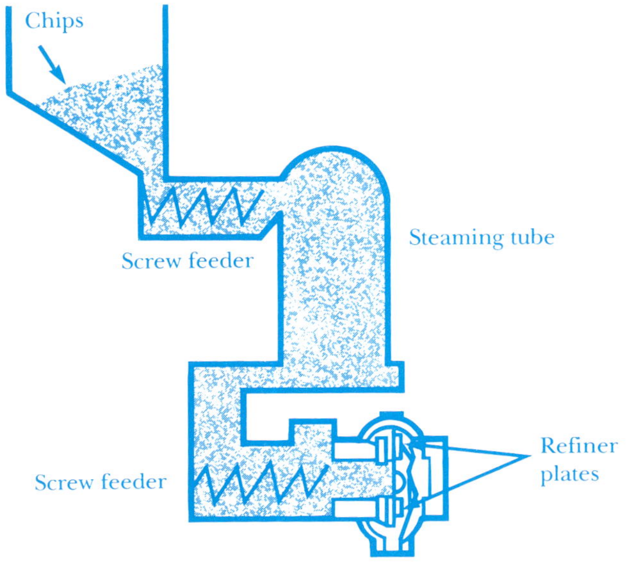

Thermomechanical pulping process.

Chemical wood pulp. In conventional pulping, peeled logs are reduced to chips and cooked with alkaline or acid materials to dissolve and remove the lignin. Recently, whole-tree chipping has been used in producing chemical wood pulp. This procedure gives a higher fiber yield, but it requires more chemicals to remove the dirt and more electric power for screening and cleaning. Chemical pulp is also being made increasingly from by-products of the lumber industry. The large logs are cut into lumber, and the slabs and sawdust are used for pulp.

Three kinds of chemical pulping will be discussed here: sulfate, sulfite, and semichemical.

Sulfate, or kraft, pulp. The word "kraft" is German and Swedish for "strength." This process produces fibers that are relatively undamaged and very strong. Sulfate pulp makes strong papers with especially good tear and tensile strength. The kraft pulping process is now the leading chemical pulping process.

The pulp is produced by cooking wood chips with sodium hydroxide and sodium sulfide. Sodium sulfide is produced from sodium sulfate, hence the name.

The sulfate process has several advantages: its greater adaptability for pulping, which includes almost every known wood species, and an efficient chemical recovery system.

The pulp is used to make kraft paper for grocery bags, wrapping paper, and corrugated board. Historically, it has been difficult to bleach, but work done in the mid-twentieth century has developed bleaching processes that yield a strong, bright pulp.

The kraft pulping process converts parts of the lignin into dimethyl sulfide, dimethyl disulfide, and methyl mercaptan—three very foul smelling chemicals. When these are discharged into the air, the "papermill smell" can be detected for miles. It has been said, probably correctly, that more attention has been paid to this environmental problem than to any other. Tiny traces, less than one part per billion parts of air, of these materials create a strong odor, and it has not been easy to reduce the material escaping from the mill to quantities less than this.

Sulfite pulp. Sulfite pulping was the first chemical pulping process. Sulfite pulps are easily bleached, but less strong than kraft pulps as the pulping process causes significant damage to the fibers.

In this process, the wood chips are cooked with sulfurous acid and one of its base salts, which may be calcium, sodium, magnesium, or ammonia. Sulfurous acid is produced by burning sulfur to form sulfur dioxide gas and reacting it with water. Next, sulfurous acid and limestone are reacted to form calcium bisulfite. This combined solution of sulfurous acid and calcium bisulfite solubilizes lignin during cooking.

Unbleached sulfite pulp has moderate strength, is soft and flexible, has a low lignin content, and is easily bleached. Its uses include supplementing mechanical fibers (as in newsprint), and making white printing and writing papers. Until the mid-1900s, it was the most important chemical pulping process. It is not suitable for pulping woods that have a high resinous content like the southern pines of the United States. Another drawback to using this process is that pollution abatement has become more stringent. It is impractical to recover the calcium base sulfite liquors, which would thereby reduce the pollution load of its effluent. Other chemical bases have evolved: sodium, magnesium, and ammonia. These bases, which are adapted to pulpmill chemical recovery systems, reduce pollution load.

Neutral sulfite semichemical pulp. Caustic soda is reacted with sulfur dioxide to produce a liquor that is nearly neutral in pH. Cooking is carried only part way, and pulping is completed by use of a refiner. The process is particularly favorable for pulping hardwoods that yield a pulp somewhat stronger and more dense than when they are pulped by the kraft process. The paper is somewhat less opaque, however. This pulp is widely used for corrugated board.

Rag pulp. There has always been a shortage of rags; in fact it was this shortage that prompted Mitscherlich to develop the sulfite process in the early nineteenth century. Cotton or linen fibers are much longer than wood fibers, and they yield a paper that is much stronger than the paper obtained from wood pulps. The expensive product is usually restricted to paper for banknotes, high-grade bond, and map paper.

New cotton rags that have never been dyed or colored yield a very strong paper that folds well. Colored rags and used rags make an inferior pulp and paper because the cleansing process weakens the fibers. Cotton linters, the fibers that remain on the seed after the cotton has been ginned, are used to make paper. The raw linters do not bond well, but after chemical treatment, they yield a strong sheet.

Cotton or linen rags, raw cotton, cotton linters, and cotton textile waste used to manufacture high-quality, permanent writing papers are given prolonged cooking with chemicals such as soda, ash, lime, or caustic soda, along with detergents. The cooked fibers are thoroughly washed and are usually refined simultaneously in a beater-type washer. During this treatment, residual chemicals, dirt, and coloring matter are removed, and the long fibers are teased out for their subsequent refining. Bleaching follows.

Recycled paper. Recycling paper as a fibrous source is not a new process. Evidence shows that it was practiced before 1637 by the Chinese.

Wastepaper is defibered by heating and by cooking in chemicals that dissolve or disperse the printing ink. When recycled wastepaper is used to make fine, white printing and writing paper, it requires deinking to remove ink and contaminants. Chipboard, the type of material used for tablet backing and for clothing boxes, is often not deinked.

Unprinted trimmings from paper plates, envelope manufacture, and computer cards contain no ink, and they are easily bleached to give a high-grade printing paper.

Chlorination and bleaching. Before wood pulp is bleached, it has a color ranging from cream to dark brown. Papers are bleached white for these reasons: printing contrast improves as the whiteness of paper increases; whiter papers are aesthetically desirable; colored papers become more brilliant when whiter pulps are used; bleaching contributes to the chemical stability, purity, and permanence of chemical pulps; and bleaching is necessary for sanitary reasons, as for food packaging papers. After the wood has been converted to pulp, the pulp is washed with water to remove the chemical solution in which the nonfibrous materials are dissolved. The pulp is then screened to separate it from undigested knots and shives.

The next step is to bleach the pulp if it is to be used for white paper. In the case of virgin pulp, it is still dark and is called **brown stock.** In the case of recycled wastepaper, color depends upon the source of wastepaper.

Unbleached chemical pulps contain residual lignin and other extractives. If chemical pulping is continued to the point of complete lignin removal, the cellulose fibers will be severely degraded. To produce white pulp, the residual lignin, which plays a major role in the pulp's dark color, must be removed or altered by bleaching. Bleaching doesn't chemically damage the cellulose.

The pulp is treated with chlorine, which reacts with residual lignin, and then with caustic. To bleach the pulp without unduly attacking the cellulose fibers, bleaching is normally carried out in several steps, with the pulp growing brighter after each operation. The removal of lignin improves the brightness of the fibers, improves their color stability, and decreases their opacity. The actual treatments depend on the type of pulp and the method of its preparation. Kraft or sulfate pulps are difficult to bleach; sulfite pulps are easily bleached.

Chlorine dioxide bleaching, the final bleaching step for kraft pulp, rapidly and selectively removes the remaining lignin and produces clean, white kraft pulp. The strength of the fibers is not destroyed, and the pulp is suitable for the manufacture of printing and writing papers.

A new bleaching agent used during multistage bleaching is oxygen. Oxygen bleaching reduces a bleach plant's pollution load.

Most of the lignin is retained in mechanical pulps. When these pulps are bleached, some of their coloring substances are removed or altered without any substantial removal of the constituents responsible for their dark color. Since high yield is one of the main advantages of mechanical pulps, it

is necessary to prevent undue loss of fiber weight and yield.

Newsprint, which typically contains 75% to 80% groundwood, is frequently sold without bleaching; however, if it must be bleached, chlorine cannot be used because chlorine reacts with the lignin. Sodium or zinc hydrosulfate and sodium or hydrogen peroxide are used to bleach groundwood pulps.

Papermaking

Stock preparation and refining. Papermaking fibers from the pulpmill are only partially prepared for papermaking. If used at this time, they would produce paper with low strength, uncontrollable texture, and a wild, uneven formation. The fibers must undergo stock preparation and refining to make them suitable for papermaking. **Stock preparation** includes fiber refining and the blending of fibrous and nonfibrous materials into the desired proportions for the papermaking furnish.

Beating, or refining, makes the fibers more flexible and increases their surface by **fibrillating** (roughening or fraying) them so that more area is available for bonding. Fibrillating generates tiny paper fibrils by abrading and unraveling the cellulose fibers. The fibers are also cut or shortened. Although cutting decreases their strength, it produces a sheet with better formation (more uniform distribution of fibers).

There are several types of equipment for refining pulp. The first mechanical refiner was the **beater.** The beater is used today as the initial refining step in smaller-capacity mills. It has an oval-shaped tub around which the pulp is circulated. The tub is equipped with a roll fitted with metal bars that rotates over a bed plate having similar rows of metal bars. The fibers are drawn between moving bars that contact stationary bars in the presence of water: this is known as beating. The fibers are fibrillated, and their surface areas are increased for greater fiber-to-fiber contact and bonding during papermaking. Refining in a beater is done in batches.

In large mills, beating pulp in batches has been replaced by continuous refining using disk refiners. Refining consists of a combination of rolling and rubbing the fibers, dispersion, and cutting.

The **Jordan,** or **conical,** refiner is used for additional refining after the beater or disk refiner. It has a conical rotor, or plug, with metal bars attached along its length, and it revolves inside a conical shell also lined with bars. The fibers enter at the smaller end of the rotating plug and are forced through the cone, passing between the opposing rows of bars. The clearance between the bars is set to cut, brush, or bruise the fibers, depending on the nature of the stock and the requirements of the paper to be produced.

Effect of refining. Pulp is refined or beaten primarily to increase the bonding of paper fibers. It increases the Mullen or bursting strength, folding strength, tensile strength, smoothness, and density of the paper. Tearing strength is increased initially, but it soon decreases. Refining always decreases

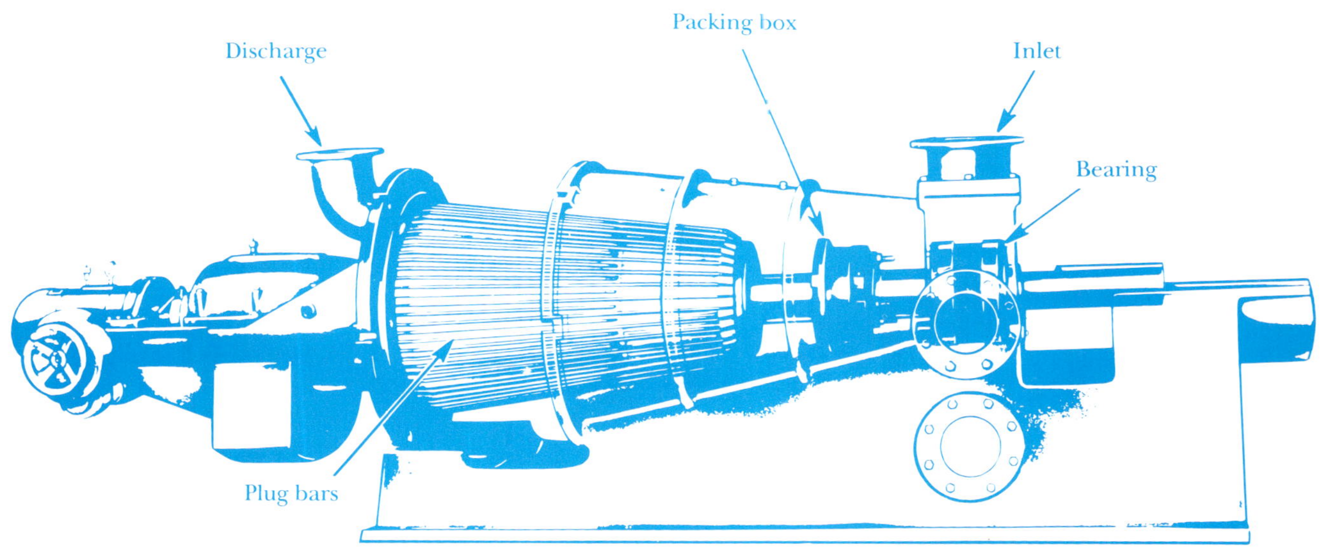

Jordan refiner.

brightness, opacity, porosity, bulk, and softness of the sheet. Carried to the extreme, refining produces a glassine paper that has high transparency, high tensile strength, poor tearing resistance, and other properties predicted from excessive beating. Paper made from unrefined pulps is bulky, weak, soft, and absorbent, has high opacity, and tends to fluff and lint.

Refining ruptures the outer wall of the fiber, and the internal fiber walls absorb water and swell. An actual chemical change occurs in which internal hydrogen bonds are broken, generating free hydroxyl groups that can form new hydrogen bonds when the paper is dried. The strength of paper depends on this chemical bonding. Cellulose sheets prepared from alcohol, acetone, or other organic materials have much less strength than papers formed in water.

The papermaker controls paper quality by controlling the refiner. If the paper machine is set tightly, it tends to cut pulp fibers, giving a very smooth, weak sheet. If the paper machine is set less tightly, the fibers are not cut and the pulp produces a paper with higher tensile strength. Various types of paper are produced depending upon the amount of work put into the paper during refining and upon the way the refiner is set. Bulky, soft grades, such as antiques require only a small amount of refining, whereas others like bonds that need rattle are given more refining. Transparent papers, such as tracing paper or glassine are refined extensively.

Paper Additives

During, or following refining, a number of materials may be added to the fibers to achieve the properties desired in the final paper.

Starch. Cooked starch is added to the paper stock furnish to increase strength and "rattle." Starch also increases stiffness, but decreases opacity. Starch increases the number of chemical bonds in the paper. The most commonly used starch is corn starch, but potato and tapioca starches are also used.

Fillers. Clay, calcium carbonate, titanium dioxide, or other pigments may be added to improve dimensional stability, opacity, brightness, and printing smoothness. These are fillers, also known as **loading.** They are used mainly because of their beneficial influence on other properties related to printability. Opacity and brightness are increased, and the print quality of uncoated papers is improved. Fillers are relatively inert to moisture in comparison to fibers, and they make paper less sensitive to changes in relative humidity and improve its dimensional stability. They also improve the printing surface, reduce ink strike-through, and decrease fiber harshness.

Clay used in papermaking originates from refined natural kaolin clay. It is an aluminum silicate, a natural product obtained from the earth and refined to remove grit and brown color. It is used primarily to make the paper smoother and to improve its affinity for printing ink. Calcium carbonate is brighter than clay and has a high affinity for ink. It is used in alkaline pulping systems. Titanium dioxide is brighter than either calcium carbonate or clay and excels in improving both the brightness and opacity of paper. Examples of other, lesser-used fillers are hydrate alumina, talc, calcium sulfate, barium sulfate, natural or synthetic silicas or silicate pigments, and zinc oxide.

The percentage of fillers used in printing and writing papers usually falls within the range of 5 to 30% of a paper's total weight. Less or no filler is used for some papers.

Fillers for papermaking have several requirements: high brightness, good light-scattering properties for increasing opacity, nonabrasiveness, and chemical inertness for papermaking and end-use requirements.

Retention aids. To improve retention of pigments, especially titanium dioxide, the papermaker may add retention aids, which are synthetic polymers or chemically modified natural polymers.

To improve fiber retention, fiber adhesion, and dry strength, additives like starches, gums, and synthetic polymers are used. Additives such as melamine-formaldehyde and urea-formaldehyde resins are used in papers that must retain most of their dry strength after being soaked in water.

Dyes and pigments. Most papers are dyed or colored to match some predetermined color specification. Adding blue or red dyes improves the visual "brightness" of white papers by overcoming the natural yellow color of the fibers. Color may be incorporated by using either a dye that attaches itself to the cellulose or by using a pigment that is retained by the sheet.

If the sheet is to be dyed a deep color, a dye may be added after the sheet has been formed, such as at the size press or the coater. Pigments are used to cover the fibers and to obtain a smoother surface.

Internal sizing. Internal sizing is added to the papermaking stock to control the penetration of liquids, primarily water. Particularly, stocks for offset lithographic papers must be sized to reduce the penetration of water. Sheetfed papers require more sizing than web papers. The most common materials used for sizing paper are alum and rosin, but synthetic sizing is also used for special purposes.

Rosin is an acidic material obtained from pine trees, and when reacted with caustic, it forms a rosin soap. The water-soluble rosin soap is added to the paper stock and "set" on the fibers with an acid salt, such as aluminum sulfate, or papermaker's alum.

When **alum** is used, the paper is slightly acidic. In addition to bonding the rosin to the cellulose, the alum greatly accelerates the aging of the paper. Where archival properties are required of paper, new synthetic-polymeric sizing agents are incorporated without the use of alum.

Sometimes **synthetic latexes** (latices) are added to increase strength, flexibility, or chemical resistance of the paper. They are more commonly added at the size press than to the papermaking furnish.

Sheet Formation

The material is now referred to as **stock, stuff,** or **paper machine furnish,** and it is ready to go to the papermaking machine. Printing and writing papers, newsprint, and most other papers and some paperboards are made on fourdrinier machines, but some tissue papers and some paperboards are produced on cylinder machines.

When the **fourdrinier** machine is used, the stock is pumped into the "head box," which is a box that maintains head or pressure to assure an even flow of stock to the "wire." The wire is actually a metal or plastic screen. Brass and bronze screens, used for decades, have now been replaced by plastic screens, which are still referred to as "wires." The stock, which has been diluted to a consistency between 0.5% and 1% fiber by weight, flows onto the wire, and the water drains through the wire.

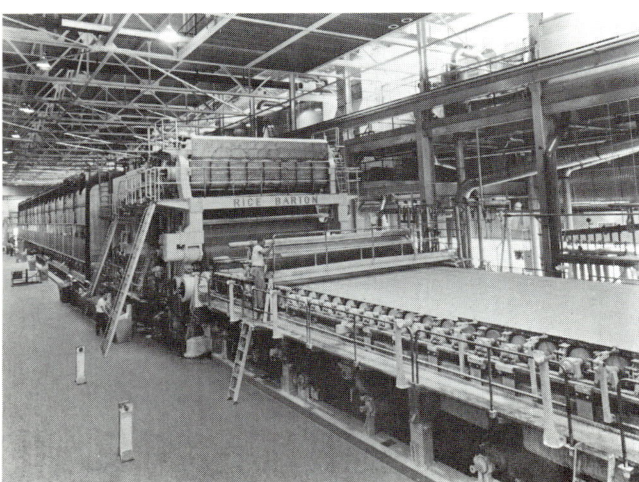

Courtesy P. H. Glatfelter Co.

Wet end of a large, high-speed fourdrinier machine.

The side of the fiber mat that is formed in contact with the wire is called the **wire side** of the paper, and the top side is the **felt side.** The felt side has more short fibers, fines, and filler than the wire side, because of drainage loss of fines from the wire side.

Modern paper machines use hydrofoils, which have arc-shaped plastic surfaces, instead of table rolls to support the wire. This reduces the amount of disturbance that occurs during drainage, thereby making a more uniform sheet. Table rolls tend to cause a greater loss of fine fibers from the wire side of the paper and make that side of the sheet rougher. Absence of the "fines" also makes the wire side somewhat stronger. Therefore, the wire side is stronger, and the top side is smoother.

Following the table rolls or hydrofoils, suction boxes provide additional drainage.

In the few seconds in which the forming sheet flows down the wire, the solids content is increased from 0.5% to about 20%. The water drained from the sheet is called "white water" because it contains fine fibers and traces of other materials added to the paper.

As the paper reaches the end of the wire, it has already achieved enough strength to be lifted off the wire and fed into the press section without tearing or "breaking." Additional water is pressed out of the sheet between synthetic-fiber blankets, which are called "felts."

After coming out of the press section, the sheet still contains two tons of water for every ton of stock, and the remaining water must be evaporated. This procedure requires high amounts of steam or energy, and it contributes significantly to the cost of paper. The paper passes through the dryer section, which consists of cylindrical dryers called "cans." Although the paper tends to shrink as it dries, the machine applies tension to the web throughout its travel. This practice means that the paper is significantly stretched during manufacture, and this is one of the factors contributing to the "grain" of the paper.

Some paper machines are **twin-wire machines.** With these machines, the stock enters between two wires and the water is drained from both sides of

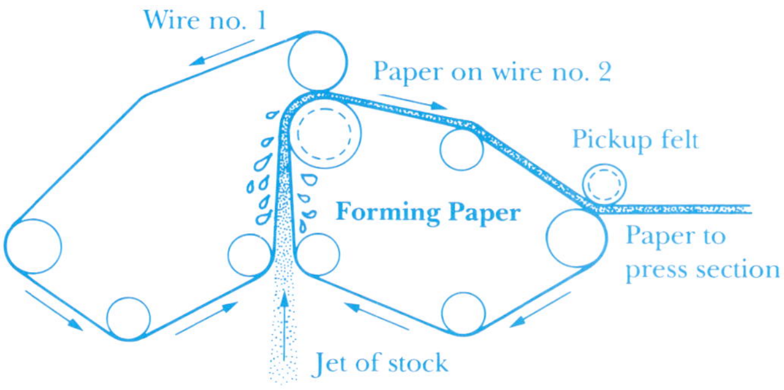

Twin-wire former (Bel Baie).

the sheet simultaneously. Twin-wire forming overcomes the limitations of one-sided drainage, which produces two-sided paper. Twin-wire machines operate at higher speeds than single-wire machines, the forming unit is usually much shorter, and the resulting sheet is more uniform.

Another type of paper-former, the **cylinder machine,** is not often used for producing printing papers. Great quantities of wastepapers are recycled into paperboard that is produced on the cylinder machine. This machine forms paper on a wire-covered cylinder that rotates in a vat of water and

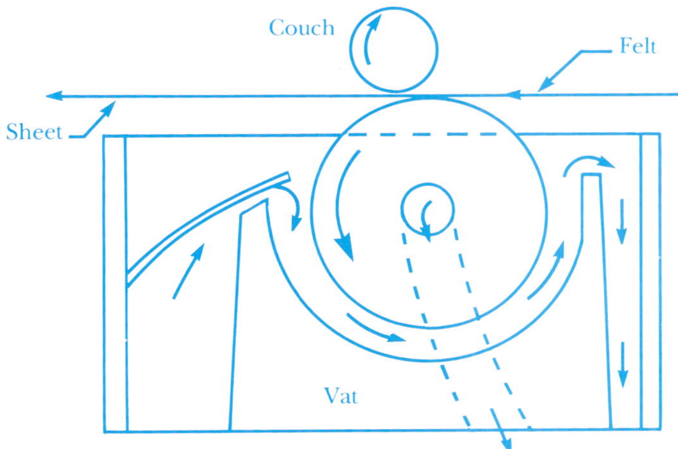

Cylinder machine.

suspended fibers. The water is drained by gravity from the outside of the cylinder to its inside. Fibers are deposited on the outer surface of the wire by drainage. Paper mats are produced on successive forming cylinders, transferred to felts, and combined to form sheets. An advantage of the cylinder machine is that it is able to make thick, heavy-weight papers that can have different composition among their individually formed plies.

Modern paper machines making tissue paper run at speeds as high as 5,000 ft./min. (25 m/s). Twin-wire machines for making newsprint run in excess of 3,000 ft./min. (15 m/s), and modern machines making fine papers run over 2,000 ft./min. (10 m/s).

The Size Press

The size press, or coating machine, is located about two-thirds of the way through the dryer section. The size press is made up of two rubber-covered rolls that apply sizing solution to the partially dried web as it enters their nip. The paper's surface will be penetrated with some of the sizing. Starch, latex, or other surface-sizing materials may be added to the sheet at this time. Sizing carried out at the size press is referred to as **external,** or **surface,** sizing, while sizing added before the sheet is formed is referred to as **internal sizing,** or **beater** sizing.

Starch is added at the size press to control ink penetration, pick resistance, dimensional stability, surface smoothness, finish, and appearance. It also reduces the tendency of the paper to fluff or lint on the offset blanket. Clay or other pigments are sometimes added to the starch for better printability and ink holdout. Starch improves the "rattle" of paper and the erasability of bond papers that are highly sized. The size press may be replaced by an "on-machine" coater that applies a pigmented slurry to the paper. The difference between a pigmented size and a paper coating is difficult to detect. The coating has higher pigment content. There are advantages to coating on the machine and also advantages to coating off the machine, and both processes are used in modern papermaking.

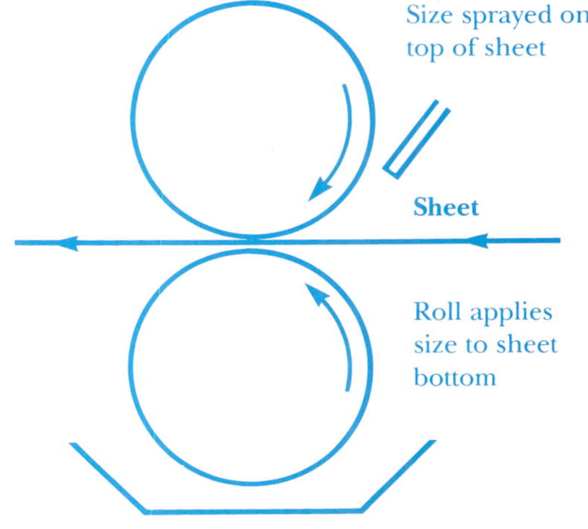

Vertical size press.

The sheet now continues through the remainder of the drying section, passes between machine calenders, and is wound up in a "log."

Before being wound, the sheet may be monitored with devices that determine the amount of water in the sheet, the amount of filler in the sheet, the caliper of the sheet, and its basis weight, brightness, and opacity. These devices can be connected to computers for a closed-loop, on-line control of properties to improve the uniformity of the paper.

The moisture content of the paper should normally be about 5% to 6% of the weight of the cellulose. That is, for an uncoated, unfilled sheet, the moisture content will be about 5%, and for a filled or coated sheet, the moisture content will be proportionately less, depending upon the amount of filler or coating present. If the paper manufacture is completed at this point, the paper is called **machine-finished.** If a higher finish is required, the paper is run through a supercalender.

Paper Coating

Pigments and **adhesives,** or **binders,** are the two principal coating materials. Pigments are used to obtain a smoother surface and to cover the fibers. Adhesives bind the pigment particles together and to the paper substrate. Final coating properties such as ink absorptivity, water resistance, gloss, and pick resistance are also controlled by adhesives. A pigment coating improves the printing qualities, and a specialty or conversion coating provides the sheet with chemical resistance and/or other functional properties. A starch/clay coating is an example of a pigment coating that improves printing qualities. A polyethylene coating is a conversion coating that gives a paper a resistance to water and grease. Pigment coatings give good gloss and ink receptivity; specialty coatings provide resistance to chemicals, water, grease, solvents, and physical damage (abrasion, folding, and scuffing).

Good quality coated paper for printing requires a good body stock. Coating will not cover up sheet defects. The body stock must have sufficient overall strength for the coating and the printing processes, and its surface smoothness and absorptivity must be uniform.

The first pigment coatings were applied by equipment resembling paint brushes or printing presses. Brush coaters brushed out coating, which then flowed onto the paper. Roll coaters applied coating to the paper much as a press applies ink. Modern equipment uses an **air-knife** or a **trailing-blade coater.**

Like printing inks, coatings consist of a pigment and a vehicle. Clay is the most widely used pigment. There are several types of clays, but for paper coating, only kaolinite is used. Kaolinite bonds easily and gives a low-cost, smooth, glossy surface. It has tiny platelet-shaped particles that shingle or slip over each other during coating and calendering. This produces good coating coverage, gloss, and ink holdout. Calcium carbonate, which may be ground limestone but is more commonly manufactured or precipitated, gives greater brightness and opacity than clay and tends to give a matte or dull finish. Calcium carbonate is acicular, that is, needle-shaped. It is often used together

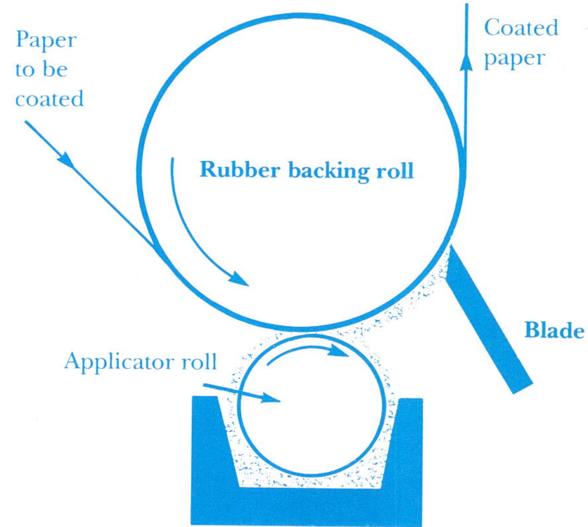

Blade coating with a trailing blade coater.

with clay to produce a coating with high brightness and a remarkable affinity for ink. Titanium dioxide has a cubic structure that cannot be calendered to give high gloss. Titanium dioxide (TiO_2) is especially noted for its brilliance and high opacity.

Pigment coatings are always applied from water. The most commonly used adhesive is starch or a starch derivative. Binders derived from natural sources are proteins, including casein and soya protein. They are sometimes used as adhesives, but synthetic polymers are now used increasingly. Polyvinyl acetate and styrene-butadiene binders are used for higher paper gloss, greater ink and varnish holdout, coating flexibility without cracking during folding and binding, and improved coating wet-rub resistance. Butadiene or synthetic rubber are the most commonly used polymeric adhesives. Acrylates are sometimes used, especially in paperboard.

Printing papers are normally coated on two sides (C2S). Papers for labels and for some other specialty products are coated on one side only (C1S). Double-coated papers receive two coatings. The first coating, perhaps an air-knife coating, prepares a smooth surface for the second coating, which may be applied with a trailing blade. Double coating produces the most desirable combination, giving precise control and a thick, smooth layer of coating.

Cast coating. An exceptionally high-gloss finish is characteristic of cast-coated papers. The process involves coating a base stock that is in contact with a highly polished, heated metal drum. For finishing and drying, the moist coating is pressed firmly against the drum surface. While it is drying, the coating is cast into a direct image of the drum. Upon drying, the paper is released from the surface to produce a paper with an extremely high gloss, and high bulk and ink absorptivity.

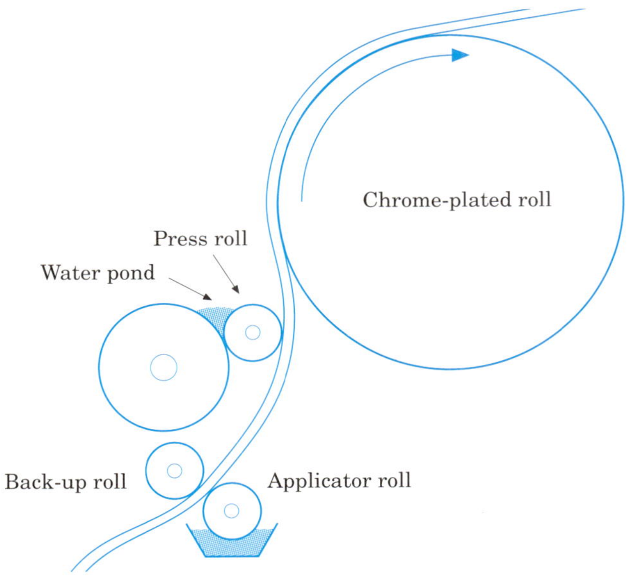

Cast coater.

Conversion coating. Polymeric coatings are applied to paper after the sheet is formed to give special performance characteristics and are used for decorative effects, high gloss, protection against chemicals, and environmental factors. The coatings comprise melted polymers or organic substances dissolved or dispersed in volatile organic liquids. Primary film formers generally are high-molecular-weight polymers such as cellulose compounds, polyethylene, and rubbers. The organic solvents include aliphatic aromatic hydrocarbons, alcohols, and ketones.

Solventless coatings are applied from the melted resin. The most common material applied in this way is polyethylene. Polyethylene-coated papers and boards are widely used for packaging. The polyethylene may be compounded with a wax giving a highly water-resistant product such as is used in manufacturing milk cartons.

Finishing

After the paper has been rolled up at the end of the machine, it must undergo a number of finishing operations. These operations include calendering, slitting and rewinding, and sheeting and packaging.

Calendering. Calendering is the final step in controlling the characteristics of paper before it leaves the paper machine. The machine calender has all-metal rolls in running contact. The dried web is sent through the nips of these rolls, and it acquires a denser, smooth surface. Also, its differences in thickness are evened out. Depending upon the finish desired, the degree of calendering may be heavy, moderate, light, or none at all. As the degree of calendering is increased, smoothness is increased and higher gloss is developed. Thickness and stiffness are reduced. Opacity is lowered considerably and brightness somewhat by compacting fibers closer together and reducing the light-scattering ability of the paper. Calendering decreases porosity and ink absorption.

Supercalendering of uncoated papers greatly improves their smoothness. The smooth, glossy appearance of enameled stock is obtained by supercalendering clay-coated paper. A supercalender is a stack of rolls supported in a frame. The rolls "iron" and polish the paper, giving it a very smooth surface. The rolls are alternately hard and soft; hard rolls are made of steel, and the soft rolls are made of compressed paper or cotton. Paper rolls are typically used for uncoated papers, and cotton rolls are typically used for coated papers.

Supercalendering paper is much like the process of pressing on an ironing board. In the calendering of paper, the soft rolls serve as the ironing board, steel rolls serve as the iron, and steam is usually used to slightly soften the paper or coating.

The bottom roll in the stack is a geared drive roll, but all the other rolls run free and are rotated only by friction, resulting in some slippage. The effect is to smash the high points and fill in the surface pits and hollow areas. The smoother the paper is initially and the heavier its coating, the smoother and glossier it will be after calendering.

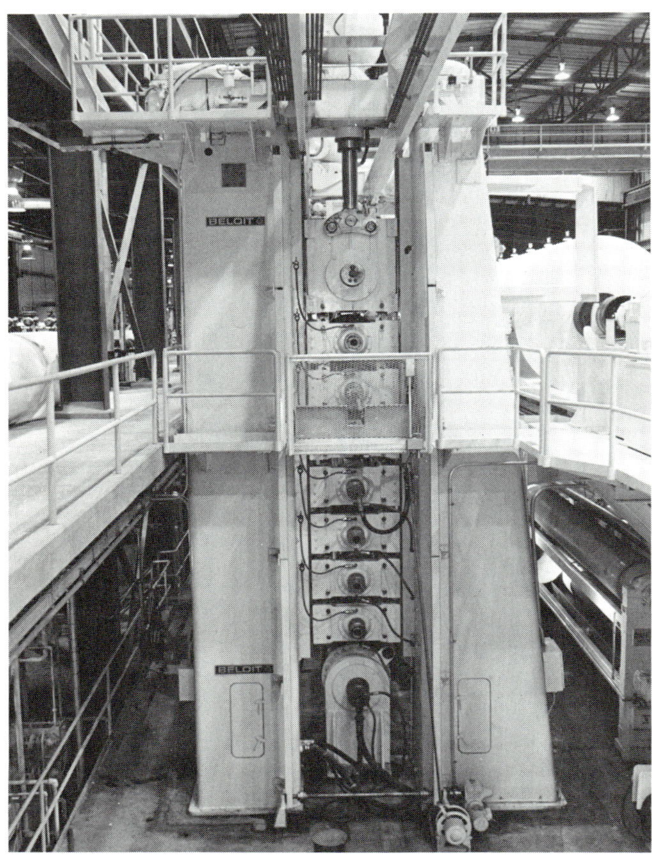

Courtesy Beloit Corporation

Supercalender stack.

In addition to smoothness and gloss, calendering increases sheet density while reducing caliper. By densifying the sheet and reducing the voids, the opacity of the sheet is lowered, as is the amount of light refracted within the sheet, thereby also reducing brightness. In fact, if too much pressure or moisture is used, the sheet becomes darkened—a defect referred to as "calender blackening."

Slitting and rewinding. Some paper machines are as wide as 300 in. (7.5 m). Since the paper they produce is wider than any press can handle, it must be slit to the specified width. The papermaker must figure out the trimmed roll widths in such a way that a maximum amount of the "log," or roll, is used. What remain are **stub** rolls, and they are sent back for recycling through the pulping process.

If the paper is to be used for web offset printing, it is essential that it be rewound very evenly. If the center of the roll is wound more loosely than the outside, a considerable jerk will occur when the inside of one roll is spliced to the outside of the next roll on the press. This jerking can cause a number of web printing problems, including web breaks.

In addition to rewinding, rewinders are used for slitting to smaller widths and specific diameters, winding on cores of specific construction, and performing operations not feasible on the paper machine winder. **Salvage rewinders** are used to rewind rolls, to remove defective paper, splicing, and other defects, and to salvage quality paper.

The paper must be of very uniform caliper. If one side of the web, for example, is 3% greater in caliper than the other side, when the roll is wound, the thicker side of the web makes one side of the roll tighter than the other. Such rolls do not feed evenly on the press. Variations in moisture content across the web also result in differences in roll tightness and paper performance on press. Use of automatic web monitoring devices discussed above reduces the variations in paper.

Sheeting. Rolls are cut into sheets on the sheeter, which consists of a single- or multiple-roll backstand, a rotary cutting unit, and a layboy, where the sheets are piled and jogged.

Rotary cutting units may have single rotary cutters or double rotary cutters. A **single rotary cutter** has a fixed-position bedknife with a second knife mounted in a rotating cylinder. When the rotary knife contacts the bedknife, the paper web is cut with a shearing action. A **double rotary cutter** has two knives; both are mounted on cylinders that rotate in synchronization. As the two rotating knives contact, they move at the web speed, and their shearing action cuts the web. The cutoff dimension, or sheet length, is determined by the speed of the rotary knife relative to web speed. The spacing between the web slitters determines sheet width. Cut sheets are transported to the layboy on traveling belts.

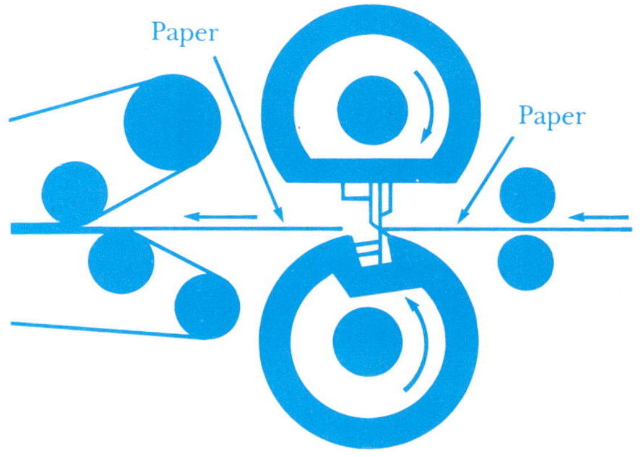

Double rotary cutter.

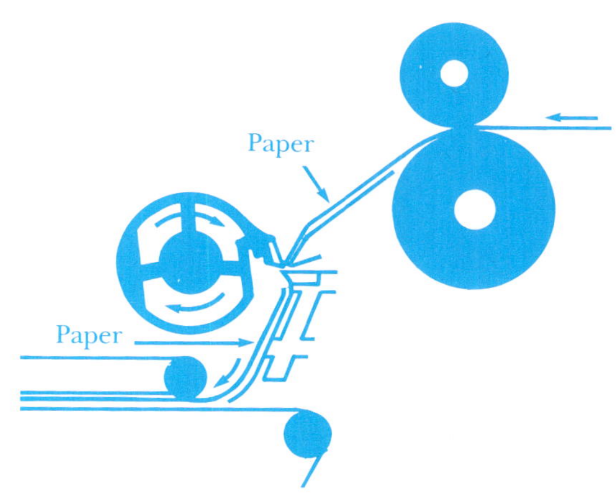

Fixed bedknife.

Several rolls of paper are usually fed into the cutter at once. The papermaker makes every effort to assure that the rolls feeding simultaneously are highly uniform. They must be from the same run of paper, the same paper machine, and the same position of the log. For example, if three rolls were used in sheeting and one of them had a different finish, then every third sheet in the skid would have a different finish.

Trimming. The sheeted paper is now trimmed on a guillotine trimmer, often controlled by computer to trim the paper rapidly and accurately. Cutting knives are kept sharp at all times. Trimming must be done by skilled operators who have been trained to exercise great care. Paper that is trimmed at the mill will be more accurately trimmed, on the average, than paper trimmed in a printing plant.

Precision sheeting. Precision sheeting machines are becoming popular because they produce paper with better uniformity at lower costs. Precision sheeters make trimming unnecessary because they cut to very accurately controlled sheet dimensions. These machines are used to make cut-size sheets, such as 8½×11 in. (216×280 mm), and they are also available for making production-size sheets. In principle, they are similar to conventional sheeting machines, except that they are designed to give very highly reproducible sheet dimensions. Each sheet must lie flat and smooth at the time it is cut. Total variation in sheet dimensions from precision sheeters is much less than that observed with guillotine-trimmed sheets. However, the observable variations in guillotine-trimmed sheets occur only from one lift to the next. Variations in precision-trimmed sheets occur from sheet to sheet, and although it may look as if the sheets have not been trimmed, sheet dimensions are very consistent throughout the load.

Statistical quality control. For many decades, top grades of printing paper were inspected and sorted by hand. However, it has been fully demonstrated that higher-quality paper is produced by the use of statistical quality control than by sorting and inspection. In addition, sorting and inspecting every sheet by hand added a great deal to the cost. Inspection and sorting can only remove defective sheets; it cannot build quality into the sheet. Modern statistical quality control in the paper mill builds quality into the sheet.

Statistical theory and analysis are used to determine the degree of long- or short-term conformance to specifications, and also to detect and correct unwanted deviations or trends in paper properties. When complaint history and feedback from the customer regarding a paper's performance are analyzed, the quality control department will benefit.

Properties Required of Printing Papers

Cleanliness and uniformity. In printing, the surface cleanliness of paper is an important consideration. This is due to several factors: the increased use of offset printing, which demands greater surface cleanliness than other printing methods; trends toward heavier ink coverage; increased press speeds; and higher gloss. Also, the consequences of stopping the press for washup too frequently are more serious in terms of cost and loss of print quality. Some of the printer's greatest troubles occur when paper is dirty or nonuniform. Trimmer dust, slitter dust, or paper or coating dust that gets into the offset press can ruin the runnability of the paper.

There are two types of contaminating materials that detract from surface cleanliness and originate during paper manufacturing. One type is **superficial,** loosely attached particles of the paper's surface. Sources for this type are lint; loosely bonded surface fibers; fibers or coating debris created by slitting, cutting, or trimming with dull or improperly sharpened slitters or knives; dirt or dust that falls from overhead structures or the air onto the paper's surface; and textile-type fibers from the

paper machine felts. The second type of contaminating material that detracts from paper cleanliness begins with foreign inclusions embedded in the surface of the paper that may be lifted out of the paper, sometimes called **pickouts.** Sources of pickouts are scale; rust; slime spots; filler agglomerates; starch spots or scale from surface sizing; and coating lumps and particles that build up on the paper machine rollers, felts, or dryers and are redeposited onto and pressed into the paper web.

Any kind of loose dust or dirt on the surface of the paper will get into the ink and cause press contamination, requiring the operator to shut down and clean up. If this occurs only after 10,000 or 20,000 sheets on a sheetfed press or after 50,000 to 100,000 impressions on a web press, the problem is not usually considered very serious. However, if the press operator must clean the press after every few hundred impressions on a sheetfed or every few thousand on a web press, the runnability of the paper is severely impaired.

As important as cleanliness is uniformity: uniformity from sheet to sheet, uniformity from roll to roll, and uniformity throughout a skid or a roll. When variations occur in finish, absorptivity, moisture content, or formation, paper will not produce a high-quality printed product. Variations in finish, for example, cause variations in absorptivity and differences in color or gloss of prints.

Short sheets, dog-ears, bowed edges, and other defects produce a product extremely hard to run. Paper rolls that are unevenly wound, telescoped, starred, crushed, or flat on one side will not perform well on press.

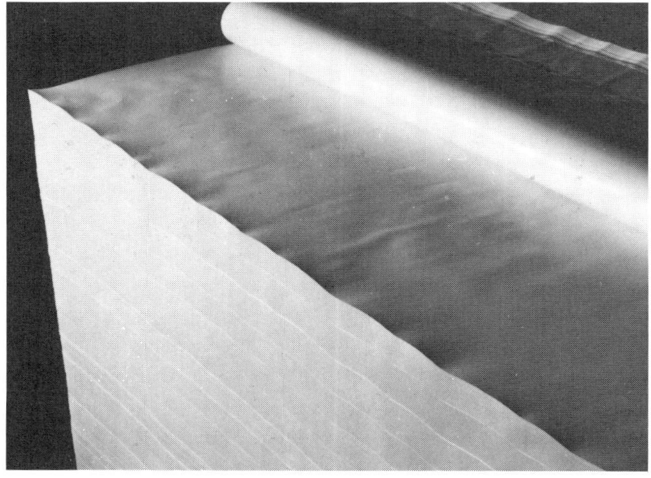

Wavy-edged piles are produced when the paper picks up moisture from the air. Control and uniformity of moisture content are important if paper is to perform well on press.

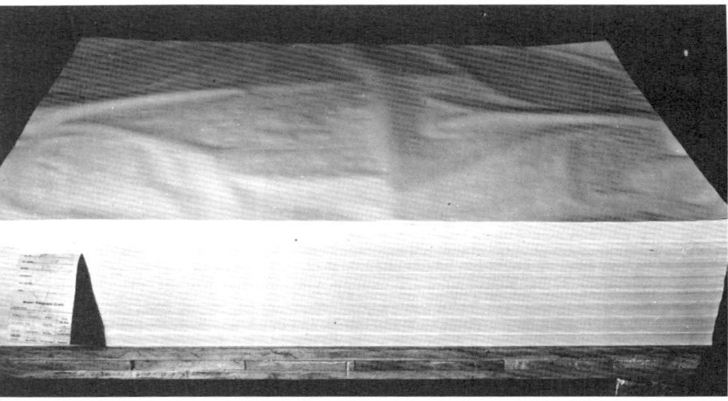

Tight-edged piles are produced when moisture is lost to the atmosphere.

Uniform moisture content. A paper's moisture content greatly influences its physical properties, its runnability on press, and its performance during operations following printing, such as folding, binding, and converting. When moisture content is increased, the fibers and coatings become more pliable. Moisture loss causes paper to become brittle and crack during folding and binding. Control and uniformity of moisture content are vitally important if paper is to perform well on either the sheetfed or the web press. Paper changes dimensions rapidly when it is exposed to a drier or a damper atmosphere than the air with which it is in equilibrium. If paper is exposed to a more moist atmosphere, it expands; if exposed to a drier atmosphere, it contracts. Unevenly distributed moisture in paper resulting from its exposure to high or low relative humidities can produce tight-edged piles or rolls with tight ends when moisture is lost to the atmosphere. Wavy-edged piles and rolls with loose ends are produced when the paper picks up moisture from the air. However, if two samples of the same length, cut from the same sheet, are conditioned, one at higher humidity, the other at lower humidity, and then brought back to the same intermediate humidity, they will not come to exactly the same length. The one conditioned at the higher humidity will be somewhat longer.

This conditioning behavior is called **hysteresis.** This dependency helps account for the fact that wavy-edged paper can never be made really flat. Hysteresis is a paper's difference in moisture content that is indicated by its ascending and descending curves for relative humidity representing opposite starting points in its conditioning history. Hysteresis explains why the equilibrium moisture content of a paper when conditioned to a specific relative humidity will differ depending upon its moisture history.

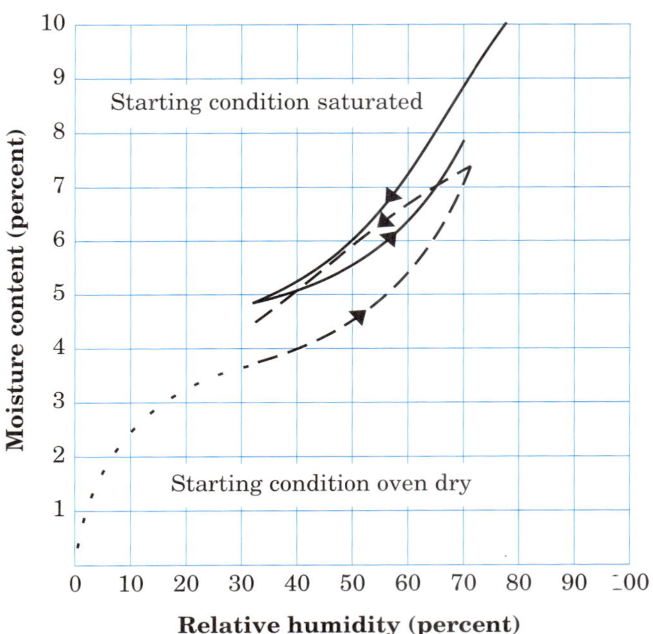

Hysteresis curve for paper.

Similar considerations explain the importance of making a uniform sheet in the first place. If the dryers on the paper machine do not produce uniformly dry sheets, the paper will not perform properly on press.

Strength. The surface strength of paper must provide adequate pick resistance. **Pick resistance** is particularly important in offset printing. The surface strength, or pick resistance, of paper makes its surface able to withstand the perpendicularly applied forces, without picking or rupturing, during the splitting of an ink film between the printed sheet and the blanket containing ink. The tackiness of inks and the thin ink films used in offset printing tend to disrupt the paper surface as the sheet or web is peeled off the blanket cylinder of the offset press. Paper is said to pick when the coating, fiber, or small bits of the paper itself are separated from the sheet as it is printed. Picking can happen in various ways: fibers can be removed partially or completely from the surface; coating fragments can be partially lifted or completely removed from the surface; the paper substrate below the printed surface can be partially delaminated, producing a disturbance that looks like a blister; or the paper surface can be ruptured. The tensile strength is closely related to the surface strength. A paper's **tensile breaking strength** is the maximum tensile stress it will withstand before breaking under prescribed conditions. Other strength properties commonly measured are Mullen or bursting strength, folding strength or folding endurance, and tearing strength or tearing resistance. Tests are performed for internal tearing strength and edge tearing resistance.

Mullen or bursting strength. Mullen or bursting strength of paper or paperboard is the hydrostatic pressure needed to rupture a sample when uniformly distributed and increasing pressure (at a constant rate) is applied to one of its sides. The test commonly used to measure bursting strength is the Mullen test.

In general, refining of paper stock, which increases tensile strength and bursting strength, decreases the tearing strength. Therefore, tensile strength and tearing strength are good examples of properties that must represent a compromise in papermaking. It is not possible for the papermaker to treat a stock mixture so as to obtain a sheet having, simultaneously, maximum tensile and maximum tear strength.

Folding endurance is the number of double folds a paper will withstand (under specified conditions and tension) before it breaks at the fold line. The folding endurance of paper degrades rapidly with age or upon heating—as in the dryer of a web offset press. Folding endurance is used to study aging of paper.

Internal tearing resistance. Internal tearing resistance is the amount of work it takes to tear paper through a fixed distance once the tear has been started.

Edge tearing resistance. Differing from internal tearing resistance, edge tearing resistance is the resistance of paper to start tearing at its edge.

Smoothness. From a printability standpoint, paper smoothness refers to surface contour and the degree to which the surface levelness approaches an optical plane such as smooth glass. Smoothness is sometimes a consideration for runnability and end-use requirements. As paper becomes smoother, its surface comes into more intimate contact with itself or other surfaces during printing. This can increase the tendency for ink setoff during sheetfed printing or "tracking" of the ink during web printing. The papermaker makes a sheet smooth through choice of fiber and filler (shorter papers produce a more level paper than do long fibers), by the use of refining, and by calendering.

Printability and runnability. "Printability" and "runnability" are terms carried over from letterpress printing, where paper could run well if it was strong, but print poorly if it was not smooth. **Printability** is the extent to which paper properties will lend themselves to the true reproduction of copy by the printing process used. **Runnability** is the paper's ability to be printed without causing problems in the mechanics of the printing operation. Since printability problems in offset lithography, such as picking and piling, required the operator to stop the press and clean up, printability and runnability are harder to distinguish in lithography. A strong, clean sheet usually runs well and prints well by offset lithography. Web offset requires, in addition, well-built rolls for runnability.

Stiffness. As customers demand lower-basis-weight sheets, the paper has become thinner and thinner. It is a fundamental relationship of engineering that the stiffness is proportional to the cube of the thickness: $S \sim t^3$.

Stiffness is the ability of paper or paperboard to resist an applied bending force, and its ability to support its own weight while being handled.

Thickness of the paper cannot be maintained indefinitely as the amount of material in the sheet is reduced. Caliper can be maintained with a reduction in basis weight by reducing sheet density, but the procedure can be carried out only to a limited extent. Lightweight sheets are very hard to handle. A web press is more successful in handling lightweight paper because the paper is held at both ends as it goes through the press.

Furthermore, the less the stiffness of the sheet, the greater is the rollout, or increase in size, as the paper is printed. Lightweight sheets, therefore, are not only difficult to feed but also to maintain register on.

Roll condition. Good roll condition is at least as important as good paper in achieving good runnability on the web press. Of course, if the paper is not well made, good rolls are hard to make. The paper web must have uniform caliper and moisture content. The rolls must be wound uniformly. If the roll is wound too tightly, the paper is stretched, and it loses some of its resiliency and breaks more readily. If the roll is not wound tightly enough, it can be telescoped while it is being handled. When a roll is **telescoped,** it has the appearance of a progressive roll edge misalignment that may be convex or concave. When an inner part of the roll slips in the direction of its axis because of a thrust force on or within its body after winding, telescoping occurs. Telescoping can happen when rolls are wound too

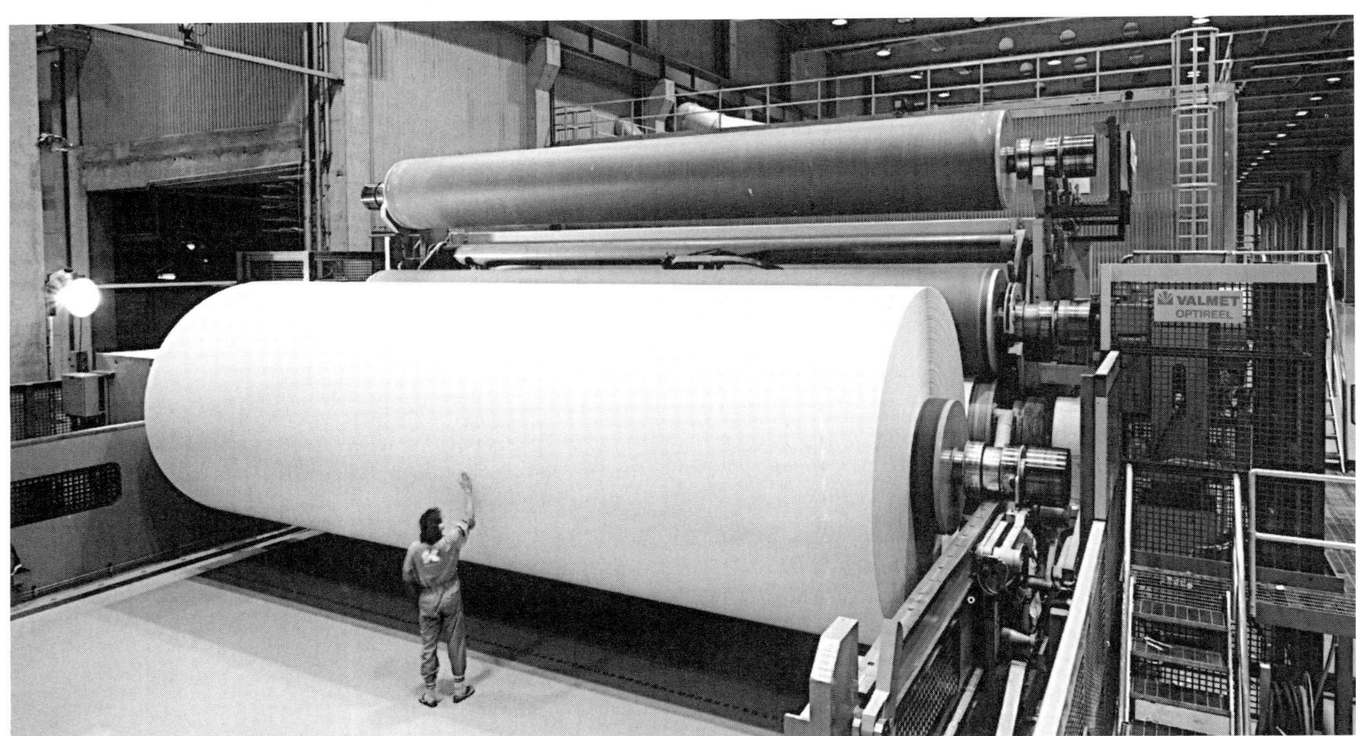

Courtesy Valmet Paper Machinery, Inc.

Optireel, which is used in the reeling process on paper machines.

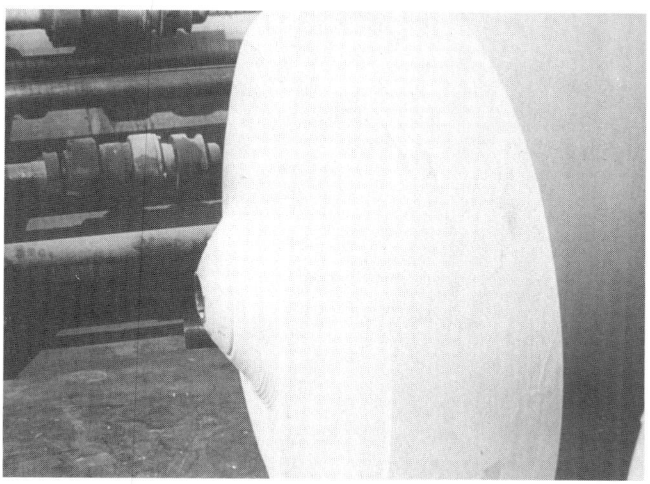

A telescoped roll.

"softly," if the cross-machine caliper is nonuniform, and if the web tension is excessive while unwinding. If the roll is wound unevenly from side to side, it feeds unevenly. If the roll is wound unevenly from inside to outside, sudden changes in tension near the splice create web breaks, doubling, and register problems. Flat spots originating during manufacture, shipping, or storage greatly increase web breaks.

Roll condition is everyone's responsibility: the papermaker's, the shipper's, and the printer's.

When the printer encounters problems with roll paper, he should report it to the papermaker. The roll card, which accompanies each roll, must be used so that good communications can be maintained.

Basis weight. According to manufacturing tolerances, papermakers supply paper within ±5.0% of the nominal basis weight. **Basis weight** is the weight in pounds of a ream of paper cut to its basic size in inches. The standard ream quantity is 500 sheets. For sheet papers that are sold by sheet count, this is satisfactory, provided the proper number of sheets are in the carton or skid. For web papers that are sold by weight, this may be entirely unsatisfactory. If the paper supplied to a printer were consistently 2% too heavy, the printer would be 2% short in the length of paper. This inaccuracy can cost the paper buyer tens of thousands of dollars per year.

For example, if a printer estimated the amount of a 50-lb. paper needed for a job but received the ordered weight of paper as 51-lb. paper, the printer would have to buy 2% more paper to complete the job.

Papermakers do, in fact, supply paper well within the 5% allowed by manufacturing tolerance, but printers must carefully monitor the paper they buy. Some papermakers indicate the length of paper in each roll, allowing the printer to calculate the usable area.

Formation and absorbency. Formation is the structure and degree of uniformity of a paper's fiber distribution as judged by transmitted light. It is affected by the type of fibers that are used, by the way they are refined, by the use of fillers, and by the paper machine. If the paper stock is not properly prepared or if the paper machine is not operated properly, the fibers clot, agglomerate, or flocculate, and the sheet is lumpy: it has a "wild formation." The longer the fibers and the greater the percent of long fibers used, the greater is the tendency to flocculate and the poorer is the formation. Paper with poor formation causes mottle and unevenness in prints or in paper coating.

Absorbency is the paper's ability to soak up the liquids or vapors with which it comes in contact. Variations in absorbency affect printed gloss and sometimes even the color of the print. If absorbency varies from place to place within the sheet because of poor formation, prints will not be uniform. The heavier the sheet, the greater the variation. It is more difficult to manufacture a uniform board than to manufacture a uniform publication paper. Variations in absorbency within a given lot of paper cause mottle or poor match in color or gloss. Variations from one lot to another make it difficult to match one job with a repeat job run later, which is common for labels and packaging.

Ink absorbency. This property determines the rate and amount of ink penetration into the paper after the press plate or blanket deposits it. Penetration is mainly that of the ink vehicle into the voids, capillaries, and pores of the paper.

Ink holdout. As a property related to ink absorbency, ink holdout concerns the printer. Ink holdout is the tendency of printing paper to resist or retard the inward penetration of the freshly printed ink film.

To some extent, the printer can overcome variations in absorbency by making the ink or varnish stiffer so that it will hold out uniformly, or softer so that it will penetrate uniformly. Sometimes the variations are too great to be handled this way, and often the problem does not become visible until the job has dried.

Flatness. Problems of flatness sometimes occur with sheetfed paper. They are uncommon with web paper. **Curl** and **waviness** originate when paper is exposed to air that has higher or lower relative humidity than that of the paper. In the wintertime, the air in North American pressrooms can become extremely dry if moisture is not added. In the summertime, paper opened in a hot, humid atmosphere can swell and develop wavy edges. More often, however, wavy edges result from condensation of moisture on cold paper. Thus, tight and wavy edges are more commonly seen in the winter than in the summer. One way to avoid wavy edges is for the printer to specify that the paper for the job be stored in a heated warehouse and be delivered on the day of the job. Another way is to keep the paper package at room temperature for a sufficient number of hours before being opened.

Curl can be caused by a difference in fiber orientation and the fibrous and nonfibrous composition of the wire and felt sides of paper made on a Fourdrinier machine. The sheet curls away from the side that is wetted because moisture causes paper to expand. When it is dry, sometimes the sheet curls toward the wetted side; this is known as **reverse curl.**

Paper undergoes various stresses due to shrinkage and tension as it is dried during manufacturing. Drying must be controlled to make residual stresses minimal and balanced for sheet flatness. Highly refined papers whose fibers are more tightly bonded to each other have a greater tendency to curl with changes in relative humidity. Papers are less prone to curl as they are made more porous and less dense.

Tight- and wavy-edged paper can also result from poor paper manufacture: the paper was made too wet or too dry. Instrumentation on modern paper machines has made this source of tight- and wavy-edged paper increasingly uncommon.

In view of the fairly simple prevention of the trouble, it is surprising how often serious problems with tight- and wavy-edged paper occur.

Other problems with flatness or curl occur when two-sided paper (paper with nonuniform sides) is moistened by the lithographic press. Since C1S (coated one side) paper used in labels is very two-sided, special manufacturing precautions must be taken, or labels will curl and fail to feed in automatic labeling machines.

With heavy stocks, cover stock, or, more commonly, paperboard, sheets will sometimes fail to lie flat after they have been sheeted. This problem is called **reel curl** or **roll set.** It is a manufacturing problem, but there are sheet decurling devices that are helpful in flattening out the curl. Roll set curl becomes greater near the roll core, especially for heavier, stiffer papers such as paperboard and cover stock.

Tests for curl and its control are conducted during paper manufacturing. The degree of curl of samples taken from various positions across the paper machine is measured. These tests are conducted after the samples have been exposed to relative humidities and temperatures of a specified value or range that is like the environment where the paper will be used.

Optical properties. It should be obvious that the color of the paper affects the color of the print, just as does the color of the ink. The optical properties of the paper must be taken into account in planning the printing job. Five properties are especially important: brightness, whiteness or hue, gloss, opacity, and fluorescence.

Brightness, whiteness, and reflectance are often confused. **Brightness** is defined as the percent of blue-light reflectance (BLR) at a standard wavelength (457 nm is used in the standard test). **Whiteness** results from the uniform reflectance of all wavelengths of light. The same amount of red, green, and blue light must be reflected. "White" should be used to indicate high and equal reflectance of all visible wavelengths.

Percent Reflected Light

	Red	Green	Blue
1. Brightness	85	85	90
2. Whitest	85	85	85
3. Most Reflectant	90	90	85

Brightness can be measured at a single wavelength, but whiteness requires a minimum of three. The table gives the reflectance of three hypothetical sheets; one has the greatest brightness, another has the greatest whiteness, and the third reflects the most light.

Of the three sheets described in the table, the first would be called a "blue" or "cold" sheet, and the third would be called a "warm" sheet. The first has a blue hue, while the third has a warm hue that favors yellows and reds.

Glossy prints require glossy paper. As described in the "Papermaking" section, gloss is achieved by

coating and by calendering or by the special technique of manufacturing a cast-coated sheet. **Gloss** is that attribute of a paper surface that causes it to be shiny or lustrous.

Opacity, the extent to which light transmission is obstructed, is obtained by reflection of light from voids and interfaces in the sheet. Opacity is an important consideration for printing papers and for the various uses of paper. If there is not sufficient opacity, excessive show-through, reduced printing contrast, and lower print quality will result. If the sheet is heavily beaten and supercalendered so that no air remains in the sheet, the product is glassine, a highly transparent paper used for windows in envelopes. The transparency can be reduced by incorporating clay or another pigment into the paper to refract light or by allowing air to remain in the sheet. This, of course, reduces the tensile strength of the sheet. Titanium dioxide produces opacity more effectively than clay.

Another effective way to increase opacity is to put a little groundwood into the furnish. If high permanence and brightness are not required in the product, groundwood improves opacity, smoothness, and formation.

Compromises in papermaking. It is often not possible to make a perfect sheet for a particular purpose, because when the papermaker changes conditions to alter one property, other properties are also changed. And, of course, improving the properties of paper often increases its cost. It has already been pointed out that decreasing the basis weight decreases the caliper and, consequently, the stiffness of the sheet. The gloss of a paper can be increased by supercalendering or by calendering. Both treatments reduce the opacity by eliminating voids that refract light. Reducing the light-refracting surfaces also reduces the brightness.

The strength of a sheet can be increased by using greater amounts of softwood kraft pulp, but this increases the roughness of the sheet and adversely affects its printability.

Selecting the best paper for a job is complicated; it requires skill, judgment, and experience. Printers should rely upon assistance from a salesperson or technical representative in making selections. However, even under the best of circumstances, faulty paper is sometimes delivered from the mill. Printers should work with the salesperson to remedy the situation.

Paper Problems in the Pressroom

Paper manufacturers report that the highest percentage of problems with paper are those resulting from mishandling or accidents. Next in order of most frequent occurrence are paper problems resulting from press contamination. These create the greatest amount of trouble because their causes are often difficult to pinpoint. Roll condition problems are the third highest category.

Mishandling problems. Mishandling often results from carelessness or lack of proper information or instruction: paper cut to the wrong size, the wrong basis weight, grain wrong, short sheets or waste in the skid, dog-ears, wrong color, and lost or late delivery.

Press contamination. When paper is dirty or contains weakly bonded or other foreign material that gets onto blankets and into the ink, press contamination results. Some of the most frequent sources of press contamination are dirty paper, slitter dust, cutter dust, or mill dirt. Calender scale, bits of coating or paper, vessel segments, and other loosely bonded particles also cause press contamination. In one press contamination problem, the cause of the contamination was identified as "calender scale," which resulted from coating that accumulated on the supercalender and broke loose. It was scattered over the web and calendered into the surface. Calendering the loose scale into the surface makes it stick sufficiently to the paper until it runs through the lithographic press.

If the dirt is truly loose, it can be removed with a sheet-cleaning device. Dirt and loosely bonded particles have been calendered into the paper, and sometimes only lithographic ink will lift them out. Calender scale and paper dust can frequently be seen by a careful and observant paper handler or press operator. If the paper mill crew is alert, they can often see the scale before the paper is shipped.

Blanket contamination. Blanket contamination occurs when any type of material becomes attached to the blanket or plate and interferes with print quality.

When material attaches to the blanket, a **hickey** may result. There are two types of **random hickeys: doughnut hickeys** and **void hickeys.** A doughnut hickey consists of a small, solid printed area surrounded by a white halo, or nonprinted

area. They are caused by solid particles that adhere to the plate or blanket and are ink-receptive in the presence of dampening moisture. Because their surfaces are raised, they print an image of themselves but prevent the area immediately surrounding them from printing. Sources of doughnut hickeys are ink skin particles, greasy dirt from the press, particles of deteriorating press rollers, and chips of paint from ceilings. The other type of random hickey, the void hickey, is caused by particles on the plate or blanket that prevent printing from occurring because they are water-receptive and ink-repellent. Because they are thick, they prevent the plate or blanket from receiving ink in their immediate surrounding area.

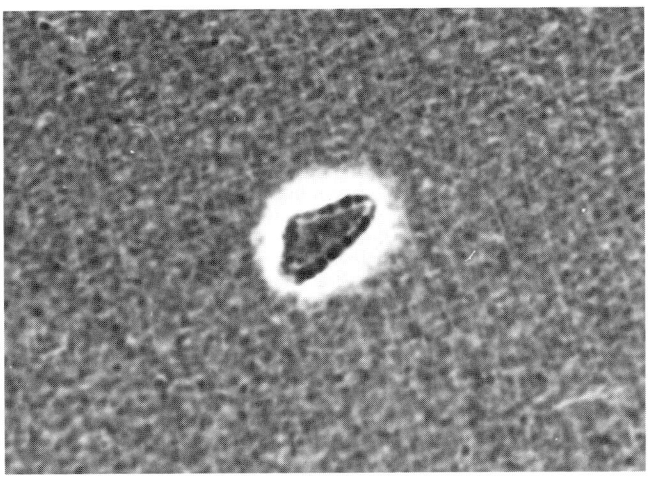

A doughnut hickey.

Paper cutter and trimmer debris generally produce void hickeys that are elongated and irregular in shape and size, and may have fibrous, fuzzy edges. Paper slitter debris often creates splinter-shaped voids. Vessel segments produce a small void hickey that is usually trapezoidal in shape.

Picking. Picking differs from paper fluff or calendered paper scale in that the pick-out is reasonably well bonded to the sheet. Picking can be caused by insufficient bonding strength in the paper or excessive ink tack. Note, in the illustration, that paper fibers have been pulled out of the surface. Picking occurs during ink transfer when the force of the splitting ink film is greater than the force required to break away portions of the surface. Obviously, the problem can be solved by going to a stronger paper, but usually it is less costly to solve the problem by adjusting the ink of the printing press. Press operators often solve picking problems by

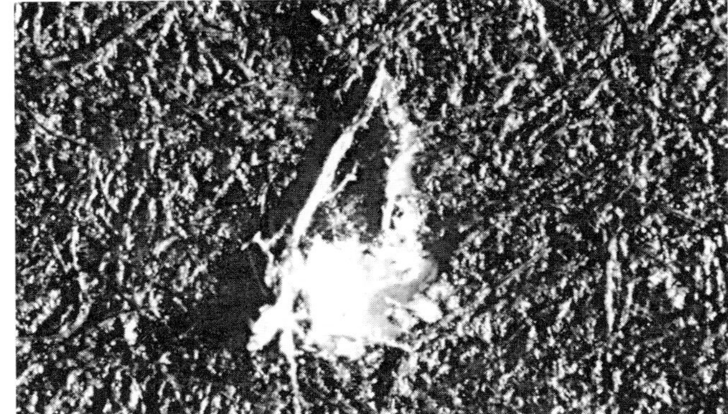

A pick-out (uncoated paper).

adding a solvent, tack reducer, or viscosity reducer to the ink. Adding materials of this sort often increases the drying time and may change color and gloss of the print, making other solutions more desirable. Reducing the speed of the press reduces the force of the ink, and reducing the pressure between the impression cylinder and the blanket reduces the force on the paper. Another way of reducing the force on the paper is to increase the ink film thickness. At first, this may seem to be incorrect, but thick films split more easily than thinner films. Thus, increasing the ink film thickness often helps to overcome a picking problem.

Linting. Like picking, linting occurs when an uncoated sheet is too weak to withstand the force of the inked blanket. Lint originates from loosely bonded surface fibers and can cause fiber buildup in the printed image areas when the lint mixes with the ink. Linting is particularly troublesome with web offset news, which contains a large amount of often weakly bonded groundwood fibers. Also, some uncoated papers may "fluff up" and some coated papers may release coating particles if web tension is excessive. It is sometimes impossible to get a linty paper to run well, but in order to help it to run and perhaps solve the problem, the press operator can decrease the ink tack, decrease the press speed, and increase the amount of water. Some blankets have better release than others, and using a quick-release blanket or other blanket with good release can help to improve the performance of linty paper.

Dusting. Dusting, or powdering, is the accumulation of visible-size particles from the paper. It is usually most readily evident on the first printing unit of the press on the nonimage areas of the blanket. Sometimes tiny bits of cellulose fiber will also

give a dustlike appearance. The dust eventually works its way into the print, filling in shadow dots or blurring lines. When the dust appears in the nonimage area of the blanket, changing the ink cannot be very helpful. Increasing water feed, decreasing the speed of the press, or reducing back cylinder squeeze can reduce dusting that occurs in the nonimage area. If dust is completely loose, a sheet cleaner may remove it before the sheet gets to the blanket.

Piling. Piling is an extremely complex interaction between ink, water, and paper. Piling is defined as the accumulation of materials on a blanket that originate from paper or ink in sufficient quantity to affect print quality, and may occur in the image or nonimage areas. It can originate from one or more of the following: inks, paper coatings, fillers, or dusting. **Image area piling** is a puttylike buildup of either paper materials or ink or both on the blanket that takes on the color of the ink. A mixture of ink and paper materials can become increasingly tacky and contribute to further piling. Because image area piling interferes with ink transfer, it causes deterioration of print quality. If the ink is poorly ground or high in pigment concentration, there is a tendency for the ink to become short or puttylike. Working water into the ink increases the shortness. Short inks do not transfer as well as long inks or lay as well on the blanket, plate, and surface of the paper. To the ink that already has a tendency to become short is now added a bit of dust from paper coating or from paper fillers, and the ink becomes too short to transfer. This reaction occurs first at the blanket-paper interface where the fibers from the paper first work their way into the ink. In severe cases, the fillers, fibers, and coatings may work their way back to the plate and cause shadow dots to fill in and halftone dots to grow. In severe cases, it works its way back to the ink rollers, causing ink caking.

If the ink becomes short and transfers poorly after 15,000 or 20,000 impressions on a sheetfed press or after 75,000 to 100,000 impressions on a web press, the printer does not consider piling to be a problem. If it occurs after a few hundred impressions on a sheetfed press or a few thousand on a web press, the paper may be considered unrunnable. Because this phenomenon is complicated, it sometimes appears to come and go almost by magic. Sometimes the problem can be solved by sending the paper back to the warehouse and getting fresh paper. Increasing the amount of ink on the press may help to wash pigment through the press and onto the paper. Reducing back cylinder squeeze, slowing the press, or reducing the force between the blanket and the paper may help to solve the problem. One research lab has identified twenty-one different factors that contribute to ink piling. Pigment filler from paper and weakly bonded paper pigment coatings are among them.

In order to produce a bright, ink-receptive sheet, the papermaker adds as little adhesive to the pigment coating as possible. However, if too little adhesive is used, the pigment can work its way into the ink, causing severe piling problems.

Roll condition. Press runnability can be greatly reduced by paper that is poorly made, rolls that are poorly wound, and rolls that are mishandled during shipping or storage. Telescoped, crushed, and starred rolls will not feed properly. **Telescoped** rolls are discussed in "Properties Required of Printing Papers." When a roll is **starred,** it has an end with a "star" pattern. This is caused by tightly wound paper surrounding loosely wound paper so that the higher tension of the outer layers squeezes the inner layers. When this type of roll is dropped, its inner layers will buckle or shift and the circular winding pattern will be transformed to a starred one. The roll has flat sections across its face that cause it to hump and unwind with jerky draws.

Paper must be slabbed off from rolls that have paper gouged out of them. This is an expensive operation. Even slabbing 0.5 in. from the outside of a 45-in. roll increases paper costs by 2.5%. One way of improving roll runnability is to install a good tension control device on the press. These devices greatly improve paper performance and print quality and reduce downtime.

Handling and shipping damage. Rolls are particularly susceptible to handling damage. Bumping, tipping, or dropping a roll only a few inches can flatten it, cause it to become starred, or bruise its edges. The result is that a portion or possibly all of the roll may become unusable for printing. Rolls should never be rolled over rough floors, nails, stones, or sharp objects, because these objects will mar the roll face with dents.

Printers should inspect paper carefully for transit damage before unloading it. Any damage should be photographed, using an instant camera to document the damage, and reported to the common carrier before the shipment is formally accepted. Otherwise, the printer pays for the damage.

Many printers equip their paper handlers with instant cameras and instruct them to routinely

take pictures of the condition of all shipments. This greatly helps in documenting shipping problems. If concealed damage is discovered while the shipment is being unloaded, the paper handler should take another picture showing the extent and nature of the problem. Damage in transit due to improper loading or inadequate packaging should be reported to the paper manufacturer and to the shipper.

Moisture problems. Moisture conditioning of paper is no longer practiced in the United States. At one time, lithographers hung paper in the pressroom or in a paper conditioning machine to bring it to the proper moisture. Paper machine controls now regulate the relative humidity of paper much more accurately, and the slow, expensive practice of paper conditioning is no longer required. If an error occurs and the paper is too dry or too moist, it must be reported to the paper supplier.

As stated previously, problems with tight and wavy edges are very common. If cold paper is brought to the pressroom and unwrapped, it will cool the surrounding air, and the unprotected edges of the paper quickly take on moisture. Moisture can condense on the edges of cold paper as it does on a glass of ice water, resulting in wavy-edged paper.

The reverse situation occurs when paper that is warmer than the pressroom is unwrapped. The higher temperature of the paper warms up the surrounding air and lowers its relative humidity. The paper's edges lose moisture to the drier air and shrink.

These two troublesome consequences emphasize the importance of temperature-conditioning all paper to pressroom temperature before it is unwrapped.

The length of time required to temperature-condition paper depends upon the volume or size of the skid, roll, or carton. To find the approximate temperature of sheeted paper, a small hole is made in the wrapper and a steel-jacketed thermometer is inserted into the pile. For rolls, the thermometer is placed between the wrapper and roll end, since it is not possible to insert it between the roll layers without damaging the paper.

Static. Static causes sheets to cling tightly to each other or to press components, interfering with the sheet pickup and forwarding mechanism of the feeder. Static also prevents sheets from advancing in proper alignment and causes variation in their positioning at the grippers and side guide. These effects in turn jam up and trip the press. After the paper has been printed, static causes poor jogging, ink smearing, sheet damage, and sheets to cling tightly to previously delivered ones. Paper with a relative humidity greater than 35% usually does not cause static problems. The basic cause of static electricity is a lack of the moisture needed for its dissipation. Static is thus observed mostly in the wintertime when paper is allowed to dry out before going to the press. The most effective means of preventing static is to maintain a relative humidity in the 40–50% range. Also, the web may be remoisturized when it is cool to combat static.

Static is somewhat less serious in lithography than in other methods of printing because the lithographic press adds water, which is usually the best static eliminator, to the paper. In unusual situations, where plastic sheets are being printed, special static eliminators can be used. These static eliminators are very effective.

Dirt held on the sheet by static forces can sometimes be virtually impossible to eliminate. The sheet cleaner combines a brush, a static eliminator, and a vacuum to reduce the amount of loose dirt on the sheet.

Problems of web papers. In addition to roll condition, web breaks, blisters, and fiber puffing cause problems on the web press. Extensive studies support the belief that web breaks are usually a 50–50 proposition between the papermaker and the printer. The paper web itself, roll condition, and shipping problems generate a great deal of trouble. Breaks, which can shut a press down for several minutes, add greatly to the printer's costs. The best runnability records have been achieved where printers and paper manufacturers maintain good communications and where each works to reduce his contribution to the problems. Poor winding, calender cuts, slime holes in the sheet, and bad splicing are the responsibility of the papermaker. Improper ink, poor tension control, and improper press adjustments are the printer's responsibility.

Blisters are not the problem they once were. **Blisters** are defined as oval-shaped, sharply defined, bubblelike formations that are visible and opposite each other on both sides of the web. Blisters never occur in uncoated paper. They occur when coated paper is subject to a sudden, sharp temperature rise in the dryer section of the web press, or when moisture in the web suddenly vaporizes into steam and ruptures or blows the paper structure apart internally. Blisters arise from the combination of many factors: dryer temperature, press speed, paper properties, ink coverage, and, even, ink color. The printer can reduce the dryer temperature; if

this means that the press must be slowed unacceptably, he can use a faster ink (one that dries at a lower temperature).

Fiber puffing, which produces a print looking like sandpaper, occurs with coated groundwood content papers that are heated too fast. Careful control of dryers will reduce this unsightly occurrence. The dryer should be used as a dryer and not as an oven. An important thing to remember is "dry the print, don't cook the paper."

Cracking. Cracking occurs when the paper has been made too dry by the dryer of the web press. When the design calls for a dark ink to be printed right over the fold, the least bit of cracking becomes readily apparent. A job that would be satisfactory in white becomes unsatisfactory in black, green, or brown. Cracking occurs more frequently with heavy papers such as cover stock and board, and these should be scored before folding. When the paper is folded against the grain, the fold is stronger, but cracking is greatly aggravated. Cracking can sometimes be avoided by applying moisture to the score line before folding.

Tail-end hook. Tail-end hook is a curl that develops at the back edge of press sheets as a result of printing heavy solids close to their back edge. Tail-end hook and waffling occur in sheetfed papers when the force to pull the sheet from a heavily

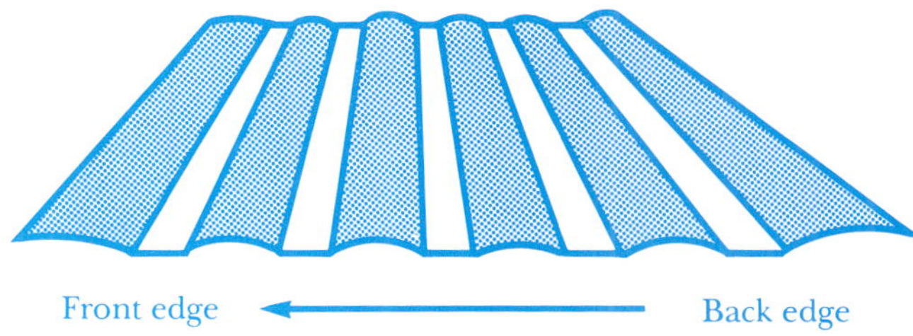

Embossing, or waffling.

inked part of the blanket stretches the sheet, and permanent waffle or embossing occurs, as shown in the accompanying illustration. The problem can occur at any part of the sheet, but it is especially bad at the tail end, hence the name. Using a stiffer sheet, improving the release of the blanket, decreasing the viscosity of the ink, or decreasing the press speed all help to prevent tail-end hook. If tail-end hook occurs anyway, the print can often be flattened with the use of a sheet decurler, a device available from a number of companies.

Setoff. Setoff is discussed further in the "Ink" chapter. It occurs when the ink does not set properly, which causes the wet ink to transfer to the next sheet in the delivery pile. Using a quickset ink helps to reduce the problem, but if the paper is not properly absorbent, the ink will not set fast enough. Setoff is most troublesome with plastic sheets. The printer can use a heavy spray of antisetoff powder, but such a spray roughens the surface and detracts from the smooth, glossy varnish film.

Misregister. Misregister is caused by unsatisfactory paper, an improperly adjusted lithographic press, a change in moisture content, or mechanical stretching. The lithographic press causes the paper to roll out and stretch, particularly as it goes through the first unit on the press. To get register on the following units, the press operator packs the press so that the first unit prints somewhat shorter than subsequent units.

Paper expands more across the grain than it does with the grain. For this reason, paper is usually fed into the sheetfed press grain long; that is, with the grain running along the axis of the cylinder. Plate and blanket packing compensate for instability across the grain.

Mottle. Mottle is discussed further in the "Ink" chapter. It arises when there are significant differences in the ink absorptivity in various parts of the sheet. A **mottled,** or **galvanized,** appearance in solid prints is defined as a visible, gross nonuniformity in ink density, color, or gloss, or any combination thereof. Mottle is found more commonly with paperboard than with paper.

If the ink cannot be adjusted to hold out uniformly, or to penetrate uniformly, it is sometimes necessary to replace the paper or board.

Paper Testing

Introduction. The basis of all quality control is an alert, observant crew. This is true in the printing plant as well as in the paper mill. Most paper mills have large, well-organized quality control programs involving a fair amount of laboratory testing. Nevertheless, the ultimate test of paper is the lithographic press. Putting the paper on press and observing whether or not it will run is the ultimate

test for most paper mills, as well as for the printer. Laboratory tests do not correlate perfectly with press performance. A battery of tests will give a profile of the paper, but interpretation is still needed. For this reason, carefully inspecting and observing the paper followed by putting it on the press to see if it will run is usually all of the routine quality control that can be justified by most printers. This section outlines additional tests that can be run for diagnostic purposes that give students an opportunity to learn how the tests are performed in the research laboratory.

Most paper testing is done with specialized instruments and under prescribed conditions. In the United States and in many other English-speaking countries, the technical standards and paper testing methods are published by the Technical Association of the Pulp and Paper Industry (TAPPI), 15 Technology Parkway, P.O. Box 105113, Norcross, GA 30092. Standards are also published by the American Society for Testing and Materials (ASTM), 1916 Race Street, Philadelphia, PA 19103; and by the American National Standards Institute (ANSI), 11 West 42nd Street, New York, NY 10036. Before starting a testing laboratory, the TAPPI, ASTM, and ANSI methods should be obtained from the associations.

TAPPI-NBS collaborative testing. Cooperation between the American National Bureau of Standards (NBS) and TAPPI in developing collaborative tests helps the testing laboratory determine which of its tests show wide deviation. Where a laboratory finds that its results deviated significantly from all other laboratories, there is presumably something wrong in its procedure or instrumentation.

Differences between laboratories are often more important than differences between different kinds of instruments. For example, nonstandard reflectance meters often give very good agreement with other laboratories in measuring brightness, while standard meters occasionally give very wide deviation and require calibration.

It is recommended that graphic arts laboratories investigate this collaborative testing procedure to make sure that their results are in reasonable agreement with others. Information is available from TAPPI.

Other countries have organizations similar to TAPPI that provide standards for paper testing. International Standards (SI) are established by the International Standards Organization (ISO). Where corresponding test methods exist, TAPPI and ISO methods are usually similar.

Sampling paper for testing. As difficult and costly as testing is, it is no more costly than adequate sampling. There is no point in testing paper unless an adequate sample has been chosen. If the sample is not representative, the test is wasted, or worse, misleading. Whether the testing is done by the manufacturer for control purposes or by a consumer for the purpose of determining whether the paper meets his requirements, it is essential that the paper sample used for testing be truly representative.

Sampling is described in detail in TAPPI Standard T 400 and ASTM D-585.

Standard conditions. When paper testing is done regularly, and the results are recorded for future reference, it should be done under standard conditions of temperature and relative humidity. The testing room should be maintained at 23±1°C (73.4±1.8°F) and 50±2% relative humidity, which is the standard testing atmosphere prescribed by TAPPI. All paper samples are conditioned in this atmosphere before the tests are made because properties of paper vary with moisture content. For more details, see TAPPI Standard T 402 for paper and paperboard; and ASTM D-685 for paper and D-641 for paperboard. Inks and oils used in testing lose viscosity rapidly with increasing temperature and must be tested at constant temperature.

A standard method must meet prescribed guidelines before it is adopted. It must give test results that are accurate and sensitive to small differences in a paper property. The method must give results from various paper laboratories, and these results must be reproducible over a long period of time. Once adopted, a standard is recognized as the authoritative method. These agreed-upon standard methods make the results of testing among laboratories comparable.

When controlled testing conditions are not available, it is possible to test an unknown sample against a test sample at ambient conditions. However, the absolute numbers are of doubtful significance and cannot be compared with tests carried out under other conditions.

Grain direction. The **grain direction** of paper results from the fact that as the water-suspended fibers flow onto the paper machine wire, they align themselves predominantly in the direction of their flow and the moving wire. Sheet paper for multicolor work should be printed grain long; that is, the grain of the paper should run parallel to the axis of the cylinder of the press. Web papers must be

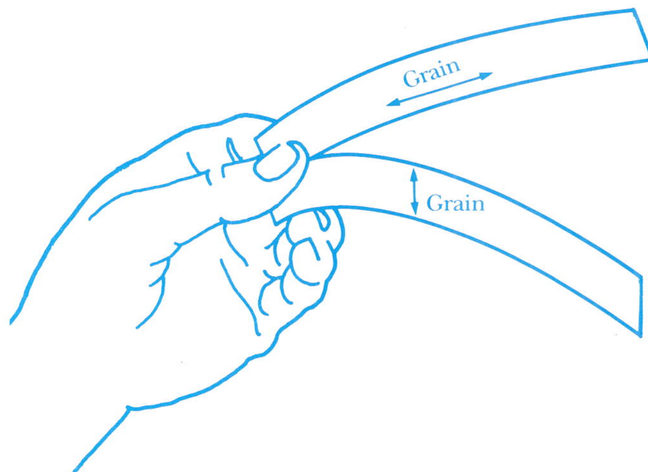

Two strips of paper of the same width cut at right angles from a sheet can show grain direction.

printed grain short; that is, the grain of the paper runs at right angles to the axis of the cylinder of the press. It is not difficult to determine the grain direction of web papers, but sheetfed papers can be cut with the grain direction either parallel to the long side of the sheet or the short side of the sheet.

One way to determine the grain direction of a paper is to determine the direction of curl. A piece of paper or paperboard approximately 2 in. square is cut from the sheet to be tested, and a line is drawn with a pencil parallel to the long edge of the original sheet. When the small square is floated on water or is moistened, it will curl away from its wetted side, and the axis of curl will be parallel to its grain direction. The **axis of curl** is the machine or grain direction of the piece. If it runs parallel to the mark on the paper, the paper has been cut grain-long. If it runs perpendicular to the mark on the paper, the paper has been cut grain-short. Additional methods are described in TAPPI Standard T 409 and ANSI-ASTM D-528.

Felt and wire sides. Felt and wire sides of paper are discussed in the "Papermaking" section of this chapter. All paper and board is two-sided. With most boards, this is obvious since they are made to be printed on one side only. The same is true of C1S papers. With papers designed for printing on both sides, the two sides should be as much alike as possible. Modern papermaking machines, which use hydrofoils to support the wire, or twin-wire machines, make paper with little difference between felt and wire sides. Consequently, it is sometimes difficult to tell which is the felt side and which is the wire side. Standard methods for determining felt and wire sides are given in TAPPI Standard T 455 and ASTM D-725.

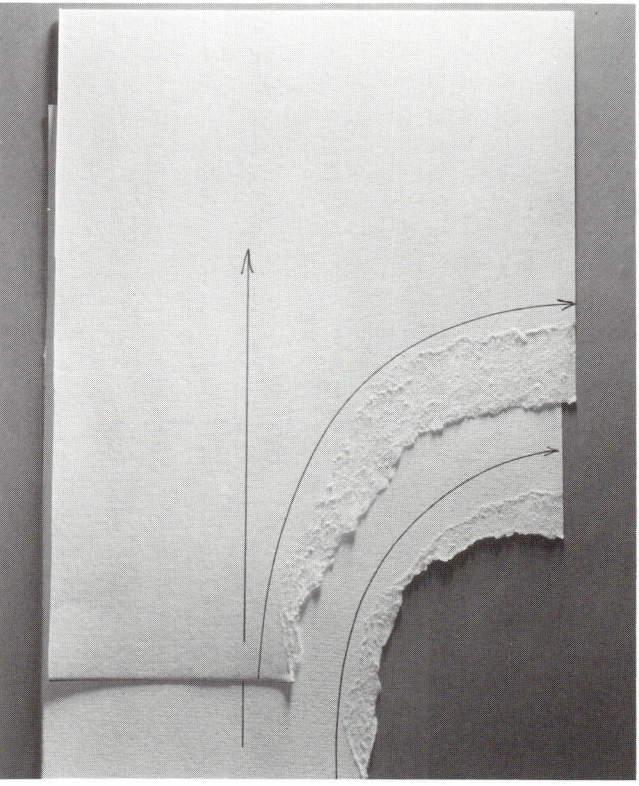

Tearing determination of wire and felt sides of paper. A tear is made first in the direction of grain and then is curved gradually to the right. The wire side (upper sample) produces a wider, feathered edge.

Perhaps the easiest way of determining the felt and wire sides is to cut two squares about 2 in. on a side, noting, of course, which side is up in the sample. The two squares are placed in a paper-drying oven: one with the same side up, and the other with that side down. After heating for a few minutes at 100°C (212°F), the curl should be observed. Paper tends to curl toward the felt side, which contains more fibers.

Moisture and relative humidity. The sheetfed printer is usually more interested in the relative humidity at which paper is in equilibrium than its absolute moisture content. Relative humidity is a more significant and precise measurement than moisture content for sheetfed paper. The relationship of paper and water is more reliably and accurately controlled as a percent moisture during its manufacture and its printing in web form.

Equilibrium relative humidity at a specified temperature is usually more significant for sheetfed

printing and some converting operations. Equilibrium relative humidity is that atmospheric humidity at which exposure of the paper will result neither in absorption nor desorption of its moisture. Absolute moisture content of paper in equilibrium with room air varies depending upon the type of paper. Uncoated paper contains more moisture than coated paper, where perhaps one-third of the sheet is pigment that does not absorb moisture.

Relative humidity of paper is determined with a hygroscope that measures whether the paper will pick up moisture from the air, whether it will lose moisture to the air, or whether it is in equilibrium with the air.

As paper is manufactured on the paper machine, its moisture content is controlled by the dryers. Automated devices measure and control the moisture content, but moisture content of the paper can change quickly if finishing rooms do not have humidity control.

The absolute moisture content of a sheet of paper is determined by drying it to constant weight at 105°C (221°F) as described in TAPPI Standard T 412 and ANSI-ASTM D-644. Strength, pick resistance, hardness, static, paper curl, and dimensional stability all depend upon moisture and moisture equilibrium.

Basis weight and grammage. Basis weight is also discussed in "Properties Required of Printing Papers." **Grammage** is the designation of paper or paperboard weight in the metric system as grams per square meter. It is the weight in grams for a single sheet of paper having an area (per side) of 1 m^2. Grammage is abbreviated as g/m^2. The measurement of basis weight and grammage of paper is described in TAPPI Standard T 410 and ASTM D-646. Sheets of known area must be conditioned under standard conditions and then weighed very accurately. From the weight and area of the sheet, the basic ream weight or grammage is calculated for the basic size.

Paper caliper and bulking thickness. The thickness of paper and paperboard and its variation is an important consideration in the manufacture and use of paper. It is described as **caliper,** which is the perpendicular distance between two surfaces of a single sheet as measured with a **micrometer,** which is an instrument that applies a specific static load for a minimum specified time. The standard procedures and instrumentation for determining thickness or caliper of paper are described in TAPPI Standard T 411 and ASTM D-645. The

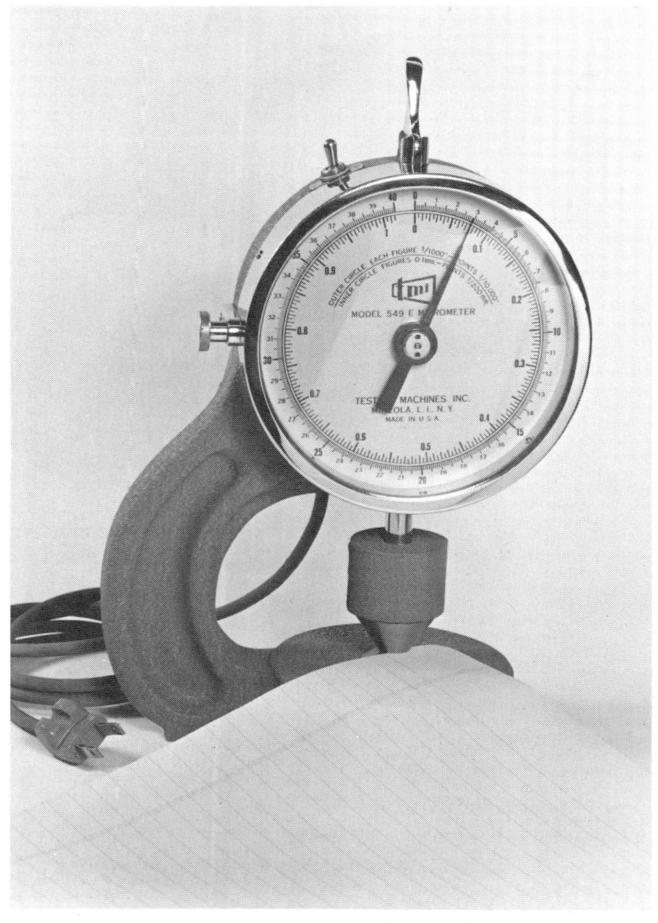

Courtesy Testing Machines, Inc.

A motor-driven bench micrometer.

thickness of paper or paperboard is the thickness in thousandths of an inch of a single sheet of paper or board. Thickness is determined by calipering individual sheets of paper or board after conditioning. A paper micrometer using standard jaws exerts a standard pressure on the paper or board.

Bulking thickness, or **book bulk,** refers to the average thickness of paper in a pile, in books and magazines, for example. The **bulking number** is the number of sheets that will bulk 1 in. (25.4 mm) under a specified applied pressure. Bulking number multiplied by 2 gives pages per inch (ppi). Bulking number and ppi are used when manufacturing and specifying paper thickness for book manufacturing. The standard procedure for determining the bulking thickness of paper is described in TAPPI Standard T 500 and in ASTM D-2175.

Squareness. Because sheets that are not cut square can create great trouble with registration and later in binding, it can be useful to observe the squareness of paper with the use of a carpenter's

square or by using a printer's layout table. The printer more frequently folds the paper together to see if the two opposite corners and edges coincide exactly. If they do not, the paper has been cut out of square.

Strength. A number of related properties are referred to as paper strength: tensile strength, tearing resistance, folding endurance, the surface strength or picking resistance, and internal bond. These characteristics depend upon the extent the paper is refined. The greater the refining, the greater the tensile, bursting, fold, and picking strengths are, but tearing strength falls off after an initial rapid rise.

Tensile strength. The tensile strength, stretch, and the general load-elongation characteristics of paper affect its ability to perform in many end-uses. **Tensile breaking strength** is the maximum tensile stress paper will withstand before breaking under prescribed conditions. As a paper undergoes tensile stress, it elongates, or stretches. Elongation, or tensile strain, as measured during a tensile test is the maximum elongation which the paper undergoes before it breaks under tension. The tensile strength is expressed in pounds per linear inch; that is, the force required to break a strip one inch wide. The tensile strength is also expressed in grams per linear meter.

The tensile strength is often converted into the breaking length, which is the calculated length of paper that weighs enough to break the sheet. For example, if a strip of 20-lb. bond paper 1 in. wide requires 4 lb. to break, the breaking length is 3,117 ft.:

a. 1 ream of bond paper = 17 in. × 22 in. × 500 sheets = 187,000 sq. in.
b. 187,000 sq. in. ÷ 1 in. = 187,000 in.

Therefore, 20 lb. of 20-lb. bond paper that is 1 in. wide has a breaking length of 187,000 in.

c. 20 lb. ÷ 187,000 in. = 0.000107 lb./in.
d. 4 lb. ÷ 0.000107 lb./in. = 37,400 in., or 3,117 ft.

The standard procedures for measuring tensile strength are described in TAPPI Standard T 404 and in ASTM D-828.

Paper stretch. Stretch is defined as the percentage elongation of a strip of paper at the time of rupture under tension. The stretch of paper is important when a web is handled under tension. Like tensile strength, the stretch is related to the toughness of the paper. Stretch affects the ability of a sheet to fold well and to resist the concentration of local stress.

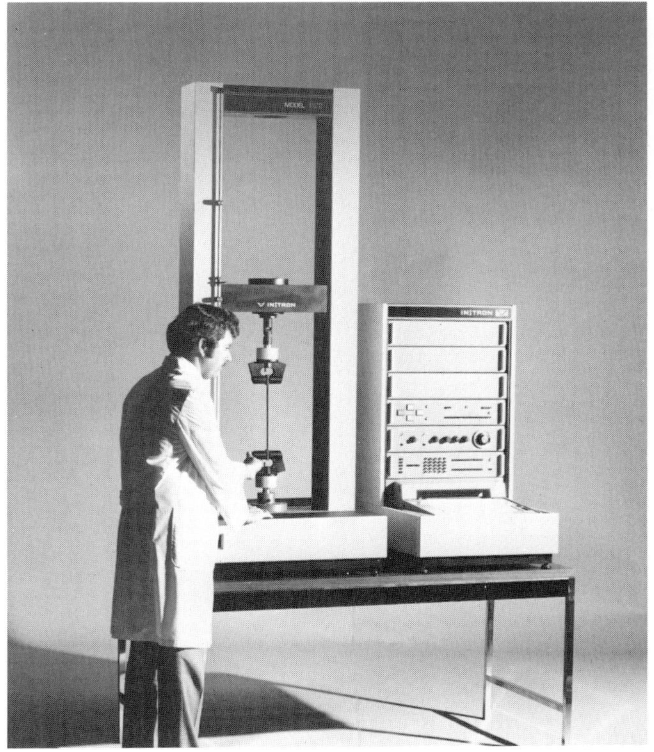

Courtesy Instron Corporation

Instron Tensile Tester.

The stretch of paper also relates to its stiffness and its runnability on sheetfed presses. In offset printing, the uniform squeeze impression and separation of paper from the blanket tends to stretch the paper in the direction of its travel. When a piece of paper bends, one side compresses and the other stretches. Therefore, it is easier to feed stiff sheets than it is to feed soft or flexible ones. Stretch measurement is described in TAPPI Standard T 457.

Load-elongation curve. The most complete information on the behavior of paper under tension is given by the load-elongation curve. The load-elongation curve is obtained with a machine that automatically plots the force, or load, applied to the strip against the increase in length or elongation of the specimen. The maximum load—that is, the load at the time of failure of the strip—corresponds to the tensile strength as measured by the tensile strength tester. In determining tensile strength, it is usual to determine also the stretch and the load-

elongation curve. Tensile energy absorption (TEA) is described in TAPPI Standard T 494.

Tensile energy absorption is the energy-absorbing capacity of paper and its ability to withstand shock.

Tearing resistance. Tearing resistance is also discussed in "Properties Required of Printing Papers." There are a number of ways of measuring tearing strength of paper, but the most commonly used one is the Elmendorf tear test, which measures the force required to tear a specimen under standardized conditions after the tear has been started. It is sometimes called "internal tearing strength." Procedures are described in TAPPI Standard T 414 and in ASTM D-689.

Bursting strength. Bursting strength is defined as the resistance of paper or paperboard to rupture as measured by the hydrostatic pressure required to burst it when a uniformly distributed and increasing pressure is applied to one of its sides. The tester used to determine bursting strength is a **Mullen Tester.** Bursting strength is an empirical test intended to define the usefulness of paper when resistance to bursting is an end-use requirement, as in packaging. Although widely used, its principal value is as a control test in the paper mill. To test a sample, it is clamped over a rubber diaphragm under a ring, and hydrostatic fluid is pumped under the diaphragm until the sample bursts. A dial shows the pressure at the time of rupture. Procedures for determining bursting strength of paper are given in TAPPI Standard T 403 and in ASTM D-774. Procedures for paperboard are given in TAPPI Standard T 801 and in ASTM D-2529, and for corrugated board and solid fiberboard in TAPPI Standard T 810 and in ASTM D-2738. Procedures for paperboard and linerboard are also given in TAPPI Standard T 807.

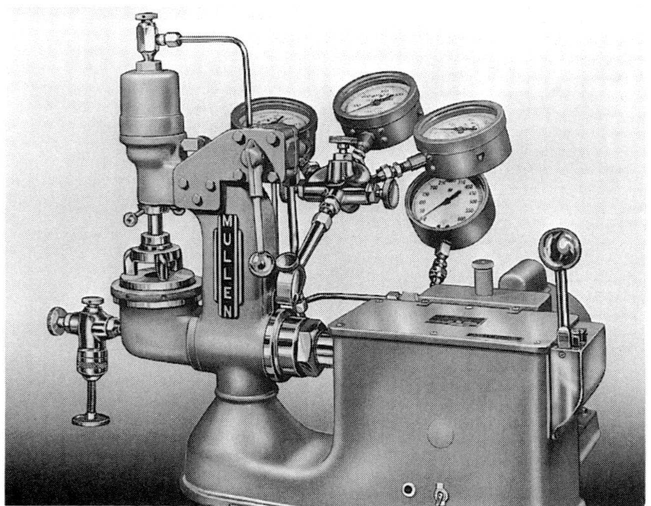

Courtesy B. F. Perkins Division

Mullen Tester used internationally for measuring the bursting strength of paper and paperboard.

Folding endurance. Folding endurance is defined as the number of folds, under specified conditions, that a specimen withstands before failure. This test measures the ability of paper to withstand repeated folding. Folding endurance is measured both with and across the grain. Generally, paper has a greater folding endurance when folded against the grain. Folding endurance can be measured by two methods: the **Schopper** and the **M.I.T.** The Schopper folding endurance test is specified in TAPPI Standard T 423 and ASTM D-643. In this method, a strip of paper is held under tension while a slotted reciprocating blade catches the strip in its middle and folds it back and forth between four rollers, folding it first toward one side, then toward the other side. The number of double folds the paper withstands before breaking is its folding endurance. The M.I.T. folding endurance test is described in TAPPI Standard T 511 and ASTM D-2176. In the M.I.T. method, a strip is clamped under tension between a spring-loaded jaw and an

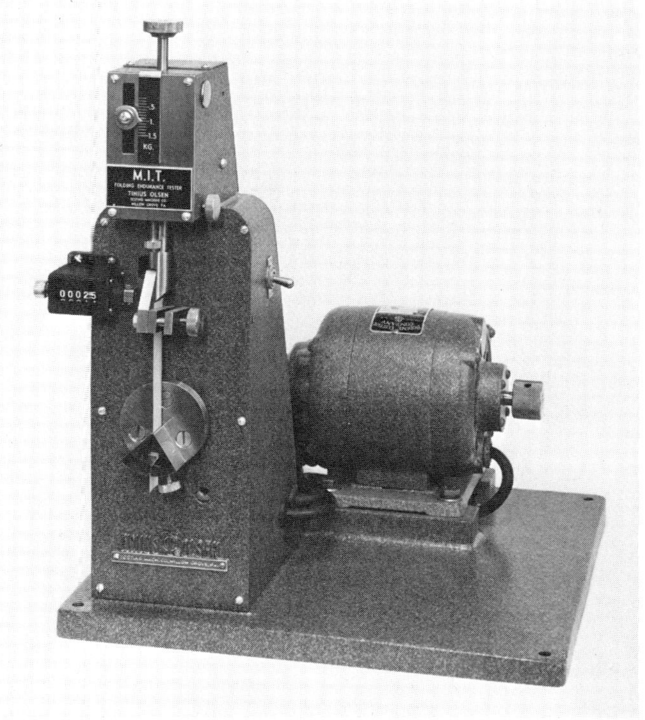

Courtesy Testing Machines, Inc.

M.I.T. Folding Endurance Tester.

oscillating folding head. As the folding head oscillates an exact number of degrees on each side of its starting position, the paper is alternately folded toward each of its two sides. The folding endurance is the number of folds the paper undergoes before breaking at its fold line. The folding endurance test is particularly sensitive to aging of the sample, and experiments on the aging and aging resistance of paper frequently involve the effect of variables on folding endurance. The stability of paper to heat is tested for by TAPPI Standard 453 and ASTM D-776.

Surface strength. There is also discussion on surface strength in "Properties Required of Printing Papers." There are a number of tests for surface strength, a property that is particularly important in lithography. Lithography places greater surface strength demands on paper than do other printing processes. Unfortunately, none of these tests adequately predict the way paper will perform on the press.

Surface strength of paper varies widely from point to point on the sheet or on the web. None of the procedures described here tests a sufficiently large area to give a good picture of the ultimate weaknesses of the paper. To learn how the paper actually behaves under press conditions, the paper mill quality control testing laboratory very often uses a production-size offset press.

Nevertheless, these tests are used for a variety of reasons, including routine quality control and laboratory evaluation of new products.

Dennison wax test. The Dennison waxes are a series of hard resin-wax sticks with graded adhesive powers. The higher the power number, the greater is the adhesiveness. They are used to determine the degree of sizing of the paper or of the coating in relation to press conditions and to determine the pick resistance. The test specimen is placed on a wooden table top or hardwood block. A stick of wax is slowly rotated over an alcohol flame or Bunsen burner to heat it. The melted end of the wax is then placed quickly on the paper surface in a vertical position and pressed down firmly. After cooling, a wooden yoke is placed around the wax, and the wax is quickly pulled away from the sheet at a right angle to the paper surface. If coating particles, fibers, or bits of paper adhere to the end of the wax at this point, the paper has "picked," or failed. If nothing adheres to the wax, the test is repeated using waxes with higher numbers. The pick resistance of the paper is the number of the highest numbered wax that does not disturb the surface of the paper. The average highest numbered wax that does not disturb the paper surface or the wax number one lower than the wax that disturbs the paper is called the **critical wax number.** Normally, both felt and wire sides are tested.

The test is used widely in paper mills, where it is performed quickly and where changes in the critical wax number suggest changes in paper properties. The test is of little use in the printing plant because the numbers obtained from the Dennison wax test have little correlation with runnability of the paper. The test is described in ASTM D-2482 and TAPPI Standard T 459.

Internal bond. Internal bond is a measure of the resistance of the paper to picking and to delamination under stress. A related property is **z-directional tensile strength,** which is the tensile strength of paper measured perpendicularly to its surface. The measurement of internal bond strength is described by TAPPI Standard T 506.

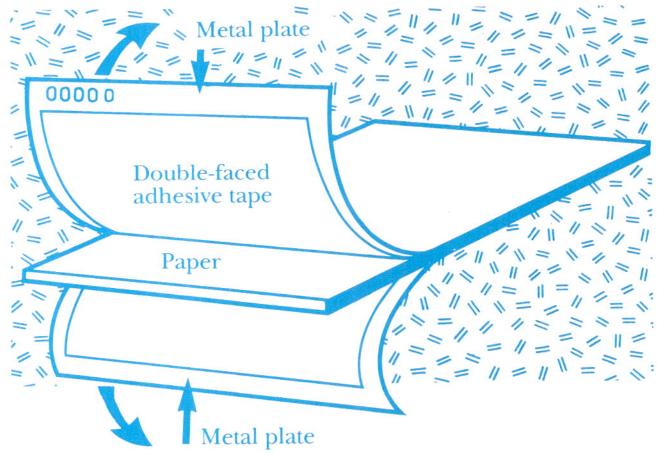

Z-directional tensile strength measurement.

IGT surface strength tester. The IGT surface strength tester, called the IGT Printability Tester, measures surface strength in accordance with TAPPI Standard T 499. It measures pick resistance of coated and uncoated papers, in a manner closely simulating the printing process, by the use of tack-graded inks, control of printing pressure, and a mechanical action similar to that of a printing press. It is possible to test both with and across the grain. In this surface strength test, a strip of the paper specimen is cut in the desired direction and mounted on a cylindrical surface. An ink film of controlled thickness is applied to the surface of a disk that rolls against the paper. The disk and cylinder are

driven with an accelerating motion so that the speed of printing varies from 0 ft./min. at the beginning of the print to over 600 ft./min. (183 m/min.) at the end of the print. As printing speed increases, the force exerted on the paper by the ink increases until picking occurs. The length of the printed strip before picking starts indicates the printing speed required to pick the paper. The product of this printing speed and the viscosity of the ink used is an index of surface strength. Viscosity rated oils or printing inks can be used for this test. The Prüfbau printability tester can also be used to measure surface strength in a manner closely simulating the printing process.

Smoothness, Porosity, and Density

Smoothness. The smoothness of paper relates to the deviations of the actual paper surface from an ideal plane. Because paper deforms and is compressible, the smoothness of a sheet as it lies on a table is not the effective smoothness at the actual time of ink transfer in printing. Smoothness, in the sense of printing smoothness, is most important in rotogravure printing, important for letterpress printing, and least important, although not completely unimportant, in offset lithographic printing.

The older and more commonly used methods of measuring smoothness of paper are the **air-leak** methods. One method involves measuring the time required for a given volume of air to leak between the paper surface and a smooth glass test plate under a specified air pressure. This method is described in TAPPI Standard T 479, and is used for the **Bekk** and the **Gurley smoothness testers.** A second method, using the **Sheffield paper smoothness gauge,** measures the rate of air flow between the paper's surfaces and an annular groove in the upper gauge head. The **Parker Print-Surf** roughness tester is an air-leak paper roughness tester designed and manufactured to operate under test conditions similar to those encountered during printing operations. It is used primarily by coating manufacturers to test the smoothness of coated paper and paperboard. Details on methods based on the rate of air flow are described in TAPPI Useful Method 518 and Useful Method 535.

There are many other methods that have been proposed for measuring smoothness of paper. Methods for comparing smoothness of papers involve printing thin ink films and judging the relative smoothness of the papers on the basis of the relative uniformity of solid or screen-tint prints. There are also profile-tracing procedures in which the profile of the paper surface is obtained by drawing a stylus that has an amplified vertical displacement over the surface. The amplified vertical displacement is automatically recorded as a trace. Another type of test measures the smoothness as the percentage of paper contacting a glass plate. The paper is held against the glass under pressure corresponding to printing conditions, and the measurement is made by light reflection.

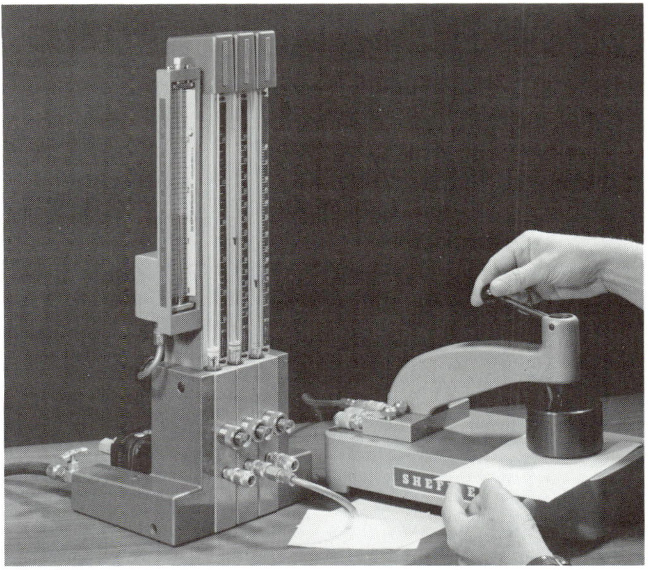

Courtesy A&M Division, Bendix Corporation
Sheffield smoothness gauge for measuring smoothness instantly.

Porosity. Porosity is defined as the ease with which air passes through paper. It may be expressed as the rate at which air flows through a given area under stated conditions. The porosity level of a paper results from its manufacture. A paper made from all long fibers will be more porous than one made from short fibers, which compact more closely together under the same manufacturing conditions. The porosity of paper is measured by its resistance to the passage of air. TAPPI Standard T 460 and ASTM D-726 determine the time required for 100 cm^3 of air under constant pressure to pass through a given area of paper. The **Gurley densometer** is commonly used for measuring porosity in this way. Another method, TAPPI Useful Method 524, measures the rate of air flow through a given area of paper. The **Sheffield porosimeter** is used in this method.

Density. Density is often confused with porosity, and there is some inverse relationship since, generally, the denser the sheet, the less the porosity.

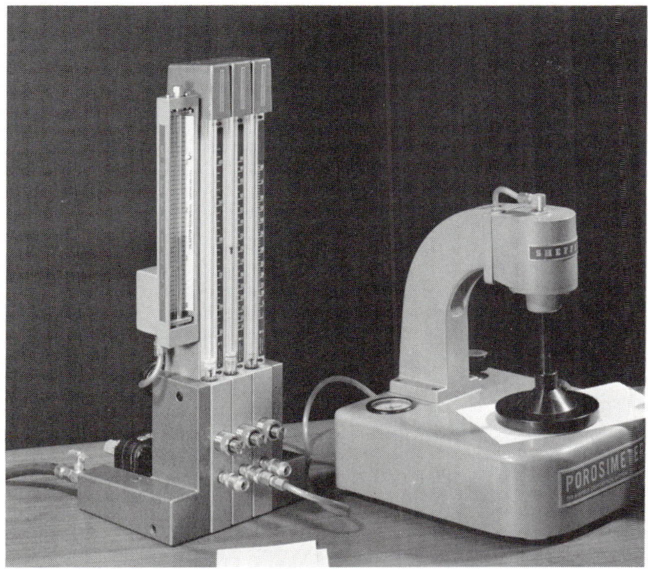

Courtesy A&M Division, Bendix Corporation

Sheffield porosimeter.

Other things being equal, **apparent density** of paper is its weight per unit volume, and it is commonly calculated by dividing the basis weight in pounds of the paper by the single-sheet thickness in thousandths of an inch.

Optical Properties

Brightness is measured with a standard brightness tester. In the United States, this tester is calibrated by monthly checks with the Institute of Paper Chemistry (IPC). As a result of continuous monitoring, the brightness test is one of the most precise and reproducible tests used in the paper industry. The brightness is measured at 457 nm, a blue wavelength, chosen because it is especially effective in measuring the yellow color that is characteristic of bleached fibers. The brightness of paper is commonly indicated by a value variously called its TAPPI, G.E. (General Electric), or IPC brightness, as described in TAPPI Standard T 452. The standard brightness test is TAPPI Standard T 452 or ASTM D-985. The instrument used for measuring brightness by this method was developed by IPC. Parallel beams of visible light at a 45° angle illuminate a pad of the paper to be tested. Reflected light is measured at an angle of 90° to the paper's surface and is filtered to measure reflected light of 457 nm.

The hue or color of a paper can be measured using a reflectance meter as described in TAPPI Standard T 524 or, better, by a spectrophotometer as described in TAPPI Standard T 442. A **spectrophotometer** measures the color of a paper by giving wavelength-by-wavelength analyses of its reflected light. Color measurement with a spectrophotometer is useful where color formulation is involved and where it becomes necessary to determine if two samples having the same color will match under all types of illumination. Reflectance must be measured at a minimum of three wavelengths. Specifying the color of paper by the Munsell system is described in ASTM D-1535.

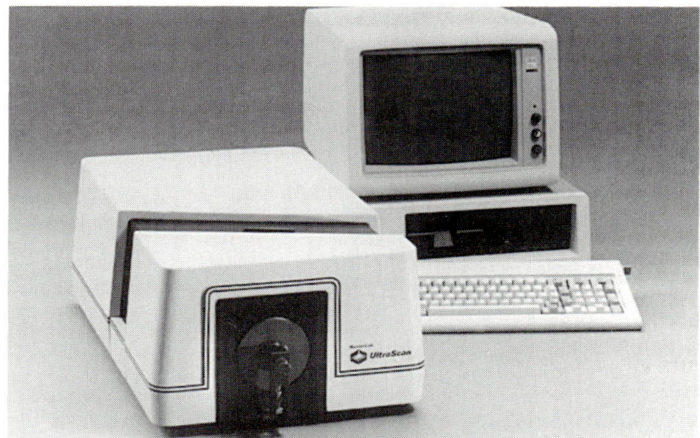

Courtesy Hunter Associates Laboratory, Inc.

Hunterlab UltraScan spectrophotometer.

Gloss is the specular, or mirror, reflectance and is measured with one of several glossmeters. For coated printing papers, gloss is usually measured at a 75° angle as described in TAPPI Standard T 480 and in ASTM D-1223. Highly glossy prints are better measured at 20°, as described in TAPPI Standard T 653.

Opacity, the extent to which light transmission is obstructed, is determined by measuring the reflectance of the paper against first a white background and then against a black background. The opacity is 100 × (RB/RW), where RB is the reflectance of the paper against the black background and RW is the reflectance against the white background. **Contrast ratio opacity,** measured in this manner, is described in TAPPI Standard T 425 and ANSI-ASTM D-589.

Fluorescence is the absorption of ultraviolet radiation, which has a relatively short wavelength, by a material that causes it to emit radiation having a longer wavelength, in the visible portion of the spectrum. Fluorescence in paper is made to occur by the use of fluorescent dyes or optical brighteners. Fluorescence of paper can be an impediment in determining the color or the apparent color of the print. It can also interfere with optical character recognition (OCR) and with instruments that mea-

sure fluorescence of inks. Fluorescence is observed with a "black light," a lamp that emits ultraviolet radiation but no visible light. A darkroom is necessary for examination except for the most brilliantly fluorescing materials. Instrumentation is used to measure the amount of fluorescence, and tests are described in TAPPI Useful Method 547 and Useful Method 548.

Paper pH. In measuring acidity or alkalinity, chemists usually report the pH; **pH** is a chemical abbreviation or symbol for the **potential of the hydrogen ion.** It is a measure of acidity or alkalinity, expressed as the negative logarithm of the concentration of hydrogen ions in moles per liter. The pH affects the drying rate of sheetfed inks, and it influences other paper properties including permanence.

Each unit decrease in pH below 7 means a tenfold increase in the acidity. Thus, a pH of 4 is 100 times more acid than a pH of 6. A pH of 7 is neutral, and each unit increase in pH above 8 represents a tenfold increase in the alkalinity.

The procedure for determining the pH of paper by hot-water extraction is given in TAPPI Standard T 435 and ASTM D-778. TAPPI Standard T 509 describes the procedure for cold-water extraction.

There are also pH meters that have flat electrodes that permit measurement of the pH of the surface of the paper, described in TAPPI Standard T 529.

The pH test may be of value in diagnostic situations and in problem solving, but it has not proved useful in routine quality control testing.

Sizing and water resistance. There are numerous tests for determining the resistance of paper and paperboard to water and aqueous fluids. These tests include the **contact angle test** (TAPPI Standard T 458), the **dry indicator test** (TAPPI Standard T 433), the **ink flotation test** (TAPPI Useful Method 481), the **ink resistance test** (TAPPI Standard T 530), the **degree of curl test** (TAPPI Standard T 466), the **Cobb size test** (TAPPI Standard T 441), and the **water immersion test** (TAPPI Standard T 491). The contact angle test is based upon the principle that the advancing angle of contact between water or writing inks and the paper's surface is a measure of its wettability by these fluids. The dry indicator test uses a water-sensitive dry indicator powder for indicating the end point of the test.

In the ink flotation test, a test sample is floated on a colored writing ink. The time for ink penetration is measured and indicates the degree of surface sizing.

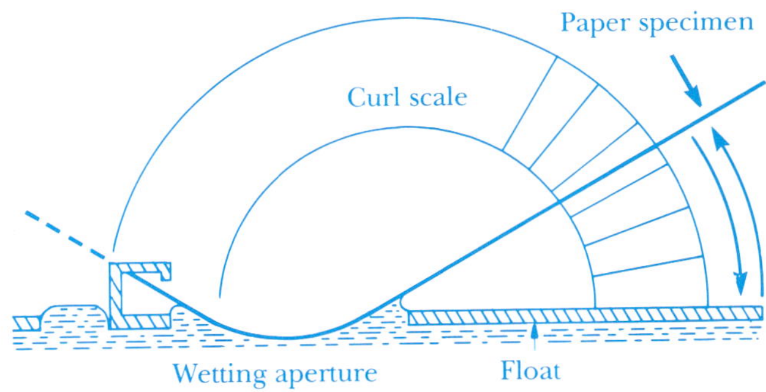

Curl test method for measuring relative degree of sizing in accordance with TAPPI Standard T 466.

In the degree of curl test, a test sample is floated on water. It will continue to curl away from its wetted side until the water has penetrated approximately halfway through the paper's thickness. Further penetration will then cause the sample to reverse its movement. Water resistance is measured by determining the time from water contact until the sample reaches its maximum curl.

The Cobb size test measures the degree of sizing of paper or paperboard by the weight of water absorbed under prescribed conditions during a specified time.

The water immersion test measures the weight of water absorbed by a paper or paperboard sample after it has been immersed in water for a given time under specified temperature conditions.

Ink absorbency of paper. The most commonly used tests to measure the absorbency of paper for printing inks are the K and N ink absorbency test, the Vanceometer method, TAPPI Useful Method 519, and those tests using laboratory printability testers or proof presses.

Ink absorbency is the property that determines at what rate and in what amount the ink penetrates the paper after the press plate or blanket deposits it. A related property is **ink holdout,** which can be defined as the tendency of paper to resist or retard the inward penetration of the freshly printed ink film. The ink absorbency of paper determines its ability to hold out the printing ink film or a varnish. Absorbency is important in controlling the setoff, finish, and gloss of the dried ink or varnish. Ink absorbency of paper is not the same as its porosity. It is primarily a surface characteristic, depending on the degree of surface sizing and on the nature of the coatings. It can be measured by the

rate at which a film of viscous oil loses gloss after being applied to the surface or by the stain remaining after a pigmented fluid has been applied to the surface.

The **Vanceometer** method, described in TAPPI Useful Method 519, depends upon the fact that immediately after a film of oil is spread on paper, its surface is highly glossy. As the oil is absorbed by the paper surface, the gloss decreases. Timing the rate of gloss decrease with the Vanceometer's glossmeter gives a measure of the absorbency of the sheet. The Vanceometer is an instrument designed specifically for this test.

The **K and N ink absorbency test** is a test for comparing the rate of ink absorption of different papers by applying a thick film of a nondrying ink to overlapped samples of different papers for a specified time, then removing and wiping them clean. The depth of stain indicates relative ink absorbency.

The K and N test is most useful in comparing the absorbency of coated and smooth-surface uncoated papers. When the test is made under standard conditions of temperature and relative humidity, it is possible to obtain reproducible results.

The K and N test is also valuable as an indication of the uniformity of absorbency of paper coatings. Mottled color or variations in density of the color of the tested area indicate nonuniform absorbency, which can result in mottled printing or mottled varnish in the finished sheet.

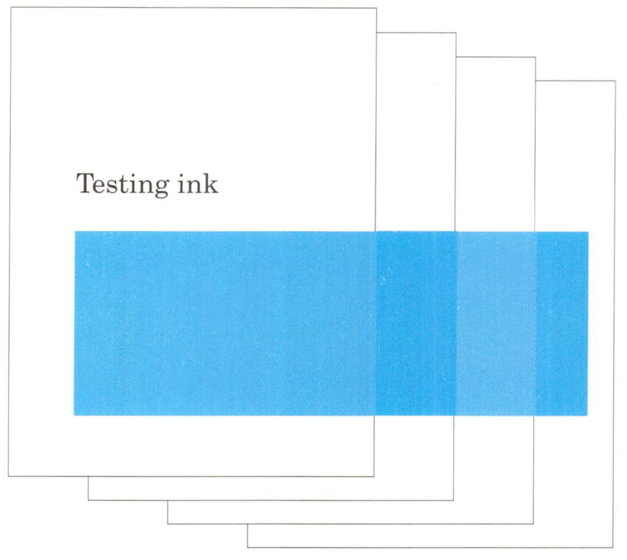

Arrangement of paper samples for the K and N ink absorbency test.

Paper surface efficiency. The print's color depends on both the absorbency of the paper and its gloss. To determine paper surface efficiency, the operator measures gloss, determines the K and N ink number, and plots them on a paper surface efficiency chart.

Paper formation. Formation is the structure and the degree of uniformity of a paper's fiber transmission as judged by transmitted light. The distribution depends on the stock used for making the sheet and on the paper machine itself. Formation is usually judged on a relative basis by comparing two sheets with each other. Since formation is difficult to judge subjectively, instrumentation has been devised to analyze and rank formation. TAPPI Useful Method 432 describes a way to compare the formation of samples with an instrument.

Ash. The percentage of ash in a sheet of paper is determined by the amount of filler or the amount of coating used. Standard chemical determinations for ash in any combustible material are applied. The paper is dried under standard conditions and ignited in a crucible in a furnace until all carbon residue is completely burned. The amount of ash is weighed and calculated as a percent of the dry paper. Determination of ash is described in TAPPI Standard T 413 and ASTM D-586. Qualitative and quantitative analysis of the ash content of paper, to identify its mineral constituents and their amounts respectively, require elaborate analytical procedures as stated in TAPPI Standard T 421 and Standard T 422.

Abrasion resistance of paper or prints. Abrasion resistance is the resistance of a paper or paperboard surface to being worn down, roughened, and disrupted by sliding frictional contact with other surfaces.

The rubbing or scuffing resistance of a printed ink film is an important consideration for packaging printing. The Gavarti Comprehensive Abrasion Tester is used to test printed paper and paperboard for abrasion damage. The Sutherland Ink-Rub Tester evaluates the scuffing or rubbing resistance of printed ink films on paper or paperboard and as described in TAPPI Useful Method 487.

Groundwood content of paper. To determine whether or not a sheet of paper contains groundwood, a phloroglucinol stain is applied to the sheet. The stain is prepared by dissolving 1 g of phloroglucinol in 50 ml of alcohol and 25 ml of concen-

both images and type are sharper. Various grades are made with matching cover weights. Some of these grades are made with pastel tints.

Cast-coated papers. Cast-coated papers have a mirrorlike gloss and are the glossiest of all coated papers. They are available in book and cover weights, such as gummed papers and folding box boards.

Cover papers. Cover papers have physical and aesthetic functions. A cover paper must have sufficient strength and durability to protect its contents adequately under normal usage while representing its contents in an attractive and appropriate manner.

Postcard-thickness papers often serve as cover papers. For instance, the heaviest coated cover paper, 20×26-in. basic size with a basis weight of 100 lb., is 10 points thick (1 point = 0.001 in.). Postcard stock may be obtained 12 points thick.

There are not many colored coated cover papers. For this reason, designers use colored coated postcard as cover papers.

Novel covers are available with special designs printed overall or with special embossing patterns, such as wood grain and leather. Pearlescence and iridescence are also used to create special effects.

Plastic laminated papers. Some cover papers are plastic-topped. The plastic coating may be dull instead of high in gloss, and it is hardy and durable.

Metallic covers. Metallic covers are made using gold, silver, and bronze. They can be plain or embossed; one-sided or two-sided. Some cover papers are made with a suede flocking as the printing surface.

Printing bristols. There are various types of bristols: printing, index, postal, and coated. Uncoated printing bristols are made from chemical wood pulp in white and in colors. Their finishes are **smooth** or **vellum.** Vellum-finish bristol is widely used for offset lithography because of its higher bulk, pleasing surface, and tendency for fast setting of ink with minimum setoff. Printing bristols are used for cover applications.

Index bristols are made with a smooth finish in white and in colors. Because they are tough, stiff, have good writing and erasing surfaces, and are resistant to repeated handling, index bristols are used for file cards and records, index systems, ruled forms, mailing cards, diecut novelties, and covers.

Postal bristol is made specifically for postcard use, in either white or a cream color. It has a smooth, uniform finish and caliper suitable for pen-and-ink writing and for handling with mail-processing equipment.

Coated bristols are available C1S or C2S and in white or in colors.

Coated-one-side (C1S) litho papers. Because lithographers are large producers of package wraps and labels, C1S litho papers are used in large tonnage. White and colored label papers are available.

Chemical wood bond papers. High on the list of papers processed in litho plants in great tonnage is sulfite bond paper. Sulfite bond looks like wove offset paper. Certain grades, generally numbers 1 and 2, are watermarked. They are high-quality papers, used for business correspondence. The grade commonly called plain bond, or number 4 bond, is not watermarked. It is used principally for one-color forms work, for long-run, direct-mail letters, and for bulletins.

Mimeograph and duplicator papers. A large percentage of mimeograph and duplicator papers is lithographed before being processed through stencil or spirit duplicating machines. Bulletin heads, letterheads, special forms, and special notes are produced in this way. Modern office duplicators are largely offset machines.

Translucent papers. Translucent papers are used as masters for copy to be reproduced on various machines. Translucent papers are often lithographed as letterheads, forms, statements, and reports to be further filled in by pen or typewriter before copies are made.

Safety papers. Safety papers are designed to prevent attempted forgery or document alteration made by mechanical erasure or chemicals. Though most safety paper is used for checks, drafts, and other negotiable documents, the product has many other uses.

Receipts, notes, business forms, licenses, permits, transportation tickets, and other legal forms requiring protection against fraudulent alteration and counterfeiting are commonly produced on safety paper.

Ledger paper and index bristol. Ledger paper is a stronger paper made for accounting and records. Its pen writing and erasure characteristics

Table of Approximate Bulks

	Basis (lb.)	Thickness (in.)
Bond		
(17×22)	9	.002
	13	.0025
	16	.003
	20	.004
Bristol—Plate		
(22½×28½)	100	.008
	120	.010
	140	.012
	160	.014
	180	.017
Bristol—Antique		
(22½×28½)	100	.012
	120	.014
	140	.016
	160	.018
	180	.020
Coated Book		
(25×38)	60	.003
	70	.0035
	80	.004
	100	.0055
	120	.006
Coated Cover		
(20×26)	50	.00475
	60	.006
	65	.0065
	80	.0075
	100	.0095
Cover		
(20×26)	50	.007
	65	.009
	80	.0105
	100	.0135
	130	.018
Eggshell		
(25×38)	50	.0045
	60	.005
	70	.006
	80	.0065
English Finish		
(25×38)	45	.0025
	50	.0035
	60	.004
	70	.0045
Index		
(20½×24¾)	58½	.007
	72	.008
	91	.0105
	111	.0135
	143	.0175
Ledger		
(17×22)	24	.004
	28	.005
	32	.00525
	36	.00575
	40	.0065
	44	.007
Offset		
(25×38)	50	.004
	60	.0045
	70	.005
	80	.006
	100	.0075
	120	.009
Super		
(25×38)	50	.0025
	60	.003
	70	.004
Tag		
(24×36)	80	.006
	100	.0075
	125	.009
	150	.011
	175	.0125
	200	.015
	250	.018
	300	.0225
Text—Smooth		
(25×38)	60	.005
	70	.0065
	80	.007
Vellum		
(17×22)	20	.004
	24	.005
	28	.006
	32	.0065
	36	.0075
	40	.0085

are similar to those of bond paper. Used for business forms, index bristols are characterized by strength and erasability.

Manifold and onionskin. Manifold and onionskin papers are essentially lightweight bond papers. These papers are used for special forms, airmail stationery, lightweight reports, and catalogs.

Cotton-content papers. Principally used for business stationery, cotton-content bond papers are also used for insurance policies, stock certificates and bank notes, certificates, and other documents when longevity is an important factor. Machine-dried cotton-content papers are free from cockle.

Tag. Tag papers are made from long-fiber sulfate pulp, have high strength, and are calendered to a smooth, hard finish. They are available in white, manila, and in various colors. Applications include tags, file folders, job tickets, jackets, heavy-duty envelopes, and covers.

Blanks. Blanks are heavy-weight stocks that range from 15 to 48 pt. (0.38 to 1.22 mm) in thickness. Coated, uncoated, and colored grades are available. Blanks are used for printed signs, point-of-purchase and window displays, posters, streetcar and bus cards, and calendar backs.

Gummed papers and heat-seal papers. Gummed papers are label papers with an adhesive coating on one side. Gummed paper is used in substantial quantities for such applications as merchandise labels, tip-ins for books, merchandise stamps, and direct-mail premiums. Heat-seal papers are coated with adhesive on one side and their sealing properties are activated by the application of heat.

Poster papers. Poster papers are used by the billboard and outdoor advertising trades.

Parchment papers. Once made from animal skins, parchment papers today are manufactured from cellulose fibers. The unsized stock is bathed in sulfuric acid to create a hard-surfaced sheet with a high wet strength and resistance to grease and dirt.

Diploma papers. Diploma papers are used for certificates, warranties, and diplomas. Some brands are 100% cotton content; others are vegetable parchment papers that resemble real parchment papers.

Basis Weights

There are many (500-sheet) ream sizes providing the basis for paper weight specifications; the most common are book, cover, bond, and metric. The basic size for **book** is 25×38 in., designated 25×38. The area of one ream is 3,300 sq. ft. **Cover stock** is 20×26, with an area of 1,800 sq. ft. **Bond** and **ledger papers** are 17×22, with an area of 1,300 sq. ft. **Board** is usually sold by the thousand square feet (1,000 sq. ft.).

Therefore, 1 sq. ft. of a 70-lb. cover, designated 20×26—70, is the same weight as 1 sq. ft. of a 128-lb. book paper, designated 25×38—128. Similarly, 1 sq. ft. of a 16-lb. bond paper weighs the same as 1 sq. ft. of a 40-lb. book paper.

All metric basic weights are expressed in grams per square meter (gsm): tissue, newsprint, book, cover, board, and the others. The 70-lb. cover has a basis weight of 190 gsm, and the 16-lb. bond has a basis weight of 60 gsm.

To convert a basis weight to the equivalent book basis weight, multiply the basis weight by 1.83 for cover stock, by 2.54 for bond, by 3.30 for board, and by 0.674 for metric. To convert a basis weight to its metric equivalent, multiply the basis weight by 1.48 for book, by 2.71 for cover stock, by 3.75 for bond, and by 4.88 for board. For example, to convert a 50-lb. book to its metric equivalent, multiply 50 (basis weight) by 1.48 (conversion factor). The metric equivalent is 74 gsm (50×1.48). To convert a 100-lb. cover stock to its equivalent book basis weight, multiply 100 (basis weight) by 1.83 (conversion factor). A 100-lb. cover has a basis weight equivalent to a book paper with a 183-lb. basis weight (100×1.83).

Paper Sampling Program

Experienced paper buyers have files of grades in widespread use. Quality changes and competitive advantages are carefully watched. Professional buyers recognize trends, sense superiorities, and capitalize on them. This technique of professional buying pays off and is highly recommended to printers. **Paper sampling** is a good way for printers to learn more about professional buying.

Lithographers must keep up with changes in the paper marketplace and learn how to use this information. Printers should indicate to suppliers which printing papers they are interested in buying—coated book, offset, cover, or others. They should ask for a complete review of samples and manufacturing data covering the latest developments, mill

by mill. Also, they should ask for a continuous flow of such information from suppliers.

Knowledge is stored using a sample system, based on standards, that considers all pertinent qualities for all paper grades, characteristic by characteristic, and that catalogs the information in a useful format.

The following sampling method is suggested, combined with the use of checklists and rating charts. Lithographers, however seasoned as paper buyers, should not be expected to be paper technicians and researchers. Their methods of recording changes in paper qualities must be based on personal preferences—whiteness, surface characteristics, and other optical values—until evidence related to runnability or end-usage supplements opinions. Any such practical shop information should be included then.

A genuine desire to keep tabs on quality changes is the only prerequisite for creating a successful and effective paper sampler.

Method of sampling changes in paper qualities. First, all samples of white printing papers on hand should be thrown away. A new file of up-to-date whites should be built. Then, a form of sampling best suited to the company's needs should be selected. This plan can be followed or adapted, depending upon individual needs:

- File whites by classification: coated book, offset, vellum and opaque, cover, text, bristol, and bond.
- Obtain a 9×12-in. three-ring binder. Dividers can be cut from heavyweight cover paper or strong bristol. Index tabs can be cut out by hand. Tabs can be labeled easily and protected by acetate, or standard dividers can be purchased. Fill the various sections—by the paper groups named above—with the single-sheet samples, the largest of which should be 8½×11 in. Then cut swatches of all other papers in the section in decreasing sizes: 8¼×11, 8×11, 7¾×11, 7½×11 in., etc. One can see at a glance the varying whiteness of different brands. It is easy to select whiteness from such a paper file.
- Ask paper suppliers to furnish the samples required. Have them all cut to 8½×11 in. Be sure to insert them in your sample book with the felt side up.
- Ask suppliers to accept the responsibility for keeping the files up-to-date. Quality and appearance changes occur frequently, so constant updating of the samples is necessary. Also, paper changes color with handling, age, and exposure to light.
- Identify and date each paper sample in the binder.
- Make a sample file for all departments involved in the purchase of papers, so that identical papers are being discussed throughout the printing plant.

Choice of standards. The evaluation of paper may be based on a set of standard qualities and characteristics for each grade. Also, choice of standards may be based on personal opinions of special values alone or grades in given price brackets. Or, the choice of standards may be based on laboratory reports provided by paper suppliers.

The two forms "Checklist for Offset Papers" and "Checklist for Cover Papers" can be used as guides to study general changes in paper qualities and to develop proper evaluation procedures.

The checklists stipulate the kind of information to seek when analyzing the usefulness of various offset and cover papers.

Checklist for Offset Papers

(1, 2, and 3 indicate standing in relation to standard that you select as first choice.)

Grade: ____________________

Manufacturer: ____________________

Merchants: ____________________

Ream Weight, 25×38: ____________________

Whiteness:	☐ Cream		☐ Blue
	☐ 1	☐ 2	☐ 3
Brightness:	☐ 1	☐ 2	☐ 3
Finish:			
☐ Smooth	☐ Smooth-Vellum		
☐ Vellum	☐ Antique		
Pigmentized:	☐ Yes	☐ No	
Bulk: Single Sheet ____________			
Opacity:	☐ 1	☐ 2	☐ 3
Dimensional Stability:	☐ 1	☐ 2	☐ 3
Likesidedness:	☐ 1	☐ 2	☐ 3
Foldability:	☐ 1	☐ 2	☐ 3
Stiffness:	☐ 1	☐ 2	☐ 3

Fiber Content:

☐ With Sulfate	☐ Without Sulfate
☐ With Old Papers	☐ Without Old Papers
☐ Groundwood	☐ Other Fibers
☐ With Titanium Dioxide	☐ Without Titanium Dioxide

Checklist for Cover Papers

(1, 2, and 3 indicate standing in relation to standard that you select as first choice.)

Grade: ______________________

Manufacturer: ______________________

Merchants: ______________________

Ream Weight, 20×26: ______________________

Whiteness:	☐ Cream		☐ Blue
	☐ 1	☐ 2	☐ 3
Brightness:	☐ 1	☐ 2	☐ 3

Color: ______________________

Finish:

☐ Smooth Antique	☐ Light Felt Finish
☐ Vellum Antique	☐ Heavy Felt Finish
☐ Rough Antique	☐ Extra Heavy Felt Finish
☐ Extra Rough Antique	☐ Laid Antique

☐ Coated ☐ Duplex ☐ Embossed

Likesidedness:			
☐ Finish:	☐ 1	☐ 2	☐ 3
☐ Color:	☐ 1	☐ 2	☐ 3
Foldability:	☐ 1	☐ 2	☐ 3
Strength:	☐ 1	☐ 2	☐ 3

Caliper Thickness: ______________________

☐ 1	☐ 2	☐ 3

Use of quality checklists. On the checklists, each paper grade is shown with its own quality points and special benefits. As each of the points is recognized for its superiority, that point becomes the standard in judging all other papers. In offset papers, brightness, whiteness, smoothness, opacity, finish, bulk, foldability, and strength are among the major points to be considered.

For example, an offset sheet chosen as a standard is more bulky than other grades tested; consequently, it has a low finish. It has good folding strength, high brightness, and rates "excellent" in likesidedness and opacity.

Smoothness, one important consideration, lends itself neither to high bulk nor strongly to exceptional opacity. Smoothness is associated with superior detail in halftone illustrations, bright colors, sharp blacks, and well-defined middletones in halftones.

Keeping up with paper quality changes. Papermakers are continuously studying the paper marketplace for changes in qualities and characteristics. Working with the sampling and study methods suggested here can pay off in competitive advantages and improved quality production.

Ordering Paper in Sheets

The checklist for ordering paper in flat sheets presents a valuable form for writing specifications. If it is followed exactly, paper suppliers—merchant and manufacturer—are provided with all the information they need to deliver satisfactory paper at a competitive price to the assigned destination at the proper time.

In the itemized list of specifications that follows, the importance of clear inquiry and order writing is emphasized.

Quantity. Specify the number of sheets followed by their total weight. For example, 100,000 sheets of 50-lb. stock, 25×38 in., is written as 25×38—50 (100M) = 10,000 lb.

Size and ream weight. Specify dimensions and weight per 1,000 sheets. To prevent misunderstanding, show ream weight in parentheses. For example: 44×64—356M (25×38—60). **M** in the size-and-weight designation means **per 1,000 sheets.**

Grade and color. Specify the grade by its brand, proprietary, or agreed-upon name, not by number or letter. Identify color in correct mill terminology. Do not write "white" when you know the paper you are ordering is made in a cream-white and in a blue-white. When in doubt, submit a sample of the color or shade you want.

Finish. Identify finish by names such as antique, vellum, wove, or laid.

If the paper is embossed, identify it by its pattern, number, or name. For deckle-edge or laid-finish papers, indicate their grain and the direction of the deckled edge or laid lines.

Intended finishing. When paper is to be varnished, lacquered, laminated, embossed, or finished in any other manner after printing, be sure to designate the finish clearly.

Many standard papers are not suited to varnishing or lacquering, but when specially treated, they are perfectly satisfactory. Give your exact requirements. Failure to mention additional paper properties necessary for effective production will create problems.

Checklist for Ordering Paper in Flat Sheets

Grade ______________________________

Quantity ______________ (sheets) ______________ (pounds)

Size & Weight ______________ M ______________ basis weight

Color ______________ Finish ______________ Design ______________

Caliper Thickness ________ one sheet ________ four sheets ________ pages to inch

☐ Watermarked ☐ Unwatermarked

Grain Direction ☐ long ☐ short ☐ optional (one dimension)

Design or Pattern Number ☐ long ☐ short ☐ optional (one dimension)

Trimming ☐ machine ☐ trimmed two sides
To one size ☐ trimmed two ends ☐ trimmed four sides
Press sheet ☐ sheetwise ☐ work and turn ☐ work and tumble

Reproduction Method (indicate which one)

☐ Letterpress ☐ one color ☐ two colors ☐ three colors ☐ four colors
☐ wet ☐ dry

☐ Lithography ☐ one color ☐ two colors ☐ three colors ☐ four colors
☐ wet ☐ dry

☐ Gravure ☐ High-gloss inks ☐ Metallic inks

☐ Finishing ☐ Varnishing ☐ Lacquering ☐ Embossing

Plant Humidity Requirements ______________________________

Intended Purpose of Paper ______________________________

Packing
☐ Reams marked in cartons ☐ Reams marked in bundles
☐ Reams sealed in cartons ☐ Reams marked on single-tier skids
☐ Reams marked on double-tier skids ☐ Reams marked on four-tier skids
☐ Felt side UP ☐ Felt side DOWN ☐ Cast side UP ☐ Cast side DOWN

Skid Specifications ☐ four-way entry ☐ two-way entry
Runners ☐ short way ☐ long way

Minimum distance between runners ______________________ inches
Maximum height ______________________ inches
Maximum weight ______________________ pounds

Note: Mark Skid Number and Order Number on Runners

Shipping
☐ siding on ______________________ RR
☐ plant can accommodate trailers up to ______________ feet long
☐ sidewalk delivery by winch truck

Most satisfactory delivery hours ______ AM to ______ AM ______ PM to ______ PM

Receiving platform closed ____________ to ____________

Special Markings on Skid Wrappers ______________________________

Special Instructions Not Identified Above ______________________________

☐ Sample for Matching Enclosed

Indicate the use of special inks. If paper is to be printed with metallic inks, high-gloss inks, heatset inks, or other special kinds of inks, be sure the paper manufacturer knows the facts. Be sure to identify the ink by maker and the number.

Grain direction. Specify grain direction—**grain-long** or **grain-short.** For example, 25×38-in. grain-long, or grain 38-in. way. When grain direction is not important, specify **grain-optional.**

Trimming. Many papers, like those for offset printing, are trimmed on four sides. Although many grades of paper are standard trimmed four-sides, do not take it for granted.

When you know that paper trimmed on one side and one end is perfectly satisfactory for the production purposes, say so. Also instruct the mill to mark the squared corner. When you need text paper with a plain edge, be sure to specify this.

Packaging. Identify packaging requirements: standard size in cartons, or junior size (10 reams of cut sizes 8½×11 in. or 8½×14 in.) in cases, or skids. Be sure to specify whether the paper is to be sealed in packages or unsealed and marked in reams or some fraction thereof.

Skid specifications consist of weight and height limitations; the number of sheets per skid; the height, direction, and distance between runners; and leg construction, location, and spacings for proper use by the printer's handling equipment.

Weight and height limitations of the shipment should be emphasized. Some printing and lithographic operations are located in loft buildings, and problems with weight and height could arise. If a skid load weighs less than the standard 3,000-lb. weight, it should be identified as such.

Elevator capacity and width of elevator or plant doors may make it necessary to pack paper on single-tier skids. Also, be sure to indicate when skids must be double-tiered.

Make the point clear if skids should be double-wrapped to maintain their moisture content. When the relative humidity of your pressroom is known, specify R.H. maximum and minimum for the time of year.

Special requirements. When special manufacturing requirements are important, itemize them property by property, characteristic by characteristic. If strength is the factor, emphasize this by listing a measured reading value for the folding strength, the tearing strength, or the Mullen strength. Be sure to include properties such as opacity, caliper, and bulking thickness.

The chance of a mistake being made is lessened when complete specifications are given.

Bulk determination scale. To determine a paper's bulk, fold a sheet of paper twice, thus making four thicknesses, or eight pages. Use a micrometer or calipers to read the thickness of four sheets in thousandths of an inch (points). In the column headed "Pages per Inch (ppi)," you will find the number of pages per inch corresponding to the micrometer reading.

For example, what is the ppi for a book in which four thicknesses measure 0.020 in. (20 points)? The answer is in the column headed "Pages per Inch" opposite 0.020—400 pages.

Bulk Determination Scale

Micrometer Reading	Pages per Inch	Micrometer Reading	Pages per Inch
.007	1142	.025	320
.0075	1066	.0255	314
.008	1000	.026	308
.0085	942	.0265	302
.009	888	.027	296
.0095	842	.0275	290
.010	800	.028	286
.0105	762	.0285	280
.011	726	.029	276
.0115	696	.0295	272
.012	666	.030	266
.0125	640	.0305	262
.013	614	.031	258
.0135	592	.0315	254
.014	570	.032	250
.0145	552	.0325	246
.015	532	.033	242
.0155	516	.0335	238
.016	500	.034	234
.0165	484	.0345	232
.017	470	.035	228
.0175	456	.0355	224
.018	444	.036	222
.0185	432	.0365	218
.019	420	.037	216
.0195	410	.0375	212
.020	400	.038	210
.0205	390	.0385	208
.021	380	.039	204
.0215	372	.0395	202
.022	364	.040	200
.0225	356	.0405	198
.023	348	.041	194
.0235	340	.0415	192
.024	332	.042	190
.0245	326	.0425	188

Bulk determination formula. To determine the bulk of a given number of pages: caliper eight pages, multiply the amount of points by the given number of pages, and then divide by eight. For example, suppose eight pages caliper 0.020 in. What will 320 pages bulk? The answer is:

$$= \frac{320 \times 0.020}{8}$$

$$= \frac{6.400}{8}$$

= 0.800 in. or slightly more than ¾ in.

To determine the ppi, caliper the eight pages, and then divide that number into 8. For example, suppose eight pages caliper 0.016 in. What is the ppi? The answer is:

$$\frac{8}{0.016} = 500 \text{ pages per inch}$$

Bulking number. Bulking number, as described in TAPPI Standard T 500, is measured in a procedure that simulates the compression applied to a book during its "smashing" and "casing in." It is the number of sheets that will bulk 1 in. (25.4 mm) after being placed in a bulk tester and having 36 lb./in.^{2} pressure applied for 30 sec. Bulking number is multiplied by two to determine ppi, since each sheet in a book represents two pages.

Bulking index. Bulking index is used to compare the bulk of different papers having the same basic size and papers having different basis weights. It is also used to calculate the bulk for other basis weights from an established thickness-to-basis-weight ratio of a given paper.

Bulking index is thickness per pound of basis weight and is calculated by dividing a paper's single-sheet thickness by its basis weight.

Ordering Paper in Rolls

There are no simple rules for ordering paper in rolls. This is because there are no established standards for paper in rolls; every order for paper in rolls is tailor-made; and operators of web presses must have the paper designed to make the most profitable use of their machinery's facilities, width cut-off, and accessories.

A manufacturer of web offset presses, talking about paper requirements for them, said, "Paper must be fitted to the job. Selection of paper should be determined by speed of the press, by the number of after-printing operations that paper must endure, kinds of ink, number of colors to be applied one over the other, area of coverage, whether printing one or two sides of the sheet, and quality of results desired."

Another manufacturer said: "Rolls that might be entirely satisfactory for letterpress printing will not get by on precision lithographic presses. Be sure the paper manufacturer knows what process of reproduction will be used and on what particular press the paper will be run. While all rolls should be wound and trimmed accurately, it is especially important that rolls for high-speed offset presses be handled with extra care and precision."

The "job-determines-the-paper" theory, therefore, is important when ordering paper in rolls. It is not unusual for roll paper to pass through several operations after printing. For instance, in addition to being printed with up to four colors, paper is punched for all sorts of business systems, numbered, perforated (lengthwise and crosswise), rewound, slit, and folded. That kind of single-flow processing represents a severe test of paper properties. In addition to having tensile, tear, surface, and bursting strength, paper for web offset must have a high degree of folding strength and resistance to blistering, delamination, and water.

Specifying Paper in Rolls

When ordering roll stock, use the checklist for ordering paper in rolls and remember the following points:

- Order rolls made to maximum diameter in order to minimize roll changes. The fewer roll changes in a run mean fewer press adjustments and a more profitable operation.
- A **splice** is an overlapping joint in the web that joins its ends together. For heatset printing, heat-resistant splicing should be requested. Splices may be made straight across or diagonally across the web. Diagonal splices distribute their thickness over a greater area in a folded signature, thus, they have less tendency to catch on some part of the press. Limit the number of splices per roll. A greater number of splices results in a greater number of press adjustments. These cause lost press time and increase paper waste. More important, there is a possibility of running into splices that are not flagged, or marked, and suffering the consequences—smashed blankets, smashed plates, and even damaged presses.

Checklist for Ordering Paper Rolls

Grade ______________________

Quantity ______________________ pounds

Maximum basis weight ______________ pounds

Maximum thickness ______ pages-to-inch ______

Maximum roll width ______________ inches

Core inside diameter ______________ inches

Type of core ______________________

Type of press ______________________

Speed of press ______________________

Maximum ink drying temperature __________

Type of delivery ______________________

Maximum roll diameter ________________

- ☐ returnable
- ☐ nonreturnable
- ☐ slotted
- ☐ nonslotted
- ☐ slots in juxtaposition
- ☐ dimensions of keyway ______ × ______

Roll winding ☐ felt side OUT ☐ felt side IN

Note: Mark Directional Arrows on Wrappers

Splicing Maximum acceptable to roll ______________________

flag

- ☐ one side
- ☐ two sides
- ☐ diagonally across roll
- ☐ use splicing material for heatset reproduction

Wrapping ☐ moisture proof ☐ nonmoisture proof

Delivery ☐ on side ☐ on end

Plant Humidity Requirements ______________________________

Special Instructions

- ☐ Rolls must be wound uniformly firm
- ☐ Indicate weight of each roll on wrapper
- ☐ Surface of paper must be free from lint and other extraneous materials
- ☐ Indicate roll number and winding direction on ends of rolls
- ☐ Provide roll cards in core of each roll
- ☐ Provide packing slips complete with roll number, weight per roll, and number of splices per roll
- ☐ Number each roll on wrapper

Shipping

- ☐ siding on ______________________________ RR
- ☐ plant can accommodate trailers up to ______________ feet long
- ☐ sidewalk delivery by winch truck

Most satisfactory delivery hours ______ AM to ______ AM ______ PM to ______ PM

Receiving platform closed ____________ to ____________

Special Markings on Roll Wrappers ______________________________

____

Special Instructions Not Identified Above ______________________________

☐ Sample for Matching Enclosed

Note: Be sure to send out-turned samples in advance of shipment.

• A manufacturing basis weight tolerance generally applies to rolls as it does to sheets. Specify the maximum basis weight required. Web papers are sold by yardage, not pounds. When ordering 17×22—20 bond paper without stipulating "not heavier than," buyers may receive 21-, 22-, or even 23-lb., paper, and consequently, decreasing yardage.
• Allow for at least 5 to 7% spoilage when estimating. The weight of the roll always includes the outside wrapper and the core. Also, in unwrapping the roll, some of the paper is invariably damaged to some degree. In transit, rolls are sometimes dropped or nicked. Almost always—depending on the weight of the paper—the 10 to 50 lb. of paper nearest the core is curled beyond use.
• Specify "free from slitter dust." Slitter dust creates spots in the prints when the job is being run. Dust piles up on blankets of offset presses and contaminates the inking systems, resulting in spoilage and lost time for washups. Most mills wind satisfactory rolls. They have overcome the slitter dust trouble by installing special vacuum cleaning units on papermaking and slitting machines.
• Stipulate **tightly wound rolls.** Soft, unevenly wound rolls are useless and likely to telescope in transit. When rolls are slightly uneven—high on one side—the paper can be run, but only carefully and slowly.
• Provide the proper information regarding the cores. There are no standard-size cores, as weights of paper and board dictate their diameter and style. Three-inch cores are in most general use. Consider whether ends with or without slots are wanted, and what the dimensions of the slotted ends should be.
• Stipulate **rewound** when rolls have narrow widths. Narrow-gauge equipment is high-precision equipment, so slitting must be exact, and winding must be firm and uniform.
• Estimate carefully. Do not take anything for granted. Allowances, or differentials between standard-packed sheets and rolls, are not standard with all paper manufacturers. Until buyers establish an expert working knowledge of mill practices, a printer is wise to investigate each purchase. For instance, some mills deduct different amounts from prices for paper packed in cartons to arrive at cost of roll merchandise. Some mills don't charge at all for winding rolls larger than 11 in. Other mills charge an additional sum for rolls between 12 and 17 in. wide. Still another charge may be added for rolls narrower than 11 in. Weight per roll also determines pricing. Some mills charge more for 250-lb. rolls than for 500-lb. rolls. It is, therefore, best to check when ordering. Nothing should be taken for granted.
• Specify **wire-side out** or **felt-side out** if there is a preference. A stronger fold generally results when the wire side is at the outside of a fold.
• Specify **directional arrows to appear on wrappers.** This detail is important to minimize roll-handling time.
• Give handling, delivery, and shipping instructions for shippers. Stipulate **load on side** or **load on end.** Delivery date required and the days and hours when the paper can be received should be included.
• Specify for what type of printing and on what type of press the paper is going to be used. This instruction may seem to be unnecessary. But nothing should be taken for granted. Also, paper manufacturers like to know on what presses their rolls are being printed.
• Tell the paper mill personnel to number all rolls and show roll weights on the wrappers, since no two rolls weigh the same. As the shipment is received, take inventory of the paper, and select rolls for running on the press.
• Ask for shipping papers that include roll numbers and weights. Shipping, stock, and accounting departments need this information.
• On the side of each roll, near the core, mark lot number, roll number, roll weight, and manufacturer's code.

Important points to remember. Paper buyers are billed for the gross weight of the roll, including paper, wrapping, and nonreturnable core. When a roll has a returnable core, there is no charge for the core. When estimating, be sure to allow for spoilage.

Determining weight of paper in rolls. An example showing the approved method for determining the approximate weight of paper in rolls is as follows: To determine the weight of a roll of *bond paper* that is 30 in. in diameter and 12 in. wide, (1) square the diameter: $30 \times 30 = 900$; (2) multiply by the width: $900 \times 12 = 10{,}800$; and (3) multiply by the factor 0.027: $10{,}800 \times 0.027 = 291.6$ lb.

To determine the approximate weight of a roll of a particular paper, use the following factors specified for each: antique finish, 0.018; machine finish, English finish, offset, bond, ledger, writing, manifold, and onionskin, 0.027; super, 0.030; coated two sides, 0.034; coated one side, 0.030; newsprint, 0.0162. These factors, an average among paper manufacturers apply for all weights.

For any given roll diameter, lighter-weight papers will bulk less; therefore, more paper will be wound on a roll.

Determining approximate linear yardage in paper rolls. An example showing the approved method for determining approximate linear yardage in a roll of paper is as follows: (1) multiply the weight of the roll by 12,000: 100 lb. × 12,000 = 1,200,000; (2) multiply roll width by basis weight: 24 in. × 50 lb. = 1,200; and (3) divide the product obtained in step 1 by the product obtained in step 2: 1,200,000 ÷ 1,200 = 1,000 yards.

Determining the number of reams in a roll of paper. The approved method for determining the number of reams in a roll of paper is to divide the approximate weight of the roll by the weight of the ream. The result is approximate because the weight of the core and plugs is not considered.

Paper spoilage allowances. In both letterpress and offset, presswork and binding spoilage is based on sheets of stock required for the job, not impressions for the job.

A work-and-turn job of 5,000 sheets printed in one color is calculated as 2,500 sheets. This is the quantity required for a work-and-turn form, which will allow two out of a sheet.

Care should be taken to make certain the correct figure is used when determining the number of sheets. For instance, 5,000 press sheets of 25×38 in. would take the 5,000 figure for presswork. This number would be 10,000 when folding is figured, or if the sheet has to be cut in half (to 19×25 in.) before the binding operation.

Based upon the experience of each plant, the paper spoilage allowances given in the following table should be modified where troublesome stocks are used. The allowances do not include waste sheets to run up color.

Paper Spoilage Allowances

	1,000	2,500	5,000	10,000	25,000 and over
Single-Color Equipment					
One color, one side	8%*	6%	5%	4%	3%
One color, work-and-turn or work-and-tumble	13	10	8	6	5
Each additional color (per side)	5	4	3	2	2
Two-Color Equipment					
Two colors, one side	—	—	5	4	3
Two colors, two sides or work-and-turn	—	—	8	6	5
Each additional two colors (per side)	—	—	3	2	2
Four-Color Equipment					
Four colors, one side only	—	—	—	6	5
Four colors, two sides or work-and-turn	—	—	—	8	7
Bindery Spoilage					
Folding, stitching, trimming	4	3	3	2	2
Cutting, punching or drilling	2	2	2	2	2
Varnishing and gumming	7	5	4	3	3

***Percentage represents press-size sheets, not impressions.**
The above figures do not include waste sheet used to run up color, as it is assumed that waste stock is used for this purpose.

Use the next higher percentage for the following papers:

1. Coated papers when the plant does not usually run coated papers.
2. Papers that caliper 0.0025 in. or less.
3. Difficult papers, such as foil, cloth, plastic, etc.

Chapter 15
Presswork

Introduction to Presswork

In all the graphic arts, with only a few exceptions, the equipment that produces the printed substrate is the focal point of a particular process. This is true even though the printed or lithographed material is often processed and the appearance of the lithographed substrate may be completely changed in order to attain its final form. All preparatory steps are designed to take full advantage of the lithographic process; however, they are governed by the capacity of the pressroom equipment. Press selection may depend upon the demands of the finishing processes, and the press should produce maximum output at the lowest possible cost.

This chapter analyzes the lithographic offset press. It stresses the capabilities and characteristics of the lithographic offset press and how it functions as a part of the closely integrated lithographic process; furthermore, specific press designs are explained. Essential press components—cylinders, inks, dampeners, feeders (sheet and roll), deliveries—are also covered, as are the more common auxiliary devices. There is, furthermore, coverage of the many control methods used throughout the printing operation. This description identifies factors to consider when planning the purchase of a lithographic offset press and explains the production of printed material.

Duplicator offset presses are widely used and capable of printing excellent single-color jobs; however, they are limited in ink-covering power, impression rigidity, and pinpoint register compared to production equipment.

Sheetfed and web press inking and dampening techniques are similar; the offset method is also the same. Feeding and delivery are quite different, except that some sheetfed presses feed paper from a roll, which is cut into sheets prior to feeding. There is a great deal in common between sheetfed and web printing so far as the offset printing method is concerned. The cylinders on a blanket-to-blanket web press function differently than the hard impression cylinders of sheetfed presses. However, many forms printing presses use hard impression cylinders.

The term **offset** describes the process of using an intermediate blanket cylinder to transfer the image from the plate to the substrate. The offset method is used in lithography as well as relief and intaglio printing. Since the offset method is the most commonly used in lithography, this chapter primarily reviews presses that print by the offset method.

Presswork is customarily categorized under three separate headings: makeready, operation, and maintenance. From a management viewpoint, this breakdown is essential in order to accurately allocate costs and determine selling price. However, it is impossible to draw a sharp line of demarcation between these three phases of presswork. Checking and setting cylinder pressures could be categorized as maintenance or makeready. A job that is already running may not print as it should, and the pressure between plate cylinder and blanket cylinder is not quite right; checking and adjusting cylinder pressure could be considered part of makeready or operation. All aspects of achieving good quality and high production on a lithographic offset press must be considered in every single step of presswork.

The material in this section covers specific points concerning generally accepted principles; however, the details of operating a particular press can be found in the manufacturer's manual.

Printing perfection is the ultimate goal; it does not take any longer to print the job right the first time. In the long run, it also costs less.

Lithographic Presses

Lithographic offset presses are typically described in terms of size, number of colors (units), sheet or roll feed, and whether they perfect (simultaneously print both sides of the substrate).

Size refers to either the maximum size sheet that can pass through the press, or the largest optimum size. Largest optimum size is seldom more than ½ in. (12 mm) smaller than the absolute maximum size, and almost always in the longer dimension. This dimension parallels the axis of the cylinders and is sometimes described as the **across-the-cylinder direction.**

Web press sizes are determined in much the same way as sheetfed press sizes. However, while sheetfed press sizes are given as the maximum size sheet that can be fed through the press, all of these presses can handle sheets that are smaller in both directions. For example, a 17½×22½-in. (445×572-mm) sheetfed press can handle a sheet as small as 8½ in. (216 mm) in the around-the-cylinder direction and 11 in. (279 mm) in the across-the-cylinder dimension. Most web presses are quite different; the around-the-cylinder direction, referred to as the cutoff, is fixed. The across-the-cylinder direction is usually given as the maximum width roll that can be handled. For example, a 22⁹⁄₁₆×38-in. (567×965-mm) press will deliver a sheet (or signature) exactly 22⁹⁄₁₆-in. in the around-the-cylinder direction, with the 38-in. dimension flexible up to a maximum of 38 in. In most cases, the shorter dimension is the cutoff length.

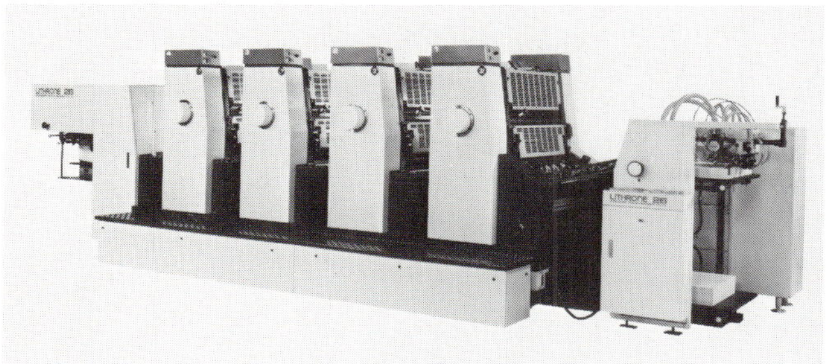

Courtesy Komori Printing Machinery Co., Ltd.

Four-color sheetfed press.

Number of colors refers to the number of printing units, if it is a sheetfed press. (The term **unit,** as synonymous with color, is not technically correct in many cases.) Each printing unit will be run with a different color, and the number of colors describes how many separate colors can be printed on the sheet with one pass through the press. However, a split ink fountain on one or more of the units results in more colors being laid down during one pass through the press.

As the lithographic process grew, multicolor presses developed primarily by the assembly of single-color units in tandem with transfer devices between units. This open-unit design was originally available only in larger press sizes, but this design is now used in multicolor presses as small as 26 in.

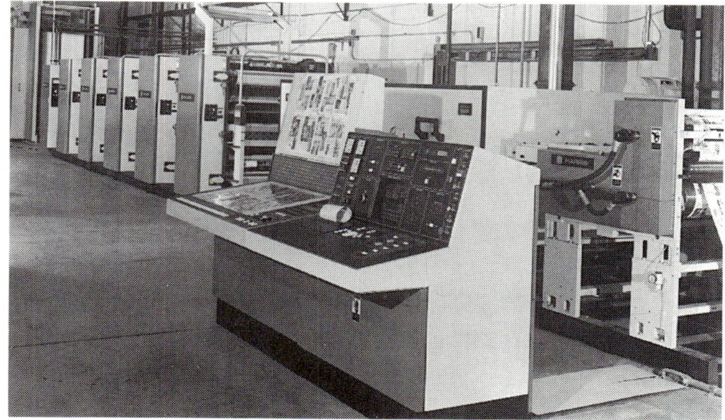

Courtesy Heidelberg Harris, Inc.

Five-unit web press.

Some two-color presses incorporate a common-impression cylinder. Others use a transfer cylinder between each of the two printing sections; two such integrally built units are set up in tandem with a transfer device between them to become a four-color press. Three such units become a six-color press. The number of colors on most presses ranges from a single color to six colors.

Feeding describes how paper enters the press and in what form. A press handles either sheets or rolls of paper. This criterion designates whether the press moves cut sheets through the feeder or is fed by threading a web of paper through the press. Hence, web press is the common term for a press that prints on paper fed directly from a roll. Sheetfed presses that use a roll sheeter in place of or to supplement a sheet feeder are best described as roll-to-sheet feeders.

Perfecting is the process by which a press prints on both sides of the paper in one pass through the press. Perfecting presses may be sheetfed or web, single-color or multicolor. Most web presses are perfecting multicolor presses of the blanket-to-blanket design. However, if equipped with the neces-

sary roll stands, these presses can be used for single-color perfecting. For example, a four-unit blanket-to-blanket press can run four colors on both sides of a single web. (Split-fountain running is not considered here.) The same press can print one color on both sides of four separate webs if the press is equipped with four roll stands. Between these two extremes, a variety of combinations is possible on the same press.

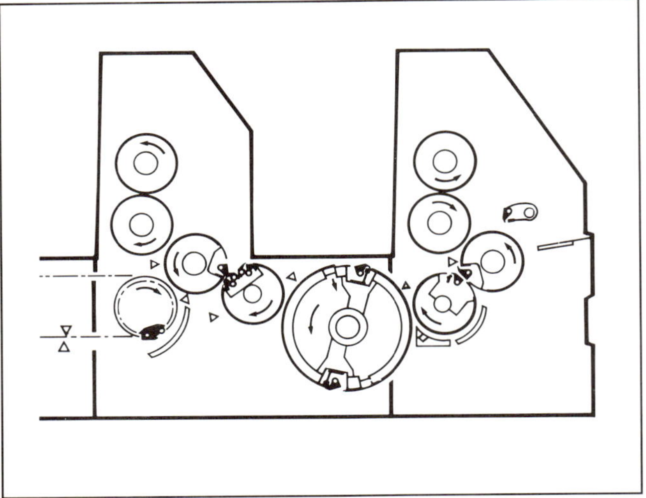

Perfecting press.

Most sheetfed perfecting presses are one-color presses. Various combinations, however, are available. For instance, it is possible to use the same press as a two-color press or as a one-color perfecting press. Single-color perfecting units may be combined to perfect multicolor during one pass.

The terms used to describe a press are generally known and yet somewhat arbitrarily employed here. There are several reasons for this. First, more and more presses are designed and built to print a special job or employ a special process. Secondly, presses may be described with respect to special auxiliary features in addition to the preceding four criteria. Furthermore, there are countless variations and combinations possible within the basic criteria. For example, a sheetfed press could print six colors in one pass, or it could be a six-color perfecting press that prints four colors on one side of the substrate and two on the reverse side during one pass. A five-unit press running from a half-width roll with a double-ender principle can print five colors on one side and five on the reverse side using split fountains on all five units. An eight-color web press usually consists of two four-color presses printing four colors on both sides of two webs and running both webs into a common folder.

Auxiliary equipment on web presses includes perforators, slitters, numbering heads, punches, rewinders, sheeters, and folders. A cutter and creaser may also be included. These attachments help produce such items as multiple forms, interleaved sets, spot-carboned leaves, cellophane-windowed pieces, insertions, and cartons.

Auxiliary equipment on sheetfed presses is somewhat limited. Units are added to lithographic offset presses and perform auxiliary operations such as bronzing, perforating, slitting, and folding.

Sheet Feeding

The lithographic offset press can be either sheetfed or rollfed. Roll feeders are most often used on web offset presses. This section is exclusively concerned with sheet feeding. The presentation is divided into two main parts: feeders and feeder setting.

Sheet Feeders

Sheet feeding is accomplished either as successive-sheet feeding or stream feeding. Either of these two methods can be combined with pile feeding or roll feeding. Therefore, the presentation is further divided into successive-sheet feeding; stream feeding; pile feeding; and roll feeding.

Successive-sheet feeders separate the top sheet from the paper supply and advance it to the feedboard, table, tapes, or ramp. The following sheet is not separated from the pile or main supply until the tail end of the preceding sheet has cleared the advancing mechanism. There is, therefore, a distinct space and time interval between sheets. Successive-sheet feeders advance the sheet by its gripper edge. The sheet must travel forward at approximately the same speed as the press operates, since one full sheet advances at a time to the registering and/or insertion device.

The sheet moves very rapidly. Special attention must be paid—especially on lightweight, large

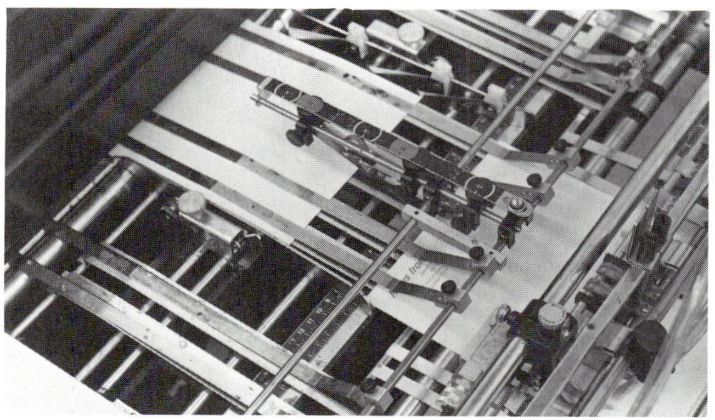

Successive-sheet feeder.

sheets—to holding the sheet down during forwarding and to keeping it moving at press speed without dragging or cocking. Successive-sheet feeders employ slow-down or preregister devices just ahead of the registration or insertion point. These devices prevent the sheet from buckling or bouncing as a result of its momentum.

Stream feeders provide a continuous flow of sheets, which are separated from the supply and advanced to the forwarding mechanism. In stream feeding, however, the separation *and* original advancing of the sheet take place at the back end of the paper. As soon as one sheet is advanced onto the forwarding devices, the following sheet is separated and also advanced. Thus, several sheets are moving forward all the time. The sheets overlap, and the forwarding speed reduces proportionately in comparison with the forwarding speed on successive-sheet feeders.

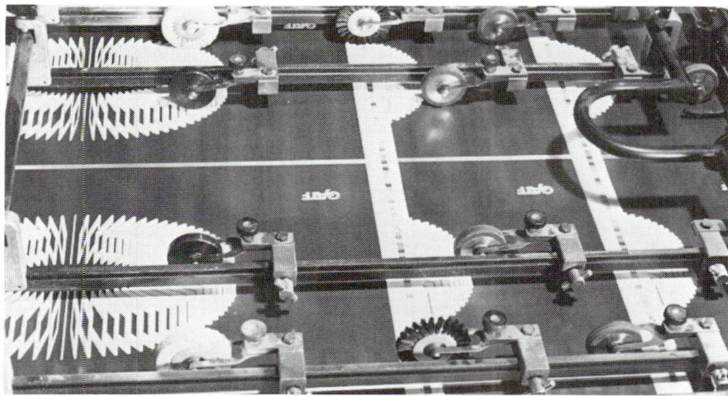

Stream feeder. Note the overlapping sheets.

Because of this overlapping, as one sheet is drawn into the nip by the impression cylinder grippers, the following sheet has only several inches of travel to reach the registering device. This slow travel to the registering position on stream feeders simplifies some of the sheet control problems prevalent on a successive-sheet feeder. Another important advantage of stream feeders is that preceding sheets tend to control the following ones as a result of their large overlap.

The guide edges of each sheet are controlled by the preceding sheet almost to the point of register. This control, coupled with slow feeding, almost completely eliminates bouncing and buckling at the register point.

Pile feeders carry the paper on a platform in the press feeder. This pile must be straight, neat, and positioned in correspondence with the register settings and insertion devices. The pile feeder raises the paper automatically to a constant level during printing.

The main disadvantage of the pile feeder is that the press must be stopped or idled during long runs for reloading. Loading a succeeding pile in the press before one pile is exhausted reduces downtime.

Continuous feeders provide a nonstop supply of paper. During this operation, a fresh load of paper is placed into elevating position on the pile feeder, while the preceding load still has some time to run. Supplementary elevator rods temporarily support the original load. The pile elevator bars lower to the fresh load and elevate it to the bottom of the preceding load. The rods are withdrawn; there is now a single pile in the feeder. If care is used in this series of operations, the pressrun is not interrupted.

Continuous feeding increases productivity. Spoilage is reduced, and consistent quality is maintained. A steadily running press maintains consistent color and eliminates off-color sheets that are produced when a press is restarted.

Roll-to-sheet feeders employ a roll of paper that is placed into running position in a sheeter. There, the web is converted into individual sheets, and the cut sheets are fed directly into the press. Some sheeters can be attached to the press as an auxiliary device to the standard pile feeder. This

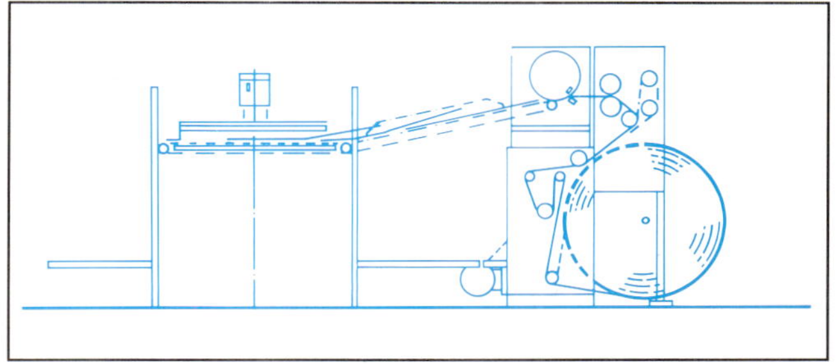

Roll-to-sheet feeder.

sheeter design allows feeding from rolls or cut stock. The press, then, retains the flexibility of running the full range of paper sizes and weights. The sheeter is used for a few standard sizes and weights, thus minimizing the roll storage problem. One of the advantages of web presses is the fact that paper bought in rolls costs significantly less than sheeted paper. In addition to the savings in paper costs, there accrues the advantage of nearly continuous operation, which can only be realized where continuous feeding is used.

Sheeters are designed for side or tandem installation. A side-mounted sheeter allows grain-long running; that is, the grain of the cut sheet parallels the axis of the press cylinders. Running grain long is desirable when register is critical, or when the sheet will pass through a press more than once.

Tandem-mounted sheeters cut paper for grain-short running. The grain aligns perpendicularly with the press cylinders. Running grain-short paper provides advantages in book work, especially where large-format books are run on large presses. Often, the imposition for such books requires running grain short. Perfecting presses eliminate problems caused by running a grain-short sheet through the press more than once.

Setting the Feeder

Loading is accomplished in several ways. On smaller presses, the paper is directly loaded into the feeder. On larger pile feeders, paper is loaded on a platform or skid, away from the press. The skid is wheeled into the feeder. The side-guide edge of the sheet is positioned so that it reaches the front guides or insertion devices within the operating area of the side guide. For example, on a press equipped with a rotary (roller) guide, the edge of the sheet must enter between the lower and upper roller so that the upper roller—when it comes down—can pinch the sheet and pull it against the face of the side guide.

Some feeder boards have matching scales near the side guide and across the front. Others have simply a scribed centerline. The paper pile must be perfectly straight and even, and sheets should not overhang at the gripper edge. Do not use paper with mutilated edges. The stock must be carefully and thoroughly winded, especially if the paper has gone through the press before. The skid or platform is now positioned in the feeder and the chains and supporting bars fastened to it.

The pile is raised to just below the normal operating height. If the feeder is equipped with pile guides on both sides of the pile, the one away from the guide side is set against the pile. Next, the devices supplied for holding the back edge of the pile in place are set. Then, the separator and sheet advancing devices are set to the operating position. On smaller presses with combined separating and advancing devices, there may be little or no setting required unless changing from a minimum size sheet to a maximum size. On other presses, one unit contains the separating device and back-edge pile controls.

Pile-height governors and two-sheet detectors control the pile prior to feeding. The pile-height governor controls the height of the paper stack. The press is idled until the pile reaches its operating height. On all feeders, this feature is automatic. Set this device in accordance with the manufacturers' instructions. The two-sheet detector, sometimes called the choke, is set (on successive-sheet feeders) by inching the press to the tripping position as indicated in the manufacturer's instruction book. A 2-in.-wide (51-mm-wide) strip of the running stock is torn to a length of 6 in. (152 mm). This strip is folded so that a single thickness protrudes 1 in. (25 mm) beyond the double thickness. The single thickness is inserted into the choke, which is then adjusted so that the single thickness of stock just slides freely under the choke but the double thickness jams, tripping the detector.

On stream feeders, several sheets are under the choke at the same time. In this case, the device is set exactly as described but with the normal number of overlapping sheets under the test strip in the choke.

Automatic feeders separate the top sheet from the pile and forward it to the guides and/or insertion device. In order for the separator devices to function properly, the pile must be at the proper height in the feeder, and the contour of the top of the pile must be reasonably flat. This is especially important on presses with the capacity to handle large sheets.

Separation and forwarding is accomplished entirely by air. Air-blast nozzles fluff the rear edge of several sheets on the top of the pile. Suckers drop down and pick up the top sheet. Another set of air-blast nozzles comes under this top sheet and floats it on a cushion of air. Then, the same suckers, or a set of separate forwarding suckers, guide the sheet into the forwarding devices at the top of the feed ramp.

The amount of air and the direction of the blower tubes or feet needs to be controlled. The sheet should float without riffling, waving, or flapping. It

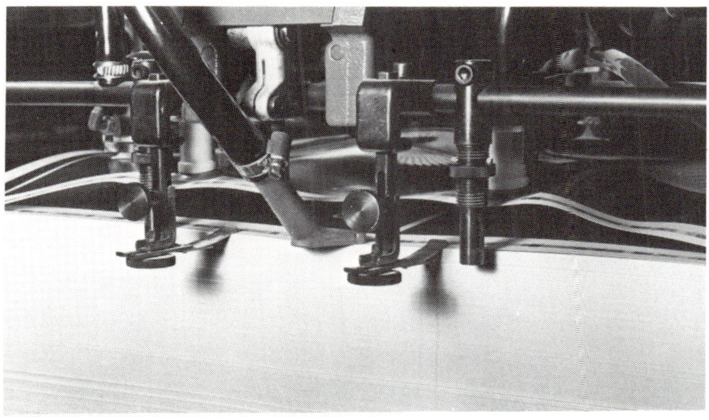

Suckers separate top sheet from pile.

must completely separate from the pile so as not to drag the next sheet, or stumble on its leading edge, especially in feeders without a blower foot. The sheet should reach the forwarding devices at the right time and in a straight position.

After the first sheet separates and advances to the forwarding wheels, inch the press and check all parts of the forwarding system for proper operation. The operator should note if the sheet comes down straight and balances on the tapes. It should be held down without dragging. The sheet is inched until its leading edge is in the side guide. It should clear the side guide but not by so much as to miss being guided. Controls allow the operator to adjust the pile slightly in either direction to correct any error in the original side pile guide setting. On smaller presses, the stock can be pushed to the proper position without seriously upsetting the pile.

The sheet is advanced by continual inching, and the operator ensures that it arrives at the guides or stops of the insertion device before the side guide starts its operating cycle.

Register and Fit

Register is the positioning of the sheet relative to the image on the blanket. During registration, the press aligns the sheet, the impression-cylinder grippers take hold and draw the sheet through the printing nip, and the front edge of the paper aligns at a set distance from the image. This distance is determined when the plate is clamped into proper position and the front guides set. One side edge also aligns at a fixed distance from the image edge. This distance is also determined when the plate is mounted and the side guide set. Every sheet must align *exactly*. With the sheets under control, and the registering devices properly set and operating, register is accomplished.

Fit describes the juxtaposition of all image elements in the printing area without regard to the sheet margin (determined and maintained as a result of registering the plate and sheet). For example, a job has front- and side-guide margins that measure exactly 1 in. (25 mm). During the run, the sheets are checked, and each one has *exactly* these margins. Therefore, the job is registering. However, further checking indicates that the image on the plate measures 40 in. across the back edge, whereas the image on the sheet measures 39.98 in. Fit is not attained. This slight variation may not significantly affect the average black-and-white job, but it could produce adverse affects on a close-tolerance piece to be diecut. A four-color job would accentuate this variation.

Front Guides and Side Guides

Guides are devices that direct the movement of the sheet. They are located at the front and side of the feedboard. Front guides are classified as multiple-stop or two-point drop guides. Front guides may act as insertion devices. Side guides operate independently of the front guides or guiding device.

Neither the design of the side guide nor the cycle of its operation is affected by the front guide, insertion device, or gripper action of the press. Side guides can be described according to their motion or by the manner in which they operate. Side guides can either push or pull. On some presses, one side guide pulls while the other side guide pushes at the same time.

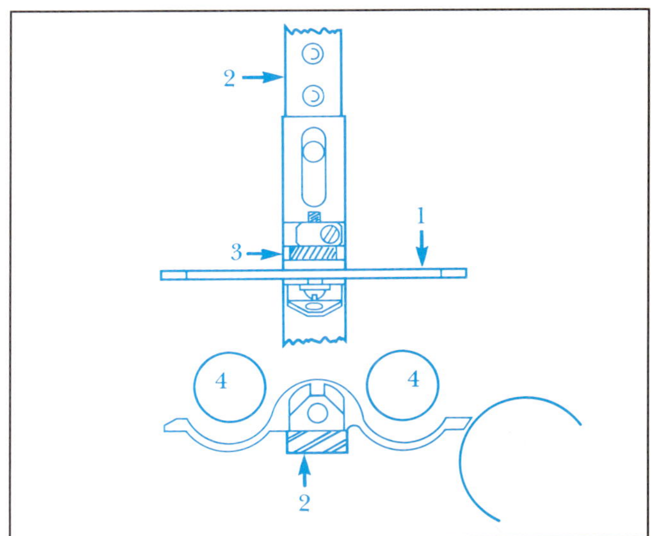

Cross-section of a push guide: (1) push plate; (2) side guide bar; (3) adjusting nut; (4) corrugating bars.

Push guides are usually found on smaller presses and those running heavy, rigid material such as metal and cardboard. They do not handle large, lightweight paper very well. A corrugating or stiffening device slightly buckles the sheet to stiffen it against the action of the push guide.

Pull guides consist of either fingers or rollers or a combination of both. These guides pull the sheet against a fixed plate after the sheet has been positioned by the front guides.

Finger pull guides advance over the sheet, close on it by pinching the sheet against a lower plate, and pull the sheet to the side guide plate. The tension is adjustable. The fingers must be adjusted so that they slip over the surface of the sheet without buckling it once the sheet is stopped by the side guide plate. The finger pull guides adjust to any stock weight.

Rotary or roller pull guides have a built-in lower roller that constantly rotates when the press is running. The sheet is forwarded to the front stops with its side edge riding over this lower guiding roller. After front register has been accomplished, a spring-loaded roller drops down and pinches the sheet against the rotating lower roll. Friction pulls the sheet against the side guide. As with the finger side guide, the tension is adjustable to accommodate a wide range of paper calipers.

Roller-finger pull guides have fingers that slide under the front-guided sheet. When this guide reaches the end of its forward movement, a spring-loaded upper roller pinches the sheet against the lower finger. Then, the finger starts to move back and pulls the sheet with it until the side edge of the sheet is stopped by the faceplate of the side guide.

Grippers

Grippers are classified either as tumbler grippers or as low-lift grippers. Presses using a three-point register system without an insertion device require tumbler grippers. Presses with either a feed roll or swing-feed (rotary-gripper) insertion device employ a low-lift gripper.

Tumbler grippers rotate through a rather large arc when they open. Then, they drop back into the impression-cylinder gap below the impression cylinder body. They must do this to clear the gripper edge of the sheet as the impression cylinder rotates to its sheet-taking position. Here, the grippers rotate into the closed position, pinching the sheet against gripper pads and pulling the sheet into the impression nip. The term tumbler is derived from the mechanism that moves the gripper shaft.

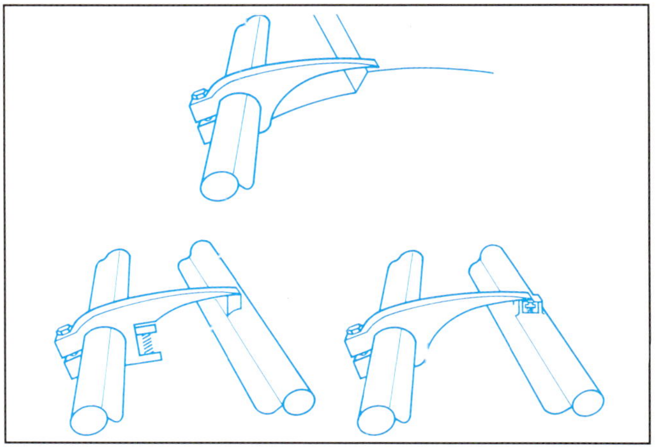

Three common forms of gripper construction. Top: a one-piece gripper; left: a two-piece spring-loaded gripper; right: a one-piece gripper with a spring-loaded gripper pad.

Low-lift grippers are mounted on a shaft that is rotated slightly through a cam and cam-roller device set at the end of the gripper shaft. (Low-lift is not a term used in the industry. It has been adopted here only for convenience.) Presses with insertion devices almost always have gripper motion in which the grippers open just enough to allow the sheet to be inserted.

Grippers may be of one-piece or two-piece design. On a one-piece gripper, the finger extends from the base or gripper clamp. In some cases, the base is a solid piece of metal drilled to fit snugly on the gripper shaft. A setscrew clamps the gripper firmly on the shaft. In other cases, the base may be split, forming an open collar around the shaft. The setscrew is threaded through both ends of the collar. When the setscrew is tightened, it closes the collar tightly around the shaft. In this case, the finger may extend from one side of the collar, or the collar is formed on the side of the gripper shaft opposite the gripper finger.

In two-piece construction, the finger and the collar are separate pieces. As the finger opens and closes, provision is made for spring-loading, which provides more uniform gripper bite on the sheet. One-piece grippers do this by spring-loading the gripper pad set in the top of the gripper post.

There is considerable pull on the sheet as it passes through the impression nip. The pressure of the gripper against the pad may not be enough. Too much bite pressure may mar the sheet. The grippers must guide the sheet through the nip; they must also hold the sheet against the pull of the nip.

Grit-faced grippers prevent the sheet from slipping during the printing cycle. On older presses,

the grippers or gripper pads may be faced with lightweight emery cloth if the spring-loaded grippers or gripper pads cannot achieve proper bite pressure.

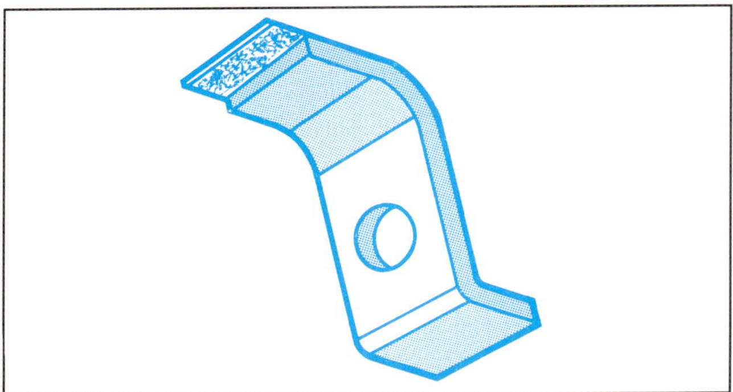

Grit-faced gripper.

Gripper pressure may be increased or decreased by adjusting the guides. This adjustment, however, should be used only as a last resort. The guides should be set to give exactly the gripper bite recommended by the press manufacturer. If the gripper-bite adjustment must be used, return the faceplate to its recommended position as soon as the job is finished. This adjustment ensures that the sheet is taken by the impression-cylinder grippers with a uniform bite across its entire front-guide edge. Proper gripper bite is essential at three points: where the grippers first take the sheet; at the impression nip; and at the point where the sheet transfers from one set of grippers to another (e.g., from impression-cylinder grippers to delivery-chain grippers).

Check gripper bite by inserting strips of tissue paper, or a 0.001-in. (0.025-mm) feeler gauge, into each gripper shaft. (The press manufacturer specifies this thickness; a thickness of 0.003 in.—0.076 mm— is common.) By feeling the pull on each strip of tissue or feeler, the press operator can evenly adjust all grippers. The tissue strip or feeler should barely pull out if everything is set right. Always follow the manufacturer's instructions for resetting and timing insertion devices.

The Three-Point Register System

In a three-point register system, the sheet is forwarded to front guides (or stops), and while it is held against the front guides, a side-guiding mechanism pushes or pulls the sheet into proper side alignment. The impression cylinder comes around to its sheet-receiving position. Simultaneously, the grippers rotate backwards (toward the leading edge of the cylinder) to the closing position. They reach the point of closing on the sheet while the cylinder is rolling in its forward motion toward the impression nip. The sheet is held motionless in its guided position. As the grippers close on the sheet, the front guides lift clear of the sheet's path to the impression nip.

Sheet control is not constant in this system. For an instant, the sheet is not under control due to the fact that the guide must clear the sheet before it starts forward. Since the gripper action and the cylinder travel are continuous, there is no way for the gripper to close firmly on the sheet before the guides are lifted. Proper timing and setting prevent loss of register during this brief instant. In addition, on presses equipped with a corrugating device, timing controls the sheet during this critical period.

The grippers jerk motionless sheets into full press speed, which may cause feeding difficulty. Insertion devices help to overcome the inertia of a large motionless sheet. Smaller presses (under 29 in.—737 mm) designed to run at high speed (over 7,500 iph) also feature insertion devices.

Front guides on the three-point register system are set across the press to align and balance the sheet while it is side-guided. The operator can move the guides across the press on the mounting shaft. They are always placed *between* a pair of grippers and not over a gripper. The stops must clear the motion of the swing or transfer assembly.

The descending guides should not bounce on the register plate or guide tongue; they should meet it gently. Where the guides are mounted with a keyway on the shaft, correct setting for easy seating is almost automatic. After the guides are set, place a sheet against them and slide it back and forth to test for smooth contact between the sheet and the front faceplate.

When setting the guide tongues or register plate, ensure that they do not cause a bulge in the paper. Such a bulge can easily wrinkle when the sheet goes through the printing nip.

Antibuckling devices have an adjustable metal plate that holds the sheet down and prevents buckling. Set the space to permit the side guide to freely move the sheet without buckling it.

Timing the front guides is accomplished by inching the press forward until the guides just begin to lift. Perfect timing is essential. The faceplate of the guide should *just* clear the sheet as the impression-cylinder grippers finally close. If the front guides are set too late, they will nick or tear the edge of the sheet. If they rise too early, misregister results.

The Feed-Roll Insertion System

Feed-roll systems employ devices that insert the sheets (directly or indirectly) into the impression cylinder grippers or an intermediate device. For the purpose of illustration, sheet travel will be followed for our operational analysis of this device.

When the sheet comes down the ramp, it is preregistered against a series of stops that are spaced across the press and mounted on a common shaft. The sheet is held against these stops and side-guided. At the proper time, the upper and lower feed rolls pinch the sheet, holding it firmly. The stops now drop out of the forward path of the sheet. The driven cams rotate and pinch the sheet against the free-rolling cams, exactly when the impression-cylinder, feed-cylinder, or transfer-cylinder grippers reach the sheet-receiving position.

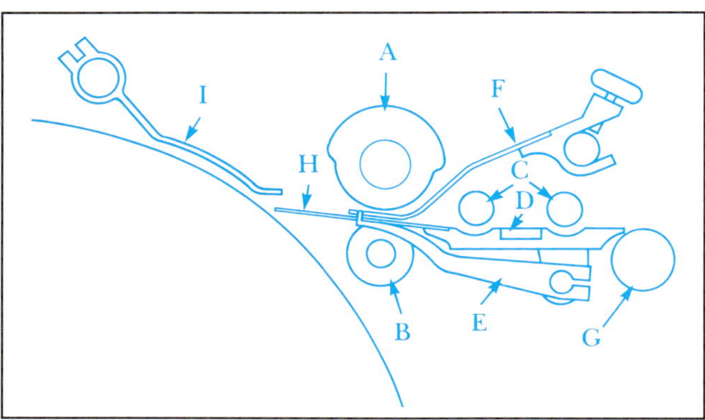

Insertion device. A: feed roll cam; B: lower feed wheel; C: corrugating bars (if push guide); D: side guide bar; E: guide stop fingers; F: upper guide fingers; G: conveyor rollers; H: feed plate; I: sheet holddown fingers.

The cams start the sheet slowly and then accelerate it to a speed *slightly faster* than the surface speed of the cylinder. As a result, the edge of the sheet is driven into the grippers and against another set of stops built into the impression, feed, or transfer cylinder, either along a separate bar or as part of each individual gripper pad. The sheet buckles slightly, just as the gripper closes.

This action is called *overfeed,* and the amount of this overfeed is adjustable to accommodate papers of varying thickness or stiffness. This forwarding and inserting method assures consistent register, because it allows the cylinder grippers to close on the sheet before the insertion device releases it. It is extremely important that the surfaces of the upper and lower rollers are absolutely clean. They should ride directly over each other. Constantly check the free-turning feed rolls; they should turn freely.

The Swing-Feed Insertion System

Swing-feed, or transfer-gripper, systems have front guides that drop *down* out of the forward path of the sheet *after* the grippers on the insertion device take hold of the sheet. The guides have less freedom to move sideways. In the three-point register system, the position of the impression cylinder grippers limit such movement. With an insertion device, additional clearances may seriously limit, if not completely prevent, such movement.

In a swing or transfer system, the sheet is forwarded down to the feedboard and brought to rest against the front stops. Then, it is side-guided. After proper guidance, the sheet is picked up by a set of grippers, and the front guides move out of the forward path of the sheet. This pickup mechanism is called a swing-feed, transfer cylinder, or transfer-gripper assembly, depending on design detail. After picking up the sheet, the mechanism forwards and inserts it into the impression cylinder grippers. In this system, the sheet is controlled during its transfer from the insertion device to the impression cylinder.

Checking Sheet Control at the Point of Guiding

When the sheet is against the stops, check the control devices. For example, on successive-sheet feeders, the tail brushes should ride on the *end* of the sheet. The drive-up wheels, or balls, should ride freely. Ensure that the sheet is held in its forward position but is still sufficiently free to be smoothly side-guided.

Impression-Cylinder Stops and Impression-Cylinder Grippers

Impression-cylinder stops are used on presses that have a feed-roll insertion device. The shaft or bar on which these stops are mounted is capable of bowing. Bowing accommodates wavy- or tight-edged paper and paper that has a bow cut into it. A wavy-edged cross-grain sheet, running grain long, tends to compress at the back end as it passes through the nip. Measure the image with a precision calibrated metal rule across the back corner marks; compare this with the measurement of the corresponding back corner marks on the plate to reveal any distortion. Bowing the stops—so that a

slightly greater gripper bite is possible toward the ends of the sheet—tends to minimize fit problems. Always start a new job by setting the stops straight and parallel to the leading edge of the cylinder, unless cross-grain wave in the paper is prevalent.

Presses that use swing-feed, or transfer-gripper, systems usually offer the option of easily cocking the gripper edge of the sheet. Do not apply too little or too much gripper bite across the sheet. To handle bowing on the larger presses equipped with swing-feed, or transfer-gripper systems, the two outer stops drop slightly away from the lead edge of the sheet (to create a concave bow) or push slightly ahead of the center stops (to create a convex bow). Some presses have a device at the back edge of the feed ramp that, when lifted slightly above the plane of the ramp, creates a convex bow at the lead edge of the sheet.

Impression-cylinder grippers require careful setting to prevent damage and maintain proper adjustment. The instruction manual carefully outlines this procedure. A gripper must firmly close on the sheet. Check this by inching the press as the grippers are closing on the sheet. Inch the press at minimum speed, and observe the motion of each gripper as it completely closes. The closing cycle must be smooth. If it is not, there is clear evidence that the gripper shaft is binding somewhere in its supports. Check each gripper for even pressure; consult the press manufacturer's manual.

Tumbler-gripper mechanisms with one-piece grippers must be evenly adjusted. One gripper that is set too tight causes the other grippers to have a looser bite.

Impression-cylinder gripper bite that is too tight adversely affects sheet transfer. A loose gripper may prematurely release the sheet. The blanket considerably pulls the sheet, especially coated stock that is printed with heavy ink coverage. If the sheet pulls out of the grippers as it leaves the nip, improper transfer to the delivery grippers or a transfer device will result.

Impression cylinder grippers are set differently from the grippers of a swing-feed or similar insertion device. Sheets are less likely to pull out of swing, rotary, or transfer grippers. The same holds true for grippers on a transfer or feed cylinder. However, there is tremendous drag on the sheet as it passes through the impression nip. The impression-cylinder grippers must hold the sheet and prevent slippage without marring the gripper edge. The grippers must firmly bite the sheet. Smoothly operating grippers should not bind or spring unnecessarily. These requirements explain why the press operator must follow the manufacturer's instructions explicitly.

Plate, Blanket, and Impression Cylinders

The printing cycle centers on three cylinders in the printing unit: the plate cylinder, the blanket cylinder, and the impression cylinder. A fourth assembly, called the delivery or skeleton cylinder, is not a conventional cylinder. It guides the printed sheet from the impression cylinder to the delivery pile.

The three printing unit cylinders on a sheetfed press are usually positioned with the plate cylinder uppermost, the blanket cylinder under the plate cylinder, and the impression cylinder below but slightly behind the blanket cylinder. One exception to this scheme is the metal-decorating press. The cylinders are mounted in a vertical row to increase the pressure between blanket and impression cylinders. This arrangement allows metal blanks to pass through the press without bending around an impression cylinder. Lithographic presses that print flexible paper employ a more compact arrangement. Placing the impression cylinder behind the blanket cylinder reduces overall height and simplifies the design for feeding and inserting the sheet. All three cylinders consist of similar materials. They are also produced and mounted similarly. The function of each cylinder differs and determines if a cylinder must be rigidly mounted in the press.

While running, the plate cylinder of a sheetfed press revolves in a counter-clockwise direction—as shown in the schematic—as viewed from the operator's side of the press. The dampening form rollers contact the plate before the ink form rollers, which deliver a charge of fresh ink to the image. During operation of a single-color press, the sheet is drawn around the impression cylinder, brought into contact with the blanket cylinder, and then transferred to the delivery chain that carries it around the skeleton cylinder to the delivery. Some presses employ intermediate or transfer cylinders between the impression cylinder and the skeleton or delivery cylinder. The last unit of a multicolor press transfers the printed sheet to the delivery chain grippers. On most multicolor presses, transfer cylinders equipped with gripper assemblies take the sheet from one impression cylinder and transfer it to the impression cylinder grippers of the succeeding unit.

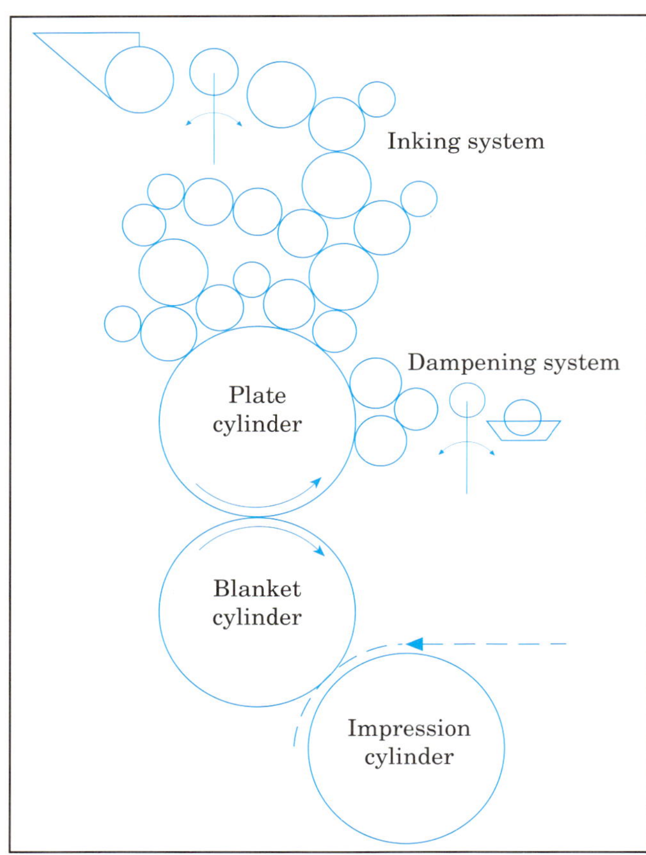

Typical printing unit.

The Plate Cylinder

As the name implies, the plate cylinder carries the lithographic plate. The plate cylinder on sheetfed presses is considerably larger in circumference than the printing plate. The cylinder surface has a gap in it that contains plate-clamping devices. These hold the plate on the cylinder.

The plate cylinder is the uppermost cylinder. Placing the plate toward the top of the press improves its accessibility. The plate cylinder is mounted in a rigid, fixed position in the press frame and cannot be adjusted for either pressure or alignment. However, it can be rotated independently of its gear.

Plate-cylinder bearers are rings of hardened steel that are attached to each end of the cylinder. Most presses are built so that the plate and blanket cylinders run on their bearers. When the impression is on, the bearers firmly contact each other.

Adjusting the plate cylinder manipulates the printed image position. The plate cylinder gear is bolted to the cylinder through slots rather than holes. This facilitates forward or backward cylinder movement to adjust the image position without opening or shifting the plate clamps. Moving the plate cylinder to adjust the printed image position consumes time and wastes paper. This movement is also limited; therefore, it is wise to establish standard print and plate-clamp margins for the stripper and platemaker to follow. Using a pin-register system reduces the time required to correctly position the plate relative to the gripper edge of the sheet. On newer presses, the plate cylinder position is adjusted from a remote control console, which saves time and improves accuracy.

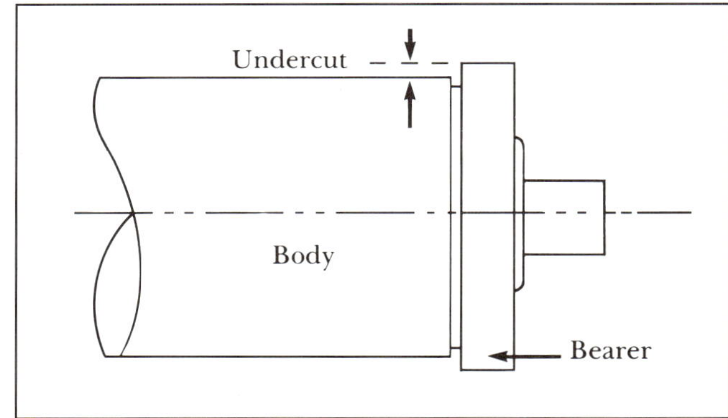

Cylinder bearer, body, and undercut.

The **undercut** of the plate cylinder is the difference between the bearer and cylinder radii. The surface of the bearer is the pitch line of the cylinder. All plate cylinders bodies are cut down below the level of the bearers. The undercut accommo-

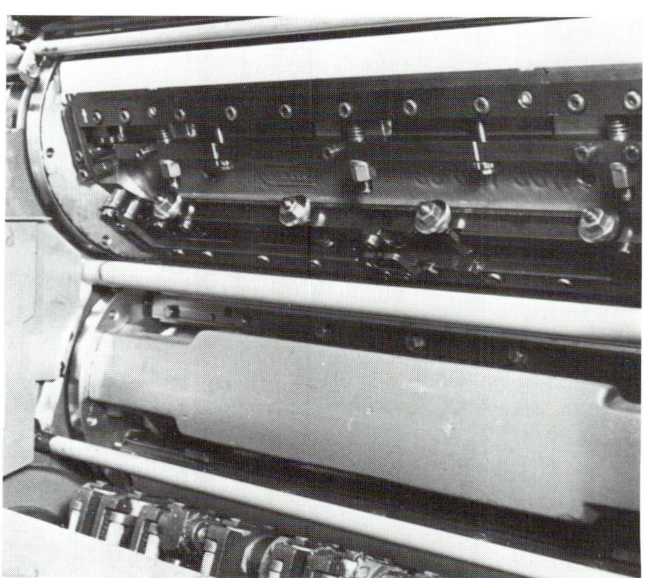

Plate cylinder with the plate locked in the clamp.

dates the plate and required packing. The combination of plate and packing that will bring the plate surface up to the correct printing height is specified by the press manufacturer. The press manufacturer has established standard undercuts for each size in the press line. However, the purchaser can specify the undercut for some special application, such as running relief plates with considerably greater caliper than the thickest lithographic plate.

Plate clamps hold the leading edge and the tail end of the plate. Both clamps allow slight sideways movement, or cocking, of the plate. This is sometimes necessary to attain proper register or fit. There is also some leeway for forward and backward movement.

The Blanket Cylinder

The blanket cylinder appears much the same as the plate cylinder, consisting of a heavy metal body with a gap across its length and with a bearer fixed to each end. The gap accommodates bars for attaching the blanket. The bar at the tail end allows the press operator to tighten the blanket. On some presses, the blanket tightens at both ends.

The blanket cylinder is mounted by means of double eccentric bushings in the press frames. On such installations, if one bushing is turned, the blanket cylinder can be moved toward the plate cylinder or away from it. This motion adjusts bearer pressure between the plate and blanket cylinders. It also achieves and maintains proper parallel alignment of the plate and blanket cylinders.

The blanket cylinder is mounted so that it can be pulled into contact or out of contact with the plate and impression cylinders while the press is operated. This feature is necessary for makeready and during running. When a sheet is missed or when the press operator idles the press, the blanket cylinder automatically moves away from the plate and impression cylinders.

Blanket-cylinder bearers are rigidly attached to the cylinder body. The blanket-cylinder gear is permanently bolted to prevent forward or backward movement. This allows for exact timing between the blanket cylinder and the impression cylinder.

Blanket-cylinder undercut is similar to the plate cylinder undercut; however, the depth of the undercut is much greater since blanket thicknesses average from 0.055 in. to 0.070 in. (1.38 mm to 1.75 mm), depending on size and ply. Lithographic plates range from 0.008 in. (0.20 mm) in the small sizes to 0.022 in. (0.55 mm) in the larger sizes. As with plate-cylinder undercuts, the press purchaser may order a special undercut. Special undercuts are very common on presses used for running paperboard; many board printers prefer to mount two blankets on their blanket cylinders. The undercut is always sufficient to allow for some packing in addition to the blanket.

The Impression Cylinder

The impression cylinder differs from the plate and blanket cylinders. Like them, it has a gap. It accommodates a gripper shaft, sometimes a gripper pad shaft, and/or a stop shaft that controls gripper bite on the sheet. However, the relationship of the impression-cylinder body with its bearers is different. Impression-cylinder design usually prohibits packing. The distance between the blanket and impression cylinders must be adjustable in order to achieve transfer squeeze on the specific paper calipers. For example, if the press is run with a transfer squeeze of 0.003 in. (0.075 mm), and if the running stock calipers to 0.003 in. (0.075 mm), then the distance between blanket and impression cylinders is set to give no clearance or squeeze between the surface of the blanket and the body of the impression cylinder under impression. No sheet is in the impression nip during this setting. When sheets are run, the caliper of the sheet will build up the required transfer squeeze. If the running stock calipers to 0.005 in. (0.125 mm), the clearance between blanket and impression cylinder surfaces under impression with no sheet in the nip would be 0.002 in. (0.050 mm).

Impression cylinder bearers are ground and polished steel rings on the ends of the impression cylinder. They are either pressed on and bolted to the impression-cylinder body, or they are an integral part of the body. However, these steel rings *do not* ride the bearers of the blanket cylinder.

The impression-cylinder bearers are used to align the impression cylinder. The cylinders are aligned by setting the space between blanket-cylinder bearers and impression-cylinder bearers so that they are exactly equal at both ends. Some foreign-built presses have plate and blanket cylinders that do not ride on their bearers. The bearers are used as reference points when cylinder pressures are adjusted and set, just as with the impression cylinder on American-built presses.

Adjust the impression cylinder to obtain correct squeeze pressure against the blanket cylinder. With the impression on—blanket cylinder in contact with the plate cylinder—the impression cylinder carries the sheet into contact with the blanket

cylinder and through the printing nip. On presses with a fixed impression cylinder, the blanket cylinder is mounted in a second set of eccentric bushings that allow for adjusting the *blanket-to-paper* squeeze without changing the *blanket-to-plate* squeeze.

The Blanket

The blanket is a rubber-surfaced fabric that is clamped around the blanket cylinder. It receives the image from the plate and transfers it to the substrate. Blankets are capable of transferring very fine images onto a wide variety of finishes, including paper, cloth, and other materials. Lithographic plates are capable of retaining and transferring high-resolution images, up to 400-line halftones. Combining the lithographic process with the offset method provides a superb printing technique.

Compressible and **noncompressible** blankets are available. A variety of blanket surface formulations are available to meet special requirements of ink formulations and solvents.

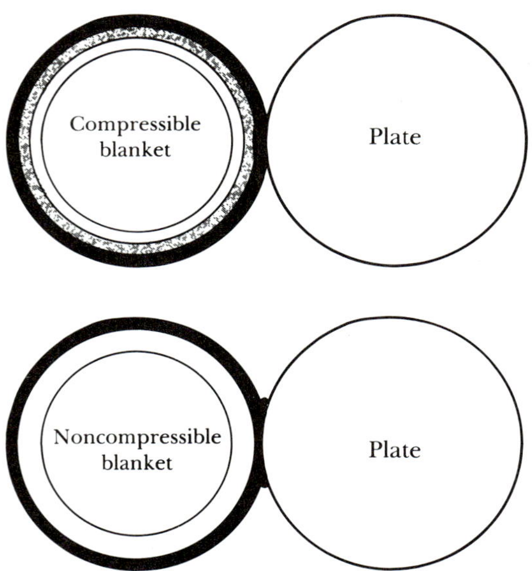

Compressible and noncompressible blankets.

The terms *compressible* and *noncompressible* describe how the blanket behaves under the squeezing action of the printing nips—plate/blanket nip and blanket/substrate nip. The noncompressible blanket when squeezed in the nip bulges out on either one or both sides of the nip. The materials cannot be compressed; therefore, they are displaced. Excessive plate/blanket squeeze causes a rubbing action against the plate as the blanket tries to recover its original shape. This rubbing action shortens plate life. In the blanket/substrate nip, excessive squeeze slurs the print.

The core of a compressible blanket will compress in the printing nips. This design accommodates greater squeeze pressures (within reason) that usually improve ink transfer.

Some blankets work better with coated papers. Specially formulated blankets must be used with some inks; heatset inks are one example. Specially formulated blankets are available in either compressible or noncompressible construction; it is the material (usually rubber) in the face of the blanket that is formulated to meet special requirements. The blanket should suit the paper and ink being run. Changing the blanket for every change of paper is not necessary. Usually, a plant that only occasionally runs a coated paper job will do well to have a special blanket available for that purpose. Consult the blanket manufacturer to determine the appropriate uses of a specific blanket.

Evaluate a new blanket before mounting it. Measure the blanket with the warp lines or directional arrows (on the back of the blanket) in the around-the-cylinder dimension to determine if it is the correct size. Make sure that the across-the-cylinder edges are square with the warp lines. Inspect both sides of the blanket for any obvious defects. Check the caliper with a blanket thickness gauge. Random measurements over the entire surface of the blanket provide an average caliper, which allows the press operator to calculate the proper amount of packing. If the caliper varies by more than a predetermined tolerance, return the blanket to the supplier.

Most blankets are mounted in blanket bars; however, some presses are designed so that the blanket, once it is cut to the proper size and squareness, mounts directly into blanket clamps built into the blanket reel bars.

Prepunched blankets that match specific mounting bars are available from blanket manufacturers. Premounted blankets are also available.

Unless otherwise specified, the holes in a prepunched blanket fall on a straight line across both ends of the blanket, at a right angle to the warp lines. The two rows of holes are parallel to each other. When a prepunched blanket is tightened on a cylinder over 35 in. (875 mm), the outer edges of the blanket may pull more than the center.

After the blanket is mounted in the bars, wash the blanket back thoroughly with water, soak it

well, and hang it up for a few days to dry. This expands all fabric fibers back to their original size, should they have been compressed in shipment or during mounting. Adjust blanket tension according to the manufacturer's recommendations.

Scrub the surface of a new blanket with blanket solvent and water using a clean soft cloth. Continue scrubbing until a smooth, even finish is attained. (Scrub with a side-to-side motion, rather than with a circular action.) Avoid soaking the ends of the blanket. Such soaking will cause the edges of the fabric to swell.

Check the levelness of a blanket by removing an amount of packing equal to about one-half of the squeeze pressure. Roll up the plate, and print on the blanket. Check ink transfer. The slightest ink film thickness deviations appear as light areas on the printed blanket. Determine if the blanket is at fault by removing it from the press and reinstalling it in the reverse position. Print on it again, in the same manner as above.

If the blanket is uneven, the deviations will appear in the same areas, and the blanket should be replaced. However, if another blanket is not available, then the one currently being used must be leveled. If this is the case, remove the rear bar and trace the low spots; use the face of the blanket as a guide. Build up low spots gradually with thin tissue, preferably 0.001 in. (0.025 mm) thick. Tear the tissue rather than cut it. Adhere the tissue paper to the back of the blanket. The feather edge of the tear prevents the edge of the patches from creating patterns in the printed solids.

Printing Transfer Squeeze Pressure

Squeeze pressure transfers printing ink from the press plate to the blanket. The height above the bearers to which the plate and blanket are packed determines this pressure under impression (i.e., the plate and blanket cylinders are running bearer-to-bearer). On presses that do not run on bearers, the clearance between their bearers—when impression is on—is the determining factor. In either case, the total thickness of the press plate with its packing and the total thickness of the blanket with its packing should coincide with the manufacturer's instructions.

Pressure transfers ink from the press plate to the blanket, and from the blanket to the paper. The cylinder surfaces must be squeezed together. Plate-to-blanket squeeze required on small presses ranges from 0.002 in. to 0.003 in. (0.050 mm to 0.075 mm). Medium-sized presses require from

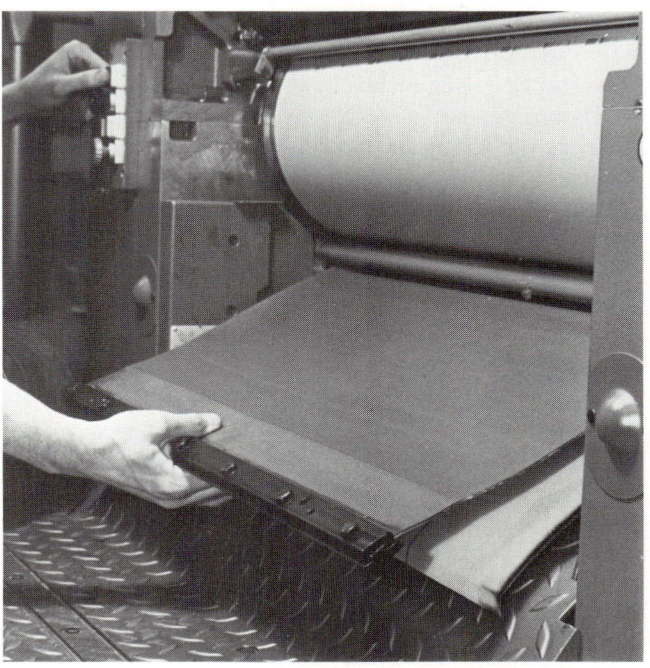

Mounting the blanket.

0.003 in. to 0.004 in. (0.075 mm to 0.100 mm) of transfer squeeze; large presses should be packed for 0.004 in. to 0.005 in. (0.100 mm to 0.125 mm) of squeeze. The above applies only to presses using conventional blankets; additional packing is required with compressible blankets. Smoother plates require less pressure than plates with coarse grain; less pressure prolongs plate life. Sufficient plate-to-blanket squeeze pressure allows the blanket to pull a full charge of ink from the plate. Plate and blanket packing alone do not guarantee adequate pressure. A press with worn cylinder journals, the play of which has not been taken up properly, cannot attain good ink transfer. The cylinders must hold together when the pressure is applied; at the same time, the squeeze pressure forces the cylinders apart. Overpacking to counteract loose or improperly set cylinder bearings (not the bearers) may adversely affect ink transfer and increase the cylinder circumferences. If the packing of both cylinders is not reasonably close to manufacturer's specifications, the cylinder circumferences will be out of balance. Although there is some leeway, any approach to either extreme of the available leeway may cause loss of fit, poor image transfer, slurring, and premature plate wear.

The **packing gauge** measures the height difference between the bearer and cylinder body. The body of the gauge is held against the cylinder body, and the gauge is zeroed. Then, the instrument is

moved so that its body rests against the cylinder body while the measuring head is over the bearer. The packing gauge also measures the exact height to which either the blanket or plate cylinder have been packed. The thickness of the packing sheets is measured using a blanket thickness gauge.

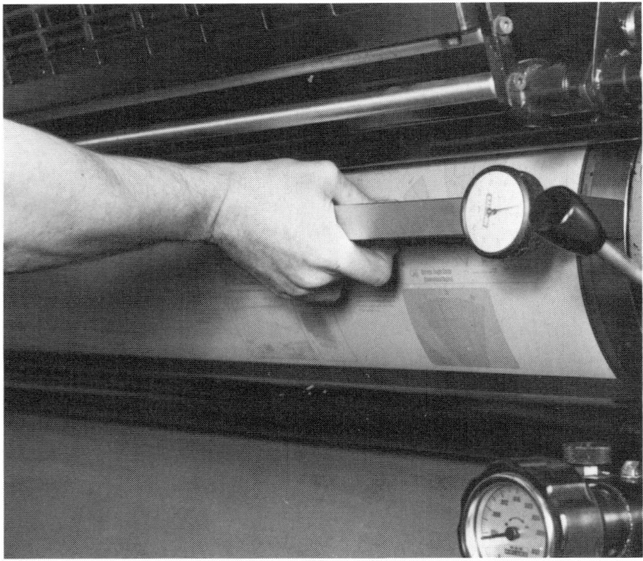

Measuring height of packed blanket.

Squeeze is determined by the combined height of the plate and blanket above their respective cylinder bearers. The undercut on the plate cylinder always exceeds the thickness of the lithographic plate. The same condition holds true on the blanket cylinder to allow for shifting the packing from one cylinder to the other in order to change the printed image size in the around-the-cylinder dimension. Transferring packing from under the blanket to under the plate maintains the proper transfer squeeze and produces a shorter image on the printed sheet, and vice versa.

The following example demonstrates how to pack the plate and blanket cylinders. The plate cylinder undercut equals 0.025 in. (0.636 mm); the plate thickness measures 0.020 in. (0.508 mm). To bring the plate to *bearer height,* add 0.005 in. (0.127 mm) of packing material under the plate. The blanket cylinder undercut equals 0.070 in. (1.778 mm), and the blanket thickness measures 0.065 in. (1.651 mm). To bring the blanket to *bearer height,* add 0.005 in. (0.127 mm) of packing material under the blanket. Since presses require additional packing to produce image transfer, add 0.002–0.005 in. (0.051–0.127 mm) of packing material. Press design dictates where to add this material. Add packing when the manufacturer specifies—at least to start the job. If, after starting, change of image size is required to attain *fit,* then shift the packing as needed. On a large sheet, the image can elongate or shorten from 0.125 in. to 0.187 in. (3.175 mm to 4.750 mm) before adverse effects are visible.

The printed lithographic image tends to be longer than the image on a flat plate. This image size increases in the around-the-cylinder direction as the plate is wrapped around the cylinder. In addition, the ironing action in the nip of the lithographic press stretches the sheet during printing. Moisture also increases sheet size. Running a heavy form also stretches the paper, because the ink pulls on the paper as it comes through the blanket/impression cylinder nip.

Determine if the press is printing the correct size on critical work by measuring the image at the beginning of the run. Checking the image size is especially important with color jobs and work to be diecut or embossed. Multicolor printing in one pass through the press will show immediately whether image length between the first- and last-down colors requires adjustment. If more than one pass is required (e.g., four-color printing on a one- or two-color press), ensure that the first-down color is printing as close to plate image size as is possible. If the first color is not printed to correct size, each succeeding color becomes more difficult to fit. Check image size on black-and-white jobs that are backed up.

The **thumbprint test** indicates whether the plate and blanket cylinder bearers are riding in firm contact. Apply a thumbprint of ink to each blanket-cylinder bearer, a few inches back from the

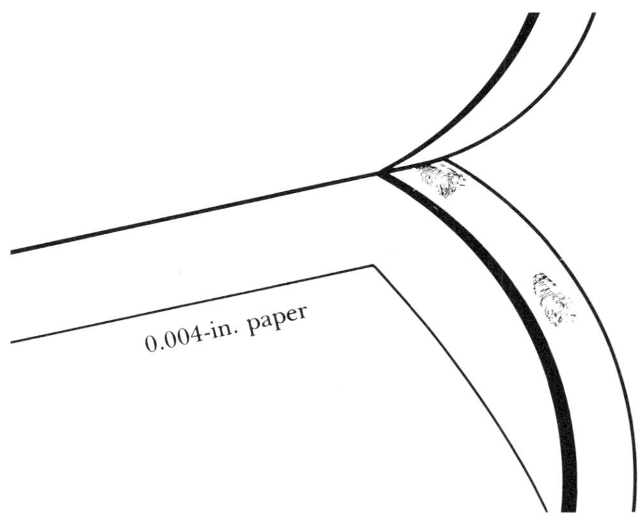

Thumbprints on one set of bearers and sheet position before test.

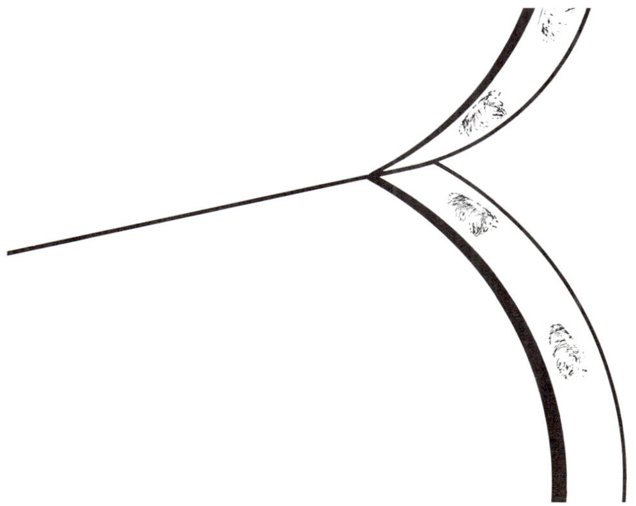

Thumbprints after test.

lead edge of the gap. The thumbprints must be equal as to amount of ink and sharpness. Place another set of thumbprints on the same bearers about 6 in. further back. Tape a sheet of 0.004-in. (0.102-mm) stock, as wide as the blanket, with its lead edge halfway between the pairs of thumbprints.

Release the tripping mechanism. Lock out the inker, and run the press for one revolution. The cylinder will trip at that point. Inch the press until the thumbprints come into view. Examine plate cylinder bearers to see whether a clear set of prints has been transferred from the sets that were put on the blanket cylinder bearers. One set of thumbprints has transferred under normal squeeze pressure and another set of thumbprints with 0.004-in. (0.102-mm) excess squeeze pressure. If both sets are not fully transferred, the bearers are not riding in firm contact. Adjust them according to the manufacturer's instructions.

Adjust impression cylinder squeeze by moving the impression cylinder toward or away from the blanket cylinder. With the impression on, and with a sheet in the nip, an experienced press operator can feel proper pressure. Calibrated scales on the press will show the amount of movement. Before measuring this movement, align the impression cylinder perfectly parallel to the blanket cylinder. Feeler gauges inserted between blanket- and impression-cylinder bearers, with the impression on, will verify parallelism. Adjust the cylinders according to the manufacturer's instructions.

Larger presses, and some smaller ones, have rigidly mounted impression cylinders, and the distance between blanket and impression cylinders adjusts at the blanket cylinder.

Transfer squeeze at the plate/blanket cylinder nip is easily and accurately measured. Measuring transfer squeeze at the blanket/impression nip is cumbersome, despite the scale that indicates this squeeze. Paper surface contributes to this difficulty. Smooth coated paper requires less squeeze to print satisfactorily than does rough uncoated stock. The press operator should back off the impression adjustment and then increase the squeeze until the print quality is satisfactory. The press operator corrects the ink film thickness before finally adjusting squeeze. The dial setting that has previously produced good printing is a good starting point.

Plate Handling and Mounting

Plate metal is very thin and is therefore easily damaged. Handle plates very carefully to avoid kinking them. Never scratch the face of the plate or expose it to any moisture. Check that the clamping edges of the plate show no signs of breaking if the plate metal has been used before. Then, caliper the plate with a micrometer.

The press operator must determine the actual thickness of the plate in order to achieve proper squeeze pressure. A micrometer measures the minute thicknesses and helps the press operator calculate how much packing is needed.

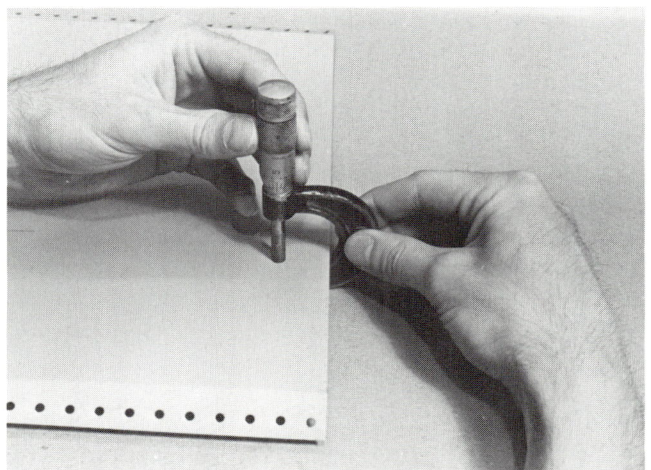

Miking the plate.

Packing thickness required to raise the plate to bearer height is determined by subtracting the thickness of the plate from the plate-cylinder undercut. The manufacturers' instructions indicate whether to pack the plate above or below bearer height. If the plate is packed over the bearer, the packing thickness is increased by the difference. If

the plate is packed below the bearer height, the packing is decreased by the thickness.

Before mounting the plate, remove any foreign material, such as paper, grease, and ink blots, from its back. Ensure that the plate cylinder is clean. Insert and lock the plate in the lead plate clamps. Then, place the packing sheets behind it so that the front edge of the sheet or sheets extends beyond the edge of the cylinder body. This locks in the sheets and prevents their shifting or wrinkling. Packing sheets with adhesive backing stick to the cylinder and maintain their position behind the plate. Use sheets that are slightly narrower than the plate. With some pull on the tail end of the plate (to make certain that the front plate clamps are up against the lead wall of the cylinder body), and with the impression on with the inker locked up, inch the press until the tail clamps are accessible. The squeeze of the blanket cylinder helps wrap the plate snugly around the cylinder. Then, slip the back edge of the plate into the clamps, and draw the plate up tight. It is not necessary to exert such a strong pull that the threads of the tightening screws are stripped or the plate torn. Inch the press off impression, and check the lead clamps to ensure that they are solidly against the cylinder wall. At this point, check the plate marks against the marks that are scribed in the cylinder, or against the scales with which some presses and pin-register systems are equipped. Inch the press forward until the tail clamps are in view, and ensure that the plate is tight and smooth completely around the cylinder.

On small presses, the angle between the plate clamps and the cylinder body is acute. In such cases, it helps to bend the clamping edges of the plate before mounting it on the cylinder. Bend the plate using a plate-bending fixture. Any plate measurements should include the amount that the clamps hold; the press manufacturer's instructions always include this distance.

The Inking System

Inking mechanisms deposit ink on the printing image. This is true in all printing processes, but on a lithographic press the inking mechanism must also perform other functions. It must work the ink by conditioning it from an essentially plastic state to that of a semiliquid. It must distribute a small, comparatively thick band of ink on the ductor roller to an even, thin film around all the form rollers. The system must deposit a uniformly even, thin film of ink on the image. It must pick up dampening solution from the lithographic plate, emulsify some of this into the ink, and evaporate the rest into the atmosphere. It picks loose particles of foreign matter from the plate and suspends them until the entire mechanism is cleaned.

The **ink fountain** is a reservoir for the ink supply. It consists of a steel roller, called the fountain roller, and a blade. One edge of the blade sets very close to the fountain roller, and the space between blade and roller is adjustable. The fountain roller rotates intermittently against the blade and draws ink through the gap set between the roller and the blade.

When the fountain roller rotates, a resilient ductor roller rests against it and picks up a supply of the ink drawn through the fountain. The fountain roller rotation and the gap set between the roller and fountain blade combine to control the amount of ink that the ductor roller picks up and carries to the distribution section. Changing the amount of

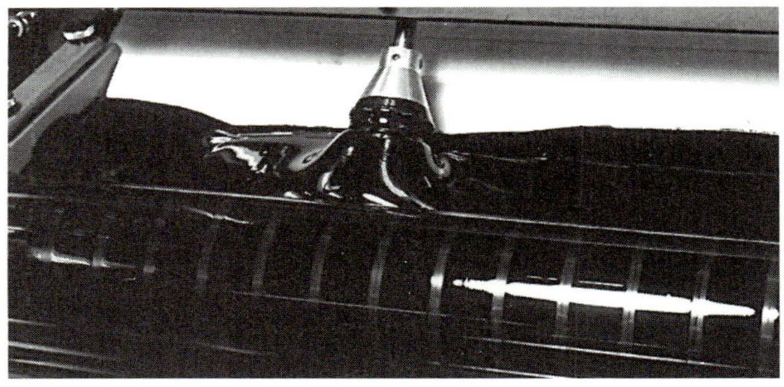

Ink fountain and agitator.

fountain roller rotation, while the ductor roller is in contact with it, governs the supply of ink across the entire roller train. Changing the gap between the fountain roller and fountain blade controls the ink flow within a specific area along the horizontal dimension of the plate.

The ink distribution section usually consists of metal oscillating rollers and a series of resilient rollers. Some smaller presses, especially duplicators, use hard rubber rollers. Many presses use copper-plated metal rollers since copper is one of the most ink-receptive metals. Roller trains always employ a resilient roller between any two hard rollers. The train is driven through gears or chains that connect the driven metal oscillators to the main drive of the press. The surface speed of the rollers equals that of the lithographic plate when it is

packed to proper printing height. All resilient rollers are driven through friction contact, directly or indirectly derived from the oscillators. Under no circumstances should the form rollers be driven as a result of friction between them and the plate. These rollers must be driven through friction between them and the press-driven oscillators.

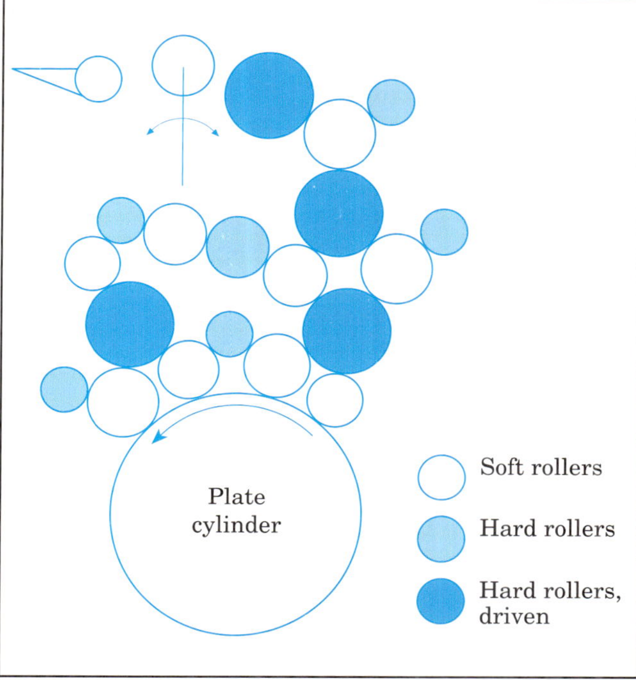

Inking system.

The fountain and distribution rollers work the ink considerably. The form rollers, consequently, receive a constant and prorated supply of properly conditioned ink for each impression.

The ink film is split each time that it transfers from one roller to another. The oscillating rollers move from side to side, which assists in working the ink. The oscillators and rollers of different diameters accomplish circumferential distribution. When the ink film reaches the form rollers that ink the plate, it is almost uniformly thick.

The form roller section consists of two to four rollers, depending on the press size. Some presses with four form rollers have an intermediate hard roller between the two pairs of form rollers. This arrangement is intended to distribute an even ink film to all form rollers at all times. The form rollers are set so that they properly contact the lithographic plate when the press is running. With some continuous-flow dampening systems, the first ink form roller applies dampening solution to the plate.

Form rollers of differing diameter help to prevent ghosting problems, especially when printing light tints. Sometimes, the diameters of all four form rollers are different. In other cases, the first and last rollers measure one size, while the middle rollers are a smaller size.

Operating the Inking System

Operating procedures include adjusting the components of the system to regulate ink flow.

Clean *all* parts of the fountain. The keys should be free of ink and solvent. The base of the fountain and such rods or bars as may be located under the fountain should also be clean and dry. Periodically, all keys should be taken out, and the keys and keyholes should be carefully cleaned. Grease the press as directed to prevent ink from drying in the side blocks.

To set the fountain blade in its operating position, start all keys in their respective holes. Turn the center key until it just touches the blade and starts to push it towards the fountain roller. Adjust all other keys similarly—working from the center out. The gap between blade and roller is gradually adjusted.

Set the blade using a 0.005-in. (0.127-mm) feeler gauge. If the gap between blade and roller appears to change at some other point than at the particular key actually being set, the blade is buckled. In this case, replace the blade since these buckles cannot be overcome by setting the keys.

After the initial setting, ink is put in the fountain and the roller turned continuously. Never set the fountain blade so tight that it actually scrapes the roller clean. This may score the roller and grind the blade, because there is no lubricating action by the ink. Regardless of how little the required ink flow may be in a particular area, it can always be achieved without ever scraping the roller clean.

Regulate ink flow by adjusting the gap between the blade and fountain roller. The distance through which the roller turns during the time when the ductor dwells against the fountain roller also controls flow.

The ductor roller must parallel the fountain as well as the ink train. The fountain is usually mounted so that it can be shifted slightly to parallel the ductor roller after the ductor roller has been paralleled to the ink train.

Adjust and set rollers according to the manufacturer's recommendations. On the lithographic offset press, the soft rollers usually adjust in two directions. In some cases, they may ride free and depend

on their own weight for proper contact. They are driven by the friction between soft and hard rollers in contact with each other, or contact between a soft distributor or rider with driven oscillator.

Set the ink rollers by inserting a set of thin paper strips. This set is made of two strips about 2 in. (50.8 mm) wide and a third strip about 1–1.5 in. (25.4–38.1 mm) wide.

Sandwich the narrower strip between the two wider strips. Insert these three strips between the rollers to be adjusted, or between roller and plate. Insert a set of strips near each end of the roller being tested. Determining the force required to remove the center strip helps the press operator to properly adjust pressure. Roller size and hardness affect the pressure required. When rollers are changed, perform this adjustment procedure before inking the press. This procedure assures sufficient squeeze between rollers to satisfactorily distribute ink. It also prevents damage to composition rollers as a result of excessive squeeze.

The system is inked by idling the press with the fountain trip on so that ink will feed into the system. When the ink film thickness on the rollers appears normal, turn off the fountain trip and bring the ink train in contact with the plate. To help assure proper roller setting, the plate must be packed to normal height.

When the plate is solidly rolled up, stop the press with the form rollers resting on the plate. Allow the press to stand for a few seconds. This procedure causes stripes to form at each roller nip. This system makes it possible to actually measure the nip widths (the widths of the stripes) and achieve accurate settings. Viewed from the operator's side of the press, the plate cylinder rotates in a counterclockwise direction, the form rollers rotate in a clockwise direction, and the oscillators rotate in a counterclockwise direction. Reverse the press, and the stripe formed between the no. 1 form roller and its oscillator will come into view. Measure the width of the stripe, and adjust the roller-to-oscillator pressure to achieve the desired line width. Set rollers of the proper durometer to give a stripe of 0.06 in. (1.59 mm) per inch of soft roller diameter. Follow the press manufacturer's recommendation for stripe widths.

A brief study of the inking system on the particular press should indicate to the press operator the easiest sequence for exposing all the form roller/oscillator nips to minimize the number of times the rollup must be repeated and should indicate which form or oscillating rollers must be temporarily removed to expose a particular nip.

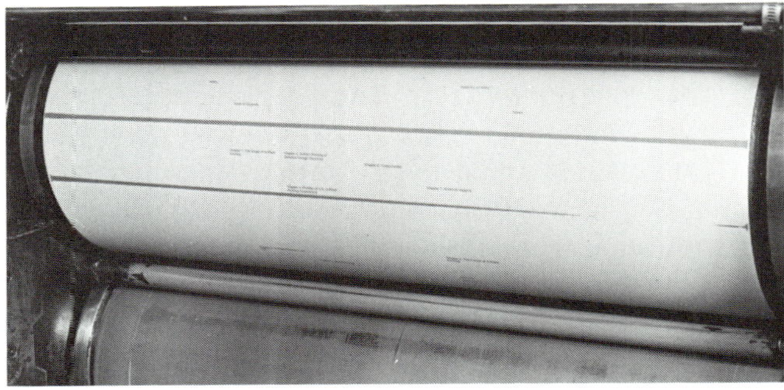

Stripes indicate nip widths.

After all form roller/oscillator nips have been set, basically the same procedure is followed to adjust the form roller/plate nip. The press is idled with the ink form rollers on the plate. When the rollup appears smooth (all earlier stripes smoothed out), stop the press with all form rollers on the plate. Permit the press to stand for a few seconds, and then lift the roller train. Inch the press to bring all of the form roller/plate stripes into view. Measure these, and adjust the required pressure settings as needed.

The form roller/plate nip should never be wider than the form roller/oscillator roller nip. A bit narrower nip is preferred to make certain that no form roller is being driven by the plate.

Composition-roller hardness is one of the factors to consider when adjusting the pressure between soft and hard rollers. Harder rollers require greater pressure. However, rollers that are too hard should be changed. New form rollers should read 25 on a durometer. Take them out of the press when they have hardened to a reading of 35. Depending on how well the inking system has been maintained, the pulled rollers may be brought back to an acceptable durometer by hand cleaning and scrubbing or surface grinding. Soft rider and distributor rollers should have a durometer of 35 when first received and will perform satisfactorily up to a durometer of 45. Consult the press manufacturer for recommended durometers.

Washup of Inking System

Washup materials and techniques reduce the need for pulling rollers out of the press for hand cleaning. Rollers also do not require washing with harsh solvents, scraping, or grinding. The materials dissolve all gum out of the roller's pores as well as remove all ink, varnish, and resin from the rollers. Consult the supplier for the proper materials and instructions.

Use more than a single solution or a one-stage procedure to thoroughly clean the ink rollers. Multistage materials are used for routine washups. These materials also prevent excessive emulsification; however, they do not eliminate the need to periodically remove and hand-clean rollers.

A prolific source of hickeys is the cuff of combined ink and solvent that forms at the ends of all rollers during washup. The cuffs should be wiped off the roller ends after each washup. Cuffs that are allowed to build up eventually chip; the chips often become ink skin hickeys. In addition, the cuffs deteriorate and crack the roller ends. As a result, the roller must be re-covered.

To thoroughly clean the inking system, apply just enough solvent at the top of and completely across the ink train to start dissolving the ink. Bring the washup blade into contact with the oscillator after the loosened ink begins to flow down the train. After the washup machine is engaged, apply just enough solvent to continue the flow of dissolved ink and solvent. A minimum amount of washup, applied in a series of steps, cleans the system more thoroughly and quickly than a large amount of solvent applied just a few times. If too much solvent is applied, it will splash in the nip. Some of this splashing results in accumulations of dried ink on tie and support bars in the train. This splashing is also a source of ink skin hickeys. Too much solvent applied at any one time causes the friction-driven rollers to skid and damages the faces of the rollers.

Roller cleaning and storage procedures recommended by the supplier should be followed. Thoroughly clean and condition spare form rollers before storing them. All that may be required is to powder the roller and stand it in the roller locker. If harsher methods must be used, follow the roller supplier's advice.

Never store rollers in a horizontal rack. Store them in an upright position. Do not bounce them on an end or drop them. Large rollers bend easily, and the slightest bend will make proper setting in the press impossible.

Store rollers in a locker, or place them in a dark, cool area. Shield soft rollers from sunlight. The surfaces of stored rollers should be protected.

The Dampening System

The dampening system on a lithographic sheetfed press applies a water-based **dampening solution** to the printing plate before it is inked. Its major objective is to provide fast and complete separation of the image and nonimage areas of the plate (i.e., to prevent ink from becoming deposited in nonimage areas). Offset press operators have to control both ink and water and balance for good results. Ink, plate, press speed, paper, temperature, and relative humidity are the principal factors that influence the need for various dampening solutions.

The **conventional** (intermittent-flow) dampening system of the lithographic offset press consists of the water fountain; the pan roller; a cloth-covered ductor roller; an oscillating roller; and the dampening form rollers. The water fountain, also called the pan, is a reservoir for the dampening solution. It functions the same as the ink fountain. Since dampening solution consists of over 98% water, local controls across the plate are crude by comparison to ink fountain controls.

The **fountain roller** revolves constantly, and part of it is always immersed in the dampening solution. The fountain roller is a metal roller, sometimes used bare and sometimes covered with cloth.

The **dampening ductor roller,** covered usually with a molleton sleeve, moves back and forth between the fountain roller and the dampening oscillator roller, which is also metal. The time during which the ductor roller dwells against the fountain roller governs the amount of water that periodically feeds to the oscillator. Fountain solutions are not always fed with each press revolution. On some presses, the fountain roller is driven by its own motor. This arrangement gives additional control over the amount of dampening solution.

The **dampening oscillator** is always gear-driven by the main drive of the press, and its surface speed equals that of the cylinders. This roller drives the dampening form rollers and equalizes the water feed across the dampening system through sideways oscillation. The oscillator drives the two dampening form rollers, which contact the plate with just enough pressure to dampen it. They must dampen the entire plate but not squeegee it.

The **dampening form rollers** contact the image and nonimage areas of the plate. The form rollers of the inking system tend to resist water, especially because they are covered with greasy ink. However, they will pick up some dampening solution. The dampening rollers lack protection because of the very slight amount of solution that they carry. Therefore, they are easily greased by the ink on the plate if the inking and dampening systems are im-

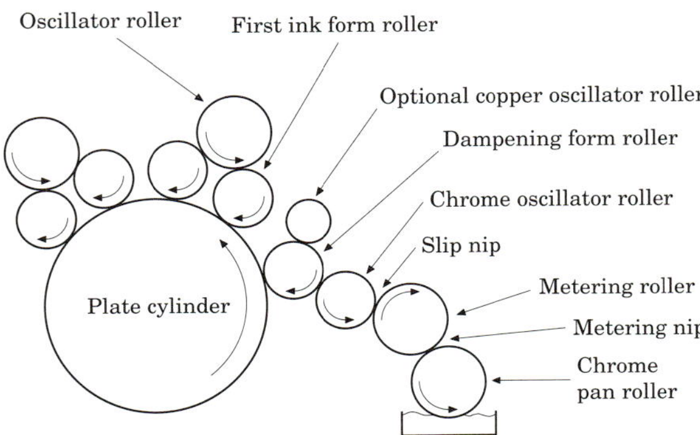

The Roland system.

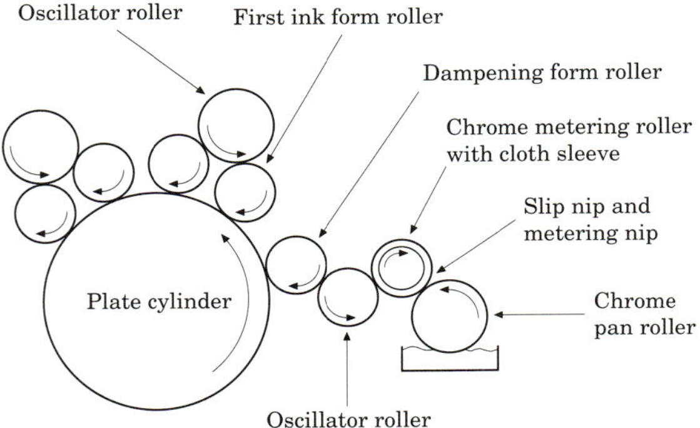

The Miller-Meter dampening system.

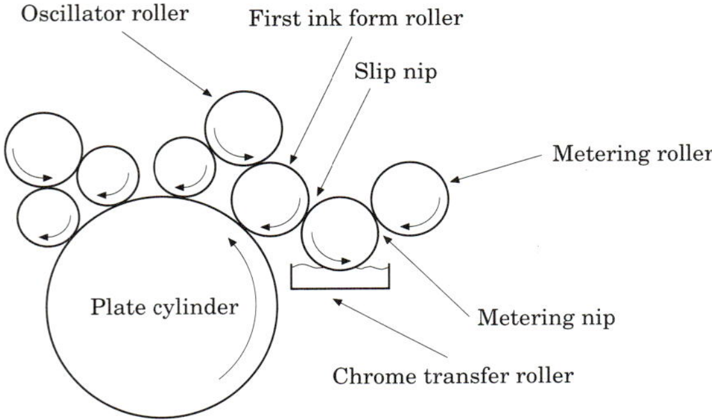

The Dahlgren dampening system.

properly set. A greasy dampening system will not function efficiently or consistently.

Dampening form rollers lack a perfectly true, even, and level surface. Therefore, and particularly if a light and even roller pressure on the plate is desired, every slight unevenness of the molleton-covered roller immediately shows up as a point of too much or too little pressure. Reasonable care when covering the rollers with molleton helps to prevent these troubles.

Check roller adjustments periodically to make sure they have held their original setting. First, adjust the dampening form rollers to the oscillator, then to the plate. The plate *must not* drive the form dampening rollers.

Dampening Roller Covers

Molleton is a soft woven cotton fabric with a very high nap, which gradually wears out. Molleton's most important characteristic is its ability to hold water. Wet molleton resists ink; however, over a period of continuous running, ink will contaminate the molleton cover. Change the rollers for each shift to minimize downtime. Keep a spare set of clean form dampeners available for this purpose. Pull the form dampeners from the press, and clean them in time to go into the press on the next shift. Do not allow ink to dry on the molleton. Clean dampeners may appear dirty; however, this appearance is due to staining and does not affect plate dampening performance. A properly maintained molleton-covered dampener will run a long time before the covering requires replacement. Such re-covering becomes necessary when the nap has worn away.

Rinse-washing freshly covered dampeners will remove most, if not all of, the lint. If a washing machine is not available, a newly covered dampener should be thoroughly soaked with water, the excess should be squeezed out, and the roller rolled out on a clean sheet of uncoated paper that has no alum content. This procedure helps to get rid of some loose fibers and lint and also tends to condition the undercover if one is used. As soon as the rollers are put in the press, adjust them according to the manufacturer's instructions. Then, idle the press, off impression, until no more lint appears on the dampener oscillator.

Prewoven cloth sleeves are pulled over specially rubber-covered or cloth dampener base material. These materials combine the advantages of paper and conventional molleton covers.

Strip coverings look and feel like heavyweight parchment paper. The coverings are a nonwoven material that absorbs water and repels ink. Originally, this material came as a 3-in.-wide roll and was applied by spirally winding the continuous strip on a soft roller similar to an inking form roller. While some printers still use the strip covering, more easily applied sleeves of similar material are available.

Dirty sleeves are easily wiped clean with a nonoily solvent. After cleaning, the roller should be rinsed and wiped clean with a water-soaked cloth. The roller may still appear dirty, but is actually only stained.

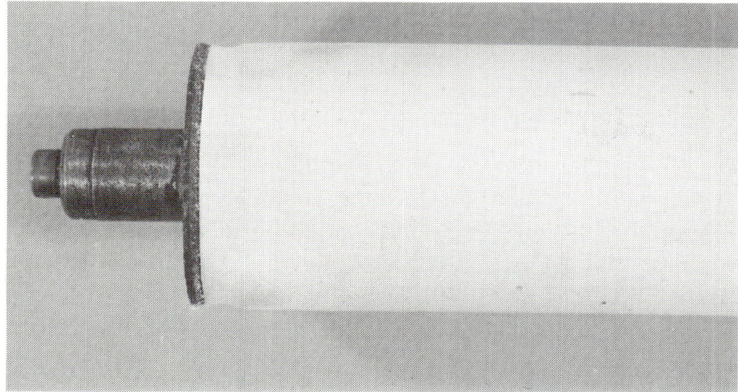

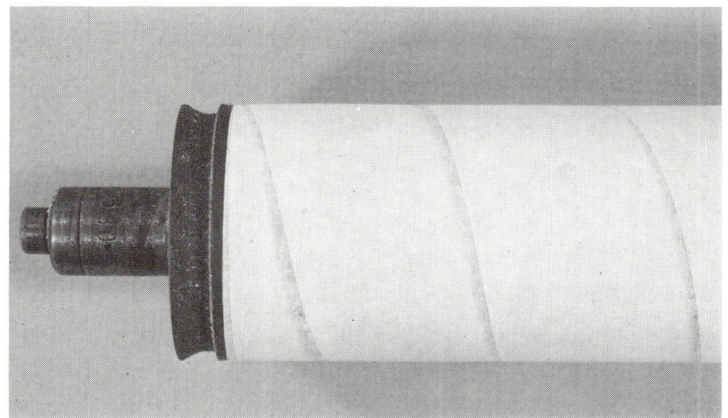

Dampening roller covers.

This covering is generally considered to have numerous advantages over cloth covers. It costs considerably less than molleton or other cloth covers despite that it wears out faster. Because the strip or sleeve cover is inexpensive and so easily replaced, there is no need to run a cover too long. Whenever a newly covered cloth dampener form roller is installed, the roller must be set for proper contact with plate and oscillator. These adjustments may have to be changed during the life of the cover because there is some decrease in overall roller diameter. Strip- or sleeve-covered rollers require no adjustment; their diameter remains stable. These dampeners lay down a more controllable thin water film, which fine-grain plates require. Reasonable care keeps these covers clean.

Best results are obtained when only the first dampener form roller is so covered. A conventional cloth-covered dampener form roller is used in the second position. This roller is set so that it touches the oscillator but not the plate. It performs the function of a storage roller. By putting it in the second position, with the strip- or sleeve-covered roller in the first position, the bead of water fed by the ductor roller is spread out before the oscillator feeds to the strip- or sleeve-covered form roller.

Dampening Control Devices

Conventional dampening system modifications have been aimed at controlling the amount of water fed across the length of the water pan roller. Press operators used to vary water feed using pieces of blanket. Squeeze rollers, metal scraper fingers, and squeegees are now used to regulate dampening.

The water level should be kept constant to maintain consistent dampening. Simple automatic devices that maintain the water level were originally developed for small offset duplicators. Their success led to the development of automatic regulating devices for larger press fountains.

One modification to the conventional dampening system employs constantly revolving hard rubber rollers or squeegees in place of the ductor, which contact the pan roller and transfer water to the oscillator. The speed of the motor-driven pan roller and the pressure of the rotating rollers against the pan roller are variable for controlling the amount of water distributed to the dampener form rollers.

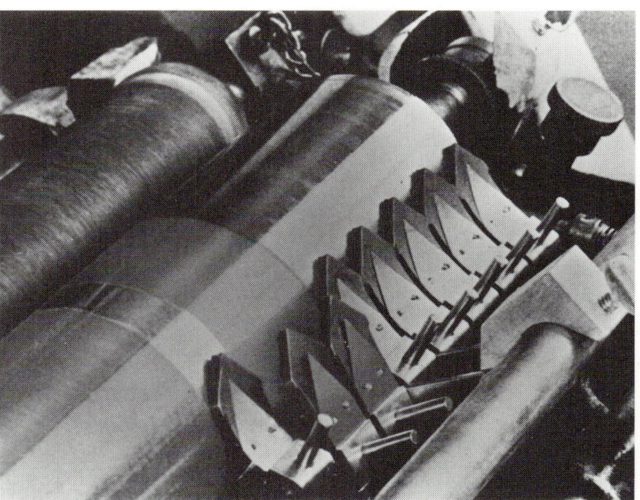

Courtesy Baldwin-Gegenheimer Div.

Water stops for variable dampening.

A similar system consists of brushes instead of rollers. One adaptation of this system employs a series of flicker fingers mounted above the brush and spaced across the full length of the brush assembly. This device allows zonal control of water fed to the plate. The pressure of individual flickers against the constantly rotating brush adjusts independently. Another method feeds water to the dampeners through a series of spinning rotors combined with vanes for directional control. A similar system uses a series of jets across the dampening system through which water under pressure is sprayed into the plate dampening section of the system.

Another water feeding system consists of a rotating shaft on which flaps of leather or molleton are mounted. This assembly replaces the ductor and pan roller. As the shaft rotates, the flaps pick up moisture and wipe it on the oscillators. There is no direct line of contact from the plate back to the water supply, which prevents ink from contaminating the dampening solution.

Continuous-Flow Dampening Systems

The other major category of dampening systems for sheetfed offset lithographic presses is the continuous-flow dampening system. It is divided into two basic categories: plate-feed and inker-feed. Plate-feed systems feed dampening solution directly to the plate. Inker-feed systems feed the dampening solution indirectly through the inking system. Some continuous-feed dampening systems incorporate features of both plate-feed and inker-feed systems. Most of the industry uses plate-feed systems.

Continuous-flow systems eliminate some of the dampening control problems associated with conventional systems, because the dampening solution is no longer supplied intermittently. A very important advantage of these systems is their rapid response to changes in fountain settings. This fast response is largely due to the absence of storage capacity in the system because the form rollers are not covered.

An **inker-feed** system is quite different from conventional and plate-feed systems. One of its principal features is using the first inking form roller as a combination inking/dampening form roller. Another feature is the absence of a ductor roller.

An inker-feed dampening system often consists of two rollers that deliver dampening solution to an ink form roller. One is a chrome-plated steel roller, and the other is a soft roller that meters (controls) the thickness of the dampening solution film on the hard roller. The line of contact between the two rollers is called the **metering nip.** Depending on the particular press requirements, either roller could be the fountain roller. They are driven independently of the press, and their surface speed is not the same as that of the plate. The hard roller rubs against the first ink form roller, which transfers the dampening solution directly to the plate. Dampening solution supply is controlled indirectly through speed control of the two rollers and the adjustable squeeze between them.

An important consideration of an inker-feed dampening system is that the dampening solution film must lay smoothly on top of the already inked form roller. The wetting properties of either alcohol (5–20% by volume) or a satisfactory substitute assist in the formation of an even film of dampening solution.

Setting the rollers on an inker-feed system is different from setting the rollers on a conventional system. The inking form roller is set heavier to the plate, because it is considerably softer than those in a conventional system. The inking form roller should leave a stripe of about ⅜ in. (10 mm) or more on the plate when the picture method is used.

Plate-feed continuous-feed systems all have *separate* dampening form rollers. As with the inker-feed system, each has a metering nip formed between a soft metering roller and a hard chrome roller. Because these two rollers are driven independently of the press, there is also a slip nip. Usually, the roller farthest from the plate can be skewed to modulate the water feed across the press. These systems have either a metering roller or a water pan roller.

Most plate-feed continuous-flow systems also require the use of alcohol or an alcohol substitute in the dampening solution. In those that do not, two of the four dampening-system rollers are covered with cloth or sleeves.

A **combination** continuous-flow dampening system incorporates features of both inker-feed and plate-feed systems. In a combination system, an oscillating or vibrating bridge roller contacts both the dampener form roller and the first ink form roller.

One combination system consists of an oscillating bridge roller and a form roller that is driven at a slower surface speed than the plate. The differential speed results in a scrubbing action on the plate, which helps to eliminate hickeys. The bridge roller can be used either as a rider or as a connection between the dampening form roller and the inking system.

Another combination system has rollers that cannot be skewed to control dampening distribution.

With this system, an air flow pattern (with water stops and an air bar) is used to evenly distribute dampening solution across and around the plate cylinder. At startup, the dampening form roller is contacting the plate (on impression), the ink form rollers are off impression, and the bridge roller is in place, feeding dampening solution to the inking system. As a result of the bridge roller carrying dampening solution to the inking system, ink/water balance is quickly achieved.

Cleanliness is one of the most critical factors in the successful operation of a continuous-flow dampener. The entire system must be cleaned periodically, at the very least when the press is shut down for a long period such as overnight or over a weekend. Additionally, every press washup should include cleaning the metering and chrome rollers.

The relative softness of the metering roller also affects the performance of the continuous dampener. The recommended durometer (Shore A) of the metering roller is 12–15. When the roller becomes excessively hard, water bonding occurs. When this happens, remove the roller. Depending on how well the system has been maintained, this roller may be thoroughly hand-cleaned, and its hardness brought back to a satisfactory durometer reading. If this is not attainable, re-cover the roller. The same holds true for the form roller. This roller, when new, should have a durometer of 25–30. The roller hardness may increase by up to ten points before this roller must be reconditioned or re-covered. These hardness/softness limits are especially critical when using alcohol substitutes.

Adhere to the manufacturer's recommended roller settings. The operator must recognize that soft roller settings differ greatly from ink roller settings. If alcohol substitutes are used, more accurate roller settings are required.

The Delivery

All sheetfed lithographic offset presses deliver the printed sheet by finally transferring it to a set of grippers moving on a continuous chain. The sheets may transfer directly from the impression cylinder grippers or through intermediate transfer cylinders. Behind and slightly below the impression cylinder (the last unit on a multicolor press) is a skeleton or delivery cylinder. The skeleton cylinder is not a conventional cylinder but a pair of sprockets that drive the delivery chains. Gripping devices prevent the sheet from rubbing, whipping, or waving between the sprockets. The sheet arrives at the delivery pile face up and with its gripper edge toward the front of the press. The chains carry delivery gripper bars; one of them is always in the taking position for each impression. On smaller presses, the delivery pile is an integral part of the press. This limits how many sheets can be placed on the delivery dolly. On larger presses, the delivery is built as an extension of the press and permits the delivery and feed piles to be the same height.

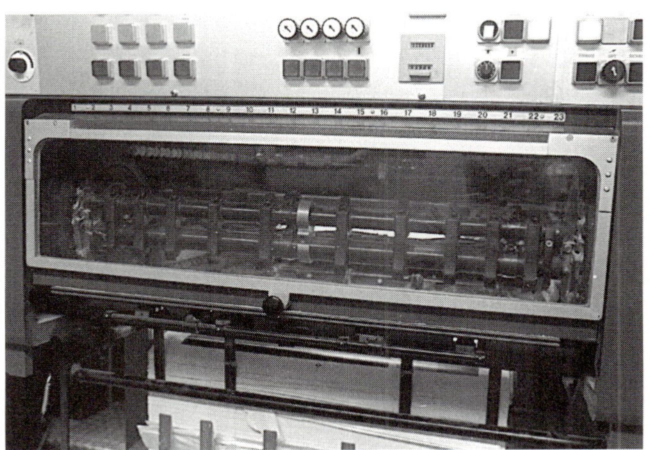

Delivery chain and grippers.

Two-pile deliveries alternately receive sheets. This allows greater ink-setting time between delivered sheets. Such a delivery setup also permits removing a printed skid load without breaking the run. Two-pile setups require extra space for the second delivery. Simple and inexpensive devices make it possible to remove a load from the delivery without stopping.

Delivery Grippers

Delivery grippers require precise timing with the insertion grippers. If any appreciable gap exists between the closing of the delivery grippers and the opening of the impression-cylinder grippers, the sheet will pull away and stick to the blanket. This action batters blankets and causes ripped paper to get into the ink train. All lithographic presses are provided with means for adjusting the delivery gripper timing. The blanket-to-impression-cylinder pressure must be adjustable in order to accommodate a wide variety of paper calipers. Adjusting the impression cylinder for change of paper thickness causes a change in the sheet transfer point. A radi-

cal change requires the press operator to check transfer timing to ensure good delivery transfer.

The delivery gripper bite must be as firm as the impression cylinder gripper bite, because the tail end of the transferring sheet may still be in the nip or trying to follow the blanket.

Design differences require press operators to follow the manufacturer's instructions for setting delivery grippers, timing the delivery grippers, and timing the delivery gripper bars. Keep bars clean, free of spray powder, and properly lubricated.

Setting the Delivery

The properly functioning delivery jogs the sheets as perfectly as possible and floats them onto the pile in such a way as to prevent smudging, smearing, or setoff. The adjustable joggers, usually on three sides of the sheet, should be set so that the sheet falls exactly between them when it drops down. Then, the sheet requires minimal movement to be jogged straight with the pile. If static is present, the sheets may drag at the back end and drop some distance from the front gate. In this case, the sheet must slide forward because of the action of the rear joggers (where they jog). Some smudging may result. Static can cause sheets to jump to the pile rather than to float down on it, and this will cause setoff.

Proper heat and humidity (i.e., 73°F, 50% RH) minimize static electricity in the pressroom. In a dry, heated but not humidified pressroom, static can create problems. Electrical neutralizing bars at the delivery help to eliminate static. Such bars may also be required at the feed ramp.

When the sheet is pulled away from the blanket, curling or tail-end hook may result. Sheet decurlers help overcome these delivery problems. One simple remedy is using stock wedges to guide the sheet without moving it unnecessarily. For example, if tail curl is present, a wedge under each rear corner of the pile helps to overcome jogging problems.

Running the Press

During a pressrun, all press units should perform properly. The ink fountain must consistently deliver the set amount of ink. The dampening system must do the same with the dampening solution. From the front of the feeder to the end of the delivery, everything should function perfectly. The press operator needs to constantly supervise the running press. Supplying paper at the right time and in the proper condition is up to the press crew, as is maintaining adequate water and ink in the fountains.

Checking the Paper before Running

Check the paper grade, size, and quality to ensure that they are correct. The paper should have been properly conditioned before the run. Under the worst conditions, the paper should be in the pressroom long enough to reach a temperature balance. This conditioning period is especially important when winter temperatures are low enough to require heating the plant.

Protect paper in moisture-proof sealed wrappings. Stock that requires cutting should be immediately resealed after cutting. Plastic covers, which are designed for this specific purpose, are available in a variety of sizes. Pile the paper on the bottom sheet; pull the top envelope over the pile, and bring the edges of the bottom sheet up around the envelope. Seal the plastic with pressure-sensitive tape. The edges of the piled paper receive minimal exposure to the atmosphere. This precaution can appreciably decrease the amount of press problems caused by tight- or wavy-edged paper. After printing, re-cover skids with the original wrappers.

Paper moisture content should equal that of the pressroom atmosphere. Paper that is out of balance with the atmosphere may still print properly in some cases. If a sheet is too dry, and if it is going to pass through the press several times, an experienced press operator knows that the edges will pick up moisture very rapidly and may become extremely wavy. The press operator also knows that the entire sheet will pick up some moisture with each printing. Additional moisture may flatten out the wavy edges; however, the sheet will expand in the across-the-grain direction. In this case, the press operator will have difficulty achieving fit on subsequent printings. Printing short may counteract this problem. The plate and blanket cylinders are packed in such a manner as to reduce the tendency of an offset press to print an image that is longer than the image on the plate, as measured on the plate *before* it was mounted.

Wet-Washing the Plate

New plates should be wet-washed with water and a sponge to remove the protective gum. A plate that

is already on the press should be washed with a mild solvent and plate cleaner on a sponge to dissolve the ink. Then, the plate should be wiped with water to remove the residual ink and solvent. After wiping with water, restart the press, and engage the dampening system before the plate dries. Roll up the plate (apply ink) for one or two revolutions. Stop the press, and carefully examine the plate. The ink should cover the image, and the background should be absolutely clean.

Registering to Paper

Successive impressions should print in the same position on each sheet. The gripper bite must be correct, and the sheets must separate, advance, and forward at the correct time and to correct position for registering. Image position may vary with press speed on a press that has a three-point register system (without an insertion device). Sheets pulled at idling speed may not register with sheets at full running speed.

Plate shifting is one method of adjusting image position. Modern pin systems eliminate most of the time spent registering to the paper.

If the plate is reasonably close to its proper sideways position, setting the side guide requires very little time. There are several means available to obtain correct front-to-back position. Shifting the plate cylinder by changing the position of the cap screws that fasten the plate cylinder to the cylinder gear takes care of gross shifts. Coupled to this feature on practically all plate cylinders is a vernier that measures fine adjustments. In this case, the cylinder can still be moved with respect to the gear, but the plate-cylinder-locking cap screw remains in the same hole. Both of these shifts move the plate image forward or back, but in a straight line. Most modern presses have remote control consoles that enable the press operator to move the plate cylinder in extremely small increments.

A third method of shifting the plate is to slide it around the cylinder by use of the space between the plate clamps and the plate cylinder body. Plate shifting at the clamps allows cocking or twisting, as well as side shifting if for some reason the side guide cannot be adjusted for side margin.

Cocking or twisting a plate affects the position in which all images on the plate will print. A plate can be twisted around the cylinder in one of two ways: Imagine that the plate is fastened to the cylinder at the exact center of the plate. When twisted, the entire plate revolves around this center point. Imagine that the plate is fastened to the cylinder at one corner, and that when the plate is being cocked, it pivots at that corner.

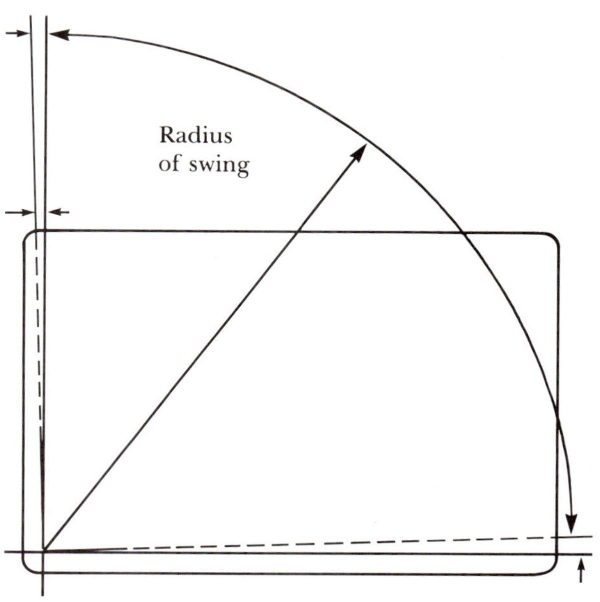

One method of plate cocking. Note that one corner is considered as being anchored and is the pivot point.

The entire plate must be cocked in order to guarantee that it will continue to hug the cylinder smoothly when the clamps are pulled up tight.

After radical packing shifts, recheck the inking and dampening roller settings. Compensate for such shifts by adjusting the squeeze applied at the back cylinder. On a first color, or the first side of a backup job, or on a once-through-the-press critical register job, check exact fit by measuring the printed image. Check these measurements against those that were taken off the plate before it went to press. If the first color or first side isn't to correct size, achieving fit on subsequent printings will be very difficult if not impossible. Radical manipulations to achieve subsequent fit reduce print quality and adversely affect plate life.

Obtain register with waste sheets. Save pulled sheets for use on the succeeding passes. Place two good sheets between every five waste sheets. Flag the alternating good and scrap sheets to separate them from the pile. Register and fit are achieved without wasting much of the printing stock. Run enough sheets to indicate how well ink and dampening fountains are functioning.

Permit the ink and water fountains to feed only while pulling sheets during the positioning. This indicates the accuracy of their settings. If the press

has a conventional dampener and stands for an appreciable time, apply extra water to the dampeners to compensate for water loss due to evaporation. When the press is stopped, the plate cylinder gap must be opposite the dampeners. If downtime will exceed fifteen minutes, gum the plate. If downtime exceeds one hour, place the plate under asphaltum., or follow the plate manufacturer's instructions

The Feeder

After the feeder is set, check the contour of the pile. It should be as flat and level as possible. Very heavy ink coverage across the tail end of a sheet will cause the sheet to curl. All of the sheets will curl the same way. Rolling out the curl while the pile is loaded in the press or on the skid may produce a reasonably flat pile at the tail end of the sheet. However, the back end may be higher than the front end of the pile. If the difference is not too great, the sheet advancing devices will still function properly. Automatic sheet decurlers use vacuum to decurl the stack while the press is running.

As the pile gets smaller, the front of the pile will reach a level higher than the recommended height. Therefore, the press operator should constantly monitor the feeder when running a pile that has been manipulated into proper contour.

Wedges may be used to bring the top or corners of the pile to correct height. The position of the wedges and the depth of their insertion will have to be adjusted constantly while the press is running, to prevent misfeeds. Do not allow wedges to get caught in the press as a result of working loose or reaching the top of the pile. Adjustable feeders that bring the gripper edge of the pile to the recommended height will have to be changed as the pile runs down.

Monitor forwarding devices to ensure that the original position has not been altered. These devices may require some adjusting if the sheets are not perfectly trimmed and flat. Observe the action of the side guide. The gripper and tail ends of the sheet should not buckle or bounce. Ensure that the tail brushes, drive-up wheels, and balls are functioning properly.

Side-guide register marks should print half off the sheet. This mark should be put on the plate at exactly that point where the side-guide edge of the sheet touches the side-guide faceplate. A mark placed at this point will always appear the same, even if the sheets are out-of-square. An elongated wedge-shaped mark at the side-guide edge makes checking even easier for register in both directions.

Inking and Dampening

The composition of the dampening solution is determined by experience, whether it be bought or formulated in the plant. The specific dampening solution must be compatible with the plate and ink. **Dampening solution pH** should range from 4.5 to 5.5, depending upon the plate etch. The term pH describes the acidity or alkalinity of a solution. It is represented by a scale that measures from 0.1 to 14.0; 7.0 is the neutral point. There are several ways of measuring pH. Indicator strips of litmus paper change color when immersed in the test solution. Each pH value corresponds to a specific color that identifies its acidity or alkalinity. These strips are fairly accurate, but their use is limited to solutions that don't mask the color of the dyes.

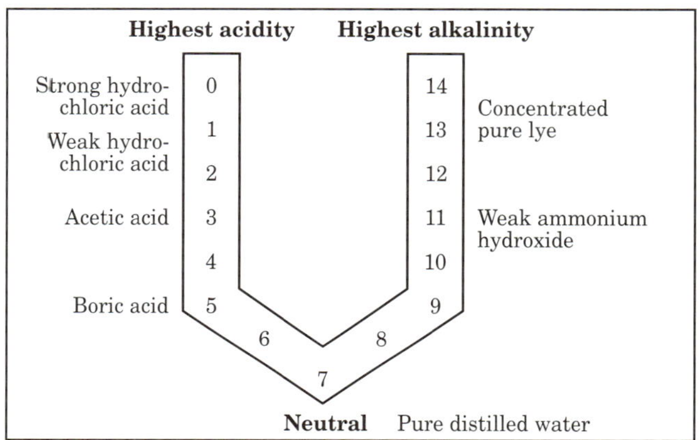

The pH scale.

Color comparators that measure pH may also be affected by solutions that mask the solutions used in the test. In addition to this limitation, the color comparator is somewhat cumbersome to use. Electronic pH meters operate with a self-contained battery. They are convenient for testing the press dampening solutions, which must be maintained at the proper pH during the pressrun.

Conductivity is a measure of the capacity of a material to conduct electricity. Extremely pure water is a poor electrical conductor. As materials dissolve or go into a solution, they form ions and the water becomes conductive. The conductivity of water increases directly with increases in the amount of dissolved matter (ions). Low (partially) ionizable materials such as alcohol and gum arabic are poor electrical conductors and usually lower dampening solution conductivity.

Pure water conductivity measures nearly 0 micromhos. Typical untreated tap water might have a

conductivity of 200 micromhos or more. As the amount of dissolved matter increases, the conductivity increases directly in a straight line. Thus, conductivity is commonly used as a measure of water purity. Soft water has a conductivity of 0–225 micromhos, and hard water has a conductivity greater than 450 micromhos. The relationship between water hardness and conductivity varies somewhat, depending upon the specific minerals and compounds in the water.

If the conductivity of different amounts of dampening solution concentrates in water is known, it is easy to measure the strength of a solution by measuring its conductivity. The following procedure can be used to develop a graph that plots conductivity and pH against concentration:

1. Measure the conductivity and pH of the water normally used to make the dampening solution. Place water in a clean 1-gal. (3.8-L) bottle.

2. Add 1 oz. (29.6 mL) of dampening solution concentrate. Remeasure conductivity and pH, and record these values.

3. Add another ounce (2 oz. total) of dampening solution concentrate, and remeasure conductivity and pH. Repeat this process until the amount of dampening solution concentrate exceeds the manufacturer's recommendations.

4. Plot these values on a graph that has concentration (oz./gal. or mL/L) on the horizontal axis and conductivity and pH on the vertical axis. A similar graph can be developed if alcohol is used in the dampening solution. New graphs must be made whenever the water or dampening solution concentrate changes. If the conductivity of the dampening solution is known, the amount of either dampening solution concentrate or alcohol can be read directly from the graph.

The most important factor in preparing dampening solution is to make sure that it is the proper concentration. Most acidic dampening solutions are buffered so that, as the amount of concentration increases, the pH drops initially but then levels off, while the solution's conductivity increases in a straight line. Thus, conductivity more accurately indicates the amount of concentrate in the dampening solution. However, pH must still be measured, because the pH must be between 4.0 and 5.5 for good printing.

With neutral dampening solutions and neutral (pH 7) water, the pH of the solution is constant, regardless of the concentration. Therefore, conductivity must be used to measure the concentration of neutral or slightly alkaline dampening solutions. Unusual conductivity readings justify rechecking the conductivity of the water and the dampening solution concentrate. Conductivity normally increases during the pressrun, because materials from the ink and paper contaminate the dampening solution. Therefore, conductivity measurements should be made before the dampening solution is used on press.

Ink/water balance describes the appropriate amounts of ink and water required to ink image areas of the plate and keep nonimage areas clean. Optimum ink film thickness on a sheetfed press ranges from 0.2 to 0.4 mil. (1 mil equals 0.001 in.) For web presses, ink film thickness should range from 0.3 to 0.6 mil.

The design of the job may require heavier ink coverage in specific areas. On multicolor presses, print heavier ink films successively to ensure proper trapping.

Running a tacky ink extremely thin and with little water may cause picking. Heavy ink coverage requires additional water. However, too much ink and water cause dot gain.

Ink agitation is required to maintain ink in a liquid state. Since lithographic ink is more like a plastic than a liquid, it will not flow without being worked. Putting the ink in the fountain and spreading it with the spatula while turning the fountain roller makes it flow. The ink is further worked by agitating it with the ink spatula while the press is running. This agitation also prevents skinning and keeps the ink up against the fountain roller. Never permit an ink fountain to run nearly dry.

Ink agitators automatically and continuously work ink in the fountain. Automatically activated pumps maintain the ink level in the fountain. These pumps eliminate the need to manually ink the press during long runs.

Ink skin and foreign matter must be removed from the ink fountain. Maintain absolute cleanliness in the inking system. Do not allow any ink skin, foreign particles, or abrasive materials to get into the fountain. Ink skin will form around the top edge of a previously opened ink can. When emptying the ink can into the fountain, the operator must be absolutely certain that no ink skin contaminates the fountain. Another possible source of ink skin is the fountain. Some ink may dry on the back end of the blade or on the faces of the side blocks. When agitating the fountain by hand, the operator should not scrape any of this dried ink into the ink supply.

Emulsification is the process by which one material becomes suspended in another. Water emulsifies into ink, and ink emulsifies into water. Some emulsification is desirable, but too much emulsifi-

cation waterlogs the ink and produces a poor print. Ink will not properly transfer between rollers and plate, between plate and blanket, and between blanket and paper. Once the ink becomes waterlogged, the press must be washed up, and the ink in the fountain thrown away.

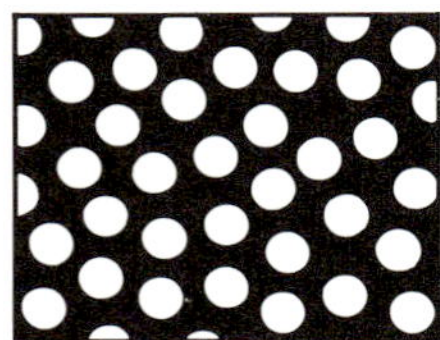

Water-in-ink

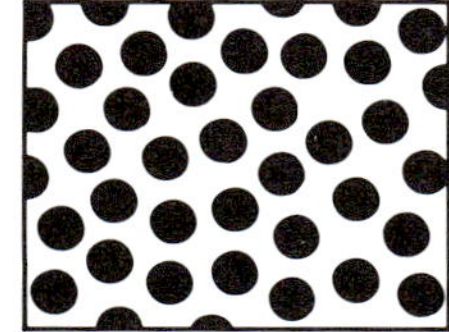

Ink-in-water

Two forms of emulsification.

To avoid this, feed a minimum amount of water to keep nonimage areas clean. Water-in-ink emulsification may not be noticed for some time. If the print begins to gray, most press operators automatically increase the ink flow. If the print begins to look fat and mushy, most press operators automatically increase the water flow. Each of these changes only serves to compound the original fault; a perfectly good plate image may be irreparably damaged before emulsification is noticed.

Excessive ink-in-water emulsification, which is usually caused by poorly matched ink and dampening solution results in tinting on the plate. Sometimes, tinting is mistaken for scumming and the flow of water increased, which aggravates the condition. **Scumming** results when the nonimage areas of the plate accept ink from the rollers. **Tinting** is a deposit of water into ink which has been emulsified, or ink pigment has deposited itself as a result of the action of the dampening solution on the ink. Surface-active materials in the paper may also cause this condition.

If a plate is tinting, the tint can be wiped off with a light touch of the finger or sponge. However, one revolution of the press *with the dampeners on* retints the same area. Scum cannot be wiped from the plate easily. When it is wiped off, it will not recur immediately unless ink contacts a dry plate.

When tinting occurs with a conventional dampening system, remove the three covered rollers and thoroughly rinse them in clear water. Empty and rinse the water pan, and clean the oscillating roller as recommended by the manufacturer. If the press starts up again with a different dampening solution and the tinting soon comes back, test the paper for the presence of surface-active material.

Automatic ink fountain controls regulate ink flow to the rollers. The press operator attains the desired color and ink/water balance. This balance is usually attained by using a reflection densitometer, which measures the density of the ink film on a reference block of the solid color printed in the trim area of the sheet. A scanning device reads the density of a target block and compares the readings on the printed sheets with the desired reading established by the press operator when the run started. Through the hookup to the fountain keys, ink feed increases or decreases automatically.

Printing Defects

Hickeys and spots are printing defects caused by particles that stick to the plate or blanket. Under magnification, hickeys look somewhat like doughnuts in reverse, although they are not always round. Once they appear, they repeat on sheet after sheet in the same places and increase in numbers as the run progresses.

Hickeys are caused by solid, ink-receptive particles that stick to the blanket or plate and do not transfer to the paper. It takes a washup to get rid of them, but unless their source is removed, they recur when the run is resumed.

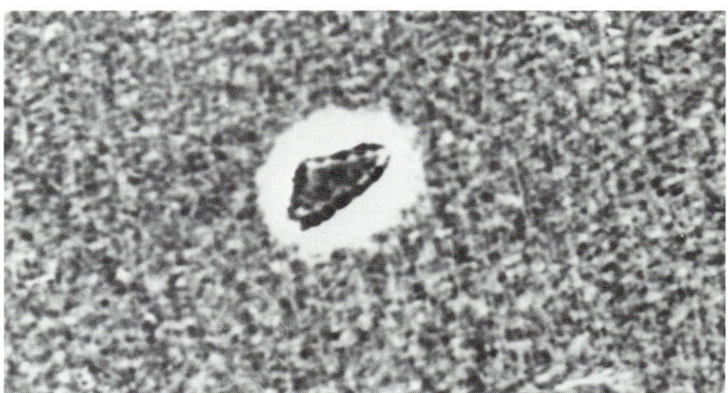

Ink skin hickey.

White spots in the image areas may be caused by particles or fibers stuck to the blanket or plate. They differ from ink-receptive hickeys in that they are water-receptive. In fact, some particles start out printing as hickeys, but as they become saturated with water the solid center spot tends to fade out and disappear.

Locate the sheet on which the hickey first appeared, and examine the spot under a magnifying glass or microscope. The main sources of particles that cause hickeys and spots are ink and paper. A dirty press, a dirty ceiling, or deteriorating rollers

are other sources. Hickeys caused by dried ink, or skin, can usually be recognized by their shape and appearance. An irregularly shaped spot with sharp edges appears inside a ring. The edges are also slightly denser than the center. Ink skin hickeys appear the same on succeeding sheets.

Locate the particle on the blanket or plate; pick it off with tape, and examine it under a microscope. Feel it with a needle; an ink skin hickey is soft and pliable, with no fibers present.

Once the particles are identified, the only thing to do is to wash up the press, discard the ink, and load the fountain with a fresh, skin-free batch of ink.

Paper particles are second to ink as a source of hickeys. They can produce hickeys as well as several kinds of spots. More knowledge and experience are necessary to identify the defects in paper that cause them. These defects are as follows:

- **Paper dust** forms when paper is slit and cut to sheet size in the mill. Some of this dust gets between the sheets. Most mills attempt to eliminate this dust by means of compressed air or vacuum. However, even if only one or two particles remain on each sheet, printing a thousand sheets can produce numerous hickeys and spots.
- **Picking** is the lifting of the paper surface by the ink. Small areas of surface fibers or coating are sometimes picked, usually in the solid areas. These fibers stick to the blanket or plate and produce hickeys or spots that repeat sheet after sheet.

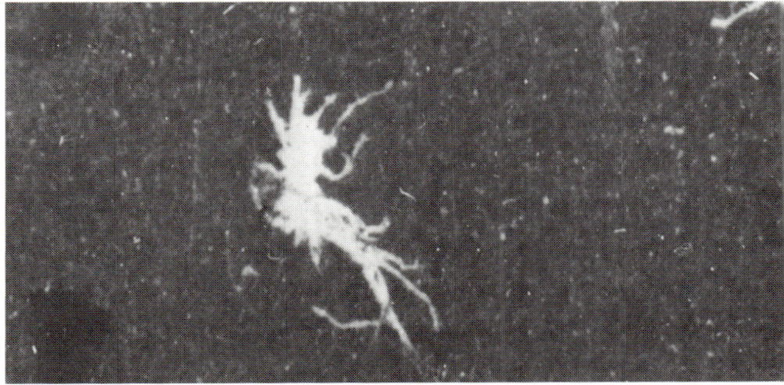

Paper that has been picked.

- **Lint, fuzz, or whiskers** result from slitting or sheeting, which sometimes releases individual fibers. These fibers become trapped between sheets. Lint, however, is usually caused by loosely bonded paper fibers. It is usually worse on the wire side than on the felt side. Ink pulls these fibers out of the sheet. They quickly become saturated with water, refuse to take fresh ink, and leave white images of themselves in the printed work. They are most apparent in solids.
- **Holes in the paper surface** result from air bubbles that form in the fiber furnish when the paper is made, or bubbles in the coating mix when the paper is coated. These holes are deep enough to prevent the blanket from depositing ink in them. Spots due to such holes occur on only one sheet and do not repeat.

Spots caused by slitter and cutter dust can be any shape from that of individual fibers to that of slivers. On the original sheet, the spot appears white and shows no evidence of picking. On succeeding sheets, the spot will be a hickey. However, the center spot appears gray or tinted, not solid. The spot lightens on succeeding sheets. This phenomenon and the absence of a sharp edge around the center spot distinguishes paper dust from ink skin.

Ink may also pick coating from the paper surface. These spots take on many shapes. Examine the sheet where the spot first appeared. Observe that the surface was picked. Hickeys appear on succeeding sheets, but their center spot lacks the sharp edge of an ink-skin hickey and prints lighter on succeeding sheets as the fibers become soaked.

Particles from other sources can also produce hickeys. Dust may fall from overhead pipes and ductwork. Clean and paint ceilings at regular intervals. Clean press parts at least once a week. They must be kept free from oil and grease that can accumulate dust and antisetoff spray or powder.

Shedding dampener covers can cause fiber-shaped spots. These appear the same as spots caused by lint or fuzz, but are much longer, since the dampener fibers are cotton. Newly covered dampeners, if not thoroughly washed before installation, can cause these spots. Old dampener covers may rot and shed fibers.

Achieving Color

Maintaining proper color and determining the amount of ink that will produce that color on the sheet require considerable judgment and expertise. Desensitize the plate by using the techniques recommended by the plate manufacturer. Include a wet-wash as described previously.

The color strength of the ink affects its printed appearance. Running excessive ink to compensate for a weak color may produce a heavier image than originally produced on the plate. At first, the job may look fine. As the run progresses, the appearance will gradually spread. When this happens, the plate has suffered damage and it cannot be brought back to its original degree of sharpness. If this is a full-color job, the finished product will show up as a

finished piece with the particular color too dark. Running a black-and-white job this way will produce poorly printed results. An entire book printed this way will vary from page to page as the binder gathers the first sheets from one signature with later sheets from other signatures.

When a plate is excessively inked, it is difficult to run clean. To eliminate this problem, run an ink with stronger color or better covering capability. Color blocks and various target and tint patterns in the trim margins of the sheet are read with a reflection densitometer. As the job is running, sheets pulled from the press are read with the instrument and checked against the recorded readings of the OK sheet. Some of the target and tint patterns are designed so that print quality factors, other than ink film thickness, can be either instrumentally measured or visually evaluated.

Preventing Setoff

Setoff is the undesirable ink transfer from a sheet in the delivery pile to the successively delivered sheet. Excessive ink film thickness contributes to setoff. The optimum ink film thickness that does not pick the paper or cause dot gain may still setoff where two or more colors overprint. The most effective way to counteract setoff is to spray **antisetoff spray powder** on each sheet in the delivery pile. Use just enough spray powder to prevent setoff.

The printed sheets must be carefully piled and jogged. Some jobs cannot be piled too high. This is especially true with varnishes, metallic inks, and high-gloss inks. Wind drying lifts in order to prevent them from sticking together.

Certain inks permit piling to full capacity but require winding shortly after delivery. During drying, some inks generate considerable heat. This process may cause sheets to stick or change color. Prevent this by constant and careful winding during the drying period.

Jog sheets without damaging the edges, especially if they have to be run through the press again. Damaged paper complicates finishing (e.g., folding, cutting, and binding). Before a job leaves the pressroom, properly flag and identify it.

Multicolor Printing

The ultimate full-color (process) printing results are attained by dry trapping colors. However, modern techniques, materials, and equipment produce high-quality printing with wet traps.

Register

Registration is the aligning of two or more printed images on the same page. Registration methods are no different on multicolor work than on black-and-white work. Color register, however, is more critical. Images must register within small tolerance.

Printing multicolor work on single-color presses complicates registration; the sheets feed through the press several times. They are more likely to develop mutilated gripper edges. They also do not stack as well on the pile feeder. Presses with two or more units print the sheet in fewer passes; however, it is more difficult to synchronize a press with two or more units and register each perfectly.

Fit

Fit describes the printed image size relative to the original image size. Ideally, the two image sizes match. However, this is not always the case. Fit is considerably affected by multicolor printing. Sheet distortion due to change in moisture content of the sheet is one of lithography's most difficult problems. Multicolor presses alleviate this problem by putting down two or more colors within a short time; the sheet has no opportunity to give or take up any appreciable amount of moisture. If the stock is kept in moisture-proof wrappings until it is put on the press, even unconditioned stock running in a nonconditioned plant will hold size satisfactorily. If the sheet is going through the press more than once, protect the stock between printings.

In multicolor work, the first color down must register and fit perfectly. Check the fit of the first color by comparing the image size on the first plate with the printed image size on the sheet. A register rule will show the amount of error. Numerous remedies include shifting the packing, bowing the stops, or deforming the sheet contour on the feedboard to attain fit within narrow limits. Condition wavy- or tight-edged stock before it is run through the press. Test the temperature and moisture balance of the stock *before* the wrappings are removed.

Trapping

Trapping describes the ability of a wet or dry printed ink film to accept a subsequently applied

wet ink film. Two prime factors that affect trapping are the paper's absorbing characteristics and the relative tack of the superimposed inks.

An inkmaker with adequate stock samples can recommend the proper ink vehicle. The Inkometer accurately determines ink tack before it goes to press. Printers should not alter an ink without the inkmaker's approval. Ink traps best when each succeeding color has less tack than the preceding one.

Counter-Etching

Previously printed colors may contaminate succeeding colors. This problem applies almost entirely to multicolor printing with wet traps. The inking and dampening form rollers contact the plate's image and nonimage areas; the blanket also contacts these areas of the plate; the paper contacts the image and nonimage areas of the blanket.

An unprinted sheet feeds through a two-color press until it reaches the first unit. Here, the first image transfers from the blanket to the paper. Then, the printed sheet passes to the second unit where it again presses against a blanket. Since full-color image elements do not always completely superimpose on each other, part of the first image presses against areas of the blanket that correspond to nonimage areas of the second plate. Some ink *always* transfers from the paper to the blanket. When this second blanket contacts its plate, the ink from the preceding impression presses against nonimage areas of the second plate.

The blanket affects the plate differently than the ink rollers. The inking form rollers *roll* against the plate without too much pressure. The blanket cylinder is squeezed against the plate with tremendous pressure. The plate also compresses the blanket, which may bring about a change in surface speed.

Variation in surface speeds between the plate and blanket surfaces causes a rubbing action. Even a slight rubbing action greatly affects the plate; the ink transferred from the first impression grinds into the second plate. If the second plate begins to hold the ink from the first image, it is said to be *counter-etched* by the first image. The water-receptive layer on the nonimage area of the plate has broken down and becomes ink receptive and prints a scum of the second color on the first.

There are three factors that contribute to good reproduction under these conditions. Inkmakers formulate inks that do not lift off when laid on the paper or over previously printed inks.

Plate research has led to the development of plates with nonimage areas that will not break down. Knowledge of dampening allows press operators to better adapt the composition of the dampening solution, as well as its pH and conductivity to the particular ink, paper, and plate.

Production planning allows the results of a multicolor job to be predicted. Do not manipulate the ink to change tone or color that was photographed in the original color separation negative. Rather, shoot the negative to produce the desired tones and colors as can be derived from the ink to be run.

The press operator adjusts ink density to match the color proof. If the multicolor job is running on a single-color press, the press operator can only adjust one color at a time. Each color should match the corresponding separation. Previously printed colors cannot be corrected. During multicolor printing on a multicolor press, any or all colors can be corrected at the same time.

Printing a test form that contains different screens and solids will show the reproduction capabilities of the press. All preparatory steps should be planned according to these capabilities.

The Lithographic Web Press

A lithographic web offset press prints on a continuous roll of paper or other substrate feeding from a roll. The operation of web offset equipment differs from that of sheetfed presses, although the general principles and practices of cylinder pressures, plate handling, blankets, inking, and dampening are practically identical.

The web press requires a **roll stand** at the infeed that holds one or more rolls. **Sheeters** cut the web and deliver flat, printed sheets. **Folders** cut the web into sections and fold them into signatures. **Rewinders** wind the web back into a roll. Some

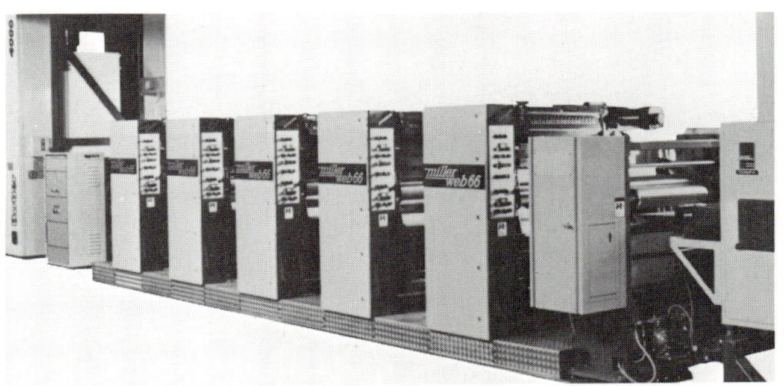

Five-unit web press.

presses also have in-line finishing devices at the delivery end. Another significant difference of the web press contrasted with a sheetfed is that the web press has much smaller plate and blanket cylinder gaps, giving a much more continuous flow of ink and water.

The Blanket-to-Blanket Press

A **printing couple** includes an inking system, a dampening system, a plate cylinder, a blanket cylinder, and (usually) an impression cylinder. In a blanket-to-blanket press, printing couples are usually stacked in pairs. One is above the other, with the web running between them. This permits simultaneous printing on both sides of the web (i.e., **perfecting**) with each blanket giving impression pressure to the other.

These printing units of two couples each are usually arranged one after the other. All sorts of webbings for various purposes are possible with a multiunit blanket-to-blanket press. A four-unit press (eight printing couples) can print four colors on each side of the web.

Various configurations allow several rolls to print simultaneously on a single press by passing one roll through each unit or combination of units.

The Common-Impression-Cylinder Press

Each printing unit on a common-impression-cylinder (CIC) press has one very large impression cylinder with four or five printing couples arranged around it.

A CIC press can perfect by having two impression cylinder units (separated by dryer and chill rolls), each with their separate color-printing couples. The web flips over between the first-unit and second-unit printings.

Another means for perfecting is called *double-ending*. This method uses half-width webs. The web is printed on one side by running through one side of the press. It then goes through the dryer and chill rollers, flips over in a turning bay, and returns to the other side of the printing unit for printing the other side.

The Press Infeed

The infeed controls the speed, tension, and lateral position of the web up to the first printing unit. It consists mainly of a roll stand and a series of rollers carrying the web into the first unit.

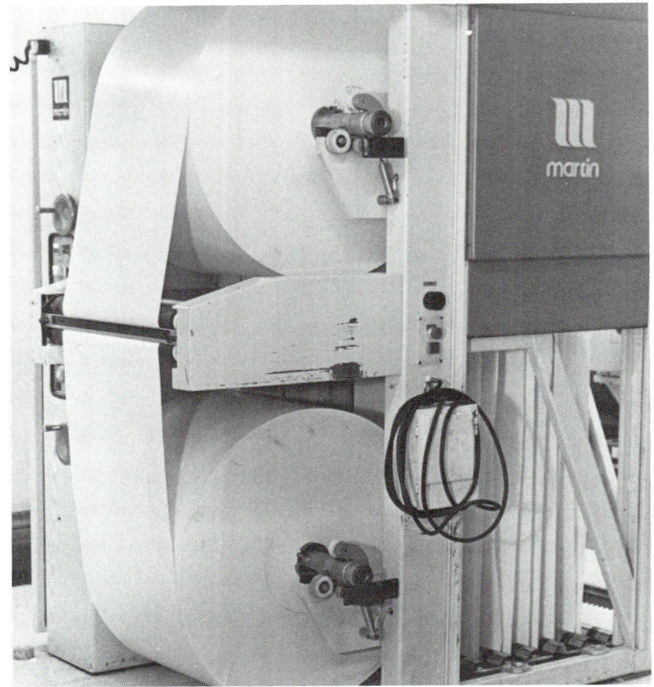

Festoon with zero-speed splicer.

Presses that accept more than one web at a time have double-roll stands, supplemented as needed by auxiliary roll stands, usually also with double-roll capacity.

Rate of paper feed is controlled by a dancer roller that actuates a roll brake to the extent needed. The dancer roller rides in a loop in the web. As the rate of roll feed varies, the web loop changes in size and the dancer, moving with it, applies more or less braking action.

A device between the dancer and the first printing unit, often a steel driven roller and a rubber nondriven roller, controls the web and keeps it taut and flat as it enters the printing unit.

The roll stand used on most web presses has an automatic splicer that splices the new roll to the expiring roll without stopping the press. The flying paster splices the paper at operating, although somewhat reduced, speed. The zero-speed splicer joins the rolls while the paper is stationary; however, the press continues to print by drawing from a festoon of paper that accumulates prior to splicing.

Dryer and Chill Rolls

A web press needs a dryer and chill rolls when heatset inks are printed. Newspaper and forms printers often use the quickest and most absorptive inks that do not require drying and chilling.

Blanket-to-blanket heatset presses require floating dryers, because the web has ink on both sides. It is supported by tension and the effects of air in the dryer. Heat is applied by high-velocity hot air.

Chill rolls, following the dryer, are driven steel drums with circulating cold water. Circulating water through a closed system minimizes mineral deposits that impair chilling efficiency.

Press operators should recognize that if the dryer/chill roll system does not prevent smearing in the folder section, the problem is not necessarily caused by insufficient dryer heat. The chill rolls may not be cold enough to harden the resins.

Delivery

Web offset presses are usually equipped to deliver a folded signature. One or more folders may be employed. Folds parallel to the grain are made by a former or chopper fold. Folds across the web, at right angles to the grain, are made by a jaw folder.

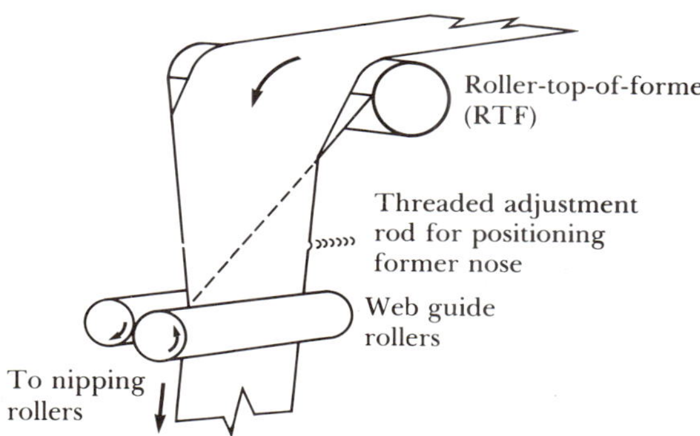

Former folder.

A **former folder** has a triangular metal former board. The web is pulled over its nose. This folds the web in the direction of web travel. The former fold is usually followed by other folds.

A **jaw folder** flows the paper around a cylinder and tucks it into the jaws of a second cylinder by means of a tucker blade from the first cylinder. A knife cuts the signature away from the web. A second jaw fold provides a double parallel fold.

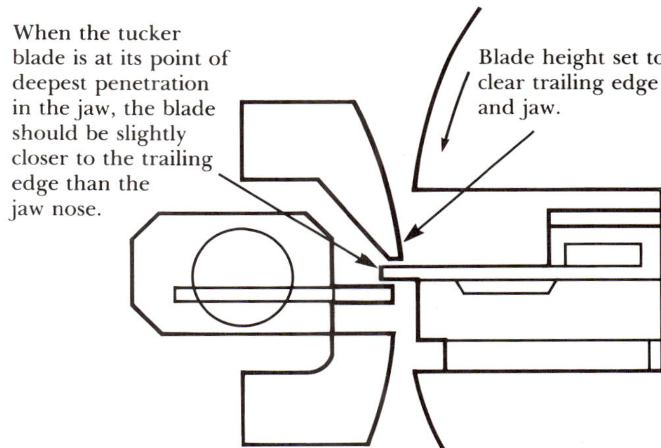

Jaw folder.

A **chopper folder** provides the last fold. The signature is conveyed from the jaw folder in a horizontal plane with the folded edge forward. It passes under a blade that pushes the signature under two rotary folding rollers. The backbone fold parallels the paper grain.

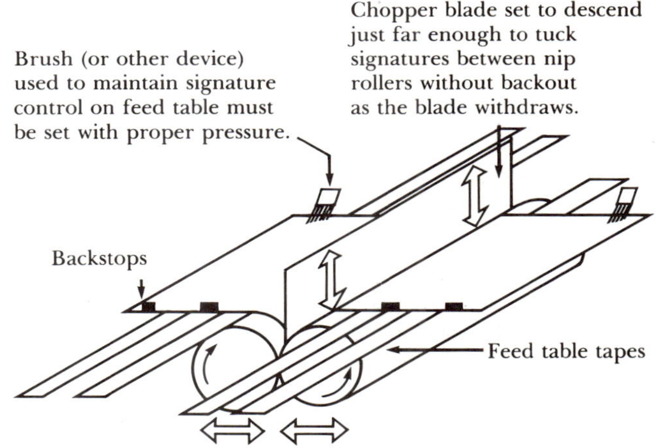

Chopper folder.

Chapter 16

Binding and Finishing

Introduction to Binding and Finishing

Binding and finishing is the final stage in creating a printed product. The work required for turning printed sheets or webs of paper into books, magazines, catalogs, and booklets is classified as **binding.** The specialized production of displays, labels, tags, packaging, and a variety of other advertising materials is classified as **finishing.** Embossing, stamping, and other decorative touches used to enhance a book's design also fall into the finishing category. Binding and finishing may be completed at a single facility or by separate suppliers of specific services. Some printers have in-line binding or finishing units attached to their presses; some purchase and use dedicated binding and finishing machinery; others rely on the services of outside firms.

Planning for Binding and Finishing

To successfully create a printed job, its production must be carefully planned and executed. Prepress (design, type or imagesetting, photography, and platemaking), presswork, and postpress (binding and finishing) are so interdependent and overlapping that the success of the final step in the production process is largely dependent on the amount of planning that took place in the early stages of the job. For example, the designer should learn all about the press on which the job will be printed; if he or she is limited in choices of paper and ink; how many colors may be used; what binding and finishing operations the job requires; and whether or not the final piece will be handled excessively. Ideally, binding and finishing procedures should be discussed before the initial design is even determined.

Imposition concerns. As the job moves into the film assembly area, the stripper must examine various layouts and dummies that will help in coordinating the different phases of **imposition,** or placing the elements on the film flat so that the job will fold correctly. The **mechanical layout,** provided by the designer, shows the general appearance and arrangement of job elements. The **imposition layout,** prepared by the stripping or binding areas, is a guide that indicates how images should be assembled on a sheet. It verifies the page sequence, margins, trims, fold marks, and cutting and scoring lines. If the job is to be printed on both sides, it must also ensure that the images on each side of the press sheet are aligned with each other.

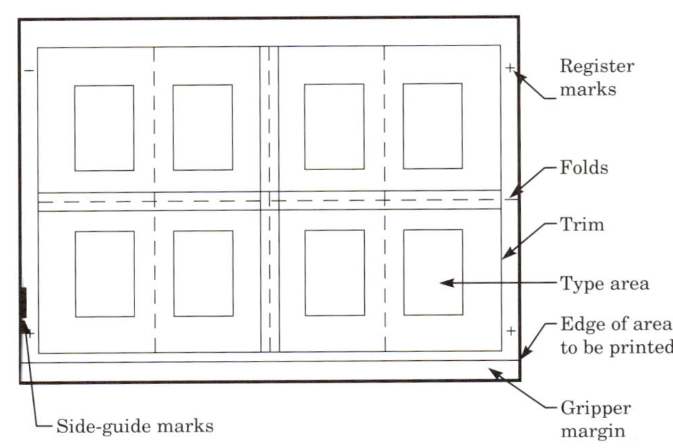

Sample imposition layout.

A **folding dummy** is a blank press-size sheet of the paper specified for the job that has been folded and marked with **folios** (page numbers) to show how the pages should be arranged as well as two Xs indicating the **gripper** (lead) edge and one X indicating the **side-guide** edge. This dummy is also

used to determine which sides of each page require single- and double-trim allowances. The **binding dummy** is very similar to the folding dummy, but it has been stitched and trimmed to demonstrate how much of the margin is lost after binding and to show the compensation needed for the outward **creep** or **thrust** of the inner pages of saddle-stitched jobs.

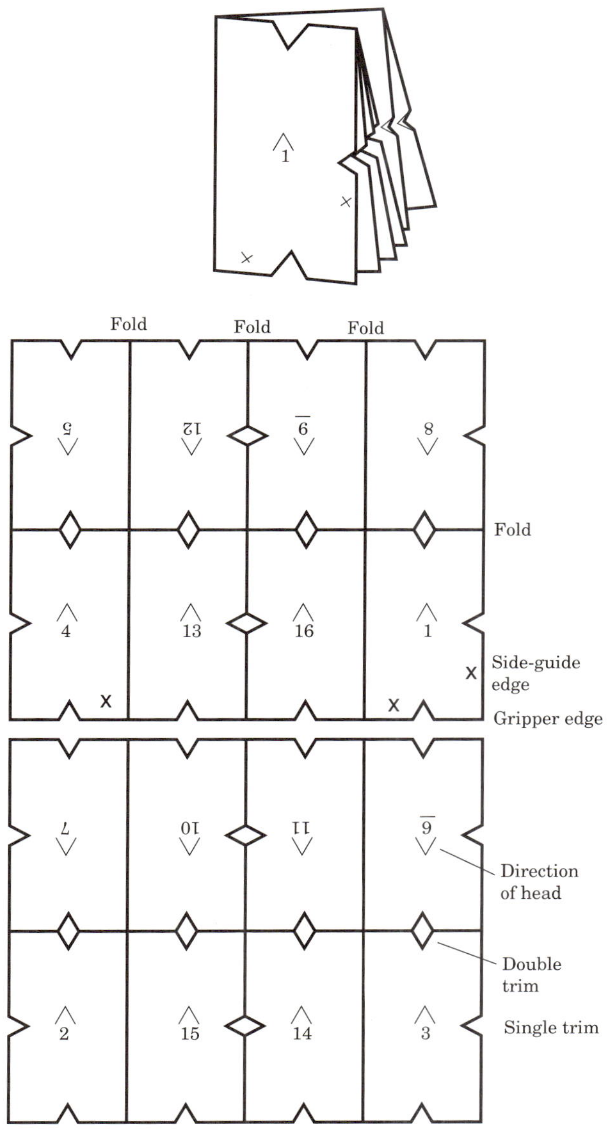

Folded dummy and open sixteen-page sheetwise layout.

The pressroom and bindery must convey information about the **press imposition layout** to the film assembly area before stripping and platemaking can take place. In lithography, standard press imposition layouts (one-up, one-side multiple, one-side combination, sheetwise, work-and-turn, and work-and-tumble) are classified as sheetfed layouts, but can also be run on web presses. The layout chosen depends on the requirements of the job and the press on which it will be run.

Simple **one-up**, single-image, single-sided **impositions** are usually prepared for smaller presses while one-side multiple, or **two-up, impositions** in which two identical images are exposed from the same negative onto a plate with step-and-repeat equipment are used on larger presses. **One-side combination layouts** combine several different forms (pages) on the same plate. This layout is sometimes referred to as a **gang-run layout.**

The **sheetwise imposition,** in which separate film flats and plates are used to print the front and back of a single press sheet, is the most common layout. The stock is run once through the press to print one side of the sheet, then the sheets are turned over and printed with a different image on the other side. The sheetwise layout is also used to illustrate imposition on the folding dummy.

With a **work-and-turn imposition format,** all of the images to print on both sides of the press sheet are exposed to the same plate. The images are placed in such a way that the same gripper and side guide edges of the paper are used to register the sheet when it passes through the press twice.

The front and back pages are also imaged on the same plate in the **work-and-tumble layout,** but the tail end of the sheet becomes the gripper or lead edge when the second side is printed.

Paper Considerations

How well a job reproduces on press and withstands folding and other binding and finishing requirements is determined, in part, by the paper, or other substrate, specified during the planning stage. The paper size chosen should be based on a sheet or web size that the press on which the job will be run can accept. Other concerns include the size and number of pages to be printed on the form and the maximum sheet size that the folder can accept, if the job will not be folded in-line.

Paper basis weight, the weight in pounds of a ream (500 sheets) of paper cut to a basic size, and **grain direction,** or the direction of the fibers that compose a sheet or roll of paper, are two more issues to consider in the planning stage. Basis weight is important in determining the number of folds per signature, because lighter papers can accommodate more folds than heavier papers. In addition, a job

should be planned so that the grain direction runs parallel to the binding edge. Otherwise, the paper will tend to buckle and crack at the spine and the pages will be stiffer and more difficult to turn. If paper with a heavier basis weight is used, the press operator will probably run the grain parallel to the axis of the press cylinder to improve results. This might conflict with binding requirements.

Folding endurance, the number of double folds a paper will withstand before breaking under tension, is another factor that must always be considered when planning a printed job. The folding endurance of different papers covers a wide range but generally is greater when the sheet is folded against the grain. Folding endurance is a good indicator of the permanence and durability of paper.

Guillotine Cutters

Guillotine cutters are used to square blank sheets before printing and separate printed sheets before binding. These machines are available in a number of models and sizes, but all have several similar components: a knife, cutting stick, table, side and back gauges, and a clamp.

The cutter's long, heavy knife, which is bolted to a bar mounted near the front of the machine, descends to the bed, slicing through a stack of paper. The knife angle is determined by the characteristics of the material to be cut. Different knives are manufactured for materials of varying hardness.

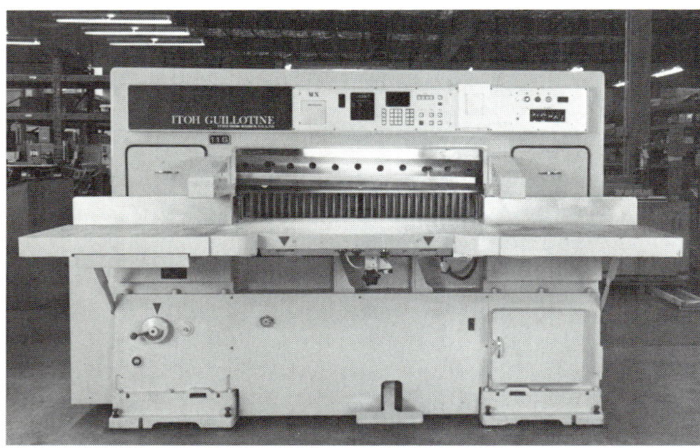

Courtesy LDR International

Itoh guillotine paper cutter.

Another important cutter component, the **cutting stick,** is inserted into a groove on the cutter table immediately beneath the cutting knife. Were it not for the cutting stick, the knife would become dull easily or even break because it would hit the metal cutting table every time it sliced through a pile of sheets.

Side and **back gauges** position sheets accurately under the knife, squaring them before cutting. The side gauges are stationary, while the back gauge can be moved to accommodate various cutoff lengths. A back gauge that is divided into two or more segments is called a **split gauge.**

The **cutter clamp** is a metal bar that runs parallel to the knife and, like it, is placed at a 90° angle to the table. It has two functions: to expel air from the pile of sheets prior to cutting and to hold the pile firmly in place during the process.

Auxiliary equipment. Automated flow systems for paper handling are among the most common add-ons to the cutter area. They enhance ergonomics while also improving productivity. A **jogger** may be used in-line with the cutter, off-line in conjunction with folding machines to jog the stock before it is loaded into folders, or in the pressroom to load printed jobs onto skids for delivery to the bindery. It squeezes air from between the sheets before cutting and tilts to align the sheets against the side-register guides.

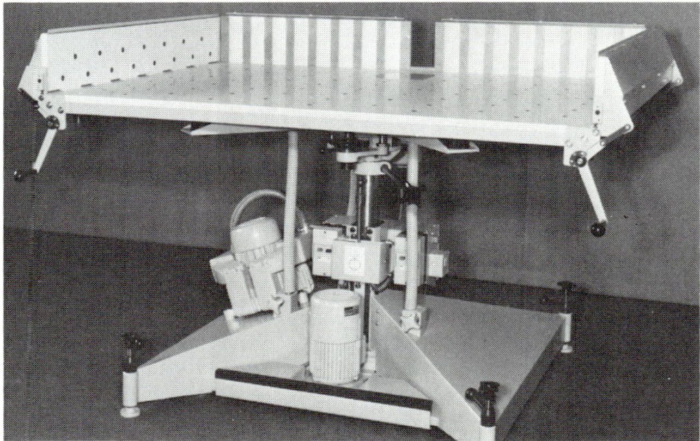

Courtesy Vijuk Bindery Equipment Co.

Paper jogger.

Lifting tables have sensors that identify the height of a pile and load and position it on the cutter. After cutting, the pile is off-loaded to another air table on the other side of the cutter and restacked on a skid. A **vertical storage system** uses air boards to lift and store as many as five or ten piles upright in the same square footage that a horizontal storage system uses to hold one pile.

Folding

Jobs that require folding include pamphlets, maps, brochures, magazines, and books. After printing, the sheets are folded into **signatures** that may consist of four pages, eight pages, sixteen pages, or some other multiple of two. These jobs are said to be **folded to print.** Press sheets with printing on only one side of the form are **folded to paper** because backup register is not a consideration.

Machine folding employs one of two basic folds: a right-angle or a parallel fold. The **right-angle fold** is made by first folding the sheet in half and then rotating it and folding it in half again. Additional right-angle folds follow this sequence. One fold makes four pages, two folds make eight pages, and three folds make sixteen pages, etc. A basic **parallel fold** is made by folding a sheet of paper twice so that the two folds are made in the same direction. For example, a sheet could be folded in half and then, with the paper in the same position, folded in half again. A variety of configurations can be made from right-angle and parallel folds, including accordion folds, signature folds, gate or panel folds, over-and-over folds, French folds, and letter folds.

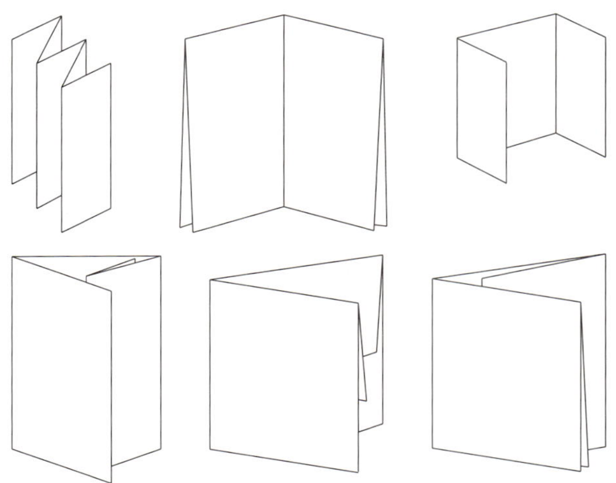

Some common folds: accordion, 8-page signature, gate, over-and-over, French (heads in), and letter.

Folding is completed on a buckle folder, a knife folder, or a combination folder, which incorporates features of buckle and knife folders in one machine.

Knife folders. Knife folding machines have individual folding units constructed in three or four levels and arranged in sequence at right angles to each preceding unit. They are designed to execute right-angle folds such as those required to produce book signatures. Printers and binders specializing in folding large sheets usually use knife folders.

After the feeder carries the sheet to the folding station, moving tapes convey it into the first fold level, where it is stopped by a gauge, positioned against a side guide. The actual knife then descends vertically and drives the sheet between two counter-revolving rollers. As the sheet passes through the rollers, it is nipped and the fold is formed. The folded sheet descends to the next level, where canvas tapes convey it to the next fold station and the process is repeated until the sheet is folded the desired number of times.

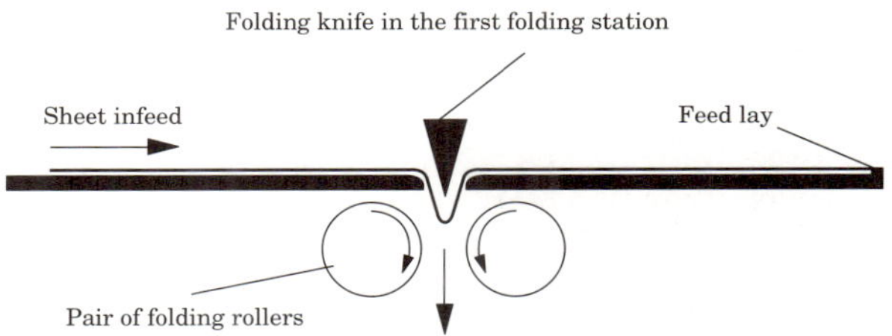

Knife folding.

The jobber, the double-sixteen, and the quadruple are three designs of knife folders. Each differs in its configuration and the jobs it can accomplish. The **jobber folder** has four folding levels and one or two parallel sections. This allows the production of up to four right-angle folds; two right-angle folds with a third fold parallel to the second; or three right-angle folds with a fourth fold parallel to the third. The jobber is the most popular knife folder because it is so flexible.

The **double-sixteen folder** is designed to produce two sixteen-page units separately, or inserted to make a single thirty-two-page unit. Adding a double-thirty-two-page section enables the production of two (smaller) thirty-two-page signatures. The double-sixteen is used mostly for publication work.

The **quadruple folder,** commonly called the quad, is designed to produce four sixteen-page units separately, or inserted to make two thirty-two-page units. The four units produced from a single sheet have closed heads. It is used mostly in edition (or case) binding, the process used to produce a thread-sewn hardcover book.

Buckle folders. The buckle folder is a versatile machine that can handle most folding assignments. Its individual folding stations are modular, meaning that new folding capabilities can be added to existing equipment. Buckle folders are used with lighter stocks and knife folders with heavier stocks. Most printers with binding equipment have at least one buckle folder. However, in Europe, the buckle folding mechaninsm is not accepted.

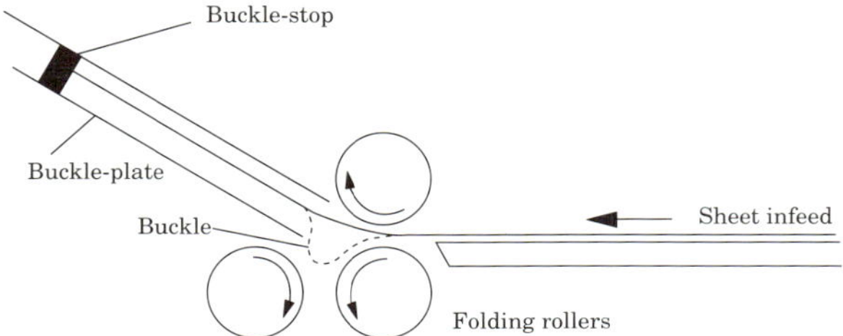

Buckle folding.

In **buckle folding,** diagonal rollers position the paper against the side guide and convey it to the folding mechanism. For each fold, two feed rollers push the sheet between two metal plates that are collectively called a fold plate. When the sheet encounters a stop placed in a preset position inside the fold plate, it begins to buckle at the entrance of the fold plate. The buckle is seized by and pulled between a third roller and the bottom feed roller. These two rollers act as the feed rollers to the next fold plate, which is inverted.

After the first fold, the sheets are carried from station to station on diagonal roller aligning tables. Each sheet is straightened and guided as it passes through. The sequence and number of folds are determined by the arrangement of folding units within the folding machine. Each folding station can hold up to six buckle plates. Buckle plates not required for a particular folding operation are bypassed by inserting sheet deflectors.

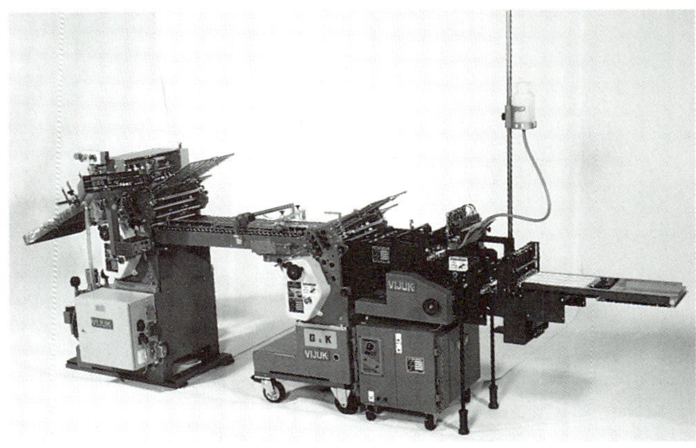

Courtesy Vijuk Bindery Equipment, Inc.

Folder.

Combination folders. The combination buckle plate/knife folder ("combi") integrates buckle and knife folding. Parallel folds are executed with buckle plates in the first folding station and subsequent right-angle folds are produced in the knife folder section. To create folds parallel to the first right-angle fold, buckle plates are also used. Conveyor tapes forward the sheets through the folder.

Combination machines are ideal for folding medium-size sheets, which often require a variety of different folds. They work well with heavier stock because the thick bulk does not have to pass through as many rollers, and paper grain direction is less of a problem.

Binding Methods

Contemporary binding is divided into four specialties: mechanical binding, adhesive or perfect binding, saddle- and side-wire stitching, and thread sewing, which involves casebinding.

Mechanical and Loose-leaf Bindings

In mechanical binding, wire or plastic coils, plastic combs, or metal rings are used to permanently join individual sheets of paper together as books or booklets, with the independent binding device often forming the backbone of the publication. The term **mechanical binding** is somewhat misleading because it is the least mechanized of all binding methods; however, in the days when most books were bound by hand, mechanical binding, with its semiautomatic aids, was a breakthrough.

Today, the category has been further broadened to include **loose-leaf bindings,** those methods of securing individual sheets in such a manner that the reader can alter the publication by adding or deleting pages at will. Like publications with mechanical bindings, loose-leaf publications have a series of round, square, or oblong holes drilled or punched through the side of the printed sheets.

Materials for both of these forms of binding are gathered, or collated, and trimmed on all four sides before the sheets are punched or drilled and joined

together. The size of the job determines whether machinery or manual methods of collating are used. In mechanical binding, two-piece covers may be collated with the text pages, while wrap-around covers

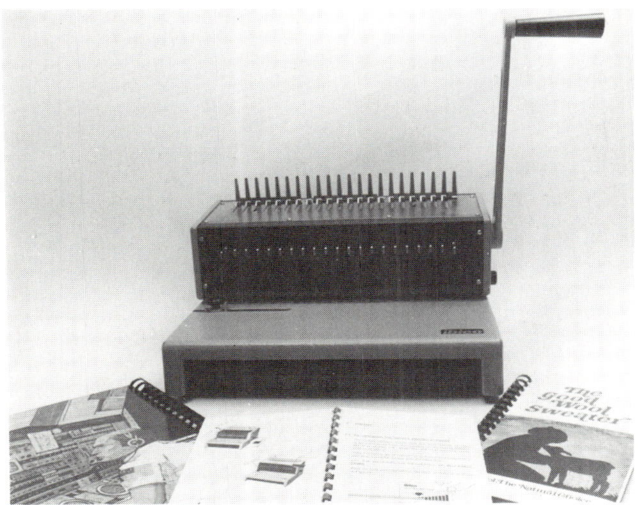

Courtesy Sprial Binding Co.
Kombo plastic binder and some of its products.

are added in a separate operation. Loose-leaf materials are always placed inside their durable binders after collating. The most important advantage of either of these binding methods is that the product lies open and flat without any appreciable strain on the backbone.

Wire and plastic mechanical bindings. To create a spiral mechanical binding with wire or plastic, a machine threads the materials through holes that have been drilled or punched in the side of a group of printed sheets. The edges of the plastic or metal binding material are then crimped on each end to secure the sheets as a single bound unit. Durable wire preformed in a spiral construction is available in various diameters. Elastic spiral coils that will not crush or crack when handled excessively are also popular.

Closed-ring and plastic strip-and-spike mechanisms are two other mechanical binding devices. **Closed-ring devices** consist of continuously connected parallel wire rings that are crimped shut by a closing die after they have been inserted through the holes punched in the side of the sheets. On **plastic-strip mechanisms,** the spikes or posts attached to the strip are driven through the holes in the sheets and attached to another strip at the bottom of the pile. With any of these independent binding devices, new pages cannot be added to or deleted from the bound copy.

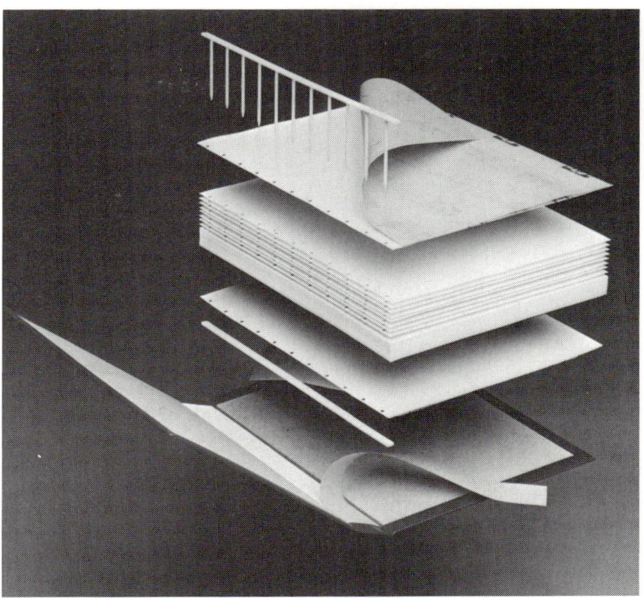

Courtesy Velo-Bind, Inc.
Plastic strip-and-spike binding with hardcover.

Loose-leaf binding. The simplest form of looseleaf binding is the **plastic slide-on clip** that, when fitted against the side of the publication and attached to a transparent wraparound cover, holds the pages together with tension and pressure. All other looseleaf binders fall into one of two categories: ring or post. **Spring-back (ring) binders** also use tension and pressure to hold the binding edges of sheets together; however, in this case, the cover is usually fairly sturdy and the binding device is almost always riveted into or otherwise attached to it. The punched pages are held in the binder by prongs or rings that can be opened or closed to interchange the sheets. **Post binders** can expand to hold a large quantity of pages very securely, but they must be completely disassembled in order to add or delete pages.

Loose-leaf (ring) binders are excellent for industrial manuals, catalogs, instruction books, financial records, or any other publications that are updated frequently. The cost of supplying updates to add to loose-leaf binders is much less than the cost of supplying a completely new edition every time information changes.

Adhesive Binding

Adhesive, or **perfect, binding** uses glue to bind the pages of a publication at its backbone. This method is used extensively to bind magazines and books that can be as thick as 2 in. (51 mm). A perfect-bound book has a rectangular backbone and

usually a soft cover of a heavier stock than the inside pages of the book. The cover is also secured at the spine with an adhesive. Thread stitches or wire staples are not used in this process, although an adhesive is used as part of the thread-sewing method of bookbinding. In perfect binding, the adhesive is the only binding material used.

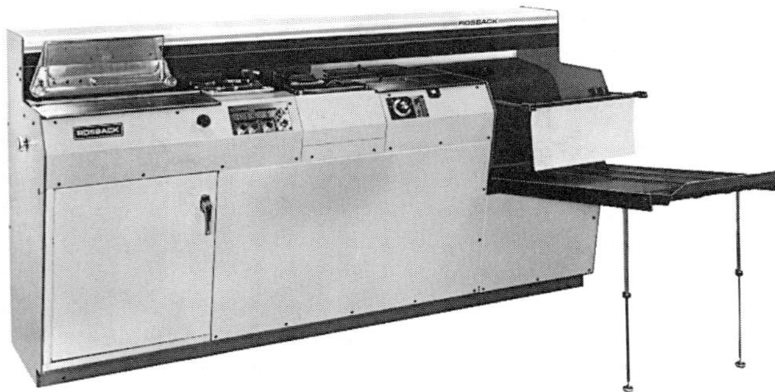

Courtesy F.P. Rosback Co.

Adhesive binder.

The largest users of perfect binding are book printers and trade binders who produce softcover, or paperback, books that have wraparound paper covers. Softcover perfect bindings are also used for telephone books and catalogs.

Perfect binding takes place in a finishing line consisting of a gatherer, backbone cutter and roughener, gluer, cover feeder, and trimmer. Trimmers are discussed in a separate section because they are used in more than one binding method.

Gatherers. Gathering is the operation of assembling signatures one on top of the other in the proper page sequence. Gatherers accept printed signatures delivered from a web press, which folds them in-line, or from stand-alone folding machines. The gatherer has a separate feeding station (pocket or hopper) for each signature. The number of feeding stations may vary from ten or fewer to more than thirty-two, depending on how many signatures make up the finished product. There are several designs of gatherer signature feeders, including rotary feeders and swinging-arm systems. After gathering, the groups of signatures, also called **book blocks,** move into the cutting and roughening area.

Backbone cutter and roughener. The book block travels along a spiral raceway that jogs and turns it from a horizontal to a vertical position. Now standing on its spine, it enters the adhesive-binding section of the perfect binder, which has continuously circulating clamps that close over it with a vise-like grip. While held in the clamps, the backbone edge of the book block extends at least ⅛ in. (3 mm) below the bottom of the clamps where the signature folds will be milled off and roughened in preparation for gluing. Knives or saws on milling or shredding units cut off or grind away the individual signature folds so that each sheet better accepts and absorbs the adhesive.

Alternatives to cutting and roughening. Notch and burst binding treat the backbone without grinding or milling away the signature folds, thereby improving glue adhesion and, in turn, the durability of the products.

In **notch binding,** large grooves are cut across the spine, removing about half of it in ¼-in. (6-mm) segments. The notches are then filled with glue, which hold all of the pages against the spine.

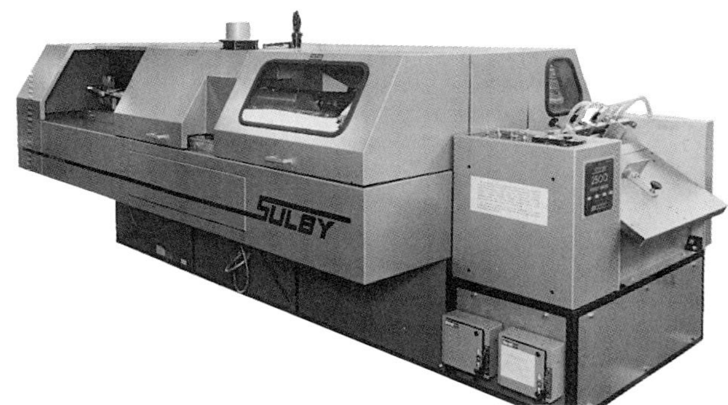

Courtesy AM Graphics

Adhesive binder.

Burst binding uses a perforating device attached to a web press or stand-alone folder that bursts through portions of the spine edge of each signature, permitting the glue to penetrate between the pages while retaining bridges of paper. **Punch perforation** is similar to burst binding. Slots cut into the binding edge just before the last fold provide a larger opening in the spine of the gathered signatures and allow the glue to penetrate easily. Both are good methods of securing the book.

Gluer. Still clamped together, the book block exits the cutting and roughening area and travels to the gluing station, which typically consists of a single glue pot with two applicator wheels. The applicator wheels force the adhesive into the exposed paper fibers, and a rotary spinner controls the thickness and uniformity of the glue coating as it meters the glue along the backbone to a thickness of approximately 0.020 in. (0.5 mm). Gluing stations with

multiple glue pots are used for jobs requiring two different adhesive formulations. Applying a low-viscosity hot-melt glue seals in all of the paper fibers, and following this with a heavy layer of a high-viscosity hot-melt helps the book block adhere to the cover. For binding thick catalogs, three coats of adhesive are often used.

Cover feeder. After gluing, the cover is applied. It falls from a hopper into a rotary or stream feeder and is scored from one to six times then jogged for proper alignment before it is pressed against the glue-covered backbone of the book block. **Nipping stations** pinch the cover around the glue-coated backbone while two plates clamp it at the score line and press its front, back, and sides against the spine of the book block. When the book block is unclamped, it drops, completely assembled, onto a conveyor that transfers it to a trimmer where its closed signatures are sliced open. Occasionally, adhesive-bound books receive hard covers in the casebinding process, which is discussed later.

Wire Stitching

Brochures, pamphlets, and thin magazines bound with staples driven through the centerfold along the backbone are some examples of items **saddle-stitched** with wire. Products **side-stitched** with wire are fastened together by inserting preformed staples through the side of the booklet or brochure parallel to the backbone. It is important to distinguish between stitching, in which wire is used, and sewing, which relies on thread to secure the signatures of a publication.

Saddle and side stitchers range from small hand- or foot-powered models to large automated machines. Signatures to be side-stitched are stacked (gathered) one on top of the other, much as signatures are stacked for perfect binding. Saddle-stitched signatures, on the other hand, are inserted, meaning that outer signatures are dropped over inner ones.

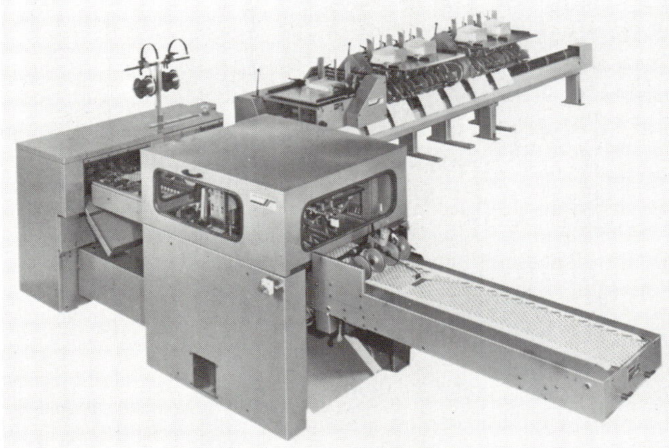

Courtesy Muller-Martini Corp.

Saddle stitching line.

Individual sheets or folded, usually four-page, signatures are transported from the gatherer to side stitcher flat on their backs or at an angle that will align the spines with the stitcher heads. The flat signatures must be placed upright and jogged, or aligned, at the head and spine before stitching. Small, raised pins on a transport chain or pusher fingers forward the signatures to the actual stitching mechanism and remove them from the stitching section after they have been secured as a unit.

Improvements in the glues used in adhesive binding have led most publishers to abandon side stitching. Bulky printed materials joined by the perfect binding method are neat, attractive, and easier to handle than those that have been side-wire stitched. Nevertheless, saddle stitching, the other form of wire stitching, remains the best method of joining publications that are up to ¼ in. (6 mm) thick, and the remainder of this section will focus on it.

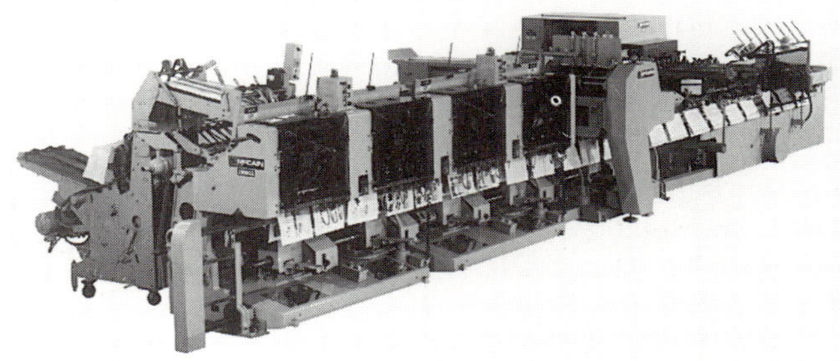

Courtesy McCain Manufacturing, Inc.

Saddle stitching line.

The three main segments of all saddle stitchers are the pockets (signature feeding stations), the stitching heads, and three-knife trimmers. Collectively, these units are referred to as a **inserter/saddle stitcher/trimmer finishing line.**

Pockets. Each folded signature is fed into the stitcher from a separate pocket, which uses mechanical "fingers" combined with vacuum suction to open it to its center before dropping it over the **saddle-bar** (sometimes called the **bayonet** or **sword**). A pin traveling along a continuous-loop conveyor chain sweeps the first signature off the

saddle-bar and pushes it toward the second pocket where the next signature drops over it and so forth on down the chain until an entire publication is formed when the cover drops from the last pocket nearest the stitching heads.

If four signatures make up a complete book, four pockets are required to feed the signatures onto the stitcher. Extra pockets can be added when needed; some saddle stitchers have over twenty-two pockets. When there are not enough pockets to handle a large magazine, an additional four, six, or eight pages are **tipped,** or glued, to a sixteen-page signature, and bound as one twenty-four-page unit called an unbalanced signature.

Stitching section. The operator sets the caliper in the stitching section to detect plus or minus deviations from the proper thickness of the job. Copies with missing signatures or double-feeds pass through without being stitched and are automatically ejected before reaching the trimmer. These signatures can be re-collated and run through the stitcher again, thus minimizing waste.

Thread Sewing

Thread sewing involves fastening printed signatures together with a needle and thread or cord. It produces strong and durable products including many encyclopedias, reference and fine art books, and Bibles. In **Smyth sewing,** the most common method of thread sewing introduced over 100 years ago, the thread is passed through the backfold of a signature and from signature to signature. This links the signatures together while permitting the book to lie flat.

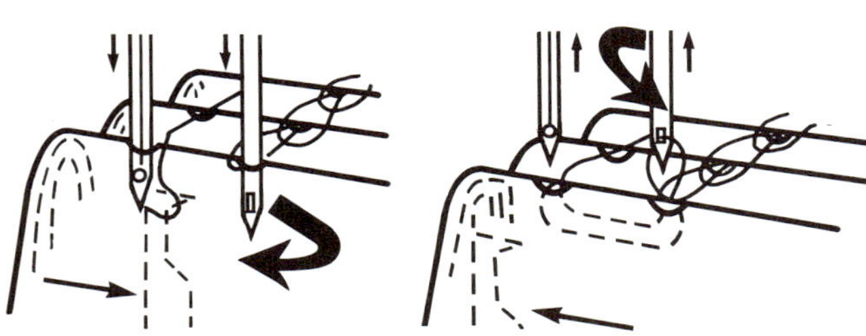

Principle of Smyth sewing.

The two forms of thread sewing are side and saddle sewing. **Side sewing** refers to securing the thread through the side of a book parallel to its binding edge (backbone). Like publications that have been side-stitched with wire, side-sewn books have very strong bindings but cannot be opened fully or lie flat. Manual side sewing is used most often for library and repair work. In machine side sewing, a needle carries a single thread through drilled holes, creating a square-stitch pattern. Double thread sewing uses a needle-and-bobbin system similar to household sewing machines, except that holes are punched through the stock for the needle to penetrate.

Saddle sewing joins book signatures together by driving the thread through the centerfold. Publications that are saddle-sewn open easily and lie flat, making this form of thread sewing more popular than side sewing. During automated saddle sewing, signatures are transferred from the feeder to the infeed saddle where a scanning head monitors movement. A roller presses the signature against the front shield of the infeed saddle, then it is taken up by the feed belt and conveyed to the sewing saddle, which swings into position. After sewing, a separating device cuts the threads before pushing the books apart and down another belt that carries them to the trimmer and then to delivery or the casebinding line.

Trimmers

Trimming involves cutting away the folded or ragged portions of a bound job to form smooth, even edges and permit all pages to open. It follows the

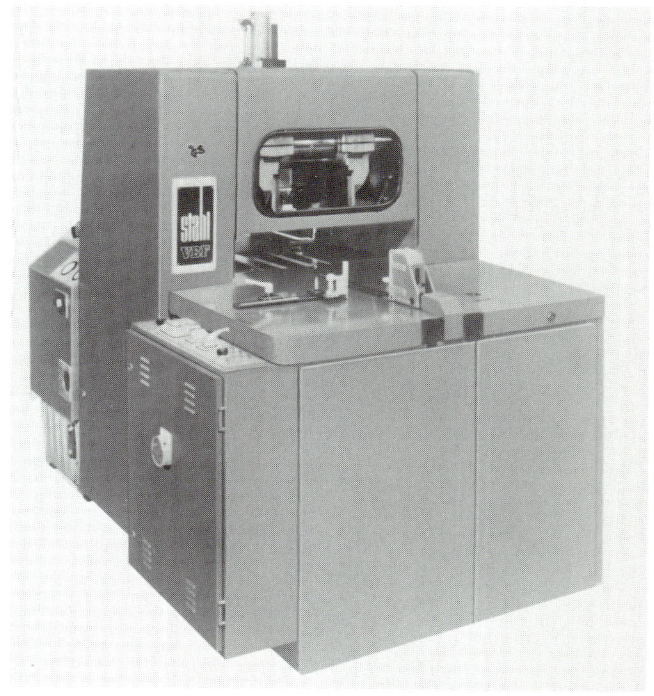

Courtesy Heidelberg USA

Stahl three-knife trimmer.

binding procedure in every process but mechanical and loose-leaf and may be included as part of a finishing line or in-line finishing system. Trimming may be completed on a guillotine cutter with a split gauge, a back gauge divided into three sections so that the book can be trimmed at the top, bottom, and on one side without changing the setting. However, most bound jobs are trimmed on three- or five-knife trimmers that are placed in finishing lines with saddle stitchers or perfect binders.

Trimmers cut signature excess from the head, foot, and fore edge of each book or magazine. As part of a finishing line sequence, the bound material is fed automatically from the binder into the trimmer, which may be trimming the front of one stack of books while trimming the ends of another. Each book block is jogged in the trimmer's infeed channel and transported to the side knives where the head and foot cuts are made simultaneously. After the side knives move out of its path, the front knife cuts the fore edge, removing the lap from the high-folio side. The delivery clamp raises the pile of trimmed publications and places them on a conveyor belt for delivery to the counter/stacker. Airblast nozzles blow trimmings off of the machine, so they do not interfere with subsequent operations.

If the job has been run two-up, two units printed and bound as one, it is cut apart with a splitting saw before three-knife trimming or, if it is not too thick, sent through a five-knife trimmer. Five-knife trimmers can also handle three-up jobs.

Casebinding

Casebinding is the process by which rigid or flexible boards are covered with cloth or leather to create a hardbound book. These covers, called cases, are produced in a step separate from the production of the bodies of the books, which are joined together by the thread sewing or adhesive binding methods. Hardbound books are covered in such a way that the cover projects beyond the edges of the pages.

Casemaking, the process of creating the book's cover, usually takes place as the signatures are gathered and sewn. Boards are slit into strips on one machine and crosscut to book board size on another before being fed into the casemaker.

To form the cover, the casemaking machine affixes the boards and backlining in place and turns the flaps of extra cloth under the boards, gluing them to the inside of the boards to shape a finished edge. Covers not preprinted may be stamped or embossed at this time after which the case is ready to be attached to the book block.

Forwarding operations are the series of steps that prepare a thread-sewn or adhesive-bound book to merge with the casebinding line where it receives a hard cover. They are performed as part of the casebinding line.

Nipping and smashing. Thread-sewn books are nipped or smashed to remove excess air and reduce the swell caused by stitching. During **nipping,** pressure is applied along the sides of the backbone; **smashing** applies pressure over the entire front and back surfaces of the book. Hard papers are nipped and soft papers are smashed.

A drive chain feeds book blocks spine downward into the nipping station. Here, spring-loaded jaws grasp each book on both sides of the fold, preventing it from snapping out of position. The smashing station compresses the book evenly across the entire surface. Smashing applies 250 tons of pressure.

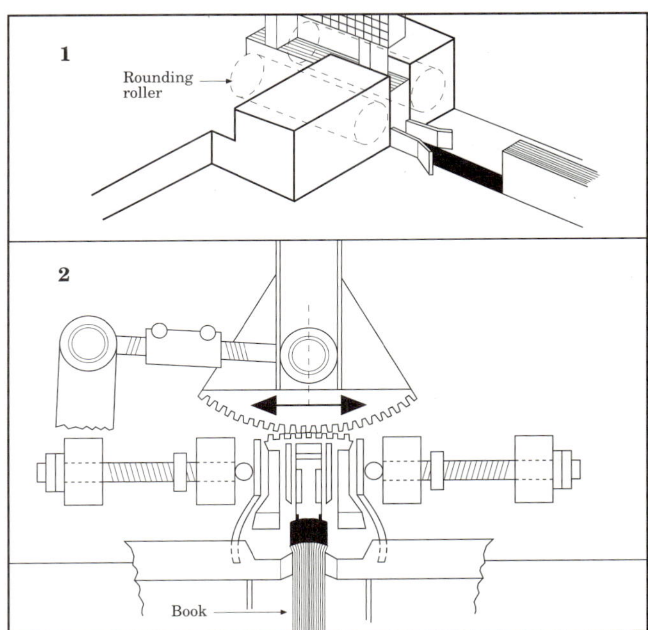

(1) Rounding. (2) Backing.

Rounding and backing. These two procedures are used with both adhesive-bound and thread-sewn books. **Rounding** is the first step in shaping a book to fit its cover. It improves a book's structure by giving it a convex spine and a concave fore-edge. This is achieved by placing the book with its spine facing forward between steel rollers rotating in opposite directions. Side-stitched or -sewn books cannot be rounded.

Backing, clamping the book's edges and flaring the back outward from the center over the edges,

provides greater flexibility and permanence for the rounded spine and creates the hinge crease for the joints of the book. It makes the spine wider than the thickness of the rest of the book to provide a shoulder against which the cardboard front and back covers rest.

Back gluing, edge treatments, and headbanding are three optional forwarding procedures. Back gluing helps a book retain its rounded shape, while edge treatments and headbanding are decorative measures. After the forwarding operations are completed, the book enters the casebinding line.

Casing-in and building-in. The casebinding process consists of two operations: casing-in and building-in. **Casing-in** attaches the cloth cover to the body of the book. The free halves of the four end papers are coated on the outside with paste and the case is placed over the book in such a way that the edges of the cover project uniformly beyond the edges of the end sheets when the two are pressed together to secure the binding.

Building-in refers to drying the case's adhesive under pressure. A series of pressure plates and heated formers press the book to set the cloth into the joints. Each set of plates and joint formers clamps the book under great pressure for a moment and then releases it. The book may pass through five or more sets of clamps and formers, depending on the amount of drying needed.

Equipment for high-volume work combines all of the forwarding and covering operations (rounding, backing, casing-in, building-in, and jacketing) into one completely mechanized production line.

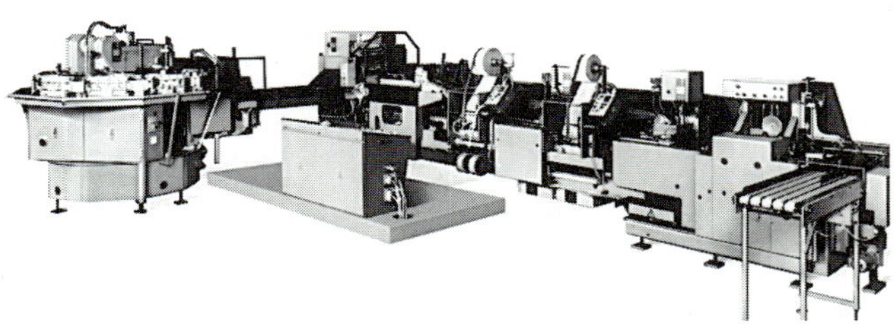

Courtesy Heidelberg USA

Casebinding line.

Casebinding categories. Casebinding can be divided into three different groupings: edition binding, job binding, and library binding. These terms refer to the quantity and the nature of the binding. Most books fall into the edition binding category.

Edition binding is the binding of hardcover books in relatively large quantities. Because edition binders use mostly automatic and semiautomatic equipment, they rarely handle runs smaller than 1,500.

Job binding is the binding of small quantities of hardcover books. It involves a considerable amount of handwork and is also used for books that cannot be handled by automatic equipment, such as Bibles bound in limp leather.

Library binding is a special service rendered to libraries and includes prebinding, rebinding, and general repair work. Library binders, like job binders, deal with small quantities and use considerable handwork. The main purpose of library binding is to provide publications that are sturdy enough to withstand the wear and tear to which books are subjected in public libraries.

Finishing

In-Line Finishing

In-line finishing includes additional operations, such as addressing, folding, and diecutting that, when performed as part of a continuous process on a web press, eliminate subsequent bindery procedures. Embossing and debossing can also be completed in-line or as part of a separate finishing line.

Publication and book web offset presses use combination folders that cut and fold printed webs into signatures for shipment to a bindery. Specialized in-line accessories, such as prefolders and plow folders can be added to increase capabilities. In-line finishing should not be confused with the finishing line, in which several binding steps are combined after printing.

Special Finishing Techniques

Point-of-purchase displays, stationery, menus, and greeting cards are among the printed products that incorporate special finishing techniques. Improvements in the technology used for embossing, foil stamping, and diecutting are discussed here. These processes may be incorporated into a finishing line or an in-line finishing system or executed from totally separate machinery.

Embossing. Embossing is the process by which dies are used to create raised, or relief, images. Blind embossed products are also impressed by dies but no decorative foils or inks are used to further enhance the appearance of the images. **Debossing**

dies produce images that are depressed (sunken) into the paper's surface.

In the embossing process, a relief die is mounted against a temperature-controlled embossing plate that is clamped to the bed of the embossing press. A counter die designed to complement the relief die is mounted in register with the platen, which also holds the substrate to be embossed. When the bed and platen are brought together over the substrate and pressure is applied, embossing occurs. Embossing can be performed with a cold die, but the use of heated dies is more common.

Foil stamping. Foil stamping involves passing the substrate between a heated die and a roll of foil fed through a stamping press. As pressure is applied, the foil is transferred to the substrate. If the substrate is flat-stamped, there is no surface emboss. **Foil embossing** combines the embossing process described above with the application of a layer of foil. Paperback books, cosmetic packages, and greeting cards are three products that are often foil-embossed or -stamped.

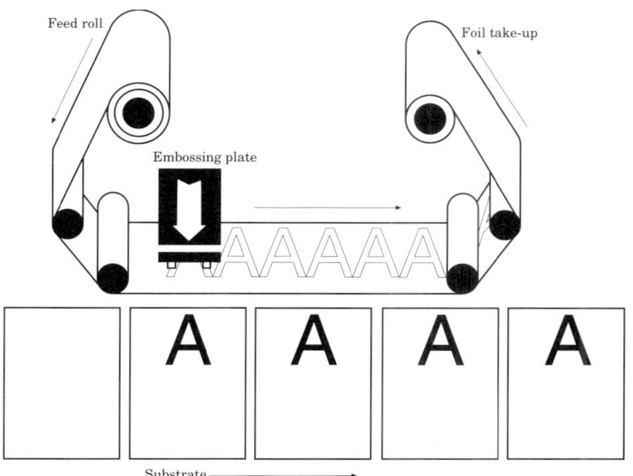

Courtesy Bobst

Typical hot-foil stamping configuration.

Diecutting. Embossing and stamping are performed immediately before or after diecutting, or sometimes as part of the diecutting process if accessories are attached to the diecutting press. Some of the items created by diecutting include labels, cartons, pop-up books, and point-of-purchase displays.

Steel-rule diecutting is a common stamping process that combines cutting, scoring, and creasing into a single operation in which automatic machines cut materials singly or in small groups of two or more.

The two varieties of diecutting presses are platen and cylinder. **Platen diecutting presses** operate on the same principle as the embossing presses described earlier. One platen holds the cutting and creasing die rules and the other holds the counter die. When the two platens are pressed against each other, cutting and creasing occurs. On **reciprocating platen diecutters,** one platen remains in a fixed position while the other moves against it. Jaw platen diecutters rely on the opening and closing motion of both platens. The cut and creased product is formed as the two platens meet. Platen diecutters can reach 9,000 impressions per hour.

Appendix

The following trade customs of the printing industry are reprinted with permission from a brochure entitled *Trade Customs of the Printing Industry of North America,* printed in June 1985 by the Graphic Arts Council of North America (GACNA).

Definition of a Trade Custom

The Uniform Commercial Code adopted by most states defines a trade custom, or usage of the trade, in Section 1-205(2) as: "Any practice or method of dealing having such regularity of observation in a place, vocation or trade as to justify an expectation that it will be observed with respect to the transaction in question. The distance and scope of such a usage are to be proved as facts. If it is established that such usage is embodied in a written trade code or similar writing the interpretation of the writing is for the court."

A trade custom, then, is any practice or method of doing business that is done so regularly in a particular industry as to justify an expectation by the parties that it will be observed with respect to a questioned transaction.

Trade customs are used by parties in interpreting their contractual relations. A trade custom may be used by the courts to translate contracts, and to further interpret an ambiguous contract.

To enforce a trade custom, the moving party must show that the other party either knew or should have known of the existence of the trade custom.

Trade Customs vs. Terms and Conditions of Sale

Unless specifically incorporated in a contract, trade customs are not part of the contract's terms and conditions of sale. Indeed, it is possible for the contract's terms and conditions to be inconsistent with the industry's trade customs. In such a case, the express terms and conditions supersede the trade customs. Further, the parties' course of dealing or course of performance under the contract, if different from the trade customs, also supersedes those customs.

Trade customs gain legal significance when a contract term is ambiguous and is not clarified by the parties' course of dealing or course of performance under the contract. In such cases, trade customs may be used as evidence of the intentions and expectations of the parties with respect to the ambiguous contract term. They may also be used to show the parties' intentions and expectations with respect to matters not provided for in a contract, or for those instances where no written contract exists.

Printing Trade Customs

1. Quotation. A quotation not accepted within sixty (60) days is subject to review. All prices are based on material costs at the time of quotation.

2. Orders. Orders regularly placed, verbal or written, cannot be canceled except upon terms that will compensate the printer against loss incurred in reliance of the order.

3. Experimental work. Experimental or preliminary work performed at the customer's request will be charged for at current rates and may not be used until the printer has been reimbursed in full for the amount of the charges billed.

4. Creative work. Creative work, such as sketches, copy, dummies, and all preparatory work

developed and furnished by the printer, shall remain the printer's exclusive property and no use of same shall be made, nor any ideas obtained therefrom be used, except upon compensation to be determined by the printer, and not expressly identified and included in the selling price.

5. Condition of copy. Upon receipt of original copy or manuscript, should it be evident that the condition of the copy differs from that which had been originally described and consequently quoted, the original quotation shall be rendered void and a new quotation issued.

6. Preparatory materials. Working mechanical art, type, negatives, positives, flats, plates, and other items, when supplied by the printer, shall remain the printer's exclusive property unless otherwise agreed in writing.

7. Alterations. Alterations represent work performed in addition to the original specifications. Such work shall be charged at current rates and be supported with documentation upon request.

8. Prepress proofs. Prepress proofs shall be submitted with original copy. Corrections are to be made on a "master set," returned marked "O.K." or "O.K. with corrections," and signed by the customer. If revised proofs are desired, a request must be made when proofs are returned. A printer cannot be held responsible for errors under any or all of the following conditions: if the work is printed per customer's O.K.; if changes are communicated verbally; if the customer has not ordered proofs; if the customer has failed to return proofs with indication of changes; or if the customer has instructed the printer to proceed without submission of proofs.

9. Press proofs. Unless specifically provided in the printer's quotation, press proofs will be charged for at current rates. An inspection sheet of any form can be submitted for customer approval, at no charge, provided the customer is available at the press during the time of makeready. Lost press time due to customer delay, or customer changes and corrections, will be charged at current rates.

10. Color proofing. Because of differences in equipment, processing, proofing substrates, papers, inks, pigments, and other conditions between color proofing and production pressroom operations, a reasonable variation in color between color proofs and the completed job shall constitute acceptable delivery.

11. Overruns and underruns. Overruns or underruns not to exceed 10% on quantities ordered, or the percentage agreed upon, shall constitute acceptable delivery. The printer will bill for actual quantity delivered within this tolerance. If the customer requires guaranteed exact quantities, the percentage tolerance must be doubled.

12. Customer's property. The printer will maintain fire, extended coverage, vandalism, malicious mischief, and sprinkler leakage insurance on all property belonging to the customer, while such property is in the printer's possession; printer's liability for such property shall not exceed the amount recoverable from such insurance. Customer's property of extraordinary value shall be insured through mutual agreement.

13. Delivery. Unless otherwise specified, the price quoted is for a single shipment, without storage, F.O.B. local customer's place of business or F.O.B. printer's platform for out-of-town customers. Proposals are based on continuous and uninterrupted delivery of complete order, unless specifications distinctly state otherwise. Charges related to delivery from customer to printer, or from customer's supplier to printer, are not included in any quotations unless specified. Special priority pickup or delivery service will be provided at current rates upon the customer's request. Materials delivered from the customer or the customer's suppliers are verified with delivery tickets as to cartons, packages, or items shown only. The accuracy of quantities indicated on such tickets cannot be verified and the printer cannot accept liability for shortages based on the supplier's tickets. Title for finished work passes to the customer upon delivery to carrier at shipping point or upon mailing of invoices for finished work, whichever occurs first.

14. Production schedules. Production schedules will be established and adhered to by the customer and printer, provided that neither shall incur any liability or penalty for delay due to state of war, riot, civil disorder, fire, labor trouble, strike, accident, energy failure, equipment breakdown, delays of suppliers or carriers, action of government or civil authority, an act of God, or other causes beyond the control of the customer or printer. Where production schedules are not adhered to by the customer, final delivery date(s) will be subject to renegotiation.

15. Customer-furnished materials. Paper stock, ink, camera copy, film, color separations, and other

customer-furnished material shall be manufactured, packed, and delivered to printer's specifications. Additional cost due to delays or impaired production caused by specification deficiencies shall be charged to the customer.

16. Terms. Payment shall be whatever was set forth in the quotation or invoice unless otherwise provided in writing. Claims for defects, damages, or shortages must be made by the customer in writing within a period of fifteen (15) days after delivery of all or any part of the order. Failure to make such claim within the stated period shall constitute irrevocable acceptance and an admission that they fully comply with terms, conditions, and specifications.

17. Liability. The printer's liability shall be limited to the stated selling price of any defective goods, and shall in no event include special or consequential damages, including profits (or profits lost). As security for payment of any sum due or to become due under terms of any agreement, the printer shall have the right, if necessary, to retain possession of and shall have a lien on all customer property in printer's possession including work in process and finished work. The extension of credit or the acceptance of notes, trade acceptance, or guarantee of payment shall not affect such security interest and lien.

18. Indemnification. The customer shall indemnify and hold harmless the printer from any and all losses, costs, expenses and damages (including court costs and reasonable attorney fees) on account of any and all manner of claims, demands, actions, and proceedings that may be instituted against the printer on grounds alleging that the said printing violates any copyrights or any proprietary right of any person; or that it contains any matter that is libelous, or obscene, or scandalous; or invades any person's right to privacy or other personal rights, except to the extent that the printer contributed to the matter. The customer agrees, at the customer's own expense, to promptly defend and continue the defense of any such claim, demand, action, or proceeding that may be brought against the printer; provided that the printer shall promptly notify the customer with respect thereto; and provided further that the printer shall give to the customer such reasonable time as the exigencies of the situation permit in which to undertake and continue the defense thereof.

Index